THE
CONSUMER
BIBLE

THE
CONSUMER
BIBLE

1001 WAYS TO SHOP SMART

BY MARK GREEN

WITH GLENN VON NOSTITZ, NANCY YOUMAN,
AND OLIVIER SULTAN

WORKMAN PUBLISHING, NEW YORK

Library of Congress Cataloging-in-Publication Data

Green, Mark J.
The Consumer Bible
p. cm
Includes index.
ISBN 1-56305-274-1
1. Consumer education—United States. 2. Shopping—United States.
I. Title.
TX336.G74 1994
640'.73'0973—dc20   94-28326
                                                CIP

Cover and book illustrations by Michael Sloan

Quotation on page 115 reprinted by permission of *The New York Times*.
Copyright © 1992 by The New York Times Company.

Workman books are available at special discount when purchased in bulk for special premiums and sales promotions as well as for fund-raising or educational use. Special editions or book excerpts also can be created to specification. For details, contact the Special Sales Director at the address below.

Workman Publishing Company, Inc.
708 Broadway
New York, NY 10003

Manufactured in the United States of America

First Printing March 1995
10 9 8 7 6 5

The views expressed in this book are those of Mark Green and not those of either the Office of the Public Advocate or the Government of New York City.

DEDICATION

To the memories of
Ann and Irving Green

ACKNOWLEDGMENTS

The Consumer Bible is, in effect, the product of thousands of advocates in hundreds of organizations over scores of years. So from Upton Sinclair to, of course, my friend and mentor Ralph Nader, I'm a megaphone for countless predecessors who spoke up and out for consumer justice.

Because of this history, up to 10 percent of the book's royalties will go to fund "$marter consumer fellowships" for summer law students, to be administered by the National Association for Public Interest Law.

This volume's midwives have been my extraordinary co-authors— Glenn von Nostitz, Nancy Youman, and Olivier Sultan—who invested a quantity and quality of effort that have distinguished their careers. They worked with me at the Department of Consumer Affairs and helped produce the pioneering studies and actions that comprised the cornerstone of our office and this book.

Other key contributors to *The Consumer Bible* include Jennifer Kohn, Amy Karas, Andy Eiler, Michael Alcamo, and Norman Schreiber—all of whom assisted so ably in their respective specialties.

I very much want to thank friends Victor Navasky and Esther Margolis, of *The Nation* and Newmarket Press respectively, who brought me and Peter Workman together to produce this collaboration. Along with Peter's early confidence, it was Suzanne Rafer's and Margot Herrera's close editing and advice that indispensably contributed to the book's coherence (such as it is).

Finally, a special note of love and appreciation to Deni, Jenya, and Jonah, a very patient family who tolerated—even encouraged!—a book and a campaign in the same year. I hope they use the result to stretch the family budget as $marter consumers should.

—M.G.

CONTENTS

A SELF-HELP MANUAL FOR THE CONSUMER CENTURY

Every day, with every purchase, consumers have a choice: Get smart—or get taken.

Some examples: If I want some 1% milk for my morning cereal, I can buy a quart within two blocks of my home in Manhattan for either 99 cents or $1.99. The same make and model VCR can be purchased for either $225 or $449 within six city blocks. A bottle of Procardia, a common heart medication, ranged from $49 to $69 on the same street. But becoming a "smarter" consumer in today's economy can be a daunting challenge. This book explains why, and what you can do about it.

First, most stores can and do outnegotiate most consumers. A business engages in thousands of consumer interactions a year, while a shopper may purchase a major product or service once in a decade (buying a home or hiring a lawyer), once a year (a vacation or appliance), or once a week (food or entertainment). As a result, the odds in most exchanges favor business—particularly if the scale is rigged, the ad misleading, the salesperson hyperbolic, or the product older than labeled.

Second, the consumer marketplace has become a teeming Tower of Babel, with not only many more choices overall but also more complicated and specialized options. Once upon a time, there was one kind of mortgage, one telephone company, and there were only three TV channels. Today fixed mortgages come with 30- and 15- and 10- year fixed terms, or you can opt for ARMs (adjustable rate mortgages); Ma Bell has many competing offspring, each with different day, evening, and weekend rates, as well as high- and low-frequency rates; and network TV has to share its audience with cable, pay-per-view, and satellite dishes.

Meanwhile, people are being deluged with consumer information and advice that can be confusing, conflicting, and overwhelming. *The Consumer Bible* was designed to be the only consumer book you'll need. It tries to tip the scales—and the odds—in favor of average shoppers by gathering in one place the best available information about your choices and rights in 64 different consumer categories.

The book is an outgrowth of my 25 years' experience as a consumer advocate, from a decade spent as a public interest lawyer with Ralph Nader in Washington, DC, to my years as the Consumer Affairs Commissioner of New York City to my present role as the elected Public Advocate, or ombudsperson, of the City. And based on the 50,000 consumer complaints my consumer office received over three years, as well as several hundred investigations, reports, and lawsuits, I've come to the following conclusions about our consumer economy: Scams are extensive and expensive—and penalties are weak. Nonetheless, smarter consumers can fight back—and, in the coming consumer century, we increasingly will.

Scams and Schemes

Although opinion leaders with cushy incomes often seem to shrug off marketplace fraud or manipulation, the average consumers whose calls flooded the hot line at the New York City Department of Consumer Affairs (DCA) were not so dismissive. Their concerns were well warranted. During my tenure, for example, the DCA found:

- Electronics store employees red-handedly using razors to cut out the word "refurbished" from cardboard boxes containing old VCRs.
- Two-thirds of all home-improve-

ment contractors failed to obtain legally required licenses.
- In an inspection sweep of 150 gas stations, one in six was caught committing "octane fraud"—deceptively selling inexpensive regular gas as the pricier premium (average overcharge per tank: $2.70).
- Supermarket scanners charged regular prices for advertised sale items 10% of the time.
- 90% of independent pay telephones illegally failed to disclose information required by the state's Public Service Commission—such as their exorbitant hidden rates.

Obviously, no one of these abuses equal the billions of dollars looted in the Savings & Loan scandal. But corner-cutting stores know that it's far easier to trick a dime out of 100,000 customers than to cheat one of $10,000 outright. Indeed, all those dimes and dollars add up to huge consumer losses: In my 1985 book, *The Challenge of Hidden Profits: Reducing Corporate Waste and Bureaucracy* (with John F. Berry), I gathered the leading studies from around the country on the costs of price-fixing, securities fraud, auto repair fraud, product defects, pollution, bribery, and kickbacks, etc. The rough total: Consumers lost $862 billion a year (in 1985 dollars) to waste, abuse, and outright fraud—a sum equal to 20% of consumer purchasing.

Suppose workers were told that, starting tomorrow, their pay would be cut by 20%. They would strike, or worse. So why should consumers in the marketplace tolerate a reduction in spending power they would never put up with in the workplace? Why work 2,000 hours a year for, say, $40,000 and then squander $8,000 on fraud and waste?

Becoming a Smarter Consumer

Consumers have two resources to get a fair deal in the free marketplace: the law and self-help.

The law, of course, consists of the rules and regulations that prohibit deceptive ads, rigged scales, phony warranties, and defective products . . . or that require price-posting, truth-in-lending, and auto performance standards.

Enacting these laws has proven easier than enforcing them. Part of the problem is that the penalties for "crime in the suites" is often so low that some companies regard them as merely the cost of doing business. "Since corporations are primarily profit-seeking institutions, they choose to violate the law only if it appears profitable," argues a classic 1979 article in *The Harvard Law Review.* "Making these costs sufficiently high should eliminate the potential benefit of illegal corporate activity and hence any incentive to undertake such activity."

Not only does the fine usually not fit the crime, but when city budgets are tight, the consumer protection agency is often the first to be cut back. And since most consumer disputes involve small sums relative to legal fees that can exceed any restitution, consumers rarely find it worthwhile to hire lawyers.

Given rights without remedies, the law alone is not sufficient to protect buyers in the marketplace. Consumer self-help is essential. No matter how strong a few *hundred* consumer officials or laws may be, they are no substitute for alert, educated consumers engaging in *billions* of weekly point-of-purchase interactions with sellers.

That was the theory that inspired a small group of academics, engineers, journalists, and labor leaders to organize Consumers Union in 1936, a time when there were few laws and no consumer officials. By providing buyers with essential information based on research and testing, they would advance the ideal of "consumer sovereignty"— i.e. informed consumers voting with their dollars could influence businesses to respond with higher quality and fairly priced goods. Today, Consumers Union publishes *Consumer Reports,* with almost five million paid subscribers.

Over the years, *Consumer Reports,* Ralph Nader, the federal Consumer Information Center, Better Business Bureaus, and national and local consumer organizations have helped to correct the traditional information imbalance between sellers and buyers in the marketplace.* By synthe-

---

*The **Consumer Information Center** in Pueblo, Colorado, distributes more than 27 million pamphlets and catalogues a year on such topics as "How to Read the New Food Labels," "Solving Credit Problems," "Nine Ways to Lower Your Auto Insurance Costs," and "How to Buy a Home with a Low Down Payment." To obtain any of their publications, either call (719) 948-4000 or write to the Consumer Information Center, Pueblo, Colorado 81009. **Consumers Union,** which is the publisher

sizing so many of these advocates' money-saving suggestions into one volume—combined with insights gleaned from years of consumer advocacy and law enforcement— *The Consumer Bible* seeks to turn readers into "$marter Consumers" and to help convert *caveat emptor—* let the buyer beware—into *caveat vendor.*

Being a $marter Consumer means more than merely complying with the Big Three of smart shopping—compare prices, ask advice from a trusted friend who's already made the purchase, and know that if it sounds too good to be true, it probably is. So this book also describes over 1,000 ways to save your money, your time, and your health. It tells how to be alert to shrinking credit card grace periods and why you need an independent jeweler's appraisal of a gem's cut, color, clarity, and carat weight before you pay thousands of dollars for it. It explains why you should avoid paying lawyers "non-refundable retainers" and why you shouldn't put down more than a third of the contract price with a home-improvement contractor. It gives suggestions on how to pay half-price for hotel rooms and commonly prescribed drugs and how to spot those pay phones that charge $10 for five-minute local calls. Each chapter provides an overview of a type of product or service, along with warnings on "What to Watch Out For." Every chapter also includes specific advice and tips on how to be a $marter Consumer and ends with a HELP box containing resources that will enable consumers to access services, get further information, or take action.

Consumer Century

A revolution is like waves lapping at a cliff, wrote French historian Henri Seé. For decades, nothing happens . . . and then the side of the cliff falls in.

Several coalescing trends are now lapping at the edges of our business-as-usual, corporate economy, which will greatly influence how consumers shop and save in the coming years.

First, there is the spreading public disdain for large bureaucracies, whether corporate or governmental. As the shrinking of our biggest "corpocracies"—IBM, AT&T, GM, Sears—shows, bigger certainly is no longer better in the marketplace. As we approach the next century, consumers increasingly reward swifter, leaner, more adaptable firms which have a market niche rather than market dominance.

---

of *Zillions,* a *Consumer Reports* for kids, *Consumer Reports on Health,* and the *Consumer Reports Travel Letter,* in addition to *Consumer Reports Magazine,* is located at 101 Truman Avenue, Yonkers, NY 10703, or call (914) 378-2000. The headquarters for the **Council of Better Business Bureaus** is 4200 Wilson Boulevard, Arlington, VA 22203, or call (703) 276-0100. The two leading consumer groups in Washington, DC, each of which have published hundreds of reports and monographs, are **Public Citizen** (2000 P Street NW, Washington, DC 20036; (202) 833-3000) and **Consumer Federation of America** (1424 16th Street NW, Suite 604, Washington, DC 20036; (202) 387-6121).

Second, the leveling off of consumer purchasing power, beginning in an era of slow economic growth in 1973, has created a kind of middle-class poverty. Today's younger generation is the first to have a *lower* standard of living than their parents—and there are ample supporting data. For example, in 1982, a full-size Chevy cost what the average worker made in four months, buying a home took about three years of solid work, and a family outing to a good steak house took about a day and a half of work. Although there are still the same 12 months in a year—in 1992 that Chevy "cost" 2.2 *more* months of work, the home requires over three *more* years of work, and even the steaks cost 25% more work, according to a study that was done by the New York City Department of Consumer Affairs.

And how do struggling wage-earners cope with the economics of this new math? By taking second jobs, by both spouses working—and by an unblinking focus on lower prices. When there's not enough money to cover the bills, clever ads and snazzy packaging aren't as likely to divert consumers from seeking bargains. That's why in recent years there's been such phenomenal growth of a wide variety of discount outlets and "superstores."

This brings us to a third trend, one that responds to the first two and sets the stage for a consumer revolution that is potentially as dramatic as the creation of advertising itself in the mid-1800s—electronic shopping.

As the information superhighway becomes a reality over the next couple of decades, couch-cozy consumers may be able to access essential information about goods and services with the flick of a remote or the click of a mouse. Or for a nominal fee, they'll be able to get on line, to learn which dealer has the cheapest Camaro or stereo, which repair store has drawn the fewest complaints, which bank pays the highest CD rates, which airline has the best fare—and which sports retailer has the five-speed bike you've been waiting for. The way Marvin Traub, the former chairman of Bloomingdales, sees it, "You'll have channels like Wal-Mart or Kmart; others will be more like Saks Fifth Avenue. And other channels might focus on, say, athletic equipment. So consumers will sort themselves out by their interests."

True, computer- or cable-illiterate consumers will not easily—probably ever—change their buying habits. But a younger generation, at ease using computers, are more capable of launching themselves into consumer cyberspace and using new, high-tech services, like these examples.

■ Consumers who currently have the ability to go on line can sample a whole range of products from the comfort of their home before deciding whether to buy. For example, a number of record companies will let you download samples of new recordings and some book and magazine companies allow you to read excerpts. Looking for a new car but hate showrooms? Shoppers can answer an electronic questionnaire that helps pinpoint their needs and then are offered a range of different vehicles that might suit.

■ According to John Markoff in *The New York Times* in late 1994, "First Virtual Holdings, a start-up company with powerful backing from the computer and financial services industries [announced] a new international system intended to make shopping with a Visa card from a home computer as secure and convenient as using a credit card at a shopping mall." The idea is to create an "automatic authorization system" that allows a user to shop and buy even though there is no previous relationship between buyer and seller.

■ "Smart Cards" are slowly coming of age to replace and expand on the numerous credit cards presently stuffed into our billfolds. These "electronic wallets" carry a computer microchip that is loaded with personal data and able to interact with computerized equipment. So a consumer could load it into her home computer to figure out bank balances, give it to her doctor to obtain medical records, or plug it into home or store computers to make and pay for purchases.

Aside from taking the schlepping out of shopping, the electronic superhighway will better equip consumers to make choices from the many options offered by more competitors. They'll be able to call up the information about products they're interested in and then compare the prices of vendors all over the country.

Hence, the coming consumer century. America's first century was agrarian-based; small farmers were the vertebrae in the spine of our economy. Our second was factory-based; the belching smokestack became the metaphor for production of goods, regardless of their net social costs or desirability. And soon, with the dawning of our new information-based global economy, buyers have the prospect of evening the odds with sellers.

Until that time when interactive TV and computers-as-showrooms fully arrive, *The Consumer Bible* provides the essential information—product by product and service by service—you need to talk back and fight back in the marketplace.

Mark Green
New York City, Febuary 1995

Food

CHAPTER 1

GROCERY SHOPPING

 Some Thought for Food

No matter how often you cook meals at home, whether you favor cooking from scratch or simply microwaving a frozen dinner, you must shop for food. You can save time, money, and your health *if* you learn to steer your way around the marketing traps of food shopping. From advertisements on television to the layout of supermarkets to marketing schemes, all of us are being urged constantly to spend our money on food that we—like Steve Martin in the remake of *Father of the Bride*—might be happier and healthier without.

Martin's character escapes from prewedding chaos by going to the supermarket to pick up something for dinner. He gets arrested in the bread aisle for refusing to pay for *twelve* hot dog buns when hot dogs come in packages of only *eight*. Martin rants about his theory of the mismatched frank and bun quantities:

"Some big shot over at the wiener company got together with some big shot over at the bun company and decided to rip off the American public because they think the American public is a bunch of trusting nitwits who'll pay for things they don't need rather than make a stink."

An extra bun here or there probably won't break your budget, but these and other marketing gimmicks can add up. According to the U.S. Department of Labor, the average household spends nearly $4,300 annually on food. By eating more meals at home, buying less processed food, selecting supermarket brands over nationally advertised ones, and reducing the amount of meat eaten, consumers could easily lop off a quarter of their bill—that's nearly $1,100 extra a year in the cookie jar.

There's other key advice to follow, such as never shopping when you're hungry—it invariably leads to overbuying, especially of food that can be quickly unwrapped and gobbled up. But there's also much more that everyone who eats can't afford *not* to know.

THE BASICS

Supermarket layout. Supermarket floor plans are designed to force shoppers to walk all the way to the back of the store to find what they

3

most often go in for—staple items, such as milk or bread. Typical are displays of "special" seasonal or new products, and colorful, fragrant fresh produce, tactics stores use to slow consumers down so that they'll stick around and spend more money. And supermarkets often place their bakeries near the entrance, filling the air with the mouth-watering smell of freshly baked bread and pastries.

Along the way to the rear of the store, shoppers are tempted by attractive displays at the ends of aisles where they may expect to find sale items. However, stores often stock these areas with high-profit items that *aren't* on sale. To encourage consumers to buy more products, supermarkets put related items near each other, such as ice cream toppings next to the ice cream freezer.

Furthermore, they place high-profit convenience foods, such as cans of pie filling and cake frosting, at eye level, but require shoppers to bend way down to find such staples as flour and sugar on the bottom shelf. Foods that companies advertise to children are also placed at eye level—kid's-eye level, that is. In the cereal aisle, there's a good chance you'll find shredded wheat on an upper shelf and Count Chocula down below. Finally, the checkout counter is loaded with candy, magazines, film, and batteries— items that many grocery shoppers might not need right then or could normally buy for less elsewhere, such as at a discount store. "I can resist anything except temptation," wrote Oscar Wilde in an axiom su-permarkets rely on when they appeal to unwary consumers.

Supermarket vs. national brands. Nationally advertised brands cost more than supermarket brands, mostly because manufacturers pass along the cost of expensive advertising campaigns. Americans could cut about 15% off their grocery bills by choosing supermarket and no-frills brands. That would amount to a national total of $27 billion, or about $110 per person a year.

Coupons and specials. Newspapers, store circulars, and Sunday-paper inserts are filled with promotions and coupons for food products. But unless an item meets your needs—budget-wise and nutritionally—a few cents off is really a lot of cents wasted. Store coupons usually have small print on them, requiring consumers to purchase a minimum amount of groceries for each coupon they use, and limiting the quantity of the item that each shopper may purchase.

To lure shoppers, most stores advertise "loss leaders," such as milk or eggs sold at or below cost. Once the shopper is there, stores then hope to sell them a lot of other items with high profit margins. To that end, according to *Consumer Reports,* stores spend some $450 million a year pitching their more lucrative items on mini-billboards on shopping carts, with in-store coupons, and through demonstrations with free tastings.

Warehouse buying clubs. Warehouse buying clubs have sprouted

NATURAL/ORGANIC: WHAT'S IN A NAME . . .

Neither "natural" nor "organic" has been defined by the federal government, though the United States Department of Agriculture (USDA) is working on a legal definition of organic.

Meanwhile, when you see food described as organic, look for more information on the label. In particular, look for products that are *certified* organic. Typically, certified organic food conforms to a state or independent certifying organization definition that means the food has not been treated with synthetic pesticides and that no synthetic pesticides have been used on the land where it was grown for at least three years. (Though some states mandate only *one* year.) Also, independent certifying organizations that review farming practices and authenticate food producers' records may give their seals of approval to some products.

But be wary of claims that mislead—many products that claim to be natural have ingredients that are anything but. Nestlé Quik claims to have "real chocolate flavor," but it also contains artificial flavors. Duncan Hines Moist Deluxe Butter Recipe Golden Cake Mix is labeled "no preservatives," but it does contain artificial colors, including red #40 and yellow #5, which some people are sensitive to. And Aunt Jemima Butter Lite Reduced Calorie Syrup Product boasts of "no artificial sweeteners" but has plenty of other artificial ingredients, including sorbic acid and sodium benzoate (preservatives), artificial maple flavors, and sodium hexametaphosphate.

up across the country, offering consumers who pay an annual fee of about $35 huge savings on bulk items in a no-frills setting. Clubs sell all sorts of items, from appliances and tires to jewelry and books. But before consumers join the buying frenzy, they should ask themselves a few questions: Do I have a lot of storage room in my pantry? Do I have plenty of refrigerator and freezer space to keep food fresh? Do I have a large family or friends to share bulk purchases with? Do I have the willpower to buy only those foods I'll really use?

Consumers who answer "yes" to those questions will probably save a lot of money shopping at a warehouse club—provided they keep these points in mind:

■ Unless consumers do a large amount of food shopping or plan to buy other non-food items at warehouse clubs, they should join only one club to make sure they save money beyond the cost of the membership fee.

- The warehouse atmosphere can encourage impulse purchases, so shoppers have to work hard to stick to their shopping lists.
- If consumers want to buy something that's not on their lists, they should be sure that they can store or use it before it spoils. A five-pound bag of rice is a better long-term investment than a five-pound block of Swiss cheese.
- As always, shoppers need to know prices—a retail supermarket's store-brand items may be cheaper, on a unit-price basis, than the name-brand product sold at a warehouse store.

Supermarket "member" cards. Some supermarkets give free identification or check-cashing cards that entitle shoppers to save money—provided they spend it at that store. Cashiers enter the shopper's ID code, and the register rings up special discounts on selected items, or charges the sale price, without the usually required coupon.

The trade-off is that a record of all purchases will be registered with the store and possibly shared with marketing companies. As a "reward" based on consumers' buying habits, the store or marketing firm may contact consumers or send them coupons. But when they apply for the card, consumers may have to report personal information, including their age, income level, marital status, and household size. Shoppers should discuss any privacy concerns with the store manager *before* signing up.

WHAT TO WATCH OUT FOR

Scanner Scams and the Case for Item Pricing

What if every time you went grocery shopping, you had to play *The Price Is Right* because there were no prices marked on any of the bottles, boxes, cans, or containers in the entire store? Actually, only a few states and localities require stores to individually price most items.

Nearly all prepackaged food products have bar codes, also known as universal product codes (UPC), on their labels. Those codes are made up of a grid of lines representing a 10-digit number that's read by electronic scanners at the checkout counter. The scanner identifies the product and charges whatever amount the store has programmed the scanner to charge.

But unless the product also has a price marked *on the package,* known as an "item price," shoppers need the memory of an elephant or the zeal of an investigative reporter—or both—to verify the price charged. Comparison shopping becomes very difficult, since shelf-pricing is often out-of-date and misplaced. And then keeping within a budget takes a mathematical genius—or a handy calculator.

According to a 1993 *PrimeTime Live* investigation, scanner scams are a national problem. In Riverdale County, California, local consumer inspectors found persistent errors when they checked scanners for accuracy at both supermarkets

HORROR STORY AT THE CONCESSION STAND

Until most movie theaters switched in 1994 to a more healthful popping oil, a small bag of plain popcorn contained nearly a full day's limit of saturated fat, and a large bag had nearly three days' worth—or what you'd get in six Big Macs. After word got out and moviegoers stopped buying popcorn, most theaters switched to canola or corn oil—and some even offer air-popped popcorn as well. Lightly seasoned, air-popped popcorn has one-third or less of the fat of the oil-popped variety.

Why the change? Nutrition activists at the advocacy group The Center for Science in the Public Interest exposed the sky-high saturated fat levels of roughly 70% of movie-theater popcorn, which for many years had been popped in tasty but unhealthful coconut oil—oil that is twice as high in saturated fat as beef fat or lard, and that is known to raise blood cholesterol more than any other fat or oil. Today most moviegoers can enjoy their popcorn without clogging their arteries.

and discount stores. When errors continued despite repeated warnings, the District Attorney filed suit against Kmart, Lucky's and Vons grocery stores; the firms agreed to stop overcharging after paying settlements that ran into six figures.

A 1991 survey in New York City also uncovered scanners regularly overcharging customers. One in 10 times an item was supposedly on sale, the scanner charged the regular price. For example, two Waldbaum's stores charged more than twice the sale price for Progresso minestrone soup—$1.55 instead of 69 cents; and an A&P charged $2 instead of the correct $1.34 for Welch's grape jelly, a 66-cent overcharge. In addition, when scanners made an error, it was ten times

more likely that the consumer was overcharged than undercharged. So unethical or careless stores can lure shoppers with sale prices—and then perhaps charge a higher price on that or another item. As a result of the survey, New York City enacted a strong item-pricing law.

PrimeTime Live found that after this item-pricing law went into effect in New York City, they weren't overcharged at any of the nine stores they investigated. "But in states where oversight isn't as strict," reported Sylvia Chase, "we were overcharged at one store after another. . . . Human mistakes are one thing, but we found a troubling pattern. We informed store management of overcharges at 11 stores, and found the same errors at eight of them the next day."

Advertising—
the Claim Game

Unfortunately, you should probably take health claims in food ads with, well, a grain of salt. A 1992 study by the New York City Department of Consumer Affairs found widespread deception and distortion in advertisements for a range of foods—from breakfast cereals and margarines to soups and cold cuts.

To clear up confusing and sometimes misleading health claims on food labels, Congress passed a law in 1990 requiring the Food and Drug Administration (FDA) to strengthen its food-labeling regulations. The USDA, which regulates meat and poultry, joined with the FDA in requiring new food *labels* to provide shoppers with more accurate and relevant information. But there's still a loophole—some food *advertisements* continue to make product claims that could not be made on labels.

With this inconsistency in regulatory control, the federal government is essentially encouraging consumers to hit the gas and brake pedals at the same time. The Federal Trade Commission (FTC) is supposed to make sure that advertisements are neither deceptive nor misleading, but the FTC has a spotty record of acting against such food ads. And even though the FTC embraced the *principles* of consistent rules in 1994 when the agency announced an advertising enforcement policy on health and nutrition claims, the weak policy still allows claims that the FDA and the USDA do not permit on labels. Until the FTC writes an advertising rule as stringent as the labeling rules, look to food labels—not ads—for reliable nutrition information.

> "*Only food labels, not advertisements, provide reliable, honest health information. Until the FTC makes the pitch and the package agree, savvy shoppers should trust the labels and ignore the ads.*"
>
> — BRUCE SILVERGLADE,
> Director of Legal Affairs, Center for Science in the Public Interest

Short-weighting
and Down-sizing

When the box says it contains 24 ounces but inside there are only 22, the company has short-weighted the package by almost 10%. Or when you ask the deli man for half a pound of ham and end up with a little less, owing to an inaccurate scale or to his not deducting the weight of the wrapping, that too is short-weighting. Every state, and many counties and cities, employs inspectors who check on the accuracy of packaged goods and grocery-store measuring devices, and these inspectors have cited large food companies and small independent grocers alike for short-weighting. If you find that you've been short-weighted, complain to either your grocer or the producer of the product or to your local consumer officials.

Some food manufacturers engage in deceptive "down-sizing"—selling food in packages that look and cost the same as the old ones but that really have less inside. Star Kist, for example, shrunk the contents of its tuna cans from 6.5 to 6 ounces but continued to charge the same price—which was, in effect, a quiet 7% price increase. In 1993, Beech-Nut Nutritional Corp. down-sized its Beech-Nut Stage 1 and Stage 2 baby foods from 4.5 to 4 ounces. Kal Kan Pedigree dog food is now sold in 13.25-ounce containers, 5% smaller than the former 14-ounce size. Scott Paper Company down-sized its Viva paper towels in 1988 from 84 to 77 sheets, then in 1991 to 70 sheets. None of the companies down-sized their prices to match. To fight this economic deception, keep an eye on the content disclosure, which is required by law, and use unit-pricing calculations to compare among brands.

Supermarket Promotions

In-store health claims that promote certain foods can be misleading. In May 1991, the New York City Department of Consumer Affairs uncovered an A&P program featuring heart symbols on shelf price tags beneath products that made many unhealthy foods seem healthy. Written inside the symbol was one of several claims, such as "low cholesterol," "low fat," and "low sodium." Although a heart symbol visually communicated the message that a product was effective

in combating heart disease, in fact many of these products were high in fat and thus would more likely cause than cure heart disease.

For example, heart symbols that read "low cholesterol" were found on tags under such high-fat products as Fleischmann's margarine and Skippy peanut butter, and high-fat diets can lead to heart disease. Hearts with "low sodium" were featured on displays of Hershey's Chocolate Syrup, Duncan Hines Milk Chocolate Brownie Mix, and Crisco Shortening; although their sodium content is comparatively low, these products are all high in fat and sugar. Eating them in significant quantities over time could increase the risk of heart disease. After being charged with violating the New York City Consumer Protection Law, A&P agreed to eliminate the deceptive tags and paid a fine.

THE SMARTER CONSUMER

Supermarket Strategies

The Golden Rule: Comparison shop. The first question to ask yourself is whether the store where you shop gives the best value for your dollars. It's easy to check—make a list of the items you frequently buy, then go to your usual supermarket and at least one other grocery store, and compare. Chances are you'll find a difference of a few percent on several items, which can add up to many dollars over time.

Keep a running shopping list. Jot down items you're running low on to make your shopping more efficient. Organize your list by type, grouping such items as fruits and vegetables, dairy products, meat, and poultry. You'll spend less time in the aisles thinking about what you may need or what you forgot. A list will also help you avoid impulse purchases, which are often costly and unhealthful. And following a list will help you avoid time-consuming extra shopping trips, which can really bust your budget if you opt for a convenience store where prices are high.

Check out unit prices. A unit price is the cost for a small unit of measure, such as an ounce, that's used to compare the cost of differently priced items in differently sized containers. Some states and cities require grocery stores to put tags listing unit prices on the shelves beneath items. If your supermarket offers you this calculation, you'll easily find the best buys. Otherwise, a calculator will come in handy.

Usually, but not always, the larger the container, the lower the unit price. According to Jewel Supermarket's unit price tags in Munster, Indiana, a box of twelve 1-ounce packets of instant oatmeal costs $4.12 per pound, while an 18-ounce carton of loose oatmeal costs $1.68 per pound—and a 42-ounce carton costs only $1.25 per pound.

Unit pricing also helps you to compare similar items made by different manufacturers, who often package products in slightly different sizes, making cost comparisons tricky. Buy the food that sells for the least amount per unit, unless you know that the quality is poor or that you don't need or can't store a large amount.

Beware of so-called "specials." Food displayed in a store as "featured" or "new"—such as cookies, soda pop, paper towels—aren't necessarily bargains but may simply be promotions of regularly-priced

FOOD DOLLARS AND HEALTH SENSE

You can save a bundle off of your food bill and do your health a favor by making a few simple changes. Eat at home more often—eating out is usually at least twice as expensive. Substitute supermarket brands for nationally advertised brands when you can. Eat less meat—the #1 source of saturated fat—and fewer processed foods, which are typically high in salt and sugar. Instead, eat more vegetables, fruit and grains, which provide dietary fiber, vitamins and minerals. You'll enjoy more money in your pocket and maybe fewer medical bills for heart disease, stroke, and cancer.

DIETARY GUIDELINES

The U.S. Departments of Agriculture and Health and Human Services jointly issue general dietary guide-lines for American consumers. In addition, the USDA developed a pyramid design to help consumers learn which types of food should be the foundation of a good diet and which types we should eat less of. Pregnant women and people with special dietary concerns or health problems should see their doctors to determine what's best for them. But the general guidelines are:

1. Eat a variety of foods.
2. Maintain a desirable weight.
3. Avoid too much fat, saturated fat, and cholesterol.
4. Choose foods with plenty of fiber.
5. Avoid too much sugar.
6. Use salt and other forms of sodium sparingly.
7. If you drink alcoholic beverages, do so in moderation.

items. To save money, buy only the special items you know you will use. When items you use are on sale, stock up. And don't be lured into buying something you really don't need just because a sign says "Limit Four Per Customer"—consumers tend to buy more when the stores impose a limit.

Try no frills and store brands. Remember, it's worth checking out alternatives to the priciest products. Buying items that are not nationally advertised but that are identical—or at least close enough—can save you a lot of money. At that Jewel Supermarket in Indiana, a gallon of Ocean Spray cranberry juice cocktail costs $3.59, 13% more than the Jewel Brand that costs $3.09, and 64% more than the store's no-frills Econo Buy brand that costs $2.19. Econo Buy saltines, toaster pastries, and pretzel twists, for example, cost only half the price of the national brand-name products Nabisco Premium saltines, Kellogg's Pop Tarts, and Frito Lay Rold Gold pretzels.

Staples such as no-name frozen vegetables or canned beans are often just as good as big-name products. Compare ingredients when they are listed on labels to determine how similar products are—sometimes, they're identical. Other items, such as dish soap, however, may be noticeably inferior. Still, take a chance; buy and try lower-cost foods—if you like them, your small "investment" will pay a high rate of return.

Scan the scanner. Scanners are fast, but you've got time on your side. If your store doesn't item-price, write on your shopping list the prices that you should be charged. Try to check the register as the cashier rings up your items, but a surer bet is to check the receipt against the items you bought when you get home. On your next visit, show any discrepancies to the store manager, who will at least correct your charge and—at some stores—may even give you the item for free.

Stick to food. Unless you know the prices are low, don't buy such health and beauty items as aspirin and toothpaste in grocery stores. You'll usually save money buying non-food items in a discount or drugstore.

Take rain checks. If your store doesn't have the advertised special you want, ask for a rain check. In some cities and states, you have a legal right to one. When the item is back in stock, you can buy it for the sale price.

Follow freshness dating. Some manufacturers put dates on food packages to ensure that their foods are not sold or eaten after they're stale or spoiled. Always buy food—especially dairy products—with the most distant date. After the date passes, the food may still be safe to eat, but be wary. And when in doubt, throw it out.

An "expiration" date indicates when the product should be thrown away. A "sell by" date is the last day a product should be sold. A "best if used by" date tells you when you can expect the quality to be at its peak. A "pack" date tells you, usually cryptically, when the food was packaged. (Unfortunately, many such manufacturing dates are undecipherable unless you know how to crack the codes. Don't hesitate to

write and ask the manufacturers—many will tell you.)

Enjoy fresh produce. Everyone agrees that Americans need to eat more fresh fruits and vegetables—and to avoid dangerous pesticides. Yet much of the produce we buy has been treated with pesticides and coated with wax. Follow these tips to maximize the health benefits of a diet rich in fresh fruits and vegetables while minimizing your exposure to pesticides.

■ Buy local produce in season. It's easiest to avoid pesticides and waxes when you buy recently harvested produce from local farmers—particularly if bought directly from them. Out-of-season produce may be imported and may contain pesticides that are restricted in the United States.

■ Buy produce that is organic, transitional, or grown under integrated pest management (IPM). Like organic fruits and vegetables, transitional produce may also be grown without synthetic pesticides, but on land where pesticides have been used too recently for the produce to be considered organic. To be sure, ask the grower or grocer what he or she means by "transitional."

Farmers who employ IPM minimize pesticide use through a variety of techniques, such as monitoring insect populations, using plants resistant to insects and disease, and releasing beneficial insects—like ladybugs and praying mantises—that eat pests on crops.

■ Buy unwaxed produce whenever

possible. Waxes often seal in pesticides and they can't be washed off—you have to peel the produce. According to a 1991 report by the New York State Attorney General's office, 85% of non-leafy produce sold in the United States is waxed. Some waxes are applied in a fine mist; even a peach that feels fuzzy can be sealed with wax. Ask your grocer to sell unwaxed produce.

■ Wash thoroughly or peel produce. To minimize your risk of eating pesticides on fruits and vegetables, wash all produce well in a pot of water with a drop of mild dishwashing detergent and rinse thoroughly.

Cherries, grapes, strawberries, cauliflower, green beans, lettuce, potatoes, sweet potatoes, and carrots are likely to have the highest levels of pesticide residue. Peel any non-organic fruit or vegetable with an obvious wax coating; discard the outer leaves of leafy vegetables such as cabbage and lettuce and the leaves on celery; and don't worry about wax on produce you peel anyway, such as bananas, melons, winter squash, and citrus fruit.

Seek out alternative grocery stores. If you're unhappy with the supermarkets near you—and even if you're not—look into what other options you have. Farmers' markets, specialty grocery stores, and quality butchers sell assortments of food you may not see even at the largest supermarkets: freshly-picked produce, ethnic items, organically grown foods, and high-quality meat, poultry, and fish. Prices may be competitive, or you may find

that the products are worth the extra money. Also, check out whether there's a food cooperative nearby. Co-ops sometimes offer members great prices and hard-to-find items in exchange for dues, labor, or both.

Read food labels. Why? To help choose foods that make up a healthful diet and reduce your risk of the leading killer diseases. For example, too much saturated fat and cholesterol raises blood cholesterol, a risk factor for heart disease. Diets rich in fiber and low in fat have been linked to a reduced risk of cancer. And too much sodium can contribute to high blood pressure, a risk factor for both heart attack and stroke.

Thanks to the revised nutrition label law, making healthy food choices has never been easier. Nearly every food sold in grocery stores must have a nutrition label and an ingredients list. And words such as "low fat" and "lite" can only be used if they describe a food that meets legal standards set by the federal government.

Decode descriptives. Here are the established definitions for common words found on food labels. The words all pertain to one serving of the food. Key to understanding the terms is the concept of *daily values*, which was created by the FDA to provide a simplified interpretation of what a person eating a 2,000-calories-per-day diet should ideally aim for. Daily values set maximum limits for fat and cholesterol, and minimum goals for essential vitamins and nutrients.

DAILY VALUES

To help consumers use food labels to plan a healthy diet, the FDA established a new term, *daily value*. These DV's are not exactly recommended intakes—use them as reference points for "average" adult diets.

- Daily values are based on a 2,000-calories-a-day diet for adults and children over four years old for fat, saturated fat, cholesterol, total carbohydrates, fiber, sodium, and potassium.
- The daily value for protein does not apply to certain populations for whom the government has established the following daily intakes: 16 grams for children one to four years old; 14 grams for infants under one year old; 60 grams for pregnant women; and 65 grams for nursing mothers.
- Daily values for all other nutrients are based on the National Academy of Sciences' Recommended Dietary Allowances.

Food Component/ Nutrient	Daily Value
Fat	65 g
Saturated fat	20 g
Cholesterol	300 mg
Total carbohydrate	300 g
Fiber	25 g
Sodium	2,400 mg
Potassium	3,500 mg
Protein	50 g
Vitamin A	5,000 IU
Vitamin C	60 mg
Thiamin	1.5 mg
Riboflavin	1.7 mg
Niacin	20 mg
Calcium	1 g
Iron	18 mg
Vitamin D	400 IU
Vitamin E	30 IU
Vitamin B6	2 mg
Folic acid	0.4 mg
Vitamin B12	6 mcg
Phosphorus	1 g
Iodine	150 mcg
Magnesium	400 mg
Zinc	15 mg
Copper	2 mg
Biotin	0.3 mg
Pantothenic acid	10 mg

Source: *FDA Consumer*, May 1993.

- *Free.* These foods can contain only a trivial amount of the nutrient. For example, "fat-free" and "sugar-free" foods can contain no more than a half-gram per serving; "calorie-free" means fewer than 5 calories per serving.
- *Low.* Foods with this term can be eaten frequently without exceeding the daily values. "Low fat" has

3 grams of fat or less; "low saturated fat" has 1 gram or less; "low sodium" has less than 140 mg; "very low sodium" has less than 20 mg; "low cholesterol" has less than 20 mg cholesterol; and "low calorie" has 40 calories or less per serving.

■ *Lean* and *extra lean*. Used to describe the fat content of cheese, meat, poultry, and seafood. "Lean" means less than 10 grams fat, less than 4 grams saturated fat, and less than 95 mg cholesterol per serving; while "extra lean" means less than 5 grams fat, less than 2 grams saturated fat, and less than 95 mg cholesterol.

■ *High.* Used when foods contain 20% or more of a daily value of a nutrient, as in "High fiber."

■ *Reduced* and *less.* Generally, these foods have 25% less of a nutrient or calories than a comparable reference food; examples include "reduced-calorie salad dressing" or "less fat."

■ *Light.* Basically, either one-third fewer calories or no more than one-half the fat (or no more than one-half the sodium) of the reference food. If "light" refers to texture or color, the label must say so, as in "light brown sugar" or "light and fluffy."

■ *More.* These foods contain at least 10% more of the daily value of a nutrient than the reference food does, as in "more iron."

Understand the health claims. The government allows health claims on labels in instances when it has determined that the scientific community is in agreement on the relationship between particular nutrients and disease. Some examples:

■ To make health claims about fat and heart disease, foods must be low in fat, saturated fat, and cholesterol.

■ Food products that make favorable health claims regarding blood pressure and sodium must be low in sodium.

■ To make claims about being cancer-fighting, foods must be low in fat and a good source, without fortification, of at least one of the following: dietary fiber or vitamins A or C.

■ To make favorable health claims pertaining to heart disease, foods must be low in fat, saturated fat, and cholesterol *and* contain at least six-tenths gram soluble fiber, without fortification.

Make the grade. The grading system for produce, dairy products, meat, and poultry does *not* refer to nutritional quality. The voluntary grading information relates to any of the following characteristics: size, uniformity, smoothness, texture, and appearance. In the case of milk and dairy products, Grade A refers to the level of sanitary processing standards.

Ingredient listings. Federal law requires food manufacturers to list ingredients in descending order of predominance by weight. So, the earlier an ingredient is listed, the more of it is in the food.

Since the FDA improved its requirements, ingredient listings have become more common and

MAKING SENSE OF NUTRITION FACTS

Serving size. *If you plan to eat the amount listed as the serving size, then simply read the rest of the information. If you eat twice the amount, double all the rest of the information, including calories, fat, and vitamins.*

Calories. *Generally, women, the elderly, and less active people need fewer calories to maintain their weight than men, younger adults, and active folks. A 5'4", 138-pound active woman needs about 2,200 calories daily, while a 5'10", 174-pound active man needs about 2,900 calories.*

Calories from fat. *Keep it low. Each gram of fat equals 9 calories. You can multiply the grams of fat in a food by 9 and divide the total fat calories into the total calories to stay below the maximum of 30% recommended by the federal government—or better yet, the 20% many health advocates advise.*

Total fat. *Most Americans eat too much fat, which contributes to obesity and disease. Recommended maximum **total fat** intake for a 2,000-calorie-a-day diet is 65 grams, of which no more than 20 grams should be saturated fat. Saturated fat is the worst kind of fat, since it can raise your blood cholesterol level. Saturated fats—butter, lard, coconut oil, etc.—are solid at room temperature; better-for-you fats like olive, corn, and canola oils are liquid.*

Cholesterol. *Found only in animal products, such as meat, poultry, fish, dairy products, and eggs. Too much contributes to heart disease; try not to eat more than 300 mg a day.*

Sodium. *Another excess in most people's diets. Keep your intake below 2,400 mg a day. Eating too much salt can lead to high blood pressure.*

Total carbohydrate. *The basis of a sound diet is plenty of carbohydrates, such as whole grains, bread, potatoes, fruits, and vegetables. But when you scan for the number of "total carbohydrate," beware—you wouldn't want most of your "carbs" to come from sugars. Read both the total grams of carbohydrates and the grams of sugar. Also, check the dietary fiber count—an average goal is at least 25 g a day. Aim for 11.5 g per 1,000 calories. Eating adequate amounts of fiber can reduce your risk of heart disease and cancer.*

Protein. *Chances are you eat a lot more protein than you need. Unless you eat a very restricted diet, don't worry about getting enough.*

Vitamins and minerals. *Eat a variety of foods to get enough of what you need. Supplement pills and powders can't compensate for a poor diet.*

Daily values. *Daily values are an interpretation of what levels of nutrients a person eating 2,000 calories a day should aim for. Use the daily values as a guide to figure out if a food is a good—or bad—source of a nutrient. Aim for low daily values for fat, saturated fat, cholesterol and sodium. Choose high daily values for total carbohydrate, dietary fiber, vitamins, and minerals.*

Nutrition Facts

Serving Size 1 cup (228g)
Servings Per Container 2

Amount Per Serving

Calories 260   Calories from Fat 120

	% Daily Value*
Total Fat 13g	**20 %**
Saturated Fat 5g	**25 %**
Cholesterol 30mg	**10 %**
Sodium 660 mg	**28 %**
Total Carbohydrate 31g	**10 %**
Dietary Fiber 0g	**0 %**
Sugars 5g	
Protein 5g	

Vitamin A 4%	•	Vitamin C 2%
Calcium 15%	•	Iron 4%

*Percent Daily Values are based on a 2,000 calorie diet. Your daily values may be higher or lower depending on your calorie needs:

	Calories:	2,000	2,500
Total Fat	Less than	65g	80g
Sat Fat	Less than	20g	25g
Cholesterol	Less than	300mg	300mg
Sodium	Less than	2,400mg	2,400mg
Total Carbohydrate		300g	375g
Dietary Fiber		25g	30g

Calories per gram:
Fat 9 • Carbohydrate 4 • Protein 4

GOOD FATS, BAD FATS

Switching from butter to margarine may not be the health bargain it was once made out to be. In 1994, Harvard researchers reported that margarine and other foods with hydrogenated vegetable oils that contain trans fatty acids could actually be *worse* for you than the saturated fat in butter and meat. Trans fatty acids are formed when more healthful liquid vegetable oils are processed to make them solid at room temperature.

Diets high in trans fatty acids may be responsible for 30,000 heart disease deaths in the United States each year. What should you do? Try to accustom your taste buds to food with less fat of any kind, and when you do eat fat, stick to healthier fats, ones that are liquid at room temperature, such as olive, canola, or corn oil.

more thorough. Many foods that were previously exempt must now disclose their contents. Certified Food, Drug and Cosmetic (FD&C) color additives must be listed by name (such as FD&C blue #1). And to help consumers who cannot easily digest dairy products, a milk derivative called caseinate must be listed on foods claiming to be non-dairy, such as coffee lighteners.

Serving sizes. The FDA has established uniform serving sizes that more nearly approximate the portions people eat—instead of the Lilliputian serving sizes that manufacturers cited in order to make their food look low-calorie and low-fat. Uniform serving sizes also make product comparisons easier. Another bonus of uniformity: Health claims and nutrient descriptions are more reliable.

How to Complain

Return spoiled food or any product you believe is short-weighted or expired to the store manager. In addition, you may want to report short-weighting and recurrent scanner overcharges to your state or local weights-and-measures department (sometimes called an agriculture, a markets, or a consumer-affairs department).

Report packaged food that is contaminated or spoiled to your local FDA office. You'll need as much of the packaging as possible, since the FDA requires certain coded information. A letter to the company is also a good idea. Products inspected by the USDA include eggs, meat, and poultry. Report any problems to the USDA office nearest you. Check the government office listing in your telephone book to find your local branch office.

A leading advocate for good nutrition and health is the Center for Science in the Public Interest (CSPI), which publishes *Nutrition Action Healthletter*, a consumer-friendly newsletter filled with food facts, research updates, practical advice, product reviews, and recipes. Improving on the USDA food pyramid, which is really a triangle, CSPI produced a three-dimensional version that separates food into three categories: those suitable for eating anytime, sometimes, and seldom. To order a CSPI pyramid or to subscribe to the newsletter, write to CSPI at 1875 Connecticut Avenue, NW, Suite 300, Washington, DC 20009-5728, or call (202) 332-9110.

Public Voice for Food and Health Policy, a research and advocacy organization, promotes seafood safety, sustainable agriculture, pesticide reduction, healthier school lunches, and consumer education. Top chefs from around the country formed Chefs Helping to Enhance Food Safety (CHEFS) to work with Public Voice on critical food-safety issues. For free tips on seafood safety, a booklet on nutrition labeling, or a list of publications, send a self-addressed, stamped envelope to Public Voice at 1001 Connecticut Avenue, NW, Suite 522, Washington, DC 20036, or call (202) 659-5930.

For a free brochure on waxes used on fresh produce, *A Consumer Guide to Waxes on Fruits and Vegetables: Safer Choices for a Healthful Diet*, send a self-addressed, stamped envelope to the New York City Department of Consumer Affairs, 42 Broadway, New York, NY 10004.

To learn how to protect yourself against pesticides, bacteria, and other hidden hazards in food, read *Safe Food:*

Eating Wisely in a Risky World, by Michael F. Jacobson, PhD, Lisa Y. Lefferts, and Anne Witte Garland (Living Planet Press: Los Angeles, 1991).

The FDA published a *Consumer* magazine special issue on food labeling. To order a copy, write to FDA (HFI-40), 5600 Fishers Lane, Rock-ville, MD 20857, or call (301) 443-3220. Call or write to your nearest FDA office for a wide range of free brochures on labeling, nutrition, and food safety.

The FDA/USDA Food Labeling Education Information Center runs a database of educational activities and can put you in touch with organizations that produce materials on food labeling. Write to Food and Information Center/National Agricultural Library, Room 304, 10301 Baltimore Blvd., Beltsville, MD 20705-2351, or call (301) 504-5719. Ask about the National Agricultural Library's 24-hour electronic bulletin board, the Agricultural Library Forum.

Direct your questions about the relationship between nutrition and cancer to the American Institute for Cancer Research Nutrition Hot Line, which operates Monday through Thursday from 9 am to 10 pm EST, and Fridays from 9 am to 6 pm: (800) 843-8114. Ask for a list of free brochures.

The American Dietetic Association sponsors the National Center for Nutrition and Dietetics Consumer Nutrition Hot Line, where registered dietitians answer calls Monday through Friday, 9 AM to 4 PM CST, and you can listen to recorded messages in English or Spanish from 8 AM to 8 PM: (800) 366-1655.

Continued on next page

HELP *continued from previous page*

■ **The USDA Meat and Poultry Hot** Line operates Monday through Friday from 10 AM to 4 PM EST, with extended hours in the days before Thanksgiving: (800) 535-4555. Ask about free USDA brochures.

■ **For information and helpful advice** on good nutrition, equipping an efficient kitchen, and cooking healthful meals, read *Jane Brody's Good Food Book*, by Jane E. Brody (New York: Bantam Books, 1985).

■ **To learn the location of the food** co-operative nearest you, call the Co-op News Network at (207) 948-6161. For a directory of over 300 food co-ops across the country, send $7 to the Network at Box 153, Unity, Maine 04988. Get information on setting up a grocery co-op by writing to the National Co-operative Business Association, 1401 New York Avenue NW, Suite 1100, Washington, DC 20005, or by calling (800) 636-NCBA.

■ **Read what parents must know** about their children's diets and learn ways to get your kids to eat more healthfully in *What Are We Feeding Our Kids?*, by Michael F. Jacobson, PhD, and Bruce Maxwell, (New York: Workman, 1994).

■ **Learn how to select and store** food for maximum enjoyment, value, and safety in *Keeping Food Fresh*, by Janet Bailey (New York: Harper & Row, 1989).

■ **Find answers to nearly every nutri-** tion question in *The Mount Sinai School of Medicine Complete Book of Nutrition*, edited by Victor Herbert, MD, FACP and Genell J. Subak-Sharpe, MS (New York: St. Martin's Press, 1990).

CHAPTER 2

FAST-FOOD OUTLETS

What Are You Getting Into and What's Getting Into You?

There was a time when most of the selection in fast-food restaurants would have warranted a Surgeon General's warning that "This Food May Be Hazardous to Your Health." In fact, some foods might deserve such a warning today—Jack in the Box sells a sandwich it calls the Ultimate Cheeseburger, which contains a whopping 69 grams of fat. That's more fat than most people should eat in an entire day.

But most fast-food chains are now adding at least a few healthier choices to their menus. Wendy's offers one of the best salad bars around; KFC sells rotisserie-roasted chicken; and McDonald's offers the McLean Deluxe, which has half the fat of its regular burgers. And along with their traditional fast-food fare, many chains now also offer salads, baked potatoes, fruit, reduced-calorie dressings, low-fat milk, and grilled chicken sandwiches.

Of course, fast-food places aren't selling these lower fat foods simply to keep your arteries clearer—many Americans are demanding more healthful food. According to a National Restaurant Association survey, nearly half of adults make a point of ordering foods that are nutritious. A diet-conscious member of a family or group of friends may veto a restaurant that doesn't offer at least some healthful choices. So fast-food restaurants have to offer more nutritious food to ensure that customers keep coming back.

Even so, it's virtually impossible to tell the good choices from the bad. Bet you didn't know that a single packet of salad dressing can have as much fat as a hamburger and fries. Thus, here are some fast food facts to digest.

> "*Choosing healthy fast foods is like walking through a mine field—be careful. Most are loaded with fat, salt, and sugar, which cause everything from obesity to heart attacks.*"
> —MICHAEL F. JACOBSON, coauthor of the *Fast-Food Guide*

THE BASICS

The $86-billion-a-year fast-food industry feeds a growing portion of the American appetite. About 20% of us eat at fast-food restaurants each day. And the U.S. Department of Agriculture (USDA) reports that half of every dollar we spend on restaurant food we spend on fast food. That adds up to an average of $340 a year—or almost a dollar a day—on fast food.

Despite some laudable recent efforts, fast food still generally tends to be high in calories, fat, cholesterol, and sodium, all of which promote obesity, heart disease, high blood pressure, and cancer.

Experts continue to focus on the relationship between diet and health and have repeatedly shown that cutting back on fat and salt can lower the risk of getting or dying from these conditions. Typically, fast-food meals are loaded with fat and sodium, but few diners realize that a fish or chicken sandwich can be worse than a burger. Without accessible, readable nutrition facts, consumers can't make healthful choices, such as:

■ Opting for a sourdough roll or breadstick (2 or 3 fat grams) instead of cornbread (13 fat grams) or a biscuit (12 grams) at KFC.
■ Having a grilled chicken breast sandwich (with 4 grams of fat), rather than a chunky chicken salad sandwich (43 fat grams) at Boston Chicken.
■ Holding off on the bacon and cheese potato topping (with 43 grams of fat) at Carl's Jr.
■ Choosing Arby's Old Fashioned Chicken Noodle Soup (2 fat grams), rather than Boston Clam Chowder (10 grams) or Wisconsin Cheese Soup (18 grams).

A Numbers Game?

In 1993, *Consumer Reports* analyzed samples of fast foods to test the accuracy of the nutrition information supplied by the companies in brochures and on posters. For the most part, the companies' numbers added up. However, some chicken salads contained several more grams of fat than the companies claimed, probably because of variations in portion size or the amount of cheese. You can avoid the extra fat by removing some or all of the cheese to make sure you don't get more fat than you want.

Consumer Reports also found that a few of the milk shakes contained more saturated fat—the kind that raises blood cholesterol levels—than the nutrition brochures state. Arby's shakes had *twice* the amount of saturated fat as the company claimed.

Kids' Meals

Kids eat fast food four out of every five times they eat out. These meals are popular because they are quick and cheap and because fast-food chains spend millions of dollars advertising on Saturday-morning television and in collaboration with movie studios and toy makers. Free dolls, toys, and colorful cups make kids want to "collect the entire set." Plus, busi-

21

BIG FATS: THE 20 MOST FATTY FAST FOODS

Chain	Food	Grams of Fat
Jack-in-the-Box	*Ultimate Cheeseburger*	*69 g*
Burger King	*Double Whopper Sandwich with Cheese*	*63 g*
Carl's Jr.	*Double Western Bacon Cheeseburger*	*63 g*
Taco Bell	*Taco Salad*	*61 g*
Burger King	*Double Whopper Sandwich*	*55 g*
Carl's Jr.	*Super Star Hamburger*	*53 g*
Hardee's	*Frisco Burger*	*50 g*
Jack-in-the-Box	*Grilled Sourdough Burger*	*50 g*
Dairy Queen/Brazier	*DQ Homestyle Ultimate Burger*	*47 g*
Burger King	*Whopper Sandwich with Cheese*	*46 g*
Jack-in-the-Box	*Bacon Bacon Cheeseburger*	*45 g*
Boston Chicken	*Chunky Chicken Salad Sandwich*	*43 g*
Burger King	*BK Big Fish Sandwich*	*43 g*
Carl's Jr.	*Bacon & Cheese Potato*	*43 g*
Burger King	*Chicken Sandwich*	*42 g*
Jack-in-the-Box	*Chicken Supreme Sandwich*	*42 g*
Jack-in-the-Box	*Mini Chimichangas, six pieces*	*42 g*
Jack-in-the-Box	*Egg Rolls, five pieces*	*41 g*
Jack-in-the-Box	*Jumbo Jack Burger with Cheese*	*40 g*
Arby's	*Italian Sub Sandwich*	*39 g*

ness from kids means business from parents, too.

Like adults, kids should eat less fat and salt and fewer calories than they typically do. Unfortunately, kids' fast-food meals aren't made up of the most healthful offerings. If you buy your children fast-food kids' meals, try to switch the soft drink for fruit juice, milk, or low-fat milk. At least that way they will get some extra vitamins and minerals.

Information, Please

Since the government advises Americans to eat less fat and

sodium, consumers need basic information about what's in the food they eat in order to make wise choices about their dollars and their health. A few fast-food restaurant chains, including McDonald's, Burger King, and Wendy's, have nutrition information available at the counter, in brochures, and on posters. But—except for Burger King's clearer posters—it is usually too difficult to decipher without a magnifying glass and a master's degree in nutrition.

Under a new federal law, words such as "light" and "low fat" on menu boards must meet the same strict federal standards that apply to packaged food. (See "Grocery Shopping," page 13, for the definitions of these and other terms.)

WHAT TO WATCH OUT FOR

If it's fried, it's fatty. Just because it's fish or chicken doesn't mean it's better than a burger. A McDonald's Filet-O-Fish sandwich has 18 grams of fat—twice as much fat as a hamburger with 9 grams, and nearly as much as a Quarter Pounder, which has 20 grams of fat. Remember that fried food, no matter what kind, is bound to be loaded with fat.

Extra crispy equals extra fatty. At KFC, an Extra Tasty Crispy thigh is loaded with 29 grams of fat and 380 calories, compared with an Original Recipe thigh, which has 21 grams of fat and 287 calories. Choosing the Original Recipe saves

the savvy diner 8 fat grams. But rest assured, neither thigh is a fat "bargain"—each derives nearly 70% of its calories from fat.

Hold the dressing. Even if you opt for a garden salad, the dressing could turn it into a fat mine.

There aren't many sure bets. Although chunky chicken salads are good choices at Burger King and McDonald's, where they have only 4 fat grams, the chunky chicken salad at Boston Chicken has ten times as much fat. And even though corn on the cob at Popeye's has only 3 fat grams, at KFC it has 12 grams. But KFC offers a decent red beans and rice side dish with 3 fat grams, while Popeye's version has 17 fat grams. Your best bet is to read each restaurant's nutrition information (if they have it) before you place your order.

Salt watchers beware. Even fast food with reduced fat and calories usually contain high levels of sodium. If you're cutting down on sodium, you may have to cut out fast food altogether. Except for plain vegetable salads, nearly every fast food is high in salt.

Even though fast-food restaurants have improved their menus, you'll still find plenty of artery-

CALCULATING YOUR FAT INTAKE

The Food and Drug Administration (FDA) advises Americans to limit their fat intake to fewer than 30% of their daily calories. "Average" adults eat 2,000 calories a day, and each gram of fat yields 9 calories, so a limit of 65 grams of fat a day (about 600 calories) is sensible. Many health experts believe that 20% fat—or about 44 grams—is a better ceiling. (See "Grocery Shopping," page 3, for more information on fat and calories.)

To calculate the proportion of fat calories in food, multiply the number of fat grams times 9 (for 9 calories in each fat gram) and divide that number into the total calories. For example, a 320-calorie Dairy Queen chili dog gets 53% of its calories from fat (19 fat grams X 9 calories/gram = 171, and 171 ÷ 320 calories = 53%)—nearly *double* the recommended guideline.

choking double-burgers with bacon and cheese, and extra-crispy (read: extra-fatty) fried chicken. The trick to eating well at fast-food restaurants is knowing how to spot the healthiest food, even when the chains give you little, if any, nutrition information.

Follow these general guidelines to make sure you eat meals that fit into the recommended lower fat diet you and your family should strive for.

■ Seek out innovative fast-food restaurants that feature more healthful food, such as grilled, skinless chicken and baked fish.
■ As a rule, smaller is always better. Don't order anything described with superlatives, such as "super," "extra," "grande," "big," "jumbo," "double," or "supreme."
■ Order baked, roasted, or broiled chicken if it's offered. Several fast-food chicken restaurants now sell rotisserie-roasted chicken. To avoid too much fat and salt in fried chicken, your best bet is to peel off and discard the fried coating as well as the skin.
■ Look for leaner versions of your favorites. Burger junkies might like McDonald's McLean Deluxe, a lower fat burger made with a seaweed extract called carrageenan. Compared to a typical McDonald's burger with 20% fat, the McLean Deluxe is about 9% fat.
■ If you eat a sandwich, skip the sauce, cheese, and mayonnaise. Instead of those high-calorie toppers, ask for extra lettuce, tomatoes, and onions to add flavor, moisture, and vitamins and minerals, too.
■ Choose side salads and plain baked potatoes instead of french fries and onion rings. Opt for a baked potato *only* if you will eat it without sour cream, cheese, and bacon.
■ Skip the saltiest and fattiest

LIGHTER FARE: THE 20 LEAST FATTY FAST FOODS

Side salads, most garden salads without dressing, and baked potatoes without toppings have three fat grams or less, and they're offered at many fast-food restaurants, including Arby's, Burger King, Carl's Jr., Dairy Queen/Brazier, Hardee's, Jack-in-the-Box, KFC, McDonald's, and Wendy's. In addition, here are some of the best offerings:

Chain	Food	Grams of Fat
Boston Chicken	Fruit salad side dish (seasonal)	0 g
Boston Chicken	Steamed vegetables side dish	0 g
Hardee's	Mashed potatoes and gravy side	0 g
KFC	Garden rice side dish	1 g
KFC	Green beans side dish	1 g
KFC	Mashed potatoes with gravy side dish	1 g
Arby's	Old-Fashioned Chicken Noodle Soup	2 g
Jack-in-the-Box	Chicken Teriyaki Bowl	2 g
KFC	BBQ Baked Beans side dish	2 g
KFC	Mean Greens side dish	2 g
Boston Chicken	Chicken Soup	3 g
Church's	Potatoes & Gravy	3 g
Jack-in-the-Box	Beef Teriyaki Bowl	3 g
KFC	Red Beans & Rice side dish	3 g
Popeye's	Corn on the cob	3 g
Arby's	LumberJack Mixed Vegetable Soup	4 g
Boston Chicken	Chicken breast sandwich without mayonnaise or mustard	4 g
Boston Chicken	White meat chicken quarter without skin and without wing	4 g
Dairy Queen/Brazier	BBQ Beef Sandwich	4 g
KFC	Vegetable Medley Salad side dish	4 g

25

BEWARE OF TRANS FATS

By 1990, most fast-food restaurants had switched from cholesterol-laden animal fats (such as beef tallow) to vegetable-based fats. That means that fried fast foods are now lower in *saturated* fats and cholesterol than they used to be. But fried foods are still laden with fat—including a kind called "trans fatty acids" that may raise your blood cholesterol level as much as saturated fats do.

In 1993, the Center for Science in the Public Interest tested several fast foods and found that some chains that boast of using "100% vegetable oil" use vegetable *shortening*, which is high in trans fatty acids. According to the group's tests:

- A large order of Burger King fries has more cholesterol-raising fat than a Whopper.
- Two plain Dunkin Donuts contain as much cholesterol-raising fat as most people should eat in an entire day.

items at salad bars, which are often filled with as many nutritionally poor choices as good ones. Avoid the bacon bits, sunflower seeds, mayonnaise-based salads, croutons, and cheese, and load up instead on low-fat bean salads in vinaigrette dressing, and fresh, sliced vegetables and fruit. Tomatoes, carrots, cauliflower, and such dark green vegetables as spinach and broccoli pack the most nutrients.

- When you top your salad, use very little dressing. A single packet of McDonald's Bleu Cheese or Ranch dressing turns an otherwise healthful salad into the fatty equivalent of a cheeseburger and a medium order of fries. Better yet, use a small amount of *lower fat* or *lower calorie* dressing. For example, McDonald's Lite Vinaigrette Dressing has only $1/17$ the amount of fat as the Bleu Cheese or Ranch.
- Instead of soft drinks—the single biggest source of sugar in our diets—wash down your meal with fruit juice, plain carbonated water from the soda spigots, low-fat or skim milk, or water. You'll avoid empty calories—a Burger King medium Sprite (18 ounces) has 14 teaspoons of sugar. Diet drinks don't offer any nutrients and are dangerous to people who can't metabolize the artificial sweetener properly.
- If you want a shake or dessert, look for a skinny alternative to a high-fat milk shake or a piece of fried pie. Check the salad bar for fresh fruit or canned fruit in its own juice, not sugary syrup. Wendy's salad bars usually have a good selection. McDonald's makes shakes and sundaes with low-fat frozen yogurt. A McDonald's vanilla shake has 5 grams of fat and 310 calories, compared to a Dairy Queen vanilla shake with 14 grams of fat and 520 calories.

Breakfast of Champions

Many fast-food outlets have tapped into Americans' desire for a morning meal on the run. If you're a fast-food eater who wants to start your day on a firm nutritional footing, it's a challenge—but not impossible. If you're careful, you can stay within the guidelines for fat, cholesterol, and sodium—and you may even take in some valuable nutrients, such as calcium and fiber. (See "Grocery Shopping," page 11, for more on dietary guidelines.)

■ Don't start your day with any version of the egg, cheese, and sausage sandwich. Whether this concoction is served up on an English muffin, a croissant, or a biscuit, it's almost always the most high-fat, cholesterol-laden, sodium-soaked choice on the menu.

■ To cut back on fat and cholesterol, order a simpler, smaller sandwich with eggs only. Ask for an English muffin or bagel—they have much less fat than biscuits and croissants.

■ Better yet, opt for pancakes. You'll get plenty of complex carbohydrates, the foundation of a sound diet. Skip the butter or margarine, and go easy on the syrup, which is high in calories.

■ Avoid scrambled egg platters—they're loaded with cholesterol and fat, especially when they come with fried potatoes and sausage.

■ Your food probably already contains plenty of butter or margarine—so don't add more. Instead, use jam or jelly—a fat-free, lower-calorie choice.

■ Choosing cold cereal and low-fat milk will also start your day off on solid nutritional ground.

■ Orange juice and low-fat milk are the best ways to wash down your meal and get valuable nutrients, to boot.

For more nutrition information about the fast food you eat, consult:

■ *The Fast-Food Guide*, **2nd Edition,** Michael F. Jacobson, PhD, and Sarah Fritschner, (Workman, 1991).

■ *Consumer Reports*, **"Can Fast** Food be Good Food?" August 1994.

■ *Consumer Reports*, **"Fast Food** Breakfasts: Good Enough to Eat?" September 1991.

■ *Consumer Reports*, **"Fast Food for** Fat Watchers," September 1993.

CHAPTER 3

WATER

Should You Be Worried About Yours?

Water, water everywhere, but is it safe to drink? Labels incorporating images of protected mountain springs and adjectives like "pure" and "natural" would have you believe that bottled water is somehow superior to regular old tap water. In most cases it isn't. And some unscrupulous sellers of home water treatment systems go so far as to come into your home to carry out sham water tests to scare you into believing you need expensive equipment to protect your family from contaminated drinking water. You probably don't.

Marketing practices like these combined with scary news reports like those about the contamination of Milwaukee's municipal water supply in early 1993 and downtown New York City's later that same year have challenged people's faith in what comes out of the faucet. The slightest brackish color, fishy smell, or funny taste to the water makes people worry.

THE BASICS

You can probably trust your tap, but don't do so blindly. Public water supplies are supposed to meet stringent standards of purity that were laid out in the Safe Drinking Water Act of 1974. The Environmental Protection Agency (EPA) enforces the law and has set maximum levels for more than 100 possible chemical, bacteriological, radiological, and physical contaminants, including lead, mercury, and benzene. To meet the law's requirements, public water supplies must be either clean to start with or purified to register within the allowable range, and municipalities generally do a good job of maintaining standards. However, the EPA's safe drinking water program has been said to be "approaching a state of disrepair" by the General Accounting Office, the main investigative arm of Congress.

While most people's worries are unfounded, some are right to be concerned about their drinking water, particularly those with immune system disorders as they may be especially vulnerable to contaminants, even at low levels. The pressures of development threaten the purity of once protected water sources; contaminants can seep into the water as it courses through the pipes or sits waiting for you to turn on the tap; and water drawn from private wells may not be subject to any state requirements for treatment and testing. The Natural Resources Defense Council documented 250,000 violations, major and minor, of the Safe Drinking Water Act in 1991 and 1992, by 43% of the nation's water systems. And a 1994 study by Ronnie Levin, the EPA chief of water safety, came to the conservative conclusion that 2 million people a year get infectious diseases from drinking water—which manifest themselves as common symptoms including uncomfortable cramps, abdominal pains, diarrhea, and vomiting. "Many outbreaks are not identified as outbreaks," she told National Public Radio. "We learned about the Milwaukee outbreak of cryptosporidiosis from drugstores there, which started running out of [diarrhea remedies] Kaopectate and Immodium."

Thousands of contaminants have been identified as unsafe—heavy metals (such as mercury and lead), radon, microbes, and industrial and agricultural pollution, to name a few. Of these contaminants, the most common and most worrisome are radon and lead.

Radon. This naturally occurring radioactive gas is often found in drinking water in liquid form, where it poses no health risk. However, radon easily converts to its potentially dangerous gaseous form, and can lead to lung cancer when excessive amounts are inhaled. If you think you may have a radon problem, ventilating the bathroom or laundry area may be all you need to do to reduce radon risk. If that's not practical you'll want to treat your water with a carbon unit or aerator, most often installed in the basement.

Lead. This toxic heavy metal is now known to be both more widely present in water and more toxic than it was once believed. Drinking water accounts for 20% of our lead exposure, according to the EPA.

Lead exposure can affect every system in the body and may contribute to high blood pressure, reproductive complications, and loss of neuromuscular control in adults. However, infants, children, and pregnant women's fetuses are most vulnerable to lead poisoning. A small dose of lead that would have little effect on an adult is readily absorbed by a fetus or a young child and can impair their mental and physical development. Fetuses exposed to low levels of lead in the mother's blood may also suffer low birth weight. Naturally, infant formula that must be mixed with tap water presents a hidden risk to infants. And even tiny amounts of lead in infants' and children's systems can affect their ability to learn; in extreme cases, lead poisoning can cause death. The

> "*With bottled water all you're paying for is a lot of marketing, a lot of hype.*"
>
> —Ian Michaels,
> New York City Department of
> Environmental Protection

blood lead level of children at age two directly correlates to their intelligence at ten, according to Dr. Herbert L. Needleman of the University of Pittsburgh and Dr. David Bellinger of Harvard Medical School, who have been periodically testing the blood lead levels and abilities of a group of 200 middle-class Boston children born between 1979 and 1981. Elevated blood lead levels in children are also associated with the incidence of attention deficit disorder and hyperactivity.

Are You Worried About Your Water?

Don't panic or make any rash purchases! First, you need to collect some information.

To find out what's in your water, request a copy of your utility company's annual water quality report. This will give you the average levels of any pollutants in the municipal water supply as well as the highest levels of any pollutants detected during the previous year.

Testing the water. Water safety problems, for the most part, escape amateur detection by sight, taste, or smell. Common complaints about unpleasant colors or tastes may be caused by such non-toxic substances as rust or sediment. Lead, however, is tasteless, colorless, and odorless—and toxic. So is gaseous radon, which invisibly escapes from its benign form, in water, into the air in people's homes when they shower, wash dishes, or run a washing machine.

The only reliable way to find out whether you should be worried about your water is to test it. Since contaminants can enter the water supply anywhere along the route from the municipal source, to your street, and your faucet, you will have to check every tap individually to fully understand what's in your water.

To start with, you might try the Nordic Ware Water Test Kit, available for about $8 at a hardware store. (A Nordic Ware mail-in test for lead costs an additional $6.) It cannot test for most toxic pollutants, such as solvents or pesticides, but *Consumer Reports* found it easy to use and accurate enough for home use.

Another alternative is a state-certified independent water testing company: Get a list from your water utility company or look in the Yellow Pages under "laboratories" or "testing." (You can also use mail-order testing companies listed in **HELP** at the end of this chapter, or call the EPA's safe drinking water hot line at 800 426-4791.) Labs will test for anything from one to hundreds of different contaminants. Since testing for a large number of contaminants will probably be expensive, narrow the list down to those you have good reason to believe may be in your water. Take into account reports from the local public works department, local news, and your neighbors.

For the test itself, the lab should have two samples from each faucet: "first draw" water, which has been standing in pipes for several hours; and "purged line" water, which

FRESH WATER AT VINTAGE PRICES

Americans buy about $2.6 billion worth of bottled water annually. In 1991 they each drank an average of 8 gallons, double what they were drinking in 1984. But at least one quarter of it is, essentially, Eau de Reservoir, according to the FDA. Bottlers simply draw water from municipal supplies, filter it, bottle it, and slap on a hefty price tag. Bottled water costs an average of only 50 cents a gallon to package, market, and distribute—and sells for anywhere from $1 to $4 a gallon. Compare those prices to the price of tap water: a New Yorker who simply turns on the tap gets 748 gallons for a dollar.

flows after the tap has run for a minute or two to clear out stagnant water. Depending on what you are testing for, you could pay from $20 to ten times that amount. Some municipal water suppliers, such as New York City, have begun offering free lead tests. And residents of San Diego, California, can get a free computer analysis of their water from the San Diego Water Utilities Product Division. If your local water supplier does not provide this service, you can get a reliable home lead test that costs $16.50 per faucet; write or call the

Environmental Law Foundation. (See HELP at the end of this chapter for contact information.)

If the test comes back positive, don't take drastic, expensive measures—yet. Ask the lab to retest your water, or send a water sample to a different lab to confirm the diagnosis. Also remember that the mere presence of a contaminant in water is not necessarily anything to worry about. The concentration of the contaminant matters most, since some are harmless when diluted. Some labs discuss testing results with consumers, others are less forthcoming; to be sure, call your local health department or the state department of health to find out whether the concentration of contaminants in your water is harmful.

Hitting the bottle. If, after testing, you are convinced that your water is unsafe, one alternative is to buy bottled water for drinking.

Since July 1993, the FDA has required bottled water manufacturers to meet the same safety standards drinking water must meet for most contaminants and an even lower standard for lead. (Because much bottled water is bought by expectant and lactating mothers or to make infant formula, it can contain only 5 parts per billion of lead, lower than the tap-water standard of 15 parts per billion.)

The FDA also set truth-in-labeling regulations that should cut down on some of the confusion about where the water in the bottle came from. The new rules set uniform definitions for "spring," "mineral," "artesian," "well," "distilled," and "purified" water and require disclosure of the water's source. If water comes from the municipal water supply, the label must say so in a type size equal to that of the brand name, unless it was processed so that it could be labeled distilled or purified. "Spring water" must come from an underground source from which water naturally flows to the surface, or would if it were not collected underground; "mineral water" must originate from a protected underground water source and must contain at least 250 parts per million in total dissolved minerals. The plan does not cover carbonated, seltzer, soda, or tonic water, which the FDA considers, and regulates as, soft drinks.

But remember that whether you get your water from a bottle or from a faucet, it all comes from springs, streams, and the ground and is subject to contamination at the source and on its way to you.

As for choosing among bottled waters, it's all a matter of taste and price. The presence and quantity of various minerals distinguish the flavor of one bottled water from an-

FINDING THE RIGHT WATER TREATMENT DEVICE

Device	How It Works	Uses
CARBON FILTER	*As water flows through the filter, contaminants stick to the charcoal.*	*Improves taste; removes odors, rust, chlorine, and such organic compounds as pesticides and solvents.*
REVERSE OSMOSIS DEVICE *(most often includes a carbon filter)*	*Water is slowly forced, under pressure, through a filter.*	*Kills microbes; removes such inorganic compounds as fluoride, lead, mercury, and nitrate.*
DISTILLER	*Boils water, then catches it as it cools and condenses.*	*Kills microbes; removes minerals and such heavy metals as lead and mercury.*
WATER SOFTENER	*Uses ion exchange to replace mineral ions with sodium ions.*	*Corrects hard water; removes minerals.*
ACTIVATED ALUMINA	*Uses ion exchange.*	*Removes lead, fluoride, and arsenic.*

Source: California Public Interest Research Group

other. You'll have to choose for yourself which you like best.

To treat or not to treat. Another alternative for dealing with tainted tap water is home water treatment.

Water treatment systems range from simple (and relatively inexpensive) carafe filters to major appliances that you'll need a professional to install. Since not every device treats every water problem, you will have to consider the nature of your particular water quality problem and the degree of the problem. The chart on the previous page should help you decide what you need.

When choosing among brands, keep an eye out for the National Sanitation Foundation's seal of approval. The independent research organization certifies water treatment devices for companies that volunteer to participate in the program and pay a fee. Products that lack a seal are not necessarily less effective than others, but the seal assures you that the device has met minimum standards of efficacy. You also might want to consult *Consumer Reports* for information and ratings about specific products.

Get the lead out. Even if your water is fine when it leaves the supplier, it can pick up lead as it makes its way to you. Lead leaches into water from pipes, chrome or brass faucets, and the solder used to join pipes. In fact, in newer homes, water is a greater source of lead contamination than paint. A University of North Carolina researcher tested 20 new faucets in 1990, and all 20 flunked. When evaluated against the stringent criteria of California's sweeping toxic-chemicals law, Proposition 65, a few of the faucets leached 50 to 250 times the legal amount of lead.

A high lead reading on the "purged line" sample of your water suggests that lead comes from a source outside your house. If the "first draw" sample of your water contains a high lead level but the "purged line" sample contains less, you probably have a problem with the pipes or faucets inside the house.

If you have a lead problem, see the above chart for water treatment devices that will effectively reduce lead. A cheap, easy-to-use alternative is the Brita Water Filtering Pitcher, distributed by the Clorox Company. It costs about $30, and replacement filters that last about two months cost $6 to $8. Independent tests show that it removes 93% of the lead in water.

WHAT TO WATCH OUT FOR

Lead heads the list. Lead in water knows no boundaries—unlike lead in paint, which is a bigger problem in older housing than in newer housing. No matter where you live, city or suburb, apartment bulding or house, lead may be leaching into your water. Have your water tested.

Anyone who wants to test your water for free. Water treatment system salespeople may come to your door offering to test your water for free. Don't trust them or their tests.

They'll almost certainly say you have something to worry about in order to sell you something.

Devices that promise totally pure water. No device will provide totally pure water no matter what the manufacturer or salesperson claims. Nor are the devices "approved" by the FDA, which neither tests or evaluates water treatment devices. If the device uses silver to inhibit the growth of bacteria in the unit, the entire unit must have been "registered" with the EPA. Registration simply means that the EPA is satisfied that excessive amounts of silver, a potentially dangerous pesticide, will not leak into your water.

Dirty filters. Don't forget upkeep. Most water treatment devices need periodic maintenance—such as cleaning or filter replacement—in order to continue doing what you installed them to do. The life expectancy of the filter depends on how much water you use and the level and number of contaminants.

Carbon filters. On their own and when they are included as part of other water treatment devices, carbon filters can be breeding grounds for bacteria—another reason to replace filters regularly. While the effects usually are not severe, bacterial contamination can lead to brief gastrointestinal distress.

Reverse osmosis. Don't waste money or water unless absolutely necessary. Reverse osmosis water treatment devices capture only 10% to 25% of the water that runs through them. The rest goes down the drain, a fact that most sales literature fails to divulge.

Expensive water. Bottled water can cost 200 times what you'd pay for tap water; some of the "fancier" waters cost 1,000 times more.

THE SMARTER CONSUMER

Let it run. When drawing water from a faucet that hasn't been used in a while, let the cold water run for a bit to flush out contaminants that may have leached into the water from pipes and plumbing fixtures. (So as not to waste water, use what you flush out to water your plants.) A minute or two should do it, but to be safe, let the water flow until it runs as cool as it gets. At this point you will know the water is flowing from its source and has not been sitting in your pipes.

Cold, cold, cold. Since hot water picks up lead more easily, use only cold water for drinking, making baby formula, or cooking.

To get rid of the taste of chlorine, let water stand in an open pitcher in the refrigerator for a few days before drinking. You can also stir water briskly or put it in an uncovered blender at a low speed—aeration makes the chlorine in water evaporate, and the unpleasant taste exits with the vapors.

■ **Colin Ingram's** *The Drinking Water Book: A Complete Guide to Safe Drinking Water* explains water quality standards, lists the kinds of pollutants or contaminants that may be in your water, and explains how to find out if you have a problem and what to do about it. It's available in bookstores or from the publisher (Ten Speed Press, Berkeley, CA) $11.95 plus $2.50 shipping and handling; (510) 527-1563.

■ **For general information about** drinking-water safety, regulations, contamination, and pollution, call the EPA safe drinking water hot line, open Monday to Friday, 9 AM to 5:30 PM EST, (800) 426-4791. The hot line provides information about regulations that apply to public water systems under the Safe Drinking Water Act, as well as publications; advice; federal, state, and local contacts for information on local drinking water conditions; information on bottled water; home water treatment units; ground water protection; and EPA-certified drinking water testing labs. (Hot line staff cannot discuss manufacturers or recommend specific brands.)

■ **Mail-order water testing services:**
National Testing Laboratories, Inc.
6555 Wilson Mills Road
Cleveland, OH 44143
(800) 458-3330

Suburban Water Testing Labs
4600 Kutztown Road
Temple, PA 19560
(800) 433-6595

■ **For a home lead testing** kit, call or write: The Environmental Law Foundation's Lead Testing Project, 1736 Franklin Street, 7th floor, Oakland, CA 94612; (510) 208-4557. Each kit costs $15, which includes materials and analysis. You'll need one kit for each faucet. No matter how many kits you order, add another $1.50 for postage and handling. Your water samples will be analyzed at one of the nation's best-regarded water testing facilities, University of North Carolina at Asheville's Environmental Quality Institute.

Clean Water Lead Testing, Inc., 29$^{1}/_{2}$ Page Avenue, Asheville, NC 28801, (704) 251-0518, sells tap water and well water kits for $17 each. Your samples will also be analyzed by UNC at Asheville's Environmental Quality Institute.

■ **To find out about the performance** of specific water treatment devices: *Consumer Reports* tested and reviewed them in January 1990. A follow-up article about lead in water and lead-filtering products appeared in February 1993. The National Sanitation Foundation, (313) 769-8010, certifies water treatment devices and also provides information about them.

■ **For more information about the** hazards of lead exposure and how to avoid them, call the National Lead Information Center Hot Line, (800) LEAD FYI.

PART 2

Health

CHAPTER 4

HEALTH INSURANCE IN THE 1990's

Stayin' Alive

"Your money or your life" was the command barked by stagecoach robbers of old, but these days health insurers may as well say it, too. Because if you're one of the 39 million Americans who can't afford health insurance, you probably can't afford to get ill.

Unfortunately, even having insurance coverage no longer guarantees avoidance of large personal medical outlays, what with growing co-payments, insurers' "reasonable cost" payments, and new rules on pre-authorization, second opinions, and excluded treatments.

How do you find affordable insurance if your job doesn't cover you or if you have been laid off? And if you now have insurance, how can you make sure you get everything you're entitled to?

Health insurance is becoming our number one consumer issue. And no wonder. The Congressional Budget Office predicts that annual national health care expenditures will reach $1.7 *trillion* by the year 2000—or one in every five dollars spent on the Gross National Prod-uct—double the $838.5 billion spent in 1992.

There are two basic models of health insurance coverage: *indemnity plan health insurance,* in which you pay a separate fee for each service that the insurer then reimburses, and *health maintenance organizations (HMOs),* in which premiums are pre-paid, so that at the time of treatment you pay nothing or only a token amount, and fill out no paperwork. If your employer offers health care coverage, you may have a choice between these two systems.

INDEMNITY "FEE FOR SERVICE" HEALTH INSURANCE

THE BASICS

Most Americans still rely on "fee for service" indemnity health insurance when serious illness strikes. "Fee for ser-

39

vice" allows you to see any doctor or use any hospital you wish. In return for this freedom, you are personally responsible for the bills, for which you must file an insurance claim form for reimbursement. In many cases the insurance company pays the provider directly—but you're ultimately liable if, for some reason, payment is not made.

Coverage Categories

Indemnity health insurance consists of three separate coverages:

Surgical/medical. This is your basic coverage for services provided by physicians and other health professionals. If you are hospitalized, surgical/medical coverage includes treatment by medical professionals not included in a hospital bill. So it could include fees for an ambulance, an anesthesiologist at your surgery, and in-home care if needed after your operation. You will probably have to pay a portion of each bill yourself, called "co-insurance"—typically 20%—although there is usually an annual cap of $5,000 or so above which the insurance company picks up the entire tab.

You will also be required to pay an annual deductible, which can range from $100 in a more comprehensive policy to $2,000 for a bare-bones policy. The average deductible is now about $250, although $500 deductibles are becoming more common.

Increasingly, insurance companies pay only what they consider to be the "reasonable and customary charge" of a medical procedure—and then only 80% of that. Although "reasonable cost" payments are separately set for each Zip code in the U.S., supposedly reflecting local costs, the amount the insurance company pays could still be significantly less than the amount on your bill, leaving the balance for you to absorb. If you disagree with a reasonable cost determination, or if your claim is rejected entirely, you can always appeal it to the company. Thereafter, your only recourse is to sue. Your chances of success in court depend to a large extent on whether you have individual or employer-sponsored insurance. You're better off on your own because state law protects you from legally "unreasonable" denials. A much less generous federal law—the Employee Retirement Income Security Act (ERISA)—applies to your employer-sponsored plan. ERISA severely limits the possible legal recovery you can get.

In 1993, *The Wall Street Journal* reported on a woman who prematurely gave birth to twins, with medical expenses amounting to $450,000. The insurer would pay only for the cost of the actual delivery because the babies had a "pre-existing condition"—they were born ill. A state court might have ruled in her favor since the plan was not clear about what it would cover. Under ERISA, however, she had no recourse, and her plan did not pick up most of the $450,000.

Hospitalization. This covers bills incurred once you are admitted to a hospital, such as the charges for the room and the operating suite, basic nursing care, and stays in the intensive care unit. It may also include a surgeon's fees for surgery done in a hospital. Usually there is no cap on the daily room rate, although some policies fully cover your room only if you are in a ward with several other patients. Your policy may also restrict payment for intensive care or rehabilitation, and maternity care may be covered only if there are delivery complications. Only gold-plated insurance policies cover those luxury suites offering *pâté de foie gras* served on bone china that some hospitals are adding to attract affluent patients.

Major medical or "catastrophic" insurance. This is supplemental coverage that kicks in once your hospitalization and surgical/medical plans have paid out $20,000 to $25,000. It's important coverage to have, especially considering how quickly medical expenses add up. In the event that you ever need long-term rehabilitation, you'll be very glad you have major medical. Major medical plans also typically have much higher lifetime limits than standard employer plans. Whereas most hospitalization and surgical/medical policies have lifetime maximum expense reimbursement of $250,000, high-limit major medical policies pay up to $1 million. Ask your insurance agent how much such a policy costs.

Cost and Availability

The cost of insurance—and whether you can buy it in the first place—depends on several factors if you are buying an individual policy or work for a small company:

Your health and age. Insurance companies do whatever they can to avoid insuring or to charge extra those who are ill or who appear likely to become ill. If you have AIDS, cancer, or another serious (and costly) chronic ailment, getting coverage will be extremely difficult, except, maybe, from one of the remaining open-enrolling Blue Cross plans. This holds true for both HMOs and indemnity plans. And the older you are, the more you'll pay.

Even if you are insured through a medium- or small-sized employer, the premiums and the quality of your coverage may be based on a procedure the industry calls "experience rating." Under "experience rating," the overall medical costs of a company's employees determines the insurance rates for its employees. If a few employees of a small firm have unusually expensive medical needs—such as regular kidney dialysis—the rates will be extra high. If you're the one driving up the group's costs, you might even be dropped from the group plan or pressured to resign.

The health insurance reform plan President Clinton proposed in 1994 would substitute "community rating" for "experience rating." With community rating, everyone pays the same premium, regardless of age, sex, or pre-existing medical conditions. In New York State, after a law requiring all health insurers to community rate for their small group and individual policyholders was enacted in 1992, rates increased somewhat for younger people and declined for many older people, although the majority of those whose rates changed experienced decreases or increases of no more than 20%. Community rating proponents call these rate adustments eminently fair since the basic premise of insurance is to spread risk (and, hopefully, we'll *all* be senior citizens some day). Opponents say community rating pits one generation against another and that many young people have trouble affording higher premiums, while senior citizens, who may be better off financially, might more easily afford the costlier coverage.

Your occupation. You may have little sympathy for doctors or lawyers, but did you know they have trouble getting reasonably priced insurance? Seems the insurers think they might make waves. People who work for lawyers and doctors also are shunned. And among other occupations whose practitioners have trouble getting health insurance are long-distance truck drivers, bartenders, and workers in restaurants, convenience stores, and parking lots.

The amount of your deductible and your co-payment. Some comprehensive policies have deductibles as high as $2,000, which significantly reduces the premium while still protecting you from financial catastrophe.

How do you find the least expensive insurance if you aren't already covered through your job?

The National Insurance Consumer Organization suggests that you first check with local HMOs (see the HMO section that follows for more information). Then try the "Blues," the non-profit Blue Cross/Blue Shield insurance company in your vicinity. Several "Blues" now offer pared-down, reduced-premium core plans, such as the Maryland Core Plan One.

In some states, the "Blues" still "open enroll" and "community rate"; that is, they take all comers and charge everyone the same rates regardless of pre-existing conditions, which they can afford to do because of special hospital discounts and tax breaks. But many of the "Blues" are in serious financial trouble; liberal enrollment practices have left them with the sicker and more expensive patients, and mismanagement has squandered millions of dollars. Consequently, some "Blues" are no longer so cheap and their service may not be up to snuff.

Finally, look into comprehensive medical policies from the major life insurance companies.

Utilization Review

Welcome to the age of the "utilization reviewers," people who have one main purpose in life: to figure out how to save the insurance industry money. Some of these folks work directly for insurance companies. Others work for one of the more than 300 utilization review companies across the U.S., a new industry that has grown up almost overnight. These firms con-

THE BASICS OF COBRA: IF YOU LOSE YOUR JOB

Massive layoffs in corporate America have been making headlines. Even financially healthy companies are shedding employees these days, simply to slim down and cut costs.

What are all of these folks doing for health insurance? Until Washington institutes a real, workable program to insure everybody, thousands of newly laid-off workers will continue to swell the ranks of the already 39 million uninsured Americans.

Brightening this bleak picture, slightly, is COBRA, the Consolidated Omnibus Budget Reconciliation Act of 1985. COBRA requires that if your employer has 20 or more employees, you can continue under your group coverage for 18 months (29 months if you are disabled). You'll have to pick up your employer's contribution (which can be considerable) to your policy plus another 2% to cover administrative expenses. Employers who go out of business have no obligation to continue coverage. You have 60 days from the date you leave your employer to opt in.

COBRA isn't *always* a bargain. Regular non-group insurance or an HMO could still be cheaper if you have no serious or chronic pre-existing medical conditions. If possible, shop around before writing your COBRA check.

One big COBRA loophole: If your employer goes out of business, you could still be left high and dry, especially if you have a chronic illness. Consider what happened to a Washington, DC, man with AIDS. He took a disability leave from his bank but kept up with his insurance payments. The bank had serious financial problems, was taken over by the U.S. Resolution Trust Corporation (RTC), and was then sold to another bank. But the man's application was rejected when he tried to sign up for health insurance coverage under COBRA. The successor bank's position was that his old employer no longer existed and that there was no obligation to sign him up under the group health coverage. It was only after he retained a prominent public interest lawyer and threatened to sue that the bank relented and agreed to cover him.

tract with insurers to pre-screen hospital admissions, decide whether a second physician's opinion is necessary before a treatment can proceed, place time limits on hospital stays, and review whether to pay for expensive medical tests. Many questions have been raised about the qualifications of the reviewers who make the actual coverage decisions; they usually aren't physicians but are called on to second guess them.

Some experts think utilization review hasn't gone far enough in reducing costs and stopping unnecessary treatment. Others think it has already gone too far and is adversely affecting public health. Stories of utilization review run amok are legion. Patients in great pain have been sent home early after serious surgery and home care patients have been denied oxygen. Doctors spend valuable time arguing individual cases with utilization reviewers.

WHAT TO WATCH OUT FOR

When shopping for a policy or selecting one from a "cafeteria" assortment presented by your employer, look out for:

"Cost containment" rules, which have been added to health insurance policies in recent years. You'll have better luck getting your claim paid if you understand the rules well before you need your coverage. So check your policy now for the following:

■ Hospital non-emergency pre-authorization. If you don't follow pre-authorization rules to the letter, you could end up paying a lot of the bill yourself.
■ Maximum payments. Find out the maximum your plan will pay *before* agreeing to any expensive procedure. For example, in Greenville, South Carolina, International Paper's plan will pay a surgeon a maximum of $1,219 for a gallbladder operation.

Dr. Neil Schulman, author of the book *Better Health Care for Less*, told of one young Georgia woman who injured her knee jogging. She spent about $2,000 on physical therapy. But since she hadn't checked her policy, she didn't know the maximum reimbursement would be only $500. If she had known this, she would have had the physical therapist teach her how to do her rehab exercises at home instead of at the therapist's office, which billed for each visit.

You might get away with spending more than the stated limit if the insurance company initially reimbursed for care and didn't specifically say to stop. But Arthur J. Dreschler, Senior Vice-President of The Segal Company, a major NYC insurance benefits consulting firm, warned us that when you're told "no more," the company means it. He cited a case where an enrollee, unaware of his insurance capitation limit, had run up a nursing home bill a few hundred thousand dollars in excess of his plan's maximum. His second mistake was to ignore the insurance company's letter saying it would no longer reimburse; he had to pay $40,000 out of pocket.

Excluded treatments. Read your policy carefully to find out specifically what is *not* covered. Some policies may also delay coverage of certain conditions for a year or more.

Find out if the policy covers

IN EXTREMIS

A 1991 story in *The New York Times* provided a particularly stark example of the excesses of the system, including utilization review. A 26-year-old woman was treated on four separate occasions for slitting her wrists at a hospital emergency room before she was finally placed in a psychiatric hospital. But a few weeks later she threw herself down a flight of stairs. Why? She panicked when she learned that her insurance company had questioned her need for the hospitalization.

To make matters even worse, the company then cited this episode as proof that the therapy wasn't working and as support of their finding that she should be discharged. It was only when the woman's family hired a lawyer that the insurance company reversed its decision.

Still, utilization review isn't always bad for patients. A requirement to get a second opinion before proceeding with an expensive medical treatment could save your money and your health. In his book *Good Operations and Bad*, Charles Inlander, who is the president of Peoples Medical Society and a faculty lecturer at Yale Medical School, reported that an estimated 10 million Americans will have unnecessary medical procedures each year.

Inlander also reports that studies show that between 15% and 20% of all second opinions on diagnoses do not agree with the original opinion and up to 80% of second opinions about what treatment to undertake disagree with the first opinion.

---

preventive care, such as regular checkups, mammograms, and cholesterol screening.

Insurers are increasingly less likely to pay for open-ended psychological and psychiatric help. You may get back only 50% of your outlay, even if your policy normally pays 80% of doctor bills, and virtually every insurance policy places time and dollar limits on outpatient therapy. So forget about reimbursement for an extended psychoanalysis. Substance abuse treatment, including for alco-holism, is often subject to the same rules.

To qualify for emotional therapy reimbursement, you might also have to say that you are unable to function on a daily basis; although medical records are supposed to be kept secret, it still isn't a good idea to have such an admission in your records if you can avoid it.

As for the long-running controversy over the efficacy of chiropractic services, many insurance companies look at insurance claims for chiropractor visits with a jaundiced eye. Dermatologist treatments are also closely scrutinized; in 1993, ABC TV's *20/20* news magazine aired a report on how insurance companies reimbursed for fancy facials in exclusive salons that dermatologists dubiously prescribed as medically necessary.

Coverage for cosmetic surgery is nearly impossible to buy. But your policy may cover it if you need plastic surgery due to an injury, to correct a birth defect, or to remove a cancerous or possibly cancerous growth.

Labor pains may not be the only pain you experience when giving birth. You could feel financial pain if your policy has unforeseen coverage exclusions, such as if you or your spouse recently started a new job and the baby was conceived before the pre-coverage waiting period had expired. Also, your policy may not cover such diagnostic procedures as ultrasound or amniocentesis. There is also a chance—especially if you work for a small company—that your insurance policy covers only pregnancy and delivery *complications*, not routine costs.

Reimbursement for assisted reproductive technologies, such as *in vitro* fertilization, is usually very limited. However, through creative (and permissible) completion of claims forms, you may get back more than you expected.

Pre-existing condition exclusions. Insurance companies don't want uninsured people suddenly signing up for coverage when they fall ill and are about to file a big claim. So they probably won't cover claims for conditions you were treated for or should have been treated for six or 12 months before you became a company subscriber. Some more restrictive policies bar claims for all pre-existing conditions, with no time limit, even if the condition hasn't needed treatment for a long time.

Sometimes specific parts of the body may be excluded from a policy if the company has the least suspicion they could lead to a claim. In their book *Winning the Insurance Game*, Ralph Nader and Wesley Smith cite the case of a Florida woman seeking health insurance who was told that the company would cover her except for her back, her left hip, and her female organs. Why these particular body parts? Because she had been treated for a back sprain after an auto accident, she had experienced left hip inflammation (even though it had been over a year since she had seen a doctor for it), and she had minor gynecological irregularities.

"Death spiral" policies. If you have an individual medical policy, you could find your premiums escalating dramatically as you pass through middle age and into your earlier senior years. This happens when a company closes your particular policy to new buyers. You and your fellow policy holders are "walled off" from younger policy holders, and the premiums for your policy rise precipitously. The industry refers to these as "death spiral" policies. Older and sicker patients are segregated so that lower premiums can be offered to induce younger—and healthier—people to buy policies with the company.

Fly-by-night insurance companies. Growing numbers of individual policy holders and employees of some small companies are being badly burned and even financially ruined by worthless policies from small insurance companies that go bust. These plans might be regulated by only a few states—maybe not yours, but sold in your state anyway—or are union-sponsored plans, which are exempt from state control. Call your state insurance department to find out if the insurance company you are considering is licensed and if it contributes to your state's guaranty fund. Be especially wary of new companies.

Get it in writing. Ask for a written predetermination of whether a proposed treatment is covered. This will avoid misunderstandings—and lawsuits.

Avoid duplicated coverage. If you and your spouse both work, figure out if you'll save money by dropping one of your coverages and joining the other's health policy. A little extra might be deducted from a paycheck if this requires conversion from an individual to a family policy.

However, you might not save money this way if your policies cross-pay—what's called "coordination of benefits." For example, one spouse's policy might cover the other's deductible or co-payment, meaning that the entire cost of a treatment is covered. Increasingly, though, insurers include non-duplication clauses in their policies.

If necessary, negotiate the fee. Try to get your doctor to accept your insurance company's "reasonable cost" payment before you go ahead with an expensive procedure. You can ask your physician to call the insurer directly to work this out.

Consider hiring a medical claims agent, especially if you have a family or are chronically ill and need to file many claims. But since medical claims agents aren't licensed, make sure you check plenty of references before hiring one.

How much do they charge? Usually an annual retainer of $100 or so and 10% to 15% of the amounts recovered. Are they worth it? Well, if you're busy and letting claims slide, then they are. Better yet, shrewd agents may be more adept than busy policyholders at getting companies to cough up more money.

Don't stop with a second opinion if your insurance company will pay for more. For major treatments, try to get a third and even a fourth opinion, and go ahead with a treatment plan only if there is a consensus. Be wary of required second opinions from a doctor chosen by the insurance company.

Consider getting a utilization review rider if you are buying an individual policy. You might have to pay for some procedures that would otherwise have been covered, but your premium will be significantly lower.

For individual coverage, consider buying a policy with a high deductible. The premium savings may more than compensate for the additional medical bills you pay out of your own pocket.

HEALTH MAINTENANCE ORGANIZATIONS

THE BASICS

Welcome to the future. By the turn of the century, it is estimated that at least nine out of ten Americans will be members of a managed health care organization. Health maintenance organizations (HMOs) are now and will probably continue to be the most prominent kind of managed health care system. The 1994 merger of the health insurance businesses of Met Life and Travelers into the nation's largest commercial health insurer, covering 13 million people, is in line with this trend. The combined entity plans to switch from traditional health insurance policies to managed-care networks.

HMOs are health insurance plans in which participating providers agree to take care of your health needs for a set, pre-paid fee. Instead of choosing any health service provider and assuming direct responsibility for the bill, as with indemnity plan health insurance, with an HMO you must use clinics or primary care doctors in a prescribed network. If you go outside the network, you may not be covered or you may have to pay a large share of the bill.

Preferred provider organizations (PPOs) are HMO variants. A company or several companies work out a deal with a group of physicians and hospitals to treat their employees at a discount. Patients have to pay out of their own pockets if they use outside doctors and hospitals.

The major advantages of HMOs are lower out-of-pocket costs and, with no claims forms to submit, no paperwork. If there is a small co-payment at the time of treatment, it is probably only a few dollars. If your HMO is in a clinic, with a range of specialists under one roof, another advantage is greater convenience. Some HMOs also live up to the name "health *maintenance* organization" by emphasizing preventive care, such as regular cholesterol tests, flu shots, mammograms, and screening for high blood pressure and diabetes. For example, of the 2.4 million members in the Kaiser-Permanente network (based in California), 99% of members' children are immunized.

In addition, as with fee-for-service insurers, HMOs practice aggressive utilization review. They might require that certain tests and procedures be conducted on an outpatient basis, even if you would feel more comfortable having them done in a hospital, or they may reject coverage for plastic surgery that another doctor would think medically advisable.

The biggest disadvantage of HMOs is that your selection of doctors is limited. So you may not want to join an HMO if you've been going to the same doctor for years and he or she doesn't participate in one. Or you may already be an HMO enrollee and your doctor may decide to leave the network.

With an HMO, you also might not be able to see the best possible specialist if he or she isn't on the list of authorized physicians. In a recent survey of 39 doctors who saw both HMO and fee-for-service patients, conducted at Georgetown University Medical Center in Washington, DC, the doctors were "more likely to refer an HMO patient to a specialist they didn't know" and "less likely to discuss patient care with specialists in HMOs."

On the other hand, there is a growing opportunity to enroll in an HMO hybrid—one that allows you to see non-network doctors of your own choice as well as network doctors. If you see a non-network doctor, you generally pay the first several hundred dollars of the fee and 20% to 50% of the remainder, with a $1,200 annual cap on your total payment. For network doctors, you pay only the usual nominal co-payment. You get the peace of mind of knowing you can visit a non-HMO doctor and be at least partially reimbursed, yet you can still enjoy the benefits of an HMO. Not

surprisingly, *The New York Times* reported in February 1994 that half of the seven million people who joined an HMO from December 1991 to February 1994 enrolled in such hybrids. Major HMO networks, such as Kaiser-Permanente, are beginning to offer this "escape hatch" option to some or all of their members.

HMO patients also complain about long waits for appointments and crowded reception rooms. The NYC Consumer Affairs Department recently questioned members of its own staff who switched HMOs, about why they had transferred. Here are some quotes from the questionnaires:

"The HIP [Health Insurance Plan, an HMO] clinic is overbooked. Patients needing a specialist wait up to four months. . . . "

"The benefits of Cigna are great, however the physicians working under the plan are not up to standards."

And an 80-year old California woman complained to the Public Citizen Health Action Group about her HMO:

"I also notice (and it's getting worse) that the doctors that check you about every three to four months only give you minimum time, and while trying to explain to him how you feel, he just walks out the door."

There is evidence that Americans prefer individual doctors over large, impersonal HMO facilities.

In a 1993 federally financed, nationwide study of 17,000 patients at Johns Hopkins University and the New England Medical Center, patients said that doctors working in their own offices showed more interest in their health than did doctors working in HMO facilities.

Are HMOs less or more expensive than indemnity, fee-for-service

---

THE DIFFERENT HMO MODELS

There are three major types of HMO:

Staff model HMOs own their clinical facilities and hire their own doctors. Except for emergencies, you will probably pay entirely out of your own pocket if you go elsewhere for care. The largest staff model HMO in the nation is Kaiser-Permanente in California.

Group model HMOs contract with separately incorporated groups of physicians who treat you in a clinic. Health Insurance Plan (HIP) is a large group model HMO in New York.

Individual practice associations contract with organized groups of physicians who work out of their own offices. They see both HMO patients and their own fee-for-service patients.

---

health insurance plans? It depends on the individual plan and the HMO. Your out-of-pocket treatment expenses will almost always be lower with an HMO, but your premiums will likely be higher. Overall, it's very likely that HMOs are cheaper, given their economies of scale, cost-saving methods, and attempts at preventive care.

How about differences in quality of care? Will you be healthier if you enroll in an HMO? There have been studies on this, but no firm conclusions. Once again, it depends on the HMO and the health insurance plan in question, although it's hard to beat a quality HMO with aggressive health monitoring and prevention programs.

Most HMOs are "federally qualified." This means that they must offer a wide range of benefits, although not necessarily including such ancillary services as dental care, optometry, and prescription drugs.

One factor that may affect quality of care is how the doctors are paid. Benefits consultant Arthur J. Dreschler gives this analogy: You can contract with your heating oil delivery company to perform oil burner repairs one of two ways: either by paying one set annual fee for service or a separate fee for each repair. Guess which method leads to frequent visits by the repairman and under which method he doesn't return phone calls?

The quality of care you receive may also depend to some extent on whether the HMO withholds part of its payment to doctors until the end of the year, releasing it only if the doctor meets a cost-contain-

HMOs: Ways to Pay

Capitated. Doctors receive a flat rate per month per enrolled patient. But since the doctor gets no extra money if you visit more often, the obvious effect of such a payment method is to discourage doctors from spending time with you. Some of the major national HMOs that pay physicians for primary care this way include U.S. Healthcare (with 1.2 million subscribers, the largest publicly traded HMO in the nation), Cigna (capitated for "routine services"), and Travelers.

Fee-for-service. Doctors are paid for each service according to a discounted fee schedule. You and/or your employer send an annual fee to the HMO. HMOs that use fee-for-service are run by Aetna, Metlife, Oxford Health Plans, and Prudential Insurance (Prucare), among others.

Salaried. In a staff model HMO, the doctors receive a paycheck that probably remains constant no matter how many patients they see. So they're under no pressure to show you to the exit and get on to the next patient. Doctors in a group model HMO may also be salaried, although they still may be pressured to limit the time they spend with you if the group's contract with the HMO provides that they are paid extra if cost-containment targets are met.

ment benchmark. Some HMOs, such as U.S. Healthcare, also consider how well a doctor does on patient evaluation questionnaires and quality benchmarks. Generally, incentive payments are more common at individual-practice HMOs.

HMOs may be either not-for-profit or for-profit. One type is not necessarily better than the other. Increasingly, as large life insurance companies start their own HMOs, they are for-profit. While you may think that for-profit HMOs would be motivated to cut a lot of corners, remember that if they don't offer a satisfactory level of care and cost, subscribers may vote with their feet—and leave.

WHAT TO WATCH OUT FOR

Advertising hype. Some HMOs spend a fortune on advertising. U.S. Healthcare, for instance, reported to the New York State Insurance Department that it spent $72.72 on advertising per member in 1991—19.1% of the total amount they spent on hospital care—compared to a national average of $17.76 per member. (You may have seen their ad with the famous movie clip of a very healthy Gene Kelly dancing to the tune "Singing in the Rain.")

Unfortunately, HMO ads offer

little useful consumer advice, such as how doctors are compensated or how much you'll be reimbursed if you see a non-network specialist. This is why you have to read all of their literature carefully, including a copy of the HMO contract, and ask a lot of questions (see the $marter Consumer, below).

A low percentage of board-certified physicians. Board-certification means that the doctor spent four years in medical school, did a residency, and then passed oral and written examinations in a specialty. Before enrolling, ask an HMO how many physicians it has and how many of them are board-certified in the specialty in which they are practicing. If less than 80% of them are board-certified, you might consider going elsewhere.

Tight restrictions on seeing outside specialists. You may have to get special permission to see the famous heart surgeon you think you need, and reimbursement for specialists not on the HMO's list might be next to nothing.

Obsolete participating provider lists. Before you call a doctor on your HMO's participating provider list, check first to make sure he or she is still with the HMO. You may also find out that your preferred doctor is in more than one HMO network, giving you a choice of which HMO to join.

Coverage gaps when you travel outside your region. If traveling to another city, you could find it difficult to get pre-authorization to use a hospital there for non-emergencies.

Fine print rules. *The Wall Street Journal* reports that courts are increasingly enforcing the fine print in HMO contracts. You'd better follow such requirements to the letter (for example, getting pre-approval for medical procedures and obtaining periodic re-authorizations for lengthy hospitalizations).

THE SMARTER CONSUMER

Read all available HMO promotional literature and, if possible, the subscriber handbook *before* you sign up. Ask a lot of questions. Among the basic information you will need to know is exactly how much of a co-payment—if any—you will be asked to pay when you visit a doctor, whether there are any deductibles, and exactly what services are included and excluded. You should especially determine whether preventive health services are included, such as an early screening program to detect colon, skin, and breast cancer; flu shots; and an effective anti-smoking program. Unfortunately, many HMOs have abandoned the original HMO premise, which was to prevent illness, not just treat it. The ideal HMO understands that promoting wellness is financially and ethically preferable to treating illness.

Internally generated scorecards issued in 1993 by U.S. Healthcare,

THE ANSWER IS "NO"

Getting an insurer to pay for alcohol and drug treatment can be as difficult as pulling teeth. In 1991, the Legal Action Center, an NYC-based public interest law firm, conducted a survey of 97 alcohol and drug treatment centers around the state, of which 94 said that an insurance company or a utilization review firm initially refused or limited payment or suggested an alternative treatment. In a majority of the cases, the review "simply second-guessed the treatment providers' medical judgment. . . . "

Kaiser-Permanente, and United Health Care—three large HMOs—revealed that the percentage of patients who receive preventive services varied significantly by HMO. For example, only 45% of United HealthCare's adult female members were reported to have received Pap smears, compared with 75% at Kaiser and 71% at U.S. Healthcare. But only 33% of diabetics received annual eye exams at U.S. Healthcare, while 60% at United Health-Care and 51% at Kaiser received them.

There are also significant differences in patient satisfaction among HMOs. In 1993, approximately 10,000 subscribers to the *Washington* [DC] *Consumers' Checkbook* filled out a survey rating their HMOs. The percentage of respondents who rated their HMOs "very good" or "excellent" in "overall quality" ranged from 46% for CareFirst and 51% for Cigna to 81% for Columbia Medical Plan and 77% for Prudential Health Plan.

Cast a jaundiced eye at an HMO's claims of superiority. Every HMO's brochure talks about their great facilities as well as their top doctors and friendly staff who minister to your every need. To find out the real story, if a clinic is involved, stop by and ask a few patients how long they've been sitting in the waiting room, how long it took to get an appointment, and how they like their doctor and the HMO. Try to examine the qualifications of all of the primary care physicians you might be choosing among and ask what the average length of practice is among the HMO's doctors.

If you have special needs, make sure the HMO can accommodate you. Find out how many pediatricians are on staff or in the network if you have children. Senior citizens might ask if any of the physicians have special training in gerontology. In other words, one size doesn't necessarily fit all.

Find out about the HMO's grievance procedures. Does the procedure impose time limits on rendering findings to make sure the process moves along quickly? Who makes the final decision? Are grievances heard by an HMO-controlled grievance committee or by an independent, outside arbiter?

Determine how the doctors are compensated before enrolling, whether per-head (capitated), fee-for-service, or straight salary. Also find out if a portion of their payment is withheld and whether they get bonuses—and on what basis they receive full payment of the bonus. It's a plus if a bonus is based on how well the doctors perform on a patient questionnaire, a minus if it's based primarily on how well the doctor keeps costs down.

Ask which hospital(s) the HMO is affiliated with. Is it a prominent regional institution or a small, general hospital that may not offer comprehensive care?

•. **For more information on** HMOs, read "Are HMOs the Answer?" in the August 1992 issue of *Consumer Reports*.

•. **To find out if a doctor is board-**certified, call the American Board of Medical Specialties at (800) 776-CERT.

CHAPTER 5

PHARMACEUTICALS AND PHARMACISTS

Prescription for Care

Americans and pharmaceuticals. It has become a stormy relationship. Miracle drugs developed in U.S. laboratories wiped out polio and smallpox and are the basis for long life expectancies of hundreds of millions of people around the world.

But with the cost of pharmaceuticals increasing at triple the inflation rate over the last decade, millions of Americans who can't afford life-prolonging drugs are going without. At the same time, millions of others are taking too many drugs or the wrong drugs or are taking potentially hazardous combinations of drugs. "Drug abuse" is not just about illegal substances. Another kind of drug abuse—the misuse of prescription drugs—is a serious national health problem.

The more you know about prescription drugs—what they do, how they're sold, their danger points—the better you will be able to afford the drugs you need and avoid further harming your health with needless or improperly taken drugs.

THE BASICS

Uninformed is Unhealthy

Americans buy some $40 billion worth of prescription drugs each year. But how much do we really know about what we're putting in our systems? Not much, according to a 1983 Louis Harris Associates poll conducted for the U.S. Food and Drug Administration (FDA) of persons who had recently filled a prescription. Only a third of the polled patients remembered being told about possible side effects, only 2% to 4% said they had asked the doctor questions about their prescription, and only 3% asked their pharmacist any questions. A mere 6% said they had received written information about the prescription while in the doctor's office.

Compare these poll results with reports that more than 125,000 Americans die each year because of poor medication practices—they failed to comply with a doctor's orders, took the wrong or an inappropriate medication, or took two medications that shouldn't have been taken together—and you begin to understand the urgent need for Americans to become much better informed about what the doctor prescribes.

Need additional convincing that there's a serious problem? The *St. Louis Post-Dispatch* reports that

FIND OUT WHAT'S WHAT

When your doctor hands you a prescription, ask these questions and write down the answers.

- What is the exact name of the drug? What is it supposed to do? What dosage am I taking?
- How and when do I take it? When do I stop?
- What foods, drinks, or activities should be avoided while taking the drug?
- What are the side effects? What do I do if I feel them?

Be sure you've told the doctor about any other drugs you are taking. You might also want to ask about those mysterious abbreviations doctors write on prescriptions. A few sample translations: QID means four times daily, TID means three times daily, PC means before meals, and HS means at bedtime.

11,000 of the 61,000 calls received at the St. Louis Regional Poison Control Center in 1992 were questions about medications and their side effects. And according to Public Citizen Health Research Group's book, *Worst Pills, Best Pills II*, recent studies among older people have revealed that "59 percent of patients were prescribed a less-than-optimal drug or one not effective for their disease . . . 28 percent of patients were given doses which were too high . . . 48 percent of patients were given drugs with one or more harmful side interactions with other drugs."

A Prescription for Savings

Increasingly, Americans obtain their medications through their health maintenance organization (HMO) or by mail order. Both sources can produce big savings. Mail order can result in savings from 5% to 40% off the average retail price of a drug, and HMOs may sell drugs to you at slightly above wholesale.

But the vast majority of people still use a pharmacy to fill prescriptions, and they choose their pharmacy because it's convenient or the service is prompt—which is why they often pay too much. Surveys around the nation have found extreme price disparities among pharmacies in the same communities for the exact same medications. The pharmacy just down the block from your home could be 50% more expensive than one a few miles away.

In 1993, the *Seattle Times* did an informal price survey of 15 drugs at

11 pharmacies, including those operated by major chains and mail-order houses. They checked prices for several short-term antibiotics and for a month's supply of a dozen medications, including birth-control pills, an antihistamine, an arthritis medication, and insulin. The market basket total of all the drugs cost $534.03 at the most expensive store and $368.73 at the least expensive, a 45% difference.

Next-to-least expensive was the mail-order drug service of the American Association of Retired Persons (AARP), which cost $384.95, and in third place was another mail order service, Costco Wholesale Corp. at $397.53. The price of 30 tablets of the hormone replacement therapy drug Premarin ranged from $9.90 from AARP to $14.95 at a Rexall drugstore. The *Seattle Times* found that small, independent pharmacies generally (but not always) had the higher prices.

Another 1993 survey, this one conducted by the NYC Consumer Affairs Department of 20 medications at 100 pharmacies, found even bigger price differences. The total market basket price ranged from a low of $571.90 up to a high of $1,146.15. On the same street—East 86th Street in Manhattan—the Department found that 90 pills of 10 mg Procardia, a common heart medication, cost $49.79 at a large chain drugstore, $52.49 at another chain store, and $69.50 at an independent pharmacy. On one block in the borough of Queens, 20 pills of the generic equivalent of the antibiotic Amoxil cost $3.99 at a major chain drugstore, $5.95 at another chain store, and $8.25 at an independent drugstore.

Why such broad disparities? One reason is that drug retailers know that people rarely comparison shop for medications. Another is that large chain drugstores are able to charge less because they buy in bulk and get a discount from the manufacturer. As a result—and also because the lower prices charged to HMOs and nursing homes have to be made up elsewhere—many small, independent pharmacies are losing business and closing their doors.

Do you figure "Why bother?" because your insurance policy covers drugs? Check your co-payment. There's a chance it's now calculated as a *percentage* of the prescription price. The higher the drug price, the more you pay out of pocket.

> "**M**y doctor prescribed me a 10-day supply (50 bottles) of Proventil, which I picked up at Duane Reade, and paid $81, less 10% for senior citizens. I went to Pathmark . . . and they told me 75 bottles would cost $45. Another drugstore quoted me 50 bottles for $90."
>
> —BEA P.,
> a Manhattan senior citizen,
> in a letter to the author

A VALIUM BY ANY OTHER NAME

Here are some of the most popular brand-name drugs and their generic equivalents:

Name Brand	Purpose	Generic
Amoxil	Antibiotic	Amoxicillin
Calan	High blood pressure	Verapamil
Cardizem	Heart medication	Diltiazem hydrochloride
Dyazid	High blood pressure	Hydrochlorothiazide triamterene
Darvon	Pain relief	Propoxyphene hydrochloride
Lanoxin	Heart medication	Digoxin
Premarin	Estrogen replacement	Conjugated estrogens
Procardia	Heart medication	Nifedipine
Tenormin	High blood pressure	Atenolol
Valium	Tranquilizer	Diazepam
Xanax	Antidepressant	Alprazolam
Zantac	Ulcers	Ranitidine hydrochloride

Senior citizens have to be especially concerned about overpaying, since Medicare doesn't cover non-hospital drugs and supplemental coverage may be unaffordable.

Save More With Generics

A new drug is first introduced to the market under a brand name by the company that researched and developed it. After a given period (usually 17 years), the company's patent expires and other companies are permitted to start making the same drug as a "generic," sold under a different name. The FDA says generics are as safe and effective as brand-name equivalents. Even though they may be a different color or shape, generics are required to have the same active ingredients and in the same amounts.

Although generic and brand-name drugs need not be *exactly* the same, most doctors believe that the only practical difference between them is price and that it is entirely safe to substitute them in the vast majority of cases. Generic drugs generally cost about half as much as their brand-name equivalents. A Minneapolis-St. Paul survey published January 24, 1993, found some generics costing 70% to 80% less than their brand-name equivalents. Not surprisingly, given the pressure from American employers to reduce health care costs, generics have gone from about 5% of U.S. prescriptions a decade ago to nearly 40% today.

Generics cost less because all of the safety and effectiveness testing has already been done; the generic manufacturer need only prove to the FDA that its product is "bio-equivalent" to the brand-name counterpart, meaning that your body will absorb the generic at the same speed and to the same extent. Generic manufacturers also spend comparatively little on marketing since the low price sells the drug without advertising.

To help resolve any remaining concerns about the safety and efficacy of generics, an FDA commission in 1988 studied the differences and concluded that there was an overall effectiveness differential of only about 3.5% between brand name and generic drugs, which is not enough to make a significant difference.

Unfortunately, generics occasionally disappear from the market. One example: Warfarin is the generic version of DuPont's blood-thinner Coumadin. When the two manufacturers of generic Warfarin stopped making it, the price of Coumadin skyrocketed, increasing 218% between 1985 and 1991.

Your Pharmacist Shouldn't Just Count Pills

Pharmacists receive years of specialized training, yet many pharmacists act merely as pill dispensers. You hand over a prescription and the pharmacist puts pills in a bottle, types a label, hands it back to you, and takes your money. Seldom do pharmacists take the time to strut their stuff.

Fortunately, this is changing. A new federal law requires pharmacists to offer counseling services and to keep records for all Medicaid prescriptions. Forty-one of 50 states have extended this law to cover all prescriptions, not just Medicaid ones. The pharmacist must record not only basic personal statistics like name and age, but also known allergies, drug reactions, chronic diseases, and a comprehensive list of all your medications. Most pharmacies have computer systems that enable them to easily record and retrieve all this data.

In addition, the new law requires pharmacists to conduct a "prospective drug review" before filling a prescription, which includes a review for possible harmful drug interactions, incorrect dosages, and serious interactions with over-the-counter drugs. Their computers are programmed to alert them to dangerous combinations.

In 22 states, the *pharmacist* must personally offer counseling each time you fill a prescription; in 19 other states an assistant may make the counseling offer. You can always refuse the advice, but if you do want it, the pharmacist should tell you about dosage, form, at what times you are to take the medication, duration of therapy, any special precautions or storage requirements, common side effects, prescription refill information, and what to do if you miss or accidentally double a dose. Mail-order pharmacies may provide counseling over toll-free phone lines. The federal agency that wrote the initial counseling legislation estimates that counseling should take two to four minutes per patient.

This new approach is a cost effective pro-consumer breakthrough—why not utilize an expert who's already at the point of purchase to educate customers about their prescriptions and their health?

Some stores are embracing the new law; the large Walgreen and Eckerd chains have added waiting rooms or counseling areas in their new or remodeled stores. But too many high-volume, deep-discount chain drugstores are dragging their feet in complying; they make money by moving customers in and out of the store quickly, and providing a customer direct contact with a pharmacist slows things down. If your drugstore is not complying, report it to your state pharmacy board. (Look under the government listings in the phone book.) In Iowa, two pharmacists at a discount chain drugstore formally complained to the state's pharmacy board that understaffing kept them from counseling patients as required by law. The store was fined $25,000 and its license was put on probation for three years.

WHAT TO WATCH OUT FOR

Inappropriate medication. The April 1992 issue of *Health Letter*, published by the Public Citizen Health Research Group, reported how physicians are bombarded with misleading pharmaceutical advertising in medical journals; 92% of advertisements in one government survey potentially violated at least one FDA regulation. *Health Letter* reported that many ads promote the use of powerful drugs for trivial maladies, cite irrelevant or weak scientific studies, or do not appropriately highlight side effects. Yet the FDA has taken almost no disciplinary action against the offending manufacturers.

How can you protect yourself? Learn as much as you can about the prescription drugs you take. Consult the Health Research Group's guide, *Worst Pills, Best Pills II* (see **HELP** at the end of this chapter) and closely question your doctor and your pharmacist about their choice of medication.

OTC and prescription drugs that don't mix. Certain over-the-counter drugs shouldn't be taken with prescription drugs. One pharmacy owner says he sometimes sees customers, who he knows are taking high blood pressure drugs, buying over-the counter cough medications. The two shouldn't be taken together. If you're on a maintenance medication, ask your doctor or pharmacist before you take an OTC product for the first time.

DRUGS AND MONEY

According to the General Accounting Office, the investigative arm of Congress, here's how much the prices of some commonly prescribed drugs increased between 1985 and 1991: Valium, 110%; Halcion, 110%; Percocet, 141%; Premarin, 160%; Tylenol III, 161%; Dilantin, 334%.

Pharmacists who don't know you. Give your pharmacist the whole picture. If you fill prescriptions at different pharmacies, tell each pharmacist all the drugs you take. Under the new counseling laws, pharmacists are required to keep track of your medications and warn you if there are two or more medications you should not be taking at the same time.

Expired medication. Although you'll rarely see an expiration date on the bottle, most medicines lose potency after a while. Liquids may partially evaporate, making the remaining medicine too concentrated to use safely. Eye drops can become contaminated with bacteria after a month. Unfortunately, most states do not require expiration dates to be placed on prescription medication packaging.

Ask your pharmacist to double-check how long you can keep using your supply of a drug. Two 1993 surveys by the NYC Department of Consumer Affairs found that 78% of 200 New York pharmacists gave bad advice when called over the telephone about medicine shelf life. For example, estimates of how long a supply of propranolol (a common medication) would last varied from six months to four years. The wrong answers stemmed in part from the druggists' failure to check the lot number to see how old the medication in question was.

Drugs from south of the border. It's tempting. Down Mexico way drugs can cost a fifth of what they do in the U.S. One 1993 survey found that 60 Zantac pills, an ulcer medication, cost $105.58 in an El Paso drugstore but only $22.02 just across the border in Juarez. But drugs made outside the U.S. are not approved by the FDA. While some may indeed be the same brand-name drugs sold here, others may be generics made in factories without FDA quality controls. So be very careful about what you buy in Mexico or other foreign countries.

While it is lawful to bring back pharmaceuticals for personal use, be aware that U.S. Customs may seize any drugs for which you have no prescription.

Use buying services and mail order. Your savings, when compared to drugstore prices, could be significant. But you'll have to take the initiative to call the mail-order company's toll-free "800" phone number for counseling if you have questions or need advice.

Follow your doctor's orders. While it's a good idea to question the initial choice of a particular drug, once it's finally settled on, *take it as directed*. Numerous studies have shown that a third to half of all drugs are not taken correctly. Typically, patients don't take the medication for the complete course, or they take it at the wrong times or with the wrong foods. Their negligence could make the drug therapy ineffective, which may lead the doctor to needlessly prescribe a stronger drug—one that may be more expensive to boot.

Get what you pay for—the patient profile, the full counseling. Remember, if you're a senior citizen or a resident of one of the 41 states requiring counseling for everyone buying prescription drugs, you're paying for that counseling; its cost has been passed to you through higher prescription prices.

Go generic. Ask your physician if there is a suitable (and cheaper) substitute, such as a generic or a different drug that accomplishes the same therapeutic mission.

Take advantage of discounts. Many drugstores give senior citizens 10% off. Ask: It may not be posted.

Keep medication records. It's smart to keep an individual medication profile for each family member. Record every prescription medication taken, how long it was taken,

the dosage, and any side effects. Include the manufacturer of the medication. Don't rely on the new pharmacist counseling laws to make your pharmacist keep all this information for you. And give the list to your family doctor periodically to review for potential problems.

Store your prescription drugs correctly. Most drugs do best in a cool, dry place, but follow any storing instructions carefully.

■ **The basic drug reference book** is the *Physician's Desk Reference*—the "PDR"—available at most public libraries.

■ **Want to know more about pre**scription drugs? For that, we suggest consulting the 772-page book, *Worst Pills, Best Pills II*, published by the Public Citizen Health Research Group, which includes information on hundreds of commonly prescribed drugs. It's available at most bookstores.

■ **The American Association of** Retired Persons (AARP) drug mail-order program can be reached by calling (800) 456-2277. You need not be a member to use it.

■ **Family Pharmaceuticals is an**other mail-order house from which anyone can order. Call (800) 922-3444.

CHAPTER 6

DOCTORS AND HOSPITALS

How to keep Your Health and Wealth

Americans spend prodigiously on health care. In 1990, our health care tab came to $2,566 per person, far greater than the $1,795 per capita spent in Canada and $1,145 in Japan, and our bill keeps mounting at more than double the inflation rate.

Waste and inefficiency in the health care system have a lot to do with our extraordinary health care costs. A study by the Rand Corporation, a well-known think tank, showed that from 30% to 50% of health care spending is unnecessary. It has been estimated that $1 billion a year is spent on needless cesarian sections alone.

And Harvard University researchers found that 25% of hospital costs are for administration. No wonder that hospitals sometimes charge $3 for an aspirin or that in August 1991 ABC News reported that one private hospital chain was charging $6.45 for a 37-cent eye patch and $47.35 for a bottle of sterile water.

No, don't scrimp on your health. Everyone wants and deserves someone like Dr. Marcus Welby as a family doctor and like pioneering heart surgeon Dr. Michael DeBakey for open-heart surgery. But better value can be extracted from our health care dollars: We can help prevent some illness from striking in the first place, we can avoid needless tests and treatments, and we can get everything we pay for from doctors and hospitals—all while continuing to have confidence in the quality of the health care we receive.

THE BASICS

Doctors

She greets you wearing an immaculate white coat, a stethoscope hanging around her neck. You deferentially address her as "Doctor," and she has the special power to give "doctor's orders" and write prescriptions.

Don't be intimidated. Yes, the doctor had many years of schooling, followed by internships and hospital residencies. And yes, she kept you waiting for an hour. But don't forget, she's *your* employee. You hired her to provide a service for you, not the other way around.

Finding one. If you're one of those people who brags about not having a doctor because you are so healthy, you'd better change your tune. If you have no regular doctor and you need medical attention, the doctor you see may have to run more tests because she is unfamiliar with you and wants to protect herself from being sued. In fact, most doctors prefer not to see new patients who need emergency care.

Start your search for a doctor by asking relatives and friends for referrals. You might also call your local medical society, where you can also ask about credentials, although such societies don't screen doctors for any other qualities.

Check credentials yourself. You'll want to know the names of the schools attended, dates graduated, and whether the doctor is "board-certified," which means she passed tests in a specialty as well as received resident training in a hospital. Find out how long she has been in practice and with which hospital(s) she is affiliated.

If you are looking for a specialist, start by asking for a reference from a primary care doctor you trust. Ask the specialist about qualifications.

Thirty-seven states now collect at least some data on individual physicians' performance. Two states, New York and Pennsylvania, have actually begun to release data on physician success rates with heart bypass operations, and it is widely expected that additional states will soon follow. California, Colorado, Florida, and Iowa are now developing statistical protocols and could be next.

New York State's Health Department began releasing heart bypass operation mortality rates by surgeon and hospital in 1991. Twenty-one different risk factors are applied to the raw mortality rates, including the patient's age and severity of illness, to reach a risk-adjusted mortality rate for surgeons performing at least 200 such operations during a three-year period. The statewide average mortality for the years 1989 to

> "**M**edical negligence kills more than 100,000 Americans every year and injures more than half a million. Yet only about 2,000 physicians are disciplined each year by state medical boards. The vast majority get a slap on the wrist— or a warning short of probation. . . ."
>
> —DR. HARVEY F. WACHSMAN,
> a lawyer and neurosurgeon
> in Great Neck, N.Y.

1991 was 3.23%, although the death rate was less than 1% for a handful of physicians and exceeded 5% for some others. Pennsylvania began releasing physician bypass mortality rates in 1992. New York will soon add results of balloon angioplasty (a non-surgical method of treating narrowed arteries).

Before the visit. How many times have you come home from the doctor only to realize that you forgot to ask an important question? This won't happen if you write down all your symptoms and questions beforehand, ranked in order of priority.

If this is a first visit, assemble any medical records you have or can get, and bring them with you. Ask how often the doctor is away or otherwise unavailable. Also ask whether the doctor accepts phone calls at any particular time of the week to answer questions. The doctor may attend numerous medical conferences, take long vacations, or split her practice among locations—in which case you'll definitely want to ask about the credentials of the doctor who covers for her.

During the visit. Take notes when you see the doctor. And ask lots of questions about alternatives to prescribed courses of treatment and tests. Don't be bashful.

Despite a new emphasis in medical schools on developing rapport with patients, too many doctors still lack a good "bedside manner." They can be terse and dismiss your questions. Some doctors speak to patients the way they talk to colleagues—in "medicalese" laced with clinical terminology and abbreviations. Remember how arrogant and abrupt William Hurt was in the film *The Doctor*, until *he* became a patient and suffered from physician condescension.

Ask about medications prescribed for you. How long will it be before it takes effect? What can (or can't) you eat while medicated? What are the potential side effects? How will it interact with other medications or over-the-counter drugs?

Physician penmanship is notoriously undecipherable. Combine this with medical abbreviations such as "q4h" (take the medicine every four hours) and the prescription your doctor hands you will probably make about as much sense as ancient Mayan glyphs. Ask the doctor to decode it.

If you need surgery, ask the surgeon how many times she has performed the operation in the last year. In this case, practice *does* make perfect.

Doctor billing. Billing can be a very sensitive subject. Most doctors prefer not to present themselves to patients as businesspeople. And they won't mention fees unless you ask.

Do check carefully and question any charges you don't understand. In one case reported in 1992 in *The New York Times,* a doctor's hospital bill for a maternity patient included a code number next to a $4,225 fee. It turned out she had been charged for total obstetric care when, in reality, the doctor provided only pre-delivery care, which cost $98.

Many a billing dispute could be avoided if doctors only disclosed to each patient the cost for standardized procedures before treatment, just as haircutters, home improvement contractors, and mechanics do.

Physician oversight—or, perhaps we should say, undersight. While most physicians are competent and some are superlative, many should try some other line of work or be put out to pasture. Trouble is, in most areas of the country, you can't rely on state authorities to weed out the problem doctors.

The non-profit and independent Public Citizen Health Research Group has been closely monitoring state disciplinary activities. Their conclusion: Most medical review boards are slipshod, take far too long to process complaints, and are very hesitant to mete out serious discipline. Public Citizen found that among states with the lowest ratios of disciplinary actions in 1991 were such major population centers as New York (ranked 49th), Massachusetts (48th), and Pennsylvania (47th). California ranked 37th.

Here are two examples of how the current system has hurt people:

■ Dr. David Benjamin had been brought up on disciplinary charges in 1990 and 1991. In 1993, he allegedly killed a woman as a result of a botched abortion. His license was ultimately suspended and he has been indicted for murder.
■ A young girl went to the hospital for a routine tonsillectomy. While she was comatose, doctors argued for 25 minutes over whose responsibility it was to administer cardiopulmonary resuscitation (CPR). The girl died. More than four years later, the case against the doctors is still being reviewed by the disciplinary board.
■ Then there's the story of 8-year-old Gussie, as told by Laura Wittkin of the Center for Patients' Rights. The Illinois child had developed an aneurysm as a result of a car accident. It went undiagnosed and mistreated for four years; doctors said the child's odd behavior was mere acting out because he was jealous of his siblings. One New Year's Eve the aneurysm burst and Gussie underwent ten hours of brain surgery—and then died. Gussie had been "acting out" because he had been in such intense pain. He would have had a 95% chance of complete recovery had the easily-detected aneurysm been treated in time. Yet according to Wittkin, ten years have passed and the responsible doctors are still practicing.

Unfortunately, the National Practitioner Data Bank—which is supposed to help keep problem doctors from restarting their practices in a new state—lets cases slip through the cracks. A few years ago, a Maine woman who had broken her nose underwent what she thought would be a simple surgical procedure to reopen an air passage. Instead, the surgeon did a radical nose job, which dramatically altered her appearance, without altering her breathing. She later learned that the doctor had been sued in Maine five times and had settled all of the cases out of court. Later, he

NICE WORK IF YOU CAN GET IT

The health care industry claims the highest paid female executive. In 1993, Turi Josefsen, executive vice president of U.S. Surgical Corporation, pulled down a cool $26.7 million.

moved to Kentucky, where he was sued twice again.

How can you protect yourself? Follow our previous advice on how to research a doctor's credentials before being treated. And lobby to make sure your state's regulatory authorities have the funds and incentive to discipline incompetent doctors.

Hospitals

Hospitals make many people so uncomfortable that they avoid visiting sick relatives. Being a hospitalized patient is an even more unsettling and disorienting experience. Yet if you find yourself about to be hospitalized, you or your loved ones will need to be alert, knowledgeable, and assertive if you are to get the best care possible.

This section is not a comprehensive consumer guide to hospitals. For that you should read *Take This Book to the Hospital With You*, by Charles B. Inlander and Ed Weiner of the People's Medical Society (see **HELP** at the end of this chapter). It tells you how to change your room,

your doctor, or your nurse; how to lower your chance of becoming a malpractice victim; how to avoid signing away important rights; and a wealth of other practical advice. Since doctors, nurses, and hospital administrators both respect and fear this volume, just setting it on your hospital bedside table might improve your treatment.

Staying out of them. It's a good idea to avoid a hospital stay if at all possible. Hospitals expose you to infections, nervous medical residents who overcompensate by overtreating, interrupted sleep, and more television-watching than you ever thought you could stand. Although major surgery still requires hospital stays, you may be surprised to learn that when it comes to lesser procedures, treatments, and especially "observation" stays, hospital overnights might be avoided.

A Harvard Medical School study of New York State hospitals released in 1990 also disclosed just how unhealthy hospitals can be. Looking at the year 1984, they estimated that 27,000 patients—3.7% of those hospitalized—were injured as a result of an "adverse event" in their medical care. In about 1% of patients, medical negligence caused the injury, which sometimes led to permanent disability or death. The Harvard report also found that "eight times as many patients suffered an injury from negligence as filed a malpractice claim in New York State."

And it's not just New York. Sidney Wolfe, M.D., director of the Public Citizen Health Research

Group, has written that 50% of hospitals around the country did not adequately monitor patients in intensive care units, 40% had safety standard deficiencies, and 51% did not adequately monitor whether unnecessary surgery was being done or was being done safely.

Comparing hospitals. There is a regrettable absence of good information with which to compare hospitals. You might find it easier to get an "A" in advanced calculus than to compare hospitals on prices, infection rates, the ratio of nurses to patients, and average lengths of stay.

Fortunately, under pressure from major employers and consumer advocates, the walls of secrecy are starting to come down. Pennsylvania led the way in 1988 by creating the Pennsylvania Health Care Cost Containment Council. The Council monitors the cost as well as the outcomes of 59 different procedures and publishes this information in periodic *Hospital Effectiveness Reports*. In Cleveland, 31 hospitals, 2,500 doctors, 50 corporations, and 8,000 small businesses have collaborated to collect information from hospitals on mortality rates and length of stay for a wide range of procedures. The information will be made public.

> "*I saw a male patient's hospital bill listing a hysterectomy and an entry for crutches on the bill of a patient who was admitted for chest pains.*"
>
> —JoAnne Fritsch, a former registered nurse, now with the Wyatt Co., a major national business consultancy

Maryland is about to collect and publish a wide variety of information about medical prices and treatment outcomes.

However, until more such information is widely available, it's a good idea to check out a hospital before you enter it, if you have a chance to do so. By calling the information hot line of the Joint Commission on the Accreditation of Healthcare Organizations (JCAHO; see **HELP** at the end of the chapter), you can find out the status of the hospital's accreditation. Although some patient advocacy groups complain that JCAHO does not release its most potentially damaging findings to the public, you should be able to get more details by writing to them and requesting all available information. It's also advisable to visit a hospital beforehand to get a feeling for how clean, orderly, and well staffed it is. If your doctor is affiliated with a hospital you prefer to avoid but recommends that you be admitted there anyway, ask if he or she has affiliations with any other hospitals and if you can be sent to one of those. If the doctor is affiliated with just the one hospital, then a referral to a suitable colleague at another hospital might be possible.

Hospital mortality rates for nine different medical procedures and eight medical conditions* can be obtained from an annual U.S. Health Care Financing Administration (HCFA) report (see **HELP** at the end of this chapter). While these rates are only for *Medicare* (that is, older) patients, they are indicative of the hospital's success with younger patients as well.

Do you need every hospital test? Probably not. Doctors trying to avoid malpractice suits sometimes practice "defensive medicine." That is, they order tests for every conceivable diagnosis so that they can prove they covered all the bases if you sue them. Sometimes, consulting physicians and "house" (hospital-based) physicians will order tests for their own use without realizing you just had the same tests done by another doctor. Excess tests are also sometimes ordered by inexperienced student residents lacking confidence.

Most tests come with at least a bit of risk, from developing a minor infection after having blood drawn to potentially serious hazards such as excessive radiation exposure (if nuclear medicine tests keep being repeated) or injury from invasive procedures like spinal taps and catheterization. Keep X-rays to a minimum because of the possible

harmful long-term effects of accumulated radiation. Since a CAT (computerized axial tomography) scan consists of many X-ray pictures, it, too, should be used sparingly. On the other hand, CAT scans are often used in place of even riskier invasive diagnostic procedures such as angiography. Ultrasound tests, which bombard the body with ultrafast sonic waves, are entirely safe. MRI (magnetic resonance imaging) is also safe (unless you have a pacemaker), since the equipment merely records the body's electromagnetic waves.

Question carefully the purpose and necessity of each and every test, starting with pre-admission testing; if you were just tested by your own doctor, you may not need a full battery of the hospital's pre-admission tests. Once you're admitted, consider asking for an independent, outside evaluation of proposed tests, particularly for tests that are expensive and/or invasive.

Going under the knife. One explanation for high U.S. medical costs is that so much surgery is unnecessary. Ask for a plain-English explanation of the need for and alternatives to any surgery. Be particularly alert if any of the following procedures are recommended:

■ *Prostate surgery.* Some 400,000 prostate operations are performed every year. In 1993, *American Health* magazine reported that the chance that a man in Iowa with an enlarged prostate will undergo surgery varies from 15% to 60% among hospitals—you have to wonder if all of them are necessary. And

---

*The procedures evaluated are angioplasty, coronary artery bypass graft, initial pacemaker insertion, carotid endarterectomy, hip replacement/revision, open reduction of fractured femur, prostatectomy, hysterectomy, and cholecystectomy. Reported medical conditions include acute myocardial infarction, congestive heart failure, pneumonia/influenza, chronic obstructive pulmonary disease, transient cerebral ischemia, stroke, fracture of neck or femur, and sepsis.

wasted money is not the only issue here. According to *American Health*, potential complications of prostate surgery include incontinence and impotence. Non-surgical treatments can often be substituted.

- *Hysterectomies. American Health* also reported in April 1993 that the chance that a woman in Maine will undergo a hysterectomy varies from 20% to 70%, depending on where in the state she lives. Local preference, not science, explains the disparity. In general, the reason for most hysterectomies is to resolve symptoms related to benign uterine fibroids. New studies show that if they aren't causing any serious and immediate symptoms, surgery is unnecessary.

- *Cesarian sections.* The U.S. Centers for Disease Control reported that in 1991 some 349,900 unnecessary cesarian sections were performed, at a cost of more than $1 billion. The rate skyrocketed from 10.4% of births in 1975 to 24.5% in 1988. Again, the issue isn't just money, although $1 billion would pay for a lot of health care for those who don't have it. Surgery can lead to infections and longer hospital stays.

- *Mastectomies.* The vast majority of women who have operable breast cancer are treated by mastectomy. Yet numerous studies have concluded that, for early-stage cancers, lumpectomy—removal of just the cancerous lump and the immediate surrounding tissue—is as effective as mastectomy when combined with radiation treatment. In 1994, it was disclosed that a Montreal doctor who supplied 16% of the data for one of the major studies

supporting lumpectomies had falsified his findings; however, according to the experts, the results would have been the same without his data.

- *Back surgery.* The better remedy for backaches may be physical therapy and brief bed rest.

Informed consent. The law requires that you give "informed consent" before undergoing surgery. You're supposed to be told in plain English exactly what is about to be done, the risks involved, the chances of failure, and the alternatives. You need not be informed of remote risks. You'll then be handed an informed-consent form to sign. Read every line carefully, and make sure you understand it completely. If you have a question or disagree, discuss it with your doctor; maybe a wording change can be worked out. Informed-consent forms are often the basis of lawsuits in which patients charge they weren't adequately informed of risks or alternatives.

Hospital billing. While all health care costs have risen in recent years, hospital costs have soared the highest, with an even steeper trajectory than for doctor and drug costs. In constant dollars, Americans spent an average of $200 a year *per capita* on hospital care in 1960—and $1,000 in 1990.

The better health insurance policies still cover your entire basic hospital bill, but some policies now make you pay up to a few thousand dollars out of pocket. Less comprehensive policies place limits on the length of your hospital stay or don't start paying until you've been hospitalized a few days.

Given the possibility that you may have to pay a portion of your hospital costs even if you have insurance, you can't afford to blithely ignore a hospital bill with the rationalization "the insurance will cover it"—especially considering that a recent survey by Congress's General Accounting Office found that over 90% of the bills reviewed had errors. And the Maryland Hospital Association reported in 1992 that billing is the largest source of patient complaints. So be sure to examine your hospital bill carefully.

The extraordinary error rate raises questions about hospitals' motivation to detect and correct mistakes in their favor. After all, they need to raise cash to cover the cost of treating poor or underinsured people who are unable to pay their way, not to mention the debt service for that newly installed state-of-the-art computerized billing system. Considering also that few patients or insurance companies double-check bills, there is little incentive to correct overcharges.

Some hospitals hire a "revenue recovery" firm to audit their billing. In 1990, experts told a U.S. Senate hearing that since these firms work on a contingency fee basis—the more they net the hospital, the more they are paid—they have a strong incentive to find and correct mistakes made in your favor but to ignore ones in the hospital's favor. After the hearing, guidelines were written to govern the industry, but they are voluntary and do not cover contingency fees.

The complexity of hospital bills also leads to inadvertent mistakes. One part of the bill is your daily room rate, which includes nursing care and meals. But everything else is billed separately, from aspirins to oxygen, echocardiograms to crutches. So an itemized bill might have 20 or 30 entries for an overnight stay, and a hospital bill for a major operation could have hundreds of daily billing entries and go on for many pages. Mistakes are made more likely because five-digit computer codes have been substituted for the names of actual medical procedures. Transposing a digit or two could result in billing for a very different —and differently priced—procedure.

What are the most common mistakes? You could be charged for more days than you stayed. There may be charges for services you never received or double charges for services you did receive. JoAnne Fritsch, a former registered nurse who now works for the Wyatt Company, a national benefits consulting firm, gave this example: Double-billing commonly occurs when a blood specimen is dropped, is inadvertently contaminated, or isn't tested soon enough and begins to clot, requiring the specimen to be drawn again. The patient shouldn't be charged for the second test, but is anyway. "It's not so serious if it's just a $75 blood test. But if it's a spinal tap, it's really expensive," she told us.

Instead of a bill for an entire procedure, you may be billed separately for every aspect of the procedure, with, for example, separate bills for drawing blood, transporting the blood, and analyzing the results of a blood test. Added up, the individual charges total more than a single "bundled bill" for an entire procedure. This could add up to real money when a doctor who performed a hysterectomy charges separately for removal of the uterus and each ovary.

Medicare and certain insurance policies take exception to itemized billing. They pay set fees for hospital procedures, regardless of how long you were hospitalized. A heart mitral valve replacement might always be billed for, say, $25,000, even if there are complications. This is called the "diagnostic-related group" (DRG) billing system. While DRG billing prevents hospitals from padding the basic bill, doctors are increasingly sending patients separate, additional bills. So it doesn't necessarily keep costs down as intended.

Fortunately, many hospitals are now trying to streamline billing and to better explain it to patients.

For example, the Cleveland Clinic has produced a brochure explaining billing and how to deal with third-party payers. And at least one state is trying to help citizens avoid recourse to lawsuits for seemingly unresolvable hospital billing disputes: In 1992, Nevada created a Commission for Hospital Patients in response to the extraordinarily high volume of billing complaints legislators were receiving. Commission staff explain bills to callers and mediate disputes.

WHAT TO WATCH OUT FOR

Doctors

Too many tests. Excess tests might be ordered if the testing laboratory is owned in part by the doctor ordering the test and she could benefit financially from them. Fortunately, as self-referrals have been banned in several states and under new Medicare rules, this practice is in rapid decline. Until self-serving referrals are banned nationwide, you might want to check whether your doctor is sending you to her own facility.

Hospitals

Extra charges. You may know that you have to pay extra for a television set in your room. But be careful about asking for anything else special—those extra pillows could get added to your bill. There's a chance that your insurance company won't cover your special requests.

PUBLIC ASSISTANCE

If you're hesitant to haggle over price with your doctor, be aware that, according to the Medical Group Management Association, in 1992 the average internist made $189,295, the average radiologist made $309,556, and the average cardiovascular surgeon made $574,769.

Outpatient surgery. Amazing advances in medical technology are leading to a dramatic shift from inpatient to outpatient surgery. You enter in the morning, have surgery, and later that afternoon you're back home relaxing on the living room sofa. It has been estimated that by the year 2000 some 70% of surgery will be done on an outpatient basis. This trend helps explain why many hospitals are converting existing wings or building new facilities dedicated to sameday service.

Most of this outpatient surgery is being performed in well-equipped, fully-staffed facilities, usually associated with and adjacent or attached to a hospital. But many outpatient surgery centers are free-standing and may not be accredited by any of the accrediting associations, even though a group of doctors runs them.

Check out an independent or non-hospital-based surgery center beforehand. Is it accredited by a professional association? What are the procedures in case of emergency? Is there an arrangement with a nearby hospital to automatically take patients who experience complications? Has your state certified or licensed the center (and not just the doctors in it)?

> "*I magine a super-market with no price tags, no lists of ingredients or nutritional information to judge value, and where prices increase 15% to 20% a year. That's the situation most of us find ourselves in when we need health care.*"
>
> —SEAN SULLIVAN,
> National Business Coalition on Health

Private, for-profit hospitals. About 15% of the country's hospitals are in this category. Be very wary of them since their chief purpose is to make money. And they do that very well. Thomas Frist, chief executive of the Hospital Corporation of America, made $127 million in 1992. Frist was first in *Business Week*'s annual report on the highest paid executives in America. He got the money as his reward in a leveraged buy-out. Guess where that money came from. You got it—patient bills.

Private hospitals respond that they offer top-rate care and make money because they are more efficient. Really? A few years ago, ABC News obtained a confidential price list from the very-profitable Humana Hospital chain that revealed their exact markups. They made at least 400% on over half the items. There were thermometers that had cost the hospital 60 cents for $11.80, an $8.35 antacid tablet, and a $47.35 bottle of sterile water.

Sleep-deprived interns and residents. Physically exhausted hospital interns and residents continue to be a safety concern, despite efforts to limit their hours. Young doctors undergoing hospital training go through a sort of baptism by fire, working 100-hour weeks and maybe catching a few winks in an unused patient bed. This system of servitude saves hospitals lots of money. But in a 1989 survey by the University of California, one third of 114 residents said exhaustion had caused them to make a mistake that contributed to a death.

So before a hospital resident begins sticking you with needles, ask when he or she last had eight straight hours of sleep. If the answer is something like "Oh, a few days ago," maybe the procedure can be delayed or a better-rested intern found.

THE SMARTER CONSUMER

Doctors

If the fee seems steep, try negotiating. If you have a limited income or recently lost your job, many doctors will give you a break.

Know where to complain. Every state has a medical board that licenses doctors and acts on complaints. But since many of these boards are ineffective, don't stop there. Also complain about a problem doctor to your insurance company, the hospital(s) where he has admitting privileges, the administrators of your HMO, and/or the local medical society.

Question all tests. Are there one or two comprehensive tests that would cover the numerous individual tests being prescribed? Are results from a test you underwent, say, six months earlier still valid? In no event should you pay for tests you did not know about. Make sure you have a complete list and update it as necessary.

Consider home-testing. Why pay a big lab fee when, for less money, you can go to a nearby drugstore and buy a home pregnancy test, a blood pressure testing kit, a urinary tract infection test kit, a blood glucose monitor for diabetics, or a fecal occult blood test?

Get free advice over the phone in order to avoid a billable visit. If you have the flu, talk to the doctor over the telephone. You'll probably be told just to drink fluids and rest. That way, you'll avoid the strain of traveling to the doctor's office, as well as the needless strain on your wallet.

Hospitals

Read the Patient's Bill of Rights (most hospitals publish one) and make use of the hospital's patient representative, sometimes called a patient advocate or liaison. Most hospitals have such a person on staff full-time. Complain if you can't get answers about medical tests that seem unnecessary, if you're left on gurneys in hallways for long stretches, or even if your roommate insists on playing *Laugh-In* TV reruns at high volume.

Ask for an itemized hospital bill. You will probably have to ask the billing office to explain the many abbreviations and codes in it. Examples: PT-PTT is a blood test for coagulation, and CBC (complete blood count) is a blood test usually done by machine. Also request elaboration on anything appearing under the all-purpose heading "miscellaneous." Remember, you have a right to know exactly what you are being charged for. Don't pay until you have had ample time to fully review and understand the itemized bill.

Challenge overcharging even if you think your insurance will pay the entire bill. One reason medical bills are so high is that everyone figures the insurance company will pay. Well, to paraphrase Pogo, we have met the insurance company and it is us! Needless claims payments are passed on to everyone through higher premiums.

Compare the itemized bill with your hospital medical records. If they don't match, find out why. An investigation into the Humana hospital chain several years ago uncovered one family that had been charged for three hours of recovery-room time after their mother had already died. They were also charged for an "O.R. implant," dated after the body had been removed for funeral preparations.

Most states require hospitals to turn your records over to you. The states that have not yet passed such a law are Alabama, Arizona, Delaware, the District of Columbia, Idaho, Iowa, Kansas, Kentucky, Mississippi, Missouri, New Mexico, North Carolina, North Dakota, Oregon, Rhode Island, South Carolina, Tennessee, Texas, Utah, and Vermont. (See **HELP** at the end of this chapter for a guide published by Public Citizen Health Reasearch explaining how to obtain your medical records.)

Keep a notebook in which you write down the dates and times of all consultations, blood tests, electrocardiograms (EKGs), sonograms, etc., assuming you are well enough. Later on, compare your records with the itemized hospital bill.

Provide your own supplies. This is one way to cut your bills for incidentals such as mouthwash. You might also try bringing your own prescription medications, although many hospitals strongly discourage patients from doing this because they are unsure of how old the medication is or of whether it has been properly stored.

Provide testing results. If the hospital will accept the results, you can cut the cost of pre-admission testing by having basic tests, such as EKGs, urinalysis, blood tests, and chest X-rays done at an outside facility rather than in the hospital, where they are likely to cost more.

You do not have to sign the informed-consent forms and patient-admission registration exactly as they are written. If you find a clause that you disagree with, suggest a change.

Be especially careful of any clause that says your surgeon *or his or her associates* can perform the operation. Since you might never have laid eyes on the associates, and you may not want some totally unknown doctor getting near you with a scalpel, you might want to cross out the words "or his or her associates."

Find out if your employer has a bill-audit program, in which you get to keep a portion of the savings from any mistakes you find on your itemized hospital bill. If your company doesn't have such program, suggest that it start one.

■▪ **The People's Medical** Society's publications, *Take This Book to the Hospital With You* and *150 Ways to Be a Savvy Medical Consumer*, have numerous helpful tips. $14.95 for the former, $5.95 for the latter. Send a check or money order to 462 Walnut Street, Allentown PA 18102. Call (215) 770-1670 to pay with MasterCard or Visa.

■▪ **To learn the status of a hospital's** accreditation, call the Joint Commission on the Accreditation of Healthcare Organization hot line, (708) 916-5800.

■▪ **To get the Health Care Finance** Agency report on hospital Medicare mortality rates, you'll have to inspect one of 14 volumes at specified local libraries or at the regional offices of the American Association of Retired Persons. For more information, call HCFA at (301) 996-1133.

■▪ **To double-check your physician's** schooling, residencies, licensing, and certification status, write to the American Medical Association's Physician Data Services at 515 North State Street, Chicago, IL 60610, or call (312) 464-5199. You can also check the AMA's *American Medical Directory*, probably in your local library, which lists every doctor in the country.

Check also the American Board of Medical Specialties; *Compendium of Certified Medical Specialists* to find out if your doctor has a hospital affiliation. To find out if a doctor is board-certified, call the American Board of Medical Specialties at (800) 776-CERT during normal business hours or check your local library for the *Directory of Medical Specialists*.

■▪ **Call the National Emergency Med**icine Alliance at (800) 553-0735 for a $4 booklet on cutting medical bills.

■▪ **The Public Citizen Health Re**search Group has published a 69-page $10 guide called *Medical Records: Getting Yours*. Order from Public Citizen, 2000 P Street NW, Suite 605, Washington, DC 20036.

■▪ **If you want to know more about** patients' rights, read the American Civil Liberties Union's 300-page handbook, *The Rights of Patients*. Send a check or money order for $8.95 plus $1.50 shipping and handling to: ACLU, Department L, PO Box 795, Medford, NY 11763.

■▪ **The *Consumer Reports* book, *How** to Be a Savvy Patient*, can help you communicate with health professionals and participate fully in your care. $14.95 from Consumer Reports Books, 9180 LeSaint Drive, Fairfield OH 45014.

CHAPTER 7

LONG-TERM CARE

 *Planning for Aging*

The good news is that Americans are living longer. The bad news? Almost half of everyone older than 65 will need help with basic daily activities such as eating, bathing, and walking. That means that when the first baby-boomers reach their golden years, several million people will require some kind of long-term care. A one-year stay in a nursing home cost $35,000 in 1993; because of spiraling healthcare costs and inflation by the year 2010, it's likely to cost nearly $150,000 a year. Skilled home care may cost $100 per hour.

Many seniors who need care—some experts estimate that as many as two thirds—move in with their adult children, other relatives, or friends. But the added stress of caring for the disabled elderly at home can break the financial backs of families already struggling to make ends meet or to handle other domestic pressures.

Take Ms. C. Her husband's sudden stroke in 1981 essentially ended their marriage. Since she could neither afford nursing home care nor qualify for state aid, Ms. C.'s life, as she described it on the CNN special "Caring Choices: Prohibitive Costs of Nursing Home Care" broadcast on February 24, 1993, has turned "into a stressful routine, centered solely around her husband." Their relationship has become more like that of parent and child than that of husband and wife.

To avoid burdening their children or entering a nursing home, a growing number of seniors who own their own homes are choosing to trade their home equity for home care. However, this trade has worked poorly for some seniors, including Jane Rood of Lincoln, Massachusetts. Unable to afford $72,000 per year for a full-time nurse, Ms. Rood agreed to sell her home to Linda Douglass in exchange for care and the right to live in her home until she died. But instead of providing care, Ms. Douglass ran a real-estate brokerage out of the house and ne-

> ## "Some consumer abuses are so severe as to raise questions about the very viability of long-term care insurance."
>
> —EARL POMEROY,
> past president of the National
> Association of Insurance
> Commissioners

glected Ms. Rood. Fortunately, Ms. Rood was rescued before it was too late and Ms. Douglass was charged with elder abuse.

Many seniors think that long-term care insurance will protect them in old age, but like Ms. O., a widow from Oregon, they can end up with hefty insurance premiums and no care when they need it. De-

spite having paid thousands of dollars in premiums for nearly ten years for two different long-term care policies, Ms. O. died penniless because her nursing home did not meet the definition of "skilled" care described in her policies' fine print.

THE MANY FACES OF CARE

There are three levels of long-term care. **Skilled care**, sometimes called **acute care**, is medical care provided by registered or licensed nurses and physicians, usually for specific curable illnesses or recoverable accidents. Skilled care also includes various "high-tech" procedures, such as dialysis and respiratory therapies. **Custodial care** is day-in, day-out assistance with such basic activities as bathing, dressing, eating, and moving around. Custodial care also includes constant supervision of those with mental disorders and dementia, such as Alzheimer's disease. More than half of all long-term care patients need custodial care, which Medicaid covers but most other government programs do not. **Intermediate care**, as the name suggests, is in between skilled and custodial care.

THE BASICS

Making the Choice to Plan Ahead

As difficult as it may be to confront the possibility of long-term disability, the only way to avoid long-term tragedy is to plan ahead. Too often, consumers make decisions based on the government programs they qualify for, rather than on the medical care they need or the living arrangements they desire. You'll feel more in control of both your health and your finances, and be a better advocate for your loved one, if you know the parlance of long-term care and can participate in the decision-making about whether and how to purchase it.

What Are the Different Long-Term Care Options?

If you need long-term care, you can opt either to live in a nursing home, which is generally categorized according to the level of care it provides, or receive care in your own home. There are several different "titles" of home care providers that do not neatly correspond to levels of care. Generally, home care workers are divided into "hands on" and "hands off" workers. Only "hands on" workers can administer medications, bathe, dress, feed, or physically touch the patient. "Hands off" workers generally maintain household finances, cook, and clean. Many states follow the federal Medicaid guidelines specifying what particular home care titles allow workers to do.

Registered nurses/licensed practical nurses/therapists. These professionals provide skilled care and "high-tech" therapies. They are professional home care workers and can charge from $25 to over $80 per hour.

Home health aides (often generically called home care workers). They can perform some "hands on" work including such minor medical tasks as taking blood pressure and administering oral medications. Home health aides charge about $25 to $35 per hour.

Personal care aides. They, too, can perform such "hands on" work as bathing and feeding, but usually cannot perform any medical tasks. Personal care aides charge from $15 to $25 per hour.

Homemakers. These workers can perform the same "hands on" tasks as personal care aides as well as provide assistance and instruction in managing and maintaining household finances. Homemakers are the only home care workers who can provide such instruction; they can charge as much as home health aides.

Housekeepers. These aides do only "hands off" work, such as cooking, cleaning, and shopping. Housekeepers are often hired at or slightly above minimum wage.

Companions. These workers offer protection by "keeping company," with patients suffering from mental dementia. Several nonprofit agencies offer free companion services, and many employment agencies refer companions for wages comparable to those earned by housekeepers.

Which Government Programs Pay for Long-Term Care?

There are three major sources of federal funds for long-term care: Medicare, Medicaid, and Title III funds from the Older Americans' Act, which together pay for barely 40% of all long-term care costs. All three programs have economic qualifications that disqualify many middle-class consumers.

Medicare. This entitlement program for all people over 65 with an illness or injury and certain disabled people under 65 pays only for skilled care, not custodial care, in a nursing home or care at the patient's home, and only after at least a three-day hospital stay. More than half of those who need long-term care do not need skilled care and so do not qualify for Medicare's long-term care coverage. Even those that do qualify are not covered for 100% of the costs for as long as they need care. The biggest gaps in Medicare's long-term care coverage are:

■ No coverage for custodial care in a nursing facility.

- No coverage for homemaker and personal care services at home.
- No coverage without prior hospitalization.
- No coverage for nursing home care after 100 days.
- Consumers must use Medicare-approved facilities.

Medicare supplement insurance (often called Medigap). This private insurance picks up where Medicare leaves off. Medigap policies still do not cover custodial care, but four of the ten policies recently standardized by the federal government will pay up to $1,600 per year for care at home if you are recovering from an illness, injury, or surgery.

Medicaid. This program provides health insurance, including coverage for all levels of long-term care, for people living at or somewhat above the poverty line. States set their own programs and qualification requirements. Since Medicaid is the only government program that pays for the custodial care most long-term care patients need, many consumers "divest" or "spend down" their assets in order to qualify.

How to Choose a Nursing Home

No one wants to live in a nursing home, but choosing the right home can turn a bad situation into a beneficial arrangement. If Medicaid is paying the bill, you must use a Medicaid-approved facility. If you're paying your own way you can choose anything from a luxury resort to a grim motel. But while stories of filthy conditions and neglect abound, if you shop around you can find both the medical care you need with a lifestyle and a price tag you can live with.

Know what kind of care you need. Since 1990, most skilled care and intermediate facilities have merged, and many custodial facilities have diversified to include "assisted living homes" (which tend to be smaller, decentralized units) and special homes for people with Alzheimer's disease, AIDS, cancer, and other specific diseases. Particularly if you need only custodial care, you may be able to find a facility attuned to your needs—if you know what they are.

Visit. Look for two things: Is the building comfortable and in good condition, and is the staff competent and cooperative? Specifically, inspect the bedrooms, bathrooms, dining rooms, recreation and therapy rooms, and all other common areas. Be suspicious if you are told that any part of the home is "off limits." Ask specific questions about the medical staff: Who are they and what are their qualifications? How many of them are on the premises or on call and how often? Also, find out if there is a social worker available to help a resident adjust to the new lifestyle.

Consider the subjective. If everything seems in order, but you just don't feel "right" about a home, go somewhere else. Observe the residents: Do they seem happy? Are they dressed? Do they use the recre-

CONSIDER HOME HEALTH AGENCIES

Pros:

- You are not responsible for paying your home care worker's salary, taxes, and benefits.
- You can go to the agency if you have a problem with your worker.
- You can more easily change your worker as your needs change.
- Most insurance and government programs cover home health services if provided by a home health agency.

Cons:

- You may not get the same caregiver every day or every week.
- Home health agencies are expensive, and the home care worker receives only a small fraction of the hourly fee you pay to the agency.
- Many home health agencies are impersonal, and if you have a problem you may have to take a number and wait in line.

---

ation areas or do they mostly stay in their rooms? Remember, you're not only looking for long-term care; you're looking for a place to live.

Consider moving to a cheaper area. Care in such states as Arizona, South Carolina, and Oregon can cost as little as one-third what you would pay for the same care in Florida or California. Unfortunately, there is no national clearinghouse for nursing home information. The cost of long-term care, however, generally mirrors the local cost of living as indicated by census statistics and the consumer price index.

How to Get Good Home Care

Most people would rather stay at home than live in a nursing home, but good home care is hard to find. You have four options:

Licensed and/or certified home health agencies provide a variety of services for an hourly fee. The agency recruits, trains, and supervises workers and technically is the workers' "employer," paying their salary, taxes, and benefits.

Nurse registries and domestic employment agencies refer home care workers for a referral fee ranging from a few hundred to a few thousand dollars. You contract directly with the worker and are responsible for wages, taxes, benefits, and, most important, supervision.

The want ads are often full of people looking for work as home health aides, homemakers, housekeepers, and even registered nurses and therapists. You take your chances but eliminate the expense and bureaucracy of agencies.

CONSIDER NURSE REGISTRIES AND DOMESTIC EMPLOYMENT AGENCIES

Pros:

- You can get the continuity of care that you often cannot get with a home health agency.
- Direct contracts with workers can cost from 30% to 50% less than agency services.
- You have more control over your home care worker than if he or she is supervised by an agency.
- Medigap policies will cover direct contract home care arrangements.

Cons:

- You have all of the financial responsibilities of an employer including supervision, which can be difficult for someone receiving care.
- You have no one to help mediate problems between you and your caregiver.
- Most states provide little protection for employers who have problems with employment agencies.

Volunteer agencies can usually provide only companion or non-health related services for a few hours of care per week. If that is all you need, these agencies may be your best bet.

How to Supervise Your Home Care Provider

Even if your worker is referred by a home health agency, you're still the boss in your own home. Most reported incidents of elder abuse are by family members and not by hired home care workers, but you should take precautions to make sure your relationship with your home care worker is appropriate.

Know what you need *and* what you, your friends, and relatives can take care of; know how many hours a day/a week you need help and

whether you want a companion as well as a caregiver or a purely professional relationship. Make these decisions *before* you start interviewing applicants.

Always interview your home care worker and check references. Whether you are going through a home health agency or an employment agency, make sure you meet and feel comfortable with your caregiver and that he or she is qualified.

Put everything in writing. Write a specific job description, including the hours, salary, vacation time, use of the phone and car, and other household rules and procedures.

Treat your caregiver like a professional. Give your caregiver periodic written evaluations and have established grievance procedures.

Long-Term Care Insurance

Given the likely odds of needing costly long-term care and the dismal odds of qualifying for government funding, it's no wonder that long-term care insurance is the fastest-growing type of health insurance. Long-term care insurance agents often promise financial security and "whatever medical care you need." But watch out—what you hear is rarely what you get.

Undercover investigations by the U.S. House Select Committee on Aging (June 1991), *Consumer Reports* (June 1991), and the NYC Department of Consumer Affairs (April 1993) all found that *every* long-term care insurance agent interviewed misled consumers about their policies. For example, eight out of eight agents interviewed by Consumer Affairs claimed that policyholders could easily qualify for benefits with a note from their doctor, but all of the policies actually required more complex procedures and had significant benefit limits. The American Express agent was particularly insistent, saying:

". . . your nursing home stay is covered when, and here's the operative language, your doctor—*your* doctor, not our doctor, not somebody else's physician [approves]. . . . We have the best claims payment record because we rely upon the individual's doctor."

This directly contradicts American Express' written policy: "We [American Express] reserve the right, as part of the review, to do a face-to-face assessment or to require you to take a physical examination paid for by us. . . . We may use an outside service to assist in evaluating your condition."

Furthermore, most of the agents assured investigators (posing as consumers) that insurance premiums would never go up, even though industry experts all agree that premium increases are highly likely. The agent for First Unum Life Insurance Company told an undercover investigator:

"[The rate at] the age at which you take it out is the rate at which it will continue. It will never go any higher. The only way it can possibly go higher is on a class basis, if they [the insurance company] apply to the State, which has never happened in the past with any company."

"With any company?" asked the incredulous investigator. "With any company," the agent replied. "Whatever you go in at—that's what the premium will be. . . . It will never happen. It will not happen." According to a U.S. Congressional report, 66 companies requested rate increases nationally in 1990 alone, and 60 of these requests were granted increases averaging 31.7%.

The lesson for consumers is clear: Do not trust insurance agents selling long-term care insurance. Even if the agent is honest, the policies themselves are riddled with problems. First, they are expensive—from $1,000 to over $10,000 per year, depending on your age and

THE PITFALLS OF PUBLIC-PRIVATE PARTNERSHIPS

Neither consumers nor the government has the money it will take to pay for the baby boomers' long-term care needs. Many states are attempting to split the difference with "public-private partnership plans" that basically promise that Medicaid will pay your long-term care tab regardless of your income and assets if you purchase a private insurance policy and exhaust its benefits. Sounds fair enough, but beware:

- Private insurance benefits won't cover all your costs; your out-of-pocket expenses may drain your assets to Medicaid levels anyway.
- Since the average nursing home stay is only 19 months and most private policies provide coverage for three years, most consumers won't be able to take advantage of the partnership benefit.
- Partnership policies are not portable, meaning that if you move to another state you won't be able to tap into Medicaid if your insurance dollars run dry.
- Finally, partnership policies have the same loopholes—and potential premium hikes—as regular policies.

the benefits you choose. Even at this price, no policy is guaranteed to pay 100% of your long-term care costs, and some policies that don't keep pace with inflation can pay as little as 30%. Having to foot 60% of the bill in addition to hefty policy premiums can quickly erode the nest egg you bought the insurance to protect.

And that's *if* you can qualify for benefits; most policies have big loopholes hidden in the fine print that can keep you from ever getting a dime. As bad, many policyholders never keep their policies until they need long-term care, because they can't keep up with the premiums. Based on estimates by the National Association of Insurance Commissioners, of every 100 60-year-olds who take out long-term care insur-

ance policies, only five still have coverage at age 80, when they are most likely to need it. A December 1991 U.S. General Accounting Office survey of insurers concurs with these estimates: On average, the insurers they reviewed "expected that 60% or more of their original policyholders would allow their policies to lapse within 10 years; one insurer expected an 89% lapse rate."

In an article published in June 1991, *Consumer Reports* found some companies "low-balling" their premiums, or charging less in premiums than they expect to pay out in claims, to attract policyholders. To pay future claims, companies will have no choice but to raise premiums substantially. If you can't pay your policy's future premium hikes, you're out of luck. Moreover, most policies do not have nonforfeiture provisions, which require payment of a portion of the policyholders' benefits, even if they had let the policy lapse.

WHAT TO WATCH OUT FOR

If, after reading this section, you decide to buy long-term care insurance, consider the following:

Too little coverage. Buy an amount that will cover all anticipated costs, or that leaves you with reasonable out-of-pocket expenses that will not drain your assets. Contrary to what some sales agents will suggest, some insurance is not necessarily better than no insurance.

Inflation eroding your coverage. Inflation protection is a must unless you buy a high daily benefit and expect to need care within a few years. Inflation protection automatically increases your daily benefit amount without increasing your premium.

The length of the elimination period. The longer the elimination period, the lower the premium. The elimination period, similar to a deductible, is the number of days of care *you* have to pay for before your insurance kicks in.

The inclusion of nonforfeiture policies. These pay reduced benefits if you qualify for care but let your policy lapse before you need care, and can be a good bet.

Too short or too little benefit duration. Benefit duration is either how much money your policy pays or for how long it will pay benefits.

Policies that don't keep pace with the actual costs of care. The more years between when you buy a policy and when you need care, the more you will have to pay out of your own pocket. If you buy your policy too far in advance, care costs may rise beyond what your policy covers by the time you need it.

THE SMARTER CONSUMER

Get satisfactory answers to these ten questions before buying long-term care insurance.

1. *Can I afford it?* A recent Families U.S.A. study reported that only one out of five Americans age 55 to 79 can afford *both* the high premiums *and* high co-payments of most policies. If you can afford it, you might be able to afford long-term care without buying insurance.

2. *When should I buy it?* Good for you, if you're thinking about long-term care in your 40s—but it may make sense to wait. The younger you are, the lower your premiums will be, but the longer you're likely to wait before you need care, allowing more time for premiums to increase and inflation to erode your benefits.

3. *Will the policy cover anticipated costs?* Compare your policy's daily

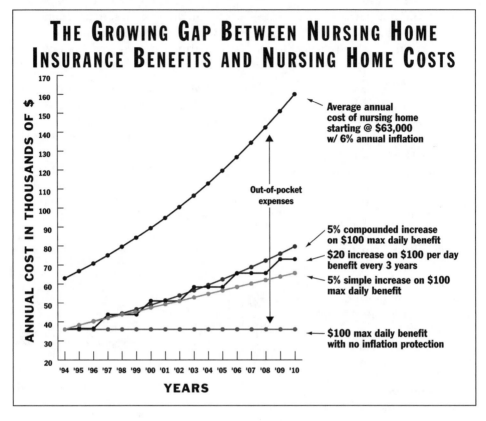

THE GROWING GAP BETWEEN NURSING HOME INSURANCE BENEFITS AND NURSING HOME COSTS

ANNUAL COST IN THOUSANDS OF $

Average annual cost of nursing home starting @ $63,000 w/ 6% annual inflation

Out-of-pocket expenses

5% compounded increase on $100 max daily benefit

$20 increase on $100 per day benefit every 3 years

5% simple increase on $100 max daily benefit

$100 max daily benefit with no inflation protection

YEARS

benefit and inflation adjustments with estimated nursing home costs (figure on 6% annual increases) when you will be 80 years old, the age at which people are most likely to need nursing home care. You'll have to pay the difference yourself—which can eat up the savings the insurance is supposed to protect.

4. *Will the policy benefits keep pace with inflation?* Currently, no policy is indexed to the actual costs of long-term care, so no policy that pays a daily benefit can guarantee to cover 100% of the costs. The best you're likely to get is a 5% increase compounded annually, which is definitely better than nothing.

5. *Will I be able to qualify for the*

policy's benefits? Look at the policy's fine print and avoid policies that require "continual one-on-one assistance to perform activities of daily living." You'd have to "be at death's door in order to meet a standard of 'continual assistance,' " according to Bill Dombi at the Center for Health Care Law. Also, avoid policies that have performance criteria for cognitive impairments. People with cognitive dementia, such as those with Alzheimer's disease, can usually perform basic physical tasks despite their memory loss, and so would not qualify for benefits. Finally, be wary of such vaguely defined criteria as "needs assistance" or "cannot perform," which makes it easier for a company to deny your claim.

6. *Does the policy provide the benefits I want at the facilities of my choice?* Most policies restrict the services and facilities they will pay for. Check whether there are facilities that meet your policy's specifications wherever you expect to live.

7. *Will I be able to keep up with the premiums?* Beware of sales agents who say that their policy's premiums will never go up. As noted above, they can and do considerably. Strongly consider nonforfeiture benefits to hedge your bet.

8. *Is the insurance company sound?* If your insurance company goes bankrupt—and hundreds have in the last decade—you can lose your coverage, or at best, pay higher premiums to a new company that takes over your policy. Ask about your company's financial ratings by calling one of the insurance company ratings services. (See "Life Insurance: Betting on Your Life," for phone numbers; page 336.) Only do business with "A+" or "A" rated companies, but beware that a high rating does not *guarantee* the company's solvency.

9. *Do I know and understand all of the policy's options?* Most policies give consumers five options: daily benefit amount, benefit duration, inflation protection, elimination period, and nonforfeiture benefits.

10. *Have I carefully reviewed the policy contract?* Do not purchase a policy without reading the fine print. Getting a second opinion from a lawyer or other expert is obviously best, but a trusted friend or family member can also ask guiding questions, like "Can you afford the premiums?" and "What will you get for your money?"

■ National Association of Area Agencies on Aging is a Washington group with an "Eldercare Locator" to direct you to the appropriate government agency or service provider in your area; call (800) 677-1116.

■ Legal Services Corporation is a federally chartered nonprofit organization that provides non-criminal legal assistance to persons who cannot afford to hire their own lawyer; call (202) 336-8800.

■ Children of Aging Parents is a clearinghouse of information about caring for the elderly. It provides support to adult children who are caring for elderly parents; call (215) 345-5104.

■ The National Association of Insurance Commissioners (NAIC), 120 West 12th Street, Suite 1100, Kansas City, MO 64105, (816) 842-3600, offers a *Long-Term Care Insurance Buying Guide.* They can also tell you whether your state has adopted the NAIC model long-term care insurance law, which sets a minimum standard for consumer protection. You can also call your state Insurance Department, many of which have state-specific buying guides and can tell you if your insurance agent has been disciplined recently.

CHAPTER 8

NUTRITIONAL SUPPLEMENTS

 No Magic Pills

"**D**evelop muscles while you sleep." "Improve your memory." "Grow healthier, more vibrant hair." "Experience an amazing energy burst."

These are some of the preposterous advertising and labeling claims made by manufacturers of nutritional supplements—vitamins, minerals, and assorted muscle pills. The virtual withdrawal of government oversight of the supplements industry during the 1980s allowed a whole new industry of purported cure purveyors to establish itself, no more honest than the infamous snake oil salesmen of the 19th century. No pill or potion will develop your muscles. Nothing you can eat will improve your memory or transform a man into a Don Juan. But Americans spend tens of millions of dollars a year anyway on nutritional supplements with names like Hot Sauce and Metabolol that promise to help make them into muscle men (or women) in short order.

This is certainly not to say that vitamin and mineral supplements have no health benefits. On the contrary, prolonged failure to obtain sufficient quantities of key vitamins and minerals definitely can lead to serious health problems. But the muscle pill industry is perpetrating an incredible hoax on those who wish to become an incredible hulk.

THE BASICS

Vitamins and Minerals: To Take Them or Not?

Vitamins are organic molecules that are essential to life. Some vitamins are fat-soluble, which means they are stored in the body and accumulate for long periods of time until needed. Among the fat-soluble vitamins are A, D, E, and K. Water-soluble vitamins do not build up in the system. They include the B vitamins and vitamin C.

Minerals are inorganic substances that are also essential to life. Among them are iron, calcium, zinc, manganese, iodine, and copper. According to the Council for

Responsible Nutrition, an industry trade group, the most commonly injested supplements are vitamins A, B₁ (thiamin), B₂ (riboflavin), B₃ (niacin), B₆ (pyridoxine), B₁₂, folic acid, C (ascorbic acid), E, calcium, and iron.

For centuries, people have known that certain foods, later discovered to be loaded with vitamins and minerals, ward off disease. Citrus fruits, which are laden with vitamin C, prevented scurvy in sailors who ate little else but hard tack and salt pork. (British sailors used to eat limes for this reason; thus their moniker, "limey.") Other vitamin-rich foods have been used to prevent beriberi and pellagra.

More recently, people have been taking vitamins because they believe they will impart special health benefits, such as preventing cancer, augmenting the immune system to fend off colds and flu, and even forestalling heart disease. The late Nobel prize-winner Dr. Linus Pauling was a great promoter of vitamin C as a cure for the common cold and even as a human immune deficiency virus (HIV) inhibitor.

While it is clearly established that a lack of one or more vitamins or minerals can lead to illness, the scientific community does not agree that taking additional vitamins and minerals above what the body normally consumes will make you healthier. Many nutritionists say that the U.S. recommended daily allowance (RDA) is all or even more than most people need. You can get your RDA from a diet with a variety of foods. Stanley Gershoff, PhD, dean of the Tufts University School of Nutrition, writes in *The Tufts University Guide to Total Nutrition,* "Most people in the United States get all the nutrients they need from the abundant food supply." On the other hand, some nutritionists point out that many Americans do not eat a mixed diet with plenty of vegetables, grains, and fruits.

Still, most people consume more nutrients than they may be aware. Milk is fortified with vitamins A and D. Iodine is added to salt. Even hamburger buns provide significant nutrition; most are fortified with extra B vitamins. While you don't need to get the full RDA for every nutrient every day, some people—especially chronic dieters—eat too little and don't get enough over time. For them, a basic multi-vitamin/mineral pill may be in order. People with unusual absorption difficulties and pregnant and lactating women may also benefit from special supplementation.

Unfortunately, much of the "scientific" evidence cited to back up the health benefit claims for taking any other nutrient-specific pills each day is not well-grounded. "Studies" referred to in product promotions often don't meet rigorous scientific standards, nor do they report whether the subjects in such studies got the vitamins from pills or from vitamin-rich foods—the latter indicating a generally healthier diet and a healthier subject. Manufacturers sometimes distort valid studies to conclude something entirely different from what the researchers intended. Even if a credible study finds some benefit, another may disagree—but the

THE ANTI-OXIDANT CONUNDRUM

Vitamins said to act as anti-oxidants—vitamins A, C, and E—have been generating much interest lately and many people are taking special supplements of them. They may be on to something. Normal cell metabolism as well as exposure to smog, X-rays, and certain other environmental hazards create oxygen free radicals, which can attack cell membranes or even damage DNA and lead to illness. Certain vitamins—beta-carotene (A), E, and C—apparently neutralize these free radicals. Vitamin E is thought to be especially helpful with preventing free-radical-caused damage to the heart; one major study found that women who took at least 100 international units (IU) a day for two years halved their risk of cardiovascular disease. And beta-carotene supplementation has been shown to reduce the incidence of heart attack and stroke.

But some experts are still skeptical. According to Dr. Stephen Barrett, author of the *Consumer Reports* book *Health Schemes, Scams and Frauds*, antioxidants can also *release* free radicals, and the latest research found that smokers who take beta-carotene actually have a higher rate of cancer. "Studies that support taking anti-oxidants are merely epidemiological and do not establish cause and effect," Barrett says.

manufacturer cites only the study that takes their side.

Some claims are complete folderol. Don't believe anything that promises to:

Make men more virile. Men have been trying since the dawn of time to find a true aphrodisiac. Our advice: Keep looking.

Provide an energy burst, as advertisements for Nature's Bounty Ener-B (a vitamin B12 nasal gel) suggest. While a severe shortage of vitamin B12 can make you feel weak, giving yourself extra does nothing.

Make your hair healthier, fuller, thicker, and make your skin supple and healthy. The ingredients in popular hair and skin formulas include a range of vitamins and minerals, such as niacin, iron, biotin, beta-carotene, and inositol. Typical of these products are the Nature's Plus lineup, including "Ultra Hair," "Ultra Skin," and "Ultra Nails." It is impossible to target vitamins or minerals to certain parts of the body. Of course, extreme serious nutritional deficiency could lead to visibly unhealthy skin or hair, but this is very rare.

Improve your memory. The claims for products making this promise are based on a study that found that taking high doses of purified phosphatidylcholine (choline) helped a few patients with Alzheimer's disease. From this, manufacturers make an extraordinary leap to assert that taking choline will help people without Alzheimer's think better. Among other ingredients that may be found in so-called memory formulas are lecithin, vitamin B6, and L-glutamine.

Help your body cope with stress. One of the most prevalent claims on vitamin shelves is that you need special supplementation if you are heavily stressed. In this frenetic society, who isn't? But you don't need to take special vitamins or minerals for it. You might need such supplementation if you have experienced severe physical stress (such as surgery), but for the emotional stresses of everyday life.

Several years ago, Lederle Labs, the makers of Stresstabs, was cited by the New York State Attorney General for deceptively claiming that this product helps the body deal with stress. Lederle agreed to stop making the claims and paid $25,000 in costs to the state. Although the company never admitted the claims were false, it agreed not to say or imply that emotional distress causes depletion of water-soluble vitamins and to start saying that people with ordinary stress can get all the nutrients they need from a balanced diet. Nonetheless, Stresstabs are still on the market, and the package and advertising still feature an image of a candle

burning at both ends, although Lederle is now careful to write on the package—in small print—that the pills are for people who have had a long illness, who drink or smoke excessively, or who follow fad diets.

Dr. Victor Herbert, a professor at New York's Mt. Sinai School of Medicine and recipient of several national awards for nutrition research, advises patients not to believe anyone who says that most disease is due to a faulty diet and can be treated with such "nutritional methods" as vitamins. According to Dr. Herbert, common symptoms like malaise, tiredness, lack of energy, aches or pains, and insomnia are usually the body's reaction to emotional stress.

There is considerable doubt as to the efficacy of supplements that claim to help relieve premenstrual syndrome (PMS) symptoms. PMS formulas contain a lot of B vitamins, and some doctors do prescribe high B6 doses to alleviate PMS. But the *Mount Sinai Medical School Complete Book of Nutrition* says, "PMS has been erroneously represented as being 'cured' by B6, when in fact the same 80 percent 'cured' by B6 are in fact 'cured' by a placebo."

A federal law enacted in 1994 curbs some of the most outrageous claims. Assertions about disease prevention or treatment will now

> "*There is no evidence that vitamins reduce stress. It's all nonsense, a sales pitch. There may be a sort of placebo effect.*"
>
> —Dr. Robert Olsen,
> State University of New York at
> Stony Brook Medical School

require Food and Drug Administration approval. Unfortunately, the law does not prohibit the much more common (yet still suspect) "structure and function" claims. A manufacturer can still imply that, since a severe lack of vitamin A could theoretically be harmful to your eyesight, a product with Vitamin A will help your vision.

"I'm Not Going to Pay a Lot for These Vitamins!"

If you are among the estimated 40% of Americans who have taken a vitamin or mineral supplement in the past month, you probably paid too much. A 1992 survey found that the price of 100 tablets of 1,000 mg of synthetic vitamin C was 3.9 cents a tablet at one pharmacy chain, 5.9 cents at another, and 6.3 cents at still another. Natural vitamin E (10 tablets of 400 IU) ranged from $4.49 at a major local drugstore chain to $7.39 at another.

Comparing prices can be difficult because the number of pills in bottles and their potencies are not standardized. If you're unable to compare exactly the same products, just remember that vitamins purchased in health food chain stores are usually more expensive than those purchased in drugstores.

Nutritional Supplements: What's in Them for You?

"A New Advanced Cell Growth Formula That Stimulates Muscle Growth Even While You Sleep!!!"

"Nothing is more powerful at adding muscle without fat."

"An Anabolic Inferno . . . the most efficient muscle building supplement. [You will] watch . . . muscles explode with incredible strength, massive size and pure energy."

What's in these products? Typical ingredient lists include choline, inositol, potassium, smilax (an extract of the Mexican sarsaparilla root), chromium picolinate, dibencozide, ginseng (it's supposed to increase stamina), sterols (made from vegetables and marketed as an alternative to animal steroids), growth hormones, and various amino acids.

There is no reliable evidence that any of these substances come anywhere near to living up to their claims. Inositol seems to have no use in the human body. The body makes more than enough choline on its own. There is no evidence that smilax does anything; in fact, it acts as a laxative, which is undesirable in athletes. Ginseng also hasn't been shown to do anything special. Nonetheless, nutritional supplement manufacturers argue that body builders and others need *more* of these ingredients than can readily be obtained from food. Nonsense.

Amino acids and growth hormones may even prove harmful. Amino acids are the building blocks of protein. Americans get more than enough protein in their regular diets, and ingesting yet more amino acids may put an extra burden on the kidneys. Moreover, amino acids are not meant to be taken free-standing, which is how

WHY PAY MORE?

Nationally advertised vitamin brands almost always cost more. Take the One-a-Day brand of multivitamins, for example. You could pay $7.29 for 100 tablets or, for the same ingredients, buy the store brand at a drugstore chain for only $1.99—a price differential of more than $300%. One hundred tablets of Centrum, a nationally advertised vitamin and mineral supplement, sold for as much as $9.99; a store brand with a bit less silicon cost only $2.99.

for their advertising claims. Some of the companies ignored the request, and others sent information consisting primarily of ingredient lists and generalized claims about effectiveness. Notably, none supplied published reports from recognized or peer-reviewed journals.

The Department charged some of the companies with deceptive trade practices. In the fall of 1993, one of the firms, L&S Research (Cybergenics), settled by agreeing to place a disclaimer on certain ads reading, "Supplement component will not promote faster or greater muscular gains."

they are often presented in supplements. Taking too much of a single amino acid might interfere in the absorption of another. And an excess of growth hormone can lead to acromegaly, in which the muscles grow in mass but become weaker and lose functionality.

In trying to escape government attacks on efficacy claims, manufacturers sometimes respond that the supplements are only part of an overall fitness program—that the products alone do not produce the benefit but work in conjunction with regular workouts. There is no credible evidence that taking supplements imparts any extra body building benefit that isn't obtained from workouts and a good diet.

In 1992, the NYC Department of Consumer Affairs asked manufacturers to provide scientific backup

WHAT TO WATCH OUT FOR

Vitamins

Overdosing. Hundreds of people overdose on vitamin and mineral supplements each year, with serious enough consequences that their mishaps are reported to the federal government. The point at which harm may be sustained is generally set at ten times the U.S. RDA for water-soluble vitamins, five times the RDA for fat-solubles, and three times the RDA for minerals.

What might actually occur?

Too much vitamin A (sustained by overdosing by more than 20,000 IU) can cause headaches, vomiting, and liver damage. One Illinois chiropractor settled a lawsuit for about $900,000 after he had erroneously prescribed hundreds of thousands of IU of vitamin A to two children with a congenital scaly skin disease.

One of the children suffered liver damage and the other one's growth was stunted.

Too much vitamin B₃ (niacin) can result in hot flashes, ulcers, and liver disorders, and excesses of vitamin B₆, sometimes administered as a PMS remedy, can lead to neurological damage.

Excessive intake of vitamin C can lead to urinary tract problems. Several people with AIDS have died from dehydration after taking massive doses of vitamin C, which had induced severe diarrhea.

Too much vitamin D can cause kidney stones.

A 1992 Finnish study found that very high iron intake can more than double the risk of heart attacks. And according to nutritionist and personal health columnist Jane Brody, although the body can handle periodic iron overdoses, chronic overdoses can result in methemochromatosis, which can damage the liver, pancreas, and heart.

> "**P**eople get all the amino acids they require by eating an adequate diet."
>
> —Dr. Douglas Archer, of the U.S. Food and Drug Administration

Marketing gimmicks. Manufacturers often make distinctions without a difference. For example, the body can't differentiate among synthetic and natural vitamin C—it's all ascorbic acid—but natural costs a lot more. "Time-release" C is also a lot more expensive but imparts no proven benefit.

Varying potencies and dissolution qualities. Unlike prescription pharmaceuticals, vitamin and mineral pills don't have to contain the *exact* quantity of ingredients stated on the label. Because these manufacturing processes are not as controlled as they are for prescription drugs, one B complex pill may contain only 90 mg of active B complex vitamin while another has 110 mg.

Variances in manufacturing and a lack of testing means that not all vitamin and mineral pills will dissolve at the same speed in the body. The United States Pharmacopeia (not a government group) is trying to resolve this problem by issuing recommended dissolution standards. For example, they propose that water-soluble vitamins be at least 75% dissolved in an hour. But these are merely recommended standards that took effect in November 1993. Products that meet the standards for potency, dissolution, disintegration, and purity will be able to display the letters "USP" on the label next to the product name.

Health food store salespeople. Their job is to sell you more vitamins and minerals, not to provide sound advice. In fact, they are prohibited by law from diagnosing medical conditions or suggesting remedies.

Eating a poorer diet because you are taking supplements. Fruits, grains, and vegetables are still the preferred sources of nutrients, and they impart other health benefits as well, such as better digestion. Scientists are just beginning to understand the complex benefits of dietary fiber, and the only way to get enough fiber is to eat food containing lots of it.

Taking vitamins for "insurance." Don't take a pill unless you analyze your diet and determine if it is deficient. "In that case," nutritionist Dr. Stephen Barrett advises, "the best course of action is to fix your diet." He adds: "If you can't correct your diet, then purchase an inexpensive multivitamin that contains no more than 100% U.S. RDA for any ingredient."

Nutritional Supplements

Hyperbolic claims. When you see the following words used on a product or in an advertisement for a nutritional supplement, remember, it just ain't so: energy enhancer, fat burner, rapid muscle growth, converts fat into energy, anabolic activator, increases lean muscle mass, lipotropic, metabolic optimizer.

"True-life" testimonials. More often than not, the testimonials come from body-builders who are paid a fee by the manufacturers or are on their regular payroll.

Try to buy vitamins with expiration dates on the bottles. Vitamin and mineral pills don't last forever. There is no government mandate to state an expiration date, but some manufacturers do so anyway.

As regards nutritional supplements, the smartest thing you can do is eat a healthy diet and not buy them.

▪ The Mount Sinai Hospital *Medical School Complete Book of Nutrition*, Victor Herbert, MD, F.A.C.P., and Genell J. Subak-Sharpe, M.S., eds., St. Martin's Press, 1990. (Herbert and Subak-Sharpe are now updating and retitling this book. The new title will be *Total Nutrition: The Only Guide You'll Ever Need*.)

▪ Read *The Health Robbers* **(Pro**metheus Books, 1993), by Stephen Barrett, MD, a prize-winning author of 23 books. His book exposes all sorts of nutritional quackery and scientific mumbo-jumbo. He also wrote *Health Schemes, Scams and Frauds* (a *Consumer Reports* book) which contains chapters on fake treatments for AIDS and cancer, phony "cures" for arthritis, "vitamin pushers," and weight control fads, among many other subjects.

To order, call the Lehigh Valley Committee Against Health Fraud at (215) 437-1795, or write to P.O. Box 1747, Allentown, PA 18105. Price: $14.

▪ The United States Pharmacopeia publishes a free guide on vitamin quality. Write for the Vitamin/Mineral Brochure, USP, 12601 Twinbrook Parkway, Rockville, MD 20852.

CHAPTER 9

WEIGHT LOSS PRODUCTS AND PROGRAMS

*The Skinny on Dieting
Deceptions and Dangers*

Are you a waist-watcher? If so, your private battle of the bulge puts you roundly in the middle of a public obsession. At any given time, about 50 million Americans are dieting (50% of all women and 25% of all men), and an equal number claim they are struggling to maintain their weight.

A $33 billion industry has grown up to feed this all-American appetite for appetite control. Fly-by-night inventors hawk gut-busting nutritional supplements that supposedly take off the pounds while you sleep. Herbalists advertise miracle concoctions, purportedly from the Far East, in the back of *The National Enquirer* and other magazines. Major U.S. corporations hire such well-knowns as baseball legend Tommy Lasorda and actress Lynn Redgrave to star in slick commercials on network television. Franchised weight-loss centers dress their staff in doctors' coats. Reputable book publishers and booksellers brazenly promote the latest fat-fighting fad.

With all this calorie counting and liquid lunching, you naturally might assume Americans were getting thinner. But if you did, you'd be wrong. Americans are fatter than ever. About a quarter to a third of all adults are now considered obese, usually defined as 20% to 30% or more over their ideal body weight, and the numbers have been increasing steadily over the last 20 years.

So Americans are dieting more, *and* getting heavier. What's behind this contradiction?

THE BASICS

Fat Facts

Losing weight is as simple, or complicated, as eating less, exercising more, or a combination of both. Any diet that includes fewer calories than you burn off will cause you to lose weight. Since about 3,500 calories make up a pound of body weight, you would need to reduce your caloric intake by 500 calories a day to lose one pound per week, assuming your weight is stable.

For this reason, virtually any diet, if followed closely, will result in temporary weight loss—purely because of reduced calorie intake, not because of any complementary combination of foods, miracle dietary supplements, or wonder gadgets.

Trouble is, the odds are slim you'll keep the weight off. The best studies have shown a failure rate of 95%—that is, only 5% of the dieters managed to keep all or most of their weight off for five or more years. In 1993 *Consumer Reports* magazine surveyed 95,000 of its readers who had recently tried to lose weight. It found that only 25% managed to keep off two-thirds of what they lost for over two years.

The human body physiologically adapts to eating fewer calories and research has shown that this may account for the temporariness of the disappearing act. Dr. C. Wayne Callaway, associate clinical professor of medicine at George Washington University and co-author of the 1990 federal *Dietary Guidelines for Americans*, testified before two congressional committees that reducing on a very low calorie diet is a form of semi-starvation that signals the body to slow down metabolism to protect against actual starvation. Thus, for example, a person who switches from a 2,000 calorie daily diet to a 1,000 calorie daily diet will most often *gain* weight when they increase their daily caloric intake even slightly, because the body is now geared to burn calories at a slower rate. Furthermore, the body compensates for under-eating by over-eating. Human and animal studies show that food can both suppress and stimulate the appetite. People and animals who have been adequately fed feel satisfied and stop eating; people and animals who've been underfed overcompensate and binge. In other words, each of us has something close to a "natural weight" that is, alas, hard to beat over time.

> ## "When it comes to losing weight, nearly all of the people who try commercial programs are being fooled nearly all of the time."
>
> —JANE BRODY,
> health writer for
> *The New York Times*

Wasteful Waist-Watching and Dangerous Diets

Fad diets. Callaway's summary of the scientific literature explains why the temporary effects of fad diets don't usually last. Whether you cut way back on carbohydrates or protein, put yourself on a fruit fast, or whatever the latest pop wisdom suggests, you'll probably lose weight simply because you're shedding water and eating fewer calories. These radical diets are hard to sustain over time, and many people never complete them because they get too hungry or too bored. Even those who get to the end find the weight creeps back once they start eating normally.

Diet pills and other diet aids. Some pills have shown some effectiveness at curbing the appetite, but they also come with undesirable side effects. Amphetamines' appetite-suppressing effect is temporary; they are also highly addictive and can be dangerous to the central nervous system and heart. For this reason, using amphetamines as a diet aid requires a doctor's conscientious supervision. And when the patient discontinues use, his or her appetite will return and weight is easily regained.

Over-the-counter diet pills such as Acutrim and Dexatrim contain phenylpropanolamine, a mild stimulant that's chemically similar to amphetamines and that many decongestant products also contain. While it is somewhat effective at decreasing appetite and may help you shed a few pounds, you'll probably gain the weight right back as soon as you stop taking the pills and your appetite returns to normal. In his book *The Health Robbers*, Dr. Stephen Barrett, a nationally

known opponent of quackery and fraud in medicine, says this drug may be dangerous to people with heart disease, high blood pressure, diabetes, or hyperthyroidism.

In a *Consumer Reports* survey published in June 1993, fewer than 5% of the people who had taken nonprescription diet pills said they were very or completely satisfied with how well the pills helped them lose weight and keep it off, and half were very or completely dissatisfied. Furthermore, people didn't like how the pills made them feel. Over 30% said they were always hungry, and over 20% at times felt dizzy or nauseated.

Commercial weight loss programs. These range from private, local clinics to massive national chains, and they all offer their own "exclusive" programs. These can include individual counseling or group meetings, specially prepared food you must buy from them, meal replacement liquids or nutritional supplements, exercise regimens, and medical and psychological exams. In general, they can be broken down into two kinds of programs: medically supervised, very low-calorie liquid fasts, in which flavored liquid formulas replace all solid food, usually for a period of months (such as Optifast, Medifast, and Health Management Resources); and non-medically supervised low-calorie regimens, in which dieters eat solid foods within a regimented meal plan (such as Jenny Craig, Nutri/System, and Diet Center). Prices vary from a few hundred to a few thousand dollars.

Generally, people who sign up with a weight-loss program believe they will receive a health-care service. But in such a commercially driven atmosphere, a pound of fat is worth a pound of profit—all too often at the expense of the dieter's health, emotional well-being, and pocketbook. Indeed, one Nutri/System Inc. franchisee said in the company's franchise brochure: "Money is the reason I became a Nutri/System franchisee. And now I have more money than I ever dreamed I could make in a lifetime."

Emphasizing sales rather than health has led these programs to overprice and overpromise, even though their plans often underestimate the risks and fail to meet the expectations they set up. A 1991 undercover investigation, by the NYC Department of Consumer Affairs, into the sales tactics of New York City weight loss programs, revealed that nine out of ten failed to warn potential customers of serious health risks and instead claimed "absolute" safety, even when investigators asked directly whether health problems could arise. In fact, there is evidence that rapid weight loss (more than three to five pounds per week) can cause gallstones and cardiac problems. Rapid weight loss can even lead to death, particularly in people who are not overweight to begin with.

After a six-month investigation into the promises of lasting weight loss made by commercial weight loss programs, the Federal Trade Commission (FTC) alleged in 1993 that five of the nation's largest commercial diet-program compa-nies—Jenny Craig Inc., Diet Center Inc., Physicians Weight Loss Centers, Nutri/System, and Weight Watchers International—deceptively advertised unsubstantiated weight-loss claims and consumer testimonials without proof that the examples represented the typical experience of dieters in the programs.

One ad for the Diet Center practically admits as much: "Temporary weight loss is usually followed by weight gain. The only effective weight-loss program is one that produces a safe and permanent result." But then it resorts to hyperbole and implies—falsely—that the Diet Center is somehow different: "The Diet Center Program provides the perfect solution."

Unsupervised meal replacement drinks. These powdered drink mixes, such as Slim-Fast and Dyna-Trim, contain protein, sugar, fiber, vitamins, and minerals and were designed to replace one or two meals a day. While many users in the *Consumer Reports* survey managed to lose weight, albeit small amounts, 20% *gained* five pounds or more. And a third said they gained back the weight they had lost as soon as they went back to solid food. Tommy Lasorda's testimonial to the contrary, you might as well eat real food.

Gimmicks. Too good to be true? You bet. Most are simply a waste of money. The effects of cellulite reducing cream, for example, are purely cosmetic and only temporary. Some gadgets are even dangerous. The Food and Drug Administration has forced a number of electrical muscle stimulators off the

FIRST, GET SOME ANSWERS

The U.S. FDA, FTC, and National Association of Attorneys General suggest you ask the following additional questions before you sign up for a commercial weight loss program:

- What are the health risks?
- What data can you show me that prove your program actually works?
- Do customers keep the weight off after they leave the diet program?
- What are the costs for membership, weekly fees, food,

supplements, maintenance, and counseling? What's the payment schedule? Are any costs covered by health insurance? Do you give refunds if I drop out?

- Do you have a maintenance program? Is it part of the package or does it cost extra?
- What kind of supervision do you provide? What are the credentials of your professionals?
- What are the program's requirements? Are there special menus or foods, counseling visits, or exercise plans?

market. They were promoted for weight loss but when used incorrectly, they caused electrical shocks and burns.

Weight Loss = Health Loss?

Worse than the waste of money and effort, losing weight may also be harmful to your health. While the benefits of losing weight are generally indisputable for truly obese people, who are at a greater risk of stroke, heart disease, diabetes, and gallstones, definitive advice for others is less clear. A June 1991 study published in the *New England Journal of Medicine* linked repeated changes in weight, no matter the person's initial weight, with a generally increased death rate and twice the chance of dying of heart disease specifically. Whether this "yo-yo dieting" is worse than stay-

ing somewhat overweight depends on your health and body type.

Although three of every four people *feel* fat, only one in four *is*, medically, fat. Indeed, recent research has shown that the number of pounds is less important than where the pounds collect in determining the health effects of excess weight. "Apple-shaped" people, whose fat collects in the abdomen and above the waist, are more at risk of heart disease than "pear-shaped" people, who carry excess fat around the hips, rear end and thighs. Men tend to be "apples" and women tend to be "pears." Given this predisposition to a certain body type and weight, it seems pointless, and possibly even dangerous, for most people to fight it.

If you are determined to do something about how you feel and look, there are two things that nobody has anything but good things to say about: increasing the amount of exercise you get and lowering the amount of fat in your diet.

You don't have to work two-hour workouts into your hectic schedule to lose weight. Instead, take exercise where you can get it: Use the stairs instead of the elevator; walk your dog instead of just letting him out the back door; park your car at the far end of the lot; allow a little extra time to walk to meetings rather than grabbing a cab.

Just lowering the fat in your diet may help you shed a few pounds, since fatty foods tend to be high in calories.

WHAT TO WATCH OUT FOR

Claims based on tantalizing words or concepts: effortless, easy, guaranteed, breakthrough, natural, burns fat away, blocks fat, blocks starch, amazing, and miraculous. It would indeed be a miracle if products pitched this way lived up to their promises, for the only "amazing results" are likely to be the promoters' amazing profits.

The claim game. Don't be swayed by testimonials or anecdotal evidence, such as startling "before and after" pictures of people who've dropped 50 pounds or four dress sizes. They skirt the fact that few studies back up short-term claims of success. Virtually no evidence supports the long-term effectiveness of commercial weight loss pro-

grams and products, according to a 1992 report of the National Institutes of Health.

Jenny Craig, for instance, ran ads that said things like "I lost 95 pounds in just over six months. And, I've kept the weight off for nearly one year!" or "I used to dream that one day I'd wake up and be slim. Thanks to Jenny Craig, it happened. I tried other programs, but the second I'd go off, I'd gain everything back, and then some. While they helped me lose weight, they never taught me how to eat in the real world and keep it off." The FTC alleges that Jenny Craig can-

WEIGHT LOSS WASHOUT

According to the *Consumer Reports* survey published in June 1993, the average dieter who used one of the commercial diet programs regained half what he or she had lost within six months of ending the diet and two thirds of it within two years. In one study published in *The International Journal of Obesity*, one-fourth of the 4,026 obese patients who went on the Optifast program dropped out within the first three weeks, and only 5% to 10% of the Optifast dieters who achieved significant weight loss were still at their reduced weights after 18 months.

A POUND OF FLESH = $100

An NYC Consumer Affairs investigation found that one Diet Center in Manhattan would have charged a potential dieter $100 per pound to lose seven pounds and maintain the weight loss. "Worse, I was only one pound away from being *underweight* to start with," said the undercover investigator.

not substantiate the implication that its customers typically are successful in reaching their weight goals and maintaining their weight loss permanently.

Is there a doctor in the house? Although many commercial weight loss centers claim their programs are "doctor-supervised," doctors may be on site only rarely, if ever. Take Physicians Weight Loss Centers, which said things like this in ads: "Our physicians, nurses, and counselors supervise your complete program. They show you how to eat for healthy weight loss, oversee your progress and well-being, and teach you new eating habits for staying slim." In fact, the FTC charges that the center physicians do not supervise participants.

Mumbo-jumbo that sounds scientific. Slim Time Weight Loss Center in New York City pushes "the secret of permanent weight loss": eating a specific combination of foods

that would increase the body's metabolic rate by forcing the stomach to digest the food quicker. No such magic combination exists.

Deceptively low prices. Nutri/System, for example, ran various price promotions. One promised, "Lose all the weight you can for only $79." Another said, "Pay only $1 per pound." However, an FTC investigation found that there are "substantial additional mandatory expenses associated with participation in the program that far exceed the advertised price."

High-pressure sales tactics used by center-based programs. These can include limited-time deals, discounts when you balk at the price, psychological manipulation ("you'll feel better if you just get started"), money-back guarantees, and follow-up phone calls that verge on harassment.

Fat-fighting frauds. Diet candies, artificial bulk-producers, starch blockers, fat blockers, and fat flushers are bogus. Some of them are even dangerous. People who have used starch blockers have complained of nausea, vomiting, diarrhea, and stomach pains. Guar gum, a bulk producer, can cause obstructions of the intestines, stomach, or esophagus, which prompted the Food and Drug Administration to take legal action against companies marketing products containing this ingredient.

All-natural products. Natural isn't necessarily better, or safe. Herbal diet pills sold by mail and in health food stores have exotic ingredient lists that give few clues as to their contents. For instance, *ma huang*, the primary ingredient in many herbal diet supplements, is ephedrine, a nervous system stimulant that acts like amphetamines and caffeine.

Expensive vitamin or protein supplements. If you are eating a balanced low-calorie diet you don't need them. If you will be eating fewer than 1,200 calories a day for a prolonged period of time, a vitamin supplement would be advisable, according to Dr. Stephen Barrett.

There is a way. It may sound too sensible, and like hard work, but if you switch to a low-fat, reduced-calorie, nutritionally balanced diet and combine it with moderate exercise you'll probably lose weight. Most doctors and registered dietitians recommend losing no more than one pound per week. While crash diets may work faster, at least at first, they often lack essential nutrients, can harm your health, and their results probably won't last. Furthermore, they do nothing to change for the long-term any unhealthy eating habits you may have. Check with your doctor before you embark on any drastic change—this goes equally for changes in your diet and exercise routines.

Before you sign up with a commercial weight loss program, check the company's reputation with the local Better Business Bureau. And before you sign a contract, make sure the costs and fees for all services, foods, supplements, and maintenance have been clearly spelled out.

■ **"Diets: What Works** —What Doesn't," *Consumer Reports*, June 1993.

■ **The Facts About** *Weight Loss Products and Programs*, a brochure available from the Federal Trade Commission, Washington, DC 20580 or the Food and Drug Administration, Consumer Affairs and Information, 5600 Fishers Lane, HFC-110, Rockville, MD 20857.

■ **"Weight Control: Facts,** Fads and Frauds," in *The Health Robbers*, edited by Stephen Barrett, MD, and William T. Jarvis, PhD, (Prometheus Books, 1993).

■ **To complain about a** weight loss program or product, contact your attorney general, the Food and Drug Administration, the Federal Trade Commission, or the local Better Business Bureau.

CHAPTER 10

HEALTH CLUBS

Exercise . . . Your Judgment

We've all heard about the benefits of exercise. But what you may have heard about are the risks of *not* exercising. C. Everett Koop, the former surgeon general, has argued that a sedentary lifestyle is equivalent to smoking a full pack of cigarettes every day. And while 26% of adults smoke, "only 22% of Americans are active today to levels recommended for good health benefits," according to the U.S. Centers for Disease Control and Prevention. More than half—54%—are "inadequately active" and 24% are "completely sedentary." The result: More than 250,000 deaths per year in the United States may be due to lack of regular physical activity.

In fact, every week seems to bring another reason to exercise. Gallup surveys indicate that those who exercise regularly feel more relaxed, experience improvements in creativity, have better social lives, exhibit more self-confidence, are more willing and able to change other health habits (like smoking and diet), feel a stronger sense of control over their health and their lives, and are even more attractive.

And these people don't just feel better—they actually *are* healthier. Regular physical activity reduces risks of coronary heart disease, adult-onset diabetes, hypertension, certain cancers, osteoporosis, and depression—and generally increases life expectancy. As much as 50% of the body's decline between ages 30 and 70 can be attributed to a sedentary lifestyle, according to 1993 data from the Canadian Fitness and Lifestyle Research Institute.

Exercising, in short, makes a lot of sense—dollars and cents, too. A 1992 study by an association of health clubs, shows benefits not just to athletes but to their employers in reduced health care costs, increased productivity, and reduced absenteeism. After one year, for instance, participants in Johnson & Johnson's "wellness program" saw their sick leave go *down* 9% while it went *up* 13% for a control group. Large companies like IBM, Microsoft, and the John Hancock Insurance Company now subsidize health club memberships for all employees; insurance groups offer rebates to subscribers who join. The Prudential Insurance Co. estimates that for every $1 spent on its fitness program, it saved 93 cents in health-care costs per employee who participated.

Fueled by such evidence and the aesthetic standards of Hollywood and fashion magazines, the '80s saw an explosion in fitness facilities where young professionals could chisel their bodies, shave off a few pounds, or simply get a little aerobic exercise. Club membership, long the preserve of young, single males, gained popularity among women, married couples, and people in their 30s and 40s. The $7 billion fitness industry has since leveled off, leading to a spate of well-publicized club closings and increasingly aggressive marketing ploys. So before exercising on the gym floor, exercise caution. If you choose the wrong health club, you're likely to lose more wallet than weight.

THE BASICS

To Join or Not to Join

A sedentary lifestyle ranks with high cholesterol, cigarette smoking, high blood pressure, and obesity as a major risk factor in heart disease and a variety of other life-threatening conditions. Government health experts now recommend that "[e]very American adult should accumulate 30 minutes or more of moderate intensity physical activity over the course of most days of the week"; things like ballroom dancing, a brisk walk home from the office, mowing the lawn, or using the stairs instead of the elevator just might do the job.

The only real question, then, should be what type of exercise is best for you. Many find membership in a health club a necessary incentive to get their juices flowing—they like the setting, they

want to get their money's worth, or they need the motivating force of a trained professional. Hence, 16.7 million Americans regularly exercise in health clubs.

Finding the Right Health Club

L et your fingertips get some exercise first: Try to narrow your choices by calling a few places and visiting the ones that seem to match your budget and your interests. Once you're there, tour the premises, ask the staff questions, and ask to be set loose on the premises so you can talk with club members to get a sense of the place. In particular, pay attention to the following:

Convenience. Location and operating hours are probably the number-one consideration. Especially if you find it hard enough to get motivated, why make exercising even more of a challenge by joining a health club 40 minutes away?

Cost. The price depends on a number of factors, including the equipment and services offered, the size of the membership, and the staff-to-member ratio. Payment plans vary, from a membership fee upfront or in installments, to an initiation fee plus monthly dues, to a pay-per-use plan. (Some clubs charge extra for specific hours or features.)

Stay away from long-term contracts. Good as your intentions may be, the world is full of ex-exercise addicts who've discovered the pleasures of being a couch potato; recent research shows that only half

WHICH CLUB'S FOR YOU?

Comparing health club memberships is no easy task. You have to consider different facilities (each offering different equipment, support staff, maintenance, etc.), terms of contract, and location, to name a few factors. Calls to health clubs in the New Haven, CT, area in May 1994 asking about a one-year basic student membership with a specific interest in weight equipment, pool/sauna, and racquetball court yielded the following results:

	Weight	Pool/ Sauna	Racquet- ball	Cost for one-year membership
Bally's Holiday Health	✓	✓		*$380/year (no student discount). Special: $15/month for 2 years*
Downtown Health and Racquet	✓	*Dry sauna*	✓	*$39/month (student fee)*
World Gym	✓			*$199/year (student fee)*
YMCA	✓	✓		*$40 joining fee + $13/month (student fee)*

the people who start exercising stay with the program six months or longer.

In addition, you may be playing into the hands of a greedy operator who'll take the money and run. That's what happened in 1991 to some 5,000 members at four Apple Health & Sports club branches in New York City when the spas shut their doors—after some members had recently paid fees of $1,000. Stay clear, in particular, of so-called "life memberships." They are illegal in most states and, as one academic notes, "For every club that opens, another one closes. A club with a large upfront fee offering a lifetime membership is a likely candidate for bankruptcy in three years."

Equipment and services. Figure out what you're interested in. Standard exercise features include aerobic equipment—such as treadmills, stationary bicycles, Stairmasters, or rowing machines—to burn calories and fat and improve circulation—and anaerobic equipment—such as Nautilus machines or free weights—that help you strengthen, tone, define, and build muscles. Other options include saunas, steamrooms, pools, whirlpools, juice bars, massage, racquet sports, tanning rooms, specialized exercise classes, private training, and nutritional counseling.

Overcrowding. Visit the club at the time you'll be using it. Ask what the number of members is and if there is a limit on membership. Experts suggest a ratio of square footage to total number of members of 10:1 to 15:1.

Maintenance and cleanliness. Visit both the exercise floor and the locker room, and inspect closely the condition of the various machines. Each piece of equipment should bear how-to-use instructions.

Staff. Find out about their qualifications—whether they hold degrees in physical education, exercise physiology, or in kinesiology; whether they are certified by a reputable organization, such as the American College of Sports Medicine or the Aerobics and Fitness Association of America, and whether they have cardiopulmonary resuscitation (CPR) training. A good instructor can help you develop the right exercise plan and motivate you to stick with your routine.

> "*If a club attempts to sell you a long-term contract on your first visit by offering you a discount, turn around and walk out.*"
>
> —Dr. William Jarvis, President, National Council Against Health Fraud

You may have other, specialized considerations. Does the club accept children or offer child care? And if you travel often, you may want to join a club that belongs to a national chain or one with reciprocal membership arrangements with other clubs—as do members of the International Physical Fitness Association. Still, be wary of such representations.

Consider Sarah Z. Three months after she had paid $240 for a two-year basic membership at a well-known health club in her Brooklyn neighborhood, she accepted a new job in San Francisco. Her club told her that she could transfer her membership to an affiliated club in California for $50. But in San Francisco, she found out that the ten local health clubs supposedly available for her use had either closed down or disavowed their affiliation with the Brooklyn club. Her calls to the corporate headquarters of the club were, of course, repeatedly ignored. Worse, she had never been told that, under New York law, she was entitled to a pro-rated refund if she moved more than 25 miles away.

Finally, run a "gut check." Do you feel good about, and comfortable with, the club? Notes fitness industry columnist John Sheehan, "People will not continue to do anything, *no matter how good it is for them*, unless it is pleasurable, unless it is enjoyable, unless it is social, unless it is entertaining."

WHAT TO WATCH OUT FOR

Blockbuster ads promising world-class facilities at bargain basement prices. Example: A Jack LaLanne print ad promised in bold letters

SIGNING UP

Before you write your chosen health club a check, check with your local Better Business Bureau or consumer agency for any history of complaints. Find out what protection you have if the club shuts down. More than 30 states, for instance, require health clubs to post bonds for this purpose. Still, since many clubs fail to do so, make a call to the office of the attorney general or secretary of state to verify that your club is actually "bonded" and that it carries liability insurance. If you buy a pre-opening membership, make sure your fee is placed in escrow.

If there is an opportunity for a try-out period, take advantage of it. Make sure, however, that the try-out fee is applicable to your long-term membership fee.

Before signing the contract, take it home and read it carefully for any hidden costs. And remember, oral promises from a sales rep are legally worthless.

The contract should include all services listed. New York State law, for example, enables you to cancel your contract if "the services cease to be offered as stated in the contract." The more specific the contract, the stronger your case. The contract should also spell out your cancellation rights and compensation provisions if the club, or some of its facilities, shuts down temporarily. Most states give health club members a right of cancellation if they move, if they are physically incapacitated for a period of time—or if the consumer dies. Some states also enable you to get out of a long-term membership short of such drastic events. Washington state law, for instance, enables you to cancel your membership, if your contract runs for more than a year, by giving 30 days' written notice. Do not sign a contract enabling the owner to change rules, hours of operation, location, or services at his or her discretion.

Finally, many states require a "cooling off" period enabling you to cancel within a few days (generally, three) of signing up.

"80% off dues at Liberty Memberships," bringing down the usual $30 per month membership to a remarkably inexpensive $6 per month. The ad, however, failed to mention an "initiation fee" of $25 to $55, "depending on the program."

Watch out for high-pressure sales tactics. Stay away from pre-opening "specials" or "discounts" that may yield surprises down the road. If the club is a legitimate operation, you'll be able to snatch a good deal when it opens up. Similarly, your scam radar should perk up if the club refuses to provide you with any information over the phone, won't let you go over the contract at home, or offers you a discount "if you sign today only."

If you haven't been exercising regularly here are a couple of important health tips:

1. Start exercising slowly—for 20 minutes, three days a week, at 60% of your respiratory capacity, suggests the American College of Sports Medicine.

2. If you are over 40 or overweight, consult your physician before beginning a program of regular exercise.

Don't get discouraged if you don't look like the Terminator after two weeks of workouts.

Personal trainers are the fastest growing trend in the health arena, increasing 25% a year for the past five years. A trainer can help you to achieve a specific goal—run a marathon, shave off 20 pounds, or get back in shape after a pregnancy—or simply help you to exercise properly or stay motivated.

MORE THAN MUSCLES AT STAKE

Getting the right contract with a cancellation provision ensuring full or pro-rated refunds is only part of the battle. In April 1994, Bally's Health & Tennis Corp., the largest chain of health clubs in the country, agreed to pay the Federal Trade Commission (FTC) $120,000 in civil penalties and to provide refunds believed to be in the hundreds of thousands of dollars to thousands of customers. The company, which operates 300 health clubs under the names Jack LaLanne and The Vertical Club among others and counts 4 million customers, was charged with overbilling, harass-ing, and ruining the credit rating of customers, refusing to cancel memberships as provided in its contract, and billing charge accounts or debiting bank accounts without the permission of the purchasers. When the FTC set up a 16-line hot line to receive customer complaints, the volume of calls was such that the telephone system crashed. Bally's also settled similar complaints in various states, agreeing to pay $63,000 in civil penalties and costs in Washington state and $138,000 in civil penalties to the Los Angeles County District Attorney's office.

Experts recommend that you work with a trainer who is a certified professional and that you stay with him or her for at least eight to ten weeks.

Don't forget the "Y"—YMCAs and the like. You'll probably pay a lot less at a Y-run health club, but the facilities and equipment may not be of the level you can get in a commercial club. Other such nonprofit organizations as hospital-based fitness centers, park district programs, or university facilities may offer low-budget memberships.

Clubs affiliated with IRSA, the Association of Quality Clubs, a self-regulating trade group representing more than 2,000 clubs, must abide by its membership pledge and code of conduct. Requirements include a ban on the sale of lifetime memberships, a three-year ceiling on pre-paid memberships, placement of pre-opening membership fees in escrow, and a ban on "deceptive, high-pressure sales tactics."

■ **To find out if a club is a member** of International Racquet Sports Association (IRSA), the Association of Quality Clubs, a self-regulating trade group representing more than 2,000 clubs worldwide, write: 253 Summer Street, Boston, MA 02210; (800) 228-4772.

■ **You'll find useful tips on select-**ing a health club and staying with your exercise program in *The Guide to Choosing a Quality Health Club*, a brochure published by IRSA. Send a self-addressed, stamped envelope to the address above for a free copy.

■ **For free brochure, with a useful** and comprehensive checklist, write for: *Health/Fitness Facility: Consumer Selection Guide*, from the American College of Sports Medicine, P.O. Box 1440, Indianapolis, IN 46206-1440, or call (317) 637-9200.

CHAPTER 11

INFERTILITY SERVICES

Deception in Conception

Every year, tens of thousands of people walk into the offices of fertility doctors and face a barrage of adorable baby pictures tacked up around the waiting rooms and offices. The implication: The high-tech techniques that are for sale have produced all those babies.

There's no question that such reproductive techniques as *in vitro* fertilization (IVF) have allowed truly amazing advances. Couples who might have given up the dream of having their own children now have reason to keep hoping because of "assisted reproductive technologies" (ARTs). The key word is *hope*. For although it would be hard to discern from the sales seminars and promotional materials, advanced infertility treatments fail far more often than they succeed. And the costs to the couples who try their luck are high—financially, emotionally, and physically.

THE BASICS

Nudging Nature

Doctors consider couples infertile if they have not conceived after a year of having unprotected sex. Estimates of how many such couples there are in America vary widely—from 2 million to 5 million, or roughly 1 in 6 couples of child-bearing age. In about 40% of the cases, infertility can be attributed to the woman; in about 40% of the cases, the problem lies with the man; and in about 20% of the cases, doctors cannot find the source of infertility.

Couples who seem not to be able to conceive and who seek advice undergo examinations to determine the cause of their infertility. If doctors can identify problems, they will recommend procedures like laparoscopic surgery to clear blocked fallopian tubes, drug therapy to coax ovulation, artificial insemination of the woman's womb with her partner's sperm, or some combination of these treatments. Couples whose problems cannot be identified may be told simply to keep trying or to take drugs to increase the woman's production of eggs.

Assisted reproductive technologies—such as IVF or GIFT—should be the treatment of last resort for people who have tried every other measure that might help them, although in certain instances it may make sense for

THE JARGON

Assisted reproductive technology (ART) is the umbrella term for a group of the most advanced treatments for infertility, including *in vitro* fertilization and its variations.

Reprotech, short for reproductive technology, is another term for ART.

***In vitro* fertilization (IVF)** is the process by which eggs are taken from a woman's body, fertilized with a man's sperm in a dish, and then returned to the woman's body. In detail, it consists of drug stimulation of the ovaries to produce eggs, ultrasound monitoring of the eggs' development in the woman's ovaries, retrieval of the eggs from the woman's body, combining the eggs with sperm in a dish, waiting for fertilization, and return of the fertilized eggs to the woman's womb.

Male factor is used to describe infertility that can be attributed, at least in part, to problems with the male partner's reproductive functions.

Gamete intrafallopian transfer (GIFT) is a variation of IVF; eggs are taken from a woman's body and put in her fallopian tubes with sperm to attempt fertilization in the tubes, where it would naturally occur.

Stimulation is the process of coaxing a woman's ovaries to produce eggs by injecting the woman with hormones.

Retrieval or egg retrieval refers to the surgical procedure in which eggs are removed from a woman's body for external fertilization; sometimes called harvesting.

Embryo transfer (ET) is the surgical procedure in which fertilized eggs are returned to the woman's body.

Pregnancy can mean two different things. A "clinical pregnancy" is a real pregnancy in which fetal heart activity has been detected. Elevated levels of various hormones indicate a "chemical pregnancy," which often can be detected shortly after embryo transfer. (A chemical pregnancy does not always result in a clinical pregnancy.)

Success rate. There is no standard definition of "success." As noted, many programs define success as a comparison between the number of clinical pregnancies or deliveries of live babies and the number of embryo transfers attempted. This overstates the true rate of success because it does not take into account all the couples who began treatment but did not make it to the transfer stage. This definition has the additional drawback of being based on the number of procedures attempted and not the number of patients involved. (See the discussion of success rates on the facing page for additional information.)

people, especially older women, to waste no time and to go directly to the most advanced procedures.

Only 10% to 14% of the couples who try to conceive using the most advanced procedures end up with a baby when it's all over. This reality contradicts the so-called success-rate statistics doctors commonly toss off about how your chances might be one in four or one in five.

Mt. Sinai Hospital in New York, for instance, distributed a promotional brochure for several years claiming that the "take-home baby rate for IVF is 20%." Thousands of people reading the brochure were led to believe that their chance of having a baby would be one in five after a single use of Mt. Sinai's advanced fertility services. But based on a New York City Department of Consumer Affairs investigation and legal charges, it turns out that the true success rate was probably half the advertised rate.

The Failure of Success Rates

Because ART procedures involve so many steps, it's easy to fudge success rates. To illustrate, take the example of IVF. One cycle comprises four stages: 1. stimulation of the woman's ovaries to produce mature eggs; 2. retrieval of the eggs (rarely is there just one) and fertilization of the eggs in the lab; 3. transfer of the embryos; and 4. a pregnancy that results in the delivery of a live baby. Each of these steps can be said to have its own success or failure rate. However, successful completion of one step does not necessarily lead to achieve-

ment of the desired goal—a child.

So let's look again at Mt. Sinai's hyped-up claim of a 20% success rate. Mt. Sinai can claim a 20% success rate only if it excludes some patients from the statistical calculation: A comparison of the number of women who gave birth to live babies (stage 4) to the number of women of all ages whose ovaries were stimulated (stage 1) shows that Mt. Sinai's success rate in 1990 couldn't have been more than 10%. Most likely, Mt. Sinai used a subset of all its patients to generate the 20% figure: the number of successful deliveries (step 4) compared to the number of women 39 or younger who made it to the embryo transfer stage of IVF (step 3). Since then, in acknowledgment that its numbers were inflated, Mt. Sinai has overhauled its program.

Most programs prefer to focus on the ratio of embryo transfers to pregnancies or births rather than the ratio of stimulations to pregnancies or births because the former creates a rosier scenario than the latter. These percentages are higher because many infertile couples never even get to embryo transfer stage in the process—even when chemically "primed," the woman does not ovulate, she produces too few viable eggs, or the eggs fail to fertilize. Whatever the case, even though the couples have attempted pregnancy with ART, their experience is not accounted for in the pool from which success rates are calculated.

These faked numbers have not gone unnoticed by federal regulators. The Federal Trade Commission (FTC) has taken legal action against

IVF Australia (now called IVF America), the Fertility Institute of Boca Raton, the Fertility Institute of Western Massachusetts, and Reproductive Genetics In Vitro of Denver—all for fudging their facts. Because desperate couples are so easily misled about success rates, laboratory standards, and credentials, Congress passed the Fertility Clinic Success Rate and Certification Act in 1992. The law establishes standard formats for success rates and requires all fertility clinics to report their rates to the federal government annually.

Is ART Worth the Price?

Since the ART process can be so costly, it's important to do your homework before you decide whether it's worth a try. Including all the medical procedures, tests, lab fees, and drugs, one cycle of treatment can cost as much as $10,000. Since it usually takes several attempts to conceive, trying to get pregnant can cost more than $30,000. In all, Americans spent $2 billion on fertility treatments in 1990.

The physical and emotional costs are also formidable. Treatment for women involves daily injections with hormones and frequent trips to the doctor's office for blood tests and ultrasound monitoring. During a single IVF cycle, there are many different checkpoints at which to feel cheered or cheated—at the retrieval of eggs, fertilization, embryo evaluation, embryo transfer, and pregnancy test, to name just a few. Couples who have been through the process describe wild swings between hopefulness and depression—which are only exacerbated by the side effects of the hormone treatments—and the terrible strains on their marriages.

Beyond all that, the long-term risk to women who use the massive quantities of hormones necessary to undergo ART is not fully known. Although there is no definitive evidence that the drugs are dangerous, there is no evidence that they are not. In fact, the thousands of women who have undergone ART in the last decade or so have not been tracked or monitored, and neither have the children who were conceived via IVF. A small, preliminary study published in the *American Journal of Epidemiology* in early 1993 suggested that the use of fertility drugs may increase by three times the risk of developing ovarian cancer. In early 1993, the Food and Drug Administration

> "We are talking about long shots. Sometimes people will get agitated and say, 'We're going to be going through all this, and those are the best odds you can offer?' What's hard for patients to understand is how incredibly complex a process approximating normalcy is."
>
> —DR. GARY L. GROSS,
> a fertility pioneer and instructor
> at Harvard Medical School

FACTOR IN THE HUMAN COST

In the March 15, 1992, issue of *The New York Times Magazine*, one woman described IVF as a "devastating limbo." Another said:

"Basically, I gave up being happy, healthy, and sane for the three years I was on it [Pergonal, a hormone to induce egg production]. Pergonal meant violent mood swings. Constant back pain. Overwhelming lethargy. Ovaries screaming to unload all these follicles [eggs]. Every day you're up at the crack of dawn for your vaginal sonogram. Every morning, there's blood work at the lab—I'd be exhausted by the time I got to work. Every afternoon, you call in to find out what your blood levels are. Every night, your husband is shooting you up in the hip with an inch-and-a-half hypodermic filled with more Pergonal. But however horrible it all was, my husband and I felt we had no choice but to continue until we were totally wiped out. At one point, I was such a basket case I had to take a leave of absence from work. In retrospect, I can't believe I was willing to risk losing a job I love for a negligible chance of getting pregnant."

began requiring Ares-Serono SA, the maker of Pergonal and Serophene, and Marion Merrell Dow Inc., the maker of Clomiphene citrate, to warn users of a possible link between these drugs and ovarian cancer.

WHAT TO WATCH OUT FOR

Keep in mind that for every success rate doctors tout, the flip side is a failure rate. If a program boasts a 15% success rate, it also has an 85% failure rate. It's not that it's inaccurate or deceptive of the program to show its statistics in the best light, but remember that "success rates" deflect attention from most people's experience.

Inflated success rates. Based on the Mt. Sinai story you may be wondering whether to believe the statistics you hear. Yes and no. ART success statistics are a perfect demonstration of the way the straightest facts can be bent to create a skewed view. Be sure you clearly understand exactly what the statistics represent.

Misleading claims. For example, success does not necessarily mean babies, even though one program uses the headline "success means babies" in its glossy brochure. But, in fact, the number of clinical *pregnancies* where fetal heart activity has been confirmed and the number of *deliveries* of live babies are both commonly used to describe success. The two are not interchangeable;

RATING FERTILITY CLINICS

You can compare one program to another by referring to the *Annual Clinic-Specific Report* published by the Society for Assisted Reproductive Technology and the American Fertility Society (see **HELP** at the end of this chapter). The *Annual Clinic-Specific Report* gives success rates for individual infertility programs around the country by breaking down success rates into four categories: women younger than 40 whose partner's sperm is fine; women under 40 whose partner's sperm is abnormal ("male factor" infertility); women 40 and older whose partner's sperm is fine; and women 40 and older with male factor infertility involved. Statistics are given for egg retrievals and embryo transfers but not for stimulations.

not all pregnancies lead to successful deliveries. In fact, many doctors counsel their patients that the risk of miscarriage is higher with ART pregnancies than with normally conceived pregnancies.

The incredible disappearing patients. To judge the usefulness of the success statistic, you also need to know to what group of patients successful patients were compared. Ask which procedures are included or omitted in the success rates. The most telling percentage is the number of successful deliveries compared with the number of ovary stimulations performed. This includes all the attempts at pregnancy that failed (but most programs won't volunteer the number). Also ask how old the women were whose experience the success rates reflect. Success rates drop precipitously for women 40 and older, and some programs may pad their numbers by excluding these women from their statistics.

Assisted reproductive technologies should be treatments of last resort because they are the most invasive and the most expensive. Investigate and try the many other treatments for infertility first, including drugs to coax ovulation, surgery to clear blocked fallopian tubes, and artificial insemination.

Only after close consultations with your physician, fertility specialists, and the staff of advanced fertility programs can you decide whether to try reprotech. The situation of every couple is different, and it's important to investigate all the alternatives for your specific case.

If doctors tell you about their "success rates," make sure you understand exactly how the rates were calculated and whether you can expect to have a similar chance at successfully undergoing treatment. The most useful statistic is one for couples within your age range with a similar diagnosis. So ask about and compare the results from several programs. And since the goal is to have a baby, look for the take-home-baby rate based on deliveries.

Look beyond the success rates when you're comparing one clinic with another. Even honest, seemingly straightforward overall success rates can be misleading. Since the success of ART procedures varies with the cause of infertility and the age of the woman, lower pregnancy success rates reported by a program do not necessarily suggest less effective care. Clinics that serve patients who are less likely to become pregnant to begin with will understandably have lower overall rates than clinics that only accept couples with better prospects.

■, **The American Fertility Society (AFS)** offers general information about infertility and also distributes the *Annual Clinic-Specific Report*, which gives success rates for ART programs around the country. Copies of the full report cost $50; partial copies covering the East, West, and Central regions of the U.S. cost $20 each or $35 for two regions. Write to the American Fertility Society, 1209 Montgomery Highway, Birmingham, AL 35216-2809, or call (205) 978-5000.

■, **Resolve is a nonprofit support and** information organization for people struggling with infertility. The national office supplies information and can direct you to a local affiliate. Resolve publishes a newsletter, recommends reading material, and can help you get in touch with other couples who have had experience with the ART programs in your area. Write to Resolve, 1310 Broadway, Somerville, MA 02144-1731, or call (617) 623-0744.

■, **The Federal Trade Commission** published a fact sheet on infertility services. Write to the FTC Office of Consumer/Business Education, Washington, DC 20580, or call (202) 326-3650.

CHAPTER 12

COLD AND FLU REMEDIES

Chicken Soup and . . .

A study conducted at the prestigious Johns Hopkins University School of Medicine in Baltimore, Maryland, found that when children with colds were given placebos or no medication, their parents said they got better just as quickly as children given cold medicine containing an antihistamine-decongestant. The conclusion: Children with colds feel better in a day or two with or without medication.

Even for adults, there is no cure for the common cold or flu. Doctors say that the best treatment is to rest, drink fluids, and let the illness run its course. Of course, you might also follow the adage to starve a cold, feed a fever. And, yes, chicken soup has been found to have therapeutic qualities, acting as a natural decongestant and expectorant.

Nonetheless, Americans still spend over a billion dollars a year on products to temporarily relieve cold and flu symptoms. These products might not speed recovery, but some of them might make you feel a little better while you're getting better, or at least knock you out so you get a full night's sleep.

THE BASICS

What Cold and Flu Remedies Do

Loosen phlegm. This is what expectorants are supposed to do. Your expectorant will probably include either guaifenesin, glycerol guaiacolate, or terpin hydrate as its active ingredient. Cough drops might work just as well and cost a lot less, too. Indeed, a U.S. Food and Drug Administration (FDA) advisory panel has concluded that all expectorants lack evidence of effectiveness—although the FDA ultimately reclassified guaifenesin as effective. The Public Citizen Health Research Group, a Washington D.C.-based advocacy organization, disagrees with the FDA's guaifenesin finding on the basis that the FDA study was seriously flawed.

Suppress coughs with antitussive drugs that act on the brain. Dextromethorphan hydrobromide is the most common one. Don't overdo it, though, because coughing has the important function of removing phlegm.

Reduce fever and relieve pain. These are the analgesics—aspirin, acetaminophen, ibuprofen, and various combinations of these with other medicines.

Decongest nasal passages. Decongestants cause bronchial passages to relax, making it easier to breathe. They help allergy sufferers or anyone with a stuffed nose by shrinking respiratory system blood vessels after histamines from pollen and other sources have dilated them and caused runny noses and itching.

Among the common decongestants are phenylephrine hydrochloride, phenylpropanolamine (PPA), pseudoephedrine hydrochloride (found in Sudafed and Actifed), ephedrine, and desoxyephedrine. Non-medicine alternatives that might work well are to breathe warm, moist air, such as the mist from a hot shower, or to eat spicy food like jalapeño peppers, garlic, or horseradish.

Ease runny noses and sneezing. Accomplished with antihistamines, which stop histamine from dilating blood vessels in the nose. The chart below lists several of the most common over-the-counter antihistamines and their effects, according to an analysis in *Consumer Reports Health Letter*, October 1989.

Many popular remedies combine

How Active Is Your Antihistamine?

Active ingredient	Antihistamine strength	Sedative effect	Nose-drying ability
TRIPROLIDINE HYDROCHLORIDE	*Moderate-high*	*Low*	*Moderate*
DOXYLAMINE SUCCINATE	*Low-moderate*	*High*	*High*
PYRILAMINE MALEATE	*Low-moderate*	*Low*	*Low*
BROMPHENIRAMINE MALEATE	*High*	*Low*	*Moderate*
CHLOROPHENIRAMINE MALEATE	*Moderate*	*Low*	*Moderate*

two ingredients in one pill or liquid; for example, an antihistamine is often combined with a decongestant to clear stuffy noses. Among the national name brands with this combination are Fedahist D, Triaminic, Dimetapp, Actifed, and Contac. Another common mixture is an expectorant and a nasal decongestant, such as Fedahist EX, or an antitussive with a nasal decongestant to relieve both coughs and runny noses, such as Triaminic DM and Vicks 44D. You may also come across an antitussive combined with an antihistamine or with an expectorant.

If you're feeling really awful, you might be tempted to take a multi-symptom reliever. Contac Cough & Sore Throat Formula, for example, combines an analgesic, an antitussive, and an expectorant. Naldecon DX mixes an expectorant, an antitussive, and a nasal decongestant. Tylenol Effervescent, Dristan, Alka-Selzter Plus, Coricidin D, and Actifed Plus combine nasal decongestants, analgesics, and antihistamines.

Finally, there are "shotgun" preparations that promise to handle almost every conceivable cold and flu symptom. They combine antitussives, analgesics, antihistamines, and nasal decongestants—all in one package. Among major national brands with all of these active ingredients are Comtrex Liquid and Tablets, Thera-Flu, Contac Severe, Medi-Flu, Robitussin NT, Nyquil, and Vicks 44M.

How Not to Overspend

First of all, know the names of the active ingredients. This knowledge will enable you to comparison shop. After all, acetaminophen is acetaminophen, whatever the brand. Then, when you are contending with drugstore shelves loaded with a wide array of bottles, nose sprays, drops, caplets, capsules, and liquids, you'll be able to compare the amount of active ingredient in each product and buy whichever is cheapest.

If you don't feel up to figuring out the relationship between active ingredients and price, then keep in mind that the generic or store brand is almost always cheaper than the heavily advertised national brand with the same active ingredients. This was confirmed in a price study of cold and flu remedies conducted in 1991 by the NYC Department of Consumer Affairs. Comparing active ingredients, strengths, and dosages showed that good old acetaminophen cost 26 cents a gram in a box that said

> "*Cold remedies of today come no closer to curing colds or shortening their duration than did folk treatments thousands of years ago. Nevertheless, today's remedies can relieve some vexing symptoms.*"
>
> —FROM THE NEW MEDICINE SHOW, a book by the editors of *Consumer Reports*

120

"Tylenol" on it, 10 cents a gram when the box said "Duane Reade" (the name of a discount drugstore chain), and only 8 cents for a box with the name "Valu-Rite." A compound containing an antihistamine and a decongestant ranged in price from 13 cents (Fedahist D) to 2 cents (Genovese brand, another chain) for each hour of relief.

Among the other findings:

■ Cold and flu remedies cost somewhat more per dose as a caplet or capsule than as a tablet, and much more as a liquid. In one price survey, Comtrex liquid was 2½ times as expensive as Comtrex tablets, yet they contain the exact same amounts of the same active ingredients.

■ Certain remedies that claim to "do more" merely add acetaminophen and charge a much higher price. You would do better to take a lower-priced medicine and a low-price generic acetaminophen tablet separately.

Another trick of the trade is to charge the same price but reduce the amount of active ingredient in the capsule or liquid—product shrinkage, if you will. You need to take a bigger dose to have the same effect, costing you more in the long run.

Since the amount of a particular active ingredient actually contained in a preparation varies considerably among brands, you have to read the label carefully for this, too. For example, the NYC Consumer Affairs Department found that Fedahist D contains 30 mg of the decongestant pseudoephedrine, while Actifed Syrup and Capsules have 60 mg and Actifed 12-hour has 120 mg.

WHAT TO WATCH OUT FOR

Overuse or misuse of certain cold and flu remedies. Taking too much acetaminophen could lead to kidney damage, according to a May 1989 study by the National Institute of Environmental Health Sciences. Too much aspirin can be irritating to the stomach. And if you take antihistamines for too long, they lose their effectiveness.

Because oral decongestants can raise blood pressure and cause nervousness, they should be avoided if you have an irregular heartbeat, glaucoma, or high blood pressure. And since appetite suppressants alone can cause hyperactivity, do not combine them with an oral antihistamine, which also may cause hyperactivity. Avoid any remedies that combine a decongestant with an antihistamine since the result could be dizziness and nervousness. Check the ingredients label before buying.

Caffeine. You get it in coffee—and in some analgesics combined with antihistamines. The caffeine is supposed to counter the drowsiness antihistamine produces. It also makes you peppier; presumably, this makes you feel better.

Chest rubs smell nice, but they aren't really effective, according to the Public Citizen Health Research Group.

THE SMARTER CONSUMER

Take only the specific active ingredient that addresses your symptoms and avoid multi-symptom preparations. If you're experiencing aches and fevers, you don't need to take a preparation also containing an expectorant. Cough suppressants are preferably taken alone. The Public Interest Health Research Group recommends avoiding products claiming to relieve several different symptoms, since, besides the medication you're after, you'll also probably end up with medications you don't need or that may actually do more harm than good.

Also, there are several hundred different cold and flu viruses out there, which means that the medication that might have worked the last time you were sick, or that a friend vouched for last month, may not work as well on your current bout. You have to match current symptoms with a specific remedy.

Don't take more than one cold remedy at a time. You could end up with an inadvisably high dosage of a medication contained in both of them.

Do not take irrational combinations, such as an expectorant and a cough suppressant; the expectorant encourages you to cough up phlegm while the suppressant works at cross-purposes by trying to keep you from coughing. Contac Cough & Sore Throat Formula, for one, contains both of these medications.

Buy big. The best value is usually with larger sizes, as is the case with most retail products.

■ **The American Academy of** Otolaryngology—Head and Neck Surgery publishes a leaflet, "Antihistamines, Decongestants and Cold Remedies." They'll send you one if you send them a self-addressed, stamped envelope to 1 Prince Street, Alexandria, VA 22314.

■ **The Public Citizen Health Re-**search Group, a not-for-profit investigative and advocacy organization, publishes a very informative monthly *Health Letter*. Among the regular features are medical device recalls, safety alerts, and the "Outrage of the Month." A one-year subscription is $18. Send check or money order made out to Health Letter to 2000 P Street NW, Washington, DC 20036.

CHAPTER 13

EYEGLASSES AND CONTACT LENSES

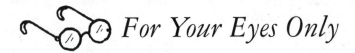 *For Your Eyes Only*

If you are one of the 140 million Americans who needs glasses or contact lenses to see well, put them on (or in) and read this chapter before you need to replace them.

And get out your magnifying glass, too, to read the fine print at the bottom of the eyewear ads in the newspaper. As chain stores like Pearle Vision Center and Lens-Crafters have proliferated, so have rebates, coupons and promotions offering two-for-the-price-of-one, more common in the grocery store. But the ads often gloss over additional charges that can send the price out of the bargain range.

LensCrafters in Minneapolis advertised: "Save up to $75." Only in a footnote do you learn you must spend at least $190 to qualify for the deal.

In a full-page ad in the *New York Post*, Cohen's Fashion Optical offers a free eye exam (no purchase necessary). But if you want a contact lens exam, that will cost extra, says the tiny type at the bottom of the coupon. In the same ad, Cohen's offers one pair of daily-wear, colored contact lenses for $79. A minuscule footnote discloses "professional fee and kit additional."

So much for eye-popping special prices.

THE BASICS

See Your Way Clear

Americans spend about $16 billion a year caring for their eyes. About three quarters of that is spent on eyeglasses and contact lenses and most of the rest on eye exams. And as baby boomers continue to move into middle age, those numbers will only rise: 90% of people need glasses by the time they reach their mid-40s. Are you one of them?

The Eye Exam

The only way to know if you need glasses is to have your eyes tested. A thorough eye exam should include collection or updating of your medical history and

THE WHO'S WHO OF EYE CARE PROFESSIONALS

You'll have to decide for yourself whether you need to see an ophthalmologist or optometrist. But since 45% of the American public, according to a Gallup poll, doesn't know the difference between them, here's what each eye care professional does:

Ophthalmologists are physicians who specialize in eyes. They can prescribe corrective lenses and drugs, treat eye disease, and perform surgery. Some also sell eyeglasses.

Optometrists have degrees in eye care from four-year colleges of optometry, but they are not physicians. They have been trained to examine eyes, detect eye disease, and prescribe eyeglasses and contact lenses. The limits of their practice vary from state to state, but in 37 states they can use drugs to treat certain diseases; for example, they can administer prescription eye drops and prescribe medication. They sell eyeglasses.

Opticians make the corrective lenses prescribed by ophthalmologists and optometrists. They cannot perform eye examinations or prescribe corrective lenses. They need licenses to operate in about half the states.

tests for eye health, visual acuity, eye coordination, focusing ability, and such common vision conditions as nearsightedness, farsightedness, and astigmatism.

The American Optometric Association suggests that babies have their first eye exam by 6 months of age and that children have their eyes examined at ages 3 and 5; that people 6 to 19 have their eyes examined annually; that people 20 to 64 have exams every one to two years; and that people 65 and older go back to annual eye exams. However, diabetics and people who have a high risk of getting glaucoma (African-Americans 40 and older and everybody older than 60) should be especially careful to have their eyes examined annually. The doctor should dilate their pupils to get the best possible view of the retina and any damage, according to the U.S. Public Health Service.

If all you need is a routine exam, an optometrist will probably be your best bet. Two 1989 studies by the State University of New York Center for Vision Care Policy found that ophthalmologists charge an average of $20 more than optometrists for the same routine eye exams and diagnostic tests. But don't let price be the only determining factor, especially if you think there's a problem.

You have the right to get your eyeglasses prescription from the doctor who examines your eyes. A 1978 Federal Trade Commission (FTC) rule requires eye doctors to give patients their prescriptions immediately after an eye examination, at no additional cost. This enables you to shop around for higher quality, better selection, lower prices, or plain old peace of mind before buying glasses. Before the rule took effect, eye care professionals often held onto prescriptions, which forced patients to buy glasses from the examiner.

Contact Lenses

The FTC's eyeglasses prescription rule does not apply to contact lenses. If you think you may not want to buy lenses from the doctor who examines your eyes, ask about the doctor's policy *before* the exam. Some doctors will give you your prescription to fill wherever you like; others will insist on fitting the lenses themselves. Lenses generally cost more to buy and maintain than glasses.

Only you and your doctor can decide which kind of lenses will work best for you. Hard lenses, once the only contact lens option, are now worn by fewer than 2% of lens wearers. Nonetheless, hard or gas-permeable lenses are often prescribed for people with high degrees of astigmatism. Consider which lens will most comfortably correct your vision problem, best suit your lifestyle, and meet your financial needs. For instance, think about whether you play active sports—soft lenses are less likely than rigid lenses to dislodge. Are you cost-conscious? Rigid gas-permeable lenses cost a bit more but last longer than soft lenses and are less troublesome and cheaper to maintain. Do you want to be able to see as soon as you

PUZZLED ABOUT LENS CARE SOLUTIONS?

Get explicit instructions about what products to use, and how often, from your eye care practitioner. Not all solutions can be used in conjunction with others, some solutions have more than one function, and not all solutions are safe for all types of lenses. Here's what the various solutions do:

■ *Cleaning solution* removes dirt, mucus, and other debris that lenses pick up during wear.

■ *Disinfectant solution* kills bacteria and germs on the lenses preventing serious eye infections.
■ *Rinsing solution* removes other solutions from lenses and prepares the lenses for wear.
■ *Enzyme solution* removes deposits of protein and other things that build up on lenses over time.
■ *Rewetting solution* lubricates the lenses while you are wearing them to make them more comfortable.

EYE ON CONTACT LENSES

Lense type	Initial price	Average annual cost	Pros	Cons
HARD LENSES	*$100-$200*	*$60-$100*	• *Sharp vision* • *Correct serious astigmatism and other problems* • *Durable (5 to 10 years)* • *Easy care*	• *Hard to adapt to* • *Cannot wear longer than 8 to 14 hours* • *Least comfortable*
RIGID, GAS-PERMEABLE LENSES	*$200-$350*	*$60-$100*	• *Sharp vision* • *Correct serious astigmatism and other problems* • *Last 2 to 4 years* • *Easy care*	• *Take longer to adapt to* • *May dislodge during sports*
SOFT LENSES	*$150-$300*	*$100-$300*	• *Easy to adapt to* • *Comfort almost from start* • *Least likely to dislodge* • *Last 2 to 4 years* • *Easy care*	• *Correct fewer problems* • *May not provide sharp vision* • *Less durable (6 months to a year)* • *Need more daily care*
EXTENDED-WEAR LENSES	*$250-$400*	*$70-$150*	• *Comfortable to wear continuously up to 7 days* • *Available as soft and gas-permeable with same advantages*	• *Increased risk of eye infection*
DISPOSABLE LENSES	—	*$500-$700*	• *Soft lenses that can be worn continuously for up to 7 days and then thrown away* • *No cleaning*	• *Less sharp vision* • *Correct fewer problems* • *Increased risk of eye infection if used improperly*

wake up? Extended-wear lenses can be worn for up to seven days without removing them.

Several companies have been testing lenses you wear for a single day then throw away. No cleaning solution to mess with means less chance of infection from wearing disposable lenses too long. The cost is the catch: about $1.50 a pair for Johnson & Johnson's version, which adds up to about $550 per year.

WHAT TO WATCH OUT FOR

There's no such thing as list **price** for eyeglasses frames—or at least there's no list you'll ever get your eyes on. Just about every optician marks up prices by at least two or three times what they pay for the frames. For instance, a Giorgio Armani frame that sells for well over $200 in L.A. (without lenses) costs the store about $70. As part of an investigation of Pearle Vision Center, the National Advertising Division of the Council of Better Business Bureaus pointed out the "special features" of the industry—"complex pricing systems, confidential price lists, limited information of comparative pricing, and consumers' reliance on the professional advice of the opticians." This can make it very difficult to know whether you are getting a good deal or an optical delusion.

Be wary of package deals and low-price offers as they may not be the bargains they seem at first sight. Your choices may be limited to a small group of frame styles, and you most often will have to pay extra for frames outside the designated group, for the oversize or high-powered lenses that may work best for you, or for the various tints and coatings you may be persuaded to buy (more on coatings later in this chapter). The Better Business Bureaus of Minnesota and Houston challenged a Pearle Vision Center program for failing to disclose the limitations of a buy-one-get-one-free promotion. Instead of getting a duplicate or similar pair of glasses, consumers were limited in the frames they could choose from, and there was an undisclosed $60 cap on the value of the "free" second pair. You might also be lured in by the promise of a free eye exam, but if the "free" exam can only be had by buying an overpriced pair of glasses from the same store, then it's not "free" at all.

Be skeptical of claims about UV absorptive coatings. A glasses salesperson may ask if you work at a computer. If you say yes, he or she may tell you about the alleged risk of exposure to ultraviolet radiation and push you to pay $10 to $20 for UV coating. But the reality is that the risk is nonexistent. Ultraviolet light is not a problem indoors—computer screens do not emit significant amounts, nor do televisions.

> **"A**s the industry is now, prices depend upon loading on extra bells and whistles, like special coatings, that most people probably don't need. If the eye exam that takes an hour is 'free,' the consumer's going to pay for it somewhere else."*
>
> —MONTE BELOTE,
> executive director of Florida
> Consumer Action Network

SUNGLASS SENSE

Ignore the hype. Most sunglasses (and many prescription eyeglasses) provide plenty of protection against harmful ultraviolet (UV) radiation. A voluntary labeling system, devised by the Sunglass Association of America and the Food and Drug Administration, tells you how much. Sunglasses called "cosmetic" must block at least 20% of the longer wavelength UVA radiation and 70% of the shorter wavelength UVB. (The shorter waves are the most dangerous to your eyes.) These are fine for everyday use. Even the cheapest sunglasses you can buy generally meet the "cosmetic" standard and can't harm eyes under normal conditions. "General purpose" means they block 60% of UVA and 95% of UVB, and are good for any outdoor activity. Sunglasses labeled "special purpose" must block 60% of UVA and 99% of UVB and are good for very bright conditions.

Anti-glare or anti-reflective coating is often overhyped. You may be told that for another $10 to $20 you can reduce glare, say from computer screens, but in fact this coating does nothing to enhance vision. It simply reduces the amount of light that bounces off the lenses, which will reduce the reflection in flash photographs or create the cosmetic effect of making thick glasses less noticeable.

THE SMARTER CONSUMER

Eyeglasses

If your eye doctor does not give you your eyeglasses prescription, ask for it. It's yours to take with you, whether or not you buy glasses from that doctor.

Don't be myopic. Many stores will try to draw you in with one-stop shopping. They offer exams and a huge selection of frame styles, and they can make glasses in an in-store laboratory within as little as an hour. It's tempting to walk in and have everything taken care of before you can bat an eye. But convenience has its price. In 1993, when *Consumer Reports* sent three staffers to price glasses at five chains, prices differed as much as 75% from store to store for the same prescription and similar frames. As with any other purchase, you'll probably do best if you shop around.

Beware of cheap package deals that supposedly include everything. The small print may say the price covers only simple prescriptions. If your prescription is more complicated (bifocals, for instance), you may not get what you need—or you may have to pay a lot more for it than you would elsewhere.

Make sure you get what you pay for. If you pay extra for impact-resistant polycarbonate plastic lenses, which are great for athletes and children, double-check to see that you haven't been given cheaper plastic lenses.

If you buy polycarbonate lenses, don't scrimp on the scratch-resistant coating. These lenses are virtually unbreakable, but they scratch easily. The coating is a must.

Contact Lenses

The basic fee for contact lenses usually covers the lenses, a lesson on wear, handling and care, and follow-up visits to check the fit and how well your eyes are adjusting to wearing lenses. But to be sure, ask your practitioner the following questions:

What tests are included in the price for the exam, and are there any additional fees you will incur? If you buy lenses from the eye doctor, ask if fitting is included in the price.

If you plan to buy lenses from the person who examines your eyes, make sure he or she offers a large selection of types and brands. The larger the selection, the more likely you are to find something comfortable you like.

Is there a refund policy? This is especially important for first-time

contact lens buyers. Some eye care specialists will refund all or part of your money if you still find the lenses uncomfortable after 60 days of trying to adapt to them.

Is an insurance agreement (also called a service agreement) included in the price? If not, can you buy one separately? Such an agreement would enable you to replace a lost or ripped lens for a reduced fee. It might also lower the price of your next exam (and updated pair of lenses) when the time comes to replace your prescription.

■ **Read the *Consumer Reports* August** 1993 cover story called "Glasses: Where to Get Them; How Much You Should Pay; Ratings of 18 Optical Chains."

■ **"Facts for Consumers on Eye** Care," is a free pamphlet distributed by the Federal Trade Commission. Write to Public Reference, FTC, Washington, DC 20580.

■ **"What You Need to Know** About Safe Contact Lens Wear," a brochure developed in conjunction with the FDA, contact lens manufacturers, and eye doctors, is available free from the Contact Lens Council. Call (800) 332-8640; Maryland residents call (301) 428-3006 to request a copy.

CHAPTER 14

GETTING THE LEAD OUT OF YOUR DIET

Dangerous Dishes

You may be trying to maintain or improve your health by choosing nutritious foods. But it's not only the foods you eat, it's also the dishes you eat your food *on* that affect your health. Many dishes are made with lead, a toxic substance that can leach from your plate into your food and your body. There is no safe limit of lead.

Manufacturers add lead to some glazes, paints, and decals for aesthetic reasons—to create a shiny look and clear colors. The use of tiny amounts of lead is not necessarily hazardous *if* manufacturers properly formulate the glazes, paints, and decals; apply them correctly; and then fire the dishes at the right temperature for the right amount of time. There's a lot of room for error, however, and since manufacturers don't need lead to make dishes, they should phase it out completely.

A 1992 NYC Department of Consumer Affairs investigation, for example, found that 16% of its em-ployees' dishes leached lead. The investigation also uncovered lead contamination in one brand of children's china tea sets and led the national importer to recall its entire china product line. Consumer Affairs also bought and tested 12 dishes made in China and decorated in traditional Chinese patterns known to be likely lead-leaching hazards. Every one of the items, including plates, spoons, saucers, and a cup, leached lead. One plate tested at *90 times the FDA limit.*

THE BASICS

You Can't Judge a Dish by Its Color

Dishes can leach lead regardless of their color, where they were made, or how expensive they are. In February 1993, Tiffany and Company recalled lead-leaching plates that cost more than $1,200 for a single place setting. Unless a manufacturer tells you that it used only lead-free glazes, paints, and decals on its dishes, you can't be certain about the presence of lead without testing.

The U.S. Food and Drug Administration (FDA) is supposed to ensure that all domestic and imported ceramic ware meets its standards regarding the amount of lead that can leach out of dishes. However, since the agency only conducts spot checks, dangerous products can and do slip by.

There were no limits at all on lead leaching until 1971, when the FDA first set guidelines. Since then, the FDA has set stricter standards. You may be using ceramic ware that doesn't meet the current guidelines. And ceramic souvenirs from abroad may not be safe for food.

The Lowdown on Lead

Lead is a highly toxic metal that people absorb through eating and breathing. Lead accumulates in the body and can be stored in the bones for more than 20 years. Exposure can cause brain damage and impair IQ levels, short-term memory, and the ability to concentrate. Lead can damage every system in the body, including the immune system. Exposed adults can suffer from hypertension, reproductive complications, and loss of neuromuscular control. In extreme cases, lead poisoning can cause death.

People of all ages are affected, but owing to their smaller size, children and fetuses are at the most risk because even small amounts of lead can harm them. A fetus exposed to low levels of lead in the mother's blood can suffer from impaired development and low birth weight. Children and adults—especially women who are or who expect to become pregnant—should minimize their exposure to lead.

WHAT TO WATCH OUT FOR

Safely Using the Dishes You Own

Be most concerned with the dishes you use most often—your coffee mug or a bowl used to store leftovers. Even though you can't tell whether lead is leaching just by looking—dishes must be tested to know for certain—there are some signs of higher-risk dishes that call for extra attention:

- Ceramic ware with a corroded glaze, or a dusty, chalky gray residue after you've washed it.
- Old china, made before the danger of lead was formally recognized by the FDA.
- Handcrafted china and pottery, whether made in this country or imported.
- Highly decorated surfaces, especially inside a bowl or in the center of a plate, where there is contact with food.
- Decorations applied on top of the glaze instead of beneath it (you may be able to check by running your fingers over the decorations or holding the item at an angle to the light).

131

If you're unsure about a certain item:

- Don't use it to heat food or drinks in conventional or micro-wave ovens.
- Don't use it to store acidic food or drinks.
- Serve only dry, acid-neutral food (such as pretzels) in it.
- Save it for special occasions.

Store food only in glass, plastic, or stainless steel containers. And minimize the three factors that cause lead to leach into food: length of contact time, heat, and acidity of the food. Acidic foods include fruit products (such as orange juice and applesauce); salsa, spaghetti sauce, and other tomato-based foods; such drinks as coffee, tea, and cola-type sodas; and salad dressings and sauces made with vinegar, wine, or lemon juice.

> *"**T**he bad news is that lead is in hundreds of millions of dishes and we can't tell which ones without plate-by-plate testing. The good news is that the problem can be solved by pure consumer choice. Why buy dishes with lead when you can get them without it?"*
>
> —DAVID ROE,
> Senior Attorney,
> Environmental Defense Fund

lead leaching from your dinner ware.

Using the same chemicals found in home kits, the Food and Drug Administration conducts spot inspections to identify ceramic ware that requires further testing. Since home tests reveal lead leaching at moderate to high levels, not in precise measurements, items tested that don't indicate lead leaching may actually leach very small amounts of lead. If you use a home test and find lead leaching from your dishes, it's best to stop using the dishes for food. If your newly purchased dishes release lead, report it to your local FDA office (listed under the Department of Health and Human Services in the government section of your phone book), or call FDA headquarters at (301) 443-3170.

Testing Your Dishes

Consider testing your dishes with a home testing kit. These simple tests are useful for identifying items that leach at least a minimum amount of lead into food. Home testing kits are not cheap, but they are much less expensive than laboratory testing. Lab tests are the only way to determine the exact level of

Buying New Dishes

Avoid the lead problem altogether by buying no-lead and

low-level lead dishes, which are widely available but not necessarily well-labeled. Few stores display dishes with information about lead. According to the NYC Department of Consumer Affairs investigation cited earlier, salespeople and store management usually know little or nothing about lead in dishes—in fact, sometimes they give the *wrong* information. Since several manufacturers make some patterns with added lead and others without it, finding out which patterns are safer takes some effort.

Plain glass (not crystal) dishes are lead-free, and plain stoneware dishes are almost always made without added lead, except for some painted decorations or decals. Stoneware has a heavy weight and a low shine compared with the high gloss of china.

If you're not buying glass dishes, your best bet is to call or write ceramic manufacturers and ask whether all the pieces from the pattern can be sold without a special warning under the California Proposition 65 law. That proconsumer, proenvironment law requires manufacturers to either meet a much stricter lead-leaching standard than the FDA's, or to put a warning on the product. Don't be snowed by manufacturers who refer to the California Tableware Safety law, which basically mirrors the FDA's looser standards. Ask about a specific pattern to get the clearest answer. Unless the manufacturer tells you that the pattern can be sold without the Proposition 65 warning, it probably doesn't meet the stricter standard. Shop around

CALLING ALL CHINA-MAKERS . . .

China and ceramic makers can give you information on specific patterns and products. Be sure to ask whether every item in a pattern can be sold in California without a Proposition 65 warning label. Here's how to reach them:

Bernardaud Limoges (212) 737-7775

Christian Dior (212) 686-5080

Dansk (914) 666-2121

Fitz and Floyd (214) 484-9494

Franciscan (800) 955-1550

Gorham (914) 666-2121

Johnson Brothers (800) 955-1550

Lenox (800) 635-3669

Mikasa (201) 392-2501

Nikko (201) 633-5100

Noritake, Inc. (210) 319-0020

Pfaltzgraff (800) 999-2811

Pickard (708) 395-3800

Portmeirion (203) 729-8255

Rosenthal USA (718) 417-3400

Royal Doulton (800) 682-4462

Royal Worcester (212) 683 7130

Sasaki (212) 686-5080

Spode Limited (212) 683-7130

Villeroy & Boch (800) 223-1762

Wedgwood (800) 955-1550

CHECK YOUR DISHES

Home testing kits cost between $20 and $30, and use different methods to test as few as eight or as many as 100 items. The Frandon system requires some mixing of solutions, but it's economical for testing as many as 40 items at once. The Lead Inspector kit is also economical for up to 100 items at once. LeadCheck swabs from Hybrivet and Carolina Environment, available in smaller packages, are cheaper for fewer tests, easier to use, and portable for travel abroad.

Frandon Lead Alert Kit, Pace Environs, Inc.
Finchene Square
Scarborough, Ontario, Canada M1X1B4
(800) 359-9000

Lead Inspector, Michigan Ceramic Supplies
4048 Seventh Street
P.O. Box 342
Wyandotte, MI 48192
(800) 860-2332

LeadCheck Swabs, HybriVet Systems, Inc.
P.O. Box 1210
Framingham, MA 01701
(800) 262-LEAD

LeadCheck Swabs, Carolina Environment
P.O. Box 26661
Charlotte, NC 28221
(800) 448-LEAD

and find a pattern you like that does. Let the manufacturer know that dishes without added lead are important to you. Consumer demand for products without added lead will help make them more available and easier to identify.

Other Ways to Get the Lead Out

Fight metal with minerals. Eat iron- and calcium-rich foods, since those minerals may interfere with lead absorption.

Avoid lead-soldered cans. Be wary of imported food and fruit juice in cans, which may contain lead solder. Kids should not eat food from lead-soldered cans, and

adults shouldn't keep food in unopened, lead-soldered cans for more than one year. To identify lead soldered cans, peel back about a half-inch of the label and look for a prominent, crimped joint with folded edges and a silver-gray smear on the outside of the seam. Safer cans either have a smooth welded seam—flat, with a narrow, gray, blue-black or black line along the joint—or are drawn, with rounded bottoms and no side seams at all, such as tuna fish and soda cans.

Crystal clarity. Crystal is made with lead—the fully leaded variety contains from 24% to 33% lead— and lead leaching can be a serious problem. Don't use lead crystal

SHOPPER'S GUIDE TO LOW-LEAD CHINA

The Environmental Defense Fund (EDF) has tested many manufacturers' china patterns for lead. The following are widely available ones that meet the stringent California Proposition 65 standards. For a full list of low-lead patterns, write EDF. See **HELP** at the end of the chapter for contact information.

Manufacturer	Brand	Pattern
FITZ AND FLOYD	Fitz and Floyd	Adobe Gold
	Fitz and Floyd	Chaumont Teal Green
LENOX	Chinastone Collection	Black Brushstrokes
	Chinastone Collection	Country Blue
	Classic Collection	Federal Gold
	Classic Collection	Federal Platinum
MIKASA	Mikasa	Bristol Court
	Mikasa	French Countryside
	Christopher Stuart	Atherton
	Christopher Stuart	Montego Bay
	Savoir Vivre	Country Delight
	Savoir Vivre	Portofino
	Studio Nova	Color Rings
NORITAKE	Noritake	Adornment
	Noritake	Eternal Blush
	Noritake	Spectrum
PFALTZGRAFF	Pfaltzgraff	Aura
	Pfaltzgraff	Juniper
	Pfaltzgraff	Sky
ROYAL DOULTON	Royal Doulton	Alton
	Royal Doulton	Matinee
	Minton	Blue Delft
	Minton	Spring Valley
	Royal Albert	Autumn Rose
	Royal Albert	Val d'Or
VILLEROY & BOCH	Villeroy & Boch	Adriana White
	Villeroy & Boch	Basket
WEDGWOOD	Wedgwood	Chinese Flowers
	Wedgwood	Provence
	Johnson Brothers	Apple
	Johnston Brothers	Peach Tree

Source: Environmental Defense Fund and California Attorney General's Office

■. **To get the Food and** Drug Administration's free pamphlet on lead in ceramic ware, crystal, wine bottles, and cans, "What You Should Know About Lead in China Dishes," write to the Office of Consumer Affairs, HFE-20, Food and Drug Administration, 5600 Fishers Lane, Room 1685, Rockville, MD 20857.

■. **For a list of ceramic ware pat-**terns that meet California Proposition 65 standards, which are stricter than the FDA's standards, send a self-addressed, stamped envelope to the Environmental Defense Fund, EDF-china, 257 Park Avenue South, New York, NY 10010.

■. **For "Dishing Up Lead: A** Guide to Poisonous Ceramics," a full-color brochure showing patterns of dishes likely to leach excessive lead, send a self-addressed, stamped envelope (at least 6" by 10½") to Hawaii Department of Health, Food and Drug Branch, 591 Ala Moana Boulevard, Honolulu, HI 96813.

■. **All children between the ages of** six months and six years should be tested for lead at least annually. State and local health departments administer lead poisoning prevention programs and provide free educational materials and information on where to have children screened for elevated blood lead levels.

every day. Use crystal decanters for serving only, and don't store wine or other liquids in them. Women who are or expect to become pregnant should not use crystal at all. Never let infants or children use lead crystal baby bottles or tumblers; such containers should be reserved for decorative purposes only, given the double danger of lead exposure and potential breakage.

The rap on wine wrappers. Wine can become contaminated when lead foil covers the bottle top and cork. Although most domestic and foreign wineries have stopped using lead foil wraps, some bottles of wine in homes, restaurants, and stores are already wrapped in lead foil, so you should always uncork the bottles carefully to reduce the chance of lead from the foil wrap getting into your glass. Follow these steps:

■ Remove the metal jacket covering the cork by cutting it below the bulge of the bottle's rim;
■ Wipe the top, neck, and cork with a cloth dampened with lemon juice or vinegar;
■ Remove the cork as you normally would, and carefully wipe again.

Also, don't drink bootleg whisky, moonshine, or homemade wine, which may have been made in lead-leaching containers. Pregnant and nursing women should completely avoid wine, as well as other alcoholic drinks.

The dirt on soil. Lead from air pollution and flaking paint can contaminate soil. If you grow food in an urban garden, get a free fact sheet on lead in urban gardens by sending a self-addressed, stamped envelope to Cornell University Co-operative Extension, 16 East 34th Street, 8th Floor, New York, New York 10016.

Heavy metal food containers. Some pewter and brass baking and serving pieces contain lead. Don't cook, store, or serve food in them unless you are sure that they are safe.

Traditional medicinals. Some folk remedies contain high levels of lead and pose a very serious risk, especially to children. Never use alarcon, alkohl, azarcon, bali goli, coral, ghasard, greta, liga, pay-loo-ah, or rueda.

Cold water only. Always use cold tap water for drinking and cooking. (See the chapter on "Water: Should You Be Worried About Yours?" on page 28 for more on this source of lead contamination.)

PART 3

Home

CHAPTER 15

HOUSES, CONDOS, AND CO-OPS

Buying and Selling the American Dream

Charles V., who spends his weekdays in the hurly-burly of Manhattan, thought he had bought his dream getaway house when he moved into a cozy, knotty pine-paneled lakefront retreat in northern New Jersey, just an hour's drive from his office. And when the engineer he hired to inspect the property discovered that the septic system was outmoded, the owner promptly knocked $10,000 off the selling price to pay for a replacement. But it was only after Charles had moved in that he discovered the defunct fuel oil tank buried under the front yard. Local regulations required that he dig down to the tank, test the surrounding soil for oil seepage, and fill the tank with gravel.

Charles was lucky; the bill came to "only" $1,000. The company that filled the tank with gravel told him it could have cost him more than ten times that much had the oil seeped.

When it comes to buying a home, there's always something else—be it a buried fuel tank, an underground stream, rotted timbers, or worse. The same goes for selling. Will the buyers turn around and sue you because the roof leaks? Will you waste a month dickering with a buyer who backs out at the last minute?

Here's how to accentuate the positive and avoid many of the negatives when buying or selling a home.

THE BASICS

Where to Buy

What makes one location more desirable than another? If you have school-age children, the reputation of the local schools may be paramount—and more particularly, say, whether they offer swim teams or free clarinet lessons. You might even consider attending a meeting of the local Parent-Teacher

141

Association or asking to be taken on a school tour to find out more about the local school system.

If the schools aren't your primary consideration, then perhaps the local tax burden will weigh more heavily on your decision. How well protected the property is by zoning laws and the quality of the police and fire departments are also near the top of many buyers' lists.

Before settling on a neighborhood, be sure to spend some time there. If you drive to work every day, test the rush hour commute. Walk around the neighborhood to get a sense of the community and to ask residents what they think of living there. Community meetings—the town planning board, the school board, the city council—can give you a pretty good idea of local concerns, and may clue you in to a major proposed development that could (adversely or positively) affect local property values, if you decide to buy.

Of course, if you are moving to a new location because you or your spouse just landed a great new job or were transferred, you might not have time to interview dog walkers or attend lengthy community meetings. So it might be better to rent before taking the big plunge into home ownership. Even though the prospect is daunting, it is preferable to move twice and get to know your new community well than to buy into a neighborhood with only scant knowledge beforehand—and maybe still have to move again because you find the neighborhood unliveable.

In other words, if you're about to make the largest consumer purchase of your life and one you'll live with (and in) for years to come, it's probably worth several days or weeks of investigation.

Zeroing In

Once you've found the right neighborhood, how do you find the right house? One way is to scan house-for-sale ads in the local newspaper. Another is to drive around looking for for-sale signs on front lawns. The easiest way, though, is to let a real estate agent (see below) steer you. A good agent will also have a good idea of which owners are serious about selling.

When you inspect a house, look at more than the physical structure. Get a sense of the sellers, too. Why are they selling? If there was a layoff or a divorce, perhaps they *have* to sell sooner rather than later; a seller under pressure will more readily reduce the asking price. Or, if the house is empty, it could mean that the owner had to move before selling, giving you an even stronger bargaining position.

Find out from the agent how long the house has been on the market and how many times the asking price has been reduced. If it's been on the market a long time at the same price, the owners might not be very serious about unloading it or about reducing their asking price.

Bring a camera on your forays. Take careful notes and photographs of the exterior and, if the seller permits it, take interior pictures, too.

WHO'S WHO AMONG AGENTS

A word of advice: Before you start a relationship, be sure to have an agent or broker clarify what type of agent he or she is and to whom fiduciary responsibility is owed.

Broker. Often used interchangeably with agent. Both need state real estate licenses. Brokers, however, must take an additional exam. Agents—also called associates or salespersons—work in offices that are managed and run by brokers. A broker will not necessarily get you better results than an agent.

Seller's agent. Retained by the seller and owes fiduciary responsibility to the seller. Usual commission is 6% of the selling price and is paid by the seller—but may be reflected in a higher price for the property.

Dual agent. Represents both buyer and seller, with fiduciary responsibility to both. The seller pays the commission.

Buyer's agent. Works for buyers only. A buyer's agent is supposed to get you, the buyer, the lowest price the seller will accept. Buyer's agents are paid by sharing in the seller's agent's commission or may receive an hourly, flat, or percentage fee from the buyer.

Subagents. Agents working for other agencies who produce a buyer but who are legally responsible to the seller; the listing firm splits its commission with the subagent.

Facilitator. Represents neither side but acts as an intermediary and furnishes advice about real estate procedures. Paid either a percentage of sales price or a flat fee. Since facilitators have no fiduciary responsibility to anyone, there can arise no conflicts of interest such as those that may occur when agents for the same firm represent both parties.

Splitting commissions. In a typical transaction, it is quite possible that the 6% commission *the seller* pays will be split among several agents: the broker who sold the house, the salesperson who did the legwork, the broker who initially listed the house, and the salesperson at that agency who listed it.

Dealing With Real Estate Agents

First and foremost, your agent should have plenty of experience in the neighborhoods under consideration. Before an agent starts showing you houses for sale, ask how many properties he or she sold in the last six months. If the answer is "none," seriously consider getting another agent. In any event, since most homes are listed with the local Multiple Listing Service (MLS)—a computer database of houses for sale available to most real estate agents in a community— make sure your agent has full access to MLS listings.

Most people don't understand that the friendly real estate agent who has been bending-over-back-wards-helpful really doesn't work for them. In fact, since most real estate agents dealing with buyers are subagents of the sellers or of a "listing" agent, their actual legal responsibility is to the *seller*. Practically speaking, this means that "your" real estate agent won't tell you, as a buyer, the lowest price the seller will accept if he or she thinks you might pay more. This is why you should not reveal any confidential information to an agent, *especially* not the maximum you are willing to pay; if you do, that is probably what you *will* pay—the agent is bound to tell the seller this piece of information.

To obtain less biased help, you might consider using a "buyer's agent," an agent who has no fiduciary responsibility to the seller. Buyer's agents usually negotiate harder for a lower selling price, and they have become increasingly common as states—44, in 1994—enact laws requiring real estate agents to tell potential buyers exactly who they represent. The one big downside: Listing agents sometimes discriminate against them. And Steven Brobeck, executive director of the Consumer Federation of America, says that while consumers are better served by buyer agents than seller

agents, you still have to be careful of a buyer agent promoting his firm's own listings or not being such an aggressive negotiator when the property is also listed with his agency, which stands to profit from both ends of the deal.

What must a real estate agent tell you about a house you're considering? Generally, in most states, it's the agent's duty to tell you about anything that affects the *physical* condition of the property. So the agent need not disclose that someone recently died in the house or that a six-lane expressway is to be built through adjacent property.

Whichever kind of agent you use, stop dealing with one who isn't willing to spend ample time with you or who keeps showing you homes $50,000 more expensive than your explicitly stated target.

Agreeing on the Price, Negotiating the Sales Contract

How much should you offer? Start to compute an appropriate bid by checking actual selling prices in the neighborhood with a real estate agent, at the local town hall, or at the county clerk's office. Be sure to take into account the cost of repairs and remodeling before you make your written or verbal purchase offer. Factor in the anticipated property tax bill and annual heating and air conditioning costs. Find out from the sellers which fixtures are staying and which ones are going. Don't ask the agent how much to offer, though. Because agents get their commission only if the house sells, they will naturally recommend that you offer enough to make sure the seller says "yes."

Within a specific neighborhood, there may be small subneighborhoods that are deemed more desirable and are therefore more expensive. Corner-lot houses cost more than houses with other houses on both sides.

Agents are required to present all offers to the owner, no matter how low. It's their fiduciary responsibility. And there's no rule against talking with the owner directly.

Reaching agreement. You'll have to agree on the price, the amount of deposit, the down payment, which fixtures are included, and on contingency clauses.

One way to resolve a negotiating deadlock is to agree to split the price difference. Negotiations can also be moved off the dime if you agree to close quickly—or to wait to close—depending on the seller's preference. Once you've decided to make an offer, the real estate agent may ask you to sign a binder. This document authorizes the agent to tell the seller your bid and, if the bid is acceptable, that a contract of sale will be executed. Since there is not yet a contract, you can still change your mind. But watch out! A binder may be a legally-enforceable contract unless it specifically states that a contract is to be signed later on.

About the contract. The sales contract (or "purchase and sale agreement") is the culmination of your home search. Among its basic elements are a legal description of the property, the price and down payment, date of occupancy, financing terms, escrow account terms, a statement of the condition of the property, what personal property and fixtures are included or excluded, the seller's warranties, an inspection clause, and who is responsible for any damage before the closing. If not written with extreme care—preferably with help from a good real estate lawyer—you could end up in financial hot water. (See page 483 to find out how to find a lawyer.)

Contracts should contain as many escape hatches (contingency clauses) as possible to allow you to not only cancel the deal but also to get your deposit back. Common are clauses that require the house to be repainted, the floors refinished, or the furnace to be replaced prior to the closing. A very important contingency clause requires that a professional inspector give the house a seal of approval before a closing can take place. To give you piece of mind, you might also make it a condition of sale that the seller disclose in writing all material defects, if such disclosure is not already required by law in your state.

One very helpful contingency clause says that the deal goes through only if you are able to sell your current home for a stated price, prior to a stated deadline. Another clause could provide that the deal is canceled unless you secure financing within 60 or 90 days of signing; you can even try to specify that you must get financing below a stated interest rate. Don't be pressured by the seller's real estate agent into dropping any reasonable clause you wish to include: remember, time is money and the agent wants to make the sale and go on to the next customer with as little delay as possible. On the other hand, if you press too hard, you may kill the deal.

If the seller fails to comply with the entire sales contract, then you may have a good case for cancellation and the right to get your deposit back. But you have to be very careful here—if the failure to comply was *your* fault, or if you fail to perform your end of the bargain, you could not only lose your deposit, but you might be sued by the seller for specific performance—that is, you could be forced to buy the house anyway (or pay money damages).

Check It Out—Very Carefully

Although you may have only limited time between the signing of the sales contract and the scheduled closing date, never buy a house without having a professional home inspector or engineer scrutinize each square foot. (An inspection should cost between $200 and $400.) The basic things to look for are the structural integrity, watertightness, and the solidity of the land the house sits on; if it's built on a former landfill, beware—it could settle. Ask to accompany the inspector on his or her rounds. Some localities actually require a report by an inspector before a sale can take place.

Some of the major items on the inspector's check-list should be:

Grounds. How good is the drainage? Are the grounds mucky for a long time after a heavy rain?

Basement. Is there any sign of seepage or dampness? Are the walls beginning to bulge?

Roof. Include drainage systems, flashing, chimneys, and skylights. Is there evidence of water penetration? Bubbling or shingle-curling?

Walls, windows, and doors. Are they straight and true? The caulking and weather-stripping should also be checked.

Heating and hot water system. How old is the furnace and hot water tank? How frequently has either been repaired during the last five years? What is the capacity of the hot water tank?

Water supply. Does the domestic water come from a well? What's the flow rate? Does the well water require filtration? You might also consider testing the well for bacteria.

Plumbing. How old is it? What is the recent repair history of the plumbing system? How good is the water pressure?

Floors. What's underneath the wall-to-wall carpeting?

Electrical system. Is it adequate? Can it support the profusion of home electronics common in so many households?

Energy efficiency. Are there storm windows? How much insulation is in the walls and the top-floor ceiling under the attic?

The inspector should be able to provide you with a general estimate of the cost of necessary repairs and renovations.

You don't think you need an inspection because you're buying new construction? Don't implicitly trust a builder, especially if you didn't get a chance to inspect the house during construction, as many single-family home buyers can do. Builders often cut corners to make bigger profits. The *Orlando Sentinel Tribune* reported on a Florida town house whose walls started to crack only four years after construction. The builder made some repairs, but the cracks only worsened. The buyer moved to California and is still unable to rent her old unit.

You can't rely on an inspection by your lender to find many of the faults and defects that could cost you a lot of money to repair. The main purpose of lender inspections is to appraise the property's value, not to determine if you'll have to repair the roof.

Increasing numbers of states now require sellers to fill out a form revealing any defects in their property. The idea, of course, is to protect buyers from hidden surprises. These forms can be very detailed. California sellers even have to disclose if there are noise problems in the neighborhood. And in the 26 states where the law does not require such forms, real estate agents may require them anyway. Actually, real estate agents are the force behind the enactment of such requirements, since completed forms shield them from prospective lawsuits by irate buyers. According to the National Association of Realtors, agents increasingly are being hit with successful lawsuits for misrepresentation or negligence.

Buyers should also check for a wide range of environmental hazards that have the potential to endanger both physical and fiscal health—they can make your new home immediately worth a lot less than you paid for it. Watch out for asbestos (used in many houses built before the mid-1970s), lead paint (used widely before 1978), lead in solder (used in plumbing in older homes), formaldehyde (used in various building materials), buried oil tanks (removing one could cost thousands of dollars if the oil leaks and contaminates the soil), and especially radon, an odorless, naturally occurring radioactive gas that comes up through the soil and rocks surrounding your house.

The National Academy of Sciences has estimated that radon contamination leads to 16,000 cases of lung cancer a year. Radon exceeds safe levels—4 picocuries per liter (pCi/L) of air—in up to 10,000,000 American homes. Levels as high as 3,500 pCi/L have been found in some homes; the average level is around 0.2 pCi/L or less. Certain geological deposits are likely to contain more radon, than others. Your state radon office (see box on the next page for phone numbers) should be able to tell you where higher levels of radon are likely to occur in your state. However, there is no particular pattern within communities. One house may have high levels of radon and a house several hundred feet away might register hardly any. Smokers who live in radon-contaminated homes greatly compound the danger.

The only way to guard against radon is to hire a firm to run a test before buying. To determine if there is a radon problem, the firm will install charcoal canisters or some other sensing equipment, such as an alpha track detector in the home, usually in the basement. After several days, canisters are taken to a lab for analysis; alpha track detectors must remain in place for two to four weeks. (Since canisters usually cost no more than $20 and can be purchased at hardware stores, you can easily use them to do an initial screening.) More accurate measurements require leaving equipment on the premises for up to a year. In 1992, it cost about

STATE RADON CONTACT NUMBERS*

Alabama	582-1866	Nevada	(702) 687-5394
Alaska	(907) 586-3543	New Hampshire	852-3345,
Arizona	(602) 255-4845		ext. 4674
Arkansas	(501) 661-2301	New Jersey	648-0394
California	745-7236	New Mexico	(505) 827-4300
Colorado	846-3986	New York	458-1158
Connecticut	(203) 566-3122	North Carolina	(919) 571-4141
Delaware	554-4636	North Dakota	(701) 221-5188
District of		Ohio	523-4439
Columbia	(202) 727-5728	Oklahoma	(405) 271-5221
Florida	543-8279	Oregon	(503) 731-4014
Georgia	745-0037	Pennsylvania	237-2366
Hawaii	(808) 586-4700	Puerto Rico	(809) 237-3563
Idaho	445-8647	Rhode Island	(401) 277-2438
Illinois	325-1245	South Carolina	768-0362
Indiana	272-9723	South Dakota	(605) 773-3351
Iowa	383-5992	Tennessee	232-1139
Kansas	(913) 296-1560	Texas	(512) 834-6688
Kentucky	(502) 564-3700	Utah	(801) 538-6734
Louisiana	256-2494	Vermont	640-0601
Maine	(207) 287-5676	Virginia	468-0138
Maryland	872-3666	Washington	323-9727
Massachusetts	(413) 586-7525	West Virginia	922-1255
Michigan	(517) 335-8190	Wisconsin	(608) 267-4795
Minnesota	798-9050	Wyoming	458-5847
Mississippi	626-7739		
Missouri	669-7236	*All calls are toll-free (800)	
Montana	(406) 444-3671	numbers for state residents, un-	
Nebraska	334-9491	less otherwise indicated.	

RADON RISK

Annual radon level (pCi/L)	If a community of 100 people were exposed to this level:	This risk of dying from lung cancer compares to:
100	About 35 people may die from radon	Having 10,000 chest x-rays each year
40	About 17 people may die from radon	Smoking two packs of cigarettes daily
20	About 9 people may die from radon	Smoking one pack of cigarettes daily
40	About 5 people may die from radon	Having 1000 chest x-rays each year
4	About 2 people may die from radon	Smoking at least five cigarettes daily

$1,200 to clean up the radon in an average home.

If your written contract with the seller doesn't allow you to fully inspect the property for such dangers, don't walk—*run* away from the deal. If you have special reason to think the locality has potential environmental problems, you might want to hire a special environmental engineer to run tests for you.

Consider what happened to the residents of Colonial Square, a town house development built in the New York City borough of Staten Island in the 1980s. Only after they purchased their homes and had been living there awhile did they learn that the abandoned landfill on an adjacent property was in actuality an inactive toxic waste dump. Their property values plummeted.

One potential environmental danger doesn't take a test to de-tect—high-tension power lines. While no one really knows the effect of electromagnetic fields (EMF) on the human body, the effect of nearby high-tension lines on a home's resale value is clearly harmful. As media accounts make Americans increasingly concerned about the possible relation of EMFs to cancer, it'll only get harder to sell homes located near power pylons.

Condominium and Co-Op Considerations

Much of the previous advice applies to co-ops or condos as well as to free-standing houses or town houses. However, there are important special considerations.

The differences between condominiums and co-ops. With a condominium, you get a deed and you pay property taxes on your unit. Cooperatives are different. You buy shares in a corporation, which owns the property and which likely has an underlying mortgage on it. The corporation gives you a proprietary lease which allows you to reside in a particular unit.

In both cases, the association or corporation maintains and sets rules for using common areas, such as hallways, elevators, and grounds. Individual owners are responsible for everything on their side of the walls. So if a toilet doesn't work, for example, and the problem isn't the plumbing inside the wall or floor, the owner foots the plumber's bill.

Co-op corporations and condo associations (sometimes called a "home-owners association") are run by boards of directors comprised of shareholders or owners elected at an annual meeting under legally-prescribed voting procedures. There are usually between three and nine directors; they, in turn, select officers from among them. Officers' terms can range from one to several years. Many boards with longer terms have the terms overlap, ensuring that there are always some experienced hands on board. One downside of co-operative and condo living is that these elections can become quite nasty and personal, yet the opposing sides are stuck living together after the election is over. So

> "*I liked it better in the old days when there was a landlord to complain to. Now the landlord is us.*"
>
> —A DISGRUNTLED APARTMENT DWELLER whose landlord converted his rental building into a co-operative

before you buy, you might want to ask several residents how everyone gets along. You want to avoid a complex that is so strife-riven that important decisions keep being deferred or, at the least, is an unpleasant place to live.

Most co-ops and condos hire an outside management company to take care of the day-to-day running of the building: collecting maintenance, paying bills, supervising staff. Still, the management company needs to be closely supervised by the owners to make sure money isn't being wasted and that services are being efficiently provided. In a series of scandals in New York City in 1994, officials of many of the city's most prominent real estate management firms were indicted for taking kickbacks from contractors and suppliers.

Once you're a member of a co-op, you might be expected to volunteer for a committee, such as a grounds or a finance committee, or one that reviews the applications of prospective purchasers.

One advantage of a co-operative is that it can be easier to finance capital improvements and repairs; the corporation can get a mortgage to pay for a new roof or furnace. In a condo, each owner may have to pay a potentially large special assessment over a short period for such capital work.

Another difference between the two—either a disadvantage or an advantage, depending on your point of view—is that co-operative boards can more carefully screen new purchasers. Co-operative boards can reject an applicant for any reason, as long as it is not on the basis of race, color, creed, or national origin. Condo residents have very little control over who buys a unit, although condo associations usually have a right of first refusal.

Condo and co-op finances. Before you buy, go over the condo or co-op's finances with a fine-toothed comb, including:

■ Annual audited financial statements for the last three years, the current operating budget, and the number of units in maintenance arrears. You will also want to check how much money the complex has in a reserve account to pay for future emergencies or capital projects.
■ Copies of the minutes of the last year's Board of Directors meetings. These could reveal a lot about the inner workings of the condo or co-operative corporation that you should know before you buy.
■ The prospectus, offering plan, or offering statement. In a condo, this may be called the declaration; master deed; or covenants, conditions, and restrictions (CCR). For both condos and co-ops, be sure to see the bylaws and the house rules.

Also, try to get a copy of an engineer's report, either one by an engineer you specially hire yourself or a recent report by an independent engineer that the complex may have hired. This is similar to a report by a professional house inspector except that an engineer will know about the more complex systems found in larger structures. Realize that if the engineer identifies pressing deficiencies and you buy anyway, a maintenance increase or special assessment to pay for repairs could be down the road. If it is a new apartment complex, it is important to check the reliability and reputation of the developer. Talk to residents of other complexes the developer has built. If anything about the developer appears the least bit shady, don't buy.

IF YOU'RE SELLING YOUR HOME . . .

Much of what you should know if you are selling a house is explained in the previous section. Just switch roles: Pretend you are considering *buying* your present house and you'll understand what a potential buyer might look for and ask about. Here are some considerations especially for sellers:

Dealing With Real Estate Agents

Do you really need one? After all, why should an agent pocket that 6% commission? Well, selling a house is not nearly as easy as it looks. A real estate agent probably knows much more about how to price your home than you do. Only agents have access to the MLS. And agents perform an important screening operation, keeping parties who are just curious or nosy away from your doorstep. Fact is, most people who try to sell their own homes eventually end up signing with an agent.

Get the right one. Try to hook up with an agent who knows your neighborhood and who sells houses like your own. If you live in a modest Cape Cod, an agent who sells only luxury estates will not be able to help you much.

Find out how many houses your agent has sold in the last six months, and ask how successful your agent was at obtaining close to the asking prices. Some real estate offices give out awards to the agents selling the most homes, and in some communities the most successful agents receive awards from the local board of realtors. But bear in mind that real estate is a second job for some agents, or they might supplement a pension with an occasional commission.

How long should you list your house? Try to keep it to 90 days or less, unless your listing has an unconditional cancellation clause, which gives you the flexibility to switch to another agent. If you agree to an "exclusive agency," only that one agency is allowed to sell the property, unless you sell it yourself. With an "exclusive right to sell," the agent gets a commission even if you are the one who ends up actually finding the buyer. An "open listing" means numerous agents list your house and only the agent making the sale gets the commission. Be careful of provisions in the listing contracts that

give the agent a commission as long as he or she delivers a bona fide purchaser, no matter if the deal falls through.

The main advantage of an "exclusive right to sell" is that the agent is likely to work harder for you than with an "open listing." The vast majority of listings are exclusive.

Is there any advantage to signing up with one of the large franchised real estate agencies, such as Century 21? No. Since the vast majority of homes are listed with the Multiple Listing Service, all agents have access to the same listings. How quickly your house sells depends to a very large degree on the abilities and initiative of the individual agent.

Most agents are honest and hard-working. But then there are others—the agents who disappear for long stretches, who gather as many listings as possible with no intention of aggressively marketing each one but who still make a decent living because they sell at least a few of them. A good selling agent will put real effort into it—not just organize an open house or place a few newspaper ads.

You can pay less and keep more. There's no law that says you must pay an agent at least a 6% commission. Some sellers negotiate a commission of only 5%. Or you can use a discount broker who charges as little as 4%; in exchange for the smaller commission, however, it could take longer to sell your house (discount brokers usually lack access to the MLS).

Get the House in Shape

Many sellers neglect the basics of presentation. Be sure to:

Clean up the place. There's no excuse for unmade beds and crumbs on the kitchen counter. Personal sloppiness sends a signal that the home isn't very well cared for, and real estate agents are less willing to show sloppy houses. It should be immaculate, even if you have to hire someone to clean. Vases of fresh cut flowers, a bubbling pot of spiced apple cider on the stove (for a wonderful aroma), and a wall of family photos are good touches.

Make minor improvements to help sell the house. Walls that could stand a coat of paint, counter tops with burn marks, and shrubbery that needs trimming are real turn-offs. On the other hand, some sellers go overboard with expensive improvements, remodeling kitchens or adding a finished basement or a deck. General rule: When the cost of renovations are added in, the market value of your house shouldn't exceed that of the more expensive homes in your neighborhood by more than 20%.

The Art of Setting the Price

Pricing a home is a very touchy subject. Emotional attachment to a home you've lived in for 20 years might lead you to overprice, which in turn might cause agents to avoid showing your beloved home, sweet home.

When setting an asking price, ask your real estate agent to prepare a written comparative market analysis. It starts with the recent sale prices of nearby houses and adds or subtracts for the special pluses (and minuses) of your house.

Learning the sale prices of these houses will give you a good idea of the strength of the local real estate market and whether your prospective asking price is high or low. (If the sellers had to reduce their prices a lot, then the market may be weak.) You should also factor in how long it took the houses to sell. If it commonly took longer than six months, then the market is weak or the sellers priced unrealistically.

You might consider hiring a professional registered appraiser. An appraiser's imprimateur on your asking price might help you get the price you want—and more than cover the appraiser's fee.

WHAT TO WATCH OUT FOR

Buyers

An overbuilt home. A massive Georgian Colonial in the midst of a neighborhood of modest ranch homes looks impressive by comparison, but the Colonial could be overbuilt. Unless you get an extraordinary price break, it's not worth buying such a house; some day, you'll have a hard time selling it.

Tampered radon tests. In a 1992 hearing, a Congressional subcommittee was told that between 30% and 40% of all home real estate transaction radon tests are intentionally or accidentally tampered with. How? Sellers or real estate agents secretly remove radon detectors from the premises for awhile, cover them with plastic bags, or purposely ventilate the test area.

Sad to say, some testing firms have had to resort to building motion detectors, barometers, and thermometers into their test equipment in order to measure changes produced by windows being opened or devices being moved. Tests using this equipment are more expensive than tests with basic charcoal canisters. Another way to guard against tampering is to conduct a surprise follow-up test; if the results vary significantly from the first test, then you can suspect tampering.

Cooperatives or condos filled with renters. If most residents rent, it's doubtful that you'll want to join a minority of shareholders or owners who are *de facto* landlords to most of their neighbors. And it can be very hard or even impossible to secure financing in such buildings for yourself or for a co-op corporation. In addition, owners who are outside investors may not be as interested in keeping the place up. And when such owners fall behind in maintenance payments, all of the other owners in a condo or co-op could end up financially responsible because the complex's full monthly bills still have to be paid.

Your real estate agent's recommendations. Take suggestions of a title insurance company, an escrow agent, and a mortgage lender with a grain of salt; the agent may have a financial arrangement with the recommended provider, although experts recommend complete disclosure of any such relationship. Compare prices and rates of reccommended providers with those you know are independent.

Buyer's agents who work in a dual agency. You've decided you need to hire a buyer's agent. Great. Just be careful if he or she works in an agency that also has seller's agents, since the buyer's agent you hire could very well end up dealing with his or her own office—a potential conflict, even if this situation is fully disclosed. It's called a "dual agency" when both sides' agents work in the same agency. You might do better with an exclusive buyer's broker, ideally one who charges a flat fee instead of a commission based on the price of the house.

Sellers

Not disclosing a defect in your home. The buyer may hold you legally liable if you fail to mention a latent defect—a defect that may not readily be apparent to the buyer but that a non-expert could discover. You might be held liable for undisclosed latent defects even if the sales contract said that your home is being purchased "as is." Minor defects that would not have affected the buyer's decision to buy your home don't count. On the other hand, obvious defects, such as a roof that is visibly collapsing, need not be specially disclosed.

Agents who misrepresent themselves. Make sure to screen potential agents carefully. Ask for a list of references, and ask those references if they would hire the agent again.

Mispricing your house. Get the opinions of at least three agents as to the market value of your house. It would be a financial tragedy if you impatiently acted on the advice of an agent who said your house was worth around $200,000 but didn't ask for opinions from two more agents—who might have said "$250,000."

Buyers

Buy or rent? In the glory days of real estate, value appreciation quickly offset closing costs and agents commissions. But in times when the housing market is in the doldrums, renting could make better sense, unless you plan to stay in a house for a long time. Closing costs usually amount to about 5% of the purchase price. As a rule of thumb, you have to stay at least five years to recoup these costs.

Negotiate, negotiate, negotiate. If something looks like it needs to be repaired—or even just painted— ask for it to be taken care of before the closing or for the selling price to be knocked down to compensate. Do you like the hallway chandelier?

Ask if it can be included in the price. And how about the seller resurfacing the driveway before the closing?

Many sellers purchased their homes at the height of the real estate market, but are selling now because they have a new job in another community or simply realize that values aren't going to return to their old levels. Such sellers could be willing to negotiate most anything, including who will cover closing costs.

Inspect the inspector. Most professional house inspectors are on the up and up. Still, keep in mind that an inspector who does the job *too* well—who finds and reports every little defect—will probably not be recommended by real estate agents for long and could end up out of work. Fortunately, some states now license home inspectors. In the meantime, make sure your inspector is a member of the American Society of Home Inspectors.

Get your lender to pre-qualify you. To get an idea of how much house you can afford, get a lender to pre-qualify you for a mortgage. This can be done informally, in a short meeting at the lender's office. Once you know how much you will likely be able to borrow, you'll know the limits of your house price.

This can also be done more formally, through a written application, which can produce a loan approval letter. You'll have to pay something—usually, the cost of the credit report—but sellers will know you are a truly serious shopper who can buy quickly, which ought to strengthen your bargaining position. Of course, only that particular lender has pre-approved you. You still might get less expensive financing for your deal from another lender.

Ask to see your lender's appraisal. According to federal law, you have the right to see your lender's property appraisal—if you ask for it in writing within 90 days after the lender has informed you of its decision on your loan or within 90 days after you withdraw your application. A copy of an appraisal has to be furnished within 30 days.

A lender's appraisal can be very useful. If the appraisal comes in low, you may be able to renegotiate the price downward before the closing. If you are purchasing property in a predominantly minority neighborhood, a low appraisal could indicate that the lender is illegally discriminating—called "red-lining"—against borrowers purchasing houses in that area.

Check into government auctions. Home prices too high for you? Maybe you can profit from the Savings & Loan crisis of the 1980s by buying failed real estate now in the hands of the U.S. Resolution Trust Corporation (RTC). Here's how:

Call the RTC at (800) 782-3006 for a catalog of nearby homes for sale and a calendar of sales. On your own, visit the homes. Some of them will be occupied, some not. Their physical condition will vary considerably. Meanwhile, attend one of the RTC's seminars (where the auction process is explained), and then attend the auction with the cashier's

check required for a down payment. *Don't* get swept away at the auction. Know your maximum bid on a property and stick to it.

Try buying a foreclosed property at a builder-sponsored auction. Less frequent lately than during the depth of the recession in the late 1980s, real estate auctions can still be a good source for a below-market price home. Generally, you have to deposit 5% to 10% of the purchase price in cash or cashier's check.

To find out about foreclosures, check your local newspaper's real estate ads or call banks directly and ask if they have a list of properties. Some of the best deals can be obtained through foreclosures; lenders just want to get their money back and aren't so interested in making a profit.

Sellers

Providing seller financing might help move your house. And, if it's feasible, it could prove a good long-term investment.

Consider renting, if worse comes to worse and you can't unload your house. This turns it into a business investment and allows you to deduct expenses and depreciation. You might even "gain" a tax loss.

Don't even *think* about tampering with a radon detector placed by a prospective buyer. Not only is it reprehensible, but you also could be sued for all you've got if the buyer finds out about it after the closing and it turns out that radon on your former property exceeds safe levels.

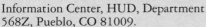

▪ For basic information, order the free booklet from the U.S. Department of Housing and Urban Development (HUD), *A Home of Your Own: Helpful Advice from HUD on Choosing, Buying and Enjoying a Home.* Write to Consumer Information Center, HUD, Department 568Z, Pueblo, CO 81009.

▪ Buy or rent? Computer software has been developed to help you compare the after-tax costs of buying and renting. Available at most computer software stores are "Buying Your Home" (Home Equity Software $49.95) and "Buy or Rent" (Real Estate Consultants, $29).

▪ To order information about environmental hazards, contact the U.S. Environmental Protection Administration (EPA), (202) 260-7751.

▪ To find out more about radon, order the U.S. EPA's booklet, *The Home Buyer's and Seller's Guide to Radon.* Write to the EPA Public Information Center, PM-211B, 401 M Street SW, Washington, DC 20460, or call (800) SOS-RADON.

▪ Is the property you're considering buying located near a hazardous waste dump? Find out from Environmental Risk Information and Imaging Services in Alexandria, VA. For $75, they'll find out. Call (800) 989-0403 to order a report.

▪ Consider leasing with an option to buy. To find out how, get the book *How Buyers, Sellers, Realty Agents and Investors Can Profit from Lease-Options,* by Robert J. Bruss. $4 from Tribune Publishing Co., 75 E. Amelia Street, Orlando, FL 32801. Bruss is a syndicated columnist who writes about real estate.

▪ To learn all you'll need to know about home inspection, borrow (at your local library) or buy *The Complete Book of Home Inspection* by Norman Becker; $12.95 from McGraw-Hill Publishing Company, Blue Ridge Summit, PA 17294-0850. Call (800) 233-1128 to order.

▪ The Fair Housing Act of 1968 makes it illegal to discriminate in selling or renting housing on the basis of race, color, religion, national origin, or sex. If you believe you have been discriminated against in buying housing, complain to the U.S. Department of Housing and Urban Development, 451 Seventh Street SW, Room 5100, Washington, DC 20410. You can also call them at (800) 424-8590, or (202) 708-1422 in DC.

CHAPTER 16

HOME IMPROVEMENT CONTRACTORS

Don't Get Hammered

Describing Harry Truman's ambitious project in 1949 to gut and rebuild the White House (then near structural collapse), biographer David McCullough noted that "little else that he was able to accomplish in these last years of his presidency would give him such satisfaction." And in 1993, David Letterman, in his CBS debut, brought on stage the whole crew who had renovated the Ed Sullivan theater to thank them for a job well done. If any proof was needed that the rich and powerful are different, these examples across the decades could easily be Exhibit A.

For most consumers, getting home improvement work done is like watching the Energizer bunny bungee-jump: a leap into the abyss that threatens to keep going . . . and going . . . and going. Anyone who saw the movies *Tin Men* and *The Money Pit* knows how contractors can cheat unsuspecting consumers. But this is one area where art only imitates life.

Stories abound of cost overruns, substandard work, missed dead-

lines, unpaid subcontractors and suppliers, incomplete jobs, and outright fraud. According to an annual survey by the National Association of Consumer Agency Administrators and the Consumer Federation of America, home improvement contractors (HICs) are, with cars, the largest source of consumer complaints; and they were the second largest complaint category for the Council of Better Business Bureaus, accounting for 10% of all complaints filed.

The victims are often among the most vulnerable consumers. Says Bill Richards, a consumer affairs official in Florida, "[t]he elderly are the major victims of home improvement fraud." Law enforcement authorities report the existence of the 20,000-strong Williamson Gang, a group of thieves also known as The Travelers, who "roam across the nation bilking senior citizens through home-repair scams." Targets also include the poor and, increasingly, immigrants.

Consider the story of Mattie H., an elderly woman living on social security in a low-income New York neighborhood. When a contractor visited her and promised to fix her porches, doors, and windows, she signed a blank contract on the spot for what she was told was $3,700, but was in fact $37,000. Sky-high interest charges tripled the cost to $119,000, or $650 a month for 15 years—payments she could not meet. Having unknowingly put her house up for collateral, Mattie faced foreclosure and homelessness. (NYC's Department of Consumer Affairs eventually got the contract rescinded.)

Home improvement fraud also involves big bucks: Americans spend over $100 billion a year on home renovations, and consumer losses can reach tens of thousands of dollars per consumer. And it is invasive, reaching into the privacy of our own homes. Consider, for example, the anguish of Sally A. of Queens, New York, who sobbed as she said, "I paid $10,000 down to re-do my kitchen. They tore up most of it but haven't come back for ten months. Where can I go to cook my meals?" Sally wound up like so many others having to lay out even more money to hire a second contractor to come in and get the job done.

> ## THE BASICS
>
> *"The cost of a home remodeling job that requires a contractor can range from a few hundred to tens of thousands of dollars. With so much money at stake, you would think that homeowners would select a contractor with more care than picking out a steak for dinner, but they don't."*
>
> —CHRISTIE COSTANZO,
> home design expert

THE BASICS

Remodeling your home can be a double benefit—enhancing both your quality of life and the value of your primary asset. But getting there from here can also be a true roller-coaster ride, interfering with your daily life and jeopardizing your savings. The process of remodeling involves turning over your home, or parts of it, to strangers for an uncertain period of time. Fortunately, picking the right contractor doesn't have to be like buying a lottery ticket; a few precautions can help.

The help you need is different depending on whether your project is a big production or a one-person show. If you're just contracting for a specific job—recovering the roof, repaving the driveway, or repainting the house—you should look for a professional in that field. If you're undertaking a more ambitious project, you should turn to a general building contractor to oversee the entire process—from helping you define the project and securing the proper permits to hiring a crew and the various subcontractors and seeing the project through to completion.

Choosing the Right Contractor

Finding a contractor isn't very complex: just flip through the Yellow Pages or write down a name on a flyer pinned on a supermarket bulletin board. As an industry insider notes, "basically all you need is a business card and a contract and you're in the home contracting business." The challenge is to find a contractor who'll do a good job in a timely fashion for a competitive price. While price is a key consideration, other factors—reputation, references, and quality of work—are just as important.

Get recommendations. Ask family, friends, colleagues, or trustworthy people in the construction industry for recommendations of local contractors that have handled jobs comparable to the one you're planning. A 1980 study by New York State's Consumer Protection Board found that consumers who relied on recommendations reported fewer problems than those who relied on radio, television, the Yellow Pages, or door-to-door sales pitches (more on those later).

Comparison shop. Get written, detailed estimates from at least three contractors after they've had a chance to visit the premises. (Find out if fees for such estimates are illegal in your jurisdiction by calling the Better Business Bureau [BBB], local consumer agency, or the attorney general's office.) Make sure that the various bids are based on the same specifics and that you're not comparing apples and oranges—or aluminum and steel. Do not auto-matically go to the lowest bidders; they may be low-balling their estimate to get the job or planning to use lower grade materials.

Check the contractors' references, background, and training. Check with your local consumer agency and BBB for records of prior complaints and to find out how long the contractor has been in business. Ask the contractor about reputable professional affiliations or certifications and for references (previous clients and suppliers).

You can also get a lot of information by interviewing the contractor. A conscientious builder should ask you plenty of questions and offer suggestions. And you'll get a sense of how well the two of you would work together.

Verify legal compliance. Prodded by the avalanche of complaints, state and local governments have taken various measures to regulate the industry and help consumers help themselves. Take advantage of the chits already on your side of the table. The main areas the regulations address are:

■ *Licensing.* As of July 1994, 32 states and the District of Columbia required some form of contracting license. These states are Alabama, Alaska, Arizona, Arkansas, California, Connecticut, Delaware, Florida, Georgia, Hawaii, Iowa, Louisiana, Maryland, Maine, Michigan, Minnesota, Mississippi Montana, Nebraska, Nevada, New Jersey, New Mexico, North Carolina, North Dakota, Oregon, Rhode Island, South Carolina, Tennessee, Utah, Virginia, Washington, and West Virginia. In addition, numerous counties, cities, and other local jurisdictions also require licenses. Licensing requirements vary greatly from state to state. California has a rigorous testing program that licenses contractors by specialty (roofing, windows, etc.) after they pass an examination. But in Iowa the only license requirement is payment of a fee.

Call the local licensing board to verify that the license is current and valid or you may end up like Michele K. of California, who hired a contractor after he gave her his business card with a contractor's license number. The contractor pocketed $2,600 to install a sprinkler system, replant the lawn, and remove a tree, but did such a shoddy job that Michele had to have the work redone by another contractor. When she contacted the board to complain about the first contractor, she was told his license number was someone else's: She was out $2,600.

A license is usually *not* a certification of professional competence or moral standing. In fact, disreputable contractors may go out of their way to get licensed precisely because it provides an air of legitimacy and tells the consumer, "See, I'm licensed. If you have any problem with me, I'll get into big trouble with the government." But it does indicate a minimum degree of accountability if you are later defrauded. For instance, New York City consumers who hire a *licensed* contractor can get back up to $20,000 from a city-run trust fund if their contractor does a shoddy job; the city awarded almost $2 million to defrauded consumers in restitution between 1990 and 1992.

■ *Posting bonds.* Many states require that contractors post a bond to compensate consumers who are defrauded. Again, this requirement is a help but no panacea: The bond may be too small to cover a large number of complaints.

■ *Cooling-off periods.* Federal law enables you to cancel your contract within three business days—except for emergency repairs and contracts solicited at "the contractor's place of business or appropriate trade premises."

Check that your contractor is insured. Unless your contractor has personal liability, property damage, and workman's compensation insurance (including coverage for subcontractors), you may be sued if someone gets injured on the job. Ask for a copy of your contractor's certificate of insurance.

Still, none of these precautions are fool-proof: Con artists learn to refine their schemes just as consumers learn the tricks of the trade. In 1993, several chimney sweeps in the New York region bent over backward to develop an aura of legitimacy, flaunting their registration or license, working by appointment only, providing customers with an "800" complaint number, and offering their cleaning services at cut-rate prices. The trick: Once on the roof, they would pry a few bricks loose and convince their customer that the chimney needed immediate repair—for several hundred dollars. They were especially hard to catch because they defrauded only selected consumers.

The Contract

Always ask for a contract, even for a small project. Once the job gets started, the contract will become your first line of defense—as long as it is carefully prepared. It should note the parties to the contract, including the contractor's name, address, telephone, and license number (if applicable), and the provisions that you and the contractor agreed upon orally—what is to be done, how long it will take, and how much it will cost. In particular, the contract should specify the following:

■ A detailed description of the work to be done, including materials. Especially when contractors are paid a flat fee, they may try to squeeze a greater profit by using low-grade or inadequate materials. Make sure that the contract spells out the types, grades, and brands of materials to be used.
■ A schedule. The contract should include the estimated start and completion dates for the project as well as completion targets of intermediate parts.
■ Financial arrangements. You can contract based on either a *flat fee* or *cost-plus* basis. The former has the great advantage of (relative) certainty. The latter, "cost-plus," means that the contractor is paid a percentage of the expenses. It is more flexible but gives the contractor no incentive to keep costs down. Most experts recommend that you avoid contractor charges based on time and materials, since overruns could send the cost skyrocketing.

The total price should be broken down by individual subcontractors and materials. A hard and fast rule: Don't pay too much in advance. One computer programmer in Brooklyn hired a contractor to do a $65,000 renovation job on his 90-year-old brownstone after he was told the house had dangerous structural problems. The contractor insisted on being paid the $65,000 cash on Monday and—guess what? —never showed up the next day to start the job.

Instead, work out a payment schedule, don't pay cash, and hold tight to your money until the job is completed. Never pay more than a tenth to a third up front, half to one third midway, and the rest upon completion, after city inspections (if required). If the project is time-sensitive—say, a summer pool or winter insulation—link payment to on-time performance.
■ Compliance with the law. Your home may be your castle, but you can't always do with your property as you wish. Construction projects must comply with local *building codes*, meaning that you'll need building permits for a lot of projects. The contract should assign responsibility to the contractor for complying with all applicable codes and obtaining all required permits, and those permits should be in the contractor's name. The National Association of the Remodelling Industry, a leading trade group,

warns, "Do not obtain your own building permit—in most jurisdictions, the individual obtaining the permit is considered to be the contractor and is, therefore, liable if the work does not comply with local building codes."

Working without a permit isn't just illegal—it can be unsafe. Joan W. of Queens, New York, who had hired a contractor to redo her basement, called her consumer agency after the work started falling apart. It turned out that the contractor had obtained none of the required permits. Electrical wires were sparking and the toilet was "dangerous and illegal," with a possibility of sewer gas infiltration. The inspector's conclusion: The contractor's work reflected "a callous disregard for human life."

■ Proof of payment for suppliers and subcontractors. If the contractor leaves workers or suppliers unpaid, they may be able to place a *mechanic's lien* on your property, a nasty legal maneuver that could jeopardize your ownership title if the bills aren't paid. A clause in the contract should enable you to withhold final payment until you have received proof of payment to subcontractors and suppliers.

■ Guarantees and warranties. The contractor should guarantee labor and material against defects or poor workmanship for a minimum of one year—agreeing to correct any shortcomings at no charge—and should give you the warranty cards for any items installed.

■ Cleaning up. Have a clear understanding of the contractor's cleanup requirements—for instance, do

you expect daily clean-up or clean-up upon completion of the job?

■ Financing. Finally, if you need financing, you should include a clause allowing you to pull out if you cannot secure financing under favorable conditions.

Don't sign the contract if any spaces are left blank and the contractor promises to fill them in "back at the office," Read it closely and in its entirety before signing. Estelle S. didn't: The contractor kept telling her, "Just read the top here to understand the job and I'll fill the rest in." The result: She signed a second mortgage on her house with high finance charges when she thought she was signing a work order to repair her leaky roof. The contractor botched the job and disappeared.

Any adjustments made to the original contract—known as *change orders*—should be put in writing, signed, and attached to the contract. You can often save yourself a good deal of money by *not* changing the project once it's started. On the other hand, *you* (not the contractor or anyone else) will have to live with the results—literally. If there must be changes, make sure you and the contractor have a clear agreement over any added costs.

Signing Off

At the end of the project, the contractor will ask you to sign a *completion certificate*—your acknowledgement that the work was completed as agreed to in the contract. Do not sign this document—

FINESSING FINANCING

Home improvements don't come cheap. The bill can quickly reach tens of thousands of dollars. Odds are therefore good that you will need financing. But can you get it?

People who moved into their home several years ago, and have seen the value of their home rise, usually find it relatively easy to get an equity line of credit or a second mortgage. But for those who've moved into their home more recently, and whose equity and value probably haven't risen much, financing is more difficult or expensive.

Shop around to find the best loan, taking into consideration the repayment schedule, interest rates, finance charges, and penalties for late or early payment.

If you're unsuccessful with conventional loan sources, you may be eligible for a Federal Housing Administration Title I loan of up to $25,000—but the interest rate for such loans can be nearly double the market rate.

Finally, a growing number of HICs and suppliers offer their own financing plans. Exercise great caution, however, because such financing has been the source of egregious consumer abuse. Look closely at the terms of the financing—the interest rate, the collateral (it could be your house!), and the financial institution that will actually be advancing the money.

Many contractors work hand-in-glove with unscrupulous finance companies to perpetuate all sorts of predatory lending practices. A smooth-talking HIC salesman shows up at the door and offers to do some remodelling—"no money down." The salesman (who is also an agent for a finance company) has the homeowner to "okay a few forms"—in fact, a contract for the work and a blank mortgage agreement. The specifics—such as interest rate and cost of the work—are often sky high and included *after* the consumer has signed the documents. The finance company then pays the contractor, who performs poor or no work. The homeowner is saddled with high monthly payments and, when she or he falls behind, faces eviction from a "legitimate" bank, which bought the mortgage from the finance company.

One reason why such schemes are able to proliferate is that redlining remains pervasive in the lending industry, making it very difficult for low-income or minority consumers to obtain loans from mainstream financial institutions. A detailed analysis by *The Wall Street Journal* in 1992 concluded that "If you live in a low-income neighborhood, chances are that many lenders have little interest in mortgage-lending in your community."

and do not make a final payment—until you've assured yourself that the work was properly
done and that all subcontractors
and suppliers have been paid.

Before signing the certificate, request that the contractor provide
and sign an *affidavit of final release*
that will protect you from liability
for non-payment of suppliers or
subcontractors.

WHAT TO WATCH OUT FOR

Fly-by-night operators. After the
flood of the Mississippi receded
from the Midwest in the summer of
1993, another kind of flood swept
the region: out-of-state scam artists
looking to make a quick buck out
of someone else's misery. The construction union in Iowa even
bought half-page ads in state newspapers warning residents against
"fly-by-night contractors from
Florida, Texas, and California."

One scenario: A "contractor"
drives around a poor neighborhood
searching for prospective victims,
finds an elderly couple sitting on
their porch, and offers to clean their
gutters for a reasonable $35 and to
inspect their roof "while he's at it."
Once on the roof, he pulls out a
(formerly concealed) hatchet, chops
a hole in the roof, and empties a
canteen of water into the hole he
created. Mr. Contractor then comes
back down, warns the couple that
they have a hole in their roof and
that "if they went upstairs they'd
probably see water on the floor"—
which, of course, they do. Mr. Con-

tractor then generously offers to
cover the roof with a "miraculous
substance" (some whitish liquid) for
a mere $6,500—payable in cash.
He does the work, drives the homeowners to the bank to get the cash,
and takes off. In the next rain, the
"miracle substance" washes away,
forcing the couple to spend another
$9,000 for a whole new roof.

Tip-offs for a savvy consumer: an
unmarked van, a post-office box address, or an answering service instead of an office. You may want to
pay a visit to your contractor's address to see whether they're working out of the back of a truck (bad)
or an office (good).

Hard-sell tactics. Be wary of anyone knocking at your door who
"just happens to be in the neighborhood" and offers to clean your
chimney or repave your driveway, or
who threatens that your house will
collapse unless you get the job done
right away.

And stay away from contractors
who call you with unbelievable
"this week only" bargains or offer
you a "special low price" for use of
your home as a "model home." Your
house might become a model, all
right—of a typical consumer scam.

Do-it-yourself? You may be able to
handle small projects yourself—
things between changing a light

bulb and changing your roof—by consulting how-to books and videos. Similarly, if you have experience in supervising large projects, you may do away with a general building contractor and act as your own owner/builder. But unless you know what you're doing, don't try this at home.

The big guns. For such major projects as renovations and additions, hire an architect to draw up plans.

Investment tips. Remember that a home renovation is also a major investment. How does the added value created by the improvement compare with the cost? Be cautious about remodeling just to increase the value of your house: According to the BBB, "when it comes time to sell, home improvements often do not pay back what they cost."

Don't overimprove. Don't turn your shack into the Taj Mahal before putting it on the market thinking you'll sell it at Taj Mahal value; you'll be sorely disappointed. Before any major investment, check with an experienced real estate agent about its potential payback.

Smart improvements are functional ones that add to the home's practicality, or low-cost cosmetic improvements that enhance your house's visual appeal.

Homeowner's insurance. Make sure to adjust your homeowner's insurance policy if the work done added substantially to the value of your house.

Complaints. You'll be able to avoid a lot of problems if you stay in constant touch with your contractor and supervise the project every step of the way. It's a good idea, for instance, to examine the materials and fixtures *before* they are installed. Don't be shy about asking questions or complaining if you find the work deficient.

If you need to complain, you'll be in much better shape if you have a solid paper trail—contract, proof of payment (such as canceled checks), written communications with your contractor, pictures of shoddy work, and agreements with subcontractors.

First, try to resolve your disagreement directly with the contractor. If you can't work things out, you have several options: You can file a complaint with the appropriate state or local agency. Or you can go to arbitration (if both parties agree) or file a lawsuit. Including a binding arbitration clause in the contract can save you from costly litigation if a disagreement occurs. Finally, you can fire the contractor—but be ready for a fight if he or she wants the balance of payment.

Emergency? The time may come when your house needs fixin' in a hurry and you don't have the chance to go through the orderly process outlined above. That's when you're at your most vulnerable, as Mr. and Mrs. C., in Seattle, Washington, found out. Their washing machine broke down—a true crisis when you have three children. They called a repairman who advertised same-day service in the Yellow Pages, who came and fixed the washer for $142—well, sort of. In fact, he rewired the electrical connections in reverse order, so the machine would spin on the wash cycle and agitate on the spin cycle. They were unable to recontact the repairman until they got his home number, when they were given another run-around. Eventually, they stopped payment on the check and got another repairman to fix the machine in 10 minutes for $50.

Before calling some name plucked out of the Yellow Pages, verify at least that the contractor is licensed. Ask the contractor about minimum charges, and before repairs begin, get a written estimate and a right of veto over added expenses. After the ordeal is over, ask your contractor to provide you with an itemized invoice. Finally, be aware that, for obvious reasons, the cooling-off period does not apply to emergency repairs.

Health alert. If the house you live in was built before 1977 and your household includes children under 6 or anyone who is pregnant, find out if the house contains lead-based paint before remodeling. Lead ingestion by children or pregnant women can cause permanent brain damage to the child or fetus.

Easy money. If your construction project will promote energy efficiency or structural renovation, you may qualify for a government grant or low-interest loan assistance. For more information, consult the catalogue of federal public assistance at your local public library or your local building department and utility companies.

■ **To obtain a list of** contractors certified by the National Association of Home Builders: Contact your state or local chapter (there are 800 in the country). You can find out how to contact your chapter by calling the national association, (800) 368-5242.

■ **The National Association of the** Remodeling Industry also offers examinations for both a general *certified remodeler* and *certified remodeler associate* designations. For a list of members in your area, to find out about NARI's arbitration program, or for a free brochure, "Selecting a Professional Remodeling Contractor," call the national association, (703) 276-7600.

■ **Under the Title I pro**gram, eligible homeowners can obtain a HUD-insured loan of up to $25,000. For approved lenders in your area, call: (800) 733-HOME.

■ *How to Get It Built*, **by architect** Werner R. Hashagen, is a treasure-trove of tips and techniques on how to build or repair your home. To order, send $24 to Werner R. Hashagen & Associates, 7480 La Jolla Boulevard, La Jolla, CA 92037; (619) 459-0122.

CHAPTER 17

THE ENERGY EFFICIENT HOME

Help Your Wallet and the Planet

Using energy efficiently is perhaps the most important aspect of being a smart, environmentally conscious consumer. Efficient energy use means we will burn less environment-harming fossil-fuels, like the oil and coal used to fuel electric power plants. Conserving energy means less dependence on foreign oil. And, of course, it will save you money.

Many people think that using energy efficiently is inconvenient, time-consuming, or complicated. Not true. A few simple measures can help clear the air—and lower your fuel bills.

Consider these two facts:

- If all Americans raised the temperature settings of their air conditioners by 6 degrees—so that cooling would begin at 76 degrees, say, instead of at 70—we'd save almost 200,000 barrels of oil a day.
- Refrigerators alone account for 7% of the nation's total electricity needs—they use the equivalent of half of the power generated by all of the nation's nuclear power plants.

THE BASICS

Home Heating

Keeping our homes cozy and warm is not without consequence. The Worldwatch Institute, an environmental group, estimates that home heating is responsible for spewing 350 million tons of carbon into the atmosphere each year—resulting in over a billion tons of carbon dioxide, the most prevalent greenhouse gas. And about an eighth of the nation's emissions of sulfur and nitrogen oxides (the leading cause of acid rain) comes from heating our homes.

Depending on where you live, heating with natural gas could save you money and help to make the air cleaner. Natural gas burns much, much cleaner, releasing none of the soot that comes from oil combustion. (It does, however, release some carbon dioxide.) Also, natural gas causes a lot less wear and tear on a furnace and so will reduce your maintenance expenses.

BUYING GREEN: DO THE RIGHT—AND THE SMART—THING

Of course, buying energy-efficient appliances is the *right* thing to do. But so is eating your spinach when you're a kid. Does that mean you'll do it? Well, you should. As the *Consumer Guide to Home Energy Savings* explains, the "wonderful thing about saving energy is that, in addition to helping the environment, you save money. It's like contributing to a good cause and ending up with more money in your pocket."

For $7.95, this little book by Alex Wilson and John Morrill contains all you need to know on the subject, including the top-rated "green" appliances by type and size and tips on how to make your whole living environment—from your house to your coffee pot—environment-friendly. Among the gems included:

- If you plan to buy a major appliance like a refrigerator, heating pump, or air conditioner soon, ask your local utility company if it will give you a rebate if you buy a more efficient model. Many utility companies will, realizing that it costs less money to conserve energy than to build new power plants.
- Front-loading (horizontal-axis) washing machines use one-third less water (and energy) than standard top-loading (vertical-axis) machines.
- You can save up to 15% in the cost of running your dryer if you buy a model that senses dryness and automatically shuts off rather than one that's controlled by a timer.

Look for the book at your bookstore or send $10 (post-age included; California residents add 8.25% sales tax) to the American Council for an Energy-Efficient Economy, 2140 Shattuck Avenue, Suite 202, Berkeley, CA 94704, or call (510) 549-9914.

WHAT TO WATCH OUT FOR

If you choose to investigate natural gas heat, you should know you're about to walk into an advertising minefield. The oil and gas industries have been battling each other in the media like latter-day Hatfields and McCoys. The gas industry pushes the cleanliness of its product; the oil industry responds with a very hard-hitting "use safe oil" advertising campaign that plays on some consumers' fears about natural gas. For example, the New York oil industry ran aggressive ads in early 1993 that came very close to deception. One commercial included the male voiceover, "Take a chance? Yeah, maybe on a lottery ticket. But gas in my house? OK, so odds are, nothing would go wrong—but I'd rather not bet on it."

By all accounts, natural gas is a clean, safe, convenient, and cheaper alternative to oil. Don't be fooled by the oil industry's not-so-subtle disinformation campaign.

THE SMARTER CONSUMER

Since 40% of the energy we use at home goes for heat, you can reduce your energy demand by implementing a home heating energy conservation program.

Treat your furnace to a tune-up. An energy tune-up costs about $50 and will increase your furnace's efficiency by about 5%. If you use oil to heat your home, ask the company that delivers it to make a service call to check your furnace. If you're paying for a service contract, you should take advantage of it; if not, you might as well take advantage of your oil company's expertise.

Keep your fireplace flue closed when you're not using the fireplace. About 8% of your heat can escape up an open damper.

Turn it down. Every degree you turn down your thermostat will cut your heating bill by 2%. By the same token, every degree you *raise* your air conditioner saves 5% in energy costs.

Insulate, insulate, insulate. Nearly half of all the energy used to heat and cool our homes is wasted. It goes out through the attic, the window, the walls, you name it. A few simple insulation steps can greatly reduce your home energy con-sumption. For example, you may want to add another 6 inches of fiberglass insulation if your attic floor now has only a few inches of it and install double-paned, insulated glass windows.

Electric and Gas Bills

Use compact fluorescent (CF) bulbs where possible. These light bulbs are a real breakthrough and only now are aggressively being brought on the market. CF bulbs last for 10,000 hours (as opposed to 750 hours for conventional incandescent bulbs). Super-efficient CF light bulbs cost more but burn just as brightly, and they significantly reduce the electricity we use. Less electricity means less air pollution and less oil we must import.

By using a CF bulb instead of a traditional bulb you'll prevent 1,000 pounds of carbon dioxide from entering the atmosphere. And you'll save a little money.

During its lifespan, the CF bulb uses about $10 worth of electricity. During the same period, you'd use about 13 regular light bulbs, which would use about $40 worth of electricity.

SPECS FOR CHOOSING EFFICIENT BULBS

Use this chart to convert your regular incandescent bulbs to compact flourescent (CF) bulbs, which last 13 times as long. For maximum efficiency, install them in fixtures that are on for an average of four or more hours a day use (but *don't* use CF bulbs on circuits with dimmer switches).

If you have this regular bulb...	Replace it with this CF bulb.
25 watts	*7 watts*
40	*11*
60	*15*
75	*18-20*
90	*23*
100	*27*

Source: New York Public Interest Research Group

CF bulbs have one other advantage: Since they give off less heat and more light, they reduce the cost of air conditioning. Consumers often don't realize how much of their air conditioning is required to overcome the heat produced by ordinary light bulbs. Substituting three 27-watt CF bulbs for three 100-watt incandescent bulbs will keep your room just as bright but will reduce a typical room air conditioner's workload by 12%.

Do a home energy audit. A home energy audit can enable you to find the trouble spots in your house where energy is being wasted. To perform one, pick a cold, windy day, take a candle, and tour the corners of your house. By watching the flame, you'll be able to tell where the drafts are and where you ought to apply weather stripping. You'll probably discover that the windows and doors are the worst offenders. Weather stripping is fairly easy to apply, and the eventual energy savings, while modest, will more than cover the cost of supplies.

Keep the filter and coils of your air conditioner clean. The air conditioner will work more efficiently if they are clean. A clogged filter uses 5% more energy than a clean one.

Use your air conditioner efficiently. Keep it in the shade. An air conditioner exposed to direct sunlight will use up to 5% more energy than one that is shaded.

Set the air-conditioner on "low cool" rather than on "high cool"; you'll use a lot less power, and you probably won't notice the difference. At night, set the air conditioner to run the fan only. The air circulation makes the room feel cooler and lets you save energy. Remember that for every degree you raise your thermostat, you'll save about 5% in energy costs. So try cooling your house to an even 76 degrees rather than to an icy 68 in

GETTING TECHNICAL ABOUT OIL BURNER TESTING

A combustion efficiency test can help you save energy from your furnace (a hot tip: have your furnace tested in the fall, before the fuel season heats up). The terms can be confusing, but here's what you need to know to converse with your mechanic.

1. *Flue gas composition* indicates how well the oil and air are mixing and how well the oil is being combusted. Carbon dioxide below the 9% to 12% range and oxygen levels above the 4% to 10% range indicate a problem.

2. *Flue gas temperature* also tells how well the oil is burning. Exhaust air above the 400- to 500-degree range indicates excessive heat loss.

3. *Draft measurement* rates the suction produced by combustion gases rising. A rating of .02 to .04 is ideal; any higher or lower is inefficient.

4. *A smoke test* shows how thoroughly the fuel is being burned. Smoke comes from incompletely burned fuel and stains a filter paper. The darker the paper, the worse the combustion.

Your furnace mechanic will measure combustion efficiency using a combination of factors. Above 80% efficiency is excellent, 70% to 80% is average, and below 70% means you're wasting too much oil and need a furnace tune-up. Tuning up the furnace can save fuel—and money!

---

the summer for environmental (and economic) conservation.

Make your refrigerator more energy efficient. Be sure the seals on the door of your refrigerator are airtight. To check, close the door over a dollar bill with half of it in the refrigerator and half of it outside; if you can pull it out easily, your seal may need replacing. Don't let frost build up in your freezer—it increases the amount of energy needed to keep the engine running. Clean the condenser coils on the back or bottom of your refrigerator at least once a year—a brush or a vacuum will do the job. You might also try adjusting the "feet" of your refrigerator to make sure the fridge is level and that the door shuts quickly and securely. (If a refrigerator leans forward a little, the door might not shut tightly.)

If your gas oven or stove has a pilot light, make sure the flame is blue, and cone-shaped. A yellow, "jumping" flame is burning inefficiently. Your local gas utility will usually check or adjust your gas stove for free.

Give your utility company a call. Its phone number is printed on your monthly bill. Many utilities nationwide are making extra efforts to conserve energy, and will even provide energy-efficient CF light bulbs at a discount or provide subsidies if you trade in an old refrigerator for a more efficient model. Call your utility and ask if it has an energy-saving program that you can "utilize" for big economic savings.

Check the seal on your oven door. Even a small gap lets a lot of heat escape.

Set your washing machine to a cold water rinse. Cold water rinses just as well as warm and saves a whole lot of energy.

Cover vents and exhaust fans when they're not in use to keep cold air from getting in.

▪ For free energy-saving tips, write or call the New York Public Interest Research Group, 9 Murray Street, New York, NY 10007, (212) 349-6460. Attn.: Director, Fuel Buyers Group.

▪ For more information on energy-saving appliances, order these booklets ($3 each) from the American Council for an Energy-Efficient Economy, 2140 Shattuck Avenue, Suite 202, Berkeley, CA 94704, or call (510) 549-9914 or fax (510) 549-9984: "The Most Energy-Efficient Appliances" and "Saving Energy and Money with Home Appliances."

▪ To learn how to weatherize your home, get these booklets ($2 each) from the Massachusetts Audubon Society, Public Information Office, Lincoln, MA 01173: "How to Weatherize Your Home or Apartment," "All About Insulation," "SuperInsulation," and "Heating Systems."

CHAPTER 18

HOME SECURITY SYSTEMS

Case Your Place

Aaaaaaaaaaaaaaaaaaaaaaaaaaaah! You just can't get a better security system than the perfect screech of Macauley Culkin in *Home Alone*!

But if you'd prefer not to leave any of your children behind when you leave the house, you can still make relatively certain your possessions are safe. "Nine out of ten household burglaries are preventable," according to the Insurance Information Institute. You simply have to take a few precautions. And they may not be as expensive as you'd think—things like keeping hedges trimmed, replacing dim light bulbs with photosensitive flood lights, and getting a noisy dog all make a difference.

If you're in the market for a sophisticated alarm system, burglar need beware—but so should buyer. Professional burglars, people who have made illicit but comfortable livings for years, told investigators from ABC News' *20/20* in 1993 that even the best, highest-priced electronic surveillance systems are

a "joke." Whether that observation is self-serving or sincere, an alarm may be worth it just for peace of mind. Besides, national crime statistics show that more and more burglaries are committed by less-hardened criminals who probably aren't as adept at slipping past motion sensors or alarms undetected. You can save yourself serious money by buying wireless sensors, which you can probably install yourself and will do many of the same jobs as a more expensive professionally installed security system.

THE BASICS

The Federal Bureau of Investigation says a burglary occurs every 10 seconds. That added up to more than three million homes being burglarized in 1992, with losses of more than $3 billion. These statistics are fueling a steady 15% annual increase in sales of locks, alarms, and other security devices.

Sensible Security Is Simple

Start with deterrence. A few simple steps might be enough to send a burglar to somebody else's house.

Trim the trees and shrubs near your doors and windows, and think twice before you build a high wall or fence around your property. Hedges and high fences add not only to your privacy but also, unfortunately, to the privacy of a potential intruder—a fence is one of the first things burglars look for (along with the darkness that so comforted the cat burglar in Alfred Hitchcock's *To Catch a Thief*).

Burglars are also on the lookout for loot. Keep yours out of sight. Even if it means rearranging the furniture, it's probably worth it to move the Van Gogh—or the VCR —out of view.

No matter how good the lock is on your front door, it's worthless if you leave your windows open or unlatched, or if the back door is unlocked. You might as well send out engraved invitations: About one in every four burglars get in through an unlocked door or window.

"Most people know these things, but they get careless," according to Detective Captain Raymond Nagel of the White Plains, New York, police department.

Fortify the door and locks. Dead bolts work best. Unfortunately, many contractors build houses with esthetics and cost in mind rather than your security. Trading up from a simple key-in-lock knob to a substantial auxiliary lock will run you from $20 to $220, depending on the lock you choose. "But even the most rugged-looking locks could be defeated by a swift kick or two unless some reinforcement was added to the door or the doorjamb," according to *Consumer Reports*. The piece that's most vulnerable is the strike plate, which attaches to the doorjamb to receive the lock's latch. You can strengthen it by replacing two-inch screws with three-inch screws, or by buying a heavy-duty strike plate or door reinforcer.

Do the windows. *Consumer Reports* has found that most window locks available at hardware stores can be foiled with a crowbar or knife. Fear not: Secure your windows simply and cheaply by "pinning" the upper and lower sashes together. Just drill a hole through the sashes where they overlap, and insert a strong nail or eyebolt from the inside. If you want to feel secure while your windows are ajar, drill a second set of holes when the window is open (not so wide that there's no point in locking it), and insert a nail or eyebolt there.

The Alarming Reality

A burglar alarm can reduce the likelihood that your house will be robbed, perhaps by as much as 80%, according to *Consumer Reports*, if you choose a reliable system and use it scrupulously. However, alarms have their downsides: Most cost a bundle; they are not always reliable; they generate false alarms that try your neighbors' patience and waste law-enforcement time; and, more than likely, they are inconvenient to those they're meant to protect.

Professionally installed systems will cost upwards of $1,500. When Michael G. and his family (of Phoenix, Arizona) looked into replacing the security system that came with their new home, they invited four salespeople (and *20/20*'s hidden camera) into their home to assess how safe they were and how much it would cost to tighten up the house's security. The assessments ranged from "It's just a cheap little system" to "You've got a good working system." The estimates ranged from $99 to $3,065.

> "**T**he golden rule of private security companies is to make a profit."
>
> —HELEN MAXWELL, author of *Home Safe Home*

What do all those bucks buy? The basic system usually includes some combination of the following: alarms on outside doors and windows, motion sensors in key areas (like the main stairway), a blaring horn and/or bright lights, and a connection to a central station.

Selecting a Security System

A reputable company will be responsive to your needs. Check various companies out with the Better Business Bureau or with friends who have used them, with the National Burglar and Fire Alarm Association (see **HELP** at the end of this chapter). They can give you guidance on which companies to avoid.

Ask several companies for itemized, written estimates. When determining the best price, take into account not only the initial investment but also any monthly service charges or routine maintenance charges. Compare warranties. And before you choose a system, ask friends or the company for references. Check with previous customers to see whether they are satisfied with the system and the service.

Helen Maxwell, author of *Home Safe Home*, for one, is certainly not satisfied. She relied on a high-priced, high-tech system. A robber slipped by it and held a gun to her temple as he forced her to walk around her home, pointing out where she kept her engagement ring, her wedding ring, and various other valuables.

WHAT TO WATCH OUT FOR

The Shortest Distance Between Two Points?

Although there are something like 14,000 home security companies in the country, there are far fewer dispatching centers.

So, if something sets off the alarm in your house in Pittsburgh, the alarm may very well be routed through Kansas or Louisiana on its way to the police precinct down the block. "Not a problem," says Dan S., a Washington, DC, lawyer whose alarm is set to summon the local po-

MAN'S BEST FRIEND

For a trusty, low-tech security system, get a noisy dog. Burglars don't worry about getting bitten; they worry about getting caught. A barking dog may grab your attention if you are home, or your neighbors' if you aren't. To burglars, the dog's bark is literally worse than the bite.

lice, after they hear about it from a central dispatching center rather than directly. "The one time we've needed them, they were here within 10 minutes."

Sounds fine, as long as you know this is the arrangement. Many salespeople will only tell you about the relay method of delivering an emergency message if you ask explicitly. One salesman told Michael G. of Phoenix that an emergency box labeled "local monitor" meant the signal went directly to the local police, when in fact it didn't.

Leasing vs. Buying

Some companies sell leased systems. You pay for installation and a monthly usage charge to borrow use of the system for a set period of time. You'll pay extra if you want a hookup to a central monitoring station. It may make sense to lease if you don't plan to stay put for long. However, if you plan to live in the house for more than two or three years, leasing most often costs more than buying.

Double-Cylinder Dead Bolts

These locks require a key to open them, whether you're inside or out. Security experts often recommend them for doors that have windows in or around them that may tempt an intruder to smash the glass, reach in, and flick the single cylinder lock open.

But think twice. You may just as easily find yourself locked in as intruders find themselves locked out; in a fire or another emergency, this can mean losing vital time. You can avoid this problem by choosing a double-cylinder dead bolt that only allows you to remove the inside key if the lock is unlocked. Better yet, since a burglar won't necessarily recognize that smashing the window is futile, use the double dead bolt and keep the inside key far enough away from the door so that a burglar can't reach it, but close enough for you to get it quickly in an emergency. And make sure everyone in the house knows where to find it.

THE SMARTER CONSUMER

Call the police before a burglar calls on you. Most police departments have crime-prevention units that will come to your house to do a free security audit. They'll tell you where your house is vulnerable and how to improve security. The police can also give you an idea of how common crime is in your neighborhood and when it's most likely to occur.

See the light. For inside lights, buy timers that turn lamps on and off. While you're at it, put the radio on a timer to create some noise that will suggest activity even when you're not at home. For outside lights, get photosensitive floodlights that turn themselves on and off in response to dusk and dawn.

Post plastic security system signs in your yard and decals on your windows. Even if you don't have the system to back them up, these lend the appearance of high-tech security and are a great deterrent. The idea is that burglars will see them, decide it's not worth taking the risk of an alarm going off, and move on.

Go wireless. Wireless alarm systems offer many of the same advantages as hard-wired systems, but at a quarter—or even a tenth—of the price. With such a wireless system, you mount battery-operated sensors on door and window frames. Then you mount the central control console someplace convenient. No wires are needed: Radio transmitters embedded in the sensors communicate with the control console. You just need to be sure the console is close enough to pick up the sensors' signals. You program the console, usually, with a tool as simple as a bent paper clip.

Another advantage of wireless systems: They are portable, which means you can take them with you if and when you move, remount them, and use them again. However, most do not give you the option of hooking into a network that will alert the police or a dispatching center in the event something—or somebody—trips the alarm.

Security upgrades can equal savings. Ask your homeowner's insurance company if you can get a discount on your policy by upgrading your home's security. Installation of dead bolts or local or monitored burglar alarms could save you 2% to 25% off your premiums.

• **Read** *Home Safe Home,* by Helen Maxwell, (New Horizon Pub., 1992). $13.95. Call (800) 533-7978.

• **Read** *Safe Homes, Safe Neighborhoods: Stopping Crime Where You Live,* (Nolo Press, 1993).

• **For more information on reputable** home security companies, contact the National Burglar and Fire Alarm Association, 7101 Wisconsin Ave. NW, Suite

1390, Bethesda, MD 20814. NBFAA also has a brochure you may find useful: *Considerations When Looking for a Home Burglar Alarm System.*

• **Write** **for** **the** **free** brochure *Home Security Basics,* distributed by the Insurance Information Institute, 110 William Street, New York, NY 10038. It's about all the things you can do to make your home more secure, short of buying an alarm system.

CHAPTER 19

FURNITURE AND MATTRESSES

Don't Take Abuse Lying Down

Neil D. went to See Ltd. in New York City and picked out a glass table. See Ltd. told him the table was in stock and available for delivery anytime; he just had to let the store know two weeks in advance. He paid $1,700 in full, plus $100 for delivery.

When Neil called See Ltd. two months later to say he was ready for the table, the vendor said the table was no longer available and had to be reordered from the manufacturer in Italy. See Ltd. offered delivery in about six weeks. Neil said this was unacceptable and asked for a refund. The vendor persuaded him to take a loaner table and wait out the shipment. Six weeks later, Neil called to ask where the table was and was assured, "The table is definitely on the boat." He could expect it in three weeks. When the time came, he called again and this time was told the table had not yet left Italy and possibly was no longer being manufactured.

Nearly five months after full payment, Neil didn't have his table, and he demanded a refund. The vendor refused. When Neil complained to the NYC Department of Consumer Affairs, the vendor quickly delivered the table—and threw in an extra table base.

THE BASICS

Neil's experience is all too typical of the problems you might encounter buying furniture, carpets, and mattresses. It's hard to know what's a fair price, and the brands are not generally fixtures of daily American life, like Levi's or Coca-Cola. Plus, once you've made up your mind, you'll most often have to wait weeks before you can begin to enjoy your new purchase. And that's if everything works out just right.

It's best to get comfortable with your rights in order to avoid finding yourself uncomfortable with your purchase. Federal Trade Commission (FTC) Rules and Guides for the Household Furniture Industry require prominent, affirmative disclosure of various "material facts which, if known to prospective purchasers, would influence their decision of whether or not to purchase." These facts include the use of veneer construction, plastic with simulated wood appearance, simulated finish or grain design, imitation leather, and the national origin and style of furniture.

For instance, all wood or wood-like furniture and ads promoting it must be clearly labeled with a description of the true composition of the piece or a statement that the material is not what it appears to be. Acceptable (if factually correct): "maple solids and veneers" or "cherry-grained maple." Unacceptable: "molded components" or "walnut finish." Similar guidelines apply to leather and imitation leather, upholstery content, and national origin and style of furniture. "Danish" and "Italian" cannot be used without qualification unless the furniture was manufactured in Denmark or Italy. (These rules do not apply to mattresses or rugs.)

WHAT TO WATCH OUT FOR

The Furniture Game

Lourdes G. bought a white lacquer bedroom set from Seaman's Furniture for $3,000. But after only seven months, the finish began peeling off. The manufacturer at first blamed Pledge, which Ms. G. used to dust her furniture, but eventually exchanged the shoddy set for a new one.

Besides endless waits for delivery and furniture that falls apart soon after delivery, typical problems include delivery of damaged furniture, delivery of the wrong furniture or carpet, and flat-out non-delivery. Is it any wonder, then, that surveys show people hate to shop for furniture, or that year after year furniture stores rank as one of the top five complaint categories, according to the Federal Trade Association and consumer affairs offices around the country?

Look beyond the surface. While problems are most likely to occur at high-volume stores that sell less expensive merchandise, "furniture games" exist throughout the industry. Don't make choices based only on style and color. Inspect the joints on the underside of tables, chairs, and dressers. Look for quality: Furniture constructed with screws will be more durable than furniture constructed with nails. Look for smooth joints, with no glue or fasteners sticking out. Try all moving parts, such as drawers and table leaves, to be sure they operate properly and smoothly.

The torture of waiting. Once you've made your selection, it's the nature of the business that you'll most often have to wait; usually the retailer must order the piece from the manufacturer. A wait of four to eight weeks is customary. The vendor should give you a realistic idea of when you can expect your furniture and keep you posted about any delays. It's not sufficient for you to be told "next week" week in and week out. One couple complained to local consumer officials

CARPETING CAVEATS

When buying a carpet or a rug, many people neglect to factor in how much foot traffic it will have to bear. Carpet on the stairs will clearly get more wear than carpet in a guest room. Buy accordingly. For dens and other areas that get a lot of use, it pays to spend more on durable carpets made of high-quality fibers. (However, stick with dense pile of medium or short height, which holds up better than high-pile carpet, which tends to get matted down.) You can probably get away with slightly lower quality in bedrooms. When judging quality, the Better Business Bureau suggests keeping an eye out for the following characteristics:

Density. The denser the carpet, the higher the quality, generally. Compare carpet samples of the same fiber type by bending the carpet and noting how close the individual tufts are to one another and how much of the backing is exposed. Press on the carpet to see how easy it is to make contact with the backing.

Twist. In higher quality carpets, the individual yarn will have "neat, tight, and well-defined" cut ends.

Heat-setting. Read the label or ask the salesperson whether the yarn has been heat-set, which locks the twist into yarns and helps carpet stand up to use and cleaning.

---

after *five months* of the retailer telling them repeatedly that their dinette set would arrive "next week." (Given the prevalence of delays, it makes sense to hang on to your old furniture until the new stuff has arrived.)

In New York City, for instance, retailers are obliged by law to give you a delivery date (or a reasonable range of dates). If a delay arises, you must be notified in writing and given a new delivery date. If the date passes without explanation and you have not received your furniture, you can ask to get your money back, choose replacement merchandise, or agree to a new delivery date.

The retailer must accommodate you on whichever option you choose.

Return policies vary from one store to another and even from one consumer to another. Retailers allow regular customers more leeway. But to be safe, you should inquire as to the return policy before you buy. What happens if the item arrives damaged? What happens if you hate the upholstery after all? What happens when you've waited around for hours for the delivery, and when your furniture shows up it cannot fit into the elevator or through the doorways of your home? In this last instance, you may very well be responsible: Prudence calls for measuring stairways, doorways and elevators *before* you buy, or arranging for the item to be assembled in your home.

Think twice about "rent-to-own" offers. If money is tight and you want instant comfort, you may be tempted. However, just remember Irene M. She told the House Banking Committee in 1993 that she paid $34.98 a week to rent a couch, chair, dining table, and four chairs. When she finally said enough was enough, she had paid $2,500 for merchandise that would have cost $1,000 to buy outright. And according to the rental company, she owed still more.

There are laws in 31 states—including Iowa, Maryland, Michigan, Minnesota, Nebraska, New York, Ohio, Pennsylvania, South Carolina, and Virginia—that protect rent-to-own consumers to varying degrees from such outrageous practices. But the laws aren't necessarily enough. An investigation of rent-to-own businesses in Pennsylvania found that the effective annual interest rate ranged from 82% to 265%, in gross violation of the state's interest rate ceiling of 18%. Most contracts do not even specify a retail price or "principal" against which to determine how much interest you will pay, making it nearly impossible to test the interest rate against a ceiling that may exist in your state. (See "Lay-Away and Rent-to-Own," page 593, for more information.)

Mattress Mania

Mattress manufacturers and retailers are in bed together, and it's quite a cozy relationship. With hundreds of permutations of mattress coils, ticking (cover material), padding, and brand names, the potential for consumer confusion is a retailer's sweet dream—and a consumer's nightmare.

One retailer may sell scores of models made by the same manufacturer that are available nowhere else, each with subtle and often meaningless differences in specifications—370 coils instead of 380, or ticking of blue clouds instead of pink flowers, for example. Take one firm called Hillside Bedding: You can buy a Sealy Posturepedic Comfort, Posturepedic Deluxe, Posturepedic Extra Plush, Posturepedic Luxury Firm, Posturepedic Firm Premium, Posturepedic Premium Firm, Posturepedic Royal Firm, Posturepedic Super Plush, Posturepedic Premium Collection I, and on and on. These are just some of the 65 different Sealy mattress models— 23 with the word "posturepedic"

> "**E**xpect a delay— don't get rid of your old bed before your new one arrives or you may find yourself sleeping on the floor."
>
> —BESS MYERSON, former Consumer Affairs Commissioner of New York City

in their name—for sale at *one* store. It's difficult to comparison-shop within one store, and since only Hillside stocks these models, it's impossible to comparison-shop among stores.

It's a little unfair to pick on Sealy and Hillside since the same kind of mind-bending model proliferation afflicts their major competitors—the network includes manufacturers like Simmons, Serta, Stearns and Foster, and major national department stores ranging from Macy's to your regional chain. One salesman openly admitted to an undercover investigator posing as a mattress shopper that the purpose of the maddening multitude of mattress models is "to stop people from shopping for price."

To add to the confusion, salespeople routinely daze consumers with conflicting claims about the superiority of one model or one type of mattress construction over another. They can get positively nasty when consumers try to write down prices and specifications in an attempt to compare one product to another. In fact, the differences among many mattresses may be more cosmetic than real. Generally speaking, the more coils the better, but a mattress's coils are only as good as the steel from which they are made. If the 380-coil mattress uses 10-gauge instead of 12-gauge steel (lower gauges are stiffer and provide more support), it could very well be better than a 400-coil mattress made with 12-gauge steel coils. The retailer selling the 400-coil mattress says it's better; the retailer selling the 380-coil mattress

naturally disagrees. Who is to be believed?

These practices wouldn't matter so much if comparable mattresses cost about the same everywhere. But in a series of shopping expeditions undertaken by NYC Department of Consumer Affairs investigators, the price for what was claimed to be the top-of-the-line, queen-size Simmons mattress set ranged from $900 at one store to nearly $2,100 at another. Similarly, the top-of-the-line Stearns and Foster set ranged from $730 to $2,020. Is the top-of-the-line mattress at one store comparable to that at another store? There's no clear answer since information is so hard to come by.

Furniture and Carpets

Know what you want. Before you go shopping, make a list of what you're looking for, measure existing furniture or the space into which new furniture will go, and measure the access routes and entry points in your home, to be sure that what you pick can fit inside. Decide how much you can spend, and set priorities in case you can't afford everything. When you go shopping, take your list, a tape measure, and samples of any carpeting, wallpaper,

No Magic Carpet Ride

Beware of carpet cleaning scams. Ads and promotional flyers may hawk unbelievably low prices—any two rooms for $19.95, for example—and, in fact, you can't believe the ads. Limitations, such as that the "any" two rooms measure less than a maximum of 200 square feet per room, (10 x 20 feet), can effectively cancel the "bargain."

paint, and upholstery you already have or chose earlier.

To avoid having the rug pulled out from under you in the store, measure the room(s) you wish to cover *before* you shop. If you're buying broadloom or stair runners, you'll probably have to buy a little more carpeting than you think to allow for installation and fitting, but you can minimize how much you have left over.

Check the store's reputation before you buy. The NYC Consumer Affairs Department took legal action against one Queens store after 20 people complained it failed to deliver merchandise, kept consumers waiting unnecessarily when it failed to cancel delivery appointments, and delivered damaged or incomplete sets of furniture. It turned out that the New York City Better Business Bureau (BBB) had

heard from another two dozen irate consumers.

Be fire smart. Ask if the item is flame-retardant. The Consumer Product Safety Commission (CPSC) has a mandatory standard for floor coverings; the CPSC "standard" for furniture is voluntary but may soon become mandatory, given recent National Association of State Fire Marshals petitions.

Before you buy furniture, check the fabric label. It should give you cleaning instructions and information about any anti-stain treatments the manufacturer has already applied. Even though the retailer may try to sell you a fabric treatment to resist stains, don't buy any additional treatment unless you need it—and if the retailer offers a warranty on the finish, make sure you understand exactly what it covers and what it doesn't.

Get an itemized receipt that breaks out every detail, no matter how small: for furniture, make and model number (be sure it's the same model you saw on the showroom floor); number of chairs or end tables; a detailed description, giving the exact dimensions, color, pattern, style, materials (wood, plastic, leather, vinyl), finish, upholstery, and any optional details; total price, including delivery, credit terms, and any additional charges; and a delivery date as close to an actual date as possible ("as soon as it comes in" is unacceptable; "four to six weeks" is okay; a specific date is best).

For carpets, make sure your receipt includes exact dimensions and price per yard for the carpet and any padding; the installation fee; the color (with code number); the type of weave and fiber by weight; a statement that the carpet passes federal flammability standards; and a guarantee of durability, resistance to shrinkage, and that dyes will not run.

The receipt will prevent the merchant from substituting lower quality merchandise, and it will protect you if he or she tries to do so anyway.

Give as small a deposit as you can, with the balance payable on delivery. Do not pay in full unless you walk out with (or take delivery of) the goods.

Everything looks different in the store. If possible, bring a sample of the carpet or upholstery home with you. Don't throw the sample out until your carpet or sofa has been delivered and you have compared the sample to your new purchase to be sure you got what you wanted—and what you paid for.

Stay away from rent-to-own. Until disclosure requirements improve or rent-to-own transactions are regulated as installment purchases and are therefore subject to the interest rate ceilings on such transactions, it's probably best to find another way to get what you need. Just about any other payment scheme works out to be cheaper, unless you need to rent the item for a very short time.

Be firm about delivery dates. Don't let the vendor string you along with the "next week" excuse.

If the estimated delivery date passes, check into the situation. If you get the runaround, complain to your local consumer office or BBB.

Double-check your delivery. Before you sign anything and show the movers out, carefully inspect your new rug or furniture. Look for defects, scratches, missing items, or missing parts. Compare fabric or rug swatches. If you aren't satisfied, have the delivery person take it back; if he or she refuses, do not sign the bill until the person writes on the bill that the item is damaged—and have him or her sign the bill, too. Then contact the store immediately. If the delivery person has to leave before you've had a chance to look at the furniture, write "subject to inspection" on the bill of sale before you sign.

Do it yourself. Stores like Ikea and Sears sell affordable furniture that you assemble yourself. Industry analysts estimate that consumers can save 25% to 50% by putting the pieces together themselves. Buying unassembled furniture means immediate gratification, too—most often, you can walk out of the store with your purchase the same day you buy it, rather than having to wait weeks for delivery.

Mattresses

Try the mattress out in the store. Since nearly every mattress sold is "firm," "ultra firm," "extra firm," or some other version of firm, these names and claims are meaningless.

Bring your mate. If you share your bed with someone else, shop together. Don't be shy about lying on the bed in your regular sleep position—it's the only way to test a product you will spend at least a quarter of each day on. Is it comfortable? Is it roomy enough?

The skinny on thickness. The thicker the mattress, the more comfortable it will be. Anything less than 7 inches between the top and bottom seams will provide less support. Keep in mind, though, that it can be harder to find sheets for extra-thick (9- and 10-inch) mattresses than for standard mattress sizes.

Reputation counts. Buy your bed in a reputable shop—one that's been around a while—and get a written guarantee that the mattress is exchangeable if you find it uncomfortable or if it loses its shape too quickly.

▪ **If you have a complaint, con**tact the Furniture Industry Consumer Action Panel, P.O. Box 2436, High Point, NC 27261.

▪ **In addition, report your com**plaint to your local Better Business Bureau. You can also consult your local BBB to check the reliability of stores before you buy.

CHAPTER 20

ELECTRONIC GOODS AND APPLIANCES

Just the Fax, Ma'am

Buying electronic goods intelligently is one of the greater challenges of the late 20th century. There is a phenomenal array of products, brands, technologies and other specifics that the average consumer—and many salespeople—simply cannot master. Take one recent item that has become as indispensable in the office as Post-it notes: the fax machine. Should you buy one now or wait for prices to come down? What is paper-curl reduction? Do you need automatic redial? A paper cutter? In addition, new technologies constantly render our "toys" out-of-date, and it's hard to keep up. Cassettes and compact discs, which forced us to shelve our vinyl records and 8-tracks, may in the not-too-distant future become obsolete as digital compact cassettes enter the market.

As if the technical hurdles weren't enough, you can count on unscrupulous merchants to ply a few tricks of their own. Some of it is just the rough-and-tumble of the free market: In midtown Manhat-tan, stores within a few blocks of each other have sold the same camera for $69 or $169. But a lot of merchant mischief is unethical or illegal, like using bait-and-switch techniques on unwary consumers or selling them refurbished goods as new: Electronics stores ranked third in category of complaints between 1990–1993 at the NYC Department of Consumer Affairs. As one expert concludes, "There's no way I know of that the average guy can work this out."

THE BASICS

Whether you're shopping for a dishwasher or a new PC, the process is in many ways the same:

Look before you leap. It's a good idea to do some research *before* you step into a store to get an idea of what you want—and what you're likely to get. For one thing, you'll be better able to figure out what features are important for your purpose and to resist being pushed into buying features you don't need.

There's no such thing as a standard price. A *New York Times* reporter shopping for a pair of portable Sony stereo speakers in Manhattan found the same items priced from $49.49 to $259.95—a range of more than 500%. In particular, don't be taken in by the "list price" or Manufacturer's Suggested Retail Price (MSRP)—a price that is often inflated far beyond what most people would actually pay.

Beware of decoys. Sometimes an advertised item may not be the same as the item sold. So be careful to get the same thing you seek in the store that you read about: Check the model number.

Stores' return policies vary widely. Many states require the return policy to be posted prominently or in writing on the receipt. If the item is defective, basic contract law entitles you to a refund or replacement, regardless of the return policy. In any case, keep your receipt—it'll make future exchanges or claims go a lot smoother.

Use your plastic. Unless you already have a high-interest debt, consider using your credit card to make electronic purchases. Under federal law, you don't have to pay a charge made on your credit card if you have a legitimate dispute with the merchant. If you believe you've been cheated, call the credit card company and stop payment.

Measure those doorways. Before buying a major home appliance—refrigerator, washing machine, etc.—make sure you can get it inside your home and fit it in a convenient and adequate space.

Extended Warranties

We've all either experienced or heard a story like this: The day after the manufacturer's warranty expires, the answering machine eats the message tape and stops functioning. When you take it to the appliance doctor, you discover that repairing it will cost just as much as replacing it with a new one. Well, the industry has come up with a solution: extended warranties.

As the hottest trend in electronics marketing right now, "extended warranties" is a fancy name to describe what are essentially service contracts. They are sold either by the manufacturer, the retailer, or, increasingly, a third party called an administrator. (Such administrators now account for 50% to 70% of the business for appliances and consumer electronics.) The contracts vary in countless ways, but there are six basic plans: date-of-purchase plans; extension plans; major component programs (on the wane); comprehensive programs; replacement programs (mostly on low-priced items); and deductibles.

Extended warranties have become increasingly elaborate in recent years. While they used to deal in straightforward parts-and-labor coverage, they now run the gamut, from maintenance (VCR head-cleaning, annual "spec checks" for audio equipment) and theft protection to insurance against freakish occurrences like lightning damage, and food spoilage insurance (for refrigerators and freezers).

The very idea of an extended warranty is somewhat paradoxical: It makes you wonder how good the product that the salesperson just gushed about really is. "If you push extended warranties, you're all but telling [customers] that the product you just told them was the best product isn't going to last," acknowledges Lee Schoenfeld, who is a senior vice-president of marketing for Best Buy.

But the industry justifies this seeming paradox by arguing that modern-day electronic gadgets have grown so sophisticated and complex that, well, nobody and nothing's perfect. Apparently, a lot of consumers are buying both the rationale and the warranties. Droves of consumers are purchasing extended warranties because it brings them peace of mind, quality service, and convenience: An extended warranty means they won't have to frantically search around for a repair store when technological tragedy strikes.

Electronics stores sell them for the same reason Willie Sutton robbed banks: That's where the money is. Says one department store executive, "One clear reason why we must sell service contracts lies in the competitive pricing structure of consumer electronics products. These contracts give us the necessary margin to keep our electronics departments in business." In other words, merchants are now dependent on extended warranties and the high profit margins they generate.

How high? Retailers generally admit to 40% to 65% profit, although Schoenfeld estimates that his legitimate cost on a $200 extended warranty is $50—a 300% profit margin. And the Financial Accounting Standards Board in Norwalk, Connecticut, estimates that large retailers spend only four to fifteen cents on actual service for every dollar collected in service-contract premiums. Needless to say, the pressure is intense to sign up customers: Industry experts estimate that salespeople receive commissions as high as 15% to 20% on the sale of extended warranties.

In short, there's no question that extended warranties are a good deal for the seller. The question is, are they such a good deal for consumers? The short answer: Don't believe the hype.

> "**B**uying an extended warranty is like making two bets: that the appliance will break down after the manufacturer's warranty expires (and before the extended warranty does) and that the cost of the repairs will exceed the cost of the contract."
>
> —*Consumer Reports*, January 1991

EXTENDED WARRANTIES: THE BASIC PLANS

DATE-OF-PURCHASE PLAN	*Runs from the time of purchase of the item, but only takes effect after the original manufacturer's warranty expires*
EXTENSION PLAN	*Begins at the expiration of the original manufacturer's warranty*
MAJOR COMPONENT PROGRAM	*Insures only the product's major component*
COMPREHENSIVE PROGRAM	*Covers all parts and labor for a specified period of time*
REPLACEMENT PROGRAM	*Guarantees product replacement if the product fails during the plan's period of coverage*
DEDUCTIBLE	*Customer is responsible for an initial amount ("deductible") for the repair, after which the coverage kicks in*

First, watch for the bad apples—companies that sell long-term warranties and go under. The Manhattan-based electronics emporium, Crazy Eddie, for instance, went into bankruptcy in 1989, defaulting on an estimated $6 million in extended-service contracts. In 1991, EWC, Inc., an Oklahoma City-based company that carried 3.2 million service contracts through retailers across the country, filed for bankruptcy protection amid allegations of financial fraud.

In response to these stories and others, the Financial Accounting Standards Board established accounting regulations for the industry that should help sellers of extended warranties operate in a more fiscally responsible fashion. And several state insurance boards have started regulating the service contract market. In Florida, for instance, sellers of extended warranties are required to meet a certain minimum of reserves, post a bond, or obtain insurance coverage for the policies. But when extended warranties are not subject to state insurance regulations, consumers have little recourse if the business extending the warranty folds. All policyholders can do: Line up in bankruptcy court.

Therefore, it's always a good idea to find out if the firm selling you the warranty is backed by a solid insurance company and if it is easy to file claims if the need arises. In addition, to protect yourself against a third-party administrator going out of business, ask the retailer selling you the product if it will assume responsibility if the administrator folds. Either way, if the administrator goes out of business, check with the retailer, who may still assume the warranty or refer you to another party that will.

Ask yourself whether the extra protection is worth the expense, even if you're dealing with a reputable company. The answer: probably not. Although as many as 40% of people who buy at electronics and appliance chain stores purchase warranties, only 12% to 20% of people who buy extended warranties ever use them.

One reason has to do with the fact that most defects in electronic goods show up within a few weeks of purchase (when the item is still covered by the original warranty) or after several years (when the average extended warranty has expired). Engineers call this phenomenon the "bathtub curve," to reflect the curve you would obtain by charting these early and late breakdowns over time. Extended warranties, in short, are expensive insurance policies to protect your goods against defects and disruptions at a time when those are least likely to occur. With the downward trend in the price of electronic goods, you may be better off pocketing the money and, if the worst-case scenario materializes, going to the electronics store and buying a brand new appliance.

Finally, an extended warranty is certainly a bad deal if it is disproportionately expensive compared with the item it is supposed to insure. The threshold amount is arguable, of course; one expert suggests that the cost of the warranty should not exceed 10% to 15% of the total value of the prod-

uct. And there are alternative ways of planning for a breakdown that don't require the purchase of a costly policy. For instance, you may be better off setting money aside in an appliance-repair fund.

WHAT TO WATCH OUT FOR

Bait-and-switch. It's the oldest trick in the world, but it still works: Cheap Tricks Electronics advertises Item A (in print, on the air, or in the store window) at an unbeatable price. Mr. Consumer, lured by the ad, goes to buy Item A but Ms. Slick Vendor pressures him to switch to Item B which, just coincidentally, has a greater profit margin, by disparaging Item A or simply claiming that it is no longer in stock. Many electronics stores play this scheme with gusto, despite laws prohibiting the practice.

Refurbished goods. These are used goods that have been "souped up" and returned to the market. There's nothing wrong with buying or selling these items—as long as the customer realizes the goods are used. But some unscrupulous merchants have figured out they can make a quick buck by removing the "reconditioned" label from the box or the goods themselves and selling them as new. In one instance, Consumer Affairs sent lawyers to serve papers on one electronics store that allegedly engaged in this practice and found employees there scissoring the word "refurbished" off of manufacturers' boxes. In fact, consumer inspectors estimate that nine out of ten stores in low-income areas sell some refurbished goods as new. Not only do you get a used item instead of the real McCoy, but most likely you won't get a manufacturer's warranty.

How can you tell the item is refurbished? Usually, you can't. But you can make sure there is a manufacturer's warranty; verify that the model number on the equipment matches that on the box; check that the product comes in a new, sealed, brand-specific box; and examine the product, front and back, for scratches or other signs of use. An "R," "B," or "X" burned onto the back of an Emerson VCR or television, for instance, is that company's code to show it's been overhauled.

Gray-market goods. Also called "parallel imports," these are name-brand products intended for sale outside the country and brought into the country by an unauthorized importer. Again, there's nothing illegal per se about selling these items, and the goods you're getting may be perfectly fine. But then again they may not: For instance, they may not operate on U.S. voltage levels or the instructions may not be in English. Some jurisdictions require stores that sell such goods to post a sign saying that "gray" goods are on sale and that they are not covered by an authorized manufacturer's warranty. Here, *caveat emptor*—let the buyer beware—is the name of the game. (For more information see "Counterfeit and Gray-Market Goods," page 598.)

THE SMARTER CONSUMER

When you shop can be as important as *where* you shop. It's often smart to buy big ticket items out-of-season—e.g., an air conditioner in November. Unless you're a gadget junkie (with disposable income), July or August may be a good time to buy certain appliances—televisions, for instance—before companies unveil their new designs with all the latest features.

Shop in "superstores" that offer huge selections at rock-bottom prices.

Comparison shop. Look for ads. Remember that products can vary by margins of 500%! Bargain with stores and hold them to their "nobody beats our prices" ads. (Be careful of restrictions, though, some of which may be of the "not applicable to items purchased between Monday and Sunday" variety.)

Your best warranty is a superior product. Buy products with proven histories of problem-free long service. It may be worth a trip to the library to look at past issues of *Consumer Reports* for performance reports, which include breakdown rates. Generally, electronic goods have a breakdown rate of 12% to 14% while "white goods"—refrigerators, washing machines and other major household appliances—have a breakdown rate of 8%.

COMPUTER SHOPPING STRATEGIES

Even if you're trying to find a bargain, it's generally a good idea to stick to established brands. The prices of personal computers has been dropping dramatically in recent years—systems that were high-end five years ago now sell for a tenth of their original price—squeezing manufacturers' profit margins. The result: The number of PC manufacturers was expected to drop 50% in 1993. If you bought a cheaper IBM *clone* (i.e., a machine that is compatible with IBM systems but retails for less) from a small manufacturer and you need servicing after they've gone under (either repair work or just technical support), you may be in for some tough times. Some questions to ask: Has the manufacturer been in business for more than five years? Is repair service available locally? Was the computer built with the same standard parts found in other brands?

One recourse may be to tune in through your modem to electronic bulletin-board networks like Prodigy or CompuServe where experienced users may be able to answer your questions.

Make sure your purchase comes with a warranty. Compare the warranties offered by various dealers or manufacturers—they come in all shapes and sizes: "Full" warranties provide comprehensive coverage, while "limited" warranties may require you to pay for diagnosis and labor costs. It may be a good idea to test all the features and controls of an appliance while it is under warranty; most defects show up during the first few uses.

Pay by credit card as often as possible, and always keep the receipt to protect yourself.

American Express and many Mastercards and Visas double the original manufacturer's warranty for up to a year if you buy an item with one of their credit cards. Citibank offers its own "Lifetime Warranty"—free warranty protection up to $1,000 per item or $2,500 a year on most major household appliances, consumer electronics, and small outdoor appliances for the "expected" life of the product—from 12 years for a washing machine to three years for an answering machine.

When a product needs repair, look for a reputable company by asking for recommendations from friends or by looking for membership in professional groups, such as the National Electronics Service Dealers Association (NESDA) or the Professional Service Association (PSA). (Contact information for both the NESDA and the PSA is listed in **HELP** at the end of the chapter.) Ask about the qualifications of the store's employees, such as whether the business employs a certified electronics technician. Make sure the company carries liability insurance to protect your goods.

If your unit is covered by a warranty, make sure that the business will honor it. If not, before you commit to a repair or even an appliance service call, ask for an estimated service charge, the expected range of anticipated costs (in writing), and whether a minimum fee is required and what it will cover. Don't neglect to ask about the warranty on completed repairs. Ask for (and save) detailed receipts whenever repairs are made on an appliance, even if no charge is involved, and ask how the repairer guarantees the services performed. If the problem recurs, you are more likely to convince the manufacturer or retailer to service the appliance again at no extra charge if you can document their earlier work.

■ **To complain about a** service/repair company or a contract/extended warranty company: Contact the company first. If you do not obtain satisfaction, contact your state attorney general or the Better Business Bureau.

■ **The Major Appliance Consumer** Action Panel, sponsored and funded by the home appliance industry offers mediation services for any complaint regarding your major appliances; contact 20 North Wacker Drive, Chicago, IL 60606.

■ **The Electronics Industries Associ-** ation Consumer Electronics Group (EIACEG) issues numerous publications regarding the purchase, use, and care of consumer electronic products, including computers. For more information, contact EIACEG, 2001 Pennsylvania Avenue NW, Washington, DC 20006, (202) 457-4977.

■ **The National Electronics Service** Dealers Association (NESDA) publishes very informative brochures regarding repair work and service dealers: *"Extended Warranty" Service Contracts: Good or Bad?*; *Getting Good Service for*

Electronic Equipment; *Consumer Complaint Checklist for Electronic Equipment Repair*. To order, send a self-addressed, stamped business-size envelope to NESDA, 2708 West Berry Street, Fort Worth, TX 76109 or call (817) 921-9061.

■ **The Professional Service Associa-** tion puts out a *Consumer Guide to Finding Reputable Service Companies*. For a copy, contact the Association at 71 Columbia Street, Cohoes, NY 12047, (518) 237-7777.

■ *The Consumer Guide to Home En-* *ergy Savings* contains all you need to know about purchasing energy-efficient appliances, including the top-rated appliances by type and size. To order, send $8.95 (California residents add 8.25% sales tax) to The American Council for an Energy-Efficient Economy, 2140 Shattuck Avenue, Suite 202, Berkeley, CA 94704.

■ **Write for** *Service Contracts* **and** *Warranties,* two brochures from the Federal Trade Commission. Its address: Public Reference Branch, Sixth and Pennsylvania Avenues, #130, Washington, DC 20580.

CABLE TELEVISION

What You Get When You Get Wired

Ronald Reagan's Federal Communications Commission (FCC) Chairman, Mark Fowler, said TV was just another appliance . . . "a toaster with pictures." But your kids certainly don't spend 20 hours a week using the toaster, and your coffeemaker won't someday be hooked up to your telephone or personal computer and able to whiz you along the "information highway."

We are living in a time of technological wizardry (and chaos) that makes it hard to watch TV without two or three remote control devices—and from all indications, this is just the beginning. You think programming your VCR or ordering a pay-per-view movie is hard? Just wait until you have to choose among hundreds of channels—and have several companies knocking on your door eager to provide those channels. Wireless and satellite programming services are coming nationwide and have arrived in a few neighborhoods already. Telephone companies are merging with cable systems. And by the time you bring home a new VCR, the cable company's next generation of gizmos may have made it obsolete.

What does all this mean, especially for the sometime couch potato who just wants to catch a ball game, *60 Minutes,* or *Sesame Street?* For now, it means the 58 million Americans who want their MTV—and Court TV, CNN and ESPN, and E! and AMC—have little choice but to enter into a relationship with one of 11,000 local cable companies—and it's a relationship that often borders on the Kafkaesque. Since most cable companies operate as lightly regulated monopolies and are the only game in town, they can charge whatever they like (within certain new guidelines), foist equipment on you that hobbles your existing equipment, and treat you rudely.

THE BASICS

For years, the phone company seemed to be the most hated company in town. Now, it's the cable company. So-called "customer service" representatives too often serve up only surliness when there's a problem—"your arrogance and lack of common decency (i.e., a return phone call or acknowledgment of your error in any way)," as one irate consumer wrote. Another unhappy consumer told of having no luck correcting a billing error after four phone calls, a cumulative total of over three hours on "hold," and a letter; the only response he got was a series of threatening phone calls from a bill collection agency. Installers or repair people never showed up—"no one ever came [to pick up the converter box], although I'd made sure someone was there all day. Two weeks later I received in the mail a bill for the amount of $667.90 for 'unreturned equipment.'"

And to add salt to the wound, prices just keep going up. Between the deregulation of prices in 1986 and 1992, cable rates rose at more than twice the rate of inflation. FCC studies of hundreds of cable operators in 1993 showed that cable systems that had competitors in their markets charged about 48 cents per channel, while those that have no competition charged 65 cents per channel. And that's just the difference in bills; no doubt there is also a sizeable service disparity. Even the reregulation imposed by Congress in 1992 that was supposed to rein in rates resulted in lower bills for a lucky few, no change for most, and even increases for some consumers.

WHAT TO WATCH OUT FOR

Equipment Equivocations

Since every cable system differs to some extent from the next, you will no doubt discover incredibly annoying quirks for yourself, but here are some common ones:

The most infuriating problem is the incompatibility of the equipment provided by the cable company with your own personal video equipment. Many cable companies distribute converter boxes to customers through which the cable signal must pass on its way to the television set. This wouldn't be so bad except the boxes have set home technology back a decade or so. Many consumers have found they need multiple remote controls just to change channels, adjust the volume, or turn on a videocassette recorder.

> "**R**oosevelt believed . . . that competition is always preferable to regulation, but if there is no competition, there should be regulation, because the worst result is an unregulated monopoly. This is what cable television is throughout the U.S. —an unregulated monopoly."
>
> —FORMER SENATOR JOHN C. DANFORTH, (R-MO), sponsor of 1992 legislation that reregulated the cable TV industry

WHY THE CABLE COMPANY IS MORE HATED THAN THE TELEPHONE COMPANY

The cable industry's response to passage of the Cable Act of 1992 secured its induction in the Hall of Shame.

Congress passed the Cable Act over President Bush's veto to address widespread dissatisfaction about incessant increases in monthly cable bills. One congressman hailed the law as "the most important consumer victory of the last 20 years."

And then the cable industry proceeded to snatch victory from the jaws of defeat. After the FCC drafted rules to enforce the new law, the nation's largest cable provider, Tele-Communications Inc., of Denver, actually encouraged its cable systems managers to use the law as an excuse to *raise* rates. In an internal memo leaked to *The Washington Post*, Barry Marshall, chief operating officer of a TCI subsidiary, urged cable systems managers to "take advantage" of the new law to raise rates for customer service calls, VCR hook-ups, and other services not covered by the new rules. "The best news of all is, we can blame it on re-regulation and the government now. Let's take advantage of it!" wrote Marshall.

"It's an outrage," Leroy Hunt, a low-income senior citizen from Plainville, Connecticut, told *The Wall Street Journal* when his bill more than doubled to $25.41 per month for service provided by a TCI cable system. "How can they get away with this?"

The FCC has since rewritten the rules. The newest rules require cable systems to recalculate their "basic" and "expanded basic" rates (which excludes such pay channels as HBO from rate regulation) according to formulas that are so complex that each cable system, indeed each cable subscriber, will be affected differently. In general, the law and the rules were intended to roll back rates charged by cable systems that have no competition to bring their rates more into line with the rates offered in areas where there is competition.

Reports in mid-1994 about the effects of the newest prices showed that prices on service and some equipment dropped an average of 7.3% in 25 major cities surveyed by the FCC.

Still others find that they cannot record one show while watching another or use their split-screen TVs without renting additional equipment—for a hefty fee.

Cable companies counter these complaints by saying they need the boxes to provide additional services to customers and to keep non-customers from stealing cable service.

ADVERTISING OR ENTERTAINMENT?

Infomercials step way over the already blurred line between commercials and the shows they sponsor: Infomercials are both. More than 2,000 of these program-length commercials have run at odd hours during the day and night, the most successful of which rake in $30 million a year. No wonder Ross Perot figured the best way to "sell" his version of America's ills in 1992 and "unsell" America on President Clinton's national health-care reform plan in 1994 was to go direct to the consumer via half-hour infomercials.

Most often, infomercials use stars at varying heights in their careers—from Lyle Waggoner (of *Carol Burnett Show* fame) to President Reagan's son Michael to Cher—in mock talk show or news formats with cheery average "Joes" and "Janes" who unanimously attest to the product's wonders. Viewers are frequently reminded that operators are standing by at the other end of 800-numbers. The top-selling infomercial merchandise includes exercise equipment, health and beauty potions, self-improvement programs, diet aids, entertainment, kitchen accessories, and real estate and money-making opportunities. And it's a huge market: In 1992, infomercial shoppers spent more than $1 billion, according to the trade magazine *Direct*.

Although industry research shows that slightly more men than women watch infomercials, women make the majority of purchases.

"The great infomercial gives a great solution to a perceived problem, and sometimes you don't even realize you have the problem," says Tim O'Leary of infomercial producer Tyree Productions in Portland, Oregon.

Anybody smell snake oil? The claims made about the products are those of the advertisers, not objective or independent evaluations. And they are not always true. The Federal Trade Commission (FTC) has challenged the accuracy of over a dozen infomercials. Said former FTC Commissioner Debra Owen: "Consumers must be reasonably able to determine what they are seeing is a commercial. The infomercial cannot appear to be an objective or investigative program."

As a result, voluntary industry guidelines require program-length commercials to be clearly identified as paid advertisements at the beginning and anytime ordering instructions are given. The sponsor's name must be disclosed, false claims or deception through omission are not allowed, the product must be available in sufficient quantity, and there must be a reasonable basis for the claims.

However, the boxes also allow you to easily buy pay-per-view programs, cable products that have the potential to provide huge profits to the cable companies.

Since all televisions sold these days are "cable-ready," don't let an electronics salesperson lead you to think this feature is anything special. Furthermore, the term "cable-ready" is virtually meaningless for people who need a converter box to receive cable service.

Reception Misperception

One of the original promises of cable television was perfect reception. In practice, however, even Dan Rather doesn't always come in loud and clear. Sometimes the problem can be traced back to the origination of the signal at the cable company; other times, the equipment that moves the signal interferes with its clarity; in other instances, your receiver (either the TV or the cable box) renders *Roseanne* even more caustic than usual. If it's a problem with the cable company's equipment, they should adjust your bill to reflect any missed service.

THE SMARTER CONSUMER

Because cable companies are essentially government-sanctioned monopolies, you're pretty much stuck with the indignities and inferior service.

You could always cancel your service—if you don't mind parting with it. If you aren't willing to go that far, here are a few suggestions:

Wait for free hook-up. If you're in no hurry, it might be worth it to wait to install cable until the cable company runs a special that includes free installation. These offers often require you to buy one or more pay channels like HBO, Showtime, or the Disney Channel for a month to get free installation. Depending on what you have to buy and for how long, it can be worth it—but don't forget to cancel your order for the pay channel when the offer expires.

Review your bill carefully. Are you getting everything you pay for? Are you paying the price you were promised?

Assess your viewing habits. Do you really need to pay extra for a movie channel when you rent movies all the time? Do you watch enough of the channels in the expanded service tier to justify paying extra for them?

Buy your own equipment. Your cable company may have foisted a converter box and remote control device on you for which you pay monthly usage fees. Check to see if you can buy the box outright—either from the cable company or from a retailer—and if that would save you money in the long run. Shop for a "universal" remote control device, which will work with many different brands of equipment and enable you to retire some of the remotes you now use to operate all your equipment. They cost about $70, but the convenience might be worth it.

Address complaints first to the cable company. If you don't get satisfaction, complain to your local franchising authority or consumer affairs office, whichever has jurisdiction over complaints about signal quality, billing errors or questionable billing practices, inadequate handling of complaints, disconnections in service, or damage to personal property. However, be forewarned that the power of local government to regulate cable companies is extremely limited. At best, the weight of documented problems might influence a municipal decision about whether to renew the franchise and under what terms.

Before their franchises were renewed in 1990, several New York City cable companies were forced to meet minimum customer service standards regarding leaving people on hold when they telephoned and setting up service appointments.

Don't get boxed in when it's time to move. Have the cable box picked up before you move. Even if you have called the company to cancel your service and a representative failed to come get the box, do not assume your responsibility ends. You probably paid a deposit for the cable equipment; if you fail to return it, you could be out not only the deposit but the hundreds of dollars the cable company says the equipment is worth. At that price, it's not worth taking the risk of entrusting this job to your landlord or the next occupant.

▪ The Federal Communications Commission's Cable Information Line operates around the clock giving consumers information about filing complaints about rates and service: (202) 418-2225; in Spanish, (202) 632-0100; TTY, (202) 632-6999. You can also write to FCC, General Cable Inquiries, P.O. Box 18698, Washington, DC 20036.

▪ Your local franchising authority is the local regulator for your cable company. Any complaints left unattended by the cable company should be addressed to the city or county government that granted the franchise. While they usually have little direct authority to intercede in individual cases, the volume of complaints about a cable operator can influence whether and under what conditions the franchise will be renewed.

▪ If you're concerned about cable rates in your area, call the FCC Cable Information Line at (202) 418-2225.

▪ To complain about dishonest or ill-identified infomercials contact the FTC, Division of Advertising Practices, Washington, DC 20580; or call (202) 326-3131.

CHAPTER 22

PETS

Pet Peeves

mericans have a love–hate relationship with domestic animals. On the one hand, there are more pets per family in the United States than anywhere else in the world, and more than 60% of American households include at least one pet. Americans own 62 million cats, 53 million dogs, 15 million birds, 10.5 million other small animals, and 95 million fish. In 1991 alone, we bought $250 million worth of goldfish and spent over $7 billion in veterinary expenses. Dog and cat owners spent more than $7 billion on pet food and $2 billion on supplies. Little pets are big business.

Yet we often treat animals as mere commodities which can be produced factory-style in so-called "puppy mills" and discarded when we need to move on with our lives. Too many Americans go through pets the way Italy goes through governments. The Humane Society of the United States (HSUS) estimates that 12 million cats and dogs are left in shelters each year, of which more than eight million are euthanized. According to the *St. Petersburg Times*, "each year an estimated 20 million to 30 million dogs and cats are killed because their owners have lost them, don't want them, or cannot afford their upkeep."

You may be tempted to run into a pet store and take home a cute and lovable furry, feathered, or finny friend. But adopting a pet means taking on important responsibilities and making a long-term commitment. Before you take the plunge, take the time to think it through—both for your sake and that of your future companion.

THE BASICS

Should You Adopt a Pet?

successful human/animal relationship offers tremendous rewards. Pets make wonderful companions; they bring fun, joy, comfort, and unqualified love. Recent studies show, for instance, that pets actually can bring down blood pressure, reduce heart disease, and provide stimulation for the old and the young that friends and family cannot.

But pets require daily attention and care. So avoid impulse buying and surprises. (The American Society for the Prevention of Cruelty to Animals [ASPCA] maintains a "no surprises" adoption policy.) Before

CAN YOU AFFORD FIDO?

Keep in mind that raising an animal costs real money. It's not as much as a car or college tuition, but caring for a dog during an average 11-year life-span costs in the range of $12,000 to $13,000, according to the American Kennel Club, while the cost of caring for a cat over a 15-year lifespan averages $5,600.

bringing home some cuddly critter, talk it through with your family and figure out who'll be responsible—who will feed, walk, and play with the pet, and insure that the pet receives proper veterinary care for the next *decade*. If it's a pet for a young child, make sure a willing adult can step up to the plate if the child can't swing it. If you're on the road often, maybe you shouldn't have a pet at all.

After deciding that you're ready to bring home an animal, figure out what pet is right for you. One way is to do as actress Ann Miller did in *Easter Parade*—get the right puppy to match your outfit. We don't recommend it. Instead, get a companion that's compatible with your lifestyle. If you live in a 300-square-foot studio apartment, don't get a 100-pound German shepherd who needs a lot of exercise. If you have young children, avoid puppies or kittens who may snap or bite at a

curious toddler's advances. If you live with a frail, older person, stay away from large, energetic, demonstrative dogs.

Can You Adopt a Pet?

There is a growing battle between pet-owner and anti-pet people in co-ops and condominiums that is becoming the modem equivalent of the rancher-farmer battles of a century ago.

Many senior citizens who urgently need the companionship of pets are being told by the governing boards of their buildings that pet ownership violates the rules of their co-op or condominium. In a recent case, a widow named Natare Narstedt bought a unit in the garden apartment complex of Lakeside Village in Culver City, California. Six months later, she was told to get rid of her three cats because she was violating the association's rules limiting pet ownership to two domestic fish in a bowl or two birds in a cage. She claimed that the rules were unreasonable since her indoor cats weren't bothering anybody.

The State Court of Appeals agreed, saying that the association had to demonstrate that the pets really did injure the living conditions or property values of other owners for the regulation to be reasonable. But in September 1994, the California Supreme Court ruled 6 to 1 that homeowner groups *can* flatly ban cats and other pets. Ms. Narstedt, having spent $50,000 in legal fees, put her pets and principles above her residence. She left Lakeside Village rather than leave her cats. "They are like my children," she explained. "They give me unconditional love, and I would rather have them than a husband or boyfriend at this point."

Where Should You Get Your Pet?

Pets come in all species, shapes, sizes, personalities—and prices. Dogs, for instance, can range from "free" to $5,000. Your first stop should be the pound—the Humane Society, the ASPCA, etc. Look in the Yellow Pages under "Animal Shelters." Other than a giveaway, it's the cheapest alternative and, except in shelters that can't afford it, the animals come neutered, with shots, fit for adoption, and healthy, even if they're a little scruffy. The ASPCA, for instance, charges a $55 processing fee for dogs and $45 for cats, which covers spaying or neutering, rabies and other shots, as well as a future visit to an ASPCA veterinarian.

If you're looking for a purebred

or pedigreed pet, the American Kennel Club (AKC) and Cat Fanciers' Association are good sources of information. The AKC in particular can suggest which breeds are best for small children or small spaces, and direct you to a reputable breeder. (To contact either group, see the **HELP** section at the end of the chapter.)

Some pet stores and variety stores sell animals as well, but for cats and dogs, pet stores are likely to be expensive—two to three times higher than a reputable breeder—and not always reliable. Some, for instance, get their animals from puppy mills where purebred dogs are raised in horrendous conditions and are often inbred and genetically defective.

What if There's Something Wrong With Your Pet?

In 1987, Eugene A. Migliaro Jr., a Connecticut legislator, bought a miniature schnauzer puppy for his granddaughter. Within days, the puppy fell deathly sick, much to the little girl's distress. Migliaro did not just get mad—he got even, with a vengeance. He took the puppy to a vet who was able to restore her good health. Then he sued the pet store who had sold him the sick puppy and won $535 in damages. And he pushed through the state legislature one of the first "pet lemon laws" in the country.

You should have no such problem if you adopt from a shelter. Most screen their animals for health and temperament problems and only offer animals they deem fit for

DOCTOR'S BILLS

Here's the mean amount that a pet owning household spends on trips to the vet each year.

Dogs	$131.84
Cats	$79.75
Birds	$34.24
Horses	$163.23
Other pets	$9.05

Source: Journal of American Veterinary Medical Association

adoption. If you run into a problem, the shelter will probably try to cure the animal (if it has a clinic on location), give you a refund, or allow you to adopt another pet.

Things get trickier if you got your animal from a breeder or a pet store. In recent years, Connecticut has been joined by a growing number of states—including Florida, Massachusetts, New Jersey, New York, Pennsylvania, and Virginia—in enacting various "pet lemon laws" that offer some degree of protection if the pet you bought turns out to be sick or deformed. These laws typically cover only cats and dogs, and vary in their details. In New York, for instance, a consumer can bring a new pet to a veterinarian within 14 days of purchase. If the vet finds the animal ill or deformed, the dealer is required to do any of three things, at the consumer's choice:

> "*The problem is that the person who pays the bill and makes the decisions is not the customer.*"
>
> —JIM KRACK,
> Executive Director, American
> Boarding Kennels Association

- Take back the animal and refund the cost of the pet and veterinary expenses;
- Exchange the pet and cover veterinary expenses; or
- Reimburse the consumer for veterinary expenses.

In New Jersey, the discovery period is six months. Contact your state's department of agriculture, attorney general, local consumer office, or, ASPCA for a copy of the law.

Some stores also offer their own refund or compensation policy. Find out what it is and what kind of health care the store provided prior to purchase—e.g. vaccinations or feline leukemia test. As always, when you sign a contract before buying a pet, make sure you're not signing your rights away.

Finally, under standard contract law, merchants in every state must sell goods that are "fit and merchantable"—whether parrots, poodles, or parkas—and most states have strong, general consumer laws that apply to pets. If you can't obtain satisfaction from the merchant, write or call your local consumer agency, state licensing agency, attorney general, ASPCA, or Better Business Bureau for help. If all else fails, you may have to take the store to court.

Caring for Your Pet

The best health care for pets, as for humans, is prevention. Ask your veterinarian for advice about diet and other pet health information. In addition, both the ASPCA and the HSUS put out helpful literature regarding animal care. Take Fifi or Felix to the vet once a year for a check-up and required shots.

A few tips about selecting the right vet: Get recommendations from friends, neighbors, or local humane societies; check the vet's record with the state licensing agency; visit the premises; ask for an AVMA accreditation; and ask about services, hours, and fees.

Millions of cats and dogs are killed each year due to overpopulation. To be part of the solution, not the problem, and for your pets' health, get them spayed or neutered, usually shortly after their seventh month.

License your dog in accordance with local laws (cats may also require a license) and make sure your pet wears a collar and ID tag at all times. Always keep your dog leashed when outdoors in an unfenced area.

If You're Traveling . . .

The federal Animal Welfare Act sets requirements for the transportation of animals. For instance: Do not ship puppies or kittens under eight weeks old; provide a sturdy, well-ventilated container; insure that your pet will be handled safely prior to departure; and, if you're planning to send Spot flying on an unusually long trip, don't assume that he too will get a cold drink and bag of peanuts on board—provide instructions and supplies for food and water.

In addition to these legal requirements, be aware that all airlines require a recent health certificate for your pet, and some ground carriers, like Amtrak, won't accept pets, even in a cage. Book your pet's flight well in advance and find out under what conditions he'll be traveling. Not all airplane cargo holds, for instance, are pressurized, properly ventilated, or temperature-controlled. If you'll be staying

in a hotel, find out the hotel's pet policy in advance. Many chains—including the Marriott, Holiday Inn, Days Inn, Howard Johnson, Residence Inn, Four Seasons, Hilton, and Westin now accommodate four-legged "guests." At the Four Seasons in Washington, DC, the general manager writes a personal welcome note to each arriving animal. Room service then sends up a silver tray decorated with flowers and bearing dog or cat toys, Evian water, a porcelain bowl, and a selection of gourmet pet treats.

If you leave your animal at home when you travel, your best bet is to leave her with an experienced friend, neighbor, or relative. Your other options: a pet sitter or a kennel. On the plus side for pet sitters: Your pet will probably prefer staying at home with an animal lover than in a narrow kennel cage with no air-conditioning and little human contact. In addition, dogs in kennels may contract "kennel cough," a form of bronchitis that requires medical treatment. For referrals, contact the National Association of Pet Sitters. Good pet sitters should visit you (and their charge-to-be) and pester you with questions about your pet's special likes, dislikes, and needs (e.g., who's the vet). They should carry some form of insurance or a bond. And check their references.

But if your critter is more Cujo than Benji, or in need of constant medical care, you may opt for a kennel. Kennels run the gamut from detention camp to summer camp. A few tips: Visit several ahead of time (look for the exercise,

WHAT WILL THEY THINK OF NEXT?

There has been an explosion of services in the pet industry in recent years. As Atlanta reporter Alan Paterneau noted in 1993, "Furry companions from purebreds to scruffy mutts are revelling in a plush lifestyle unknown to their ancestors." The reason, many experts believe, is that many Americans, living alone or without children, now consider their animal companion a full-fledged family member.

You can now send Rover to a luxury pet hotel in Bedford, Texas, with $21.95-a-night suites and a kitchen preparing hot meals for its furry guests. Kamer Canine College in North Hollywood, California, offers an eight-week acting class for Lassie wanna-bes, and Animal Behavior Consultants in Brooklyn offers therapy for dog phobia. The Pet Set, a beauty salon in Atlanta, offers soothing oatmeal baths, whirlpool treatment, organic dip with citrus oil, and a full groom and cut. Here again, a healthy dose of skepticism may be warranted.

confinement, and food preparation areas); ask about health care arrangements and supervision; and inquire about possible add-on costs. The kennel *should* require proof of immunization. Call the Better Business Bureau for a background check. The American Boarding Kennel Association, the American Pet Boarding Association, your vet, or a friend are good sources for referrals.

About Pet Health Insurance . . .

Health care costs for animals are *also* on the rise, primarily the result of increasingly sophisticated care, from computed tomography scans to chemotherapy. In response, several insurance companies now offer pet health insurance. Medipet, for instance, offers two policies with varying premiums, coverage, and deductibles. For now, such policies are probably not cost-effective: premiums and deductibles are high, and many things are not covered.

Fido's Final Send-Off

What happens when your pet dies? There are a number of options, depending on state regulations and local ordinances. The simplest: The city can collect the animal and bury it in the city dump. Or you can take your animal to an animal shelter or a veterinarian, who'll dispose of him or her for a small fee. You may be able to arrange a cremation by calling a crematory directly or with your vet's help. If you have a garden, some localities still permit you to bury your pet on your property.

Finally, Stephen King's book and film notwithstanding, from 1% to 2% of pets are now buried in pet cemeteries, and the number of such cemeteries has shot up from 400 in 1990 to over 650 in 1993, according to the International Association of Pet Cemeteries (IAPC). A pet burial can run up in the hundreds of dollars, but the cemetery will let you organize the ceremony of your choice, from a simple cremation to an elaborate funeral, including viewing, gravesite service, and a marker. Members of the IAPC are supposed to adhere to a strict code of ethics, but scandals occasionally occur. A Long Island, New York, couple was awarded $1.2 million in damages after they discovered that their beloved sheepdog had been buried in a mass grave instead of in a private plot.

Such departures aside, a pet cemetery may turn out to be less than an eternal resting place: unlike human cemeteries, pet cemeteries do not have to be protected from future development. The IAPC or a local ASPCA or Humane Society should be able to help you locate a pet cemetery in your area.

WHAT TO WATCH OUT FOR

Vets who won't let you inspect surgery or kennel areas. As Donna Marsden of the Humane Society warns, "If vets will not let you in their back rooms, do not use them. Their operating areas should be as clean as hospitals and without odor."

Dogs and cats from pet stores. Unless the store has a co-operative arrangement with a shelter, chances are the pet is from a mill. Animal mills are notorious for horrible breeding conditions and inbred animals are prone to genetic defects.

Dog trainers with no credentials. Anyone can call himself—or herself—a dog trainer. Ask for qualifications and recommendations from a shelter or an AKC affiliation.

THE SMARTER CONSUMER

Affordable dignity. To bury your animal without the expenses of a cemetery, but with more dignity than the landfill or the vet, consider having his or her remains cremated—it costs as little as $30.

Short-term pet cemeteries. Will your animal's burial truly provide him or her eternal rest? Twenty-two years after burying her collie Laurie, Doreen T. of Sunnyvale, California, got a letter from the graveyard requesting an additional $300 for the next 20 years—or the late Laurie would be dug up and reburied in a common grave.

Co-ops vs. pets. Especially since the *Narstedt* decision, be sure to check your co-op's or condominium's by-laws on pets *before* moving in. But if it's too late and the rules ban your pet, check with a lawyer whether you can claim that you'd be disabled under the Americans with Disabilities Act without kitty because of your therapeutic reliance on her. "We're getting a lot more pet owners claiming disability," said Karl Scheuerman, a chief attorney with Florida's Department of Business and Professional Regulation, to *The New York Times*.

■ For an animal shelter near you, check your Yellow Pages under "Animal Shelters" or contact the Humane Society of the U.S., 2100 L Street NW, Washington, DC 20037, (202) 452-1100.

USA ($9.95), which lists lodgings where pets are allowed and veterinarians in all 50 states; to order, call (800) 255-8038 or *Pets-R-Permitted* ($11.95), which lists hotels, motels, kennels, pet sitters, and useful travel tips; to order, call (800) 274-7297.

■ Various insurance companies offer pet health insurance. For information about the Animal Health Insurance Agency/Medipet, (800) 528-4961; DVM/Veterinary Pet Insurance Co., (800) 872-7387; American Pet Care association, (800) 538-7387.

■ If you're leaving Toto behind on your next trip and can't arrange for a friend, neighbor, or relative to take him in, you can hire a professional pet sitter or send him to pet camp—the kennel. For pet-sitting referrals, contact the National Association of Pet Sitters, 1200 G Street NW, Suite 760, Washington, DC 20005; (202) 393-3317. For kennels, contact the American Boarding Kennel Association, 4575 Galley Road, Suite 400A, Colorado Springs, CO 80915, (719) 591-1113 or the American Pet Boarding Association; send SASE to P.O. Box 931, Wheeling, IL 60090, (708) 634-9447.

■ For more information about pet cemeteries, call the International Association of Pet Cemeteries, (800) 952-5541.

■ If you plan to travel with your pet, you may want to consult *Take Your Pet*

■ If the pet of your dreams is pedi- greed or a purebred, the AKC and the Cat Fanciers' Association are good sources. The AKC, the principal registry of purebred dogs in the country, can be reached at 51 Madison Avenue, New York, NY 10010, (212) 696-8200. The Cat Fanciers' Association is the largest registry of pedigreed cats in the world. To contact the Association, write to P.O. Box 1005, Manasquam, NJ 08736-0805, (908) 528-9797. In addition, your local shelter may occasionally have purebred animals available for adoption.

■ To help you organize your animal's next flight, write for the Air Transport Association of America's brochure, *Air Travel for Your Dog or Cat*, at 1709 New York Avenue NW, Washington, DC 20006-5206.

■ The American Veterinary Medical Association (AVMA) puts out a useful brochure to help you figure out the right pet for you. To obtain *The Veterinarian's Way of Selecting a Proper Pet*, write to the AVMA Public Information Department, 1931 North Meacham Road, Schaumburg, IL 60173.

CHAPTER 23

LAWN CARE

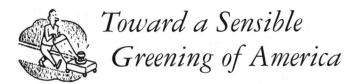

Toward a Sensible Greening of America

Have you ever been tempted to let your lawn "go natural?" Many Americans would, if they weren't worried about their neighbors' reactions or their home's resale value. After all, there are many better things to do with your free time than water, spread fertilizer, and kill crabgrass. And as for mowing—well, grass just grows back!

Still, we persist. Grass—fescue, bluegrass, or Bermuda—is America's biggest crop, covering an estimated 25 million acres. Lawns consume prodigious amounts of water and money—up to 60% of precious municipal water supplies in more arid areas of the country and about $25 *billion* a year in upkeep costs. And this is not to mention that we apply tons of environmentally unfriendly weed and insect fighters.

No, I'm not advocating letting your lawn become a weed-filled meadow nor paving it over. By putting in just a reasonable amount of work and money and by using alternatives to possibly hazardous weedkillers and polluting fertilizers, you can still have a respectable looking yard that will keep the peace with your neighbors.

THE BASICS

Economy, Ecology, and Safety

Watering. With the price of municipal water rising and supplies dwindling, we can't afford to waste it. Established lawns require only about an inch of water a week (about an inch and a half if your soil is sandy). Since this amount of water is provided by Mother Nature in much of the country, you probably don't need to begin watering until about two weeks have passed with no substantial rainfall. Then, water infrequently, but regularly. Water enough to make sure the soil is thoroughly wet, not just the grass; too much water is a waste and just encourages the weeds.

Water your lawn only when the soil around the roots has dried out. The best time to water is in the morning; about 30% of water applied later in the day merely evaporates, and morning watering gives the surface of the lawn all day to dry off. Second-best is early evening watering.

If you're conscious about water use, don't worry too much about moderate browning in the heat of the summer. The lawn is merely dormant and it'll come back. You might also invest in a drip-irrigation system, developed by the Israelis to make their deserts bloom. A drip irrigation system is a water miser, substituting for wasteful sprinklers and delivering just the right amount of droplets directly to root systems. If you're putting in a new lawn, choose with an eye on water consumption. New varieties of grass are being developed that require much less water.

Mowing. Most people cut their grass to about 1 to 1½ inches. But letting your lawn grow longer helps shade the actual blades of grass and reduces water use. A Smithsonian Institution test found that a 3-inch lawn looked "acceptable" and that a 2-inch lawn didn't look much different than a 1-inch one. Higher grass also helps smother weeds. A rule of thumb: Never cut off more than a third of the blade. But don't let the grass grow *too* high; grass higher than 4 inches tends to lean over and block essential sunlight.

Leaving the clippings on your lawn not only saves you the hassle of removing them, but their presence as a kind of mulch helps retain moisture and reduces the need for fertilizer. Of course, if you neglected mowing for a long time and you've got what could pass for hay, remove the clippings. The best time to mow is the morning or early evening, not midday, when temperatures are higher.

Thatch is a thick interwoven mass of roots, stems, blades, rhizomes, and other accumulations that builds up above the soil. Too much of it can prevent water, air, and necessary fertilizer from penetrating, and it can harbor insects. Prevent excessive thatch build-up by raking, clearing away excessive clippings, and aerating the lawn at least once a year.

If you can minimize the size of your lawn or mow less frequently, you'll help the environment considerably. Lawn mowers emit a lot of pollution. According to the California Air Resources Board, annual pollution emissions from such lawn power equipment as mowers and edgers in that state are equivalent to the emissions of 3.5 million late-model cars driven 16,000 miles each. That's why California implemented regulations in 1994 to limit lawn-equipment emissions, to be toughened in 1999.

> "**Y**ou can have a beautiful lawn without using a lot of water. For example, there are some tall fescues—good in the Northeast and Midwest—that stay green during dry summers."
>
> —MARIA CINQUE,
> Cornell Cooperative Extension
> Agent, Plainview, New York

Fertilizing. Your lawn probably doesn't need as much fertilizer as you think, especially if you leave the clippings. Grass makes its own food, in its blades. (Which is one of the reasons not to mow it too short.)

Still, your lawn could probably stand a moderate fertilization once in late spring, about the time that the spring growth spurt has started to slow down, and, even more important, in early fall, to strengthen the lawn for its long winter dormancy. Early spring fertilizing might also be considered if your lawn comes through the winter very weak and stunted. In the South, fertilization in midspring and midsummer is recommended.

Remember, if you overfertilize, much of it will run off and could pollute nearby streams and ponds. To help the local ecology and save money, you might get away with just a fall application if you leave the clippings from spring and summer mowings. Even better, apply mulch or use compost as fertilizer. If your lawn looks good and you've used alternatives, you might try skipping commercial fertilizers altogether.

What's the difference between organic and synthetic fertilizer? Synthetic works through chemical reactions that give your lawn a quick nutrition fix. Organic fertilizer, made of non-chemically processed minerals or animal or plant matter, works slower and usually costs more, but its "time-release" feature means you might only have to apply it once a year. Maybe your best bet would be one of the "bridge" fertilizers that incorporates both.

Weed and insect fighting. Perfect lawns aren't the traditional American way. It wasn't until after World War II, with the increase in the use of weedkillers and pesticides, that the "monoculture" lawn—lawns with just one kind of plant—became the ideal. Now, to meet our heightened expectations for a flawless lawn, we pour on the chemicals.

But no one really knows how safe these chemicals are. Very few have been fully evaluated. Yet there's plenty of anecdotal evidence that lawn chemicals can make you ill.

U.S. Senate hearings in 1991 on the issue of residential pesticide safety heard from several witnesses who got very sick from lawn chemicals. Christina Locek, a concert pianist, was sunning herself in her back yard when a lawn care company began spraying the neighbor's yard. Wind blew the spray onto her, and she immediately got very ill and collapsed; she is now blind in one eye. Her cat died in only a few minutes, and her dog died later in the day.

The National Cancer Institute reports that dogs whose owners use the broadleaf weed killer 2,4-D, developed by the military, have an increased rate of immune system cancer. And the insecticide diazinon was banned for golf courses because it kills birds. It is still available, however, in 1,500 weed-killing products sold for residential lawns.

Avoid using lots of chemicals by adopting integrated pest management (IPM) techniques for your lawn, shrubs, and trees. IPM involves careful year-round monitoring of the yard, shrubs, and trees for pests. When needed, chemicals are applied on the affected spot rather than broadcast over an entire area, which means that fewer chemicals are used overall.

After chemicals have been applied to the lawn, keep kids, pets, and yourself away until the lawn is thoroughly dry. About half the states in the U.S. require lawn care services to notify you when applying pesticides. Usually they tell you directly or post warning signs on the lawn. In Connecticut, the lawn care company must also tell your neighbors. Unfortunately, most notification laws do not require the lawn service to say *what* is being sprayed.

Rethink Your Lawn

There's a growing (excuse the pun) movement to let lawns grow longer and to allow more native species, including grasses and weeds, to intrude. If you can't stand to let your entire lawn go shaggy, try restricting the perfect, weed-free section of lawn to just around

IT AIN'T NECESSARILY SO

Just because pesticides are registered with the U.S. Environmental Protection Agency (EPA) doesn't mean they're safe for humans and other living things:

■ The EPA studies only the active ingredients that actually kill weeds and pests, not inert ingredients, which might also be harmful.
■ The EPA registration is a "balancing act, a cost-benefit analysis," according to Phyllis Spaeth, an assistant attorney general in New York State. If a particular pesticide is deemed necessary for agriculture, that factor weighs heavily in the registration process.
■ The EPA is currently considering 18 major lawn chemicals for reregistration, and it takes years to analyze tests of environment and health effects. In 1994, the U.S. General Accounting Office concluded, "Until reregistration is completed, the safety of the 18 pesticides will be questionable, while the approximately 2,100 lawn-care products containing them will continue in widespread use."
■ The test data the EPA relies on are produced by labs hired by the manufacturer, which are more likely to be biased.

Nonetheless, pesticide makers trumpet EPA registration and imply that it means their pesticide is safe.

Also remember: Pesticides sprayed on lawns do not always stay where they were applied. The wind carries them away and they run downhill, especially if it rains soon after application.

(maybe only in front of) your house.

It's a matter of altering your mind-set about what looks good. Environmentalists are concerned about the ecological impact of chemicals that farmers apply to their fields, but homeowners use ten times more chemicals per acre than farmers do. Keep this in mind whenever you gaze on a "perfect" lawn and you'll start thinking differently about what looks good.

If you're worried about what going natural will do to your property, consider "xeriscaping" or "naturescaping," where you replace lawn with native ground covers, flowers, and shrubs that need much less water. Xeriscaping also involves grouping together plants that need more water—to avoid having to apply a lot of water to the entire yard—and keeping such thirsty plants out of hot, unshaded areas. A side benefit of xeriscaping is that it takes less maintenance and saves money. The Planting Fields Arboretum in Oyster Bay, Long Island, adopted xeriscaping, and Assistant Director David Barnett was quoted in a local newspaper: "We have forty acres of lawn and haven't watered one bit in eight years."

WHAT TO WATCH OUT FOR

Lawn care services. The basic service is fertilizing and controlling weeds. Add mowing, reseeding, and soil aeration—for more money.

But service can be unreliable. Lawn care companies have been known to skip promised treatments, to fail to show up when they're supposed to (and show up when they weren't expected—perhaps when you had planned an outdoor party), and to overbill. Protect yourself by getting ample references and written bids and contracts before you hire. The bid and the contract should specify in detail exactly what services will be provided, where the clippings will be taken if they are removed (preferably off the premises), and exactly what products will be spread around. Check to see if the service is a member of the Professional Lawn Care Association of America. And, of course, make sure the service carries personal liability insurance.

Weed killer and pesticide safety claims. According to draft charges by the Federal Trade Commission, the Orkin Exterminating Company falsely claimed that its lawn products are "practically nontoxic" or have lower toxicity than many common household products like suntan lotion or shaving cream. Orkin went so far as to claim, "We'll keep weeds and harmful bugs out, using environmentally safe, biodegradable products that are neither harmful to you nor your soil." Not true. In March, 1993, Orkin agreed to stop making such claims.

And, in another case, the nation's largest lawn-care company, ChemLawn Services Corp., agreed in 1991 to stop advertising that its products were non-toxic and to pay the state of Pennsylvania $20,000 in a legal settlement. ChemLawn got into trouble when its employees told state agents posing as "shoppers" that its products were so safe that children could crawl around on a just-treated lawn. ChemLawn reached a similar agreement to stop advertising non-toxicity with New York State in 1990.

Mowing injuries. The U.S. Consumer Project Safety Commission estimates that from 1983 to 1990 emergency rooms treated 549,000 injuries caused by lawnmowers. Avoid becoming one of these statistics by never mowing a wet lawn (you might slip and hurt yourself) and by clearing the lawn of sticks and stones before you start.

Carefully consider the safety of any lawnmower you buy. The June 1993 issue of *Consumer Reports* includes a comparison of lawn tractors and riding mowers. The testers found that three of the tested tractors had an unsafe design—one of the mowers could easily do a backward "wheelie" when climbing a hill. The June 1994 issue rated 35 push (non–self-propelled) mowers for ability to mulch, bag, and discharge. With push mower prices ranging from $170 to a hefty $650, it makes money sense to read *Consumer Reports* before you buy.

THE SMARTER CONSUMER

Test your soil. Find how much or what kind of fertilizer you might need by having your local co-opera-tive extension service test your soil. They'll also check for acidity to see if you should apply lime.

To sod or not to sod. If you want an instant verdant carpet of lawn around your house, sod is the way to go. It can be installed in spring, summer, or fall. It can even be placed on slopes. And weeds don't have much of a chance with it. This all comes with a cost—sod isn't cheap. And it may need plenty of attention and water; until well established, it can dry out quickly, and it may need aerating to prevent thatching.

To protect your lawn against grass diseases naturally, sow a variety of grass types. This way, if a disease attacks one kind of grass, the others may still survive.

Take these basic safety precautions when hiring a lawn-care company: Get copies of labels for any pesticide mixture they are using. Be sure to find out how long you should wait after they are applied and what you should do if it rains right after an application. Make sure you know about any pesticide application well in advance so that you can take precautions—e.g., removing a wading pool or toys, or covering your vegetable garden before the lawn is sprayed.

Keep your mower blades sharp. Dull blades rip the grass, exposing it to diseases and insect damage. In addition, sharply cut grass looks better. And change your mowing pattern each time you mow. Constant mowing in one direction discourages grass from standing upright.

■ **The U.S. EPA's free** booklet, *The Citizen's Guide to Pesticides*, tells how to properly choose and use pesticides and how to handle an emergency. Write to Environmental Protection Agency, Office of Pesticide Programs H7502C, 401 M Street SW, Washington, DC 20460.

■ **Find out the real story about** your weed killer. Call the 24-hour National Pesticide Telecommunications Network at (800) 858-7378. Operators can also advise you in case a pet appears to be poisoned. This service is partially funded by your federal tax dollars. Another good information source is the National Coalition Against the Misuse of Pesticides, call them at (202) 543-5450.

■ **Take care of your lawn** the organic way. Order these two books from the National Coalition Against the Misuse of Pesticides: *Least Toxic Control of Pests* and *Organic Gardening: Sowing the Seeds of Safety*. Price: $3 each or $4 for both. Send a check or money order to National Coalition Against the Misuse of Pesticides, 701 E Street SE, Suite 200, Washington, DC 20003.

■ *Rodale's Chemical-Free Yard & Garden* (Rodale Press, $26.95) explains natural insect, disease, and weed control.

CHAPTER 24

MOVING COMPANIES

A Moving Experience

Psychiatrists list moving as one of the top trauma-creating circumstances, right after death and divorce. Indeed, the words "moving experience" too often take an unfortunate dual meaning. But they don't have to. In fact, with advance planning, some consumer savvy, and a bit of luck, you just may be able to beat the odds and have your next move be— well, if not quite a pleasant experience, at least a successful one.

Americans are a people on the move. One in five families—or 43 million people—relocate each year, according to the U.S. Census Bureau. One third of people in their 20s change their addresses every year. Studies show that you and I will move an average of eleven times in our lifetime. Thus, it's not surprising that the moving industry generates $7 billion a year in revenues and employs an estimated 450,000 workers.

This constant coming and going doesn't come cheap. Transporting 10,000 pounds (the typical weight of goods from a three-bedroom house) from Los Angeles to New York costs about $5,000. And it doesn't come easy either: Complaints against the industry in New York nearly tripled from 1989 to 1993, the result of what one state investigation called "a law-of-the-jungle competition."

Movers operating across state borders are regulated by the Federal Highway Administration (FHA) of the Department of Transportation (which took over from the Interstate Commerce Commission in January 1996). In 1980, the federal Household Goods and Transportation Act partially deregulated the industry, increasing competition and, in many cases, lowering prices for consumers. Interstate movers are still required to obtain a license from and file their tariffs with the FHA, but they can now offer discounts, additional insurance, and binding estimates that guarantee a fixed price.

Movers operating within a state are regulated by that state—typically the department of transportation or public utility commission. Because rules vary greatly from state to state, this chapter deals primarily with *interstate* moving.

Even Bill Clinton, hours after his inauguration, was heard greeting the movers from United Van Lines driving up to the White House with a relieved "Y'all made it, huh?" While you can't eliminate the trauma of dislocation and relocation, you can save yourself a lot of grief and money by planning early and doing your homework.

THE BASICS

Picking the Right Company

To do the job well, plan early—*Consumer Reports* suggests getting started eight weeks before your anticipated moving day. When selecting a mover, the two key factors are reliability and price.

Reliability. First of all, make sure the company is licensed by the FHA (if you're moving interstate) or by your state for intrastate moves. If your state does not require a license, make sure the company is adequately insured. (Ask for a copy of the policy to insure that it covers your losses, not just the mover's.)

The FHA requires every interstate moving company to compile and make available to consumers an "Annual Performance Report" that includes information about the number of claims they received for loss or damages, how often they delivered late, and how often they *incorrectly* estimated the final cost of ship-

> "**Y**ou have people wanting to move all their earthly possessions, and they just look in the Yellow Pages and call somebody. It's amazing. The truck pulls over; they take everything and drive away. That's fantastic faith in your fellow human beings. A lot of people just don't do enough checking."
>
> —GEORGE E. BENNETT, American Movers Conference

ment. In addition, ask family, friends, coworkers, or a reputable real-estate agent for recommendations, and check with your consumer agency or Better Business Bureau.

Price. The American Movers Conference (AMC) recommends that you get written price estimates from three different movers. Don't accept phone estimates. Glenn M. had a textbook experience of everything that can go wrong when moving: His first inkling that he was in for trouble came when the foreman, after loading up the truck, told him his bill was $2,200 when he'd been given a phone estimate of $1,300. Unfortunately, there's little you can do when your furniture is in their possession.

Don't reflexively go to the cheapest company. As George Bennett of the AMC notes, "be leery of the lowest one . . . the cheapest company could have old equipment, people who aren't trained movers, inadequate insurance, whatever." If one company vastly outbids the others, find out why. And remember that interstate rates—and intrastate rates in half of the country—are fully negotiable.

The FHA and most states enable you to ask for a binding or non-binding estimate.

■ Binding estimates are guaranteed final prices. Companies may charge you for this option. Make sure to tell the mover about special conditions—walk-ups, narrow doorways that require heavy lifting through the windows, etc.; appreciate that new arrangements may void the binding estimate. At your request, some movers will weigh your shipment even under a binding estimate option and, if the weight-based rate is less than the binding estimate, charge you the lower amount.

■ Nonbinding estimates are just that—the mover's best guess. The final cost will be determined primarily by the actual weight of the shipment multiplied by the distance traveled. Interstate companies are required to post their rates with the FHA but can offer discounts of up to 50%. (For short-distance intrastate moves, costs may be determined by handling time and required personnel.)

Consumer Reports recommends binding estimates, "even though they can run slightly higher than nonbinding ones." Nonbinding estimates, on the other hand, give you the flexibility to alter your plans at the last minute. In either case, show the mover everything you're planning to take, including long-forgotten relics in the garage, under the bed, or in the attic. Ask about any potential extra charges. Some movers, for instance, may charge you an extra $55 to move Aunt Rosie's Steinway, and another $45

to get it to your fifth-floor apartment. There may be extra charges for additional stops, parking far from the front door, or a non-elevator apartment building.

For an interstate move, the company you selected should give you an "Order for Service" detailing the estimated charge, terms and method of payment, all special services ordered, and agreed-upon pick-up and delivery dates (or spreads of dates). Don't accept a promise that they'll move you "as soon as possible." The company should also give you a pamphlet describing its procedures for handling complaints and questions as well as a brochure the FHA requires that it distributes to customers, *Your Rights and Responsibilities When You Move* (see **HELP** at the end of this chapter). Know that you can cancel the order without penalty at *any* time, up to the day of the move.

Packing Up

You can save hundreds of dollars by doing your own packing and unpacking . . . and a few extra bucks by getting your own boxes. (The mover will charge you premium rates for *their* boxes.) Consider at least packing non-breakable items—books, linen, clothing. Better yet, leave soft items like clothes inside drawers and tape the drawers shut. Pack heavy items (books) in small boxes. But you may want to let the movers pack the breakable stuff—dishware, electronic equipment, etc. Then *they'll* be responsible if anything happens. (Although not an FHA requirement, some companies accept responsibility for items you packed as long as you did so carefully.) But be aware that 55% of those who paid their mover to pack for them in a *Consumer Reports* survey reported damage, against 32% of those who did their own packing.

The movers must keep an inventory describing the nature and condition of the goods they pack. If you packed, they should still do an inventory of boxes and goods. Check it carefully before signing: It will prove an invaluable document down the road if you need to file a claim for items lost or damaged. Make sure it is specific—if you're moving your favorite Rembrandt or a first-edition King James Bible, it shouldn't just say "painting" or "book." If you disagree with a description, ask the movers to change it. If they refuse, photograph the item in dispute and make your own notation on the inventory.

Carry with you irreplaceable items like fine art, jewelry, and family photos. Also, it's a good idea to have one box of essentials—bed linens, coffee pot, towels, favorite toys, a phone—set aside to get you through the first few chaotic hours.

Weighing the Merchandise

If you are moving interstate, you will usually be charged based on distance and weight (more rarely on volume) plus packing and other services. The mover may require a minimum weight—usually 500 pounds or more—and should inform you if your shipment falls below that. You should be given a "weigh ticket" identifying the "tare weight" of the vehicle without shipment (including necessary moving equipment) and the "gross weight" (with shipment), so you can figure out the "net weight" of your shipment. You can ask to—and should—be present at the weighing. If weight is measured prior to the trip ("origin weighing"), you can ask that the truck be reweighed at destination at no extra charge; but if the second weighing is higher, you pay the higher price. A rule of thumb from the FHA: If the average weight per article ranges between 35 and 45 pounds, don't bother reweighing—it's probably on the mark.

If no scale or certified weighmaster is available, the trucker will compute the bill based on an assumed weight of 7 pounds per cubic foot of van space used.

Loading Up

Before loading up, the mover must give you a copy of the "bill of lading," the contract of transportation. It should include much of the same information as the Order for Service—price estimate and method of payment, special services ordered, time and place of delivery—plus the tare weight and where you can be reached in case of delay.

Again, read the contract carefully before signing and work out all disagreements before the movers load up, or you might fall prey to what New York Magazine calls "a basic law of consumer physics: Once somebody has all your worldly possessions on his truck, you must give him whatever he wants."

The bill of lading should also include the company's liability policy. Companies usually offer the following three options: released value liability, added value protection, and full value protection (see the chart on the next page for details).

Before selecting added or full-value protection, check that your homeowner's insurance does not already provide you with coverage, or that your insurance company does not offer such coverage for less than the moving company. If you do select either option, make sure to note on the shipping papers items of extraordinary value (over $100 per pound). Otherwise, the mover may be able to elude liability.

Delivery and Payment

Delivery date. The mover is contractually bound to pick up and deliver your shipment on the terms set in the bill of lading. Usually movers provide a range of dates within which they'll deliver your things. (You may have to purchase a "liquidated damages" policy to arrange a specific date.) But a 1990 *Consumer Reports* survey found that 12% of respondents received their goods after the last promised delivery date. The mover is required to notify you by telephone, telegram, or in person if pickup or delivery will not be on schedule. Make sure you can be reached at all times, lest your goods be put in storage—at your expense.

If you incur any expenses as a result of the delay (e.g., hotel stay or restaurant meals), you should be able to recover them, unless the mover can present a "defense of *force majeure*," circumstances that are both unforeseeable and beyond its control—say, a hurricane. Some companies will be receptive to your "inconvenience" or "delay" claim; others will force you to litigate. And some may require that you purchase a "guaranteed service" option obliging them to pay you a fixed per diem fee if they miss the promised date. Such per diem fees often preclude a separate inconvenience claim. Find out your moving company's policy. In either case, save all receipts of expenses.

Payment. The bill of lading will specify the terms of payment. Most movers require payment before unloading and accept cash, certified checks, money orders, travelers checks—and, sometimes, credit cards—but *not* personal checks. If you opted for a nonbinding estimate and the mover asks for more than the estimate, you are only responsible for paying the estimate plus 10% before unloading, and the balance within 30 days. You are also responsible for any services not included in the estimate. (If you refuse to pay because you disagree with the final bill, the mover may lock your goods in storage and stick you with an extra bill for storage and redelivery fees.)

Receipt. You will generally be asked to sign a receipt or delivery paper. Before you do so, make sure all your goods have arrived safely. At a minimum, open up boxes with breakable items or boxes that look

LIABILITY OPTIONS

RELEASED VALUE LIABILITY	*Interstate movers are responsible for damages or losses up to 60 cents per pound, regardless of the item's value. (That is, you get $6 if the mover shatters your 10-pound Ming Dynasty vase. To get this cheaper option, you must ask for it. Otherwise, you'll automatically receive—and be billed for—added value coverage.*
ADDED VALUE PROTECTION (ICC PLAN)	*This plan enables you to recover the actual value of the lost or damaged item: replacement cost minus depreciation. If the value of your shipment exceeds the mover's maximum liability, you can obtain additional liability protection—at an extra cost, of course—by declaring your shipment at its real value.*
FULL VALUE PROTECTION	*Companies may offer alternative protection plans for the full current cost of replacement or repair. Such plans usually cost about 90 cents for every $100 of coverage with no deductible. (The higher the deductible, the lower the cost.) As always, read the fine print carefully for any restrictions or deductibles.*

damaged and inspect fragile items—look for rips on your leather sofa. If you find any damage, write it down on both sets of delivery papers (yours and the mover's) before signing. If you discover damage after the driver has left, leave the item in its packaging and contact the moving company.

Claims

Nearly half of all people who move report some damage. If something goes wrong with your move, ask for a company claim form, complete it ASAP (the law gives you nine months from delivery to file), and return it to the mover via return-receipt-requested mail. Try to get independent esti-

mates of the goods—the company may do so as well—but don't overreach. In addition, you are entitled to recover transportation charges proportional to the portion of the shipment that was lost or destroyed.

The company must acknowledge your claim within 30 days, and either deny it or offer a settlement within 120 days. (The majority of claims are settled within 30 days.)

If all else fails, you may have to take the mover to court (within two years of the company's response or lack thereof) or request that your case go to arbitration (within 60 days): the American Movers Conference offers binding arbitration for interstate disputed loss and damage claims involving its 1,500 mem-

LEAST REGULATED STATES

	Limited or no regulation for household carriers	No intrastate license requirement
ALASKA	X	X
ARIZONA	X	X
COLORADO	X	X
DELAWARE	X	X
FLORIDA	X	X
HAWAII		X
IDAHO	X	X
MAINE	X	X
MARYLAND	X	X
NEW MEXICO		X
VERMONT	X	X
WISCONSIN	X	
WYOMING	X	

Source: American Mover's Conference

state. Most rate regulations are based on time, weight, or distance. To find out regulations in your state, contact your state public utilities commission, department of transportation, or attorney general's office, or the American Movers Conference.

An unregulated field is fertile ground for what one exposé described as "estimate-lowballing, tip-extorting, chandelier-dropping, wedding-album-losing scam artists." This provides all the more reason for asking family, friends, and colleagues for recommendations, discussing bids from several movers, and going over the contract with a fine-toothed comb to catch all the tangles. A committee of the New York State Senate conducted a two-year investigation of the industry. Among the dozens of horror stories in the report is that of Thomas B., who received an estimate of $598.50 for moving about 100 miles, from Manhattan to New Paltz, New York. When he refused to pay the final bill of $1,518, the crew drove off with his belongings—including family jewelry and Christmas presents for his children.

bers—if both parties agree in writing. Written arbitration by mail is free, but in-person proceedings require a small fee.

Moving Intrastate

Moving intrastate is a lot cheaper and a lot less complicated. But it is not regulated by the FHA; regulations vary from state to

THE SMARTER CONSUMER

Look closely at the moving companies' annual performance reports. Track records (on giving out non-

STASHING IT AWAY: MINI STORAGE WAREHOUSES

If you're moving overseas or to a smaller or already-furnished home, you may want to consider sending some of your belongings on a trip to mini-storage land. Two pointers:

■ Inspect the premises before you arrive with all your possessions. Check that the security is good and the place seems well run. "If the place is unkempt with trash all over you might not want to rent space there," suggests a senior executive from one of the largest companies in the field.

■ You're probably aware of all the calamities that can happen to your goods while in storage: theft, fire, heat, rats, to name a few. In a perfect world, each of these could be dealt with through security systems, sprinklers, and pest and climate control. And it's a good idea to find out about these various options when you visit the premises. But in the world of mini-storage warehouses, these things do happen. If you go to the trouble of getting a storage space for your possessions, you may want to go the extra mile and get insurance as well.

binding estimates, for instance) can vary greatly. In 1992, North American Van Lines low-balled its estimates 50% of the time; Mayflower Transit, 33%; United Van Lines, 30%. In contrast, Atlas, Bekins, and Global Van Lines ended up charging customers at or below the estimate in 95% to 99% of cases.

If you sign a guaranteed service agreement binding the mover to a specific pick-up or delivery date, read the penalty provisions carefully. The mover may offer you a per diem compensation that precludes other compensations, such as costly hotel accommodations.

If you choose a full-value protection plan, read the fine print very closely. Many plans only cover inventoried items that are either lost or not delivered.

Travel light. Go through your belongings and figure out what you need and what you can sell, offer at a garage sale, give to charity, or throw away. (Remember to get receipts: Charity donations are deductible from your federal income tax.) Think of your new space and what's not going to fit in.

Do your own packing and save up to one third of moving expenses. But unless you know what you're doing, it's often best to let the movers pack fragile items—like your great-aunt's china. Ask about the company's policy on liability for self-packed cartons.

If you have the energy, time, and person-power, you may save up to 50% by doing your own move. Jonathan Elias, a TV news reporter who landed a job in Minneapolis, decided to do just that after receiving bids of $3,500 and up to move him from Sacramento, California. Total cost of the do-it-yourself operation: $2,000, including dinner for a "crew" of four friends.

But consider carefully whether it's worth it. Factor in all expenses involved (rental and insurance for the truck, pizza, chips and gallons of soda for your friends helping out) —and the effort. If you do go ahead, Ryder, U-Haul, and other truck rental companies have booklets suggesting the furniture capacity of their various trucks. U-Haul will even give you a free video detailing packing and loading procedures if you buy your moving boxes from them.

Keep records of all moving expenses—they may be tax-deductible. Call the IRS and ask for Publication 521 for tax deductions for job-related moves.

Avoid moving during the summer. More than half of all moves in the United States are completed from May to September. Service may therefore be slower—and prices higher. You'll also do well to avoid the last four or five days of the month. And remember to start your move early in the day to avoid overtime costs that some movers charge after 5 PM.

If you are moving at your employer's request, find out what portions of your expenses the company will pick up.

■. **The Federal Highway** Administration requires interstate movers to distribute a detailed booklet, *Your Rights and Responsibilities When You Move.* The FHA will answer very basic questions about interstate moving companies. The recent dismantling of the Interstate Commerce Commision has left consumers with less government oversight of movers than in the past. The phone number for the FHA is (202) 927-5520.

■. **The American Movers Conference** publishes various useful brochures to help consumers prepare their moving arrangements: *Guide to a Satisfying Move; Moving and Children; Moving With Pets and Plants.* Send a self-addressed, stamped envelope for free copies, 1611 Duke Street, Alexandria, VA 22314.

■. **Consumer Reports** published a comprehensive article in August 1990 on moving and the industry, replete with company rankings, consumer surveys, and useful tips and schedules.

■. **For information regarding the** American Movers Conference arbitration program, write to Dispute Settlement Program, 1611 Duke Street, Alexandria, VA 22314.

PART 4

Automobiles

CHAPTER 25

NEW CARS

*Don't Get Taken for
an Expensive Ride*

Very few of the roughly 27 million Americans who buy cars each year are prepared to do battle on an equal footing with the salespeople who seem to be constantly searching for suckers. As a result, Americans spend about $4 billion more a year than they have to, according to James R. Ross, author of *How to Buy a Car: A Former Car Salesman Tells All*. Is it any wonder, then, that there are few things people hate to do more than shop for cars?

It doesn't have to be so bad. With a little preparation, you can learn the basics about the cars you can afford and how to drive a hard bargain. And if you want to avoid showroom shenanigans altogether, new automobile shopping services will dicker over the sticker for you.

THE BASICS

Safety First

All cars must meet the safety standards set by the U.S. government. Given that 40,000 people die in car accidents every year and millions more are injured, it makes no sense to buy anything less than the safest car you can afford.

Safety equipment and crash protection. It's taken 20 years, and untold lives (approximately 4,000 avoidable deaths in 1991 alone), but finally air bags are here. In 1993, two out of three cars sold had at least one air bag on the driver's side, and by the 1998 model year, all new cars will be required to have both driver and passenger air bags, along with manual lap-and-shoulder safety belts. For now, federal law requires manufacturers to equip all new cars with something—air bags, seat belts, or other new equipment—that will automatically protect the driver and front-seat passenger in a collision into a fixed barrier at 30 miles per hour.

Air bags used in conjunction with seat belts give the best all-around protection. An air bag on the driver's side increases by 29% the driver's chance of surviving a frontal collision, according to a recent study of fatal crashes by the Insurance Institute for Highway Safety, the insurance industry's auto-safety organization. Between 1974 and 1976, General Motors installed air bags in over 10,000 cars that traveled more than 600 million miles, and "the death and injury rate of the occupants was 50% lower than the rate for non-air bag cars," according to *The Car Book*, by Jack Gillis, who is a former automotive information officer at the U.S. Department of Transportation (DOT).

Whether you are driving or going along for the ride, you should always wear a seat belt, regardless of whether the car has air bags. Air bags do no good in side and rear collisions; they pop out only in front collisions of force equal to hitting a solid wall at about 10 miles per hour. Plus, many cars have air bags only on the driver's side, which does nothing to protect passengers.

By automatically pumping the brakes, anti-lock braking systems (ABS) prevent you from skidding out of control when you stop short. Even if you are braking, you will still be able to steer. This safety feature, along with dual-side air bags, is strongly recommended by auto safety advocates, even though it

> "*When I began my one-year stint selling cars, the first serious advice I got came from a veteran salesman who said, simply, 'Tell them what they want to hear.' Another pro described the typical car sale as a 'lying contest': 'The customer lies to you, you lie to the customer, the customer lies to you, you lie to the customer, and so on. . . . The better liar prevails.' "*
>
> —DEBRA SHERMAN,
> a former car dealer

might well add a few hundred dollars to the purchase price of the car.

Crash test performance. Since 1979, the U.S. DOT has been test-crashing cars to see how well they protect drivers and passengers who are wearing seat belts. DOT releases the data to the public through the National Highway Traffic Safety Administration (NHTSA). *The Car Book* analyzes the government data and presents the results, using a "Crash Test Index" number that makes it easy to compare the crash test results of cars of comparable size—the lower the number, the better the car protected its occupants. Even so, the data is limited by the narrowness of NHTSA's test conditions: The straight-ahead collisions they create rarely happen on the road, and NHTSA does not test for side, rear, or angled collisions, rollovers, or how a car would do in a collision with a bigger or smaller vehicle. However, by 1997 (when a new law takes effect), auto makers will be required to assure the safety of their vehicles in side collisions and NHTSA will test to be sure the makers are making good.

Child safety seats. Every state requires them—for good reason—for kids up to a certain age or size (requirements vary from state to state). Once infants get beyond the first few weeks of life, car crashes are the leading cause of death and serious injury for children. The middle of the back seat is the safest place for children in car seats.

Driving a Hard Bargain

Timing. If you can, shop for a car when the dealer is likely to need the sale. The biggest sales slump is in the weeks just before and after Christmas. (Exception: Do not let on that you are buying the car as a Christmas present or the salesperson is likely to hold out for a higher price with the knowledge that you need the car by December 25.) The end of any month is often a good time to buy because only a few days remain for the dealer and salespeople to meet their monthly quotas; any additional sales mean an extra bonus. Hungry for sales, they are likelier to sacrifice profit than their bonus.

Do your homework. Go into the showroom with as much information as can be had. You'll even the playing field with the salesperson if you know how much you can spend, have a promise of financing at a reasonable rate from a bank, and know how much the dealer paid the manufacturer for the car and options. Don't share all these thoughts with the salesperson, but keep them in mind as you shop.

To find out what the dealer paid for the car, consult the *Consumer Reports* annual car buying issue (published every April). The ratings charts give cost factors for every make and model. Multiply this factor by the sticker price on the car to get an idea of the dealer's "invoice price," which is what it costs the dealer to buy the car from the manufacturer. You can get more exact price information about any make, model, trim line, options, and factory rebates from *Consumer Reports* Auto Price Service (see **HELP** at the end of the chapter). If the dealer challenges your research, ask to see the manufacturer's invoice. If you're getting the straight story on what the car costs dealers, they have nothing to lose by proving it.

Don't get your heart set on only one car. You probably don't need the exact make and model rated highest by *Consumer Reports*; you want one that scores near the top. Many cars have nearly identical twins or corporate cousins that go by different names but are essentially the same car. For instance, the Ford Taurus is similar to the Mercury Sable, and the Geo Prizm is practically the same as the Toyota Corolla. Keep in mind that a twin with a higher price tag may also come with more standard options. If they are the options you want, you might get a better deal than if you outfitted the lower-priced car with the same extras.

Don't let high-pressure sales tactics get to you. Ads are designed to bring you into the showroom. Read them very carefully and be on the lookout for footnotes. Car dealers may be hiding information in small print that they would be just as happy to have you gloss over. A price that's good today ought to be good next week. Don't leave a deposit unless you've got a firm agreement; it will just pressure you into returning to buy the car. If you leave a deposit, make sure you get a written receipt that also says it's refundable.

Take the car for a spin. To test the car's performance, you'll want to tool around town, navigating through traffic, and cruise down the highway (within the speed limit, of course). Does the engine run smoothly? How does the car do going up steep hills or passing another car on the highway? Try stopping short and taking a variety of turns. And try it all again with the air conditioner on to make sure the car's engine can both keep you cool *and* meet your standards.

You'll spend many hours in your car, so get in and make sure you're comfortable. Is there enough headroom and legroom? Can you get in and out without bruises? Try the back seat, too. (Don't forget that your gangly teenager may one day be driving his basketball teammates home from practice: Will he and his tall friends fit comfortably?)

Comparison shop. More than one dealer sells the cars that you have decided best fit your needs, and each of them may offer you a different price. Don't be shy about reminding the dealer of this—and your willingness to drive down the road for the better deal you found

last weekend. Remember, they know what their cost is and how low they'll go. The only way you can find out their bottom line is to negotiate in its direction.

WHAT TO WATCH OUT FOR

As with driving a car, you can't take your eye off the road when you're shopping for one. But like those dangerous S curves, there are some trouble spots where you need to be especially careful.

Extended Warranties or Service Contracts

This is one of the most expensive options you can buy and—not coincidentally—a major source of profit for car dealers. Consumer advocates say these contracts generally aren't worth the one-time $250 to $1,000 they typically cost. The company offering the contract is betting that making necessary repairs will cost them less than you paid for the contract; otherwise, they wouldn't be in business. Nationwide, about 2 million consumers are overcharged a whopping $300 million annually on service contracts. One Chrysler dealer charged $1,620 for a contract it paid only $125 for, according to a 1990 investigation by the New York State Attorney General.

The Car Book suggests that you put the money that you would have spent on the service contract in a special savings account and draw on it if your car needs a major repair.

You'll probably have plenty of money to cover the mechanic's bill.

Add-Ons for Gimmicks

Avoid buying rust-proofing, paint sealant, fabric protection, and other services. Most cars don't need them. If you want them, you'll almost certainly pay less if you have the work done elsewhere.

Dealers often try to tack on additional charges for these services after you have agreed on a price. Take Olympia Z., who agreed to purchase a car for $11,411. After she signed a contract to buy the car, various salespeople tried to sell her options she wasn't interested in. She asked for information about some options, but never agreed to purchase any. Nevertheless, when she picked up the car, the invoice said she owed $14,140 for the car and options she did not want, nearly $3,000 more than she had authorized with her signature on the sales contract.

Some dealers will say that available cars have an option or two you don't want—a cassette deck, for instance, or up-front door lock controls. If you want the car, be clear about your willingness to buy it— and equally clear that you won't pay for the extras you didn't request. You may be able to negotiate the purchase without paying an extra cost.

> **"Never under any circumstance buy a car based on monthly payment. Know what the total purchase price is."**
>
> — JIM MILLER
> Managing Editor,
> Road & Track Specials

The No-Dicker Sticker

In recognition of consumers' distrust of car salespeople and dislike of the bazaar-like atmosphere in many showrooms, more and more dealers have abandoned bargaining in favor of a pre-set, take-it-or-leave-it price. This takes a lot of the pressure out of the process.

Witness the success of General Motors' Saturn Corporation, which sells all its cars this way; it can't manufacture the cars fast enough to keep up with demand. However, pleasantness has its price. *Consumer Reports* tested both haggle-free and haggle-*si* dealers and found that "people who are willing to do their homework and bargain hard can save somewhere between $200 and $300 doing it the old-fashioned way."

Warranties

Government standards for "full" manufacturers' warranties require car makers to cover all aspects of the car's performance. For this reason, most manufacturers offer only "limited" warranties, which cover the costs of making repairs that are necessary to correct defective parts or assembly during the warranty period. Warranties do not cover problems resulting from routine wear and tear, nor do they cover the costs of routine mainte-

SECRET WARRANTIES

Manufacturers deny they exist, but there has long been a quiet tradition of auto makers paying for repairs of problems resulting from design defects, even after the warranty has run out. Manufacturers prefer to call such repairs "policy adjustments." Sounds reasonable, except that since auto makers do not notify all car owners, the policy applies only to people who complain the loudest. In other words, squeaky wheels get free grease, and everybody else has to pay for their own. For in-

stance, General Motors extended the warranty on the power steering units on millions of its front-wheel drive cars from model years 1982 to 1986 (to five years or 50,000 miles from one year or 12,000 miles) after it discovered they were wearing out faster than expected. GM notified dealers and put out a press release but did not contact owners directly.

Only Virginia and Connecticut require auto makers to notify consumers of post-warranty adjustments.

nance. And they are void if problems result from misuse of the car, negligence, accidents, of if you fail to maintain the car as recommended in the owner's manual. If you have routine maintenance done somewhere other than the dealer's shop (which is a good idea, since alternatives will almost always be cheaper), keep records so that you can prove you've kept up with the manufacturer's prescribed maintenance schedule.

Dealer-added options can sometimes void your warranty. If you have any questions, contact the manufacturer before you have options installed.

Tricks of the Trade-In

Most people have no idea what their current car is worth and as a result get taken on their trade-

in. It's more work, but you'll almost always get more for your old car if you sell it yourself.

Rule 1. Whether you want to trade it or sell it yourself, you need to know what your old car is worth. To find out, either call the *Consumer Reports* Used Car Price Service or look it up in the National Automobile Dealers Association *Official Used Car Price Guide* or in the *Kelley Blue Book*. With this information you should be able to negotiate a fair price for it with an individual or with a dealer.

Rule 2. If you're going to trade in the old car, keep the negotiation for the new car separate from the negotiation over the value of your old car. If you let on that you want to trade in your old car too early, the salesperson can shave a bit off the price of the new car and make up for it by giving you less than your old car is worth.

Financing the Car

Car dealers often try to entice buyers into the showroom with the promise of low monthly loan rates. Be on your guard. The favorable rates may apply only to cars the dealer wants to unload or to more expensive cars than you had in mind. Also, don't let the salesperson give with one hand and take away with the other by making up for a good deal on the purchase price with a bad deal on the financing, or vice versa.

If the price is right, by all means take it, but shop around. You might find a bank or credit union willing to give you a better deal. (For more information on installment credit, see the chapter "Installment Loans," page 583.)

Leasing

While leases are in many ways similar to installment credit purchases—both call for monthly payments over a fixed period—the monthly cost of leasing a car will be cheaper than financing. However, other long-term and hidden costs can sour the deal. And, keep in mind that you will own a car at the end of a finance period, whereas you will have nothing but a potential headache at the end of a lease. Even so, leasing makes sense for some people, especially those who couldn't otherwise afford to drive as nice a car as they'd like. (For more details, read the chapter later in this section, "Car Leasing: Look Before You Lease," page 242.)

Lemon Laws

State laws vary, but most have "lemon laws" that will help you get a refund or a new car if you buy a car that doesn't run right. For specific information on the law in your state, contact the Attorney General's Office. Generally speaking, a new vehicle is usually defined as a "lemon" if it has been in the shop at least four times for the same problem or has been out of service for a total of 30 days during the first year you own it. Attention, leasing customers: Lemon laws do not necessarily apply to leased vehicles.

THE SMARTER CONSUMER

Get all agreements in writing. Oral promises are virtually impossible to prove should a dispute arise.

Pay as little as you can get away with over the dealer's cost. Most often this will mean a profit of $250 to $350 for the salesperson, which is reasonable, except if the car is in unusually high demand. Shop around until you find a dealer who will go along with your terms.

Compare the sales contract to the invoice. Don't let the dealer add charges after you have agreed on a final price.

FUELING UP FOR LESS

How much difference does fuel economy make? Even among cars of similar size, fuel economy varies all over the lot. Say you pay $1 per gallon of gas. If you drive 15,000 miles a year in a car that gets 34 miles to the gallon, you'll pay $441 for gas. Compare that to the $682 you'd pay if you drove a gas guzzler that gets only 22 miles to the gallon.

The EPA tests and approximates new cars' gas mileage—the "22 mph city and 30 mph highway" familiar to TV commercial viewers. But as the car ads point out, "Your mileage may differ," and you should expect it to. Because fuel economy depends upon driving conditions and your car's condition, both of which are likely to be inferior to the EPA's test conditions, your mileage will probably be something less.

Inspect the car before you drive it off the lot. Do not settle for inspection of a similar car. Make sure your car has all the options you have paid for and no nicks or other visible damage. And by all means take it with you once you've inspected it. If you leave it overnight, you may find the AM/FM radio turns out to be AM only or some other mysterious transformation or disappearing act.

Think twice about extras. Don't buy anything but the car from the dealer. Extended warranties, security-alarm systems, and chemical treatments may not be necessary. If you decide they are, be aware that they certainly cost less at shops whose primary business is selling these items or services.

Shop around for financing. Arranging your own financing might be cheaper than the dealer's financing, and having a finance guarantee can give you leverage when you are negotiating a real price—the salesperson will know you are ready to buy, and you can just as easily take your business elsewhere if you aren't offered a fair price.

Buy a fuel-efficient car. It will be good not only for your wallet but also for the environment. The Environmental Protection Agency (EPA) suggests a manual transmission (it can save 6.5 miles per gallon over an automatic transmission), a smaller engine (which runs more efficiently and burns less fuel), radial tires (which can improve gas mileage 3% to 7% over bias-ply tires), and using the air conditioning as little as possible because it eats an additional three miles per gallon in city driving.

Never put a child's safety seat in the front seat of a car equipped with an air bag on the passenger side.

The Car Book: The De-
finitive Buyer's Guide to Car
Safety, Fuel Economy, Main-
tenance and More, by Jack
Gillis. New York: Harper
Perennial, 1993. This
guide covers all aspects of
car buying: safety, fuel
economy, maintenance,
warranties, show-room strategy, insurance, tires, and how to complain. Available in bookstores or from the Center for
Auto Safety, 2001 S Street NW, Washington, DC 20009, or call (202) 328-
7700. The Center receives a portion of
the profit if you buy it from them.

Consumer Reports Annual Auto
Issue, published in April of each year,
available at the library year-round, at
newsstands in April, or for $5 from
Consumers Union, 101 Truman Avenue, Yonkers, NY 10703; call (914)
378-2000 to order.

Consumer Reports Auto Price Ser-
vice can tell you exactly what the dealer
paid the manufacturer for any make,
model, and trim line you are interested
in. For $11, you will get a printout list-
ing the standard equipment, list price,
and dealer cost of the basic car, along
with an itemized list of the dealer
cost and list price of every individual
option and options package along with
and current information about factory
rebates. It costs $20 for two cars; $27 for
three, and $5 for each additional car; call
(800) 933-5555.

How to Buy a Car: A Former Car
Salesman Tells All, by James R. Ross,
(St. Martin's Press, 1992,) $6.95.

The Lemon Book: Auto Rights for
New and Used Cars, by Ralph Nader
and Clarence Ditlow. Mount Kisco,
NY: Moyer Bell Limited, 1990.

The Gas Mileage Guide,
published by the Environ-
mental Protection Agency,
lists estimated fuel economy
by make and model. Avail-
able for free from the U.S.
Department of Energy's Conservation and Renewable Energy Inquiry and Referral
Service; call (800) 523-2929.

The National Highway Traffic
Safety Administration's Auto Safety
Hotline, (800) 424-9393, provides useful information on cars, child safety
seats, or tires you may be considering;
the results of government crash tests,
and uniform tire quality grades. You
can also use the hot line to protect
others by reporting any safety problems
you discover.

Insurance Institute for Highway
Safety publishes a booklet, *Shopping for a*
Safer Car, which lists the safety features
that come with many different 1994 car
models. To get this free booklet, send a
stamped, self-addressed envelope to the
Insurance Institute for Highway Safety,
P.O. Box 1420, Arlington, VA 22210;
or call (703) 247-1500.

To avoid negotiating for yourself,
call CarBargains, a service offered by the
non-profit Center for the Study of Services. For $135, you tell CarBargains
which makes, models, and style of car
you want to buy, and they will get firm
price quotes from at least five dealers in
your area who know they are competing
against one another. You will receive the
prices and additional information about
the dealers' costs and options, and can
choose from among them. Send a check
to CarBargains, 806 15th Street NW,
Suite 925CB, Washington, DC 20005.
To use Visa or Mastercard, call (800)
475-7283.

CHAPTER 26

USED CARS

Buy a Peach, Not a Lemon

I f you saw Robin Williams try-ing to sell a used car to a griev-ing widow at her husband's funeral in *Cadillac Man*, you know why this section is necessary.

What's more, Americans are turning to used cars because new cars cost more than many can afford. The average new car cost $19,500 in 1994, an increase of 70% since 1984. During the same decade, me-dian incomes rose only 40% and prices for goods and services other than cars tracked income. And with so many vehicles coming onto the used car lot after original car leases run out, there are plenty of good bargains to choose from.

THE BASICS

Much of the same advice about buying a new car applies when buying a used car (see the pre-vious chapter), but there are even fewer objective standards of com-parison and additional potential trouble spots.

Finding a Reliable Brand

A wealth of sources exists to help you investigate worthwhile prospects. The *Consumer Reports* an-nual car-buying issue (published every April) can tell you which used cars to seek and which to avoid based on their repair records. And Jack Gillis's *Used Car Book* rates cars based on their relative complaint records and their government crash-test performance when they were new.

New and used car dealers. You'll pay top dollar for a used car at a new-car dealership, but it might be worth it for the selection of late-model cars, service, and war-ranty. Dealers who sell only used cars offer cheaper cars but are po-tentially riskier. Before you go, find out about the dealer's reputation from your local government con-sumer office or Better Business Bureau.

Auctions. Cars that have been abandoned by their owners or re-possessed are often auctioned off. Look for ads in local papers. But exercise extreme caution. A NYC Department of Consumer Affairs investigation showed that consumer complaints, rather than cars, zoom off auto auction lots. For instance, one man paid $2,256 for a 1987 Renault; it was only later he discov-ered the car would not run in re-verse. The auctioneer refused to

236

give him a refund. Another woman paid $2,550 for a 1988 Mitsubishi with 55,000 miles on the odometer; two days later the car started to smoke and needed repairs that cost $860, and the auction house refused to reimburse her even though New York's Used Car Lemon Law holds the auction house responsible for paying.

Other consumer abuses include cars sold without titles, cars that immediately break down or are in unsafe condition, cars with the odometers turned back, and salespeople who deny buyers the chance to thoroughly inspect car interiors and engines.

Individuals. The price may be right, but you have to choose carefully. If possible, buy from someone you know. Someone you're acquainted with is theoretically less likely to lie, and you may be able to double-check their version of the car's history.

Car rental companies. Call the companies to find out if they periodically sell off their cars to the public. Rental cars often have been driven for under a year and for relatively short distances. However, since they are not driven by their owners, they are subject to greater abuse.

> "**D**espite all the laws, your best warranty is a skilled, independent mechanic or an American Automobile Association diagnostic test center. . . . If the used-car dealer won't let the mechanic check out the car, don't buy it."
>
> —JANE BRYANT QUINN, consumer finance columnist

Is the Price Right?

Prices vary based on mileage, condition, and geography. Since every used car is unique, figuring out a fair price can be tricky. Good places to start are the various guides available at libraries, book stores, and newsstands, such as the National Automobile Dealers Association *Official Used Car Guide, Kelly's Blue Book* (popular in California), and *Edmund's Used Car Prices*, which list prices you can expect to pay for various cars and optional equipment. Use the difference between the wholesale and retail prices as a range within which the price you pay should fall; clearly, you don't want to pay anything higher than the average retail price, and the dealer probably won't let you go any lower than the average wholesale price.

One caveat: Since the mileage and condition of each car are unique and market conditions vary from one area of the country to another, you might also want to compare prices in the guidebooks to prices advertised in your local paper. For specific price information, you can also call the *Consumer Reports* Used Car Price Service, which gives updated price quotes for cars in your area and reliability information. (See **HELP** at the end of this chapter for more information.)

The new-car leasing boom of the early- and mid-1990s could very well result in a buyers' market for used cars later in the decade. Whereas a million cars came off lease and into the used car market in 1994, more than 3 million will become available in 1997, projects the Ford Motor Co. Since so many two-, three-, and four-year-old cars will be on lots, prices should be very favorable—particularly for the cars most often leased, like the Ford Taurus and Toyota Corolla.

Warranties and Used Car Lemon Laws

The Federal Trade Commission's "Used Car Rule" requires any-body other than a private individual who's selling a used car to display a "Buyer's Guide" sticker in the window. The sticker will tell you if the car has a warranty, what it covers, and how long it lasts, and also lists any major problems the car might have. If a car is sold "as is," as are most used cars, there is no warranty, and you will be responsible for all repairs. Connecticut, Kansas, Maine, Maryland, Massachusetts, Minnesota, Mississippi, New York, Rhode Island, Vermont, West Virginia, and Washington, DC, restrict or prohibit "as is" sales.

Six states have Used Car Lemon Laws—Connecticut, Massachusetts, Maryland, Minnesota, New York, and Rhode Island—which protect consumers in the event the used car they buy needs a major repair. The laws vary; the New York State Used Car Lemon Law requires the dealer to offer a 90-day/4,000 mile warranty (whichever comes first) for cars with up to 36,000 miles on them; 60 days/3,000 miles for cars with 36,001 to 79,999 miles; and 30 days/1,000 miles for cars with 80,000 to 100,000 miles. If the dealer cannot repair the defect after three attempts, or if the car's accumulated "down" time is more than 15 days (not necessarily consecutive), consumers have the right to request a refund or a replacement. In New York, it is illegal for a dealer to disclaim responsibility for major repairs. To get information about your state's law, call your State Attorney General's office.

A Lemon Law won't save you from the hassle of dealing with a heap, but it could save you a lot of

WHAT'S A FAIR PRICE?

The *Consumer Reports* Used Car Price Service quotes prices, based on where you live, for all vehicles built since 1982. You'll get an idea of what you should pay and, in many instances, a reliability report on the cars you are considering. Have ready your ZIP code, the car's model name and year, mileage, major options, and approximate condition. Call (900) 446-0500; the charge for calls ($1.75 per minute) will appear on your phone bill. Expect to talk for at least five minutes.

money. One woman bought a 1986 Buick from a used car dealer for $3,500, plus the value of the 1975 Chevrolet she traded in. Shortly after she bought it, the car began shaking violently while she was driving. When she tried to stop the car engine, it wouldn't cut off immediately. The dealer agreed to fix it. After four trips to the dealer the car still wouldn't run smoothly. New York's Used Car Lemon Law allowed her to demand a replacement car, which the dealer gave her.

WHAT TO WATCH OUT FOR

Never forget that since it's easy to just plain lie or temporarily camouflage a clunker by simply painting over rust or replacing the power-brake fluid, used cars will rarely appear used up—even if they are.

Missing and Misleading Prices

It's rare to see a price tag (even in states where they are mandatory). Leaving prices off the cars allows the salesperson to size you up and juggle the price accordingly. Don't give the salesperson too much information: For instance, if you say you can spend $5,000, you'll be shown cars that will cost $5,000, even if they are worth only $4,200.

And be wary when you see prices advertised or slapped on the window of the car. Dealers may try to lure you into their lot with insincere offers. When you get there, you find out the car has "already been sold."

Remember that the price marked on the windshield or first quoted by the salesperson is always negotiable.

Used Rental Cars

Used car dealers often sell used rental cars, which might be called "program," "executive," "slightly used," or "manufacturers' auction" cars. Buy with care or you could end up like Donna S. In July 1992, Donna bought what she was told was a used 1991 Chevrolet Lumina with an odometer reading of 8,229 miles. She inspected the car when she got home and found a rental car agreement in the glove compartment, even though the salesman told her it had been used only as a "courtesy" car. What's worse, the rental agreement showed that the odometer had been turned back! The car had been rented in January 1992 with an odometer reading of 17,762. Donna was lucky the dealer was sloppy—she found the rental agreement and demanded her old car and all her money back, and got it. But we can't all expect to be so lucky.

Because dealers have not been completely straight with consumers about their cars' backgrounds, two states (Missouri and New York) now require dealers to get signed statements from customers to show that they have been told the car was once owned by a rental company.

Lies and Misinformation

Everybody wants to buy a car with low mileage that has been driven little more than back and forth between home and the office 15 minutes away by a mild-mannered middle-aged bachelor. Hence, a used car salesperson is likely to tell you that, *mirabile dictu*, this is just the background of any car you show interest in.

Know your rights. Frank S. of Brooklyn paid $2,723.25 cash for a 10-year-old Cadillac with 84,000 miles on it. The dealer claimed the car had been inspected and erroneously asserted that this made it ineligible for warranty coverage. Frank signed a form that absolved the dealer of any financial responsibility for car parts and labor used in the repair of the engine and brakes.

Within a week, the engine started smoking. "There is no way this car could have passed an emission inspection, much less a New York State safety inspection," Frank complained to the NYC Department of Consumer Affairs. Frank had a mechanic examine the car and was told the engine had been tinkered with and that the valves were shot. The dealer agreed that the engine was bad, but only offered to pay half of the cost of fixing it. Frank accepted the deal even though he had a right to more.

Don't buy from a car dealer who doesn't affix the mandatory Buyer's Guide to the window.

Keep a copy of the bill of sale. In many states, it must list the name, make, serial number, year of manufacture, and total price, including all finance charges.

No two cars are the same. Even if you've chosen a specific model, inspect the individual car carefully, inside and out, before buying. Do this in daylight. Look under the hood, inside the tailpipe, and under the body for stains, soot, dents, rust, and breaks in the frame. Hold a piece of paper behind the tailpipe and rev the engine. If it comes out sooty or splattered with oil, the car has costly problems. Check the inside of the tires (they may simply have been turned around). Look to see if the upholstery is worn, a sign of heavy wear and tear. Test every light, knob, and button to be sure they work.

Take the car for a spin over varied terrain, both on and off the highway. Listen for funny noises, be sensitive to odd vibrations or bad-bump performance, and watch the gauges. After the drive, re-check the power steering and power-brake fluid to make sure the short ride didn't deplete the supply.

Have a professional look it over, if the car passes your inspection. Don't buy a car if the dealer won't let an independent mechanic examine it. Use a mechanic you trust or one who participates in the American Automobile Association's diagnostic test center program.

If you can, talk to the previous owner. Ask whether he or she had any trouble with the car, how it was used, what kind of gas mileage it got, whether it was ever in any major accidents, and whether it was maintained as suggested by the manufacturer.

Get written certification from the dealer that the car is in safe condition at the time of the sale.

Get the recall history for the make and model of any used car you may buy. It's available from the National Highway Traffic Safety Administration Auto Safety Hotline (see **HELP** below).

Keep records of *everything*. Retain all receipts from repair shops, the dealer, the dealer's mechanic, the tow service, etc., as proof of the problems you've had with the car. They will come in handy if you have to take advantage of your warranty or local Used Car Lemon Law.

Skip the lemonade. If a dealer or an individual sells you a lemon, take advantage of your state's Used Car Lemon Law.

■ *The Used Car Book: The Definitive Guide to Buying a Safe, Reliable, and Economical Used Car*, by Jack Gillis, New York: Harper Perennial, 1993, $11. This guide rates hundreds of used cars based on safety, maintenance, insurance costs, fuel economy, and price ranges. It also provides checklists, negotiating strategy, and maintenance tips.

■ *The Lemon Book: Auto Rights for New and Used Cars,* by Ralph Nader and Clarence Ditlow. It is available for $15.95 from the Center for Auto Safety, 2001 S Street NW, Washington, DC 20009.

■ *How to Buy a Car: A Former Car Salesman Tells All*, by James R. Ross, (St. Martin's Press, 1992,) $6.95.

■ **The National Highway Traffic** Safety Administration's Auto Safety Hotline, (800) 424-9393, provides useful information on the safety recall history of used cars.

CHAPTER 27

CAR LEASING

Look Before You Lease

At first glance, car leases seem little different from installment contracts. Once a month you write a check that enables you to drive a car you can't afford to buy outright. At some point you don't have to write the checks anymore. But that's where the similarity ends. With an installment contract, after you've paid off the loan, you own the car. Since a lease is basically just a long-term rental arrangement, once you're paid up you have to return the car and start again.

That's why car companies push leases on the public. The theory goes that if they keep you happy enough, you'll return the car and lease another one . . . and another one . . . and so on. The theory is working pretty well. The number of people leasing vehicles has skyrocketed to more than 2.5 million, an eight-fold increase since 1983, according to the Federal Trade Commission. In 1994, that was about one out of every four car sales, and for luxury cars like Jaguars, three out of four customers choose to lease.

The appeal is clear. The monthly cost of leasing a car usually appears cheaper than financing—allowing people to drive a classier car than they could afford to buy. And many people like the idea of getting a new car every two or three years.

However, over the long haul, hidden charges add up, usually making leases more expensive than installment contracts. Just when car purchasers heave a sigh of relief—when they finally make the last payment on their car loan—lease customers are most likely to groan in disbelief. "You mean I'm responsible for 'excess wear and tear,' and it's going to cost how much? Who defined this and how? What do you mean there's a clause in the contract that essentially requires that I return the car in condition such that I'd have had to garage it rather than drive it for three years?"

The answers to these and other crucial questions are buried in the leasing contract—and could cost you thousands of dollars unless you read your contract carefully before you lease. For instance, one driver returned a well-maintained van at the end of its lease term and was told he owed nothing extra. He drove away from the dealer satisfied, in a newly leased van. A month later he got a bill for just under $3,000, the finance company's charge for "excess wear and tear."

In addition to rooting out

242

charges that would be otherwise hidden until the lease ends, you need to deconstruct the contract to figure out: how much you would be paying for the car and whether the price is fair, the percentage your monthly lease payments are based on, and how much you would owe if you bailed out of the lease early.

THE BASICS

The Come-On

You can't judge a lease by its attractively low monthly payment. The low rates touted in lease ads are just the bait. And it can cost an unexpected bundle to extricate yourself from the camouflaged traps. Low monthly payments almost always mean a high payment at one end of the lease or the other. The true cost is buried in the advertisement's foot-notes—hefty "capital cost reductions," which are fancy words for a down payment; "no money down," except for the three payments you have to pay up front to qualify; "other restrictions may apply," including penalties for driving more miles than the lease allows.

Tri-Honda Advertising Associa-

> "**A**uto lease ads promote an attractive monthly payment in large type and then bury a notice of large down payments with asterisks and small-type footnotes, which are very difficult to read. Consumers rarely read these footnotes, but if they did they would see that they contradict and confuse the message of the ad."
>
> —ROBERT ABRAMS, former New York State Attorney General

tion of New York, New Jersey, and Connecticut took this tactic to the extreme. A Honda Accord LX lease was advertised for a price of $5 a day, or a low $149 a month for 24 months. A footnote, in small type, revealed that buyers would have to put down $2,750 to qualify for the deal, which had the effect of raising the actual monthly cost to over $263 if you factored in the down payment over the life of the lease. That's 77% more than the large type in the ad trumpeted!

There is no such thing as a standard leasing contract. Few rules regulate the advertising and marketing practices of the leasing indus-try, and whatever rules exist are lim-ited and not stan-dard from state to state. In this regula-tory environment, it's not surprising that the boom in car leasing has led to a boom in car leasing complaints made to consumer officials around the country. After a 1992 investigation, the New York State Attorney General's Office charged a dozen car makers and dealers with misleading and deceptive advertis-ing that touted artificially low monthly payments in newspaper ads and television commercials. The auto makers and dealer associations—including BMW, Mazda Motor Co., Mitsubishi Motors Corp., Isuzu Motors Ltd., Alfa Romeo Inc., Tri-Honda Advertising Association, and the Upstate New York Lincoln-Mercury Dealers Association—have since agreed to disclose any down payment required and make the footnotes more noticeable and easier to read. In Florida, the attorney general's office found some sort of deception or fraud in 10% of 15,000 leases it reviewed. And in 1994 a group of Washington state auto dealers paid several hundred thousand dollars to settle a civil complaint brought by the state.

If you are really interested in a good deal, there's no way to avoid comparison shopping. Since the real price of a car lease depends upon the internal and unique financing structure of the agreement, the only objective way to evaluate one lease is to compare it with another lease or with a purchase contract. You have to gather all the key financial information from several potential lease or purchase agreements and then make your decision.

WHAT TO WATCH OUT FOR

Hidden Net Capitalized Cost

This number (often referred to simply as the capitalized cost) is the total of the cost of leasing the vehicle, license and registration fees, taxes and insurance, minus your down payment and the value of your trade-in.

Unfortunately, leasing companies will rarely give you the capitalized cost; hiding this number makes it easier for them to disguise other financial traps. But you can usually calculate it from other financial disclosures in the lease. Here's a formula:

Net Capitalized Cost = (average monthly depreciation x number of monthly payments) + (the estimated end-of-lease value of the vehicle, i.e., its residual value)

Always insist that a leasing company itemize amounts included in the capitalized cost for any fees and services above the cost of the vehicle. Otherwise you can't calculate what you are being charged for the vehicle and compare it to what you would pay to buy it. Also insist that the leasing company put the net capitalized cost in writing. If a lessor refuses to provide the numbers that you need to compute this cost, take your business elsewhere.

Are you being charged too much? Use the capitalized cost to compare the lease price of the car with the purchase price:

Loan Terminology	Lease Terminology
Total selling price	= *Gross (total) capitalized cost*
Down payment	= *Capitalized cost reduction*
Amount financed	= *Net capitalized cost*

LEASING LINGO

If you are considering leasing a new car, learn to speak the specialized language you'll soon be hearing.

Capitalized cost. Simply put, this is what you agree to pay for a car, less any down payment, including license, registration, fees, taxes, and insurance. This term is analogous to the "amount financed" if you purchase the car on an installment contract.

Capitalized cost reduction. Your down payment.

Deposits. Money you pay up front toward fees you may owe when the lease ends. (Deposits *do not* reduce the capitalized cost.)

Depreciation. The value the car loses over the term of its lease. It's the difference between what you agree to pay for the car and the car's value when the lease ends.

Excess mileage and wear and tear charges. Money you owe at the end of the lease.

Gap coverage. Insurance sold by the leasing company that covers the cost of replacing the car if it is totaled or stolen. The "gap" is the difference between how much you would have to pay the leasing company to the end of the lease and how much the insurance company will pay to replace the car.

Lease charges. The money you pay to lease the car in addition to the capitalized cost. This fee is comparable to the "finance charge" you would pay in an installment contract.

MSRP. Manufacturer's Suggested Retail Price, i.e., the "list" price.

Purchase option. Gives you the right to buy the car from the leasing company when the lease ends and a formula for calculating the price.

Residual value. An estimate of the value of the car at the end of the lease, which you agree upon at the outset of the lease. This is what you would pay to buy the car when the lease ends.

Early termination charge. What you would have to pay to end the lease ahead of schedule.

When you make these comparisons, don't forget to adjust the sticker price for any manufacturer's rebates or dealer discounts. If the cost of the car under the lease is much higher than its purchase price, bargain harder for a better lease deal—or buy the car with a finance contract.

Keep in mind that all key financial terms of the lease, such as monthly payments and early termination charges, will be set in direct proportion to the net capitalized cost. Thus, the more you are charged for capitalized costs, the more you will pay for early termination and monthly lease charges.

Unrevealed Lease Charges

This charge is comparable to the finance charge you pay in an installment credit arrangement. But while creditors are required to disclose the total finance charge and the interest rate, lease companies are not, and they rarely do. However, you can often calculate the lease charge from the other disclosures made in a lease. Here's the formula:

Lease charge = total of monthly payments − total depreciation

Early Termination Rights and Obligations

Before you sign a lease agreement, ask what happens if you need to end your lease early for any reason—perhaps because the car is stolen, or totalled, or because you no longer need it. Since about half of all retail car leases terminate early, it's as likely as not that this clause in the contract will be critical later. You need to know about two things—if you have a *right* to terminate the lease early and how much it will *cost* you. What you might owe varies greatly from one lease to another.

The right. Avoid a lease that bans early termination with a clause such as "You may not terminate this lease before the end of the term. This lease will terminate early only upon default." Under this lease, you would be in default even if the lease had to be terminated early because of the theft or destruction of the car. Look instead for a lease that in-

cludes a clause specifically entitling you to terminate ahead of schedule without a penalty—for example, "Providing I am not in default, I have a right at any time to terminate this lease. . . ."

The cost. The early termination charge—the amount you would have to pay to end a lease ahead of schedule—is the costliest and usually the best-concealed trap in a lease. There are huge differences among lessors in how much they charge at early termination.

Avoid any lease that would require you to pay all remaining monthly payments in total to terminate the agreement prematurely or you could be stuck in an expensive bind. For instance, one woman who unwittingly agreed to an unfavorable lease tried to terminate her lease early after paying $9,240. She was told she owed an *additional* $16,000 for a car with a manufacturer's suggested retail price of only $14,927, a legitimate bill within the contract's terms—if wholly unscrupulous.

In most cases, a consumer's early termination obligation is determined by a formula stated in the lease. When comparing early termination terms, there are a few things to look for:

■ Ask if the lease uses the "actuarial method" of computing a rebate on unearned lease charges. Put the question in these words, and if the answer is yes, get it in writing. The actuarial method is the cheapest and fairest method of computing liability for future payments. Steer clear of other computation methods, such as the "rule of 78ths," the "sum of the digits," or "net present value," which will usually end up costing you much more.

■ How will the value of the car be determined at early termination? Look for a lease that gives you the option to use a professional appraiser or allows you and the lease company to agree on the value of the vehicle before termination.

■ Are there any other specific fees and/or any additional number of monthly payments that have to be paid at early termination? If so, what specific amounts would be owed?

■ To see how the early termination terms compute and to compare one lease with another, ask salespeople to compute how much you would owe if you terminated after making exactly half of the monthly payments, before crediting the value of the vehicle. For example, ask what you would owe if the lease ends after you have made 24 payments on a four-year lease.

In one 1989 study, the charge for early termination of lease agreements for similar vehicles differed by $5,200. The study looked at the leases of ten major companies in a typical situation—a consumer leases a new $15,000 car for 48 months at a monthly charge of $347.98. The study assumed that the car would be worth $6,000 at the end of the lease. The table on the next page shows the balance the consumer would owe if he or she chose to terminate the lease after 24 months and returned the car (with an estimated value of $9,000).

Estimated Residual Value

This is what the car is expected to be worth at the end of the lease. Be sure it is stated as a specific dollar amount, not a vague valuation such as "the market price."

Don't be fooled by an inflated estimated residual value, a common pitfall. An inflated residual value estimate lowers your monthly payments, thereby making the lease *appear* more affordable, but an inflated estimated residual value will mean a higher early termination payoff. And, if the used car will sell for less than estimated, the leasing company will almost certainly try to make up for the loss by tacking on high end-of-lease charges for things like excess wear and tear, disposition fees, and excess mileage.

End-of-Lease Charges

If the lease end signals the beginning of trouble, it's too late to do much about it. Without realizing it, you may have signed a contract requiring you to return the car in mint condition—in perfect running order with no nicks or scratches—after driving it for four years. Or you may be required to pay exorbitant "disposition fees," which the lessor collects to dispose of the car.

Look for at least the following items in each lease (but be sure to ask if there are any other end-of-lease charges):

■ How much of a *disposition fee* would be required at the end of the lease if you return (rather than buy) the vehicle?

THE CHARGE FOR EARLY TERMINATION OF A LEASE

NORSTAR	*$7,366*
BARCO	*$5,352*
G.E.C.A.L	*$4,023*
OXFORD	*$3,316*
MARINE MIDLAND	*$3,016*
WHEELEASE	*$2,966*
CURRY	*$2,923*
CHASE MANHATTAN	*$2,566*
CHRYSLER	*$2,295*
GMAC	*$2,090*

Source: New York State Attorney General's Office, 1989.

■ What *excess mileage* or other "use charges" are included in the lease? How much would be owed for each? Be realistic about your driving habits and don't take a car with a lower annual mileage limit than you are likely to need. If you do go over the limit, you will usually be better off if the penalty is a fixed charge per mile rather than an amount to be determined at lease end.

■ What *wear and tear charges* could be imposed based on the condition of the vehicle at lease end, including for *excess wear and tear* or for *mechanical malfunctions*? If you are responsible for mechanical malfunctions (a standard requirement), be sure to keep the car in tip top shape

or you may have to foot the bill for costly repairs. Check if the lease includes procedures you can use to contest the lessor's claims, such as the right to seek an independent appraisal or third-party arbitration.

Purchase Option and Option Price

About a quarter of consumers who lease end up buying the car. The purchase option should be clearly spelled out in advance. Check for the following:

■ Does the lease entitle you to buy the car, at your option, at the end of the lease? If the car is worth more than the leasing company estimated, you might want to buy it. If it's worth less, don't even think about buying.

■ Avoid purchase option prices based on a vehicle's undefined "fair market value" at lease end. Such vague language allows the leasing company to charge whatever it likes, which is likely to be much more than the car is actually worth. The fairest purchase option price is the vehicle's estimated residual value, which is what the lease sets as its lease end value. Alternatively you might opt to use another objective standard such as a well-known used-car price guide like the *Blue Book* or *National Automobile Dealer Association Guide*; both guides are widely available. Ask the dealer for a sample of the book if the lease refers to it, and take note of the range of published values for *trade-in, loan value, wholesale value,* and *retail value* for the car.

Liability on the Casualty Loss of the Vehicle

Before you sign a lease, find out how much you would owe if the car is destroyed or stolen. If there is a gap between what you would owe and the amount the insurance company would cover, ask if you can buy additional insurance to cover this gap. Of course the best lease is one that does not hold you liable for the gap, but barring that, try to get one that makes insurance available at a reasonable cost. Charges for "gap coverage" vary widely, so shop around.

Much of the same advice that applies when buying a car also applies when leasing one. Thus, you will probably want to refer to "New Cars" (page 227). In addition:

Know what you're signing. Do not sign a lease unless you are certain you understand every word. If you have any doubts, hold off. Do more reading (see **HELP** at the end of the chapter), talk to a knowledgeable friend or relative, and keep shopping for an agreement you *do* understand.

Be wary of newspaper ads or television commercials promoting unbelievably low monthly lease payments.

Figure out the early termination clause in the lease. These clauses are "commonly written in mind-boggling legalese and are beyond the comprehension of virtually all consumers," found former New York State Attorney General Robert Abrams.

Be realistic about mileage. Assess your driving habits before signing a lease agreement that allows only low mileage (typically 12,000 miles a year or less).

If you want gap insurance, *Consumer Reports* says you shouldn't pay more than a couple hundred dollars. The price is probably negotiable; some leasing companies provide it free. Read the policy carefully and make sure that it truly closes the gap between what you would pay and what the insurance company covers.

Choose your car wisely. Cars that lose their value slowest often make the best lease deals—e.g., luxury cars like the Lexus or Mercedes-Benz. Since the leasing company will be able to sell the car when you are finished with it for a significant price, your monthly payments will be proportionately lower.

Make a larger down payment. Since it will reduce lease costs and monthly payments, it can be worthwhile for you to make a larger down payment. To check how different down payments affect lease costs and monthly payments, ask the leasing company to compute the financial terms using various down-payment scenarios.

Keep deposits down. Since security deposits do not lower costs or the size of monthly payments, keep them as low as possible.

Find out when a required deposit is refundable and under what conditions. Also find out what charges a lessor can automatically apply against the deposit and how to resolve disputes that may arise over charges against the deposit. Remember, the easier it is for a lessor to apply charges against a deposit, the harder it will be to get any money back at the end of the lease.

■ **To complain about a** problem with a car leasing company, write or call your state attorney general's office.

■ **If the leasing company** is a financial institution, such as a bank or credit union, you can also complain to:

Office of the Comptroller of the
  Currency
250 E Street SW
Washington, DC 20219
(*National banks*)

Board of Governors of the Federal
  Reserve System
  Consumer and Community Affairs
20th and C Streets NW
Washington, DC 20551
(*State member banks of the Federal
  Reserve System*)

Federal Deposit Insurance
  Corporation
Office of Consumer
  Programs
550 17th Street NW
Washington, DC 20429
(*Non-member federally insured
  banks*)

Office of Thrift Supervision
Consumer Affairs Program
1700 G Street NW
Washington, DC 20552
(*Federally insured savings and loans and
  federally chartered state banks*)

National Credit Union Administration
1776 G Street NW
Washington, DC 20456
(*Federal credit unions*)

■ **Check out "Should You Lease?**
Maybe, But Beware of the Fine Print,"
Consumer Reports, April 1993.

GASOLINE

Pay Less to Drive More

Americans enjoy some of the cheapest gasoline in the world. We pay a third or one fourth as much as folks in Europe or Asia do. Yet millions of American motorists still pay more than they have to. They buy premium gas when their car doesn't need it, or they get low-octane fuel from high-octane pumps. They don't get the maximum fuel efficiency from their cars, or they believe bogus claims about the advantages of expensive brands.

Getting every last mile out of every fuel dollar is more important than ever. New taxes and requirements for cleaner gasolines that cost extra are now kicking in. Regional pull-outs by major oil companies, industry consolidation, and a one-third decline in the number of service stations since 1980 are making price wars by neighboring gas stations a thing of the past. Yet average fuel efficiency for the nation's cars hasn't improved since 1987.

THE BASICS

Is All Gas Created Equal?

Each of the major oil companies spend a fortune trying to convince you that its gasoline is better, that you'll feel a new-found power surge as soon as you fill up, or that their brand will clean your engine better than the others.

In fact, the only appreciable difference may be in the ability of detergent additives to prevent deposits on engine intake valves. In 1990, *Consumer Reports* asked oil companies if their gasolines could pass a rigorous 10,000 mile valve-deposit test established by the auto maker BMW. Most passed or would soon be reformulated to pass.

Claims that an advertised brand's cleaning power is superior to all other brands are therefore basically meaningless, since any of the many brands that passed the tough BMW test are perfectly acceptable for even the most discriminating engines. Unfortunately, you can't easily find out if the gas you regularly buy passed the BMW test since the law doesn't require pumps to disclose detergent abilities as it does octane levels.

One independent retailer of discount gasoline told us that when a refinery production problem caught one of the "majors" short of supply, it simply bought gasoline from his company for several weeks. He visited one of the major company's service stations after it had been selling his company's "cheap" gas for a while and asked motorists what they thought of its gas compared to gas from his company. He heard comments like, "Oh, I would never buy gas from [his company]" and "I only buy gas here."

How Much Octane Is Enough?

Octane is a measure of a gas's ability to prevent knocking, which occurs when a portion of the fuel detonates spontaneously and prematurely in the cylinder. Higher octane gas better resists knocking.

The chart below shows the octane levels of gas sold in most American service stations. Federal law requires that the octane level appear on a yellow label on the pump.

Gasoline advertisements in recent years have claimed that premium gas provides more power, faster acceleration, and cleaner engines. These ads have been very effective: The market share of premium gasoline doubled during the 1980s, even though premium costs an average of 18 cents a gallon more than regular and the vast majority of new-car owner manuals recommend using regular gas.

But, contrary to the premise of the ads, most premium gas buying is unnecessary. A 1990 study by Public Citizen, a Washington, DC-based consumer advocacy organization, found that while 20% of gasoline sold is premium, only 3% of cars actually need it—cars such

as Jaguars, Mercedes-Benzes, Ferraris, and Rolls Royces. Premium does not improve performance for 97% of cars, and it doesn't clean engines any better since virtually all gasoline now contains the same detergents in the same concentrations. In 1991, the Federal Trade Commission ordered Sunoco to stop advertising its 93.4 and 94 octane gas as superior to lower-octane gas in providing engine power and acceleration because the company could not substantiate the claims.

Public Citizen concluded that Americans waste $3 billion a year on premium gas—about $95 per vehicle. Of course, the oil industry disagreed. An industry spokesperson responded that while there are no advantages in "overbuying" octane, 25% of cars on the road, including cars that have traveled more than 15,000 miles, need higher octane levels. But the oil industry is self-interested; premium gas produces bigger profits than regular gas does.

Are You Getting What You Pay for?

It's bad enough that many Americans needlessly buy premium gas. But too often the gasoline

REGULAR UNLEADED	87 octane
REGULAR LEADED	89 octane
MID-GRADE UNLEADED	89 octane
PREMIUM	91 to 94 octane

THE INCREDIBLE MAGIC GAS PUMPS!

Octane fraud is easy to perpetrate. A 1990 Congressional study described a gas station that had just one underground tank—but that tank somehow dispensed regular, plus, and premium gasoline. This type of highway robbery is especially common in localities that rely only on the Federal Trade Commission and the Environmental Protection Agency for consumer enforcement rather than on their own octane accuracy testing programs. Unfortunately, only 25 states and a few local governments had testing programs in 1992.

flowing out of the premium pump is less than premium grade, as retailers try to pass off lower octane gas as higher, figuring the public will never know the difference.

How widespread is octane fraud? A 1990 Congressional study found that Americans are being overcharged a total of $600 million a year for octane they never receive. Separate investigations in five states since then have found up to an 18% octane mislabeling rate. In 1990, the New York City Department of Consumer Affairs found a 16% rate; by 1993, a stepped-up enforcement campaign against gas cheats had reduced it to 4%.

Greener Gas—but Less Green Stuff in Your Wallet

You don't have to live in Southern California to know that gasoline produces smog. Finally, though, something is being done about it. In November 1992, in order to meet federal Clean Air Act rules, 39 cities started to require gasoline sold in winter to contain a new additive, either ethanol or methyl tertiary butyl ether (MTBE), which boosts gasoline's oxygen content, making it burn more completely and reducing carbon monoxide (CO) emissions. (Oxygenated gas is required only in winter weather because the inversion layer, which traps pollutants, is much lower.) In some areas with more severe pollution, oxygenated gasoline is sold from early October to late April. A gas pump label is supposed to tell you the dates when it is pumping oxygenated gasoline. While oxygenated gas also seems to reduce fuel efficiency by 2% to 3%, this sacrifice is worth the health benefits oxygenated gas provides.

In 1995, federal law will require gas stations in nine metropolitan areas with severe summer ozone problems—Baltimore, Chicago, Hartford, Houston, Milwaukee, New York, Philadelphia, San Diego, and the smog capital of the nation, Los Angeles—to sell a specially reformulated anti-smog gasoline, which will add another 5 cents to 8 cents per gallon to the pump price. California will have its own special formula, which is expected to add 15 cents to 25 cents per gallon to the pump price there.

Alternative Fuels—When?

Remember the long lines at gas stations in the late 1970s after oil exporting countries slapped us with an oil embargo? That crisis encouraged research into alternative fuels, which is just starting to bear fruit. Cars fueled by methanol or natural gas are coming on line.

As an inducement to buy alternative fuel vehicles, you can get a federal tax deduction of up to $2,000 for buying a car fueled by ethanol, methanol, natural gas, or propane, and a deduction of up to $4,000 for buying an electric car. California and Massachusetts offer additional tax breaks.

It's not so easy to find one of these cars, but that's changing. Chrysler will soon offer a natural gas version of its popular minivans, and Ford is beginning to produce a methanol-powered Taurus. Filling stations for these cars have just started to appear, encouraged by President Clinton's plan to increase by 50% the federal government's purchase of alternative-fuel vehicles. But a practical electric car that can travel more than a few hundred miles before a lengthy battery recharge or one that can go faster than 70 miles per hour still

> "For the vast majority of cars, there's no reason to buy premium gasoline. None. Contrary to everything you learn from advertising, it will not make your car run better; it will not make your engine cleaner; and it will not provide more power."
>
> —JOAN CLAYBROOK,
> president, Public Citizen

hasn't been produced. A public–private effort, The U.S. Advanced Battery Consortium, has more work to do on developing affordable and usable batteries for electric cars. Meanwhile, existing cars work fine on gasohol, which is 10% ethanol, although there is a fierce debate on whether ethanol is, on balance, unfriendly to the environment. Despite these encouraging developments, gasoline is likely to remain the primary fuel for at least the next few decades. All of the other fuels have disadvantages: Methanol can blind or kill if swallowed and is highly corrosive; ethanol is expensive; natural gas refueling takes two to three times longer than gasoline refueling and the tanks are bulky; and, as mentioned, electric cars still have limited range and speed. Reformulated gasolines with additives that improve efficiency and reduce emissions may give this old standby a new lease.

WHAT TO WATCH OUT FOR

Octane fraud. You can reasonably suspect octane fraud if you fill up with your usual octane and you hear knocking or pinging sounds. Other

CRYSTAL CLEAR NONSENSE

You might have seen some TV ads touting Amoco's clear Ultimate gasoline. "...there's nothing like crystal clear Amoco Ultimate...for unsurpassed performance and a cleaner environment," the narrator intones.

Don't be fooled. Fact is, burning a gallon of any gasoline produces plenty of carbon dioxide and other air pollutants such as benzene. That's why, in the winter of 1994, the Center for Science in the Public Interest (CSPI), a consumer advocacy group, awarded the Amoco ad a Harlan Page Hubbard Lemon Award. (Hubbard was a notable snake-oil salesman in the late 19th century.) CSPI gave the award for Amoco's claim that the Ultimate gasoline helps create a cleaner environment, when gasoline is the leading cause of urban air pollution.

Scott Denman, Executive Director of the Safe Energy Communication Council, calls the ad "another example of corporate greenwashing that's ultimately so egregious and ridiculous that it reduces consumer confidence in anything else."

---

signs of too-low octane: a lack of power and the engine's continuing to run after you turn the car off.

Oxygenation drawbacks. Oxygenated gasoline can cause hard starts, stalling, and rough idling. This is a particular problem with poorly maintained cars.

Gas savers. According to Jack Gillis, author of *The Car Book*, out of 100 "gas-saving" products tested by the federal government, only six actually saved gas, and then only a little. Among the worthless products were air-bleed devices, fuel line devices, fuel additives, ignition devices, engine modifications, mixture enhancers, oil additives, and vapor bleed devices. Those that do work somewhat were a gadget that shuts off your air-conditioner when you rapidly accelerate, a buzzer that alerts you if your car has been idling too long, and a device to circulate heat from the engine to the passenger compartment, which can keep you warm in cold weather after you've shut off the engine.

THE SMARTER CONSUMER

Don't buy more octane than necessary. To find out your car's optimum octane level, try this simple test recommended by Jack Gillis: When your tank is empty, fill up with your usual gasoline and drive

WORTH ITS WEIGHT IN SAVINGS

Each year, the average car emits hundreds of pounds of carbon monoxide, hydrocarbons (forms smog), nitrogen oxides (leads to acid rain), particulate matter (better known as grime and soot), and carbon dioxide, a major contributor to global warming. About 30% of carbon dioxide emissions in the U.S. come from motor vehicles.

The federal government could require the average car to get 40 miles per gallon. Energy saving technologies, including the use of four valves per cylinder, low-friction rings and pistons, and overhead cams, now exist. Mandating such efficiency just takes political will power.

radial tires are quite flexible, their treads are very stiff and strong.

■ *Air conditioning.* Uses up to 3 miles per gallon in city driving, but in highway driving at constant speed AC use doesn't matter.

■ *Transmission.* Automatic transmissions generally are less fuel-efficient than properly used manual ones.

■ *Engine condition.* A tune-up—still possible in older cars where ignition timing can be manually adjusted—can improve mileage up to 20%.

■ *Driving practices.* Avoid sudden accelerations when possible. In a traffic jam, inch along instead of stopping and starting.

■ *Car weight.* Don't carry unnecessary cargo in your trunk. An extra 100 pounds of stuff can reduce your gasoline consumption by up to a mile per gallon.

ten or so miles. Stop. Now accelerate rapidly. If your engine knocks, then you should use a higher octane. If it sounds fine, the next time you fill up, switch to a lower octane and repeat the test.

Improve your car's fuel efficiency. Doing so will help your pocketbook and the environment.

■ *Tires.* Poor alignment and insufficient tire pressure can cost two miles per gallon. Radial tires are more fuel efficient than bias-ply because, even though the sidewalls in

■ **If you follow just a few of the** 300-odd tips in *How to Get More Miles Per Gallon in the 1990s* by Robert Sikorsky, the $7.95 price should be more than recouped. Order book no. 157754-8 from McGraw-Hill Publishing Co., Blue Ridge Summit, PA 17294-0850, or call (800) 233-1128.

■ **Jack Gillis's *The Car Book* has** the latest fuel economy ratings and helpful hints for increasing your fuel economy.

CHAPTER 29

AUTOMOBILE INSURANCE

 *Drive Down the Cost*

The rising cost of automobile insurance has made and broken political careers. Former governor of New Jersey Jim Florio was elected in 1989 partly on a platform of slashing the highest auto insurance premiums in the nation. California, with the third highest premiums, recently switched from an appointed to an elected insurance commissioner . . . who fast became one of that state's most visible politicians.

No wonder. There are few places in America where you can get by without a car. And virtually every state in the union requires drivers to purchase automobile liability insurance. So if you drive, you have to deal with an insurance company.

And dealing with an insurance company may be enough to give you a migraine. You might find yourself surcharged for no apparent reason. You might not be able to renew your policy because of a few too many speeding tickets. Or the cost of replacing your totalled car may be a lot higher than your insur-

ance payment. The quality of customer service varies from prompt and courteous to a version of the creaking bureaucracy in the old Soviet Union.

Making the business even more complicated and frustrating are the wide and sometimes inexplicable differences in premiums among states and among communities within states, as well as among different car models, driver ages, and gender. The total annual payments for a 55-year-old driving a sedate sedan in Nebraska could be as low as a few hundred dollars a year, while a 23-year-young New Jerseyean who drives a sports car will probably pay at least $2,500 just for a bare-bones policy—if he or she can find a company willing to write up a policy.

Still, no matter where you live or what you drive, it always pays to spend time shopping around for a lower premium and a better company. You could save hundreds of dollars a year on premiums and a few dollars on headache remedies.

THE BASICS

Types of Coverage

First, learn the coverage terms in the declarations page (cover sheet) of your auto insurance policy. Each coverage category charges its own separate premium. Added up, they equal your total premium.

Bodily injury liability. If you're in an accident and someone else is hurt, this covers your legal liability to them. Typically, this coverage has "split limits," which means that there is a coverage maximum for an entire accident and separate maximums per individual in the accident. It's described in terms of tens or hundreds of thousands of dollars. So, for example, "100/300" coverage would provide up to $100,000 coverage per person and a total of $300,000 for everyone injured in an accident.

Most states require minimum coverage, ranging from 10/20 to 25/50. These limits are absurdly low, of course. If you ever lose (or settle) a liability lawsuit, and it's your fault, you can be sure that you'll have to pay much more out of your own pocket. Coverage of at least 100/300 is recommended.

Property damage liability. If you're in an accident and someone else's property is damaged, like the plate glass of a store window you drove through, this is the part of your policy that covers you. It also covers the car that you hit when you tried to back out of the plate glass window. Bodily injury and property damage liability are the two most expensive parts of your policy.

Uninsured motorist. This coverage pays for injuries, including pain and suffering, if you're in an accident with an uninsured motorist or with a hit-and-run driver. Your claim will be paid only if the other person was at fault.

Underinsured motorist coverage. This covers you when the other driver was at fault but didn't have very much coverage. Mandatory coverage levels of $10,000 to $25,000 don't go far these days.

Collision coverage. Covers the cost of car repairs or replacement. With body shops charging hundreds of dollars for minor fender benders, this coverage may account for as much as one third of your total premium.

Collision claims are paid in one of two ways. Either you get the cash value of the car if the company determines it's not worth repairing or you get the amount needed to repair or replace it. A lot of drivers get steamed when the company pays cash value because the market value of the car is usually a lot less than the cost of a suitable replacement vehicle, especially when the company considers how much your car depreciated and deducts an additional charge for unusually high mileage.

Medical expense. The policy will pay medical expenses for accidental injuries to you and your passengers. It also covers funeral expenses. In these cases, fault doesn't matter.

Comprehensive. This kind of coverage includes theft and vandalism, as well as forces of nature, such as hail and earthquakes.

Personal injury protection (PIP). This additional coverage is required by law in no-fault states. It pays for medical expenses and some earnings, regardless of who was at fault. In New York, for example, such coverage must be in place for at least $50,000 per person.

Under no-fault, you get to sue only if a damage threshold has been passed. The threshold may be monetary or verbal. With monetary thresholds, you can sue if your medical costs exceed a base amount. Verbal thresholds allow you to sue if there are serious injuries or death. Property damage compensation is not included under the laws of most states with no-fault.

The states with some form of mandatory no-fault insurance accompanied by restrictions on liability lawsuits are Colorado, Connecticut, Georgia, Hawaii, Kansas, Massachusetts, Michigan, Minnesota, New York, North Dakota, and Utah.

Other possible coverages include towing and labor, umbrella coverage (pays when all of your other coverage is exhausted), and special endorsements, such as for built-in camper equipment.

The Insuring Agreement

There is an insuring agreement attached to the declarations page. Read it carefully because it includes important definitions, such as exactly who the policy covers and under what conditions a claim will be paid.

The people who are covered are known as the "insureds." They include the individuals specifically named on the declarations page, other household residents, and occasional users of your car (with your permission). Non-permissive drivers—such as car thieves—are not covered if they, and your vehicle, are involved in an accident. But you are covered if you have an accident driving someone else's car, as long as it is with their permission.

The insuring agreement also lists any exclusions, that is, whatever is specifically not covered. Read these before you sign, not when you file your first claim.

The Factors That Determine Your Premium

Winston Churchill called Russia "a riddle wrapped in a mystery inside an enigma." The same might be said for the way insurance premiums are computed.

Your premium is figured by multiplying a per-unit rate by the amount of insurance (the number of units of insurance) you wish to buy. Your rate is computed by taking into account the factors described below. As explained later, surcharges or discounts may then be applied to your premium.

Your state of residence. No one can entirely figure out why, but some states, like New Jersey and California, have much more expensive auto insurance than others. One reason may be that heavily urbanized states have more cars, more

SOME NO-FAULT PROS AND CONS

Pros	Cons
Since it dispenses with lawsuits, there are supposed to be no legal fees. All the money goes to the parties, none to lawyers.	*You forfeit your right to sue except in the most serious cases. The most restrictive no-fault state is Michigan, where there must have been death, severe disfigurement, or a serious impairment of a bodily function in order to sue.*
Accident victims' bill are paid promptly. Since justice is slow, it can otherwise take years for a case to come up in court.	*In the more restrictive states, you lose the right in most cases to collect for pain and suffering.*
Reduces auto insurance premiums. Less money goes to lawsuits, more of each premium dollar goes to compensating the parties.	*Accident victims in effect end up compensating the party at fault in an accident.*

traffic congestion, and therefore more accidents, raising the cost of providing insurance; New Jersey is the most densely populated state in the union and Southern California traffic is legendary.

Where you garage your car. If you live (and park) your car within the zip code of a heavily urbanized area, you can pay two or three times as much as your twin sister who happens to live (and park) in a rural area some miles away, even if you both have perfect records and drive the same model car. Suburban drivers' premiums tend to be somewhere between the premiums paid by urban and rural drivers. Premiums tend to be highest in lower-income, inner-city neighborhoods.

According to a 1992 article in *The Los Angeles Times*, a 30-year-old driver with one ticket who only wished to obtain the mandated coverage would have paid Farmer's Insurance Company $1,058 in Los Angeles, $594 in San Bernardino, and $458 in Northern California.

The insurance industry calls the system of figuring rates based on a car's home address "territorial rating." How fair is it? Not very. Premiums decline as you age, but you have to physically relocate to reduce a premium based on address. The poor pay more because low incomes and racial discrimination in housing keep many people from moving into areas with cheaper premiums. And territorial boundaries tend to be arbitrarily drawn. Besides, how fair is a system where your premium could be cut 25% just by moving a few blocks into a different territory?

The amount of coverage you are buying. In California, raising coverage from the minimal state-mandated level to, say, 50/100 will raise your premium an average of about 34%. In Rochester, New York, a $211 annual Geico premium for mandated liability insurance increases by $48 to $259 (a 22% increase) if the liability coverage is raised to 100/300.

Your age, how long you've been driving, your sex, and marital status. There's no denying it: Younger male drivers tend to have more accidents— *many* more accidents—than more mature drivers. So it's not unreasonable for male drivers under 25 to pay 100% to 200% more because, unlike racial or gender discrimination, all young drivers can escape this classification by successfully aging. If you have been driving for only a few years, you'll pay a surcharge regardless of your age. Generally, you have to have been driving from five to ten years before this surcharge is entirely erased.

You'll probably pay less if you're married—insurance companies believe that married drivers have fewer accidents. Unfortunately, the use of marital status as a factor inherently discriminates against unmarried hetero- or homosexual couples, whose domestic partnerships the law doesn't recognize, and against lower-income drivers, who are statistically less likely to be married.

Your driving record. Logically enough, people with poor driving records pay surcharges. There may or may not be a small surcharge of about 5% for your first ticket if you are an otherwise good driver. If you have a small accident, though, you can expect at least a 25% increase in your premium. Your premium could double or your insurance might not be renewed at all if you get one or more drunk-driving tickets.

Your car model. If you drive an armored personnel carrier and a compact sedan runs smack into you at 30 mph, chances are that your vehicle will hardly be dented and you won't be filing a liability claim. While it's illegal to drive an armored personnel carrier, you can save a lot of money if you buy the safest car possible—and you might just save your life.

A car that is costly to fix is costly to insure. A 12-cylinder Jaguar is a wonderful car, but insurance may cost a lot more than it would for a basic Dodge or Ford. Comprehensive coverage for cars

> "*The market—so effective in most industries in forcing companies to provide high quality goods at competitive prices— has not worked well in private passenger automobile insurance.*"
>
> —FROM THE NATIONAL ASSOCIATION OF Attorneys General Model Automobile Insurance Information Disclosure Statute

CITY SLICKERS GET TAKEN

Urban drivers pay far more for the same coverage than rural, and even suburban, drivers. In 1992, an Allstate policy that cost $726 a year in densely populated Brooklyn, New York, cost $474 in suburban Long Island 20 miles away, and only $256 in bucolic upstate Jefferson County. Even within a small state, the differences can be significant: in Delaware in 1991, Aetna Casualty and Surety Company charged a married female (25 to 49 years old) $340 in the city of Wilmington, $302 in New Castle County, and $248 in the rural Kent and Sussex counties.

that are both expensive to replace and popular with thieves, such as sports and luxury cars, is, of course, more expensive.

How you use your car. A car used for business costs more to insure because it is driven more and the chance of an accident is therefore greater. You'll also probably pay more if you commute a long distance to work or if your commute is entirely within a heavily urbanized area. But you'll enjoy a reduction if your car is used solely for "pleasure." "Farm use" is cheapest of all. Your agent might ask you how many miles you drive a year, and you could be surcharged if you drive a lot more than the annual average of 12,000 to 15,000 miles.

Besides using these factors to figure the premiums, the company will use them to decide whether to accept you in the first place. The process of making this determination is called *underwriting*. While the insurance agent makes the first cut by deciding whether to do business with you at all, it is the insurance company underwriter who reviews the application, makes the decision whether or not to insure you, and sets the premium. The underwriter determines if you are a preferred, standard, or nonstandard (i.e., high) risk driver. A standard risk driver usually pays about 20% more than a preferred driver. A nonstandard risk driver's application may be rejected or heavily surcharged.

Underwriting is more art than science. While a computer could apply a formula to place you in any one of hundreds of possible insurance classifications based on the factors listed earlier (such as "female driver over 65 living in suburban territory driving a full-size sedan"), the underwriter tries to get a "feel" for your riskiness, perhaps giving a little extra weight to one or another factor in a particular application. Among the subtle factors that might help determine if a company will accept you is your occupation. For example, insurance companies don't seem to favor police officers, firefighters, and bartenders.

Premium Discounts

Once your premium is figured you may be eligible for a discount. Be sure to tell your insurance agent about any of the following factors that might apply. But don't let discounts alone decide which insurer you'll use; a company that offers only a few of the following discounts might charge a low basic premium.

More than one car. Most companies offer a discount for bringing all your auto insurance business to them.

Safety equipment. If your car comes equipped with such passive restraints as air bags, you may be entitled to a large reduction on your medical coverage premium.

Anti-theft devices. City dwellers trying to get a full night's sleep loathe car alarms, and their effectiveness in stopping theft is dubious. Who actually does anything promptly about a wailing alarm? Still, car alarms can reduce comprehensive coverage premiums in some states, as can more neighbor-friendly devices like Chapman locks and other ignition cut-off devices.

Lots of driving experience. Mature drivers, usually drivers over 50, may enjoy a 10% discount. Insurers presume that older drivers drive less than they used to.

Good grades. Young people pay through the nose for auto insurance. But if your high school or college student gets good grades, usually a "B" average or better, a "good student discount" may be available. Some companies apparently assume that good students are more likely to be studying at home than out cruising for adventure.

Nonsmoker. People who smoke have more accidents. Perhaps the smoke gets in their eyes, or they take their hands off the wheel when lighting up. Or perhaps people who take fewer risks with their health also take fewer risks behind the wheel.

Driver safety course. Taking a defensive driving course may reduce your premium 5% to 15%.

Car pool. Presumably you're driving your own vehicle less and exposing yourelf to less risk if you car pool.

Shared Markets and Assigned Risk Pools

The basic concept of insurance is to spread risk. The driver who has never filed a claim subsidizes the hapless fellow who backed into the light post at the mall parking lot.

Of course, coverage obtained through shared markets is much more expensive than voluntary market coverage. So drive defensively and don't get soaked in the assigned-risk pool.

Cancellation and Non-Renewal

Nothing makes motorists angrier than being cancelled or non-renewed without so much as an explanation.

Cancellation. Basically, after the first 60 days of coverage, insurers can cancel your coverage only if you don't pay your premium, your license is revoked, or if someone covered by the policy is convicted of driving while intoxicated. Before the first 60 days, they can cancel your policy pretty much at will.

Non-renewal. Much more frequent and problematical is the insurer's refusal to renew your policy. An insurance company can decide not to renew your policy for any reason, except for age, sex, occupation, or race in the states where non-renewal for such reasons is specifically prohibited. In many states, the insurer doesn't have to tell you why you were dropped.

WHAT TO WATCH OUT FOR

The wrong information from the agent. According to one survey, applicants who ask agents for premium comparisons get the wrong answer one third to one half of the time. To find the right information, first try your State Insurance Department; a few of the more consumer-helpful departments issue guides with a comparison of premiums among companies for various driver classifications. You might also call or have a friend call an agent back later to double-check a premium quote.

Sloppy service. Price isn't everything. The least expensive insurer may provide lousy service. So ask friends and relatives about an insurer's reputation before applying. Also, an insurance company operating on the edge of solvency isn't likely to offer very good service. Find out about their financial health through a research service (see **HELP** at the end of the chapter).

A misleading or incorrect C.L.U.E. report. Most drivers haven't a clue about C.L.U.E., the Comprehensive Loss Underwriting Exchange. It's a new national database run by Equifax Inc., with up to five years' worth of claims histories on some 107 million drivers covered by liability insurance. Insurers use C.L.U.E. to decide whose premiums to raise, whose policies not to renew, and whose applications to reject.

Few motorists have checked the accuracy of what their C.L.U.E. file says about them. Yet there could be irrelevant or outdated claims. And entries could be misleading, since there are no facts describing the circumstances of any of the claims, other than the claim amount. A major controversy has recently arisen about the accuracy of credit reporting files. (See the chapter "Consumer Privacy: Who's Watching?" on page 562.) The fact is, there is little reason to believe that C.L.U.E. files are any more accurate.

One unwary consumer found out her auto insurance application was rejected by Allstate and she ended up in the assigned risk pool because of her C.L.U.E. report. Allstate found 10 claims totaling $11,362 on it, even though she had never been in an accident and had never had a moving violation. But a closer inspection revealed that two of the biggest claims were for vandalism and theft and were no longer relevant; she had moved several years earlier from the old neighborhood where the incidents occurred to a much safer area.

The woman contends that another claim listed as an accident was a spurious accusation that she had knocked someone's mirror off in a parking lot. Since it was cheaper for the insurance company to pay than to defend against a wrongful claim, the claim went into the database unexplained.

To get a copy of your report, call Equifax at (800) 456-6004. You will need to have available your driver's license number, date of birth, social security number, and, if you can, a 14-digit reference number that appears on the notice from your insurance company, if that's what prompted your call.

Expensive subsidiaries of major insurance companies. Robert Hunter, former head of the National Insurance Consumers Organization and now Texas Insurance Commissioner, told us about one law school dean who was "fat and happy because he had State Farm" as his insurer. His neighbor told him that he also had State Farm and that he paid several hundred dollars less than the dean. The dean looked into it and found out that he was insured by State Farm Fire and Casualty, which as it turns out, is more expensive than his neighbor's insurer, State Farm Mutual. His

agent had signed him up with the more expensive insurer to earn a higher commission. When the dean threatened to sue, he was switched to State Farm and got back his extra premium payments.

Such costlier subsidiaries are supposed to insure only higher risk drivers. But you might not really be a higher risk driver and still end up with the expensive subsidiary. Check to see if you're insured by the company's more expensive subsidiary, if it has one.

THE SMARTER CONSUMER

Shop around. Yes, it takes some work. But different insurance companies have very different premiums, even in the same zip code area. Three examples: In San Diego, the 1992 six-month premium for the same driver, coverage, and car varied from $278 at 20th Century Insurance Group to $563 at State Farm Mutual. In Wilmington, Delaware, the annual premium for a driver aged 25 to 49 was $340 at Aetna Casualty and Surety, $444 at Travelers Indemnity Company, $596 at Allstate Insurance Company, and $626 at Colonial Penn Insurance Company. And in Syracuse, New York, a few years ago, the basic legally mandated package for an unmarried 35-year-old male ranged from $193 a year at United Services

Automobile Association to $371 at Progressive Casualty Company.

Just because a company has high premiums does not mean it offers good service. And a company with low premiums does not necessarily offer bad service. Some insurance companies, like GEICO, have lower premiums because they specialize in insuring good, low-risk drivers. You might also find that an insurance company that sells directly—like State Farm and GEICO—rather than through an independent agent is cheaper.

Drop unnecessary coverage. Examine your declarations page carefully for coverage that you can reasonably reduce or eliminate. The most promising area for saving money may be your collision and comprehensive coverage. You may decide that this coverage is no longer worthwhile when your car is four or five years old. If you're in an accident, chances are that the company will "total" rather than repair your car—that is, give you what they calculate to be its cash value—which won't be much for an older car. The general rule is to drop collision coverage when the premium is 10% of the car's market value.

You might also reduce medical coverage, particularly if you already have a health insurance policy.

Reducing your liability coverage could be risky. Remember, if you are sued you'll want the company to defend you in court, and they're much more likely to put up a strong defense if they might have to shell out $1 million rather than $10,000.

Uninsured motorist coverage is especially advisable if you live in a state without no-fault coverage. If you don't have it, you'll have to pay all of your expenses above your medical coverage if you are in a hit-and-run accident or if the other driver doesn't have insurance.

Raise your deductibles. Consider this: You're probably not going to file a claim for a minor fender-bender, because if you do, your premium will most certainly go up, probably offsetting any amount the insurance company paid out to you. So if you're not going to file small claims, then why not raise your collision and comprehensive deductible to, say, $1,000 and put the premiums you save in the bank?

Robert Hunter, Texas Insurance Commissioner, in effect self-insures. He has high deductibles and puts his premium savings in a separate bank account, which he uses to pay for any fender-bender damage.

Report any changes in status that might reduce your premium. Say you start car-pooling or you install an alarm system. Tell your insurer immediately.

Ask about a "first accident allowance." If you have an accident after many years of driving accident-free, some insurers will overlook it and not surcharge you.

Drive a safer car. Logically enough, larger and heavier cars tend to be safer and therefore less expensive to insure (though they are more expensive to drive).

Put your kids on your policy if they drive your car less than half the time. It's a lot cheaper than buying them separate insurance. If they have their own policies, then they are "principal," as opposed to "occasional," drivers, which are cheaper to cover. If they go to school more than 100 miles away (*without* your car), you'll also get a discount.

Buy your homeowners and auto insurance from the same company. You could get a discount of about 10% on your auto policy.

¶ Where to complain. The insurance industry is regulated entirely by the states. Most states have a consumer services division in their insurance departments where you can report your insurer if you think you have been mistreated. Check the government listings in your local telephone directory.

¶ Are you driving a thief's favorite model? Find out for free from the Highway Loss Data Institute, 1005 North Glebe Road, Arlington, VA 22201, (703) 247-1600. Surprisingly, some older models are favored because of the great demand for their parts.

¶ Should you maintain collision coverage? Check the market value of your car with the National Automobile Dealer's Association. Most public libraries have their price book.

¶ If you suspect insurance fraud, call the National Insurance Crime Bureau hot line at 800-TEL-NICB. Remember that insurance fraud, like shoplifting, raises costs for everyone.

¶ For answers to your insurance questions, try the National Insurance Consumer Helpline at (800) 942-4242. This service is paid for by the insurance industry, so take what they say with a grain of salt. Another industry organization that can answer basic insurance questions is the Insurance Information Institute, 110 William Street, New York, NY 10038; call (800) 331-9146.

¶ Check out an insurer before applying. Call your state insurance department to find out if a company has been the subject of government disciplinary actions.

CHAPTER 30

CAR REPAIR

Take Your Car in Without Getting Taken In

In 1941 and again in 1987, *Reader's Digest* reporters took a car that was in perfect working condition into repair shops around the country to see how many would make expensive, unneeded "repairs." The result: 63% of shops did unnecessary work in 1941 and 56% in 1987.

This worthless work costs you dearly. In 1979, the U.S. Department of Transportation found that American consumers paid $26.5 billion for unnecessary car repairs and related costs—about half of what they spent at the garage. And things haven't gotten much better: Out of the $100 billion Americans now spend annually on auto repair, Ralph Nader estimated that Americans now shell out more than $40 billion unnecessarily.

One New Jersey woman, for example, was forced to pay $1,000 in cash to retrieve her car from the repair shop. As she drove away, she realized she'd paid a lot for nothing—the car had not been repaired. In another example, thousands of Sears Auto Repair customers paid anywhere from a few dollars to $500 for unnecessary repairs before

California's Bureau of Automotive Repair cracked down in 1992.

Don't let these stories or a phobia of car dealers and mechanics scare you into submission. You don't have to take it—if you take care when selecting a mechanic and overseeing repair jobs.

THE BASICS

Routine Maintenance

Since routine maintenance greatly increases the life of your car, it's prudent to follow the maintenance guidelines.

Easier said than done. In a sort of duel of the maintenance schedules, manufacturers suggest one thing and dealers another.

A 1992 investigation by *U.S. News & World Report* found that 80% of auto dealers surveyed performed more services than the manufacturer recommended, and 63% of dealers replaced parts that manufacturers said had plenty of life left in them.

For instance, the owner's manual for a 1992 Ford Tempo suggests a return trip for service after 7,500 miles, unless the car gets "hard use" (such as police or taxi work, towing trailers, or lots of trips shorter than 10 miles in subfreezing weather). Hard use requires oil and filter changes at 3,000 miles and again at 6,000 miles, when tire rotation is also recommended. However, one dealer told a Ford Tempo driver whose car did not get "hard use" to bring the car in after 3,000 miles for an oil and filter change and again after 6,000 miles for the same service, plus a tire rotation and other "therapeutic" treatments.

It's hard to know whom to believe. Manufacturers may underprescribe routine maintenance like oil and transmission changes to make their cars seem cheaper to keep. Dealers have an incentive to overprescribe, because they make money every time you bring your car in for service; the bill for the Ford Tempo driver's 6,000-mile check-up, which the manufacturer said was unnecessary, came to $130.

Various car experts and the American Automobile Association recommend changing the oil more frequently than the manufacturers suggest—every 3,000 to 5,000 miles—and following the manufacturers' guidelines for other services.

> "*Consumers can— and should— seek a second opinion if they have doubts about the {car repair} advice they are receiving. . . . Some all-inclusive offers may include unnecessary service, while others may be too limiting for your particular needs.*"
>
> —JIM CONRAN,
> director of the State of California
> Department of Consumer Affairs

To be really safe, the AAA recommends that car owners use the "frequent service" schedule recommended by manufacturers for the cars they produce.

Not only is regular service good for the car, it's also essential if you want your warranty to cover major repairs. Most manufacturers' warranties are void if you haven't kept up with the prescribed maintenance schedule.

Finding a Repair Shop

You have a number of options when choosing a repair shop. Here are some things to consider.

Car dealers. As the profit in selling cars has decreased, dealers have become more reliant on their service centers to be profit centers. Just 11% of dealer profits came from the service department in 1983, according to the National Automobile Dealers Association. Ten years later, only 14% of their profits *don't* come from repairs. While the prices for nonwarranty work will be high, the dealer's mechanics have been trained to understand thoroughly your car's quirks. Furthermore, dealers are often the only convenient supplier of the diagnostic equipment necessary to understand bugs in your car's complex computer system.

Specialty shops, franchise shops, and department store auto centers. Service is usually fast and convenient and prices reasonable. Different chains specialize in particular services, such as muffler repair or tune-ups, and often know little about other systems in the car.

Independent service stations. Services and prices vary. The main attractions are convenience and customer satisfaction. There's a good chance you can have the same mechanic service your car time and again, and he or she will know your car, which can help you to feel more confident about diagnoses and price estimates.

Choose a shop based on the kind of repair you need. For work covered by the warranty, go straight to the dealer. For routine maintenance, the automotive center at the local department store will probably do just fine, as will one of the chains, such as Jiffy Lube, that specializes in what you need. For routine repairs and individualized attention, try your local mechanic.

WHAT TO WATCH OUT FOR

The problem? You may not know what kind of service you need. If this is the case, you need to find a full-service shop you can trust. As with most other things, the first thing to do is ask your friends, neighbors, and relatives whom they recommend. If that nets

nothing, you're on your own. Here's what you should look for:

Credentials. Seek out repair shops endorsed by the American Automobile Association; the AAA holds them to rigorous standards and guarantees their work for AAA members. AAA will also mediate disagreements between its members and repair shops it has endorsed.

Look for certification by the National Institute for Automotive Service Excellence. Certification is no guarantee of quality, nor is it legally required, but it is an assurance of experience. The institute certifies mechanics in eight repair areas, and mechanics who are certified can advertise this fact. Ask if the mechanic is certified to do the work your car needs: A mechanic certified in, say, brake repairs isn't necessarily better than the garage down the block if your car needs a new transmission.

Poor service. Although Americans spend $100 billion a year on automobile parts and service, every third car repaired requires a return visit to the shop, according to automotive consultant J.D. Power and Associates. It's no wonder, then, that auto repair consistently rates as a top complaint category at local consumer affairs agencies and better business bureaus.

Unnecessary repairs. When the NYC Department of Consumer Affairs took in test vehicles—rigged by expert mechanics with small problems that should have cost little to fix—more than half of the transmission shops wanted to do

REPAIR AD ABSURDUM

What would you do if your mechanic jacked up your car, with your wheelchair-bound wife in it, and tried to extort $1,000 from you before you could get your wife or your car back? Sounds like a *Saturday Night Live* skit, right? This is exactly what happened to Robert and Shirley A. of Canoga Park, California. They brought their RV into a dealer that had offered a free lubrication and oil change. What they got instead was a demand for $1,000 "ransom" before the dealer would take the mobile home off the jacks. Robert had no choice but to pay. When he got home, he stopped payment on the check. The RV dealer had to repay the couple $1,300 and eventually went to jail.

receiving a slew of complaints, the State of California's Bureau of Automotive Repair (BAR) went undercover and found Sears selling unnecessary service and parts 90% of the time. In some cases, undercover inspectors were overcharged as much as $550 for unnecessary repairs. BAR inspectors also found that Sears pressured employees to meet daily quotas for the sales of alignments, springs, shock absorbers, struts, and brake jobs with the threat of cutting back employees' work hours or transferring them to other Sears departments. Once caught, Sears changed its compensation system to remove the incentive to do unnecessary work.

Charges for work that wasn't done. Lisa C. of New Jersey has a classic story. One rainy day, she couldn't get her car to start. The next day, the car started fine, but just to be safe she took it in to a repair shop for a check-up. She was told that necessary work would cost $1,000. When she came back to pick up the car two days later, the mechanic asked her to pay in cash and would not let her test-drive the car first. Since she needed the car, she had no choice but to pay. She took the car to another mechanic who told her that no work had been done and that the job should have cost only $50. The car had a cracked spark plug; when plugs get wet, they can keep a car from starting.

Misleading ads. Beware of commercials promising unbelievably low prices for repairs. The low prices often do not include all the necessary parts and labor. Meineke

unnecessary work, ranging in price from $75 to $1,133; a third of the muffler shops wanted to charge $60 to $325 for superfluous service.

Mechanics in franchise stores frequently work on commission or have quotas to fill. The more work they do, the more money they make. That means they may be tempted to line the pockets of their jumpsuits by performing unnecessary repairs on your car. California's 1992 investigation into Sears Auto Stores provides a glaring example. After

Discount Muffler Shops Inc. was charged with deceptive advertising by the NYC Department of Consumer Affairs several years ago for touting nonexistent muffler deals for $18.93 to $26.95—in fact, they cost as much as $150.

The captive consumer. Some garages will try to strong-arm you into letting them repair your car. Don't let them; you have a right to choose your own mechanic. Take the case of John G. His van was stolen, recovered by the police, and—without his knowledge or approval—towed to a garage. When John went to the garage to claim the van, he was told he could not have it unless he authorized the garage to do the necessary repairs. The garage claimed that some work had already been done and that parts were on order. But because John had not authorized *any* work, he refused to pay. Until local consumer officials intervened, the garage refused to release the van.

In many states, by law, you can only be charged for repairs if you sign an authorization. Do not be coerced into paying for repairs that were performed without your consent.

Towing tricks. Tow services are another consistent source of consumer complaints. Once they've got your car, it can be difficult to get them to give it up. Even if you would prefer to have your regular mechanic make the necessary repairs, towers may try to strong-arm you into having their shop work on your car.

William S.'s story is typical of how towing companies pad their bills. He was driving home from work when his car broke down. When he asked the tow truck driver who responded to his call how much the tow would cost, he was told $130 for 27 miles, which he then authorized. The next day, William clocked the trip and found that it was only 19 miles. When he looked at the bill he noticed charges for "motor trouble" and "wrecked vehicle" that did not apply to his case. He calculated that this modern-day highway robber overcharged him by $55—for a tow that should have cost only $75.

Warranty waivers. Many dealers insert clauses into their warranties stating that if something goes wrong as a result of repairs done by a facility other than the dealer's service center, the cost of fixing the problem will not be covered by the warranty. Don't let the dealer use this clause to persuade you that *all* routine work, such as oil changes or 10,000-mile check-ups, must be done by the dealer in order to keep your warranty. You can save money using independents or chains for routine services—or by doing simple maintenance yourself—and the dealer must still honor your warranty for bigger repairs.

"Service notices." Don't be fooled by mailings from your dealer that look like official service notices from the manufacturer. One local Mazda dealership mailed notices to 5,000 Mazda owners in Palm Beach County, Florida, telling them to bring their cars to the dealership to have the timing belt inspected and possibly replaced. The mailing referenced "Mazda and Service Notification TTB #46A, May 1992" and said, in part: "This is to notify you of a Special Vehicle Maintenance Inspection regarding timing belt replacement on most 1984–1989 Mazda models." As official as the letter sounded, the directive had not come from Mazda of America but from Mazda of Palm Beach County—it was just a sneaky promotion concocted to drum up repair business.

Choose the right shop for the job. Routine maintenance jobs are easily and inexpensively handled by franchised chains and department store repair shops. Dealers will charge top dollar. Be sure to use a shop that specializes in what you need.

Do your own maintenance. It's relatively simple and the cheapest by far. But keep receipts for oil or filters you buy so that you can prove you adhered to the manufacturer's maintenance schedule if you ever need to.

Get a second opinion, unless you're sure of the mechanic. This is particularly important if you've been towed to a shop you know nothing about. You may have to pay for another tow and a couple of

estimates, but in the end you may save hundreds of dollars.

Talk directly to the person who will work on your car, whenever possible. If it's the only way to describe the symptoms, have the mechanic take a test drive with you.

Get an estimate and tell the garage not to begin repairing the car until you have approved the repairs at the estimated price.

Know what you're paying for. If work was performed without authorization or if you were charged for work that wasn't done, don't pay for it. Complain to the garage, and, if the matter is not resolved satisfactorily, complain to local consumer authorities.

Don't sign a service order until you know what will be involved. At the very least, the service order should describe your car's problems specifically; ideally, it should state exactly what work will be done. Tell the mechanic not to do any additional work without getting your explicit approval.

Rebuilt parts are as good as new ones, and, at as little as a quarter of the price, a better buy. Ask ahead of time—otherwise the mechanic will probably put in the more expensive new part. One catch: Rebuilt parts come with shorter guarantees than new parts.

Don't pay for work that was never done. If you had parts replaced, ask to see the old ones. Some states even require mechanics to give you the parts they remove from your car—in Maryland, for instance, consumers are not obligated to pay for repairs if key parts are not returned to them.

Keep a copy of the bill for your records. It may come in handy if you are the unlucky one out of three people who needs a follow-up visit to get things running right. You might also need it to prove that you have been maintaining the car properly and qualify for the warranty.

Know your warranty. Before you take your car to an independent mechanic, check if the repair work would be covered by the warranty if you took the car to the dealer. Conversely, for routine maintenance or a repair, take your car to the dealer only if the warranty covers it.

Avoid garages that accept only cash. It may be a sign they won't stand behind their work. Taking this precaution would have protected Lisa C., the car owner we met earlier, whose car was released only after a $1,000 cash payment. If she had paid by check, she could have asked the bank to stop payment; if she had paid with a credit card, she could have asked the credit card company not to pay the charge until the dispute was resolved. The credit card company cannot charge you interest or penalities until the problem is settled or resolved in court. If you need to do this, write a letter to the credit card company and garage explaining the problem, and be sure to keep copies.

. **If you have a problem** with a garage that has been endorsed by AAA, report it to the organization. Garages can lose their standing with AAA if the problems are common or serious enough.

. **The State of California Bureau of** Automotive Repair investigates every complaint it receives and mediates between mechanics and car owners when necessary: In California, call (800) 952-5210 (7 AM to 5 PM weekdays). Residents of other states, call your state department of transportation to see if anything similar is available where you live.

. **For a list of the 1,800 tires rated** by the National Highway Traffic Safety Administration; call the agency's Auto Safety Hotline (800) 424-9393. For a list of long-lasting tires, send a stamped, self-addressed envelope to the Center for Auto Safety, 2001 S Street NW, Washington, DC 20009.

. **The Center for Auto** Safety can also send you a list of lawyers in your area who specialize in helping consumers with car repair problems. Send a stamped, self-addressed envelope to the address above.

. **For more advice, consult** *The Car Book* or *The Used Car Book*, by Jack Gillis, New York: Harper Perennial, 1993. They are available in bookstores, but if you buy them from the Center for Auto Safety, this non-profit group gets a portion of the profits. Write to 2001 S Street NW, Washington, DC 20009, or call (202) 328-7700.

PART 5

Finances

CHAPTER 31

CREDIT CARDS

Still Expensive After All These Years

Millions of Americans breathed a sigh of financial relief when credit card interest rates began to moderate in 1992. For nearly a decade, rates had remained steadily at record heights, even as earnings on deposit accounts plummeted to their lowest levels since automobiles had tail fins. Throughout the 1980s, consumers had a common question and complaint: If what banks *paid* for their money fell from 16% to 3%, why did what they *charged* for their money stay at 19.8%?

If you have a decent payment history, at this point you should have no trouble getting a credit card with an annual interest rate below 16% and a full 25-day grace period, which is a significant improvement on the recent 19.8% norm. If your credit is very solid, you may qualify for a card with interest below 12%.

But the news isn't all good. Much of what card issuers give you with one hand—namely, the lower interest rates and annual fee waivers—they take back with the other, through a confusion of new fees, shrunken grace periods, and costlier methods of computing finance charges. Despite slightly lower interest charges, card issuers still rake in major profits both because of fees and because of the continuing enormous gap between the cost of the money they lend you and the interest rate they charge.

Do credit cards have you confused yet hooked? If so, you're not alone: Millions of Americans remain expensively addicted to plastic. The number of credit cards in circulation doubled during the 1980s, despite punishingly high interest rates and proliferating fees. Visa and MasterCard are now accepted at thousands of supermarkets and medical offices, and 82% of college students in the U.S. carry at least one credit card.

THE BASICS

Credit Card Jargon

Surveys have shown that many cardholders lack basic information about the plastic cards filling their wallets. Here are the definitions of the basic terms:

Credit cards and charge cards. They're not the same. With credit cards, you are borrowing money when you choose not to pay your entire outstanding balance. Most credit cards are sponsored by banks, although department stores, oil companies, and large corporations like General Motors and General Electric sponsor them, too. Charge cards (also called travel & entertainment cards) do not charge interest and require you to pay your entire balance each month. American Express, Diner's Club and Carte Blanche are charge cards.

Annual membership fee. This fee, which ranges from $15 to $55 for a basic card, is automatically charged to your account once you've used the card. For "gold" cards, the annual fee ranges from $40 to $100.

APR. You are charged interest on your outstanding balance for the use of the issuer's money. This rate is expressed as an APR, or annual percentage rate. The actual APR is usually higher than what the bank says it is because finance charges are added to your outstanding balance, so you pay interest on your interest and your balance. A 16.4% rate, for example, actually becomes 17.69% if you revolve a $100 balance for one year, make no other purchases, and interest is compounded monthly, as it is with most cards.

Grace period. The time the issuer gives you to pay off the new balance before assessing finance charges is the grace period. It's often measured from the close of the billing cycle to the payment due date. You owe finance charges if your entire outstanding balance is not paid during the grace period.

Fixed-rate and variable-rate interest. With variable-rate cards the interest rate is adjusted automatically (usually every quarter) and is keyed to an index, typically the prime interest rate. Fixed-rate cards maintain the same interest rate—unless, of course, the issuing bank decides to change it, which it's supposed to tell you about in advance.

How to Find the Cheapest Card

Compare interest rates and fees. If you are among the approximately 28% of cardholders who always pay the entire monthly bill, then you are what the industry calls a "convenience user." Technically, you shouldn't care if the interest rate is 100%, so long as the card has a sufficient grace period to give you plenty of time to pay without

---

ENJOY NOW . . . PAY LATER

Credit card spending totaled $225 billion in the U.S. in 1991—almost three times the $80 billion spent in 1981. The number of credit cards outstanding has jumped from 556 million in 1980 to more than 1 billion in 1992.

EVERY LITTLE BIT COUNTS

Interest rate*	6 months	12 months	24 months	36 months	48 months
19.8%	$1,096	$1,186	$1,349	$1,490	$1,611
18%	$1,087	$1,168	$1,312	$1,434	$1,534
16%	$1,077	$1,148	$1,272	$1,375	$1,455
14%	$1,067	$1,128	$1,234	$1,319	$1,380
12%	$1,057	$1,109	$1,197	$1,265	$1,311

*On a loan of $1,000.

incurring a finance charge. Look for a card with a low or no annual fee.

If you usually have an outstanding balance, then the annual fee will not be nearly as important as finding the lowest possible interest rate. If you virtually never pay off your entire balance, opt for a card with no grace period; such cards usually impose the lowest interest rates of all.

What if you do both—pay it all off some months, revolve charges in other months? You might want to carry both a low-interest rate credit card and a charge card. Reserve the credit card for major purchases you know you will have to pay for over a long period and use the charge card for purchases you plan to pay off right away.

You can save a lot by switching to a lower-rate card. Say you use a Visa card to buy a $1,000 refrigerator. If you make only minimum payments, in this case 2.8% of the monthly bill, and your card issuer charges 19.8% annual interest, the true cost will be $1,349 after two years. If you had charged it on a 12% card, you would have paid only $1,197. The $152 savings would be enough to stock that refrigerator with groceries. The chart above shows how much you'd spend on finance charges on $1,000 over varying periods of time for several different annual interest rates.

Switching cards isn't difficult. Most banks offer free transfer checks. But be wary of low "teaser" rates offered to card switchers. Often, these rates last only several months and then jump to not-so-low levels. For example, a recent Bank One Visa card mail solicitation trumpeted a 5.9% APR guaranteed for one year. It was only in the extremely small-print, mandatory truth-in-lending disclosure chart inserted with the glossy promotional literature that you learned that there is a $15 annual fee and that, when the introductory year ends, the interest rate skyrockets to an above-average 16.8% variable.

In addition, make sure the low interest rate on the balance you carried over from your old card is the same for new purchases, not the higher rate charged for cash advances. Don't fall for direct-mail or telephone solicitations for "low-interest" credit cards, *especially* if solicitors ask you to send them money. As for "900" phone numbers that promise low-rate credit cards, you may be charged as much as $50 if you call. There's a good chance that all you'll get from any of these offers is a *list* of cards and maybe some application forms.

Increasingly, issuers pick and choose among their customers when setting interest rates. Their best customers—people who charge a lot or those who pay off their entire balance every month—are being rewarded with percentage-point rate reductions. Cardholders with somewhat checkered payment histories or those who don't use their card often aren't told about the new rates. Citibank, Sears Discover, and American Express Optima are among the card companies with such tiered rate structures.

If you still pay a top rate and think you deserve better treatment, and if your bank has tiered rating, call the customer service number and ask for a reduction. If your credit record is pretty good, threaten to switch to another issuer unless they give you a reduction.

An increasing proportion of credit cards charge variable interest rates. Is a variable- or fixed-rate interest card best? Variable-rate cards, which typically have lower interest rates because you assume the interest rate risk, can make it harder to budget—with the rate changing periodically, you can never be sure just how much that refrigerator will end up costing, especially if you take a long time to pay it off. In addition, while issuers must notify you in advance of any rate change for a fixed-rate card—giving you time to cancel the card—the only way you'll find out about a variable-rate change is by looking for the rate at the bottom of the monthly statement. With interest rates trending upward lately, variable-rate cardholders have to keep a close eye on this. So, if you're not the gambling type, stick with a fixed-rate card. But choose carefully—the interest rates on many fixed-rate cards have remained just that, *fixed*, at high levels.

Compare fees. When assessing which card will cost you less, be sure to take into account the various fees that may be charged. These can include:

■ *Annual membership fee.* Most card issuers charge annual membership fees, now typically $20 for a basic card. They justified these fees when first imposed in the early 1980s because they were "losing money" on all the people who paid their full balances each month. This argument conveniently ignored issuers' revenue from their share of the "merchant discount" retailers pay them, which now amounts to about 8% of credit-card revenue.

With the credit card industry becoming more competitive of late, some issuers have dropped the annual fee, at least for the first year.

Also, sometimes an issuer will waive the fee (again, usually just for a year) if you threaten to switch to someone else's no-fee card. So don't be shy—call the customer service number and ask. If the customer representative says no, speak to a supervisor.

■ *Over-the-credit-limit fee.* If you don't keep close tabs on your spending and accidentally exceed your credit limit, even by only a few dollars, most issuers will slap on a fee of $10 or $15. What's worse, a few issuers charge a separate fee for each over-limit purchase.

■ *Late payment fee.* Most issuers now charge a late fee of $10 or $15 if your payment arrives after the payment due date (it's printed on your monthly statement). With over-limit and late fees, you can effectively pay double interest—after all, the bank is charging you interest on the amount by which you exceeded your balance or didn't pay on time. To add insult to injury, interest is usually also charged on the fees.

If your payment was just a few days late and you were charged a fee, call the customer service number and ask for a waiver. There's a good chance they'll say "yes" if you aren't a late payment recidivist.

■ *Transaction fees* for writing a check against your credit card or for a cash advance are typically 2% to 3% of the total, generally with a $2 minimum and sometimes with a $10 to $20 cap. So use your credit card to get cash only as a last resort. And don't cash the cash advance "convenience checks" some banks will send you if you are a new cardholder. They're really just a convenience for the bank to charge you fees and cash advance interest rates, which may be higher than interest rates for purchases.

■ *Minimum finance charge.* No matter how small your outstanding balance, in most states you'll always pay at least 50 cents. You can avoid this small indignity by being sure to pay your entire bill. There's probably no good reason to have an outstanding balance of only a few dollars.

Banks are coming up with new fees all the time. No wonder fees (not including annual fees) contributed 11% to 1992 and 1993 credit card issuer revenues, up from 6% in 1991. One bank actually charges a fee for *closing* your credit card account. First Deposit National Bank of San Francisco imposes finance charges on what you *might* charge on their Visa gold card; you pay a fee based on the amount of your credit line. In early 1994, the Center for Science in the Public Interest (CSPI) awarded First Deposit one of its Harlan Page Hubbard Awards (Hubbard was a famous 19th century snake oil salesman) for advertising that claimed "no annual fee" and "low interest rates." According to CSPI, the monthly credit line fee "often exceeds the annual fee and interest charges assessed by most Visa cards."

Examine balance computation methods. The Average Daily Balance method is the most common

	Average daily balance method, including new purchases	Average daily balance method, excluding new purchases
ANNUAL PERCENTAGE RATE	*18%*	*18%*
PREVIOUS BALANCE	*$400*	*$400*
NEW PURCHASES ON THE 18TH DAY	*$50*	*$50*
PAYMENTS	*$300 on the 15th day (new balance=$100)*	*$300 on the 15th day (new balance=$100)*
AVERAGE DAILY BALANCE	*$270*	*$250*
FINANCE CHARGE	*$4.05*	*$3.75*

way card issuers figure the balance on which you pay finance charges. You are charged interest on the total you owed each day during the monthly billing cycle, divided by the number of days in the cycle. New purchases are included and payments are subtracted.

Whether the average daily balance method your issuer uses includes new purchases in calculating finance charges also affects the cost of credit, as the chart above illustrates.

A much costlier method adopted by some card issuers, including Sears Discover Card and General Motors MasterCard, is the two-cycle average daily balance method. This method may hurt you if you pay off your entire balance some months and revolve it others. As the non-profit advocacy group Bankcard Holders of America explained in a 1992 report, *Credit Cards: What You Don't Know Can Cost You!*:

"The two-cycle method appears to be designed to recoup interest for those months in which a consumer did not pay off her new purchases in full, but was charged interest on those new purchases because she paid the previous month's balance in full. In other words, if a consumer starts the month with a previous balance of zero, all new purchases will not accrue finance charges in that billing cycle. If those purchases are not paid in full by the due date, the issuer using the two-cycle method will include them in the average daily balance for the current month (like other issuers do), but will *also* figure an average daily balance for the previous month, and assess a finance charge for that balance as well."

Be sure to find out if this method is used before you sign up for a new card.

Another way banks are upping your outstanding balance is by charging interest from the date of your purchase rather than the date your purchase is *posted* to your card account, which can be a difference of several days.

Don't take the bells and whistles too seriously. When all card issuers charged interest rates greater than 18% and had similar annual membership fees and grace periods, there wasn't much to distinguish one Visa or MasterCard from another except the design on the face of the card. So issuers had to create some differences—special credit card deals known in the industry as "bells and whistles." As this term implies, they frequently do not offer much real value. Stay focused on the interest rate, balance calculation method, and annual fee when choosing a card and consider the "bells and whistles" when you can't decide between two otherwise competitive cards.

■ *Price protection.* The issuer guarantees that you'll pay the lowest available price for merchandise. But Citibank, for example, requires you to jump through hoops to be reimbursed: You'll need to show a print ad or catalog entry for the *exact* same item, the ad must have run within 60 days of your purchase, you have to submit your credit card receipt with your claim, and claim amounts are limited.

■ *Purchase protection.* The issuer promises that you'll be reimbursed if you break, lose, or suffer the theft of any merchandise within three months of charging it to the card. Sounds great—until you actually file a claim and have to deal with the required proofs and paperwork. One major issuer's long list of items not covered includes "losses from abuse, fraud, or hostility," whatever that means.

■ *Frequent flier miles.* Most major airlines have hooked up with banks to issue co-branded Visa or Master-Cards. These can be good deals. You usually earn one frequent flier mile for each dollar you charge on the card. Your primary concern should still be with the basic interest rate and annual fees. The value of a free ticket after charging $25,000 worth of merchandise (i.e., to earn 25,000 frequent flier miles) may be more than offset by a high interest rate and annual fees. (A $50 fee instead of a $20 fee—that's $30 extra right there. If it takes two years to accu-

TWO-CYCLE SLEIGHT OF HAND

According to Bankcard Holders of America, the two-cycle method of computing credit card financing charges can cost cardholders three times as much as the least expensive method. One woman complained that the two-cycle method increased her monthly interest from $25 to $80.

mulate 25,000 miles, then that's $60 extra in annual fees.) Citibank AAdvantage (American Airlines) imposes a hefty $50 annual fee, while many cards now have no annual fee. The NationsBank–USAir card was charging 17.9% (16.9% Gold) at a time when many credit card issuers were charging under 15% interest. And some issuers cap the number of miles you can accumulate.

■ *Collision damage waivers.* This one might actually save you real money if you travel and rent cars frequently: The card issuer picks up the cost of car rental companies' collision damage waivers. (See page 465 for a full discussion.)

■ *Miscellany.* Be skeptical of the value of offers for travel accident insurance, lost luggage assistance, emergency roadside help, and extended warranties. You probably will never need these services or you have them already. And there could be a lot of paperwork for you to fill out when you do use them.

What to Do About . . .

Lost cards. If you lose your credit card, you are not liable for any charges—as long as you notify the issuer before any unauthorized charges are made. You also pay nothing if someone fraudulently used your card number and you still have the card.

So what do you do if you lose your card, then learn that the finder took it to Tiffany's for a spending spree? No problem. The most you're liable for is $50, as long as you report the loss by calling the customer service number on your statement. There's no time limit. It's not legally required, but it's a good idea to follow up with a written notification to the issuer.

If you discover that someone else has used your credit card number, Bankcard Holders of America recommends that in your letter to the issuer, you say that an "unauthorized charge" was made; if you don't use these words, it may be treated as a billing error, and restrictive rules (explained below) will apply.

Most issuers try to persuade you to sign up for a credit card registry service when they send you new or replacement cards. For a fee of about $15, you make only one call to this service; it will cancel all your cards and order replacements. Since it should take only a few minutes to cancel a card yourself, this service is hardly worth it unless your wallet is chock full of credit cards or you're too busy to take the time.

Billing mistakes. If you find an error on your bill—say you did not get the promised credit for the $2,500 crystal chandelier you bought on a whim and returned—the law says you have 60 days from the date that the bill containing the error was mailed to dispute the charge *in writing* to your card issuer. It's a good idea to use certified mail, return receipt requested. You do not have to pay the disputed portion of your bill, and you can still use your card while the issuer investigates. The issuer has 30 days to acknowledge in writing receipt of your letter. Within two billing cycles (or a maximum of 90 days), the issuer must have conducted a reasonable investigation and either corrected any mistake or explained why *you* are mistaken. When writing, state your name, account number, the amount of the mistake, and the reason you think the bill is in error. The creditor cannot impose a finance charge on the disputed amount pending an investigation.

Defective merchandise. If your problem is with the *quality* of goods or services, and if the cost was at least $50 and they were bought in or within 100 miles of your home state, different rules apply. Depending on your state's law governing your right to withhold payment to a merchant, you might be able to withhold payment from the credit card issuer, as long as you made a good-faith attempt to resolve the problem with the merchant. In fact, the card issuer may very well have charged back the amount to the merchant, so your dispute will be directly with the merchant.

If you regularly pay off your entire balance, you should withhold the disputed portion and immediately raise your claim with the merchant and the card issuer. One of the advantages of revolving charges is that—since you haven't fully paid for the merchandise yet—you preserve the leverage to withhold payment from the card issuer.

Avoiding Fraud

Massachusetts' practice of imprinting social security numbers on drivers' licenses led to six months of bureaucratic misery for Susan P. after she used her license as identification for a check written at a store. A thief saw her social security number, memorized it, then used it to order a new MasterCard, giving her first name as Susan and attributing a different last name and a new address to a recent marriage. After charging several thousand dollars worth of purchases, the pseudo-Susan figured the coast was clear and ordered credit cards from two department stores on which she racked up even more charges. Eventually, the imposter used Susan P.'s good credit to buy a new car—with a $14,000 loan from the General Motors Acceptance Corporation (GMAC).

Susan P. learned about the thefts only when she ordered a copy of her credit report to apply for a mortgage. All of the borrowings were in default and it took Susan six months to clear her record. The credit bureau repeatedly ignored her letters and put her in what she called "voice mail hell" when she telephoned them directly. The Massachusetts Attorney General's office said they couldn't help; even the local police department said they could do nothing.

In desperation, Susan phoned "Call for Action" on Boston radio station WBZ. The Attorney General's office was suddenly much more accommodating when WBZ called on her behalf, and put her in touch with the Cambridge Consumer Council and the Massachusetts Public Interest Research Group. They advised her to get in touch with the creditors and, through GMAC, Susan tracked down the imposter and eventually straightened it all out. She learned that the thief had been borrowing off her good name for three years.

NEW CARDS ON THE BLOCK

Several non-banks introduced their own credit cards in recent years, including the Sears Discover Card, AT&T Universal MasterCard and Visa, General Motors MasterCard, and General Electric Rewards MasterCard. Another recent development is the "co-branded" card, which carries the names of a major corporation and a bank, such as the Ford Citibank MasterCard or Visa and the Shell MasterCard from Chemical Bank. Most charge a variable interest rate, which shifts rate risk to *your* shoulders.

Many of these cards are distinguished by their givebacks, such as GM's rebate of 5% of everything you charge—applicable to purchase or lease of a GM car. But the real value of the givebacks may not be enough to make them a better deal than lower-rate and no-fee cards available elsewhere. The Shell MasterCard from Chemical Bank gives rebates, but the annual variable interest rate is prime plus 9% (16.4%, as this is being written) and there is a $20 annual fee (waived the first year). The lower rates and waived annual fees of plenty of other cards might more than offset your rebate. The GE Rewards Master-Card rebate is 0.5% for balances of up to $2,000 and 1.0% for balances of $2,001 to $4,000. A much larger rebate of 2.0% is provided on balances of over $6,000. But with the average U.S. credit card racking up just $2,500 a year in purchases, the cash rebate is likely to amount to only $15 or so. And GE's interest rate of 10.9 points above the prime rate (8.9 points above prime, for the more credit-worthy customers) is no bargain. The Discover Card's touted year-end rebate would amount to only $15 if you charged a total of $3,000.

In a different category are "affinity cards"—issued by a bank in conjunction typically with a museum, college, or charity. Each use of the card generates a donation to the organization. Usually it comes to very little, maybe 25 cents per transaction. If you regularly pay finance charges, you may very well qualify for a card elsewhere with a significantly lower interest rate; it might make more sense to write a check to the organization you wish to support than to pay needless interest charges on one of these cards.

Unfortunately, Susan P.'s story is not unusual. Fraud cost credit card companies more than $1.5 billion in the United States in 1992.

Retailer Credit Cards

There's one big exception to the recent trend in slightly lower credit card interest rates: cards issued by department stores and oil companies. Although they impose no annual fees, most such issuers still charge interest rates several percentage points above even the costlier Visa and MasterCards. For example, as this is being written, Burdine's still charges 21.0% a year and Macy's and Bullocks charge a phenomenal 21.6%. If you need to buy on credit and your department store or gas station accepts Visa, MasterCard, Discover, or Optima, use these cards and keep your store-brand card in your wallet where it can't hurt you.

WHAT TO WATCH OUT FOR

The incredible shrinking grace period. A "full grace period" used to mean 28 to 30 days—that is, an entire month. A few years ago, card issuers started to redefine "month" as only 25 days. And 20-day grace periods may be on the way. Robert V. discovered this when he was paying his "Citibank AAdvantage" Visa bill and just happened to notice that the "Payment Due" date was five days earlier than usual. In fact, his payment was due the next day. Knowing that a late payment would trigger hefty finance charges on his entire outstanding balance, which he fully paid each month, he called Citibank to complain. "Don't worry," he was told, the payment date would be moved back. He had merely been randomly selected for a "test" in which payment due dates were moved several days earlier.

Cardholders had not been specially notified of the change because the very fine, light print on the reverse side of the monthly statement disclosed that the grace period "is not less than 20 days"—although the bank had been allowing 25 days. So keep an eye out for shifting payment due dates on your monthly statement and read all the small "mouse type" in your contract and on your statements.

Some issuers effectively reduce grace periods simply by taking their time putting your bill in the mail. The end of the billing period might be, say, the 16th of the month, but when you check the postmark you might notice that your statement did not leave the issuer's office until the 23rd of the month. Before you realize it, your promised 25-day grace period has been reduced to a mere 18 days. Add the three or four days it may take the statement to reach you, and your effective grace period is now only 15 days. With normal postal delays, it's a good idea to mail your payment at least five days before the due date, further compressing your effective grace period into about a week.

Or issuers might effectively reduce the grace period on the other end by not crediting your payment right away. Bankcard Holders of America has heard quite a few complaints about this technique. If you suspect this is happening to you, send your payment by certified mail a few times to prove when you mailed it and to show the issuer that you're watching.

Minimum and skipped payments. Card issuers love it when you charge up a storm and then send them only the minimum payment each month. That's how they make their money. And they make it exceedingly easy to pay very little, typically requiring that you send only a minuscule portion of the total monthly balance. In fact, the average minimum payment percentage has been reduced from 5% to less than 3% since the mid-

1980s. But don't take the bait. You'll be paying for what seems like an eternity and forking over a lot more interest. For example, if you buy a $2,000 dining room set at a 15.9% interest rate and make only minimum monthly payments of 2.083%, it'll take you 207 months (more than 17 years) to pay it off, and you'll fork over $2,944 in interest. The dining room set will end up costing nearly $5,000.

The following chart, prepared for this book by Mark Eisenson, author of *The Banker's Secret*, shows what a major difference a slight difference in the minimum payment makes in your total payout. The chart assumes you borrowed $2,000.

You have to wonder how total interest or very similar costs for cards with the same annual interest

WHAT A DIFFERENCE THE MINIMUM PAYMENT MAKES*

Card	Interest rate	Minimum payment	Total interest cost	Months to payoff
CHASE**	19.8%	2.000%	$7,636	502
FCC/FIRST	19.8%	2.083%	$6,271	425
CHASE	17.65%	2.000%	$4,479	353
FIDELITY	17.15%	2.500%	$2,332	210
FCC/FIRST	17.1%	2.083%	$3,636	298
AMALGAMATED	12.25%	2.500%	$1,141	133
AFBA	10.15%	3.500%	$589	106
WACHOVIA	10.15%	3.000%	$714	122

*On a loan of $2,000.
**Although Chase credit cards are no longer routinely offered at 19.8%, interest on cash advances is still generally 19.8%.

GRACE BE UNTO YOU

Responding to the desire of many cardholders to make purchases without worrying about the grace period, the new Optima True Grace Card from American Express gives you 25 full days interest-free after the close of the account cycle, even if you carried over an outstanding balance. On top of that, there is no annual fee if you use the card at least three times a year. What's the catch? Well, the interest rate is only so-so—a promotional rate of 7.9% the first six months, prime plus 8.75% (16.5% as of this writing) thereafter for purchases, and prime plus 10.9% (18.15%) for cash advances. If your credit is good, you could do better than that elsewhere. On the other hand, you'd still have to be careful about losing your grace period unless you *always* pay the full balance.

your January and February card payments. Be careful! They're playing more Scrooge than Santa. Such "deferred payment" programs are a trap—you'll still accrue interest on your entire outstanding balance during the skipped months and end up with even more to pay off.

Instead, try to pay off as much principal as possible. *The Banker's Secret* explains that paying just $50 a month more than the minimum payment against $2,000 in credit card charges (at a 20% interest rate) would save more than $6,500 in interest and cut 30.5 years from the payment period. At the least, try to make your payment just after receiving your bill in order to lessen your average daily balance and the impact of compounding of finance charges.

Transfer tricks. If you're transferring an outstanding balance from your current high-interest-rate card to one with a lower rate, make sure the low interest rate on the transferred balance is the same as for new purchases, and not the higher rate sometimes charged for cash advances.

rate differs so much. The answer is in the hidden aspect of credit card math: the minimum percentage payment.

Moral: *Always* pay more than the minimum you can get away with because even a very small difference in your minimum payment makes a big difference in total interest cost and payoff period.

Around year-end holiday time, some issuers suggest that you skip

Tear into small pieces every unwanted credit card application. Otherwise a thief—maybe one of the people the industry refers to as a

"dumpster diver"—may find it in the garbage, fill it out with a supposedly "new" address, and get a card in your name. Organized dumpster-diver rings exist in many areas.

Be aware of the date your monthly statement usually arrives. If it doesn't show up within a few days of when it's supposed to, prevent "account takeover" by notifying the issuer immediately. Someone could have stolen the statement from the mail and used the information to order first-class plane tickets to some far-off locale.

Never disclose your account number in response to a call, postcard, or ad you receive. Give your number over the phone only to a reputable business that you call. For similar reasons, destroy anything that may have your credit card number on it, like travel ticket stubs and copies of charge slips. If you have to give your card number to make reservations, for example, try to get the name of the person asking.

Never write your address, phone number, or social security number on a credit card slip (or your credit card or social security number on a check), even if a merchant insists. There is no legal requirement to provide this information; your signature is enough.

Destroy your expired cards to prevent anyone from altering and using them.

Check the issuer's reputation before applying. Many cardholders are under the mistaken impression that Visa or MasterCard issue credit cards. They don't. And since it's the bank that actually issues and services the card, one Visa or MasterCard is not like another. The quality of service varies.

Judy H. learned this the hard way when she opened her monthly statement and noticed a charge for a rental car—in Hawaii. She called her card issuer, a medium-sized bank, to complain that she had never set foot in the Aloha State. They agreed to drop the charge once she showed them that she had incurred charges in her hometown on the same date she was supposedly driving around Hawaii. She was told to deduct the rental charge from her bill and that everything would be fine.

But it wasn't. The bank didn't remove the car rental charge until three more billing cycles. And Judy—who scrupulously paid her entire balance every month—started to accumulate finance charges on everything she charged on the card since she had not paid the bank her *entire* outstanding balance. When she called and wrote to the bank to complain about the finance charges, the bank deducted from her next bill only the finance charges pertaining to the car rental, but not the charges accrued on the rest of her outstanding balance. When more phone calls and letters still didn't resolve the problem, Judy threw up her hands and resignedly paid the remaining outstanding finance charges. Then she cancelled the card.

The second lesson of this story: You will become a "revolver" and owe finance charges on your entire outstanding balance unless you pay off *every penny* of your balance by the due date.

Use your grace period. One good way to take full advantage of your grace period is to make major purchases at the very beginning of your billing cycle. This allows you to add the one-month billing period *and* the grace period and therefore effectively borrow money for up to 45 days interest-free. Of course, this works only if you paid off your previous balance in full and therefore don't incur finance charges.

If you want to cancel your card, the law provides that you do not have to pay an annual fee as long as you notify the issuer in writing within 40 days of receiving the statement containing the fee.

Avoid a rejection complex. Since retailers' cards are often easier to get than a regular Visa or MasterCard, you might start to build a credit record by getting a card from a department store you regularly patronize. (Just don't take long to pay your balance; retailers' rates are very high.) If you have had a good payment record for a year or more, you might "graduate" to a Visa or MasterCard. But be sure not to apply for two or more cards within several months of each other; issuers have access to your credit records and may get nervous that you are overextending yourself and may not approve your application.

Another route to building your credit record is through a secured card. Secured cards look just like regular Visa or MasterCards, but they are secured by a bank account deposit equal to the amount of the card credit limit at the issuing institution. On the downside, you will not be able to draw on this account as long as you use the card. And interest rates may be higher than for regular cards; First Deposit National Bank, for example, charged 19.8% a year with *no grace period* plus a $35 annual fee. But these cards do offer one way to establish a solid credit history.

Merchants aren't supposed to impose a minimum credit card purchase requirement. Many—perhaps most—merchants do so anyway, even though it violates credit card company agreements with issuing banks. You're not getting full value out of your card if the store won't let you charge a $15 purchase on it. For three of the major cards issued, you can report the offending retailer by writing to Visa, U.S.A, Minimum Purchase, P.O. Box 8999, San Francisco, CA 94128; MasterCard International, P.O. Box 1288, Radio City Station, New York, NY 10101-1288; American Express, Executive Consumer Relations, 200 Vesey Street, New York, NY 10285-3130. MasterCard asks that you include the name, address, and telephone number of the merchant and a receipt from the purchase, if possible, which is a good procedure to follow for all three.

Depending on the law in your state, merchants may be prohibited from charging extra if you buy with a credit card. Call your state's Attorney General or consumer protection agency to find out.

■. **Where the cards are.** Probably the best listing of cheaper cards is by Bank-card Holders of America. For $4, this group will send you their latest list of Low Rate/No Fee credit cards. Write to 560 Herndon Parkway, Suite 120, Herndon, VA 22070; or call (800) 553-8025. In addition, RAM Research issues CardTrak, a monthly newsletter, with lots of credit card rates and tips, (800) 344-7714. RAM also sells a list of secured cards for $5.

■. **Swimming in credit card debt?** For just $15, Bankcard Holders of America will send you a Personal Credit Card Payment Plan. A computer program organizes your credit cards and details exactly which ones you should pay and when to pay them in order to retire your card debt as fast as possible. (See previous address.)

■. **You can dramatically** cut your credit card interest payments by paying even a few dollars more than the minimum payment every month. To order a newsletter, *The Banker's Secret Quarterly*, explaining the virtues of early payment of principal on all kinds of consumer loans, call (800) 255-0899. Also available is a computer program to help you calculate the best early payment scenarios.

■. **To help you avoid fraud, Visa USA** will send you a free booklet on card fraud and personal credit management; call (800) VISA-511 to order.

CHAPTER 32

BANKING ON BANKS

 *The Safety and Soundness of Your Accounts*

Y ou've probably seen one of those newspaper or TV bank ads depicting cheerful consumers saving money and time because their bank is so convenient and the staff so helpful. Unfortunately, feel-good bank ads rarely reveal anything very useful, such as the monthly checking fee or the early withdrawal penalty on a certificate of deposit (CD). And their pricing claims can be misleading. "Low minimum balances" can be a lot higher than the competition's, "free" checking can turn out to be expensive, and a savings account can fast become a "losing" account once hidden fees are paid.

You can save quite a bit of money by shopping around for a bank as carefully as you would shop for a VCR. For example, a 1993 ranking of 50 local banks based on fees and interest rates by the NYC Department of Consumer Affairs determined that when interest earnings and fees were totted up, a hypothetical customer with a consistent yearlong balance of $2,600 would have *made* $80.67 at the cheapest bank and *lost* $107.97 at the most expensive one.

THE BASICS

Checking Accounts

L et's start with checking accounts. There are two basic kinds, regular and NOW (negotiable order of withdrawal).

You might have opened your first checking account in high school or college. If that was in the 1970s or earlier, chances are you weren't charged more than 10 cents for each check you wrote, plus a modest check-printing fee. Since then, however, checking account fees have increased geometrically. A certified check that cost only 25 cents in 1979 will now set you back $2 or $3.

Still, if you check around for checking, you needn't overpay. The minimum balance to avoid a fee on a regular checking account could be as little as $100 or as much as $3,000, and the monthly service fee could range from only $1 to as much as $10.

"Regular checking" is the best choice if you have only a few hundred dollars in the bank, because the minimum balances to avoid fees and the fees themselves tend to be lower than for NOW "interest on checking" accounts. NOW checking accounts have significantly higher fees because interest is paid—although the interest may not amount to much, since interest rates plummeted in the early 1990s. Some NOW accounts pay a higher rate if you keep a bigger balance; these are called tiered interest rates.

Some banks offer what they call "relationship banking," which lets you add together all your account balances to reach the free-checking minimum.

How much can a NOW account cost? In 1993, Bank of America's relationship account required a combined $4,000 balance to avoid a $9 monthly fee. New York's Citibank, a national price leader, required customers to have an astounding $10,000 in combined balances to avoid paying $12 a month and 35 cents per check or automatic teller machine (ATM) withdrawal. A few banks have even started charging you for failing to use your ATM card within a certain time period. Not surprisingly, a CFA study found that ATMs generated $2 billion in profits for banks in 1993, and that banks made 78 cents pure profit for each ATM fee dollar.

Monthly and per-check charges aren't the whole fee story. Increasingly, fees are charged for the use of ATMs. Because ATMs save banks money, they were free when the machines were introduced in the late 1970s. But by the mid-1980s, as banks felt the pressure to make up for both their huge real-estate and third-world loan losses, they began viewing ATMs as revenue-producers in their own right. Besides charging up to 35 cents for a withdrawal or transfer if you fail to maintain a minimum balance, most banks now also charge special fees of up to $1 to use another bank's ATM in a shared network like NYCE or HONOR.

Some banks even charge $1 or $2 for the privilege of phoning to find out how much of your money they have.

Stop-payment order fees also are often hefty, ranging from $5 to $20. Be sure to ask the bank how long the stop is effective for. Usually, but not always, it'll last six months. Also, most banks put stops into effect immediately, but some take up to 24 hours.

How do you find the checking

> "**B**anks have a four-part strategy to earn fee income by gouging consumers. First, they are raising fees. Second, they are coming up with new fees. Third, they are making more people pay fees by raising the balances to avoid fees. And fourth, they are changing those balances from averages to minimums."
>
> —EDMUND MIERZWINSKI, Consumer Program Director, U.S. Public Interest Research Group

account that will cost you the least? Look first at savings banks. Generally speaking, savings banks—especially smaller, neighborhood banks —offer better deals than big commercial banks with many branches. The bigger banks used to be able to say that the convenience of having so many branches outweighed their higher costs, but now that even small savings banks have joined shared ATM networks, this argument is not as persuasive.

Next, calculate your average monthly balance and the number of checks you wrote each month for the last year or so and apply this experience to the different checking accounts at the banks you are considering. How often would you have fallen below the minimum balance for free checking? How much would you have paid in monthly, per-check, or ATM withdrawal fees? Use your final cost figures to compare competing banks. If two banks' costs are close and you're considering a NOW account, then include in your calculation how much you would earn on your money.

Debit cards. A new and increasingly popular way to access the money in your checking account that avoids checks altogether is the debit card. Debit cards look like credit cards, but they deduct the amount of your purchase directly from your checking account.

There are two kinds of debit cards: on-line and off-line. On-line debit cards work like an ATM card. Once you've punched your personal identification number (PIN) into a terminal in the store and the bank's computer verifies that you have enough money to cover the purchase, the sum is deducted from your checking account immediately. And there's the rub. Immediate deduction means you lose the interest you would get during the several days it can take a check to clear (i.e., you lose the "float"). The "float" could be as long as 45 days if you pay with a credit card (billing period plus grace period).

Some banks' ATM cards now double as on-line debit cards. In addition, Visa and MasterCard have rolled out on-line checking account debit services as add-ons to your bank ATM card. MasterCard calls its on-line service "Maestro" and Visa calls its service "Interlink."

Off-line debit cards, which are sponsored by Visa (Visa Debit) and MasterCard (MasterCard Debit) are accepted in the same places as the corresponding credit cards. Your debit card goes in the same machines to process your payment. Since it usually takes several days to clear the charge, you still enjoy a brief "float."

Debit cards aren't free. Issuing banks usually charge $10 or $15 a year for off-line debit cards. You might be charged as much as a dollar per transaction when you use an on-line card. You may also have a daily purchase limit of several hundred dollars.

How long to clear a check? Every bank should do the same thing when it comes to clearing a check. Because banks use your money for days without making it available to

YOUR MONEY...ALMOST

Item	Day funds are available	Day available for deposits over $5,000 and for new or problem accounts
LOCAL CHECKS	*2nd business day following day of deposit*	*7th business day following day of deposit*
NON-LOCAL CHECKS	*5th business day following day of deposit*	*11th business day following day of deposit*

you, the federal Expedited Funds Availability Act now limits how long banks can take to make deposited funds available to you. What the law requires is outlined in the chart above.

Cash, electronic payments, and certain low-risk checks (such as government checks) must be made available the first business day following the day of deposit.

Savings and Money Market Rate Accounts

There are two kinds of savings accounts: passbook accounts and statement savings accounts. With the former, you get a passbook in which your current balance and interest earnings are recorded. With the latter, you get a monthly or quarterly statement instead of a passbook, and you can access your money through an ATM; you may also be able to have your account status included on a monthly statement that presents the status of all your accounts at a bank.

The two most common methods of figuring how much interest you earn are "day-of-deposit to day-of-withdrawal" and "average daily balance." Day-of-deposit to day-of-withdrawal is better—you earn interest on every dollar every single day. The average daily balance method pays interest on the average daily balance for the month or quarter, depending on the bank. In addition, market rate accounts sometimes offer tiered interest rates; you earn at a lower rate if your balance goes below a minimum.

Money market rate accounts differ from savings accounts because they allow you to write checks, although usually no more than three a month. Banks introduced these accounts with interest rates higher than savings accounts to keep customers from defecting to money market funds. But these accounts still pay less than real money market funds, because they are insured by the Federal Deposit Insurance Corporation (FDIC).

Good news for all "deposit account" (savings, checking account, money market rate account, CD) customers: The federal Truth-in-Savings Law requires banks to adopt a uniform manner of disclosing how they figure your fees, interest rates, and yields, including minimum deposits and balances, and they must tell you this when you open your account and on periodic account statements after that. You now can compare banks through their APYs—annual percentage yields.

Certificates of Deposit

CDs tie up your money for a set period of time in return for a higher rate. As a general rule, the longer the term, the more you earn.

Shop around for the highest possible yield. Many local newspapers publish CD rate charts comparing area banks. Since you cannot deposit into or withdraw from a CD once you open it without paying a penalty, bank convenience should not be a major factor in your choice. In fact, it's not even necessary to visit the bank—in many cases, everything can be handled by mail.

When you compare one CD to another, compare the yield, not the rate. Interest on CDs is not necessarily compounded. Some CDs, such as those bought through brokers, pay only simple interest: For example, if the rate is 4% and you open a one-year CD for $1,000, you'll have $1,040 when it matures. CDs may also compound interest daily, weekly, quarterly, or even semiannually.

Don't worry about CD fees; there aren't any. But the penalty for early withdrawals is usually three months' interest on CDs of less than one year and six months' interest on others.

Banks have devised many clever new CD products to lure you away from other investments. These special CDs might promise to keep pace with increases in college costs or to double the average return of a stock index. Others offer variable rates—the rate could be indexed to U.S. Treasury bills and adjusted monthly, for example. Rule of thumb for these innovative CDs: No bank simply gives away money.

Take Citibank, for example. It is offering a "Stock Index Insured Account." This CD, available for retirement savings, promises to pay two times the average percentage increase in the Standard & Poor's 500 Stock Index over a five-year term. Sounds unbeatable, doesn't it? But in a critique in *Time* magazine, popular financial adviser Andrew Tobias explained that the bank holds onto the stock dividends and doesn't double the five-year gain (if there is one)—but doubles the Standard & Poor *average* annual gain over five years. The declines over five years could reduce the advances, perhaps to nothing.

Credit Unions

Credit unions are financial institutions open to people who have a "common bond." No, a passion for blues music or bungee jumping does not qualify. You usually have to belong to a sponsoring labor union or work for a particular employer to join. Approximately 37 million Americans belong to federally chartered credit unions.

The rationale for credit unions is that people gain financially when they pool their money and lend directly to one another without shareholders to siphon off profits. A 1992 survey by the publication *Bank Rate Monitor* bore this out: Credit unions pay about one percentage point more on CDs, and their rates for auto loans, credit cards, and personal loans are, on average, below the national average.

To top it off, credit unions also typically charge lower fees *and* have ATMs. They managed to avoid the banking industry crisis of the 1980s because they made relatively few of the types of commercial loans that got banks into such deep trouble.

One indication that credit unions must be a pretty good deal is that the banking industry is accusing them of competing unfairly and wants Washington to regulate and tax credit unions more severely.

Bank Account Insurance

It used to be that each account at a bank was insured for up to $100,000. If the bank failed, you could have a million dollars in your name at one bank and you wouldn't lose a dime, as long as it was divided into at least ten different $100,000 accounts.

It's not so simple anymore. Now the FDIC adds up every dollar you have in the bank in a *separately titled account* in each *ownership category* and reimburses you only for a maximum $100,000 per title (i.e., owner name(s)) in an ownership category at each bank. The most common ownership categories are individual accounts, joint accounts, trust accounts, and retirement accounts such as individual retirement accounts (IRAs) and Keoghs. You still can hold several accounts and each will be covered, as long as each account is in a different ownership category or your name appears along with a different name on each account.

You also used to be able to count on the government to bail you out if your bank failed and your deposits exceeded the $100,000 ceiling. But in 1991, Congress passed a law making it harder for the government to reimburse depositors for amounts exceeding the $100,000 insurance cap. Besides slowing depletion of the Bank Insurance Fund, the idea behind the law was to get large depositors to pressure banks into operating more soundly—which seems an unfair expectation of the not untypical middle-class American family that just sold its house and is parking the proceeds at a bank for a while.

So you have to be careful. Over 8,500 depositors lost a total of $108 million when American Savings Bank of White Plains, New York, failed in the early 1990s. The *Wall Street Journal* reported on one depositor, Helen Patterson, who had saved more than $100,000 to buy her retirement home. The FDIC didn't fully reimburse her.

How can you avoid Ms. Patterson's fate?

Several warning signs should tell you of a serious problem with your bank before the local TV news program shows panicky depositors lined up at its front door. If you

COVERING YOUR ASSETS

Here's how "Bonnie" and "Clyde" can deposit $600,000 in the same bank and still be protected.

INDIVIDUAL ACCOUNTS
Bonnie $100,000
Clyde $100,000

JOINT ACCOUNTS
Bonnie and Clyde . . . $100,000

JOINT ACCOUNTS
Bonnie as trustee
for Clyde $100,000

RETIREMENT ACCOUNTS
Bonnie $100,000
Clyde $100,000

read in the business pages of your local newspaper that the bank has been losing money for several quarters, that its problem loans come very close to or exceed its loan-loss reserves, or that the bank's capital ratio has dropped under 5%, then you should start to be concerned.

Unfortunately, there's no free phone number to call to learn if the bank holding your nest egg is about to fold. The FDIC keeps lists of problem banks, but they won't tell you if your bank is on it because that could start a bank run. But for $10 you can learn how your bank rates on a soundness scale. (See **HELP** at the end of this chapter.)

Even if your savings account is fully FDIC-insured, you should still be concerned about your bank's soundness. It could take a while to get your money should your bank fail. Or your bank could be taken over by another, stronger bank you do not care for, perhaps with higher fees and/or lower interest rates. Weak banks are tempted to raise fees and lay off staff, which can mean worse service.

Bank Safety

Banks lose billions of dollars a year through fraud. Thieves with the right information can pilfer personal accounts—a social security number can be used to order new checks sent to a "changed" account address. Easy access to your credit reports (see "Consumer Privacy," page 562 for a full discussion) can provide thieves with even more information that's useful for impersonating you. Or, if thieves have your ATM card and somehow learn your PIN, they can go on a spending spree with your money.

Should you become an ATM fraud victim, don't panic. The chart on the following page shows how much of a loss from your bank accounts you can be liable for. (If your state's law or your contract with the issuer provides for lower limits, those limits apply instead of the limits in this chart.)

Banks are reluctant to release figures on ATM crime. But it's clearly a problem. Crooks know you have money when you're leaving an ATM, and they can force you to withdraw up to the daily maximum. Almost any kind of card with a magnetic stripe can open an ATM vestibule door.

In response, New York City en-

IF YOU LOSE YOUR ATM CARD

When you report card loss to the bank	Monetary limit on your liability for unauthorized use
BEFORE FINDER OR THIEF USES IT	*Responsible for no charges*
WITHIN TWO BUSINESS DAYS AFTER YOU REALIZE IT IS MISSING	*$50*
AFTER TWO BUSINESS DAYS FROM WHEN YOU REALIZE IT IS MISSING	*$500*
MORE THAN 60 DAYS AFTER RECEIVING THE BANK STATEMENT WITH THE UNAUTHORIZED ACTIVITY	*The sky's the limit. (Don't forget that a thief with your ATM card might also be able to access your overdraft line of credit.)*

acted an ATM safety law that could become a model for the nation. ATMs are required to have surveillance cameras, rear-view mirrors and door locks that only the bank's own ATM cards can open. Other localities are now considering similar laws. Also, Chicago and Los Angeles are pioneering a new concept: ATMs in or around police precinct buildings, locations that provide potential customers with greater security.

WHAT TO WATCH OUT FOR

Checking Accounts

New fees and tricky rules coming down the pike. Banks are thinking up new fees every day. A few have started charging a fee for each day your account is overdrawn. Some banks are reportedly thinking about charging an annual fee for your ATM card. In 1994, 85% of banks charged a fee if you unwittingly deposited a check that bounced—up from 35% in 1991—and some banks charged for closing a checking account within six months of opening it. There may also be a "dormant fee" if the account is inactive for six months.

ChexSystem. Big Brother is watching you. When you open an account, most banks will check you out with ChexSystem, a national computer database, to see if you have previously bounced checks or engaged in some sort of financial shenanigans. Since about the only notice of this review that many banks give you is a small ChexSystem sign somewhere in the branch, you may be incorrectly or unfairly listed and not know it—and thus not know to challenge it. (See **HELP** at the end of this chapter for contact information.)

Many banks will automatically

reject you if your name was added to the ChexSystem database during the last five years. Consider this story from San Francisco Consumer Action about Amy L.: She had a joint bank account with her husband, who had bounced $8,000 worth of checks. Although they were later divorced and she paid all the bounced check fines, she was turned down for a checking account because *her* name was listed with ChexSystem.

Non-return of cancelled checks. Rising numbers of banks offer lower-cost "truncated accounts" that send you only an "image" of your check and only if you ask for it and pay a fee. Be sure to ask before opening the account if you get your cancelled checks—or at least copies of them—back automatically.

Stopping payment on a check. Sure, you're angry that the VCR is still broken after you spent good money on a repair. But think twice before stopping payment on the check you gave the repair shop. It could then be treated as a bounced check, with potentially unpleasant legal and credit-rating consequences for you.

Leaky debit card security. Security may not be as good with debit cards as with checks or credit cards. The applicable law says that you could be liable for a somewhat bigger portion of unauthorized withdrawals than you would be with a credit card—up to $500 if you don't notify the bank within two business days of learning that your card is missing. The sky's the limit

if you don't notify them after more than 60 days. Don't forget, a thief may also access a credit line linked to your checking account.

Savings and Money Market Rate Accounts

Savings accounts were pretty basic in the '70s. You needed only $1 to open a passbook account, and if you were a kid and earned $200 for a summer of chasing toddlers or pushing mowers, you didn't have to worry about the bank whittling away most of it by the next summer. Now you have to be careful.

Balance minimums. If your savings account balance falls under a minimum level, you are likely to be charged monthly or quarterly penalty fees—and to forfeit interest. The fee itself could be as high as $5 a month.

Stiff check fees. Money market rate accounts may charge a stiff per-check fee if you write more than three checks a month.

Certificates of Deposit

Low interest rates. You can no longer rely on three- and six-month CDs to pay a significantly higher rate than savings accounts.

Bank takeovers. If another bank takes over your bank, the CD interest rate might be reduced. You'll be notified of this and given a period of time within which to withdraw your money without penalty.

Automatic rollovers. The bank will automatically roll over your

CD for the same term if you ignore the maturity notice. You might not want this to happen if the new rate is lower or if you need the money.

Hidden tiering. Tiered-rate CDs pay more if you deposit more. The new Truth-in-Savings law requires deposit accounts, *except for CDs*, to disclose tiering. Ask, or you might lose the chance to get a better rate by depositing a few dollars more.

STEALING COOKIES FROM A BABY

In 1994, ten-year-old Ryan Lorraine Cobb told a panel of Congress members what happened to the $54.50 she had earned for selling 109 boxes of Girl Scout cookies. The State Department Federal Credit Union charged her $12 when a check someone had given her bounced. She was charged another $12 when it didn't clear a second time. And she was hit for another $15 for bouncing a $7 check she had written because she didn't know the deposited check had bounced. Word got around, and besides testifying before Congress, Ryan appeared on the David Letterman Show. The embarrassed credit union gave Ryan back her $39 in fees and donated an additional $100 to the Girl Scouts.

Credit Unions

Few mortgage bargains. Mortgage interest rates tend to be the same as they are at banks in the same markets, since all mortgage originators (including credit unions) unload their mortgages on the same secondary market.

A limited number of offices. Unlike banks, most credit unions don't have a lot of branches, and their locations might not be convenient.

A credit union isn't *always* cheaper. Some savings banks are very competitive, and rates and fees vary among credit unions.

Bank Safety and Soundness

Warning! Don't come too close to $100,000 in one account. Interest earnings could propel you above the limit by the time a CD matures. (You can get around this by asking the bank to send you periodic interest checks.)

Private deposit insurance. Almost anything can be insured these days, including the possibility that you'll lose money in a bank failure. This insurance is of limited value: The company that offers the policy is choosy about the bank, rejects all savings and loan institutions, the policies last only six months, and can be cancelled with only 30 days notice. Perhaps the only plus of such a policy is that, if it is not renewed, you'll have been alerted that your bank may be having financial problems.

THE SMARTER CONSUMER

Checking Accounts

Check into check-printing fees. You'll probably pay less if you don't use the bank's designated check-printer. (See **HELP** at the end of this chapter for alternatives.)

Consider overdraft protection. You'll pay a high interest rate, but you only pay if you use it. As long as you are overdrawn for only a few days, an overdraft loan will probably still be significantly cheaper than the bank's bounced check fee.

Ask about lower-cost accounts. "Lifeline," senior citizen, veterans, and student accounts may allow you to write from six to eight checks a month for one relatively reasonable flat monthly fee. But look for a potentially steep per-check charge if you exceed this limit. Under the 1994 New York lifeline account law, the bank can treat your account like a regular account for the months when this occurs.

Demand a waiver of unwarranted bounced check fees. If you wrote several checks one day and every one bounced, the bank may have played a little game with you—clearing the largest one first and treating it as an overdraft, thereby ensuring that the others also bounce. This generates a separate bounced check fee for each check.

Demand to know which check cleared first and ask for fee waivers if it was the biggest. Banks engage in this tactic with increasing frequency. *American Banker,* an industry publication, reported one bank executive exclaiming, "Since we started clearing the largest first, our income in our small bank has gone up over $80,000 a year!"

Actually read the pamphlets banks stuff in your monthly checking statement, especially anything printed in small type and black and white—it's probably telling you about a fee increase or a money-costing rule change.

Savings Accounts

The fee/interest rate balance. Evaluate whether you are going to keep enough money in a savings or market-rate account to offset fees. You might find it makes more sense to keep all your money in an interest-bearing checking account—or even a regular checking account—if the fees and interest forfeiture would eat into your savings.

Certificates of Deposit

Analyze the yield. When CD-shopping, ask the bank how much money you will have at the end of the term instead of relying on the annual yield to compare offerings. Advertised yields are good only for one-year CDs. If you are buying, say, a six-month CD and you let it roll over when it matures, the rate could drop later in the year and the actual one-year yield could be a lot less than you had anticipated. Odd-length terms, like 11 months and 15 months, make it especially difficult to use the annual yield to compare banks' CD offerings.

Diversify your CD maturities. If you want to put a lot of your money into bank CDs, buy a mixture of short- and long-term ones. If rates decline, some of your CDs will still be earning excellent yields. If rates go up, you'll have funds to reinvest at the new yields.

Shop the nation for a higher yield. (See **HELP** at the end of this chapter to learn how.) Another way to earn more is with insured bank CDs bought through stockbrokers—although the broker takes a small fee and the market price of your investment may go down if CD rates rise. On the other hand, you avoid early-withdrawal penalties (there may be a small early-withdrawal service charge). If you go through a broker, ask for the name of the CD's bank(s) and check if they are financially sound, by checking the warning signs mentioned on page 298, or by calling Veribanc (see **HELP** for contact information).

If you opt for a variable-rate CD, make sure it has a high minimum interest rate (i.e., "floor") and be sure to find out the index it is keyed to so you can follow it in the newspaper.

Credit Unions

Ensure that you're insured. Double check that the credit union is insured by the National Credit Union Administration (NCUA). If it is among the 95% or so that are insured, you'll enjoy the same degree of deposit protection as if you were at a federally insured bank.

Bank Security and Safety

One reason to put money in a bank instead of under a mattress is to keep it safe. But if you aren't careful, the mattress could turn out to be the better depository.

Immediately report any unusual transactions that appear on your monthly statement.

Try to use ATMs during the day. If you must use an ATM at night, make sure it is well-lit—both inside and out—and in a well-traveled location. Stay clear of ATMs with people loitering about.

Opt for a unique PIN. Make sure your ATM PIN does not match any other numbers you carry, like your birth date or the first digits of your social security number. Don't write the PIN anyplace where someone might see it.

Don't leave your ATM receipts behind. Crooks can get useful information from them, like your account number and balance. If they also get your PIN, real damage can be done. PINs are sometimes obtained by sharp-eyed people hanging around ATMs and even by people using binoculars to watch your hand movements as you punch in your number.

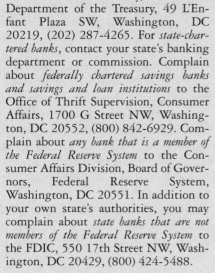

▪ If you get nowhere with the bank branch manager, take your complaints to a higher authority. For *federally chartered commercial banks*, complain to the Director of Consumer Activities, Comptroller of the Currency, Department of the Treasury, 49 L'Enfant Plaza SW, Washington, DC 20219, (202) 287-4265. For *state-chartered banks*, contact your state's banking department or commission. Complain about *federally chartered savings banks and savings and loan institutions* to the Office of Thrift Supervision, Consumer Affairs, 1700 G Street NW, Washington, DC 20552, (800) 842-6929. Complain about *any bank that is a member of the Federal Reserve System* to the Consumer Affairs Division, Board of Governors, Federal Reserve System, Washington, DC 20551. In addition to your own state's authorities, you may complain about *state banks that are not members of the Federal Reserve System* to the FDIC, 550 17th Street NW, Washington, DC 20429, (800) 424-5488.

▪ Cheaper checks. Current Inc. sells 200 basic checks for $6.95; call (800) 533-3973. Checks in the Mail also has low prices; call (800) 733-4443—you can get all the rainbow and scenery designs you want.

▪ Certificates of deposit. To find the highest-paying CDs, check business sections of major national newspapers like *USA Today* and *The Wall Street Journal* or the weekly financial paper, *Barron's*. Or subscribe to the newsletter, *Highest Yields*, by calling (800) 327-7717.

▪ Bank soundness. To get a $10 safety rating of your bank, call Veribanc at (800) SAFETY-3 or (800) 44-BANKS. The ratings are updated every three months. If you know how to read financial statements, for $2.40 you can order your bank's quarterly balance sheet, called a "Call Report," from the federal government; call (800) 843-1669 to order.

▪ For further explanation of how to figure out how safe your bank is, read the book, *How to Keep Your Savings Safe*, by Walter L. Updegrave, an editor of *Money* magazine (Crown Publishers, 1992). $19.00

▪ Need help finding a credit union? Call (800) 356-5710. (In New York State, it's (800) 342-5710.)

▪ See if you are listed with ChexSystem, and why. You are entitled to a free report as well as to insert a 100-word rebuttal in it. Write to ChexSystems, Inc., Attn: Customer Relations, 1550 East 79th Street, Minneapolis, MN 55425.

CHAPTER 33

MUTUAL FUNDS

A Good CD Alternative?

Millions of Americans have responded to low bank deposit rates by voting with their feet—fleeing banks for alternative investments. Savers long accustomed to certificates of deposit (CDs) paying 6% and 7% annually are not easily accepting 3.0% during the 1990s.

But banks haven't given up. They've been selling other kinds of investments, typically mutual funds, which have the potential to perform better than CDs—hence Citibank's advertising slogan, "Wall Street Comes to Citibank."

Independent mutual fund companies have also stepped up their advertising campaigns targeted to dissatisfied bank depositors. Increasing numbers of Americans are coming to associate "Magellan" with a popular mutual fund rather than with a 16th-century explorer and, thanks to prime-time TV ads, the Dreyfus lion is becoming as well known as MGM's. All of this marketing muscle being put to work helps explain why mutual fund assets increased 600% from $370 billion in 1984 to $2.2 *trillion* in 1994!

Of course, Americans have also been drawn to mutual funds by the promise of lucrative returns. According to one analysis, from 1988 to 1993 you would have enjoyed a return of only 38.75% if you had a six-month CD and kept rolling it over, compared to 78.12% for the balanced-mutual fund index and 91.9% for the growth mutual fund index, provided all dividends were reinvested.

But past performance is no guarantee of how a fund will do in the future. Millions of investors learned this the hard way when some 93% of the mutual funds listed in *The Wall Street Journal*'s daily charts lost money in the first half of 1994. The dangers of "derivatives" contained in mutual funds—complex contracts that "derive" their value from underlying investments and whose value can fluctuate wildly— have also been in the news. So with the bloom off the mutual fund rose, the industry's meteoric growth is slowing as cautious investors and savers reconsider alternatives.

Be cautious, but don't be scared away. Many mutual funds remain superior investments. The trick is knowing how to read prospectuses and ask questions of the fund's customer service representatives so that you'll understand exactly what a fund is investing in and the true amount of risk you're taking on. Invest your time before you invest your money.

THE BASICS

What's a Mutual Fund?

Maybe you always were interested in playing the stock market but weren't confident enough of your investment prowess to jump in. Well, mutual funds allow you to participate in the financial markets and leave the heavy thinking to the experts.

This is possible because you pool your money with other investors by buying shares in a mutual fund corporation, not in individual investments. The fund managers then buy bonds, stocks, or money-market securities. A fund portfolio could include a few dozen or a few hundred different stocks, bonds, or other investments. So besides getting professional management, mutual funds may be advantageous because your portfolio, and therefore your risk, is diversified. With one in four U.S. households now invested in mutual funds, there now is more money in mutual funds than in FDIC-insured bank accounts. There are 6,000 dif-

> "**P**eople are pouring money into mutual funds to the tune of $1 billion a day. . . . By some estimates, the funds could top $4 trillion by the end of the decade."
>
> —*Business Week,* January 18, 1993

ferent mutual funds—more than the number of stocks listed on the New York Stock Exchange.

It's easy to buy into a mutual fund. Just call a mutual fund company or broker's toll-free "800" number to order a prospectus. You can also buy through a financial planner. Most funds require an initial investment of $500 to $3,000.

Increasing numbers of investors buy mutual funds at banks. It is estimated that banks sell as much as 30% of all mutual funds, up from virtually zero in the early 1980s. Why such growth? People trust banks, and it's easy to buy mutual funds at the same place you have your checking and savings accounts. A few of the big banks even sell mutual fund shares through their ATMs. And some banks have taken to posting bond yields next to the usual charts of CD rates. To make it even easier, banks are conveniently beginning to report the status of your mutual funds along with your other accounts in one monthly mailing.

Now for an issue of prime concern, especially to people thinking of investing in a mutual fund for the first time: risk. Like the securities they are comprised of, mutual fund values can go down as well as up. You own "shares" in a mutual fund corporation, not absolute dollars. If you must have complete safety and if you need to know exactly how much you'll have earned a few years hence, keep your money in a bank account.

But if you can take some volatility in the short term, mutual funds give you a better chance of realizing significant long-term gains.

Types of Mutual Funds

Money market funds invest in short-term debt securities in the money market, such as CDs and U.S. Treasury bills. Risk level is considered the lowest among mutual funds.

Bond funds, naturally, invest in corporate and government bonds. What's the risk in a bond fund? Bond fund values can tumble if interest rates jump, because investors earn better yields in new issues. The basic principle is that bond yield moves inversely to prices on the

bond market. The risk is magnified by the effect of group psychology. If yields begin to climb strongly, many bond investors—especially neophytes who have been switching from bank CDs in large numbers— could get ice-cold feet and pull out of the bond market in a hurry, further depressing prices and scaring still more investors into leaving, creating a downward price spiral.

Of course, you get your entire principal back if you hold onto an individual bond until maturity as long as it doesn't default, although you might not if you bail out of a bond fund at a time of rising interest rates. Still, bond funds tend to be less volatile than equity, or stock, funds (see below).

Municipal bond funds are popular in high-tax states because you don't have to pay state or local taxes on the earnings. But bond-rating agencies are downgrading some local government bonds because the politicians are either not raising taxes or cutting spending enough, leading to chronic budget deficits and reduced investor confidence.

What are the chances of a bond defaulting? Pretty remote. And with lots of different bonds in a fund, you spread your default risk even wider.

Some bond funds are much riskier than others, which is why you should always understand exactly what is in the bond fund before you buy. Many people who bought into First Investors "Fund for Income" learned this the hard way. Some of the investors didn't understand they were actually buying junk bonds. Kenneth and Mary

CONSUMER SAVINGS

Year	% of funds in mutual funds	% of funds in banks
1983	15%	85%
1985	20%	80%
1987	29%	71%
1989	34%	68%
1991	39%	61%
1993	53%	47%

W. of Barkhamsted, Connecticut, lost most of their life savings, amounting to over $60,000. A sales representative had told them the fund was "very secure." When they expressed concern, the company representative assured them that the fluctuation would "correct itself." It didn't.

U.S. government securities are, of course, backed by Uncle Sam; if he defaults then we're *all* in deep trouble.

Equity (stock) funds tend to be more volatile than bond funds. Some stock funds emphasize high dividend-paying equities, while others stress earning high market gains. Sector funds specialize in the stocks and bonds of particular industries; they are especially volatile. If you want more stability, think about buying an index fund. These invest in the stocks included in well known stock indexes, such as the Standard & Poor 500.

International funds invest in foreign stocks and bonds. The level of risk depends on the type of investment. Generally, though, foreign funds are riskier. Some foreign markets are not as tightly regulated as ours, markets in some foreign countries tend to be more volatile, and currency fluctuations might erode fund value.

Gold and precious metal funds. If you're a pessimist and believe we're about to face a major war or a domestic uprising, you can always retreat to these investments—as well as to your fortified mountain re-

doubt. But risk is high the rest of the time.

Funds can also be "load" and "no-load." A "load" is a flat upfront sales commission of about 3% to 6%, although 8% is not unheard of. Most of the funds sold at banks and through brokers are load funds. No-load funds are usually purchased direct from the fund company and charge no commissions, although some discount brokers also sell them. A "back-end load" fund charges fees (ranging from 0.5% to 6.0%) when you sell your shares. Often these fees decline the longer you hold the fund. Generally—and especially if you are investing short-term—you should favor no-load funds, because all of your money goes to work for you right away.

Several different indicators can be used to compare fund performance. You will often see fund ads touting the yield. This is computed by dividing total dividends for a time period by the current price per share. Yield is important, but a more comprehensive and potentially useful indicator is *total annual return*. It takes into account yield as well as changes in market value. A fund with a high yield may have shrinking asset values and, therefore, a reduced total return.

Some other indicator terms you may hear include *net investment income* (or loss), which is what the fund is earning in dividends and interest, after expenses, and *net realized and unrealized gains* (losses). *Net asset value* (NAV) is the price per fund share, which is the same

WHAT YOU DON'T KNOW CAN HURT YOU

In November, 1993, *American Banker*, an industry publication, spot-checked ten New York City bank branches for compliance with new mutual fund consumer disclosure rules. In only two of the branches did the staff volunteer that mutual funds, unlike bank deposits, are not federally insured. Mutual fund fees were seldom mentioned and inappropriate investment recommendations were also heard.

count and administration fees of 0.2% to 1.0%. There also may be a Section 12b-1 fee (named after a section of the securities regulation) of as much as 0.75%, which is the percentage of the fund assets spent on marketing. Try to pick funds with 12b-1 fees below 0.25%.

When comparing funds, be sure to consider the expenses charged by the fund, as measured by the total expense ratio. Stock funds tend to have higher ratios, usually around 1.5%, because of the work involved in picking stocks. Basic bond funds should charge around 1%. Remember that with the long-term effect of compounding, a slight difference in expense ratio really mounts up over time.

Mutual funds specialize in a particular investment strategy. You choose among funds based on how well the fund matches your financial goals and your tolerance for risk. The chart on the next page summarizes the most basic major mutual fund objectives categories.

as total fund assets divided by the number of shares, after distributions. Both the NAV and changes in NAV from the previous day are reported in daily newspaper quotations of mutual fund performance.

To decide which stock fund to buy, start by comparing the fund's performance (without dividends reinvested) over the last several years with one of the stock indexes, such as the Standard & Poor 500 and the Dow Jones Industrials. There are several well-known bond indexes to use for comparing bond fund returns with, such as the Shearson Lehman Government-Corporate Bond Index.

Be sure to find out about redemption fees of 1% to 2% of assets for early withdrawal, transaction or exchange fees, management or advisory fees of 0.2% to 1.6%, and ac-

WHAT TO WATCH OUT FOR

Tricky advertising. The Securities and Exchange Commission has fairly strict advertising rules, but due to understaffing, the rules are not enforced very well. So take mutual fund ads with several grains of salt.

That's what the New York City Department of Consumer Affairs did when in 1993 staff reviewed over 50 mutual fund advertisements that ran in daily newspapers

Fund Objective	What It Invests In	Pros and Cons
AGGRESSIVE GROWTH	*Stocks of companies expected to have extra-high earning potential, including new and small companies.*	*High risk, more volatility, and low dividend payments, but high potential for excellent long-term growth.*
GROWTH	*Equities of companies expected to increase in value, especially larger and blue-chip companies.*	*Relatively high-risk; may have bigger "net realized and unrealized" gains—or losses—than with less growth-oriented funds. Dividend income is likely to be small.*
INCOME	*Income-producing securities that provide sizeable periodic payments; includes bonds as well as stocks that pay dividends.*	*Medium risk; when stock market drops, loss is cushioned.*
REASONABLE INCOME WITH MODERATE GROWTH— "BALANCED" FUNDS	*Stocks that have the potential for rapid increase in value and bonds, which provide a steady income stream and are not as volatile.*	*Income is reasonable—so is risk level—but growth potential is not as great as with riskier funds.*
SAFETY	*CDs, U.S. Treasury securities, commercial paper.*	*Low risk, but earnings are lower, too.*

and financial magazines. They found some very serious problems, including these gimmicks:

■ Misuse of the words "guaranteed" and "insured." An ad headline for Franklin's *Valuemark II* fund claimed, "Retirement Income Guaranteed for Life." The guarantee was provided by an insurance company, which promised that future payments would continue if the mutual fund went sour. But the "guarantee" in the ad was really

only as solid as the insurance company that made it. A Franklin customer service representative recently admitted to the Department of Consumer Affairs that *Valuemark II* "has some risk."

■ Exaggeration. One Dreyfus ad trumpeted, "High Yields Without High Risk." Not exactly.

■ Claims of "no fees." The *Vanguard Small Capitalization Stock Fund* advertised, "the Portfolio does not pay investment advisory fees." But the prospectus said the fund pays 0.06% in "management expenses" and a $10 annual account maintenance fee. When it comes down to it, no fund generously provides the public with a free service.

Sales spiels. As confusing as the ads themselves are the claims you hear when you call a fund's "800" number for information. A well-rehearsed representative may tell you your money will be safe because the fund has performed extremely well —which is no assurance at all of future performance. Or, if you ask about fees, they'll omit a few. Some will try to sell you investments that are inappropriate for your financial circumstances. Others cite high historical total returns; further checking might reveal that returns were extraordinarily high a decade earlier but that recent returns have been lackluster, although the average of all the years—the figure cited—still sounds impressive.

Brokers aren't necessarily more straightforward. A broker might steer you to a fund with a higher commission—good for the broker but maybe not so good for you. Nonetheless, it's not all that difficult to choose a fund if you follow the advice in this chapter.

In defense of brokers, many do have real investment expertise and familiarity with a wide range of funds. If you're a novice, a broker might provide some comforting hand-holding, too.

Believing the fund is government-insured. A 1993 survey for the American Association of Retired Persons and the North American Securities Dealers Association found that a disturbing 39% of consumers whose banks offer mutual funds incorrectly responded that the FDIC insures mutual funds —and another 43% said they did not know. Some banks are only sowing more confusion by attaching names to their funds that could make people believe the bank and the fund are insured as one. NationsBank sells *NationsFunds* and Boston's BayBanks has *BayFunds*, for example. If you buy a fund at a bank, remember that mutual funds are not insured by the government, despite the FDIC decal on the bank's door.

Banks call it "cross-selling" when they deploy their usual staff, accustomed to marketing CDs and checking accounts, to push alternative investments. Watch out! Cross-selling can get quite aggressive; staff earn commissions, and even the tellers might be awarded $10 bonuses for successfully referring you to a sales agent.

And if you are told the fund is

EXPERT ERRORS

In September 1992, *Money* magazine interviewed 32 of the practitioners listed under "Financial Planners" in the Santa Rosa, California, Yellow Pages. *Money* reporters asked a series of questions about professional practices and knowledge. More than half of them answered at least a third of the questions incorrectly.

insured by the SIPC—the Securities Investor Protection Corporation—know that this only protects you if the brokerage goes belly up, not if the investments themselves perform poorly. It's nothing at all like FDIC deposit insurance.

Departure of a star manager. The fund manager who was responsible for the stellar returns that attracted you may leave for another fund. You might want your money to follow.

THE SMARTER CONSUMER

Always read the prospectus before buying. Don't buy a fund based solely on an advertisement or on what a sales agent or broker said. Yes, these 15- to 20-page documents are about as reader-friendly as an advanced economics textbook and often bury or obfuscate important information, such as whether the fund invests in derivatives, the degree of market risk, and the fees charged. Still, if you know what to look for and are patient, you'll find important information about the fund's past performance, objectives, and risk. To summarize:

■ *The investment objectives* section says what the fund is primarily interested in—for example, growth or current income—and describes its principal investments.

■ *What the fund invests in* tells you about the kinds of bonds or stock it buys. You'll find out here if it buys low-investment grade bonds. It could take some digging, but you should also be able to discover if a fund invests in derivatives. Derivatives are very complex and possibly risky investments—usually traded over-the-counter—that derive their value from underlying assets, which could be anything from a stock index to a rate. And this value can change dramatically. Most major funds say somewhere, somehow that they can use derivatives. Among indications that it does: The prospectus says the fund "may invest" in other securities, such as "options, futures, forwards, swaps." Or derivatives could be disguised with terms like "income-enhancement opportunities" or "portfolio investment techniques."

Also look out for "asset-backed securities"; some funds were badly eroded in the first half of 1994 because their investments in mortgage-backed securities went down when interest rates went up.

■ Under *the investment risk* section you'll find important statistics that indicate how volatile the fund has been over the years, how much it has paid out (dividends from net investment income), how much was earned from trading securities (distributions from net realized capital gains), and change in net asset value (the change in a share's purchase price).

■ *The summary of fees and expenses* is also very important; high expenses could turn a potentially good investment into a mediocre one.

■ *Description of managers' experience* is supposed to tell you the manager's name, how long he or she has been managing the fund, and business background. But funds managed by a committee need not disclose names. And, unfortunately, prospectuses tell you barely any more than the most basic information about managers, often omitting their academic degrees or their responsibilities at their previous jobs.

Look for longer-term gain. Don't necessarily buy a fund based on one or two high-return years. Sure, fantastic performance in the last year or two may show that the fund managers have real savvy, and maybe they'll repeat their feat next year. Or it could have been luck. Unless you really know what you're doing, it's best to go for funds with solid returns over several years—the longer the better.

Get more information. You might request a free Statement of Additional Information (SAI) and the fund's annual report before buying. You will find a detailed list of its investments and learn more about the fund's investment strategy, which is useful to know before you sink real money into any fund.

Don't put all your eggs in one basket. Protect yourself by diversifying as much as your investment objectives allow. You can do this by investing in one fund that in turn buys shares in an array of other funds that invest in a variety of areas and have different investment objectives. Or you can devise your own spread of mutual fund investments, perhaps with the advice of an independent financial planner.

▪▪ There are many ways to find out about a mutual fund's past performance. *Business Week* magazine publishes an annual survey. Or, for $35.95 you can get *The Mutual Fund Encyclopedia*, which comes out annually and rates over a thousand funds. Call Dearborn Financial Publishing at (800) 326-6941 to order. An old standby is *Morningstar Mutual Funds*, a newsletter that costs nearly $400 a year but that you might be able to read for free at your local library. A cheaper, truncated *Morningstar* newsletter that might be all you need is available for $65 a year; call (800) 876-5005.

▪▪ If you want to know more about mutual fund risk, perhaps the most comprehensive yet understandable explanation is found in a chart in Jane Bryant Quinn's book, *Making the Most of Your Money* (Simon & Schuster, 1991).

CHAPTER 34

RETIREMENT NEST EGGS

 IRAs, 401(k)s, and Annuities

Will Social Security benefits have to be scaled
back someday when
baby boomers retire *en masse*? Will
the federal government insure your
woefully underfunded pension?
Will Social Security and a full pension together be adequate to maintain the lifestyle you've come to
expect?

If questions like these keep you
awake some nights, then you ought
to think about creating a special
nest egg. Three options for doing so
are individual retirement accounts
(IRAs), 401(k)s and annuities.

Indeed, you may have no choice
but to manage your own retirement
fund, which could require learning
about these investments. Increasing
numbers of Americans are self-em-
ployed or work for companies that
have abandoned the traditional
defined-benefit plans. In such a traditional plan the employer contributes a fixed amount each year
and you are entitled to a fixed pension for the rest of your life. In
many current plans, employers
leave it up to the employees to
determine how best to invest the
company's contribution to the retirement program.

If you're thirtysomething, it isn't
too early to start planning for the
"golden years." The earlier you start
saving, the less you have to salt away
each year in order to provide a secure
retirement.

THE BASICS

Individual Retirement Accounts

Americans weren't saving
enough. That was the premise
of the 1981 law that created IRAs.
Congress believed that tax incentives would encourage Americans to
save and invest more money.

It worked—almost *too* well.
IRAs became such a drain on the
federal treasury that the IRA law
was revised to restrict deductibility.
But IRAs may still be a very good
deal. Here are the basic rules:

■ You and your spouse can each invest up to $2,000 a year from

(NOT) RISKY BUSINESS

Recent declines in interest rates have left some major private pension funds underfunded. In December 1993, the U.S. Pension Benefit Guarantee Corporation revealed that, at the 50 most under-funded private pension systems, there exists a $38 billion gap between what companies have agreed to pay out and how much money they have to pay it.

You needn't worry too much about this, though, since the Guarantee Corporation would likely bail you out if your company goes belly-up. And the gap could narrow as interest rates go back up. So don't give up on your company's pension plan. After all, the investment risk is still with the company.

earnings in a range of investments, such as bank certificates of deposit (CDs), stocks, bonds, and mutual funds. If your spouse doesn't work, you can invest $2,250 a year.

You've probably seen full-page newspaper ads and television commercials for IRAs just before April 15th every year. They're telling you that you can still open an IRA with a lump sum up until April 15th and, if you're eligible, deduct your IRA contribution from the previous year's tax return.

■ If you don't participate in a company pension plan, you can deduct the full amount you contributed to an IRA. If you do participate, you can still deduct the full amount if your adjusted gross income is no more than $40,000 (married, filing jointly) or $25,000 (single). You can deduct some of the IRA contribution if your income is under $50,000 (married) and $35,000 (single).

■ Whether you can deduct the contribution or not, you defer paying taxes on earnings until you start withdrawing money at age 59½.

■ You can move your IRA investments from one account to another, from one bank to another, or between bank accounts and other types of investments.

The downside of IRAs: If you withdraw the money before 59½, you pay a hefty 10% penalty and the taxes owed—although there are a few loopholes, such as if you become totally disabled or if you take "substantially equal periodic payments" over the course of your life.

In addition, you'll have to pay taxes if you don't start withdrawing by April 1st of the year after you reach 70½. Then you must withdraw enough each year to empty your account during your life expectancy, which is based on Internal Revenue Service (IRS) mortality tables. (Life expectancy tables are in IRS Publication 939.) If you die before your predicted longevity and your surviving spouse is your beneficiary, she or he is allowed to roll over the entire amount into her or his own IRA with no adverse tax consequences. If you have already started taking required distributions because you are at least 70½, your surviving spouse can continue to take them. Since these are only the basics, ask your IRA custodian or your financial advisor for details.

In the event you didn't start taking required minimum distributions, your surviving spouse can take distributions based on her or his life expectancy. Alternatively, she or he can take a full distribution by the end of the fifth year following your death. More special rules apply if the beneficiary is someone else; again, follow up with your financial advisor or IRA custodian for details.

401(k) Retirement Plans

Named after a section of the tax law, 401(k) plans are available to people whose companies establish them. Twenty million Americans have invested in 401(k) plans. More than 95% of companies with at least 5,000 employees, approximately 75% of companies with 1,000 to 5,000 employees, and more than half of those with 500 to 1,000 employees offer 401(k) plans. Quite simply, your employer sends a certain amount of your paycheck to your 401(k) account. You invest it in one of several different investment plans your employer offers. You might be able to choose among a money fund, a guaranteed investment contract (in which insurance companies agree to pay a definite interest rate), a bond fund, a stock fund, a "balanced" fund containing both stocks and bonds, and, less

commonly, an international fund and the company's own stock. The money fund and guaranteed investment contract present the least amount of investment risk; the international fund and the company's own stock, the most.

If you have a chance to join a 401(k) plan, grab it. To all of your company savings plans, including a 401(k), you and the company can together annually contribute either up to 25% of your net salary or $30,000, whichever is less. The maximum pre-tax 401(k) tax deduction increases slightly each year; it was a very substantial $9,240 in 1994. Earnings on additional contributions are tax-deferred.

As with IRAs, your 401(k) earnings are also tax-deferred. You can start making withdrawals when you reach 59½, and you must begin to withdraw by 70½ or pay a 10% federal tax penalty, with certain limited exceptions.

You direct this investment. You can change your investment allocations, usually quarterly. In addition:

■ When you leave the company, you can roll over your 401(k) savings into an IRA.
■ The majority of companies offering 401(k) plans match part or all of your contribution. If yours does, then you're throwing free money away if you don't sign up.
■ Since your contributions are made through payroll deduction, if you never see the money, you won't be tempted to spend it.
■ If you need cash, it is possible to borrow from your 401(k) fund at most companies.

Tax-Deferred Annuities

Tax-deferred annuities are investments sold by insurance companies that allow you to defer taxes on the income until later in life. You pay one or a series of upfront lump sum payments to start, with no limits on how much you can invest and still receive full tax deferral. The company puts your money in CDs, a mutual-fund-type account, or other investments.

During an "accumulation period," you pay no taxes on your earnings, which leaves you with even more money to reinvest. You pay taxes during the payout period, by which time you'll presumably be retired and the tax bite will be relatively modest on your reduced income. You can withdraw one lump sum or periodic payments.

You can invest in either a fixed-rate or variable-rate annuity. Fixed-rate means the rate is guaranteed for a period of years, usually from one to ten. After that, the company can adjust the rate at will, but most promise that it will remain competitive. There is a floor below which the rate can't drop, although it is always very low. Usually, the longer the commitment period, the higher the interest rate. The insurance company guarantees repayment of your principal. (Remember, though, this guarantee is only as sound as the insurance company itself.)

With variable-rate annuities, you get to select the annuity's investments, which means that the rates can change and that *you*, not the insurance company, therefore assume all the rate risk. (See page 310 in the previous chapter for a discussion of mutual fund investment risks, which are similar to the risks you would assume if you invest in a variable-rate annuity.) Your principal may also go up and down, although its return is assured in the guaranteed death benefit; even if the insurance company loses, say, half the principal, your beneficiary will still get everything that you had invested when you die. One of the nice things about variable-rate annuities is that you may be able to invest with your favorite mutual fund company.

Unlike investing in a mutual fund, though, you can't transfer money from a poorly managed family of funds to funds elsewhere. You're locked in, because, in return for the tax breaks, Uncle Sam imposes a 10% tax penalty on your interest earnings if you take money out of an annuity before you turn 59½.

To compensate for the loss of future fees, you will also probably have to pay the annuity company a surrender charge, as much as 7% of your investment initially and diminishing to nothing over succeeding years. Usually, new surrender fees are imposed for each additional cash withdrawal. Most fixed-rate annuities allow withdrawal of up to 10% of the principal each year without paying surrender fees.

One advantage that annuities have over IRAs is that you don't *have to* take your money out of an annuity at any particular time, while IRAs require you to start withdrawals by age 70½. But investing in annuities does not allow you to deduct any of your contribution from your income.

You can buy annuities directly from insurance companies or through financial planners, stockbrokers, and, increasingly, banks. More than 40% of banks now sell them.

WHAT TO WATCH OUT FOR

Individual Retirement Accounts

Withdrawal penalties for certain kinds of IRAs. Banks usually charge an early-withdrawal penalty on CDs. Mutual funds may have minimum withdrawal requirements. Before you get to the point of withdrawing, be sure to check early withdrawal penalties or restrictions. And if your IRA is in a CD, avoid a bank penalty by withdrawing, transferring, or rolling over your money on the day the CD matures.

Before you invest in an IRA, check the IRA contract to see if there are any special fees for withdrawals; they could amount to an extra $30 or so.

The 60-day reinvestment time limit. Your IRA can be paid to you if you choose to withdraw it, but to keep all the benefits, you must put it back into another IRA within 60 days. You also need to watch out for institutions that are slow to pay out; after all, you're no longer their customer—what do they care if they inconvenience you?

Other pitfalls. There are numerous tax traps aside from the 10% penalty for early withdrawal. For example, there's a 15% excise tax if you exceed the $150,000 annual retirement benefit withdrawal ceiling. Consult your tax advisor. (If you want to go it alone, IRS instructions booklet 590 explains IRA tax issues.)

401(k) Plans

Risk. Many companies have turned to 401(k)s because they don't want to be in the business of managing funds. And, under a Labor Department rule that took effect in January 1994, your employer no longer has any legal responsibilty for 401(k) losses you may incur, as long as they offer at least three broadly diversified investment options, provide ample information on the offerings, and allow you to shift your investments at least once a quarter. This rule should encourage employers with only one or two plans to beef up their offerings. But it also means that if you goof, you lose.

Management fees. The mutual fund you invest in will charge you management fees, deducted from your return. This usually amounts to about 1.5% of the fund assets each year.

Annuities

There's no free lunch. The insurance company sponsoring the annuity is not doing so out of goodwill. Management fees, mortality expense, and administrative fees of up to $60 can add up to as much as 3% of your cash infusion. There may also be sales commissions. If such

THEN, THERE'S SOCIAL SECURITY

When planning for your retirement, it's a good idea to send away for your free Social Security benefit record. You'll find out exactly how much you'll receive at a stated retirement age, as well as how much you'll get if you are disabled, and how much your beneficiaries will get if you die. You'll also see an historical accounting of your earnings subject to Social Security tax and the amount of Social Security taxes you paid each year. Your benefit record will also tell you if you've worked long enough to qualify for benefits. How to get one? Call (800) 772-1213.

Note: A new law (it takes effect in 1995) requires the Social Security Administration to automatically mail a benefit statement to anyone who is about to turn 60.

A+ by a rating service, such as A.M. Best or Standard & Poor.

While annuity contributions are tax-deferred, they are not tax-deductible; contributions to an IRA or 401(k) plan may be.

Individual Retirement Accounts

Consolidate your accounts. Don't keep several small IRA accounts at different institutions. Avoid potential maintenance fees as well as the annoyance of keeping track of several accounts.

Need money from your IRA? You can get it without paying a tax penalty if you set up a schedule of "substantially equal periodic payments" for the rest of your life. You must withdraw on a fixed schedule *only* for at least five years and until you are 59½. Doesn't sound too practical for most people. But if you are in your 50s and need extra money for your kid's college tuition, this may be the way to do it.

Another way to get at your IRA money, at least temporarily, is through a "tax-free rollover." You close down your IRA and maintain tax deferment by putting it in another IRA within 60 days. Meanwhile, you have 60 days to use your money. Before you try this, though,

charges are high enough, you'll offset the benefits of tax deferral, meaning that your annuity must have a very good rate of return to make it worthwhile.

The guarantee is only as solid as the annuity company. Since fixed-rate annuities "guarantee" a rate, always look for insurance companies that will live up to the guarantee. Your best bets are those rated A or

make sure you'll definitely reinvest the full sum on time.

401(k) Plans

Invest the maximum in a 401(k) plan, especially if your employer also contributes. They are a good deal—they combine large deductibility with tax-deferral. And you're contributing pre-tax money.

Take your money with you. If you leave your job and your plan is fully vested (allowing you to remove the entire amount saved), roll your money over into an IRA account or into your new company's 401(k) plan. It's important to put it into another retirement account to preserve tax-deferral. You have 60 days

from when you remove the money to do this.

Annuities

Ask about annuity surrender charges. If the surrender charge never disappears or is higher than that charged elsewhere and is not offset by a higher interest rate, then go elsewhere—unless you're absolutely sure you'll never take the money out early.

When choosing a fixed-rate annuity, be sure to factor in the length of the guaranteed rate period and the interest rate offered. For variable-rate annuities, take a good look at their total returns for three years or more.

▪ For the ins and outs of retirement investing, read *Making the Most of Your Money*, a very detailed book by Jane Bryant Quinn. (Simon & Schuster, 1991). $27.50.

▪ Want to know a lot more about annuities? Read *All About Annuities: Safe Investment Havens for High-Profit Returns*, by Gordon K. Williamson (John Wiley & Sons, Inc., 1993). $19.95.

▪ Independent Advantage Financial provides an annuity shopping service; call (800) 829-2887 for more info.

▪ Morningstar Variable Annuity Performance Reports tells you how most of the major funds have performed. $15 per issue; call (800) 876-5005 to order.

▪ IRS pamphlets and brochures may be obtained by calling your local IRS office or (800) 829-1040; TDD consumers should call (800) 829-4059.

▪ The Variable Annuity Research & Data Service tracks variable annuity performance data. Each thick issue is $49. Call (404) 998-5186 to order.

CHAPTER 35

MORTGAGES AND HOME EQUITY BORROWING

Financing Your American Dreams

I f you're like most Americans, you want to own your home—preferably a 14-bedroom mansion—but you'll most likely settle for a comfortable Cape Cod. And if you haven't inherited a small fortune, you will need to borrow a substantial amount of money to reach your goal.

So how do you (legally) get your hands on, say, $100,000? Are ads touting low interest rates and "no points" to be believed, despite the lengthy fine print disclaimers? How about the TV pitchman who "says yes" when your bank "says no"?

MORTGAGE BASICS

Different Kinds of Mortgages

S tated simply, a mortgage is an installment loan on your home. A lender gives you a large lump sum which you add to your own money to buy a piece of property. Then over a period of years—called the term—you pay the lender back in monthly installments until you've repaid all the principal and the interest. Your monthly payments consist of the principal, interest, and extra money that sometimes is required to be deposited in an escrow account to cover property taxes and insurance.

In the early years of the mortgage, the lender makes sure it will profit from your loan by applying most of your monthly payment to interest charges. If you default after only a few years, you'll still owe practically the entire principal. Later in the term, most of your monthly payment will reduce the principal, as the chart on the facing page illustrates. It assumes a $75,000 mortgage, an annual interest rate of 10%, a 30-year term

(360 months), and a monthly payment of $658.18.

While mortgages come in infinite combinations of terms, rates, and special features, there are two basic types: fixed-rate and adjustable-rate.

Fixed-rate. The interest rate and the amount of the monthly payment is set for the entire term of the loan. The advantage is that you'll always know how much you owe. Also, if you're lucky at predicting the future course of interest rates, you might be able to lock in a low rate and pay less than you would if interest rates go up. Fixed-rate mortgages have become more popular as home buyers and refinancers have taken advantage of the low interest rates of the early 1990s.

With some fixed-rate mortgages, your payments increase slightly each month. The object of these "growing equity mortgages"

is to pay off the principal sooner and thereby potentially save thousands of dollars in interest.

Another variation is the "graduated payment mortgage," designed to make it easier for you to qualify for a mortgage. You pay less than normal amortization for the first several years of the mortgage and more later on. The reduced payments are arranged by deferring interest. Of course, a big disadvantage of such a mortgage is that you may be too optimistic about your future earnings potential and be unable to afford the larger payments down the road. Another disadvantage is that graduated payment mortgages generally end up costing more over the entire term. Furthermore, they are not a wise choice if you are thinking of keeping your house for only a few years because you will pay off too little interest; when you sell, you'll have to pay off *more* than what you borrowed.

360 MONTHS OF MORTGAGE PAYMENTS

$658.18 Payment	Interest Paid	Principal Paid	Remaining Balance
1ST	$625.00	$33.18	$74,966.82
2ND	$624.72	$33.46	$74,933.36
3RD	$624.44	$33.74	$74,899.62
358TH	$16.16	$642.02	$1,296.91
359TH	$10.81	$647.37	$649.54
360TH (last)	$5.41	$649.54	$0.00

Then there are "balloon mortgages" in which you still owe a substantial portion of the principal at the end of the payment period; it was not fully amortized. At the end of the term, you would presumably refinance, if you can. The advantage to the borrower is that the monthly payments are lower than if it was a fully-amortizing mortgage, although the interest rate when you finance years later could be high.

Adjustable-rate. In the early 1980s, banks began to transfer interest rate risk to borrowers by introducing adjustable-rate mortgages. The rate changes at regular intervals, usually once a year, and is tied to a published index, such as the rate on U.S. Treasury securities. The margin is usually 1 to 4 percentage points above the index.

What's in it for you? The initial interest rate is lower than for fixed-rate loans. And, if national interest rates go down, so do yours. What's in it for the lender? If national interest rates go up, so do yours.

Adjustable-rate mortgages aren't completely unpredictable. Most include a "lifetime cap," typically 6 percentage points above the initial rate that the rate can never surpass and a "payment cap," which is the most the rate can increase in any adjustment period and is usually set at about 2 percentage points. Never get a mortgage without both caps.

How Much Will It Cost?

Borrowers are often shocked when they get their mortgage commitment letter and see for the first time how much the loan will end up costing when all the interest is paid. So compare carefully the interest annual percentage rate (APR). What is APR? It includes interest, "points" (explained later), and other mortgage closing costs and presents them as if they were paid over a one-year period.

In addition to the APR, factors that affect how much the mortgage will ultimately cost include:

Term. The most common term is 30 years, although 15-year mortgages are becoming more popular. A longer term mortgage may be appealing; by stretching out payments, each monthly installment is lower. But, because you are using the lender's money longer, you end up shelling out more interest.

The chart on the facing page illustrates our point: Assume a $100,000 loan. The interest rates are the same, but when all is said and done, the 15-year mortgage will save you $99,540 in interest—no small change.

If you send the lender more money every month, you're reducing the outstanding loan balance on which 8.5% interest is due—and that's like putting the extra money in an 8.5% certificate of deposit. Also, you are increasing your equity in your home; if real estate values go up, that's a good investment, too. Another plus: Interest rates on 15-year mortgages are usually slightly lower than on 30-year mortgages because there is less risk in the shorter-term loan.

However, several factors can offset much of the seemingly enor-

Percentage*	Term	Monthly Payment	Total Interest Payment
8.5%	15 years	$985	$77,300
8.5%	30 years	$769	$176,840

*On a $100,000 loan

mous gain in the chart above. First, if you take the 30-year mortgage instead of the 15-year one, you might be able to invest the difference between the $769 monthly payment and the $985 payment in something that pays better than 9%, especially if interest rates climb.

Second, tax write-offs partly offset the interest burden. However, Marc Eisenson, author of a book on the advantages of mortgage prepayment, *The Banker's Secret*, says that the tax benefit is often overstated because many homeowners opt for the standard deduction anyway ($6,200 if married and filing jointly). He adds that even if joint filers itemize, "the first $6,200 squandered on wasted interest doesn't buy a nickel on tax deductions." As New York City tax specialist Curtis Arluck put it, "In deciding between a shorter and longer term mortgage, tax implications are the tail and the amount of money you pay is the dog."

So selecting a term depends on your own psychological makeup (do you have such a strong aversion to debt that is it *important* to you to shed this obligation in only 15 years?), financial situation (a shorter term locks you into making larger monthly payments no matter what happens to you financially), and al-

ternative investment options. And remember, almost every 30-year mortgage allows you to send in larger-than-billed payments to reduce your principal and your total interest payments. So the best alternative in the chart above could be to take the 30-year mortgage and write a $985 check every month anyway, with the extra payment earmarked for principal reduction.

Fees. Lenders charge for everything imaginable. For openers, there's the application fee of anywhere from $50 to several hundred dollars and a property appraisal fee of $200 to $400. You may think your prospective dream home is perfect, but the lender will still want to have an engineer inspect it for structural problems and termite damage, and you'll foot the bill. (Of course, the engineer's report is very helpful for you, too.) You also may have to pay for your own credit report. These fees usually are not refunded if the loan application is rejected.

There's more: A recording fee of as much as $12 is charged for each document that has to be officially recorded. You have to pay your own attorney anywhere from $150 to $500 to represent you at the closing, plus you'll have to pay for the lender's attorney. Lenders also

KEEP ON SHOPPING

A small reduction in the APR can produce enormous savings over the life of the loan. For example, after 30 years, a $100,000 mortgage will cost you a total of $245,584.80 in interest and principal if the annual interest rate is 7.25%, but only $239,511.60 if the rate is $7.00%. Decide for yourself if saving $6,073.20 is worth a few extra hours spent mortgage-shopping.

require title insurance, which protects you and the lender by insuring that the seller is conveying clear title to you—that no other ownership claims, easements, liens, or judgments are filed against the property. Title insurance reimburses you in case the title searcher makes a mistake and overlooks something. The fee for it is based on the amount you borrowed; for a $50,000 loan, it can range from $150 to $300.

The biggest fee could be "points." One "point" equals 1% of the amount financed, so two points on a $150,000 loan comes to $3,000. While fees are generally non-tax-deductible, points are generally regarded as interest and are fully deductible as mortgage interest on an original home purchase. On a refinancing, points must be amortized over the life of the loan, according to Curtis Arluck.

You'd think these levies (except for your own attorney's fees) would be included in your interest payments. After all, points were originally allowed in order to enable creditors to recover their costs and keep the interest rate below the legal usury ceiling—and loans rarely approach the usury ceiling these days. But banks lure you with a lower loan rate and then take hundreds—maybe thousands—of dollars up front.

Taxes. Depending on where you live, the tax man may want to take a bite. Mortgage taxes won't vary from lender to lender since they're set by the government. But keep in mind that they could total hundreds of dollars. For example, New York's mortgage tax is 1.75% of the amount borrowed.

How to Find a Mortgage

Start by gathering mortgage information from your local newspapers and by telephoning lenders. Organize the information into a worksheet. You can put several mortgages you wish to compare in separate columns on the same worksheet, as in the sample on the next page.

For each mortgage, the worksheet should report the APR, points, fees (including application, credit check, appraisal, bank's attorney), term, and the loan-to-value ratio. For adjustable rate mortgages, add the index, margin, payment cap, lifetime cap, adjustment frequency and period, whether the loan is convertible to a fixed-rate, and if there is a fee for doing so. For both kinds of loans you might also add pre-payment penalties and allowable debt-to-income ratio. For an adjustable rate mortgage, also take into account the duration of any low introductory "teaser" rate—usually it's for just a year.

Now it's a matter of comparing the offerings for similar mortgages and answering such questions as:

■ Is an adjustable-rate loan with a lower APR a better deal than a fixed-rate loan with a slightly higher APR? The answer depends on how long you plan to keep the home, whether the adjustable-rate mortgage has a low enough lifetime rate cap, and what direction you predict interest rates will go.

If you expect to move in only a few years, an adjustable-rate loan is preferable: You'll benefit from the lower rate for a while and if the rate goes up, you won't be stuck with it. If your loan adjusts once every three years, it's possible that you'll have sold the house before the adjustment.

Also consider the lifetime and

MORTGAGE WORKSHEET			
	Mortgage A	Mortgage B	Mortgage C
APR			
Points			
Total fees			
Term			
Loan-to-value ratio			
Index*			
Margin*			
Payment cap*			
Lifetime cap*			
Adjustment frequency*			
Adjustment period*			
Convertible?* When? Cost?			
Pre-payment penalties			

*For adjustable-rate mortgages.

payment caps of an adjustable-rate loan. Be a pessimist and calculate the monthly payment if the interest rate climbs to the capped rate. Could you afford it? For how long? On the other hand, if you have a mortgage that caps the monthly payments, and the rate goes high enough, you could end up negatively amortizing (explained in **What to Watch Out For**).

■ Should you take a 30- or a 15-year loan? The answer may be decided for you if you can't make the higher monthly payments required with a 15-year mortgage and *have* to take a 30-year term. This might not be such a bad alternative if the 30-year mortgage has no pre-payment penalty, which would enable you to pay extra and reduce principal when you can.

Nonetheless, a 15-year mortgage may be preferable because the interest rate is often slightly lower. The choice all depends on your specific circumstances.

■ What's the best index for an adjustable-rate mortgage? Some indexes, such as the commonly-used Treasury bill rate, are more volatile than others. Higher volatility means wider rate and payment swings.

■ How much of the cost of the loan do you want to pay up front? If you're planning on staying in your new home for quite a few years, points and fees are less important, since you're spreading their cost over a long period. But if you think you might keep the home for only a few years, you might consider paying a slightly higher

interest rate in exchange for fewer fees and no points.

How to Apply for a Mortgage

You can apply for mortgages at commercial banks, thrift institutions (savings banks and Savings & Loan Associations), mortgage bankers (they are licensed by your state, funded by private investors, and offer only mortgages), and credit unions. Nearly half of U.S. mortgages are arranged through brokers who will, for a fee, find a mortgage for you and help you qualify.

Start by getting copies of your credit reports. If there are errors, get them corrected *before* you apply for a mortgage. (See the **HELP** box, page 571, in "Consumer Privacy" to find out how.) Next, you'll want to figure out how much you can afford to borrow. As a rule of thumb, lenders require that your payments not exceed 28% of your monthly gross income or 36% of your gross after monthly payments for other debts are considered. As for your down payment, 20% is standard. If your down payment is less than 20%, you'll probably be required to buy private mortgage insurance to protect the lender, and the interest rate could be higher.

Your application must be as complete as you can make it. Lenders will not help you fill your information gaps. So to avoid mortgage application processing delays, have all your documents ready for submission with the application, including several months of bank statements (to show where your down payment and closing costs are coming from), all of your bank account numbers, at least two years' worth of W-2 tax forms, tax returns from the last two years, the name(s) of your stockbroker(s) and recent account statements, a list of all your debts with documentation, any alimony and child support payments, and a letter from a relative if they contributed some or all of your down payment.

Should you co-sign a mortgage with a relative? Generally this should be avoided in all but the closest families. If the buyer is unable to make the payments, the co-signer becomes fully responsible for every penny. By the way, parents who give (or loan) their kids money for a down payment may be subject to taxation according to IRS rules specifically covering such generous gestures.

The lender will want to know where any sudden cash infusions in your checking account came from to make sure it isn't laundered money or a temporary loan from a helpful friend. If you are buying a co-op, bring the corporation's recent financial reports, prospectus, and by-laws. For a house, supply a copy of your sales contract.

Should You Refinance?

Interest rates plummeted in the early 1990s. If you were unlucky enough to get your mortgage when rates were high, you might consider refinancing (although, as this is written, rates are rising). As a general guideline, you will benefit from refinancing if there is a difference of more than 2 percentage points between the interest rate on your current loan and a new one.

How much could you save? Say your current $100,000 30-year loan is financed at 11.25%. The monthly payment is $971.27. If you refinance for 30 years at 7.0%, the monthly payment would be only $665.31, giving you an extra $305.96 a month. Even if you refinanced into a 15-year mortgage, you'd pay $898.83 monthly, still a significant reduction. Better yet, you would pay only $161,789.40 in interest and principal over the term of the new, shorter loan, compared with $349,657.20 interest and principal paid over the term of the original loan.

The 2% rule on refinancing is not hard and fast. Be sure to consider how long it will take to recover closing costs such as points, as well as appraisals and application fees. Application fees for refinancings can be as high as 1.5% of the amount borrowed; this high fee is intended to discourage you from applying to several lenders simultaneously. Refinancing probably makes no sense if you're planning to pull up stakes relatively soon, but if you're staying for more than a few years, refinancing might be worthwhile even if the reduction in the basic rate is only one percentage point.

You should also consider the time and effort necessary to complete the paperwork. There's about as much of it as for a new mortgage since your existing mortgage has probably been sold to another lender who doesn't know much about you or your property and has to find out. Finally, if the value of your home has declined, you may have to pay off a large chunk of your mortgage before refinancing. If you already have that money in a good investment, removing it could offset the benefits of refinancing.

HOME EQUITY BORROWING

Let's say you own a home and you're intrigued by ads urging you to tap the equity in your home to take a cruise or finance your kids' college bills—perhaps you're tempted by one of those ads picturing houses with U.S. currency bursting out of windows and the chimney. In this a good move?

Many Americans have used the equity in their homes to pay for home improvements or college tuitions they otherwise would have foregone. Interest is tax-deductible on up to $100,000 worth of borrowings, while deductibility has been phased out for credit cards. (See your tax adviser for more information.) And home equity interest rates are generally lower than credit card rates.

Not surprisingly, lenders are more than willing to help get you into debt. They've made application forms simple. Turnaround is fast. And if you are approved for a home equity line of credit, you'll probably be given a checkbook—or even a credit card—to encourage you to spend. Not surprisingly, more than

$350 billion worth of home equity loans are now outstanding.

But home equity borrowing has enormous disadvantages. Home, sweet home is the collateral. If you fall behind on payments, you could lose it to foreclosure. And it's *always* a bad idea to finance immediate consumption or depreciating purchases like cars with a long-term loan such as a home equity loan. Nonetheless, a 1992 Gallup poll found that home equity loan borrowings are used primarily to pay taxes, consolidate credit card debts, buy a car, or just for spending money.

Home equity borrowing has declined recently as homeowners raise extra cash for tuition or a swimming pool by refinancing their mortgages with larger ones instead of with a home equity loan or credit line. Still, home equity borrowing may have several advantages over refinancings. Application processing usually goes faster, closing costs may be less, and you can draw on a line of credit periodically and only as you need the money.

HOME EQUITY BORROWING BASICS

The two basic types of home-equity lending are *home equity loans* and *home equity lines of credit.*

With home equity loans (HELs), also known as closed-end, fixed-rate loans, you receive the entire amount you borrow at the loan closing. The term is generally up to ten years. Fixed interest rates are usually a little higher than variable rates.

About a third of home equity loans have variable rates.

Home equity lines of credit, also known as open-end, variable-rate loans, typically allow you to draw on a credit line, usually by writing checks, during an "access period" of the first five to ten years. Then you have another five to fifteen years to pay it all back—with interest, of course. During the access period you are required to pay only the interest on whatever you've borrowed. Paying principal is optional during this time.

The interest on home equity lines of credit is typically indexed to banks' prime lending rate, as published in *The Wall Street Journal*. The law requires a lifetime interest rate cap but lets the lender set it.

A home equity line of credit is preferable to a HEL when you have periodic payments to make, such as college tuition, since you pay no interest until you actually write a check or use a linked credit card. You may prefer a HEL when you are making only a few big payments over a short time, such as to a home improvement contractor.

How much are you allowed to borrow? Generally, up to 75% of the appraised value of your home, minus the value of any existing mortgage.

What about fees? Home-equity loans involve many of the same fees as mortgages, including application fees, credit check fees, title insurance, and points. These fees may be waived or reduced for home equity "lines of credit" of less than $50,000. Or they can mount up so high that several percentage points

are added to the effective annual interest rate.

WHAT TO WATCH OUT FOR

Mortgages

Negative amortization. This occurs when your billed monthly payment is insufficient to cover the interest due. Negative amortization happens most frequently when monthly interest payments on adjustable-rate mortgages fail to keep up with the interest due, say because you can't afford the increase or because there is a lag between an increase in the interest rate and the increase in your billed monthly payment. The difference gets added to the principal and you end up owing more each month than the month before.

Lowballing and bait-and-switch. You're elated when your phone search uncovers a lender whose rate is a full point below its competitors. Be careful. The rate may be guaranteed for only ten days, which is obviously insufficient time to close on the property. Always ask how long a low rate is locked in.

Also be on the lookout for bait-and-switch artists. After you've handed over hundreds of dollars in nonrefundable fees, you're told that a small problem has been found with your credit history and the lender requires only sterling credit records. Then you are offered a somewhat costlier loan. You might not even realize that you were baited and then switched.

Dishonest mortgage brokers. The vast majority of brokers are honest and hardworking. Mortgage brokers can save you a lot of time and effort. With their help, you fill out just one application, and the broker does the hard work of searching for the best mortgage.

But some consumers have run into problems with mortgage brokers. Some of the less honest operators take a fee up front, produce nothing, and fail to give a refund. Another scam is to inflate your credit worthiness in order to get you the loan—and the broker his or her commission. But you may end up with a bigger loan than you can handle.

Still other brokers charge "junk" fees. The only fees you should pay up front are for property appraisal, your credit check, and the basic application fee. Since mortgage brokers are paid by the lender, you shouldn't be charged any more than if you went directly to the lender.

Conversion fees. Some mortgages allow you to convert from an adjustable-rate to a fixed-rate mortgage without reapplying. Ask how much the fee will be for converting. But bear in mind that the fixed rate you convert to may be higher than the market rate for similar kinds of fixed-rate mortgages.

Mortgages provided through home improvement contractors. A scam has swept the nation, called "equity fraud." At a 1993 U.S. Senate hearing on the subject, experts testified that tens of thousands of homeowners—mostly in minority neighborhoods—have been victimized by dishonest contractors working hand-in-glove with home finance companies. The homeowners usually did not understand that they had agreed to a mortgage, and the work was rarely done properly.

Lesson: Don't sign any legal documents until you have had plenty of time to read them carefully, and be sure to request and receive copies of anything you sign. Alarms should sound if the documents include a retail installment obligation or mortgage application.

> " *S ome people who have a home equity line available to them are using it like unemployment insurance. If they get thrown out of work, they borrow up to the hilt on their equity credit line to provide the money to see them over what they hope is a temporary embarrassment.*"
>
> —JOHN P. LAWARE,
> Federal Reserve Board Governor,
> April 1992

Home Equity Loans

Too much debt. A large home equity loan may make it harder to move up, and when you sell your home and pay off the loan, you have less money to reinvest.

Higher interest rates on no-fee loans. Choosing a bank loan can get pretty complicated: Some loans have no fees but a higher rate; others have moderate fees and mid-range rates; and still others have full fees but considerably lower rates. Compare carefully, remembering that thousands of dollars may depend on a few hours of research.

Teaser rates. Low interest rates may be in effect for only a short time. A 1989 law requires lenders that mention interest rates in their ads to also reveal other key costs and terms, such as how long the rate is in effect. Still, small-print disclosures can be confusing.

THE SMARTER CONSUMER

Mortgages

Beware of ads for "guaranteed" mortgages. One scheme advertising mortgages with a "money-back guarantee" requires calling an "800" number for information. The caller is told to send in an advance fee of several hundred dollars which will be "applied to the loan." The scamsters disappear once the mark sends the money.

Check out brokerages before paying them money. Find out how long a mortgage broker you may use has been in business and check its state licenses (most states license them) for administrative actions and consumer complaints. Learn if it is a member of the National Association of Mortgage Brokers. Try to patronize a broker that a friend or relative has had good results from.

Ask how many lenders the mortgage broker represents—it should be more than a handful—and get a written breakdown of your broker's fees.

Once a broker has found you a lender, double-check the rate and terms with the lender directly to make sure the broker isn't overcharging you.

Ask if an escrow account is absolutely required. An escrow account is set up to guarantee the lender that property taxes and insurance will be paid. As a borrower, you pay into this account an extra amount on top of the regular monthly mortgage payment.

Avoid escrow if possible. Depending on the law in your state, you might not earn any interest on an escrow account. Even if you do, you could probably earn more on your money investing it elsewhere.

Tax escrow should be avoidable if your cash down payment was 30% or more of the selling price or if you have a low loan-to-value ratio. You might be able to get the insurance escrow dropped too.

Check into Federal Housing Administration (FHA) and Veterans Administration (VA) mortgages that are available from participating lenders. The rates may be lower because the government insures repayment. FHA loans may require only

3% down, and you can finance your closing costs. You must have excellent credit to qualify, however, and the most you can borrow for an FHA loan is about $100,000 to $160,000, depending on the locality; these loans are meant for houses moderately priced for their communities. VA loans have somewhat higher borrowing limits and might even let you waive the down payment. But only veterans—which includes National Guard members and reservists—are eligible. The law requires an escrow account for taxes and insurance with both kinds of loans.

Choose your own insurance providers. You don't have to use the title insurance recommended by the lender. You might find a cheaper one if you ask around. The same goes for homeowners insurance.

Get a copy of your appraisal. A new federal regulation says that, if you request it in writing, the lender must show you the property appraisal it relies on in reviewing your mortgage application. If your application was rejected, you could use a mistakenly low appraisal as a reason to ask for a second review. In addition correct low appraisal could be used to bargain with the seller for a lower price.

Under a special new program, you can pay as little as 3% down with some lenders, including GE Capital and Norwest Mortgage. To be eligible, you must earn no more than the median income for your region, as determined by the federal government.

If You Already Have a Mortgage

Consider pre-paying your mortgage to save big on interest, especially in the mortgage's early years. In his book, *The Banker's Secret*, Marc Eisenson, the apostle of loan pre-payment, explains how small pre-payments of only $25 a month toward principal can save more than $34,000 in interest on a 30-year, 10%-rate, $75,000 loan. Pre-payment works because the bank computes the interest due on your outstanding balance each month. By shrinking the balance, you reduce your interest outlay. The bank no longer collects the compounded interest on the amount you repaid. His book also answers tax questions about pre-payment.

Growing equity mortgages—in which monthly payments are increased annually, with the additional money going to principal—and bi-weekly payment mortgages have much the same interest-eliminating effect as pre-payment, but they are less flexible. With simple pre-payment, you can send in $100 extra one month and only $10 extra the next if you wish.

Beware of payment mistakes. Recent disclosures that lenders have made hundreds of millions of dollars worth of errors in calculating mortgage payments should make you a bit wary if you have an adjustable-rate loan. If you are concerned that your outstanding principal doesn't seem to be declining fast enough when you've made principal prepayments, that you are paying more than your latest adjustment would seem to warrant, or that you are paying too much into escrow, ask the lender for a complete payment history. If this doesn't help, consider paying a professional to check your payments with a computer. (See **HELP** at the end of this chapter for names of companies that will check your payment for mistakes.)

Don't be a mortgage payment scam victim. With mortgages bought and sold like scalped tickets to a hot concert, thieves have figured out how to cash in. There have been cases where official-looking letters were mailed from a "company" claiming to have purchased mortgages and directing the homeowner to send future payments to them. The letters gave an excuse for why a certified check or money order should be sent instead of a personal check. You can avoid becoming a victim if you send money to a new company only after the old lender sends you a letter saying the mortgage is being sold. And send only personal checks.

Home Equity Borrowing

Use home equity loans and credit lines judiciously. Obtain them for home improvements, education, and other capital investments with long-term benefits rather than for clothes, vacations, and eating out.

Home equity credit lines linked to credit cards. In a 1993 survey conducted for the Consumer Bankers Association, 18% of 93 interviewed lenders said they issue credit cards that allow holders to borrow on their home equity credit line—up from 10% a few years prior. Danger! Such linked cards make it far too easy to overspend on eating out and vacations, and you risk losing your home. Even more common are banks that allow you to draw on your credit line through a cash machine—almost as much a temptation to go on a spending spree as a linked credit card.

If the disclosed terms of the loan change before it is finalized, you can refuse to take the money. You are also entitled by law to a complete refund of all fees.

▪ Find the lowest rate. For $20, HSH Associates will send you a list of rates, terms, and fees for 25 to 50 lenders that make loans in your area. To order, call (800) 873-2837.

▪ Check your rate adjustment. Several companies will run a computer check to find out if your lender has correctly adjusted your mortgage payment. One is LoanCheck, which charges a flat $74; call (800) 477-6166. Another is Mortgage Monitor, which charges a third of your recovery; call (800) 283-4887.

▪ *The Banker's Secret* by Marc Eisensen (Villard Books, 1990) explains principal pre-payment. To order, call (800) 255-0899.

CHAPTER 36

LIFE INSURANCE

Betting on Your Life

They bet on your life. That's what insurance companies do when they sell you a life insurance policy.

While it's a pretty good bet for them—they have decades of experience figuring probabilities—is it a good bet for you? Do you need life insurance? If you do, what kind of policy? And will the insurance company you choose be around in 20 or 30 or 40 years to pay off?

THE BASICS

Americans spent $6.5 billion on life insurance premiums in 1992. Unfortunately, they probably spent too much. Most policyholders do not fully understand what they buy or realize that the price of the same insurance protection can vary by 100% among insurance carriers. Life insurance is usually bought when an insurance agent comes calling, before the purchaser has a chance to analyze her or his insurance needs and competing policies.

In all fairness to confused consumers, life insurance is very complicated. While there are only a few basic kinds of policies, there are literally hundreds of variations, hybrids, and permutations, and it's difficult to understand all the various points. If you're considering buying life insurance, use this chapter as a primer, but make sure you also investigate thoroughly any policies you're considering before you write a check.

Do You Need Life Insurance?

Consider the purpose of life insurance: to protect the financial well being of the people you name as beneficiaries in case you—the insured person—dies. The basic rule of thumb is that a family of four should have coverage of at least seven times the principal breadwinner's annual income. But if your survivors can easily handle the immediate funeral and post-funeral expenses and support themselves for an indefinite time without insurance, then you don't need it.

Senior citizens usually don't need life insurance to replace lost income. Nor do young, two-income couples with no dependents.

Factor in all of your financial resources that will be available to your beneficiaries after you die. There may be Social Security; bank, credit union, stock brokerage, and mutual fund accounts including Individual Retirement Accounts, annuities, Keough accounts, sellable real estate other than your home, pension plan death benefits, and so on. If you find that your beneficiaries will have ample resources to cope with the loss of income, you may not need coverage. But think of *every* possibility. There may be uninsured medical expenses. You may want your survivors to be able to immediately pay off a mortgage or credit card balances. A spouse's domestic responsibilties are certainly worth plenty in monetary terms if the survivor has to hire domestic help. If you're supporting an elderly parent, life insurance could pay to hire helpers to look after them if you die. Factor in the cost of your childrens' college educations. And remember that spending a little on life insurance now can help offset substantial estate and other taxes later. Consider talking to your tax or financial advisor about the tax benefits of life insurance.

Some life insurance—the cash-value kind discussed later—is an investment. It's a tax-deferred investment, since any earnings on a cash value policy aren't taxed until withdrawn. And the proceeds payable when you die for any kind of insurance policy are not taxable income either.

The Jargon

Term insurance is the simplest type of life insurance. Your beneficiaries are covered for a particular period of time (or "term")—anywhere from one to 70 years—as long as you keep up with the premiums. You buy a designated amount of coverage, and if you die during the term, your beneficiaries are paid that amount in a lump sum.

If it is "straight term" insurance, the policy ends at the end of the term. You have to buy a new policy if you still want life insurance.

Renewable term insurance—either annual renewable or multiyear renewable—provides either that your renewal is automatic or that the company has a right to order a medical checkup at renewal time, called the "re-entry" feature. With automatic renewal, your premium will go up because you aged and your chances of dying are greater. A "re-entry" policy could be cheaper because, if the checkup concludes that you're still healthy, you get a special rate. If you're not in such great physical shape, though, your premium may climb dramatically. Robert D. Stuchiner, an industry analyst with the Ascott Alliance Group, calls the re-entry feature "a bad buy since you're saving a few bucks today with the possibility of paying a horrendous amount more tomorrow."

Among variations on the term insurance theme are:

■ *Decreasing term* insurance. This coverage is often linked to a mortgage. You designate the term, say 19 years, to correspond to the term of the mortgage. You pay the same premium throughout the term, but your coverage is reduced over time, as your debt decreases. Decreasing term is often called family income or mortgage insurance.

■ *Level term policies.* These are policies in which your premium is the same for five, ten, or 15 years and then suddenly shoots upward. The future premiums can be either projected or guaranteed.

The biggest advantage of term insurance over the cash-value policies (described later in this chapter) is that term insurance is much more affordable when you're young, during the first several years of the policy. A $100,000 term policy on a 35-year-old can be purchased from a reliable carrier for as little as $140 a year, while a cash-value policy will cost several times that. Another advantage of term insurance is that you can easily drop it when it's no longer needed.

A disadvantage is that annual premiums climb rapidly as you move into middle age—although by 60, you could probably safely reduce your coverage and moderate your premiums. Generally speaking, term insurance is not a good buy for senior citizens. In fact, according to Stuchiner, in New York State "you can't even hold term insurance after age 70. It's prohibited because it's not in the consumer's best interest."

Another disadvantage of term insurance is that you have to find new insurance at the end of the term, unless it is a guaranteed renewable policy or a convertible (into cash value insurance) policy. Your temporary insurance need could have become a longer-term need and you could be left out in the cold.

Of course, the biggest disadvantage of term insurance is that all of the premiums will have been wasted if the insured doesn't die while the insurance is in force—and only around 8% of term policies actually pay death benefits.

Most insurance agents won't try very hard to sell you term insurance; it pays them smaller commissions than other kinds of policies. Yet most term policies will meet your basic need for protection.

To compare which term policy will cost less, look at more than just annual premiums. With inflation, premiums in the later years of a policy are paid for with cheaper dollars. So a policy with very low early-year premiums and very high later-year premiums could be preferable to one with more level premiums. The "interest-adjusted cost index" takes this time value of money into account. The law in 38 states requires insurers to make this index available—stated as a cost per $1,000 of insurance.

If you'd rather have someone else do the shopping, you might consider calling a telephone quote service. After you've told them about your age, health, and the kind of policy you're looking for, a computer will spit out the names of the five best buys. (See **HELP** at the end of this chapter for quote service names.) Still, remember that this is a limited service and you won't learn much about the policies; you have to know what you're looking for.

Finally, check the term policy comparisons published in the July 1993 issue of *Consumer Reports.* The price disparities were substantial. For a $250,000 annual renewable-term policy, a 45-year-old woman would pay only $275 a year for the "Valuterm I" policy from Golden Rule—*Consumer Reports'* all-around highest scorer—or $575 a year for a similar policy from Lincoln National.

Cash-Value Policies

Whole life insurance is a whole lot more complicated. As long as the premiums are paid, a whole life insurance contract continues for the insured's "whole life" or until the age of 100. Part of your premium pays for the "mortality charge"—the cost of the insurance protection. The rest goes into a reserve fund.

To keep premiums level year after year, you, the insured, pay more in your younger years than the actual cost of protection and less in your later years. The extra cash you accumulate in the reserve fund earns interest. The "cash surrender value" of the policy is the amount of money you would get back if you dropped your coverage.

To illustrate: Let's say you are "30-something" and you buy a $100,000 whole life policy. For the duration of the policy, the annual premium stays at a level $1,500. Right after you buy the policy its cash value is zero and the death benefit is $100,000. In the policy's sixth year the cash surrender value has gone up to $6,400—$6,400 is what you would get if you gave up the policy then. The death benefit remains at $100,000. And the company is now exposing itself to $93,600 in risk: $100,000 minus $6,400. This exposure is called the "amount of protection." By the policy's 26th year, your cash surrender value would be up to $37,600. Since the death benefit always remains at $100,000, the "amount of protection" is now down to $62,400.

Most policies guarantee at least a minimum return, but you have to ask the insurer what the actual interest rate is. Most whole life policies also pay dividends, sometimes referred to as "excess earnings." These can be paid out, applied to help build up cash values, applied to premiums, or used to buy more insurance. Dividend-paying policies are called "participating" policies. Dividends are paid depending on the yield on the company's investments, how much it has paid out in death benefits, the company's expenses, and, naturally, on the particulars of your own coverage.

An insurance agent will probably show you charts illustrating "projected earnings" of a cash value policy over the years. These figures are typically exaggerated to convince you that a policy is a good investment. One enterprising agent testified before a U.S. Senate hearing in 1992 that he personally checked the state insurance department filings of 20 major insurance companies and found that 80% admitted they could not meet the earnings assumptions used in their projection charts. They could not meet even the first two years of their cash-value policies.

This is a long-standing abuse—a scandal, really—and a testament to the weakness of insurance industry oversight. (For more on this, see **What to Watch Out For** later in this chapter.)

One reason some people consider buying a whole life policy is that the interest earned is tax-deferred until it's withdrawn. And at that time, taxes will be paid only on the portion of the amount withdrawn that exceeds the premiums you paid plus dividends. Another positive feature is the ability to borrow against cash value—perhaps at a comparatively favorable interest rate—directly from the insurance company. One New York insurance and planning expert gives this rule of thumb to help decide whether to buy insurance as an investment: Compare the expected return on the insurance policy with the return on alternative tax-free investments, assuming you have the discipline to keep up that non-insurance investment plan. But also consider, he adds, that with insurance you're also buying coverage.

Universal life. Universal life is like whole life, except it is much more flexible; you decide how much to pay in premiums, whether to skip premiums, or whether to pay extra for a few months. You can structure the policy so that for, say, eight years, you pay large enough premiums to make sure that your cash value entirely covers premiums thereafter. You can also change the death benefit.

Your universal life premiums go into an "accumulation fund," on which you are paid interest. Periodically, "mortality charges" (the cost of insurance protection), adminis-

tration expenses, and commissions are deducted. An annual statement breaks down how much has gone to mortality charges and expenses and how much is in your accumulation fund. You can stop contributing to the accumulation fund for a while or even make extra payments to your account. It's also possible to increase your coverage without incurring a new "load" (payments for expenses), although this may require some evidence of good health, perhaps a medical exam.

Some policies pay only the death benefit. Others, which cost more, pay the death benefit plus whatever is in the accumulation fund.

About surrender charges: If you have a "front-load" universal policy, administrative fees as well as the agent's commission will be subtracted from your premiums. However, most policies these days are "back-load," which means that the charges, fees, and commissions are together called "surrender charges" because they are deducted from the cash surrender value if you discontinue your policy. During the first few years of such a policy, most of your accumulation fund could (and probably would) be wiped out by surrender charges. The charges diminish later on and disappear altogether with some policies.

Most policyholders are told next to nothing about surrender charges. Jim Hunt, an actuary and director of the National Insurance Consumer Organization (NICO), said that one of his clients was sold an annual premium universal life policy as a substitute for an IRA.

After two years—when he had invested $4,000 and wanted to take his money out—he discovered to his consternation that the cash surrender value was down to only a few hundred dollars. To add insult to injury, since he was single and had no dependents, he really didn't need life insurance in the first place.

A common variation on universal life and whole life is single-premium insurance. With single-premium, you make one large up-front premium payment. Earnings on this single payment augment the cash value over time. The main reasons to buy such a policy are to defer taxes and to build collateral to borrow money.

Variable life. Variable life insurance is cash-value insurance that allows you—rather than the insurance company—to decide where to invest the savings component, called the "separate investment account." You circumvent the insurance company's reserve account.

The most positive thing about variable life insurance is that you might do better than the insurance company would in choosing investments. This could be a down side, too, since you might make bad decisions and there is typically no minimum interest guarantee. Risk also extends to the value of the death benefit, although there is usually a minimum below which it can't fall.

As with universal life, variable life policies impose substantial surrender charges as well as mortality and administration charges.

Your Premium

If an insurance company has reason to believe that you are a bigger risk, you'll pay more. Age is the initial determinant; inevitably, your chance of dying increases as you grow older.

Then comes health. Insurers find out how healthy you are from your medical records, which can be accessed from the Medical Information Bureau (MIB), an insurance-industry–sponsored national computer data base. (See page 569 for more about the MIB.) If you are asking for a substantial amount of coverage and are middle-aged or older—around 45—the insurance company will probably ask you to submit to a medical exam. If you have a chronic health problem like high blood pressure, you might still be able to buy a guaranteed acceptance policy. But you'll pay through the nose for these heavily promoted policies; benefits may be limited and you might do just as well paying the higher rate for a regular insurance policy. Unfortunately, people who are seriously ill, such as people with AIDS, probably can't get any insurance at all.

Tobacco companies may claim that smoking isn't bad for your health, but insurance companies beg to disagree. Nonsmokers pay up to 50% less for life insurance than smokers. Don't lie about smoking on a life insurance application; the urine taken during your insurance physical will probably be tested for nicotine, among other chemicals. And if you die from lung cancer and lied about smoking on

CREDIT LIFE INSURANCE: GENERALLY NOT A GOOD DEAL

Credit life insurance is insurance you may buy when you purchase something on an installment payment basis. It pays all unpaid installments on the loan if you die. Auto dealers, finance companies, and others selling installment credit aggressively promote credit life insurance not only to make sure they get paid—but to make themselves extra income on the side.

Stephen Brobeck, Executive Director of the Consumer Federation of America (CFA), calls credit life insurance "the nation's worst insurance rip-off." On average, in 1992 it paid out only 43 cents on each premium dollar, while consumer organizations recommend a ratio of at least 70 cents. (New York and Maine are exceptions; payout is up to at least 70 cents on the dollar there.) And the coverage often has loopholes that get insurers off the hook if a claim is filed. CFA estimates the total overcharging at $500 million to $1 billion a year.

Sometimes consumers unwittingly buy credit life insurance because its price is automatically included in the monthly loan payment. But you don't *have* to buy it. The loan papers can be rewritten to exclude it. So read installment loan documents carefully and ask the seller or lender if credit life insurance is included. If you still believe you need this kind of protection, buy a good overall life or disability insurance policy instead.

your application, your survivors may get a reduced benefit.

Another risk factor is alcohol consumption. For larger amounts of requested coverage, the company will probably check your driving record for driving-while-intoxicated (DWI) convictions. If you're in a hazardous occupation like lion-taming, fighting forest fires, or if you fly your own aircraft, you'll pay more. Potentially dangerous hobbies, such as scuba diving and rock climbing, could also cost you extra.

Gender is another consideration. Women live longer than men. Unless the company has unisex rates, men pay extra.

Once they've amassed all the information they need, if they agree to take you on, the company applies a complex scoring system to place you in one of three risk categories: preferred, standard, or substandard. The vast majority of policies are written at standard rates.

Insurance Company Soundness

"Like a good neighbor," will they really be there? Are you and your family truly "in good hands?" Is your insurer as solid as the Rock of Gibraltar?

These are important questions, as almost a million policyholders learned in 1991. Within a few months, six major life insurance companies were seized by regulators. Accounts were frozen. Some customers were not allowed to cash in their policies or borrow against them, except in cases of extreme hardship.

Many retirees on fixed incomes were hurt when one of these companies, Executive Life Insurance, began paying only 70% of benefits in group pension plans. The *Providence Journal-Bulletin* reported in 1991 that at Landmark Medical Center in Woonsocket, Rhode Island, more than 400 nonunion and 50 union employees had annuities in a group pension plan with Executive Life, and the hospital had no plans to make up the 30% benefits shortfall.

Why the sudden difficulties in an industry long seen as a paragon of stability? Answer: junk bonds, bad commercial loans, and unwise real estate investments. Like commercial banks and savings and loans, insurance companies also cashed in on the boom of the 1980s. And like their cousin financial institutions, they've suffered from a bad hangover.

The problem is that there's no FDIC to protect the policy-holding public. Consumers are protected by individual state insurance guaranty associations, and the amount of maximum guaranteed death penalty payment ranges from a low of $100,000 up to $500,000. How-

ever, the guaranty funds do not protect you at all from cash surrender and borrowing prohibitions that could be imposed if your company gets in trouble.

To protect yourself, do your own research. Check a company's financial soundness ratings with the five major rating companies: A.M. Best, Moody's, Standard & Poor's, Duff & Phelps, and Weiss Research (see **HELP** at the end of this chapter for contact information). The rating agencies look at the company's capital base and surplus, its reserves, its profit history, management record, and intangible factors, such as how well-run the company appears to be. Find out if the company you are considering has been downgraded in recent years. If it was rated triple-A for four years and in the fifth and most recent year it was only double-A, then there was a change in the company that triggered the downgrade. Generally, you should buy only from insurance companies with the highest ratings for the last five to ten years. And bear in mind that small firms may not be sufficiently diversified to withstand an economic downturn. Industry analyst Robert D. Stuchiner also suggests reading the report on which the rating is based. It'll say which way the company is likely to go. Be on guard if it says something like "downgrade implications." These reports, usually costing around $25, can be obtained through your agent or by calling the rating company direct.

Understand, though, that the ratings are carefully nuanced and that the rating agencies avoid giving a bad sounding grade. So, for example, Duff and Phelps gives seven levels of "A" (AAA, AA+, AA, AA-, A+, A, and A-), and their worst grade is CCC.

Where Should You Buy Life Insurance?

The biggest disadvantage of buying life insurance from an insurance agent is the large commissions they earn, especially for cash-value policies. Not only do commissions erode the funds you want to have working for you, they may affect the agent's choice of which policy to recommend, with the policy paying *them* the most urged on you, instead of the policy that pays *you* the most. Agents answer that they provide a valuable advisory service and that they would lose their customers if they didn't serve them well.

Many insurance policies have A and B versions, with the B version charging maybe 20% less. A few brave agents might pull the B version out of the drawer, even though they're supposed to use it only to win big sales.

You might save a lot of money by dealing with an insurance company directly—by phone, mail, or through financial planners—and avoiding agents altogether. Insurance consultant Glenn Daily, author of *Low-Load Life Insurance*, says that with agent-purchased cash-value insurance, commissions, administration costs, and other fees typically run 100% of the premium in the first year, 10% to 15% for the next three or four years, and then

about 5% until the tenth year. In contrast, you'd pay only 20% the first year and a few percent a year for ten years with policies charging lower-than-usual loads, called "low-load" policies.

Why doesn't everyone buy low-load? Because the projection charts used by agents to sell full-load policies so often exaggerate future return. Since low-load issuers don't normally use these tricks and subterfuges, their policies often don't look any better than load policies, and consumers figure they might as well buy from an agent. And, as Daily puts it, "Most people don't affirmatively buy life insurance. They buy when approached by an agent, maybe a golf partner. People don't like to think about death, so they don't learn much about the subject."

The National Insurance Consumer Organization (NICO) recommends two companies, USAA Life and Ameritas. Both operate over the phone, and can also serve as a benchmark to measure other companies against.

You can also buy life insurance in a bank. Savings banks have been selling term insurance for decades, and commercial banks are now getting into the insurance sales act.

One of the better deals could be term insurance purchased through your employer. Group rates tend to be lower and, as part of an employee group, you might not have to undergo a medical exam.

Still, going through an agent has many advantages. A good agent can tell you the pros and cons of various policy options, review your insurance with you every few years to make sure you're keeping up with any changes in your family or financial situation, and identify companies that are more likely to accept you if you have a medical condition.

Buying the right life insurance can be a complicated matter. Not only are there numerous insurance and policy variations, the tax implications can be complex. You can unwittingly forfeit enormous benefits and tax savings if you don't choose the best policy or most expedient policy owner or beneficiary.

WHAT TO WATCH OUT FOR

Illusory illustrations. Benjamin Disraeli's aphorism, "There are three kinds of lies: lies, damned lies and statistics," applies perfectly to life insurance marketing. Americans are deceived in droves by insurance company computer-produced projection charts full of statistics of future earnings and death benefits of cash-value life insurance policies. Small-print disclaimers in these charts, like "projected earnings" and "based on current assumptions," are used to make cash-surrender values look better than they really are. In fact, it is virtually impossible to project what might happen 15, 20, or 30 years down the road.

Some policy illustrations assume, with no basis at all, that administrative expenses will be cut five years hence. Or they assume,

again with no basis, that life expectancy will improve. And some insurance companies could just as well predict future interest rates by throwing darts.

In other words, projection illustrations are utterly worthless for purposes of comparing policies.

In 1992 and 1993, former Senator Howard Metzenbaum (D-Ohio) held hearings of the Senate Judiciary Committee Subcommittee on Antitrust and Monopolies to highlight the deceptions. One witness described how he and his father were sold a policy with projections showing that the policy would be all paid up in five years. He called the company after five years and was horrified to learn that his father still owed thousands of dollars in premiums to. Since his father was suffering from terminal cancer, he wouldn't be able to get insurance elsewhere. He had no choice—pay or go uncovered.

Forbes magazine reported in 1992 on a Denver couple who had to fork over nine instead of six $12,000 premium payments after their insurance company's interest rate fell from 10.75% in 1988 to 10.1% four years later.

NICO director Jim Hunt says that many people who were sold "vanishing premium" policies during the 1980s when interest rates were high began panicking in the early 1990s. With rates having plummeted, many policyholders discovered that they will have to pay premiums for many years after they were to have vanished.

Jolted by the Metzenbaum hearings, the National Association of

Insurance Commissioners (NAIC), the body that coordinates state insurance regulation, formed a working group to study the deception problem and issued a report that corroborated many of Metzenbaum's findings. The NAIC is considering prohibiting the use of projection illustrations, but the insurance industry is gearing up to fight any such move to the finish.

Lapse-basing: very low cash-surrender values in earlier years. Agents trying to sell you a cash-value policy point to the generous cash surrender value in, say, the 21st year, and gloss over the extremely parsimonious cash surrender value in early years that may be eaten up by high surrender charges. Most people don't realize—and agents certainly never reveal—that agents earn a total 55% to 105% commission on premiums paid during the first few years of a policy.

Insurance companies know that most customers let their policies lapse after only several years. This lapse-basing encourages insurance companies to "churn" policies; that is, to get you to replace your policy after only a few years with something "new and better." But with a replacement policy, you again pay big early-year commissions and fees, accruing very little if any cash surrender value for several years. According to Jim Hunt, about half of all cash value policies are dropped in seven or eight years— causing a loss or only a small gain for these policyholders. Hunt told Metzenbaum's hearing that he figured that not even one out of ten

policy replacements in the 1980s were in the best financial interests of policyholders.

The difference between gross and net yields on cash-value insurance. Which policy would you choose? One policy has a 12% annual return. Another policy returns only 8%. Annual premiums on both are $1,000. You'd choose the first policy, of course. But what if surrender charges on the first policy came to $600 and to only $300 on the second? The second policy may then become the better deal. It's a common deception to tell potential policyholders about only the *gross* and not the *net* yield.

Combination term and whole life. Such policies have a whole life component, say for $50,000, and a term component for, say, $200,000. The agent explains that over time the dividends from the whole life portion of the policy will pay for the term insurance, or that the dividends go for "paid-up additions" to your whole life component's death benefit, and, eventually, the term insurance is replaced by the whole life. The trouble is, future dividends are often exaggerated.

Paying insufficient premiums on a universal life policy. If the earnings assumptions are too rosy and don't pan out, you could easily pay too little to cover the premiums on the term insurance component without being aware of it. And you'll be left unprotected.

Riders that take you for a ride. According to NICO, insurance companies make big profits on certain riders, which is why they often are a poor value. Some examples:

■ *Premium waiver riders.* You can skip premiums if you are disabled and can't work, and your insurance will remain in force. Generally, if you can't work in your usual occupation, such waivers keep you covered for two years. After that, they apply only if you can't work in an occupation for which you are reasonably fitted. But check carefully how the policy defines this. And compare the cost of this rider with a good disability policy.

■ *Double-indemnity riders.* Such riders provide for double benefits to be paid in case of accidental death. In the 1944 movie "Double Indemnity" Fred MacMurray is an insurance agent who falls in love with Barbara Stanwyck. Together they conspire to murder her husband and make it appear like an accident in order to collect on his double-indemnity rider. If you think you might be married to a Barbara Stanwyck type, think twice about purchasing such a rider. The other reason not to buy one is that the vast majority of deaths are not accidental, and this extra coverage is usually overpriced. Plus, if your survivors really need the cash, why limit the extra benefits to this one cause of death?

■ *Guaranteed insurability rider.* You can purchase additional cash-value insurance without undergoing a new medical exam. The premium is very high for this option; you're likely better off buying more insurance in the first place.

Insuring your children. Insurance companies promote buying insurance on your children. Unless your child is a prodigy who has been supporting you in a style to which you would like to stay accustomed, there is no good reason to buy it.

Meaningless names. Many policy names do not include the important descriptive words "whole life," "universal life," or "variable life." Instead, they go by such unhelpful names as "lifetime protector" or, "heritage extra." Be sure to ask exactly what kind of policy you are being sold.

Life insurance targeted at seniors. A bad deal. You give them $5 a month, they give you next to nothing—maybe only a few hundred dollars coverage as you get older. And there are exclusions, like you have to die in an accident during the first few years of the policy.

Life insurance policies sold as a retirement plan. Metropolitan Life got into hot water in 1993 when authorities learned that company agents were selling Florida nurses whole life insurance policies disguised as retirement plans; most takers thought they were getting some kind of a tax-deferred annuity. Met Life is offering refunds to tens of thousands of people who were deceived, and is paying millions of dollars in fines.

Various states are investigating other insurance companies who appear to have been doing the same thing as Met Life. The best way to avoid becoming a victim is to understand the basic kinds of policies—and ask a lot of questions.

THE SMARTER CONSUMER

Keep up with the payments. If you buy level premium term insurance, try not to let the policy lapse before the end of the term. Such policies are structured so that the premium is a good deal only if you keep the policy in force for a long time.

Think twice before buying a cash-value policy. Consumers Union doesn't think very highly of cash-value policies, generally. IRAs and 401(k) plans could be preferable from an investment and retirement planning point of view. (See "Retirement Nest Eggs," page 315, for more information.)

Still, Jim Hunt believes that in light of their tax advantages, cash-value life insurance policies "can be a good investment, provided that you buy in a good company and you commit to keep the policy for 15 or 20 years in order to amortize the huge up-front costs over a longer period of time and to give the tax advantages and ability of companies to invest well to overcome those high front-end costs."

If you do buy cash-value insurance, at a minimum ask for:

■ All variables, including surrender charges, dividends, interest rates, mortality charges, and administrative fees.

■ An illustration that shows projected and guaranteed values of both cash and death benefits to at least the age of 90. It is most important to see the early years because all policies will show great numbers after 65.

■ The agent should sign the illustration when you are handed the policy, confirming that the illustration corresponds to the policy actually issued.

■ An internal rate-of-return analysis to age 85. This figure is computed from a formula used to determine your investment return at any given point in the policy. The analysis takes into account the premiums paid, the cash value accumulation, and the time value of money. It compares the amount of premiums paid against the ultimate death benefit promised or the cash value.

■ If buying from an agent, make sure he or she is well-qualified, licensed, and has not had the license suspended. At the least make sure the agent sells insurance full time and is a "CLU" (Chartered Life Underwriter) or a "ChFC" (Chartered Financial Consultant).

And if you have a medical condition, make sure the agent has a good grounding in the medical science behind insurance underwriting. One of the consultants for this chapter suggest that you ask your prospective agent what elevated liver enzymes are. If he or she doesn't know, consider going to someone else.

■, **Rating agencies. The** major rater is A.M. Best & Company, which each year publishes two volumes of *Best's Insurance Reports*, one rating life insurance companies and the other rating property-liability companies. These volumes are

probably available at your local library. Weiss Research, considered the toughest grader, will give you a rating over the phone for $15; (800) 289-9222. Standard & Poor's, (212) 208-1527; Moody's, (212) 553-0377; and Duff & Phelps (312) 368-3157 give out their ratings for free. A.M. Best charges $2.50 a minute to call (900) 420-0400, but call (908) 439-2200 to get the insurance company's identification number first.

■, **You should also call your state in**surance department and ask if a company you're considering has faced any regulatory action regarding its solvency. And ask if the company has had problems paying their claims.

■, **Among the free term insurance** comparison shopping services: Term Quote, (800) 444-TERM; SelectQuote (800) 343-1985; and Insurancequote (800) 972-1104. A $50 fee is charged by Insurance Information, Inc., (800) 472-5800, since they don't earn anything by selling policies; the $50 is refunded if you don't save $50 through their service. Quotesmith charges $15; (800) 556-9393.

■, **The National Insurance Consumer** Organization (NICO) recommends buying your low-load universal life policies direct from two Texas companies, USAA Life, (800) 531-8000, and VEST Insurance Marketing Corporation, which sells an Ameritas policy, (800) 552-3553. Geico, (800) 841-3000, and Amica Mutual, (800) 242-6422, are two others. A new, free,

low-load quote service is offered by the Wholesale Insurance Network (WIN), except in Oregon, which requires only fee-paid advisors to sell insurance; call (800) 808-5810.

■, **Clear explanations of** life insurance can be found in *How to Save Money on Life Insurance*, published by the National Insurance Consumer Organization (121 North Payne Street, Alexandria, VA 22314; (703) 549-8050 and Joseph Belth's *Life Insurance: A Consumer Handbook* (University of Indiana, 1988). Belth is a nationally known and feared industry watchdog. In-depth explanations of the tricks of the trade can be found in *Save a Fortune on Your Life Insurance*, by Barry Kaye (1991, Simon & Schuster) and in *Life Insurance: How to Buy the Right Policy From the Right Company at the Right Price*, by the editors of Consumer Reports Books with Trudy Lieberman (1988, Consumers Union).

■, **For an analysis of a policy's rate**-of-return (after fees and expenses), contact the National Insurance Consumer Organization at the address given above. NICO will compute the real rate of return on the cash value part of a policy—minus all the charges—and tell you if you could do better investing your money elsewhere. Price: $35 for one policy and $25 for additional policies. Send the sales illustration of a policy you might buy or the inforce ledger of your current policy to NICO.

■, **For $100, Beacon Company will** compare a policy illustration you provide with its own performance benchmarks; call (800) 824-1274.

■, **Answers, please. The American** Council of Life Insurers has a helpline, (800) 942-4242, but keep in mind that this is an industry group.

CHAPTER 37

HOMEOWNER'S INSURANCE

Covering Your Castle

Private property. It's the American way. And to protect their private property from fire, hail, lightning, theft, burglary, vandalism, and floods, Americans spend over $17 billion a year on homeowner's insurance premiums.

With significant disparities in premiums among insurance companies for the same coverage, it's easy to overpay. Yet comparison shopping for the least expensive policy isn't very difficult; you just have to know what to look for.

THE BASICS

The Standard Policies

Wherever you live in the United States, you'll find these same basic policy categories:

■ HO-1 (Homeowner's 1) is basic protection for the most common perils: damages from fire and lightning, smoke, hail/windstorm, explosion, vehicles, riot or civil disorder, vandalism, and for theft,

burglary, and glass breakage. It covers your personal property as well as your home.

■ HO-2 adds additional coverage to HO-1 policies for falling object damage; roof collapse due to ice, sleet, or snow; collapse of your home generally; damage from an electrical surge or short circuit; and damage from frozen pipes or an air conditioning system malfunction. It doesn't cost much more than HO-1.

■ HO-3 is even more comprehensive. All risks to your house, except for a few specific exclusions, like floods, earthquakes, and wars, are covered. You will also be reimbursed for damaged trees and shrubs and for debris removal. HO-3 is the most commonly purchased protection.

■ HO-4 is for renters. It covers personal property and liability.

■ HO-6 is designed for condominium or co-operative apartment owners. It covers personal belongings, liability, and can also be written to cover physical improvements you made to your apartment, like adding an expensive parquet floor.

■ HO-8 is for valuable or unique older homes. Its coverage tends to be restricted because of the high cost of replicating the original.

While your homeowner's insurance covers your personal property anywhere in the world you take it, you will be reimbursed only for the *current market value* of the personal property, not what it would cost to replace, and for a maximum of 50% of the face value of the policy. That old TV destined for the dump will fetch next to nothing. You can purchase additional "replacement-cost coverage" for an extra premium.

The typical policy also pays your additional expenses for alternative lodgings if damage to your house forces you out. These expenses must be "reasonable," so no resort living while your house is made habitable.

Homeowner's insurance policies also cover you for liability—the chandelier falling on your boss at dinner, your dog taking a small chunk out of the newspaper girl's leg. The standard coverage is for $100,000, which is probably not enough; you can buy more for a small addition to your premium.

How Premiums Are Figured

How much you actually spend depends on the cost of replacing your home and personal property. The insurance company will do an appraisal for free. If you want an independent appraisal, you'll have to spend a few hundred dollars on your own appraiser.

The big bad wolf couldn't blow down the little pig's house made of brick, and insurance companies charge less for houses of brick or stone than for wooden ones. (Straw houses are probably uninsurable.)

Location is critical. Insurance companies compile loss statistics for neighborhoods, and you'll pay more if losses are high in your vicinity. They also assign your neighborhood to a fire protection class. You may pay extra if your neighborhood is served by a volunteer fire department or lacks hydrants.

Extra liability coverage also adds to the premium bill. But raising the deductible to above the usual $250 will yield significant savings.

There are numerous discounts to ask about. Since so many fires are traceable to lit cigarettes, many companies offer a nonsmoker discount. Smoke detectors and burglar alarms can earn you a discount, too. You can also get a break if you are a loyal customer or if your house is new. And you can save on your home and auto insurance if you buy from the same company.

How Much Insurance Do You Need?

Six months after Hurricane Andrew devastated parts of South Florida in 1992, a *Miami Herald* survey found that 17% of policyholders who had filed claims believed they should have had more coverage.

The general rule is that if you buy coverage for at least 80% of your home's replacement cost, you'll be fully reimbursed for claims other than for total rebuilding, such as for repairs to a fire-damaged kitchen. The problem is, what happens if the entire house burns to the ground? If rebuilding costs $200,000, the company will pay only $160,000; you'll have to come up with the rest. So avoid the common mistake of buying only for 80% of replacement cost and get full coverage.

Better yet, buy a guaranteed replacement-cost provision—called an "endorsement"—for your policy. No matter how much it costs to rebuild your home, you're covered. The additional cost of this endorsement is usually minimal, yet its value was well learned by the people who lost their homes in the 1991 Oakland firestorm. But be very clear about exactly what "guaranteed replacement" means. In Oakland, insurance companies maintained that "guaranteed replacement" did not mean that insurers have to pay to meet new, more stringent building codes prompted by recent California earthquakes. However, under pressure from the state—and from the many influential burned-out citizens who banded together as United Policyholders— 34 insurance companies ultimately upgraded retroactively hundreds of policies. Great for them, it's true—but it's unlikely that you could garner such clout all by yourself.

> **"The biggest challenge with insurance is trying to cover all possible situations with all kinds of people, and I've never seen anything designed by man to do it."**
>
> —IRVING LEPELSTAT,
> Brooklyn, New York,
> insurance agent

Exclusions and Limitations

Before plunking down your first premium, read carefully the policy's sections on exclusions and limitations. Here is a partial list of what most homeowner's policies will *not* pay for: earthquakes and floods; damage from a nuclear meltdown; damage from freezing or vandalism after the property has been vacant for several weeks; damage from an area-wide power failure; slow and constant water seepage; normal wear and tear; breakage of personal property; property belonging to a roommate (only your *personal* property is covered). Sorry, pet lovers, neither Fifi nor your piranhas are covered. And your liability coverage won't apply if you intentionally hurt someone in your home.

Typically, homeowner's policies place dollar limits on reimbursement for such personal property as cash and securities, coins, bank notes, deeds, passports, bookkeeping records, tickets, jewelry, furs, watches, and the family silver. You have to buy extra protection to fully cover such items.

A homeowner's policy wouldn't have helped Noah; flood insurance has to be bought separately. Flood policies can be purchased through the National Flood Insurance Pro-

STUPIDITY INSURANCE?

Coverage expectations can be pretty unreasonable. One broker related the story of a woman who once hung wet dungarees over a live fire in her fireplace to dry. When they started to smoulder, she extinguished them—by beating them against her new wall-to-wall carpeting, making a terrible mess. She asked if her homeowner's policy would reimburse her for the $3,000 cost of her carpet. The broker's answer: "Your policy doesn't cover stupidity."

gram (NFIP), which is available to an estimated 11 million homes in designated communities where flood risk is high. In return for NFIP coverage—the government guarantees that participating insurers' premiums will cover all losses—the community has to take flood prevention measures. Unfortunately, only 10% of eligible homeowners sign up for this subsidized coverage. Thousands of homeowners displaced by the 1993 Mississippi River floods sure wish they had bought it. Insured losses came to less than $300 million, compared to more than $15 *billion* for Hurricane Andrew in Florida a year earlier.

Earthquake coverage also has to be bought separately, or you can buy a special earthquake endorsement on your policy. When it comes to earthquake protection, the third little pig had it backward. Earthquake endorsements cost less for wood houses, which better withstand quake stresses, than for houses made of brick.

Unfortunately, those enormous Hurricane Andrew payouts (and the Hurricane Hugo claims in the Carolinas before that) have prompted many insurers to get out of the homeowner's insurance business in certain high-loss geographic areas. Thousands of homeowners in affected communities are, in industry parlance, being "non-renewed," and others are facing astronomic rate hikes. In Florida, the insurer of last resort is the state-sponsored Resident Property and Casualty Joint Underwriting Association. It offers bare-bones coverage and costs about 25% more than the non-renewed coverage. It may not be much, but it's better than nothing.

Condo Insurance

Your condominium apartment association has insurance on your apartment complex—or at least it's supposed to. But the coverage may be insufficient. In case of severe damage, the condo association might be forced to impose an assessment on all owners to cover an insurance shortfall. Your share could come to thousands of dollars.

So if you own a condo (or a co-op), it's a good idea to buy an individual policy to cover shortages in the condo association's coverage and your own special improvements, like the designer kitchen you created. It will also cover you for liability, cover your personal possessions, as well as pay for a modest condo association damage repair assessment.

To avoid overpaying or underinsuring, get a copy of the condo association's policy and compare it to an individual policy you might buy. You can tailor your individual policy to coordinate benefits with those of the association's.

WHAT TO WATCH OUT FOR

Buying coverage based on the market value of your home and property rather than on the replacement cost of just the house. The cost of replacement, of course, has little to do with a home's market value: It keeps rising no matter what. A guaranteed replacement cost policy ensures that you always have enough coverage to rebuild.

Inflation creep. The cost of rebuilding keeps going up. If you don't have a guaranteed replacement cost policy, then you could become underinsured over time. Automatic inflation protection is a second-choice alternative to guaranteed replacement cost. But don't assume that your policy has automatic inflation protection. It does not have it unless it says so.

Overpriced insurance. Most lenders require home buyers to insure the property. Many borrowers simply buy the insurance from the company the lender recommends. But you might pay less for the same or more coverage by shopping

around. You may also get a discount if you buy from the same agency that sold you your other insurance. You might also get better service when you file a claim if you are a "regular customer" who has more than one policy.

Insufficient insurance. Don't rely on your mortgage lenders to make sure your home is sufficiently insured. Your lenders couldn't care less about your home's contents. They just want to be sure the house itself is covered.

Too little liability coverage. Make sure your policy has enough liability coverage. Most experts recommend buying enough to cover as much of your net worth as possible. The standard coverage of $100,000 might not do it. Additional coverage up to $300,000 will probably cost less than $30 a year. You'll probably have to buy a separate policy for coverage above $500,000.

THE SMARTER CONSUMER

"The check is in the mail." Don't buy homeowner's insurance solely on the basis of price. Ask friends and neighbors about their experiences, especially about how long it took to pay a claim, and only sign up with a company with good references.

Before you renew your policy, shop around for lower premiums, as rates change frequently.

The Fair Access to Insurance Requirements (FAIR) plan provides protection against insurance red-lining. Red-lining is when an insurer figuratively or even literally draws a red line around a neighborhood where policies will not be written—often neighborhoods with predominantly minority residents. FAIR was created to ensure coverage for residents of areas insurance carriers have historically shunned. Ask your insurance agent about it; 31 states and the District of Columbia offer FAIR policies.

Homeowner's policies usually cover you for up to $500 in unauthorized credit card purchases. If you lose your credit cards and the "finder" takes them on a spree, the law says you are liable for a maximum of only $50 per card if you report the loss promptly. If you carry a lot of plastic, you could be out several hundred dollars without homeowner's insurance.

Keep a running inventory of valuable possessions. Record the date of purchase and how much you paid. It'll make filing a claim easier. Ask your insurance agent for an inventory form. When you're filling it out, record the serial numbers of appliances. Don't keep these documents or film, video, or photographic records in your house.

The higher the deductible, the lower the premium. You can reduce your premium by 10% or more by raising your deductible from $250 to $500 or above.

■ For information on federal flood insurance, call the Federal Emergency Management Agency, Federal Insurance Administration, at (800) 638-6620 or write to them at 500 C Street SW, Washington, DC 20472.

■ insurance questions? Call your state insurance department or the Insurance Information Institute, (800) 221-4954.

■ Live in a high-crime area? Buy cut-rate Federal Crime Insurance. This program survived many attempts by the Reagan and Bush Administrations to "zero it out." Take advantage of it while it lasts. You will be guaranteed coverage for burglary and theft as long as you install basic protective devices. Call (800) 638-8780 for more information.

■ For help in finding a public adjuster, call the National Association of Public Insurance Adjusters at (410) 539-4141, or write to them at 300 Water Street, Baltimore, MD 21202.

CHAPTER 38

DEBT COLLECTORS

What They Can and Can't Do

Intimidating phone calls at odd hours. Calls to your coworkers—and even your boss. Nasty and profane language. Threats of putting you behind bars. These are some of the hardball tactics used by a disturbingly large number of the nation's debt collectors, despite the 1977 federal Fair Debt Collection Practices Act, which Congress enacted to stop such abuses.

Decidedly not-nice collection tactics are becoming more common as increasing numbers of Americans during hard economic times fall behind in payments on their credit cards, mortgages, home equity, and personal loans. With lots of encouragement from lenders looking for big profits during the go-go 1980s, consumers more than doubled their personal debt tab from $2 trillion in 1980 to $4.4 trillion in 1988. Many consumers suddenly had trouble repaying that easy money when the economy dove into a tailspin at the end of the decade.

Everybody should pay their bills promptly. But if you don't, there is still no reason to put up with abusive collection tactics. The 1977 federal Fair Debt Collection Practices Act (subsequently called "the Act") gives consumers potent weapons to turn the tables on any strongarm collection agency that comes calling.

In addition, many innocent people who really don't owe money can get caught up in collection nightmares. The creditor or collection agency may have been in error, the merchandise might not have been provided, or the purchaser may have been the victim of misleading advertising. The Act protects them, too.

While the Act is tough, it isn't much help unless you are prepared to invoke it in confrontations with bill collectors. If you don't stand up for your rights, the collectors will know they have little to fear, and they will squeeze every possible penny out of you.

THE BASICS

The Fair Debt Collection Practices Act

Applicability. The Act generally covers debts arising from consumer transactions, such as goods or services bought on credit for personal, family, or household use (e.g., appliances or car repairs). Broadly speaking, it applies to anyone who regularly collects consumer debts for other creditors, like the Tight-fist Collection Agency that tries to make you fork over money owed to the doctor, furniture store, or any other creditor.

The Act does not usually apply to the tactics of creditors, like department stores or banks, collecting their own credit card bills. However, it does apply to creditors who try to collect their own bills under an alias. Under a 1986 amendment, the Act now also applies to attorneys who regularly collect debts.

Who can be contacted, and how? A bill collector's stock-in-trade is making contacts to pressure debtors into paying. Bill collectors used to have a free hand to contact debtors or anyone else they believed could be used to pressure debtors into paying. One collector actually parked a black hearse with the inscription "A deadbeat lives here" in front of a debtor's house.

But not anymore. The Act puts collectors on a short leash, allowing them to contact only a few persons about an individual's debt. These restrictions almost completely bar all contacts with "outsiders" that collectors could previously count on to pressure or embarrass you into paying, like relatives, friends, or employers.

When calling others in trying to locate you, bill collectors must identify only themselves (i.e., their names)—not who they are collecting for—unless specifically requested to do so. They must also call only to confirm or correct location information. This prohibits a collector from calling your office and saying, for example: "Hi, I'm Sam Jones, calling from the Acme Collection Agency. Could you tell me if Mary Jones still works there?" They cannot even print the agency's name or a phrase like "Open immediately. Overdue bill inside" on the envelope.

How can't a bill collector contact you? What can't they say or do? The Act gives collectors a fairly free hand in how they can contact you about a bill, such as by mail, telephone, telegram, or in person. But they cannot use a postcard. And they can't reveal in any way that they are trying to collect a debt

FACING THE FACTS

- In a 12-month stretch ending September 30, 1991, individual bankruptcy filings zoomed from 685,000 to 849,000 nationwide, a 24% increase.
- The number of individuals or families who sought help from Consumer Credit Counseling Service offices has nearly doubled, from 211,000 in 1987 to 400,000 in 1990.
- In New York City, for example, the Department of Consumer Affairs reported that the number of complaints received against debt collectors jumped from 258 in 1990 to 425 in 1992—a 65% increase.

COLLECTION PROTECTION: WHAT THE ACT PROVIDES

The 1977 federal Fair Debt Collection Practices Act basically allows collectors to contact only the following persons about a bill:

- The debtor (including the debtor's spouse). Collectors cannot contact you in a way that would let someone else in on your financial troubles, such as by mailing a bill with the collection agency's name on the envelope to your place of employment.
- The debtor's attorney.
- A consumer reporting agency, as permitted by law.
- The bill collector's own attorney.

A collector can, however, contact "outsiders" in the following circumstances:

- The debtor specifically allows it. (The law doesn't require you to say "no"; you only have to avoid saying "yes.")
- The collector needs to locate a debtor. That's called "skip-tracing" in the trade, and the Act strictly limits how collectors can do it.
- A court specifically authorizes the contact.
- The contact is made to implement a post-judgment judicial remedy, like a wage garnishment.

when communicating by telegram or the mails.

In addition, they are not allowed to contact you at inconvenient times or places. This usually means before 8 AM and after 9 PM, unless, of course, the collector knows you work at night. If they know you are represented by an attorney, they cannot contact you directly, unless your attorney fails to respond within a reasonable time—usually within 30 days. And they cannot contact you at work if the collector knows (or should know) that your employer disapproves. When they do contact you, they are supposed to identify themselves and make clear the purpose of their call—no anonymous, intimidating calls.

"Can you spell harass?" taunted one abusive debt collector when William P. of Queens, New York, asked him to stop harassing his wife about an overdue American Express bill. The collector then told William P. that his physical disability was just an excuse not to pay and that he was going to "have the sheriff come to [his] house and pick [his] wife up at her place of employment and arrest her." One of the most important prohibitions in the Act is against abuse or harassment. This bill collector's behavior egregiously violated the law.

Collectors are also not supposed to coerce or intimidate consumers, such as by threatening criminal acts or violence, publishing lists of debtors with your name included, or repeatedly telephoning you. Audrey S. told the NYC that National Financial Services called her several times a day and told her she'd be sued not only for the $2,000 balance but also for legal fees as well, and that her name would be published in the newspaper—a no-no.

When they contact you, collectors are also prohibited from making false or misleading representations, such as:

■ Implying they represent a government agency, or that they are employed by a consumer reporting agency. Manuel A. complained to the NYC Consumer Affairs Department about collectors from International Collection Agency who claimed to be police officers. One of them had a gun and the other held out handcuffs and threatened to take him to jail.

> "**H**e said he didn't care if he harassed me enough to give me another heart attack, he was going to get his money."
>
> —BOB D.
> of Morganton, North Carolina

■ Misrepresenting the character, the amount, or the legal status of a debt. For example, collectors can't claim that a creditor has obtained a judgment when she or he has not, or that the debt is secured by collateral the creditor will repossess when in fact he or she has no collateral covering the debt.

■ Making bogus claims about what they can or will do to collect the bill. They cannot, for example, threaten to garnish your wages unless it is actually legal to do so.

■ Using misleading communications, such as official-looking documents, that make you think you are being sued.

They also can't use a wide range of unfair or misleading collection techniques. Examples of such practices include:

■ Collecting any amounts or imposing charges that are not expressly authorized under the agreement involved or by law. For example, a collector cannot impose a collection charge unless the agreement you signed specifically permits it, which is extremely unlikely. Once a bill is past due, however, the creditor would usually be entitled to charge interest at the rate set by your state's law.

■ Taking or threatening to take your property when there is no present legal right to do so, when they do not intend to do so, or when the property is legally exempt from repossession.

What must collectors do to identify a debt? Unless a collector has already done so or you pay first, within five days after you are first contacted, a collector must send you a *written* notice stating:

■ How much you owe and the name of the creditor.

■ What you can do if you dispute the debt.

BAD TIMES MEAN GOOD TIMES FOR DEBT COLLECTORS

The collection business has boomed. The National Collectors Association (the industry's main trade organization) reports that in the decade from 1980 to 1990, debts handled by collection agencies jumped from $14.5 billion to $66.6 billion, a 360% increase. In 1992, there were approximately 6,000 credit reporting agencies in the United States, up from 5,100 a decade earlier.

■ How you can ask the collector to verify the debt.
■ What the collector must do if you ask for verification.
■ That the creditor will assume the debt is valid unless you dispute it within 30 days after receiving the written notice.

At the very least, this written notice identifies the debt and tells you about key steps to take to enforce important rights. These written particulars can help you confirm that the collector is really authorized to collect the bill for the original creditor.

Even if you owe the money, never discuss or agree to payment arrangements until you get this written notice. Waiting for this notice also gives you some breathing room to figure out how you can deal with the collector if you do owe the money.

What if you dispute the bill or can't identify the creditor? The Act helps you stop debt collectors in their tracks if they try to collect bills you dispute or that you can't identify. It entitles you to demand that a collector verify the identity of a creditor or the debt that you dispute. To make it count, you must send the collector a written notice within 30 days that you dispute all or some portion of the debt or to ask the collector to identify the name and address of the original creditor if it is different from the current creditor.

The written request for verification is your way to tell collectors to get lost until they can show you who you owed the bill to or that you owe it.

You must make this demand in writing within the required 30-day period. One of the biggest mistakes consumers make is not putting this demand in writing. Consumers instead simply ask collectors verbally. This mistake telegraphs at least two things to collectors: First, the consumer does not know what the law requires. Second, the consumer may be too lazy or too afraid to stand up for his or her rights as the law requires. In either case, it's a green light for the collector to ignore the law.

The Act does not spell out what counts as verification of a debt other than a judgment. It would, however, usually be at least a copy of the contract you signed or some other written documentation showing that you in fact owe the money.

Can you stop collectors from contacting you? You certainly can. The Act entitles you to tell a bill collector to stop all further contacts. This is your fail-safe in any confrontation with bill collectors.

You can use this defense any time. To make it count, you must notify a collector *in writing* and indicate either that you refuse to pay the bill or that the collector is to cease communicating with you. Since the notice is binding on the collector upon receipt, always send it by certified mail, return receipt requested. You then have proof of the exact date after which the collector must comply.

Once a collector receives your demand to stop communications, he or she can contact you one more time to tell you that all further communications will be stopped. Collectors can't use this communiqué to make idle threats, however. They can say they may sue, for example, but only if they usually do so in cases like yours and intend to do so.

Laura H. didn't mail any written notice at all. Like many recent college graduates contending with small salaries and large bills, Laura had trouble paying back her student loans. But she did make some payments over a period of years, demonstrating her intention and at least a limited ability to pay, and unfortunately encouraging two collection agencies, Windham Professionals and Superior Credit Ser-

vices, to call her daily and sometimes several times a day with such threats as "this will not go away."

Of course, telling a creditor to stop communicating with you merely stops collectors from using nonlegal recourse to collect. It does not keep them from taking you to court.

Using the Act Against Abusive Collectors

The threshold question to answer before tackling any bill collector is: Do I owe the bill? Your answer will determine what parts of the law can help you the most and what parts you can use most forcefully against a collector. Here's how:

Bills you are unsure about. If you are unsure whether you owe a bill, immediately send the bill collector a written verification request. Make clear you will not discuss the debt or make payments until the collector verifies the debt. Also make this clear in the letter you send requesting the verification.

Once you receive the required verification, you must decide whether you owe or should dispute the bill.

Bills you dispute. If you're sure you don't owe a bill or it's one that you dispute, there is little point in beating around the bush with the collector.

Clearly state the reasons why you dispute all or part of the bill. It could be that you already paid it and the seller or creditor is trying to collect again; the bill may be for goods or services that you ordered but did not receive; maybe it's not your bill; or perhaps the original seller did not live up to the contract and you are entitled to withhold part of the bill.

If you are disputing the purchase, you should already have taken up the dispute with the seller. Explain the steps you have taken to the collector, and send along copies of documents and letters that back up your claims.

Insist on written confirmation of any settlement you propose. If you

THE PENALTY BOX

Violations can cost collectors plenty. The best part? It could be money in your pocket. A collector who violates any part of the Act could be liable for the sum of the following amounts:

■ All losses you had because of any illegal actions the collector took, such as loss of a job, expenses you incurred, or mental anguish that was caused.
■ Up to $1,000 that a court could award for violations even if you had no actual losses. The law allows consumers to collect this money to punish collectors who violated the law when seeking to collect a debt.
■ The cost of the legal action plus your "reasonable" attorney's fees (determined by the court).

know you owe part but not all of a bill, you could send a "payment in full" check and write on the back of the check that it can be accepted only as payment in full of the disputed amount. (One trick here is to offer to pay a few dollars more than the amount you admit you owe. Cashing the check will then almost certainly legally bar the creditor from trying to collect more.)

Your leverage for getting a favorable response is to tell collectors that you will order them to cease all further communications unless they respond favorably to how you asked them to take care of the disputed bill.

If the collector responds by pressuring you to pay instead of trying to resolve the disputed bill as you proposed, the only practical alternative is to order the collector to cease further communications. If the collector insists on not listening to you, it's a waste of time to keep shouting. Tell the collector to get lost.

Alternatively, you could order a collector to cease communications as your initial step. Doing so, however, prevents you from settling the dispute. You could be sued—but that may be exactly what you want if you are absolutely certain you don't owe the bill.

Bills you owe. If you owe the bill but lack the money to pay, it is important not to evade the issue by making up woeful tales or using nitpicking legal technicalities. The collector has likely heard it all before (and then some), and you won't win any sympathy no matter how hard you try.

In all such cases, your first step is to insist that the collector identify the bill as required by the Act. This gives you time to decide what you can do about the bill. Your next and most important step is to decide what you can realistically afford to pay toward the bill. The only thing that helps is to be straightforward about what you can do to pay and demonstrate that you will make a determined effort to do so.

The most important rules here are: Never say you *will* pay if you can't; never say you *can't* pay when you can pay at least something. Ignoring the rules is the surest way to trigger the full collection treatment.

WHAT TO WATCH OUT FOR

Post-dated checks. A debt collector might pressure you into writing post-dated checks. Then with a stack of post-dated checks in hand, collectors can pressure you to pay by threatening criminal prosecution under bad-check laws. The Act contains specific, limited provisions for taking post-dated checks.

Charges for communications, such as for long-distance collect calls. Collectors sometimes use a ruse such as claiming there is an emergency involving a relative to get you to accept collect charges for phone calls. If you're being hounded by bill collectors, be on guard for this.

Not getting it in writing. We repeat: Get a written confirmation that the collector has accepted pay-

ments lower than those called for by your agreement. If you are already in default on a bill, paying less than you owe without a written agreement could lead to problems later, even if you have an oral agreement with the collector.

Don't ignore debt collectors. They won't go away; they'll just come at you harder, convinced you are a deadbeat.

Keep records. Hang on to any written materials collectors send you to document their actions. Document the dates, times, and places of any oral communications, and write up a summary of what happened. Take notes of any discussions, and keep written records to help you prove what happened. In addition, the Act requires that you use written communication to trigger certain rights. Doing otherwise is the same as throwing away the rights the Act created for you. Of course, you should keep a copy of any letters you send a collector.

Deal calmly with collectors. Most encounters with debt collectors will be of the oral kind, whether in person or over the phone. Always stay calm and stick to the point. Be polite but always firmly insist that collectors strictly toe the lines drawn in the Act. Here is an example of how to make collectors heel to when they try to browbeat you in oral confrontations:

"You must be aware that the Fair Debt Collection Practices Act prohibits you from [describe the illegal tactic the collector uses]. . . . If you keep that up, we are not going to have much more to talk about." That's a veiled threat that you will exercise your right to order the collector to cease all further communications.

Making clear you won't even talk about payments until you receive the required five-day notice under the Act creates leverage to get the collector to send it. If you still have not received the notice within a few days after the five-day period, there is a good chance the collector has violated the law. Pointing to such violations and the penalties the collector could face gives you leverage in future confrontations.

Never give collectors post-dated checks, no matter how convincing they are. The postage you save by not having to mail each check will be trifling compared to one bounced-check charge.

Answer any lawsuit summons. Otherwise, the creditor will get a default judgment and with it the power to use judicial collection remedies like garnishment and repossession of property. If you appear in court, you may be able to work out a payment settlement with your creditor's attorney on the spot.

▪ If you have serious financial problems, seek professional help. Call the National Foundation for Consumer Counseling to locate the credit counseling agency closest to you; (800) 388-2227.

▪ Where to complain. The Federal Trade Commission is primarily responsible for enforcing the Fair Debt Collection Practices Act against collection agencies. Send any written complaint to Debt Collection Practices, Federal Trade Commission, Washington, DC 20580.

▪ Many states also have their own debt collection laws that are often based on the Fair Debt Collection Practices Act. Check with your State Attorney General's Office to find out about your rights under your state's law.

CHAPTER 39

TAX PREPARERS

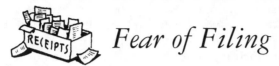

Fear of Filing

E ven before Chief Justice Marshall declared in 1819 that "the power to tax is the power to destroy," taxes had been this country's great obsession. Political careers are lost for supporting them; millionaires go to prison for evading them. And the rest of us—the "little people" in Leona Helmsley's immortal words—are left to sweat and fret as April 15 looms near. When asked shortly before Super Bowl XXV if he was afraid of the other team's quarterback, New York Giants coach Bill Parcells replied, "Let me tell you what I'm scared of: spiders, snakes, and the IRS."

Some 115 million Americans dutifully file their income tax return with the Internal Revenue Service each year. Slightly over half choose to go through this painful ritual alone, sitting at the kitchen table one Sunday afternoon and measuring the extent of the damage. The rest, due to fear or financial complexity, seek solace or savings by hiring a tax preparer.

Finding the right professional can truly be a taxing task. As Leonard Sloane of *The New York Times* notes, "the industry . . . is diffuse, unstructured, and virtually unregulated." There is no national standard or educational require-

ment: All you need to do is click your ruby shoes together three times and murmur, "I am a tax preparer"—*et voilà,* you can hang out a shingle and get to business. Only California and Oregon have qualifying guidelines.

And while fiscal laws are in a constant flux, one in seven preparers has in recent years canceled subscriptions to tax information services that help keep accountants up to date. The result: U.S. taxpayers demanded $100 million in damages from certified public accountants (CPAs) in 1992, according to the chief insurance liability underwriter for the accounting industry. As one industry insider notes, "Most accountants are three to five years behind the laws and regulations. . . . It's like doing carpentry without a hammer."

Therefore you need to take some time to find the right person to take care of your financial health, if you choose not to do it yourself.

THE BASICS

S tep one is to decide if you'll prepare your tax return yourself or go for professional help.

If your tax situation changed

365

little since last year, or if you have only a few pieces of information—one or two W-2s, some interest and investment income, and a mortgage deduction—consider sitting down at home one weekend with pen, pencil, coffee, and calculator and slogging through until it's done. As one business journalist who has done his own taxes for 20 years explains, "I go it alone because of an absolute conviction that no outsider will take as much care with my return as I will, no matter how big the fee. Keeping that fee in my own pocket is a big attraction, too, of course. And then there is the buzz that comes from taking on Uncle Sam and his troops at the IRS." Even if you don't enjoy that "buzz," you should be able to knock off your return in an afternoon: According to the IRS, it takes the average taxpayer 3 hours and 27 minutes to prepare a 1040 Form, plus two more hours for forms listing itemized deductions and capital gains and losses.

> "*People get frightened when they look at the forms and booklets. But if a person's situation is fairly simple—just wages, interest and dividends, and no itemizing—there's no reason why he can't do his taxes himself.*"
>
> —JOEL S. ISAACSON,
> Weber, Lipshie & Company,
> Accounting firm

If you decide to go it alone, the IRS offers free help with publications, phone hotlines, and walk-in centers. While telephone assistance has been notoriously unreliable—one commentator suggested that "you have a better chance of getting accurate information by dialing 1-900-WEATHER"—the rate of technical accuracy had reached 89% by 1993, up from 78% in 1991. If you can show that an error in your return was due to erroneous IRS advice, you'll still be responsible for back taxes and interest, but no penalty. Therefore, keep track of the person's name, date, and time you spoke to him or her, the question you asked, and the answer you received.

In addition, call your local IRS office to find out about Volunteer Income Tax Assistance, a program that offers free assistance to low-income taxpayers, the disabled, non-English speakers, and, in conjunction with the American Association of Retired Persons, low- and moderate-income citizens 60 years and up.

Consider also investing in a tax guidebook or, if you have a computer, a software program. The best programs are relatively cheap (around $40 to $50, with big discounts available by buying directly from the manufacturer), easy to use, and they enable you to try out various scenarios to come up with the lowest taxes. *Money* magazine tested several in 1993 and recommended Kiplinger's TaxCut for its "exceptional clarity," as well as Andrew Tobias's TaxCut and TurboTax.

A Good Tax Preparer Is Hard to Find

If your tax return is reasonably complex or if you need professional back-up, help is available. But not all tax preparers are equally qualified—or equally expensive. Each year, *Money* magazine asks 50 tax preparers to calculate taxes owed by a hypothetical household. In 1993, 41 respondents submitted 40 different answers, and no one got the figure calculated by the magazine's experts—$35,643. Only two came within $500 of the target tax. One (a CPA) came up almost $40,000 in excess, at $74,450. In addition, preparers' fees varied by 860%, from $375 to $3,600.

A few pointed queries should help you come up with the right person for the job. First, find out about prospects' professional background. Look for someone with experience (experts suggest five years or more), expertise in your field, and a recommendation from someone in a comparable financial situation. Ask how preparers stay current on tax developments—do they read specialized journals or attend seminars?

Stay in contact with your preparer year-round, and make sure he or she will be available if you're audited. Find out if your preparer shares your financial philosophy—whether he or she will aggressively push the legal envelope or act in a conservative fashion. Finally, ask how the fee is computed. Storefront preparers generally charge based on the number of forms; enrolled agents and CPAs, on a hourly basis. Steer clear if the fee is calculated based on the size rather than the complexity of your return. Don't forget to ask if your preparer will reimburse you for errors that result in interest or penalties.

Most important, look for someone whose skills match the complexity of your return. Just as you wouldn't hire Albert Einstein to tutor your child in 4th-grade math, you don't need a CPA from one of the Big Six accounting firms to file a 1040EZ (for "easy") form. At the same time, you don't want to hire a rookie if you're playing in the big leagues. Tax professionals break down into four categories:

■ *Storefront preparers* provide the best bang for the buck if your filing is fairly straightforward (only a few documents). Because anyone can claim to be a tax preparer, make sure to check a prospective preparer's qualifications, as suggested above. You're probably in good hands if you go to one of the large national chains. H&R Block, which files one in eight U.S. tax returns, requires all its employees to complete annual 11-week courses. For an average of $50, you can expect a solid, straightforward job—but no fancy accounting to jazz up your refunds. H&R also offers an "executive tax service" for taxpayers earning $40,000 or more. The benefit: nicer amenities—including a private office—a continued relationship with one agent, and year-round planning tips. The down side: double the fees for the same quality of service.

Unlike enrolled agents, CPAs, and tax attorneys, storefront operators cannot represent you at an IRS audit; large chains, however, will generally send a preparer to accompany you to the IRS if your return is audited.

For business returns or complicated personal returns—if you sold a house, got married or divorced, want to claim depreciation of assets, or had partnership income last year—consider going to a more thoroughly trained professional. There are three kinds:

- *Enrolled agents (EAs)* are certified to practice before the IRS after having either worked at the IRS for a minimum of five years or passed a rigorous two-day exam (only 30% pass). They are skilled at navigating the system and can handle most functions a CPA would serve, including complex tax returns, financial planning, and representing you at an audit, often for up to one-half to one-third less than a CPA would charge.

Enrolled agents must complete 72 hours of continuing study on tax law every three years. Members of the National Association of Enrolled Agents (NAEA) meet more stringent requirements (minimum of 30 hours of training a year). Ask your EA to show you an enrollment card and number that you can check with the IRS.

- *Certified public accountants (CPAs),* like enrolled agents, should be considered for complex filings—especially if your situation involves large investment portfolios, business interests, trusts, or self-employment plans. CPAs may be especially valuable for financial and tax planning. But while all CPAs have some tax training, not all are experts on individual returns. And while they are required to take 80 hours of continuing education courses every two years to maintain their CPA designation, they may do so in a field unrelated to your needs. (Members of the American Institute of Certified Public Accountants [AICPA] must undergo 40-hour brushup courses on tax law each year.) Make sure that your CPA specializes in your area.

- *Tax lawyers* are the industry's 800-pound gorillas. They generally do not assist in the preparation of individual returns but rather intervene in complex issues like divorce settlements or more adversarial IRS audits.

Once you decide on the level of expertise you need, narrow your selection to three possibilities. Start the process before January 1, or the right person may not be available to give you the attention you require. Check their history with your local consumer office or Better Business Bureau; the IRS maintains a list of "problem preparers" whose clients face a high chance of being audited.

Tax preparers should be able to give you an estimate of their fee based on your previous year's return and basic information about your current financial situation. You can bring the fee down and make everyone's job easier by keeping careful records year-round and organizing your documents ahead of time instead of dumping a shoebox filled with papers in your tax preparer's lap on April 14. And to avoid trouble down the road, *never* sign a blank return or one written in pencil, and make sure that both you and your preparer signed your return (with his or her social security number) and that you understand what you're signing: As the IRS warns, "you are still responsible for the accuracy of every item entered on your return. If there is any underpayment, you are responsible for paying it, plus any interest and penalty that may be due."

So found the clients of the Tompkins Square Tax Savers (TSTS), a Manhattan tax preparation service. They got an unpleasant surprise in April 1991 when they called TSTS and got a recording saying that the IRS had seized its records *and* their returns after arresting the owner for claiming refunds that taxpayers were not entitled to, apparently after forging his customers' signatures. The message warned that TSTS clients were likely to be audited and that they would be well advised "to consult with your attorney."

Finally, you are entitled to—and by law must receive—a copy of your return as well as any accompanying documents.

Electronic Filings and Refund Anticipation Loans

Since 1986, taxpayers can file their federal returns electronically through an authorized filing service; 12.3 million taxpayers did so in 1993. Many tax preparers also

AUDIT TIME

Getting an audit letter from the IRS is about as welcome as getting a "go directly to jail" card would be in real life. Fortunately, less than 1% of returns are subjected to this nerve-wracking process. If fate or fraud singled you out, and if a tax preparer was involved in the return, he or she should generally be involved in the audit as well.

If the issue is straightforward—eg, justifying a high deduction with the canceled check—there's no need for an expert. In fact, 80% of taxpayers who face office audits go it alone; half face field audits (conducted at home or their place of business) without professional assistance. IRS Publication 556, "Examination of Returns," can help. Key tips: Never lie. Don't volunteer information. And don't rule out a settlement.

If the issues are complex, go to a professional—an enrolled agent, a CPA, or a tax attorney. In particular, you will need a tax attorney if fraud is alleged and also perhaps if the audit involves complex matters like trusts, estates, charitable foundations, or partnerships.

offer refund anticipation loans (RALs), which are loans advanced by a bank to a consumer based on an anticipated refund from the IRS.

Filing electronically cuts down the refund time by half—from six to eight weeks to about three weeks, or two weeks if your refund goes directly to your bank. And you can usually get a RAL within five days of filing. In addition, returns filed electronically have a substantially lower rate of error.

But while these programs have grown popular in recent years as recession-plagued taxpayers have needed quick cash, most financial experts agree with *Newsday* reporter Jerry Morgan, who argues that "unless you need cash right away—within five days of filing your return to ward off creditors—filing electronically to get a RAL doesn't pay." Suppose, for instance, that you are charged $30 to file electronically and another $30 to get a RAL of $1,000. The fee amounts to 6% of the loan over a four-week period—or an exorbitant 72% annual interest rate! In addition, some experts believe that electronically filed returns are easier for the IRS to scan, review, and thus, audit. If you go ahead anyway, shop around. A 1993 *Newsday* survey found prices for electronic filings ranging from $25 to $75.

WHAT TO WATCH OUT FOR

Tax preparers often advertise refund anticipation loans as "rapid refund."

They are not—they are short-term loans at exorbitant interest rates. Following legal action by NYC's Department of Consumer Affairs, H&R Block branches in New York have agreed to stop advertising their RALs as refunds and to disclose both the lending institution and the fact that a fee or interest is being charged. Similar actions in Connecticut, Florida, and other states led to the same result.

Some preparers also misrepresent the fee they charge for a RAL. In 1992, the NYC Department of Consumer Affairs took action against Beneficial National Bank, a company that made RALs through hundreds of tax preparers for a $29 fee. Beneficial claimed that its interest rate on a $500 loan was 2.5%—but over a ten-day period, that worked out to an astronomical 225% annual rate.

Stay away from preparers who claim a special relationship with the government or who base their fee on the size of the refund they can get you.

THE SMARTER CONSUMER

Look for a tax preparer before January 1st so that you get the right person for you and to ensure proper attention from him or her.

Organize your documents before visiting your tax preparer. You'll save time—and when you're being billed on a hourly basis, time is money.

Familiarize yourself with tax regulations that apply to you even if you hire a professional to do the calculations and fill out the paperwork.

Never agree to have your tax refund sent to your preparer. It should always be sent to you.

Come out of hiding. If you are among the 10 million Americans who failed to file in the past, don't stay in hiding. The IRS doesn't prosecute taxpayers who voluntarily come forward. But if you don't, you may be getting yourself in more trouble—and missing out on a possible refund. (Three out of four persons who file tax returns receive refunds, but refunds must be claimed within three years.)

· **To get free assistance** from the IRS, call (800) 829-1040 or your local IRS office. Deaf consumers with TDD equipment should call (800) 829-4059.

· **For a list of members** of the American Institute of Certified Public Accountants in your area, call (800) 862-4272.

· **For a list of members in the National Association of Enrolled Agents** in your area, call (800) 424-4339.

· **The IRS puts out over a hundred** useful booklets including Publication 1, *Your Rights as a Taxpayer*; Publication 17, *Your Federal Income Tax*; Publication 910, *Guide to Free Tax Services*; and Publication 579S, *Como Preparar la De-*

claracion de Impuesto Federal for Spanish speakers. Call (800) 829-3676 for free copies.

· **Many newspapers publish** special tax sections in February or March with useful tips and information on filing your tax return and where to get help.

· **Several organizations—such as** *Consumer Reports*, H&R Block, Ernst & Young, etc.—put out annual tax preparation guide/helpers. For $15 to $20, these guides can help you prepare even moderately complex returns.

· **If your tax preparer fails to send** you a copy of your tax return, write to the IRS Director of Practice, 1111 Constitution Avenue NW, Washington, DC 20224.

What You Wear

CHAPTER 40

JEWELRY AND WATCHES

All That Glitters Is Not Gold

Everyone should have it as easy as Holly Golightly when she skipped breakfast to go shopping at Tiffany's. She walked out of the store with full knowledge that the ring she just had engraved was made of plastic and came out of a box of Cracker Jacks. Meanwhile, most everyone else is left to wonder whether they've gotten their money's worth for the jewelry or watch they bought. The most common problems involve junky jewelry that breaks after the second or third wearing, deceptions about the quality of gemstones or the gold or silver content, and phony appraisals.

Buying jewelry is like buying works of art: The uniqueness of each gem or piece of jewelry makes it inherently difficult to evaluate without a trained eye. One unhappy man complained about a string of "cultured" pearls he bought as a graduation gift for his daughter. He paid $350 (supposedly 80% off the regular price) and was given what he was told was a "certified appraisal" indicating that the necklace

was worth $1,575. An independent appraiser found that the necklace was made of imitation pearls and worth $75.

A suburban couple complained about an appraiser on 47th Street—the heart of New York's well-known jewelry district—who had worked in cahoots with a neighboring jeweler to prop up the jeweler's claims about the quality of the diamond engagement ring they had just bought. Independent appraisers found the ring to be worth two thirds of the $11,000 the couple had been led to believe it was worth. When they confronted the jeweler, he refused to take the ring back or return their money.

THE BASICS

Find a Jeweler You Can Trust

Before you buy anything, ask your friends and relatives for the names of jewelry stores where they have had good experiences.

375

You can also check with the Better Business Bureau (BBB) in your area to find out if the stores you are considering have complaint records. If you buy something from the first store you walk into, you could end up like the 1993 *Primetime Live* undercover producer who paid $3,700 for a diamond ring at Diamond City in Manhattan that an independent expert said was worth not even half that, only $1,700. The store's owner had appraised the diamond at $5,800, more than three times its actual value.

Purchasing diamonds and other true gemstones is tricky business. Each stone offers a unique combination of the 4Cs—cut, color, clarity, and carat (weight). The average consumer may have a very hard time seeing or gauging these characteristics and therefore judging a stone's true value. Since no two stones are alike, it's hard to comparison-shop even among stones of comparable weights. And since most consumers probably aren't gem experts, you are dependent upon the jeweler's expertise and honesty to make sure you don't get ripped off on a fifth C—cost.

For this reason, a trustworthy, reputable jeweler is a necessity. Many people in the jewelry industry recommend shopping at well-known, established stores, if not at showplaces like Tiffany's or Cartier. You'll definitely pay more, but you'll almost certainly get exactly what you pay for. And if you don't, you can be sure you'll be able to settle the dispute quickly and satisfactorily. Well-tended reputations depend upon it.

The Jargon

The key to shopping for jewelry is understanding the terms used to describe and value it.

Quality mark. This represents the percentage of gold or silver alloyed with other metals, such as copper and brass. Jewelry industry guidelines require that jewelry marked silver or sterling silver contain 92.5% silver. On gold jewelry, the quality mark is expressed as the number of karats. The higher the number of karats, the higher the gold content. No jewelry is made from pure gold (24K) or pure silver because neither element is strong or durable enough by itself for long wear.

Manufacturer's registered trademark. Federal law requires this mark to identify the manufacturer if an item has been stamped with a quality mark so that you will know the name of the entity that stands behind the quality of the item.

Gold-filled. A thin layer of gold of at least 10K is bonded to the surface of a base metal, and the gold content is at least 20% of the total weight of the metal. This term must be accompanied by a quality mark.

Gold electroplate. A base metal has been coated with gold. The gold can be as thin as seven millionths of an inch. This term must be accompanied by a quality mark.

Layered in gold. This term is completely meaningless; purveyors who offer such items hope that

KARAT COUNTING

Quality Mark	Gold Content	Notes
24K	*100%*	*Too soft to make jewelry from*
18K	*75%*	*Standard in Europe*
14K	*58.5%*	*Standard in the U.S.*
10K	*41.6%*	*Lowest percentage that legally can be called gold in the U.S.*

consumers simply won't ask what it means.

Solid gold. Do not confuse this term with "pure gold." Solid gold means simply that the jewelry has not been hollowed out and tells you nothing about the amount of gold in the piece of jewelry. For example, a 10K solid gold ring cannot be hollow inside. This term must be accompanied by a quality mark.

Four Cs. This is shorthand for the four qualities of gemstones—especially diamonds—that determine their value.

■ *Cut* (also known as the facet). This refers to the small flat surfaces on gems, not just the shape of the stone. The quality of the cut affects brilliance, beauty, and the value of the stone. The price of two stones of similar color and clarity can vary 30% to 50% because of variations in cut.

■ *Color.* Diamonds are graded from colorless (the highest grade) to light yellow or brown (the lowest grade) on a scale between D and Z. D means the diamond is flawless and brilliantly clear. Z means it's yellow in color. Gems other than diamonds also vary in value depending on color.

■ *Clarity.* This scale from F1 (flawless) to I (imperfect or inclusion) grades the stone on the kinds, number, and placement of imperfections. Federal Trade Commission (FTC) rules prohibit any diamond from being called flawless unless no imperfections are visible to a trained eye in good light under 10-power magnification.

■ *Carat.* This is a standard measurement of the weight of the stone. One carat weighs 200 mg. Carats are divided into 100 units, called points. Thus a half-carat diamond is the same as a 50-point diamond.

Kinds of gems. "Natural" gems are found in nature; "synthetic" gems are essentially the same in composition and brilliance qualities as their natural counterparts, but they are made in a laboratory or factory. "Imitation" gems are made of different materials and resemble natural and synthetic gems only in appearance; they must be labeled imitation or simulated.

Watches. "Mechanical watches" are operated by a spring inside the watch. "Quartz" or "electronic" watches are operated by a battery.

Appraisals are opinions as to the value, authenticity, quality, and design of jewelry or watches. Since they represent opinions about unique items, there can be a certain amount of variation among competent appraisals. There are two types:

■ *Insurance replacement value* gives you the approximate cost to replace an item, taking into account current market prices, materials, and other costs. You need it to insure your jewelry against loss or damage.
■ *Estate value* estimates what the item would fetch on the open market and is usually lower than the insurance replacement value.

WHAT TO WATCH OUT FOR

All that glitters is not gold. Check the quality markings on both the clasp or hook *and* on the jewelry itself. Each should have a quality mark. A common trick is to put a good clasp on junky jewelry. If you check only the clasp for a quality mark, you may end up with a great clasp—and an inferior bracelet.

It is illegal to mismark jewelry. Most merchants are reliable, but a few may stamp 14K on jewelry that isn't anywhere near it. If you discover that an item you purchased was mismarked—usually through a

professional appraisal—you can complain to law enforcement authorities, the local BBB, and consumer affairs officials.

Street vendors. Avoid buying jewelry on the street or take extra precautions. These vendors often use the mismatched markings trick, hoping you will check only the quality mark on the clasp and pay a dear price for cheap jewelry. Be skeptical of street peddlers who offer deep discounts on designer or famous name watches—counterfeits are plentiful (see "Counterfeit and Gray-Market Goods," page 598).

Beware of jewelers hawking "wholesale" prices. It's just a come-on. By definition, wholesale involves sales to merchants; if a consumer buys something, it is a retail transaction.

Be skeptical of ads that claim an item is discounted by some percent or discounted from "list price." Ask yourself, 40% off what? Merchants that sell brand-name jewelry—a Bulova watch, for example—can honestly say they are selling the watch at a discount (if in fact they are). But in the case of diamonds or other natural, non-synthetic gems, the discount is meaningless. Watch out for dealers touting discounts off a "list price." Each stone is unique, made by nature, and Mother Nature doesn't set list prices.

Never buy gemstones by phone. Many people have been taken in by telemarketers who sell "investment stones," buying them sight unseen. For instance, Newport Gems,

DIAMONDS MAY BE FOREVER, BUT PEARLS ARE MORE POPULAR

The value of pearls is based on shape, color, luster (also called orient), size, surface perfection, and rarity. Since it is a difficult and long process to grow a pearl, larger pearls are rarer and generally more valuable. More symmetrical pearls fetch higher prices, and pink pearls are more valuable than white, which are more valuable than gray. Measurements are across their diameter, expressed in millimeters.

A mollusk produces a pearl when an irritant lodges in its body and deposits of a crystalline substance called nacre form around it. "Natural" pearls result when the irritant gets there by accident (they are virtually unavailable on the market). "Cultured" pearls are formed when an irritant is placed in a mollusk. Anything else that resembles pearls was manufactured, and the FTC requires that it be labeled "simulated" or "imitation." Here are the most common kinds of cultured pearls, according to the Jewelers of America trade association:

- *Akoya* pearls are grown in pearl oysters off the coast of Japan and are the most familiar cultured pearl.
- *South Sea* pearls are large pearls grown in oysters off the coast of Australia. They are usually silvery and less lustrous than Akoya pearls.
- *Fresh water* pearls are cultivated in mollusks other than oysters in fresh water lakes and rivers. They most often come in elongated, irregular shapes.
- *Biwa* pearls are fresh water pearls cultivated in a mollusk found only in Japan's Lake Biwa. They are smoother and more lustrous than fresh water pearls from China.
- *Burmese* pearls are large and grown in oysters off the coast of Burma. Their color tones are warmer than those grown in the South Seas and they are rare and expensive.
- *Mabe* pearls are large hemisphere-shaped pearls; because of their shape they are usually mounted on rings, earrings, or brooches. They are less expensive than spherical cultured pearls.

When you buy pearls, don't expect any two to match perfectly in size and color—unless they're marked imitation or simulated. However, if you roll a well-strung strand along a flat surface, it should roll evenly without any wobbling. Also, knots between each pearl in the strand will protect you from losing more than one pearl if the string should break.

RIME Inc., and Palm Gallery, three California telemarketers, paid $1.2 million to settle 1990 charges by the FTC that they had exaggerated the resale value of semiprecious stones they sold and underplayed the risk of the investment.

Return policies. Before you plunk down any serious money, find out about the store's return policy. Don't buy from anybody who won't accept a return or be there to take one, i.e., traveling trunk shows at hotels or convention centers.

THE SMARTER CONSUMER

Look for the quality mark and the manufacturer's registered trademark when you're shopping for gold or silver jewelry or watches. Karat quality marks are not required, but most jewelry has been stamped with a quality mark. If there is a quality mark, the National Gold and Silver Stamping Act requires the manufacturer to stamp its registered trademark on the item as a guarantee of authenticity. (Exceptions: antiques and foreign pieces.)

Do not buy a gem without an independent appraisal unless you feel absolutely sure of yourself and your jeweler. A good jeweler who has dealt with you honestly should have no hesitation about allowing you to take a piece of jewelry to an appraiser of your choice. Ask the jeweler if you can charge the item on a credit card and return it if the independent appraisal contradicts what the jeweler told you. Keep in mind that jewelry appraisal is a subjective science; the dollar values don't have to match exactly, but they should be within a reasonable range (about 10%) of each other.

Do not use an appraiser recommended by the jeweler. Find an independent appraiser who has a gemologist's certificate from one of the four major certifying groups— American Gemological Society, American Society of Appraisers, Accredited Gemologist Association, and National Association of Jewelry Appraisers. Using an appraiser from any of these organizations is no guarantee of honesty but it's a good place to start. Get a very specific appraisal, including a written description of the item, an enumeration of each gem's cut, color, clarity, shape, carat weight, and position, and diagrams of all stones. Pay a flat fee or an hourly rate; do not pay an appraiser based on the appraised value of the stone.

When you buy, insist on a detailed, written receipt. The seller should be willing to put on paper every detail promised—the type of setting, quality of the gold or silver, and quality of the gem (specifying each of the 4Cs). An honest jeweler should be willing to give you a money-back guarantee that you've bought what you were told you bought. Get it in writing; he or she has nothing to lose if you get an independent appraisal.

Ask for an independent quality report for each piece of fine jewelry you buy. If the jeweler does not have one, ask him or her to submit the item to the Gemological Institute of America (GIA), and get a written guarantee that the jeweler will refund your money if the GIA report shows anything different from what the jeweler promised. Don't try to get the GIA report yourself; the GIA accepts gems only from jewelers.

The best reports include a standard diagram of the stone with its unique internal flaws plotted on the diagram by the gem grader. Since every stone is different, you can use these reports to identify your stone. In a story told on ABC's *Primetime Live*, a Philadelphia woman took a ring with a high-quality diamond to a jeweler for enlarging. When she picked the ring up later, her good diamond had been replaced with an inferior stone. She used the quality report to help prove her case.

Let your budget be your guide. Because high-end jewelry stores want to force potential buyers to talk to a salesperson who can then steer them to even-higher-priced items, they do not mark their jewelry with prices. While a few jurisdictions require that at the very least a range of prices be posted in every display case, most do not. Don't get shifted out of your price range until you're sure there's nothing within it that suits your taste.

Ask about a watch's warranty before you buy. What's covered and for how long? Who will repair it? Where can you get spare parts once the warranty runs out?

▪ The Jewelers Vigilance Committee tries to help resolve consumer complaints. Write to: Jewelers Vigilance Committee, 401 East 34th Street, Suite N13A, New York, NY 10016-8578.

America, your jeweler has to submit items to GIA's Gemological Trade Laboratory. For information, call (800) 421-7250. GIA created the standardized rating system that is widely used in the U.S. to grade gems.

▪ The trade association for jewelers has several free, helpful pamphlets on buying gold, silver, and gems. Write to Jewelers of America, 1185 Avenue of the Americas, 30th Floor, New York, NY 10036.

▪ To get an independent quality re-port from the Gemological Institute of

▪ The Federal Trade Commission will not intervene in individual disputes, but it will take legal action if it sees a pattern of misrepresentation. Send the FTC copies of your complaint letters to jewelers, manufacturers, or local consumer law enforcement authorities: FTC, Public Reference, Washington, DC 20580.

CHAPTER 41

COSMETICS

The Truth Isn't Even Skin Deep

"For good skin," one dermatologist told the NYC Department of Consumer Affairs, "you don't need much more than a mild soap to wash away the dirt and grime of the day. You don't need masks, scrubs, peels, pore openers, pore closers, etc. It's all bull." Despite all the hype and hope, no cosmetic can iron out wrinkles, crow's feet, or a furrowed brow. Nor can any concoction dissolve those cellulite bulges on the hips and thighs. These changes are natural and irreversible parts of the aging process. Pay no attention to the $2.4 billion-worth of advertising that toiletries and cosmetics manufacturers circulate each year to convince you otherwise. None of the lotions, lathers, or cleansers for sale can do anything more than temporarily alter the appearance of the skin. It's that simple.

THE BASICS

The Skinny on Skin and Skin Care

The skin's job is to act as a barrier to bacteria and harmful substances in the environment. At around age 25, the skin begins to age as the naturally occurring collagen fibers that give skin its strength and flexibility begin to deteriorate. The skin then begins to dry out, and gravity's pull creates sagging and wrinkles. Exposure to sunlight and/or ultraviolet (UV) rays hastens wrinkling (and increases the risk of cancer). Avoiding the sun will delay the onset of wrinkling, but it's impossible to completely prevent wrinkles. Only cosmetic surgery and Retin-A (tretinoin) can temporarily stay this process—no cosmetic can.

You'd never know it, though, from the pseudoscientific language and fantastic claims peculiar to cosmetics advertising and promotional pitches at department store counters. In a brazen attempt to distinguish one similar product from another, manufacturers transform creams in bottles into genies in bottles by implying that various substances like proteins, vitamins, RNA, aloe, and collagen have healing, rejuvenating, or reconditioning powers. A quick flip through some fashion magazines turned up the following typical examples:

■ Clarins Hydration Plus "effectively neutralizes dehydrating aggressors that stress and sensitize facial skin. Key natural ingredients include reflective rice bran extract, skin-softening linden, nourishing wheat germ and ginseng, vitamins B, C, and E."

■ Oil of Olay Hydro Night Renewal Gel is "so brilliantly effective at helping prevent moisture loss, it actually accelerates skin's own moisture recovery."

■ Lancôme Niosôme Plus is a "perfected age treatment . . . blocking age-causing free radicals before they can damage surface skin."

Based on 148 undercover inquiries at 14 cosmetics counters at Macy's, A&S, Bloomingdale's, Lord & Taylor, and Saks Fifth Avenue, the NYC Department of Consumer Affairs found that salespeople stretch the truth about cosmetic lotions beyond recognition more than a third of the time. Among the worst sales pitches were:

■ Clarins Concentrated "Cellulite" Control Gel. A salesperson described the gel to an undercover investigator as "a natural diuretic" that helps decrease water retention in the area to which it is applied. "It's like medicine," said the salesperson.

■ Lancôme Durable Minceur. The salesperson said that rubbing the cream on in a circular motion would help the body flush cellulite away and that it would work even if the consumer didn't exercise, although not as well as it would work *with* exercise.

In reality, these and similar products are little more than high-priced moisturizers, and moisturizers accomplish only limited results. They do not actually add moisture to the skin; they work by forming a seal that prevents water already contained in the skin from evaporating. Moisturizers all include the same basic ingredients:

■ Water.

■ An emollient to prevent moisture from escaping through the surface of the skin, such as the commonly used petrolatum (better known as petroleum jelly or Vaseline) or lanolin (a sheep's wool extract).

■ Natural moisturizing factor, a group of ingredients that naturally exist in the body and seem to bind or hold water to the skin, such as urea, lactic acid, collagen, hyaluronic acid, mucupolysaccharids, NaPCA (sodium pyrrolidone carboxylate), and hydroxy acids.

■ Other ingredients (such as aloe, jojoba oil, and allantoin) and triglycerides (such as apricot kernel oil, cocoa butter, and wheat germ oil).

Although you may not like the look of dry skin, it does not cause wrinkles; it only makes them more noticeable. So despite the advice dispensed at cosmetics counters and in glossy ads, using a moisturizer does nothing to prevent aging.

Safety: More Questions Than Answers

While most cosmetics appear to be safe for short-term use, no one knows conclusively how the sustained use of cosmetics or their constituent ingredients will affect the user. Few rules regulate the manufacture and sale of cosmetics. The Food, Drug, and Cosmetic Act, passed in 1938, gives the U.S. Food and Drug Administration (FDA) jurisdiction over the industry but very little real authority. Scientific advances, however, have shown that the skin is not the impermeable protective layer lawmakers assumed when they wrote the law, which does not require affirmative proof of safety before products go on sale. Skin absorbs many chemicals and cosmetic ingredients, allowing some substances whose dangers have not been investigated to enter the body.

Regulations governing the manufacture and sale of cosmetics are nowhere near as stringent as those for food and drugs. While drugs must be proven safe and effective before they can be marketed, the FDA does not approve cosmetics for sale and does not require manufacturers to test products before they hit the market. Nor do manufacturers have to give the formulas for their products to the FDA or even register their existence with the agency. And no rule requires manufacturers to report consumer complaints, cosmetics-related injuries, or adverse reactions to the FDA.

This is not to say that manufac-turers do not test their products for safety; since they are selling little more than an image, and a flimsy one at that, most manufacturers safety-test their products to minimize the likelihood of adverse reactions, adverse publicity, and costly lawsuits. Two problems: These tests are not sufficient to establish that the products or ingredients are not toxic over the longer term; and no regulatory body reviews the tests or results for adequacy or accuracy.

So what rules does the cosmetics industry have to follow? The Food, Drug, and Cosmetic Act defines cosmetics as "articles other than soap which are applied to the human body for cleansing, beautifying, promoting attractiveness, or altering the appearance." Any product that qualifies under this definition is not allowed to contain a disease-causing microorganism or any other substance known to be harmful; it must not be adulterated or stored in unsanitary conditions; it can contain only FDA-approved color additives; it must be labeled with the name of the product, its weight, the name and address of the manufacturer, and an ingredient list organized in descending order of predominance. In addition, manufacturing plants are subject to FDA inspection. Although cosmetics

> "*These anti-aging products were developed under the pressure of the market, not according to scientific principles. . . . There is just no evidence they work.*"
>
> —FDA OFFICIAL
> (insisting on anonymity) to the
> New York City Department of
> Consumer Affairs

Don't Get Burned—or Tanned

Virtually any exposure to the sun contributes to burning, wrinkling, and all forms of skin cancer. Thus the American Academy of Dermatology recommends that, regardless of your skin type, you use a sunscreen with a sun protection factor (SPF) of at least 15 year-round—and local and national weather services have added a "solar risk index" or "ultraviolet index" to their weather reports to help you schedule your outdoor activities. No wonder the market for sunscreen has more than doubled since the early 1980s.

Sunscreens shield you from ultraviolet-B (UVB) radiation, which causes sunburning, tanning, and skin cancer. The FDA-approved SPF system refers to the amount of extra time you can spend in the sun without burning if you properly apply the sunscreen. For instance, a person whose unprotected skin burns after 10 minutes in the sun could spend 20 minutes in the sun while wearing an SPF of 2, or 150 minutes in the sun while wearing an SPF of 15.

More and more products also provide a degree of protection from harmful ultraviolet-A radiation (UVA), which penetrates deeper than UVB rays into the base layer of skin and may contribute to melanoma. To be on the safe side, look for a sunscreen that provides "broad-spectrum" protection, which is the catch phrase for UVA protection.

When choosing a sunscreen products, keep in mind that *Consumer Reports* research has shown one sunscreen to be as good as the next. Furthermore, SPF protection does not increase proportionally with the SPF number. While an SPF of 15 shields you from 93% of sunburning rays, raising the SPF to 34 adds only an additional 4% to the protection. That said, it makes sense to buy the cheapest waterproof or water-resistant sunscreen of SPF 15 or higher that you can find.

The protective value of the sunscreen was established assuming a uniform and liberal application of goop. Trouble is, most people use about half as much sunscreen as they need to get the protection level promised on the package. As a general rule, the average bathing-suit-clad body needs about an ounce of sunscreen to achieve the advertised SPF.

Interestingly, sunscreens have never been shown to prevent human skin cancers; the only sure way to prevent skin cancer—or at least curtail the risk of getting it—is to avoid the sun altogether and to wear hats and protective clothing when you're outdoors between the hours of 10 AM and 3 PM.

THE DANGERS OF SKIN LIGHTENERS

Don't misuse skin-lightener creams. An investigation by the NYC Department of Consumer Affairs showed that many of these products, which are pitched primarily to African-Americans, promise more than they can deliver and do not carry adequate warnings about the dangers of long-term use or exposure to the sun. High doses or prolonged use of the active ingredient, hydroquinone (HQ), can lead to a disfiguring skin condition called exogenous ochronosis in which blue-black blotches develop deep in the skin. Citing this disease, South Africa banned over-the-counter sales of skin bleach in 1990. Preliminary research by the U.S. Department of Health and Human Services suggests HQ also may be carcinogenic. The FDA's position on HQ is, according to the agency, "under review."

If you are going to use skin bleach—which, for safety reasons, we do not recommend— dermatologists and the FDA agree it should only be applied in very small amounts to limited areas of dark-brownish discoloration, spots, or blotches. Always use a strong sunscreen to prevent re-darkening, an important step that most products fail to highlight.

labels must list the product's ingredients in descending order of quantity, the ingredients of specific flavors and fragrances need not be listed. In addition, the ingredient lists of make-up need only list the colors that *might* be in the product; thus, some colors that are listed in fact may not be in the product at all.

WHAT TO WATCH OUT FOR

Be alert to the technobabble that makes a cosmetic sound like the Fountain of Youth. The government permits puffed-up claims, no matter how meaningless or confusing. However, if a manufacturer makes a therapeutic claim, such as "heals dry skin" or "removes dandruff," the product has strayed into the over-the-counter drug category, and the FDA will demand either retraction of the claim or research proving the product's safety and efficacy. In 1987 and 1988, the government challenged 22 cosmetics companies to prove claims that their products could reverse the process of aging. Given the choice of rewriting the ads or submitting their products to the long, expensive process of FDA testing and approval, the companies, not surprisingly, toned down the rhetoric. But manufacturers still throw the following terms around:

Allergens. Ingredients to which some people have allergic reactions. Any ingredient can cause a reaction, but fragrance is the most common allergen; lanolin, coal tar dyes, and preservatives can also cause allergic reactions.

Hypoallergenic. This is virtually meaningless. No regulatory or even voluntary standard has been established for what this means. Products with this label are believed by the manufacturer to have fewer allergens than other products. Hypoallergenic does not mean the product will not cause an allergic reaction. The same warning goes for terms such as dermatologist-tested, sensitivity-tested, allergy-tested, and non-irritating.

Fragrance-free. Contrary to what you might think, products with this label can still contain fragrances. A more precise term would be "smell-free"—and to achieve this effect the manufacturer probably had to add some fragrance to mask the product's original smell.

Natural. There are no standards for this term; it can mean virtually anything to anybody. Natural cosmetics contain pretty much the same ingredients as the rest, including preservatives. Adding "natural" ingredients like milk, honey, avocado, algae, and vitamins have not been shown to enhance effectiveness.

No animal testing. Products that claim not to have been tested on animals may be splitting hairs. While the product itself was "tested" only on people, the *ingredients* were most likely tested on animals. Both FDA and industry officials say that companies making these claims use well-known ingredients that have already been proven safe—most likely with animal tests, since there are almost no cosmetic ingredients for human use that weren't first tested on animals.

Other ingredients. This catch-all term appears often in ingredient lists and refers to substances that the FDA has allowed manufacturers not to divulge because they are trade secrets.

THE SMARTER CONSUMER

Before you next choose between a no-name 19-cent-per-ounce moisturizer and a luxurious $40-per-ounce cream with a designer label—or decide whether to dispense with cosmetics altogether—keep the following in mind:

Don't be taken in by empty promises that a product will "lift the eyes," "firm," "nourish," "recondition," or "retrain" the skin; "relieve," "remove," or "reduce" cellulite; "target" trouble areas, "wash away" free radicals, or "prevent" aging. Cosmetics affect only the outermost layer of skin to temporarily change its appearance. The collagen molecule, for example, is too big to penetrate the outermost layer, the epidermis, to reach the dermis below where it might rejuvenate the skin. A surgeon can lift sagging eyes; a cream cannot.

Price says nothing about quality. The beneficial ingredients are quite cheap and vary little from one product to another. When you buy expensive products, you pay for advertising, fancy packaging, free samples, perfumes, and all the other razzamatazz that contribute to the creation of the fancy image.

All you need to maintain healthy skin is to wash with mild soap; to avoid overexposure to the sun or wear a sunscreen; to eat healthy foods, drink plenty of liquids, and exercise regularly; and to refrain from smoking.

If you have skin problems, consult a dermatologist. Do not rely on salespeople or anyone else frocked in a white lab coat at a cosmetics counter for a diagnosis.

Use cosmetics that are widely distributed and marketed by a well-known firm. At least you'll know the product has a multitude of users who have apparently used it without significant side effects.

A cosmetics reading list:

■ *Being Beautiful: Deciding for Yourself*, selected readings on beauty products, health, and safety, with an introduction by Ralph Nader; published by the Center for the Study of Responsive Law, 1986.

■ *Save Your Money, Save Your Face: What Every Cosmetics Buyer Needs to Know*, by Elaine Brumberg (Facts on File and Perennial Library, 1987).

■ *The Look You Like: Medical Answers to 400 Questions on Skin and Hair Care*, by Linda Allen Schoen and Paul Lazar, MD, sponsored by the American Academy of Dermatology; published by Marcel Dekker, 1990.

■ *The Cosmetics Trap: When Truth is Only Skin Deep*, an investigative report by the New York City Department of Consumer Affairs, June 1992, available on request from NYC Department of Consumer Affairs, 42 Broadway, New York, NY 10004.

■ *A Study in Hype and Risk: The Marketing of Skin Bleaches*, an investigative report by the New York City Department of Consumer Affairs, August 1992, available on request (address above).

■ You can look up any cosmetic ingredient to determine whether it is safe in *A Consumer's Dictionary of Cosmetic Ingredients*, by Ruth Winter (Crown, 1984).

CHAPTER 42

DRY CLEANING

Don't Get Hung Out to Dry

Everyone seems to have a tale of woe about a favorite item of clothing that went to the cleaner wrinkled and slightly soiled and came back with a conspicuous spot or mysterious tear. One woman tells of picking up a white linen dress from the cleaner and finding blue stains where the receipt had been attached—the ink had bled through the paper. Another day, a favorite rayon dress came back with a hole in the fabric under the arm (not in a seam, where it could be easily fixed). "That was my favorite dress. Every week, it's something else. And the cleaners say it's not their fault," she complains.

Sound familiar? Dry cleaning disputes are one of those common annoyances you probably can't avoid entirely, but you can minimize them pretty painlessly.

THE BASICS

Check the Instructions

If you want to lower your dry cleaning bills, look for the care label before you buy. The Federal Trade Commission (FTC) Care Labeling Rule requires clothing manufacturers and importers to sew care labels into most garments. The label must be easily found, designed to last as long as the garment, and give instructions for washing, drying, pressing, and bleaching. All parts of the garment must be able to withstand the recommended care procedure. If an article of clothing cannot be cleaned, the label must also disclose this fact explicitly.

This said, the labels are not always accurate. When the New York School of Dry Cleaning surveyed 12,000 garments that had been damaged during cleaning, it found that mislabeling caused half the problems. The case of Bonnie & Company Fashions is typical: It sold imported off-white cotton and ramie sweaters with leather appliqués on the front. The care label told consumers to dry clean the sweaters, but many of the sweaters came back from the dry cleaner damaged. Bonnie & Company paid the FTC a fine of $10,000 for failing to give proper care instructions.

In the unhappy event that a garment does not withstand the care recommended by the manufacturer on the label, the manufacturer is responsible. Your best bet is to return the item to the store where

389

you bought it. In most cases the store will give you a refund or exchange and then settle up with the manufacturer. The FTC will investigate if it learns of a pattern of mislabeling.

Which Pieces of Clothing Go to the Cleaner?

If you follow the care instructions and the item comes back damaged, you have a right to press your case. If the cleaner followed the care instructions, and they proved to be flawed, the manufacturer must replace the article of clothing (usually accomplished through the store where you purchased it). If the cleaner deviated from the instructions (which they are unlikely to admit), it is responsible. Either way, you're not at fault.

If you want to save the considerable sums dry cleaning bills amount to—and are willing to take the chance, however slight, that you'll ruin the garment—try hand-washing it yourself. Since manufacturers want to avoid liability for replacing clothing that doesn't withstand the prescribed cleaning instructions, the labels are often overly cautious. Thus, many items that say "dry clean only" can probably be safely hand-washed.

In fact, the FTC is currently considering revising its care label rule to require manufacturers to tell consumers when garments can be hand-washed or wet-cleaned. Meanwhile, it's difficult to guess which ones will hold up and which won't. The fabric content will give you a clue as to how careful you need to be, but it's

no guarantee that the item won't shrink and the dye won't run. And unfortunately if you override the care instructions and your glad rag turns into a dust rag, you have no recourse.

What the Dry Cleaner Does

The cleaner uses solvents rather than soap and water to remove stains from fabric (hence the term

TO WASH OR NOT TO WASH

The dyes and fabric finishes used by manufacturers give clothes luster and sheen, minimize wrinkles and shrinkage, repel stains, and create softness or stiffness. They also make it difficult to generalize about which fabrics can stand up to hand-washing and which can't.

Use the following as a rough guide. Fabrics made of a mixture of natural and synthetic fibers tend to be stronger than natural fibers alone and stand up to hand-washing better. In addition, many woolen and linen things, some rayon, and even a few silks can be hand-washed. However, be extra careful with silk, which is delicate and discolors easily. Never use water on cotton or silk velvet, unless you like it permanently flat.

"dry" cleaning). Since no water is used, dry cleaning is appropriate for items that would otherwise shrink, fade, or run if they were washed in water.

Perchloroethylene ("perc"), the solvent most dry cleaners use to clean garments, is toxic and has been linked to cancer and liver and neurotoxic disorders. People who work in dry cleaners or live very near them are at the greatest risk; if the clothes were properly dried (the solvent evaporates very quickly), it probably poses no risk to the dry cleaning customer. As required by 1990 amendments to the Clean Air Act, the Environmental Protection Agency has asked dry cleaners to reduce perc emissions by 1996. In New York City alone, 5 million pounds of the chemical are released into the air each year.

If you are environmentally conscious, you may want to cut back on your use of dry cleaning services to minimize your perc contribution. Alternatives include hand-washing (be careful, as noted above) or using a spot remover to clean stains. However, many spot removers contain perc or other toxic solvents and must be used exactly as instructed to avoid exposure and fires.

Another way to minimize perc pollution is to use dry cleaners that have installed new machines that do not release perc into the air and that dispose of toxic perc filters responsibly.

Look for the "We Care" emblem at cleaners that have contracted with Safety Kleen to remove and recycle used perc and filters. Safety Kleen picks up the used perc, re-moves the clay-like residue, which it turns into pellets that are used to fuel cement kilns. The purified perc can then be reused for dry cleaning. The process costs the cleaner a little more, and the surcharge may be passed along to you. Decide for yourself if the extra expenditure is worth the environmental benefit.

Out, Out, Damned Spot!

Come clean—or your favorite pants may stay dirty.

When you bring your soiled garments to the cleaner, be truthful about where the spot came from and what home remedies you've tried. The cleaner will decide, based on what you say, how to treat the spot. An oily stain on silk gets treated one way, but an oily stain on silk that you tried to remove with soap and water calls for different treatment.

In general, you have a better chance of getting rid of a spot if you bring the garment in to the cleaner as soon as you can. And with greasy stains (which means most food stains), there's no point trying to remove them yourself.

If you absolutely can't resist, it's probably safe to blot coffee, tea, or alcoholic beverage spills on non-delicate fabrics, but do so only with cold water, seltzer, or club soda and a white cloth towel. Don't use a napkin—the fibers can migrate to the garment. Don't use soap, detergent, alcohol, or home remedies, since they'll leave residue or rings. And last of all, don't rub, which can cause fading or weakening of the fabric.

WHAT TO WATCH OUT FOR

When buying clothing, and especially when bringing it to the dry cleaner, be on the lookout for trim, buttons, beads, and belts that may require special treatment or that make dry cleaning inadvisable. Polystyrene buttons, for instance, cannot be safely dry cleaned because they dissolve in the solvents, and the cardboard or glue sometimes used in belts may not hold up. If you have a question about buttons or other decorations, point them out to the cleaner, who'll decide whether dry cleaning them is safe.

And just because you can't see any damage from the lemon-lime soda you spilled on your tie—or the coffee you think you removed—don't assume there is no stain lurking there. It sounds like an oxymoron, but dry cleaners say some spots are invisible until the heat from cleaning brings them out. You can avoid nasty surprises when you pick up your clothes by telling the cleaner about spills, even if there's no visible damage.

Have all matching pieces cleaned together. This way any fading or color change will be uniform and the pieces will still match.

Don't go directly to the manufacturer. If an article of clothing did not hold up under the cleaning process recommended by the manufacturer on the care label, return it to the store where you bought it. The store must reimburse you and then settle with the manufacturer.

Be especially careful when buying clothing made from a combination of materials. Talk to your cleaner about whether and how to clean them. Sequins often do not stand up to machine cleaning, and hand-cleaning them can be costly.

Keep your receipts for garments that call for dry cleaning. Should you ever have a dispute with your cleaner over replacement of a damaged or lost item, you will be in a better position to request and receive a refund if you can prove how much you paid for the item. And if the problem was not the cleaner's fault, the retailer will be more likely to reimburse you for a damaged piece of clothing if you can prove you bought it there.

Inspect your clothing before you leave the dry cleaner. Point out any wrinkles or spots that did not come out. Cleaners are usually happy to take the item back to try again—sometimes the problem can be solved on the spot. If you notice any damage, bring it to the cleaner's attention immediately. Be courteous and firm. Ask to be reimbursed.

GREEN CLEANERS

Check to see if anyone in your neighborhood offers a wet cleaning process that uses only heat, steam, and natural soaps and that won't harm you or the environment. The Environmental Protection Agency has found one such process, called Ecoclean, financially competitive with dry cleaning and just as effective for many garments. While it's not a complete substitute for dry cleaning, one wet cleaning establishment reports that it uses Ecoclean regularly to clean everything from wool to silk to leather. Further EPA-funded studies are testing other alternatives to dry cleaning in Chicago, Indianapolis, and Los Angeles. If you're looking for an environmentally safe spot cleaner (that's safe for your clothing, too), try Aveda fabric cleaner made from plants and herb extracts or Ecover wool wash. Both are available in natural foods stores or, if you live in New York City, at the Ecomat environmentally safe laundries.

Most often, cleaners will give you the "current value" of the item and not a full reimbursement of what you paid or what it will cost to replace the item. The cleaner will decide the item's "current value," based on how long you've owned the garment, its condition, and the original purchase price, but negotiating the estimate can be difficult. If you're not satisfied, say so—and take your business elsewhere. As a last resort, you can complain to local consumer affairs officials or go to small claims court.

If you and the cleaner disagree about who's at fault, ask the cleaner to have its trade association's textile analysis lab examine the garment. You cannot send the garment yourself: only the dry cleaner, Better Business Bureau (BBB), or retailer can. If you don't get satisfaction, complain to your local consumer affairs office or BBB.

To be on the safe side, air out your dry cleaned garments in the yard, garage, or a spare room. Take them out of the plastic wrapping as soon as you get home and let any leftover gases from the solvents escape before you hang your clothes, uncovered, in the closet or in a breathable fabric garment bag.

Keep used plastic wrapping out of the reach of children, who may be tempted to play with it and can asphyxiate themselves. Some cleaners have begun to shun plastic. They wrap dry cleaned clothes in reusable garment bags. Ask your cleaner about it.

Bring spare wire hangers back to the cleaner. They will be reused.

▪ If you have a complaint about a dry cleaner, contact:

International Fabricare Institute, a trade association of dry cleaners in the Washington, DC, and surrounding areas, offers textile analysis to its members; call (301) 622-1900.

Neighborhood Cleaners Association, the trade association for dry cleaners in Connecticut, Delaware, Florida, Massachusetts, New Jersey, New York, Pennsylvania, Rhode Island, and West Virginia, offers textile analysis to its members and a complaint mediation service between consumers and cleaners. Main office: (212) 967-3002.

Northeastern Fabricare Institute, 343 Salem Street, Wakefield, MA 01880; call (617) 245-6688.

▪ If a dry cleaning problem arises from a manufacturing defect and you can't get the retailer to take the item back, ask the retailer for the name of the manufacturer or find the RN number, usually located on the care label. If you tell them the RN number the FTC can give you the manufacturer's name. The International Fabricare Institute suggests sending the item and an explanation of the problem to the manufacturer via registered mail with a return receipt.

▪ For more tips on dry cleaning, read *Better Business Bureau A to Z Buying Guide*, (Henry Holt & Co., 1990).

▪ For more information on the haz-ards of dry cleaning and safer alternatives, contact the Pollution Prevention Information Clearinghouse, U.S. Environmental Protection Agency, 401 M Street, SW (PM-211A), Washington, DC 20460; (202) 260-1023.

PART 7

Telephones

CHAPTER 43

TELEPHONES

The High Cost of High Technology

Telephone technology is changing at warp speed, as they would say in *Star Trek*, and in ways that inventor Alexander Graham Bell couldn't possibly have foreseen. You can immediately learn the number of a caller, trace phone calls, forward your calls to anywhere in the world, and even be assigned a phone number for life. Before long, your phone line will transmit movies that you can watch on your television set, giving you more choices than ever.

But these amazing conveniences don't come cheap. There's a hefty fee attached to each one of them. And, if time is money, then you can spend a lot of "money" just trying to figure out the new services.

THE BASICS

Equipment

Let's look first at the hardware—phones—before tackling the profusion of telephone line services—the "software." You can either buy your telephone or lease it from the phone company. The only advantage of leasing is that if the phone breaks down the phone company delivers another one. But de-

cent phones usually cost about $30; just buy another and it'll likely be cheaper than leasing charges in the long run.

When buying a phone, beware of $10 to $20 models since they probably won't last long and sound tinny. A built-in speakerphone will add another $10 and multi-line features add about $15 more.

Over half the phones now sold are cordless models. Cordless phones work better than they used to, but wired phones often still have superior sound quality. Cordless phones can't be used if the electricity fails (they plug into an outlet), and they stop working if the battery hasn't been recharged. Check if buying an inexpensive longer cord for your existing telephone will give you enough roaming room before plunking down a hundred dollars or more on a cordless.

Cellular phones are no longer a status symbol. There are more than 12 million cellular phone subscribers nationally, in a booming industry that didn't even exist until the 1980s. The major types of cellular phones are the small, low-powered, battery-powered folding ones you can carry in your pocket and the more powerful (three-watt) car phones, some of which can also be carried outside the car with a battery pack. For most people, especially in urban areas with plenty of cellular transmitters, the lighter, more portable pocket models are sufficient, despite the need to keep recharging the batteries. Cellular phones can cost as little as $100 to purchase, although, with an average annual bill of over $800 in the last half of 1992, operating one could take a hefty bite out of your budget.

Line Services

Phone services are like car options—the vendor makes the big profit on the extras, not on the basic product. So the cost of service options promoted in advertising inserts with your monthly statement can really add up. Yet a survey in 1992 by the Consumer Federation of America and AT&T found that most consumers knew that these services exist but did not know how much they cost.

The fact is that you could pay up to an extra $135 a year if you order just three services—touch tone, call waiting, and call forwarding—and initial hook-up fees may be additional. The annual cost of "the works" could be $400 or more.

Still, while most people probably don't need very many of these services, they may be handy for a few. This guide will help you to decide whether to order one. If a service is not yet offered in your area, it probably will be available soon. (The fees cited below don't include one-time hook-up charges.)

Touch-tone service. There are two basic types of telephone service, pulse (which includes rotary phones) and touch tone. A clicking sound is heard when you make a call on a rotary phone, a tone pitch when you make a touch-tone call. You probably got by for years just fine with a plain old rotary (pulse) phone.

Still, touch-tone calling is faster than pulse calling, and it is required to use certain computerized phone company services like call answering. (You will probably also need it to access your answering machine.) Touch-tone phones also allow you to access electronic answering systems ("Press 1 for the accounting department, 2 for customer service . . ."), although you'll still be connected to an operator if you have a rotary phone.

Call waiting. Phone companies report that this is the most popular of the special line services. You avoid missed calls by taking a second call while you're already on the phone. The fee comes to around $50 to $60 a year. Yet many people consider it rude to put someone on hold on their home phone . . . and then have to choose which call is the more compelling.

Call forwarding. For about $40 a year your phone calls will follow you wherever you go. You can also order that only selected callers be forwarded.

Speed dialing. Is it worth paying from $30 to $50 a year to be able to press just one or two numbers for frequent calls? Your call. But re-

CELLULAR PHONES SEEM SAFE

How safe are cellular phones? In January 1993, questions were raised when a Florida resident, David Reynard, said on TV that his wife died of brain cancer because of her incessant use of a cellular phone. Reynard sued the phone's manufacturer, NEC Corp.

In December 1993, the National Institute of Health released a major study that concluded that there is no danger. So it is safe to say the phones are OK for normal use.

member that many push-button phones allow you to program ten or more numbers into their memory; you can call these numbers by pressing just one or two buttons.

Call answering. This works much like an answering machine, but with two advantages: calls can be answered while you are on another line (similar to call waiting) and it doesn't break down. On the negative side, call answering services cost from $70 to $80 a year plus a hook-up fee of about $20; a decent answering machine costs only about $60 and ought to last far longer than a year.

Call connection. In many localities, after the directory assistance voice tells you the number, it asks if you would like to have the number called; you then just say "yes" or press 1. Not just a courtesy—the connection fee in New York and Chicago is 35 cents.

Priority ringing. You add one or two new incoming lines electronically, without new wiring. Each number produces its own distinctive ring. You could give one number to, say, your kids and keep the other for your own calls. Or, if you work at home, you could have a business line and a personal one. In New York, one extra number costs $5.14 a month and two cost $7.22 a month.

Automatic call-back. You can return the last call you received, whether you answered it or not. This service is also called "call return." Fees could be up to 75 cents per use.

Repeat dialing. Is the number you called busy? This feature will automatically repeat the last number you called for up to half an hour and complete it once the line is free. Cost: 75 cents per use or $35 to $60 a year. While many phones are equipped to repeat-dial a number if you press the pound (#) button, with the repeat dialing service offered by the phone company you leave the phone while the repeat dialing continues—or you can make and receive calls in the meantime. It rings you back when it has made the connection.

Three-way (conference) calling. Being able to talk to two parties at once can cost $40 to $50 a year.

Caller ID. For $70 to $85 a year this service displays on a special monitor next to your phone the number of the party calling you. This way, you'll know exactly who is calling and can decide whether to answer. Of course, the call screening feature on most answering machines accomplishes much the same goal, although it doesn't reveal the identification of callers who choose to remain anonymous.

Privacy advocates are concerned that caller ID could lead to an invasion of privacy. How would you like to have *your* phone number displayed on a monitor whenever you place a call? Fortunately, many states have required phone companies to offer a free blocking service in which you can prevent anyone with caller ID from learning your number. You can order either total blocking or per-call blocking. The cost of offering free blocking has prompted some companies to delay offering caller ID.

Call screen. This service blocks calls from certain numbers in your service area that you program into the phone. A loophole is that someone who really wants to bother you, such as a bill collector, can simply call from a different number. The cost is around $40 a year.

Call trace. At your request the phone company will trace the number of the last call and notify the police. The cost ranges from $2 to $5 per trace. Obviously, this service is of limited value if the harasser calls from pay phones. And it works only on calls that originate within your local service area. An alterna-tive would be to change your phone number; the phone company may waive its usual fee if the reason is to avoid a harassing caller.

Lifetime phone number. You keep the same social security number for life. How about keeping your phone number too? You can with "700" number service. For $7 a month AT&T will assign you a new lifetime ten-digit phone number including a "700" prefix. You use this number in addition to your regular phone number.

Callers dial the "700" number; it's directed to your home phone or forwarded to a number you punched in on your phone. It's like call forwarding, except that you keep the same number forever, even if you move several times. You can also arrange for people to call you toll-free when they dial a code.

Voice dialing. No need to re-member or look up numbers. You can program up to 50 phone num-bers, then say the name of the per-son you're calling into the receiver, and the phone company does the rest. Works from any home phone. NYNEX (as New York Telephone is now called) charges $4.50 a month for 30 different numbers, $5.50 for 50 numbers.

Calling Rates

Phone companies usually offer two kinds of billing: flat rate billing and measured billing. With flat rate billing, you pay one set fee each month and make all the local calls you like. Calls outside your local calling area (sometimes called the "home region"), which are still handled by your local phone company, cost extra. Some companies restrict flat rate billing to "life-line" services reserved for eligible fixed- or lower-income customers.

The industry is moving increasingly toward offering just measured service. With measured service, your basic monthly service charge is probably about half of what it is for flat rate service. But a flat charge is also imposed for each call within your local calling area. This may seem obvious from the plain meaning of the words "measured service"; but in the 1992 Consumer Federation of America–AT&T survey mentioned earlier, only 28% of the respondents knew that measured service meant that the more calls you make, the more you are charged.

With measured service, calls outside your local calling area but within the Local Access and Transport Area (LATA) are timed and billed in one-minute increments; the rate for the first minute may be substantially higher than for each additional minute.

You may know that evening and night long-distance rates are lower, but did you know that local service also has time differentials? If you're a penny pincher, you might want to wait until 11 PM to call Aunt Maude, even if she's on the next block. Check with your local company for the details. A typical rate discount schedule for local calls (Pacific Bell/Los Angeles) is: Weekday (full price) 8 AM to 5 PM. Evening (discount) 5 PM to 11 PM. Nights/weekends (bigger discount) 11 PM to 8 AM.

Schedules and discounts vary considerably around the country. New York's NYNEX, for one, charges the full weekday rate between 8 AM and 9 PM and the evening rate from 9 PM to 11 PM. Southwestern Bell's schedule is the same as Pacific Bell's, except that the evening rate is charged on Sunday evenings instead of the night/weekend rate. On weekdays, Illinois Bell charges the full rate from 9 AM to 11 AM and 2 PM to 8 PM—because of the lower volume of lunchtime calls, the rate is discounted 5% from 11 AM to 2 PM. Consult the instruction pages at the beginning of your local phone directory for the rate schedule in your area.

The percentage discount also varies considerably. NYNEX offers one of the steeper discounts: a 40% reduction in regular rates during evening hours and 65% for night/weekend calling. But Southwestern Bell in Houston gives only 25% off for evening calls and 40% off for night/weekend calls. In Los Angeles, Pacific Bell's discounts are 30% and 60%. Some companies offer automatic volume discounts. For example, Illinois Bell provides residential customers with volume discounts of up to 33% when the total local bill exceeds a certain amount.

If you can't wait until the monthly bill comes to learn how much a call costs, you can always ask the operator for "time and charge," that is, to tell you how long you talked and how much it will cost. You must dial the operator first to ask that this be done and the operator will stay on the line until the end of your call. Of course, there's an additional charge for this operator-assisted call.

Cellular phone calls are considerably more expensive than calls placed through regular lines. Phone companies may charge an activation fee of up to $100 to turn your service on, an access fee of about $30 a month, air-time fees of as much as 80 cents a minute during peak times (usually 7 AM to 9 PM), and "roaming fees," which are incurred once you leave your basic service area. Every region has two companies licensed to carry cellular service signals. One of them is the same company that handles your area's local phone service. The other is independently owned. Sign up with the provider offering the best combination of price and quality.

Billing

Telephone industry deregulation has made phone bills infinitely more complicated. Your local telephone bill is separated into these sections:

The local carrier. This covers the basic cost of regular monthly service, which may include the FCC line charge (covers the cost to connect your phone to the network), the exchange access line, special line services like touch tone, and state and local taxes.

Included in the local portion of your phone bill are calls within your local calling area, which means your town or city and maybe some areas a mile or two beyond the limits. Also included are calls past the

local calling area but still included in the LATA, which could be 40 or 50 miles from your local calling area. Most states have at least two LATAs; New York has six and California, with 11, has the most. Within most LATAs, non-local calling area calls are automatically routed to your local phone company, although it is usually possible to dial an access code for another carrier—and those calls would appear on a separate page in your bill. In a few years most states will probably allow customers to pre-designate the carrier which automatically gets intra-LATA calls, just as is done for inter-LATA calls.

Usually listed separately is a call break-down if you have measured service. How many minutes you called to different rate zones and whether you called during day, evening, or night/weekend hours are reported here. Also listed are calls made with your local company's calling card, directory information request charges, and service order charges.

Your primary long-distance carrier. If your primary long-distance carrier doesn't bill you separately, then this page itemizes your long-distance calls. All of this information is provided by your primary long distance carrier.

Other providers. Local telephone companies are required to provide a billing service to long-distance carriers and other telephone service providers. There may be a separate page with the trademark of another long-distance carrier if you used one and had calls charged to your home phone, such as with a calling card. Additional pages may be for operator service providers and for "900" calls placed from your phone.

Calling Cards

Calling cards, which are issued by both local phone companies and long-distance carriers, are cards you use to charge local and long distance calls to your home phone.

You can use your local phone company calling card for local and long distance calls. A service charge of about 40 cents is imposed on each direct call charged; it may be higher for longer distances. You use a local company's calling card by dialing "0" before the number called, which is different than for long-distance calling cards, and can also be accessed by dialing a special five-digit code (explained in the next chapter).

"With credit cards, at least you are limited to $50 in liability if you report unauthorized use in time. Not so with calling cards. . . . People don't appreciate that calling cards are really money."

—FRANCES FELD, Executive Director, Communication Fraud Control Association, Washington, DC

Alternative Pay Phones

Have you ever placed a calling card call from a pay phone, only to be billed several times the amount you expected? If so, you've got lots of company. Such charges are not out of the ordinary. A four-minute collect call to a phone only four blocks away billed through a national company named "Integretel" cost one caller an incredible $6.21. A six-minute credit card call to a phone only a few miles away cost another caller $6.73.

The problem here is not with "Bell" company phones operated by your local telephone company (local companies are called "local exchange carriers"). At issue is a new kind of pay phone, called a COCOT—for Customer-Owned, Coin-Operated Telephone —that can look just like a regular pay phone but sure doesn't charge like one. Tens of thousands of COCOTs have sprung up in places like hospitals, hotels, beauty salons, airports, and convenience stores since the divestiture of AT&T in 1984.

A COCOT-providing company is essentially a reseller of telephone services provided by the local exchange carrier and by long-distance companies. The local exchange carrier supplies the phone line, and a merchant, such as a restaurant owner or hospital, contracts with one of the COCOT providers to have a phone installed. Merchants like them—COCOT phones yield commissions to the merchant, which can be much higher from each call than with a pay phone provided by the local phone company.

For long-distance services,

COCOTs presubscribe with an Operator Service Provider (OSP) company, much as you might subscribe with Sprint or MCI for home long-distance service. These OSPs perform switching functions, verify credit and calling cards, and perform all the other functions of a long-distance carrier. They might surcharge you $1 or more if you use a calling card, and the total charges for a call placed through an OSP could be a few times more than through AT&T, Sprint, or MCI. (See the next chapter for more about OSPs.)

Responding to out-of-control "Wild West" conditions in the new COCOT industry, a 1990 federal law required COCOT companies to file rate information with the Federal Communications Commission. But the law didn't limit how much a COCOT can charge.

Many states have also enacted COCOT restrictions and information disclosure requirements. Generally, these require signs to be posted on or next to the COCOT disclosing the name of the owner, the phone numbers for refunds, repairs and directory assistance, and the names of the alternative operator service the phone uses.

Despite the new laws, there is still a long way to go before you can let your guard down when using one of these phones. A 1992 survey by the Pennsylvania Public Utility Commission found that 87% of the COCOTs surveyed at rest areas on a major toll highway had inadequacies, such as price gouging, unreachable COCOT providers, and inadequate informational postings.

The COCOT industry defends its surcharges and high rates by blaming what they call the excessive fees they have to pay the local exchange carriers for the "dial tone." And they complain that every time you use a calling card, the local exchange carrier gets a big cut of their surcharge.

WHAT TO WATCH OUT FOR

Push-button phones that are really pulse models. Just because it has push buttons doesn't mean that it's not a pulse phone—in effect, a dial phone with push buttons that takes almost as long to use. To find out for sure, inspect the FCC registration number imprinted on the phone. If it ends in "T", it's a tone phone. "E" means it can be both pulse and tone.

Cordless phone interference. Since they have only one or two channels, the cheaper cordless phones can be subject to interference from a nearby neighbor's cordless phone. To avoid this, purchase a 10-channel model on which you can switch channels or which automatically switches your call to a clear channel.

Wire maintenance fees. For about $10 to $15 a year, you can sign up for wire maintenance service. This means that you won't have to pay the company's expensive repair fees if the phone company has to fix the lines within your house. The repair fees generally are at least $35 just to show up and another $15 to $20 for each additional 15 minutes the repairers are at your home.

Still, wire maintenance service is probably not a good deal. How often does a wire break? You can probably fix it yourself if it does. Wire maintenance fees are a big phone company profit generator.

Deposits. You may have to pay a deposit to get your phone turned on if it had been shut off because of non-payment. A deposit might also be required if you failed to pay at least half the amount due in two consecutive bills. The deposit is usually for the cost of two months estimated usage. Terms may be easier for senior citizens.

Non-published number fee. You might reasonably think this would be free, but it can cost up to $2 a month *not* to have your number listed in the phone directory and/or given out by directory assistance.

Busy signal verification fee. You could be charged up to one dollar when you ask an operator to verify that a line is busy. There is an additional fee if you then ask for a call to be interrupted.

COCOTs in disguise. COCOTs usually look like any old pay phone. Some even adopt the same color scheme and graphics as the local exchange carrier pay phones. You can tell the difference by looking carefully for the name of the servicer on the phone. If the name of your local exchange carrier, like Pacific Bell or Illinois Telephone, isn't on the phone, then it's a COCOT.

Higher-priced Operator Service Providers. If you require operator assistance to call from a COCOT,

you'll be hooked up with an OSP rather than an operator from your local phone company. OSPs generally charge more for their operator assistance services—sometimes a great deal more.

Difficulties getting refunds. Ivan Kotcher, who handles complaints about California COCOTs for the Tele-Consumer Hotline, says that the overwhelming majority of the complaints he receives are about refunds. Rather than an operator offering an immediate refund or credit, COCOT callers sometimes are asked to leave a message on an answering machine or they must contend with an automatic complaint-handling system. He suggests that callers test the refund number posted on the phone before placing a potentially expensive call.

Higher coin call charges. The law in most states sets the maximum charge for the initial period of a coin call, usually five minutes. Thereafter, the company can charge whatever it likes—with a COCOT, you could end up emptying a pocketful of change into the phone for a call just a mile away.

Ask your local phone company for a free customer service record. It will tell you exactly what services you are paying for and how much they cost. You may see a service listed that you don't remember ordering or use rarely and could easily cancel.

Check into economy and low-cost "life line" service plans. Your local phone company probably offers "economy" or "basic" service plans. For example, customers of C & P Telephone in Washington, DC, can order a bare-bones service for which they may receive unlimited calls but pay for each outgoing call; touch-tone and special line services are unavailable. C & P's senior-citizen plan is even cheaper—it allows for 60 outgoing calls a month, after which a per-call charge is imposed.

If you receive Supplemental Security Income (SSI), a Veterans Disability Pension or Surviving Spouse Pension, or local public assistance, your local company may also offer a reduced rate "life line" plan.

Know where your local calling area is. If you have measured local service, be sure to know the boundaries of your local calling area, which is where a flat, untimed rate is charged per call. If you call just over the border, you'll pay by the minute and the total charge will be much higher.

Get a credit for wrong numbers or poor connections. After you hang up, immediately dial the three-digit credits number (it's listed in your local phone book).

Don't immediately say "yes" to phone solicitations for special line services. What's the rush? Read all the fine print in the phone company's brochure. Compute just how much the new service will cost for an entire year and ask yourself if it is worth it.

Avoid becoming a victim of calling card fraud. Imagine opening your phone bill and seeing hundreds of dollars worth of calls to Pakistan, Hong Kong, or France. It could happen to you if you aren't careful when placing a calling card call at a public phone. Snoops with amazing eyesight and hearing abilities may learn and memorize your identification number as you dial or recite your number to an operator. Then they sell the number on the street. There are public pay phones in New York City where queues of alien residents line up to call home for a discounted flat rate with a calling card number provided by a numbers thief standing nearby.

Services for the deaf. Most local phone carriers provide discounts for users of Telecommunications Devices for the Deaf (TDD). There are also relay calls, in which TDD users can reach non-TDD users by a telephone company Communications Assistant, who will complete the call, relay the conversation, and type a response on your TDD.

Install an inexpensive network interface, which allows you to determine if a phone problem is due to the wiring inside or outside the house. The interface is installed at the point where the outside wiring (the phone company's responsibility) meets the inside wiring (your responsibility if you aren't paying a wire maintenance fee). If you plug a phone into the interface and it still doesn't work, the problem is outside the house. Why would you want to know? Because if the phone company comes to fix your phone and the problem is in the line inside your home or with your phone—rather than with the outside line, which the phone company must fix—you'll have to pay a visit charge of at least $35 anyway. You can buy interface parts for less than $25 at most electronics stores. Included should be instructions for how to mount it near where the phone line enters your house or apartment. AT&T will provide free installation instructions if you call them at 800-222-3111.

Call the COCOT's information number to learn how much a call will cost *before* placing it. The 1990 Federal law requires phone companies to post on or near the phone their name, address, and a toll-free number consumers can call for information, along with the address of the Federal Communications Commission informal complaints office, which is where consumers can take grievances. On top of this, many states have passed even stricter information posting requirements.

If you call for a rate, be sure to ask the operator about surcharges imposed on top of the regular timed rate; ask how much the call will cost with *all* of the fees included.

Make long distance calls on CO-COTs through your regular carrier. It is now against the law for a COCOT/OSP to prevent you from dialing your preferred carrier's access code. (See page 411 in the next chapter for a list of these codes.)

Margaret S. learned this the hard way when she used her NYNEX calling card for a two-minute daytime call from New York City to Santa Monica, California. A month later her phone bill had a $9.90 Oncor Communications, Inc. charge for the call. Why so much? She hadn't initially accessed her preferred long-distance carrier. The calling card surcharge was $5.33 and the operator surcharge was $2.50. The per minute rate was 69 cents. Fortunately, Oncor offered to drop all but the per-minute charge when she called its customer service line.

▪ **The Tele-Consumer Hotline is a** toll-free number you can call for answers from trained counselors to questions about telephone concerns and to receive publications on those issues. Information is available on a wide variety of subjects, from calling cards and bill dispute handling to telephone fraud and phone features for disabled people. Call (800) 332-1124. *Available only to customers of Bell Atlantic, NYNEX, Pacific Bell, and Southwestern Bell.*

▪ **Want to complain? Check the** government listings section of your phone directory for your state's public utilities commission. They handle complaints about local residential service and pay phones.

CHAPTER 44

CALLING LONG DISTANCE

Phone Home for Less

Few consumers gave much thought to their long-distance carrier before a federal judge in 1984 ordered the break-up of the AT&T-regulated telephone monopoly. Now there are several major carriers and together they spend billions of dollars a year on advertising to get you to think a lot about long distance.

The ads—soft focus "feel-good" appeals and hard-hitting criticisms of competitors' service quality and rates—have one major goal: to get you to switch carriers. And to lure you, each of the carriers has introduced a long list of special discount plans.

Trouble is, the ads and the discount plans have led to a profusion of confusion. Sprint says it offers over 30 different calling plans; AT&T has about 20. New discount plan variations, each with its own special rules and prices, seem to be introduced weekly.

Our major conclusion: Unless you spend at least $10 a month on long distance, it makes very little difference which carrier you select.

It's a matter of nickels. Even long distance bills of about $25 a month don't present much opportunity for real savings; a 15% reduction would amount to $45 a year, which may not be worth the effort required to compare the many rates and arcane calling plan rules. Still, don't skip this chapter if you aren't a heavy caller, because you probably *can* save substantially by taking advantage of your current carrier's discount plans, which we discuss here.

THE BASICS

How to Pay Less for Domestic Long Distance

When it comes right down to it, no one can say which firm among the five major nationwide carriers—AT&T, Allnet, LDDS/Metromedia, US Sprint, or MCI—is the cheapest. The cheapest carrier is the one that costs the least for *your* particular calling pattern. This was the conclusion of a 1992 survey by the NYC Department of

Consumer Affairs, which found that, while the five major carriers' charges for a mixed market-basket of calls were close, when individual calling patterns were considered, certain companies were better deals than others. For example, light callers who talked only 45 minutes a month found Metromedia to be just as cheap as MCI.

If you think it's worth the effort to find the least expensive carrier for your calling pattern, start by dialing each of the major long distance carriers' toll-free information numbers (provided below) and ask for rate charts and brochures describing their discount plans. You might have to be insistent about getting rate charts, but you'll need them if you're going to compare companies. You might also check the Yellow Pages directory for names of regional long distance carriers.

The rate charts will provide per-minute rates (initial and additional minutes) broken down by "mileage band" for the carrier's various calling plans. The 24-hour numbers, as of this printing, are shown below.

MCI	(800) 444-3333
AT&T	(800) 222-0300
US Sprint	(800) 877-4646
Allnet	(800) 631-4000
LDDS/Metromedia	(800) 275-0100

You might have to wait. We were on hold with AT&T for ten minutes when we called one weekday morning. MCI put us on hold for eight minutes shortly thereafter.

We listened to Allnet's "elevator" music for 23 minutes one Saturday afternoon and for 15 minutes on a Sunday afternoon before giving up both times—which didn't make us feel too good about their customer responsiveness.

Next step: Gather your last four months' long distance bills and assess how many minutes you usually call during a typical month, the time of day you usually call (day, evening, or night hours), and whether there are certain parties or areas you call especially often (you might get a lower rate). Then apply your typical calling experience to each carrier's rate schedule, taking discount plans into account. You'll have the answer after you add up how much each carrier would have cost you over the course of the four months.

You can also send copies of a few typical phone bills to each of the carriers and ask them to figure out how much they would charge you, taking into account their savings plans.

Discount programs are generally worth looking into if you spend at least $10 a month calling long distance, although they might require you to make your calls during specified hours to benefit.

Described here are some basic examples of discount programs:

Volume discount. As of mid-1994, Allnet, for example, offered 5% discounts on evening and night/weekend rates for customers who spend between $10 and $25 a month and 10% if you spend more than $25. AT&T's True USA

Savings gave 10% off monthly bills that exceed $10 and 25% off bills that exceed $25. In addition, when the bill tops $30, AT&T's Simple Savings program offered 25% off calls to a selected area code and 15% off other calls. Sprint offered an automatic 20% off regular rates if your monthly bill is at least $30 and greater discounts for higher monthly bills. A variation on this theme was Sprint's "Most" program under which you get a 20% discount on all calls to the person you talked to most during the month, or 36% if that person is also a Sprint customer.

Hourly discount programs. You pay a flat monthly rate for an hour or so of calls anywhere. It may take patience to calculate whether these plans, offered by AT&T, Sprint, and MCI, are appropriate for your usual calling pattern.

A few AT&T examples illustrate our point: The AnyHour Saver Plan gave you a full hour of out-of-state calls for a monthly flat fee of $10, whether you call during the day, at night, or on weekends. The half-hour plan gave half an hour of long distance calls anywhere in the nation for a flat $4 a month. Then there was the AT&T Evening Plus plan—a $7.50 monthly fee for the first hour of calls after 5 PM. And the AT&T True Rewards program presented yet another variation: if you make at least $25 in long distance calls in a month, you earn points good for frequent flier miles on three major airlines or for "free" long distance minutes.

MCI had two plans—Prime-Time and AnyTime—each with its own first-hour flat rate and per-minute rates thereafter. Sprint also offered Select State-to-State calling plans, which charged $8.60 a month for the first hour of calls.

With hourly discount programs, remember that you'll be charged the full flat fee even if you make very few calls in a month.

Discounts in return for a monthly fee. The Sprint Day PLUS plan, for example, gave a 15% discount for a monthly fee of $1.95. MCI offered "Easy Rate," a variation for out-of-state calls that charged $3 a month, 23 cents a minute during the day, and 12 cents a minute other times.

Discounts for calls to pre-listed phone numbers and designated area codes. MCI calls it their "Friends and Family" program. You get a 20% discount on calls to a "circle" of up to 20 people who are also plan members. But to sign on you have to give MCI the names of plan candidates. For a $1 fee, the MCI Best Friends program gives 40% off calls to one particular person who also uses MCI, or 20% off if that person is not an MCI customer. Yet another option was added in 1994. The new Friends and Family II Sure Save program costs $3 a month and gives a 40% discount on calls to *all* MCI customers—if you bill at least $25 a month in calls.

AT&T's SelectSaver option basically provides, for a fee of $1.90 a month, lower per-minute rates for direct-dialed calls to the one area code you dial most frequently. Plus you get a 5% discount on all other AT&T out-of-state calls.

Yes, discount programs *are* complicated. It seems to us that the carriers could do everyone a favor by simply reducing basic rates and vastly simplifying the discount programs. But it increasingly makes sense to sign up for one. When AT&T inaugurated its True Savings volume discount program in 1993, callers spending less than $10 a month got a base-rate increase. Competitors were expected to raise their base rates, too.

Non-carriers have also gotten into the long distance game. Here are two more special deals:

Working Assets Long Distance. Working Assets donates 1% of your charges to such progressive citizens groups as Greenpeace and the Children's Defense Fund, and every month they send you information on some current topic, such as the national health insurance debate. This actually doesn't amount to much—a $2 contribution if you charge $200 all year. And while Working Assets' standard calling rates may be very competitive, the major carriers may have cheaper discount plans.

There's one unique benefit, though. Working Assets allows one free call a month to a designated Senator or corporate executive regarding the issue discussed in the monthly newsletter.

American Express "Connect-Plus." Using the Sprint system, you can get a 10% discount on any call charged on your American Express card. Charges appear on your monthly American Express statement.

The company you designate becomes your "primary carrier." But you don't always have to use your primary carrier. The 1984 decree ending AT&T's long distance monopoly mandates "equal access," meaning that you must be afforded full opportunity to use any long distance company that serves your area.

It's referred to as "casual calling" when you use a company other than your primary carrier. Why would you want to "casual call?" Perhaps to test the quality of a carrier's service before you sign them on as your primary carrier. Or you may "casual call" if your primary carrier is experiencing technical difficulties—or if its circuits are loaded to Florida on Mother's Day.

If you're the type who makes a sport out of saving nickels, you can use alternative carriers at times when their "casual calling" rates are lower than your primary carrier's after you consider your current discounts. Be sure to request the carrier's rate charts first, and check the casual calling rates before you dial, since they might differ from the carrier's regular rates.

You need not set up an account with a carrier to place a casual call. Just dial these "equal access" codes; that's all there is to it.

Allnet	*10 + 444*
AT&T	*10 + 288*
MCI	*10 + 222*
MetromediaUS	*10 + 488*
Sprint	*10 + 333*

The charges you incur will appear on a separate billing page in your monthly phone bill.

Finally, when settling on a carrier, decide if you want to have your bills mailed separately or included with your local telephone company bill. Some carriers offer separate billing.

Collect Calling

Amazing technological advances are allowing long distance carriers to offer services no one imagined just a few decades ago. One of these is residential toll-free 800 service. Anyone can call you toll-free, rather than collect. Of course, there's a monthly fee no matter how many or how few calls you get. Sprint, for example, charged a flat $5 a month for its "Residential 800" service. MCI calls its 800 service "Home Connect" and charges $3.95 a month for it, and the monthly charge for AT&T's "True Ties" 800 service is $4.50. But be aware that per-minute rate variances among carriers could offset any monthly fee savings.

Of course, anyone can call *you* collect without talking to an operator by dialing an 800 number: for MCI, (800) COLLECT; for AT&T, (800) OPERATOR; and for Sprint, (800) 877-8000. It is generally cheaper, however, to use a calling card if you have one. For instance, AT&T's calling card surcharge is 80 cents per call, compared with the (800) OPERATOR surcharge of $1.50. Still, calling collect via an 800 number is probably your best bet when using an off-brand pay phone not provided by the dominant local carrier. You'll always be routed to your major long distance company, bypassing the potentially very expensive intermediary that the pay-phone company might be connected to. These often have high calling card surcharges.

Long Distance Calling Cards

Local calling cards were briefly discussed in the previous chapter. But long distance calling cards actually started back in the 1950s. There are now about 15 different kinds—even a card in Braille.

Basically, to use a calling card you dial an access code, then the number of the party you're calling, followed by your calling card number. Charges show up on your phone bill. Calling cards are essential if you don't want to pump buckets of coins into a pay phone. They are very useful for travelers, who can use the card to avoid the hotels' high direct-call surcharges.

Calling card providers offer many new services, like teleconferencing and speed-dialing. They also offer special message-forwarding services. If you make an AT&T calling card or Universal Card call and the line is busy, you can dial a few digits and leave a message with a service. For $1.75 ($2.50 if person-to-person) the service will automatically keep dialing the number for four hours. If there is an answer, your message is played. MCI's similar service is called "Messenger."

Sprint offers a voice-activated card. No need to punch in a personal identification number or the

JUST SAY NO

Thieves are constantly developing new *modus operandi* to get your calling card number. According to Frances Feld, Executive Director of the Communications Fraud Control Association, thieves have lately been telephoning calling cardholders and, posing as phone company employees, they ask for personal identification numbers, "just to verify it is you." Many naive consumers gladly comply, especially college students.

numbers of your most frequent calls. You dial an 800 access number, a computer identifies your voice (it might ask a few identifying questions if it can't recognize you), and you simply say "call home" or "call office." You can program up to ten voice-activated call commands. But the fees can add up: the domestic per-call surcharge is $1, compared to 80 cents for the regular calling card. Sprint also charges $5 a month (it's free if you charge at least $50 a month in calls).

It probably makes sense to get basic calling cards from each of the major carriers—they're free and you might get a special discount just for signing up. To order, call AT&T at (800) 225-5288, MCI at (800) 999-4400, Sprint at (800) 795-5978, Allnet at (800) 631-

4000, and LDDS/Metromedia at (800) 275-0100.

The newest variation is the prepaid long distance calling card. You access the long distance line by calling an 800 number. Then you punch in a personal identification number followed by the number you're calling. At the end of your conversation, an automated voice tells you how much credit you have left. There's a time warning one minute before your money is used up. One advantage over regular calling cards: no per-call surcharge. Where can you get them? Call (800) 505-1115 to order Sprint's FON-CARD, which comes in increments of $5 up to $50; they can also be purchased in some convenience store chains. Call (800) 374-0909 to find out the nearest place to buy Western Union's Phone Card. Allnet's card comes in $24, $36, and $48 amounts and is valid for six months. (Call their 800 number, given in the previous paragraph.) TLC sells "PhoneCash" cards in convenience stores (800-925-4119 for more information).

WHAT TO WATCH OUT FOR

Switchover fees. Your local telephone company will charge a service fee, probably $5, to switch your long distance carrier. Allnet and Metromedia credit you for it. Before you sign up, ask the others if they will, too.

Directory assistance fees. Each carrier charges 60 or 65 cents for a long distance directory assistance inquiry, which is more than for local directory assistance. To get a phone number, call 1 + the area code + 555-1212.

The "round-up." You are generally charged for a full minute, even if you spoke for only three seconds of it.

Higher charges for calling cards. Long distance calling cards are a great convenience. But for Sprint, MCI, and AT&T, there is a surcharge on domestic interstate calls of 75 or 80 cents, although most carriers will provide you with a special discount if they are your primary carrier and you also use their calling card. For example, for $2 a month, AT&T Reach Out America customers can apply their calling card calls to the plan and the 80-cent calling card fee is waived during non-peak hours.

Being charged even after you defect. A few years ago many consumers complained to the authorities about being charged for monthly flat-fee calling plans, even after they had switched to another carrier. This problem seems to have subsided, but keep an eye out for it anyway.

> "*One person had a small microphone hooked to the back of his watch that he was speaking into. . . . Another wrote the number down, and another person looked like he was mouthing the numbers to memorize them.*"
>
> —JAMES SNYDER, an MCI Communications Corp. lawyer, describing how calling card number thieves who hang out near public phones do their work

Being switched without knowing it. Mrs. Bowers didn't understand that "no" can sometimes mean "yes." She thought that AT&T handled all of her long distance phone calls. But one day she opened her phone bill and noticed a $5 service charge from a different long distance company. As it turned out, she had opened an account with a new long distance carrier without realizing it when she had talked with a very persistent telephone salesman a few weeks before. She thought she had said "no" but the salesman interpreted what she said as "yes, connect me." In telephone industry parlance, she had been "slammed."

The practice of "slamming" was specifically outlawed in 1991 by the Federal Communications Commission. But even with newly required customer confirmations for carrier changes, many Americans still end up switching companies without completely understanding what they're doing. This is because competition in the long distance industry for new customers has become so cutthroat that sales representatives are sometimes less than clear about what they're asking people to do. There was even a case in Texas where people were switched by

ROOM SERVICE COSTS

According to *The Wall Street Journal,* in 1994 the lodging industry will collect an astounding $1.8 billion worth of phone fees. What kinds of fees? Potentially enormous surcharges if you dial long distance directly from your room. Some hotels fail to pass along the carrier's evening and night discounts. Others don't print the duration of the call on your bill, preventing you from checking the bill's accuracy and easily enabling overcharging. Some hotel chains charge a fee of a dollar or so if you try to bypass hotel surcharges by using your own calling card—and some hotels block card calls altogether. And most hotels charge fees of 50 cents or $1 for local calls. What to do? If in doubt about how much the hotel will tack on, don't call from a hotel phone.

ing an unfamiliar carrier (i.e., one not among the five major carriers), you'll know you're being serviced by an OSP—and that the sky's the limit on how much the call will cost. Examine pay phones before calling long distance to see if they are connected to your usual long distance company; federal law requires pay phones to have a sign disclosing their long distance company connection. Or you can find out from the long distance operator by dialing "00" or by calling the switchboard (of a hotel or hospital, for example, if that is where you are calling from).

You can also ask the "00" operator for rates and surcharges for the call you are about to place. If you are calling from a pay phone or a residence, call (700) 555-4141 (toll-free) for a recording stating the name of the carrier the phone is connected to.

If you want to use your regular carrier from any phone, just dial your equal access code.

Discount plan start-up fees. AT&T, for one, charges a $5 order processing fee for its half-hour flat rate plan.

Sales spiels and sniping. When you call carriers for information about their services, they launch into their sales pitch and may make disparaging remarks about the competition. An MCI representative informed us that AT&T charges a $30 hook-up fee for its personal 800 number and MCI charges none. An AT&T representative responded that the charge was only $10 and it would be deducted

entering a long distance company's sweepstakes, providing their effective consent. So unless you're really on the ball, you could end up with a new carrier without even knowing it.

High-priced operator service providers (OSPs). If you place a long distance call on a phone other than your own and hear a voice identify-

THE $MARTER CALLER

DAY RATE	*Monday through Friday, 8 AM to 5 PM*
EVENING RATE	*Sunday through Friday, 5 PM to 11 PM (10 PM for AT&T)*
NIGHT/WEEKEND RATE	*Sunday through Friday, 11 PM (10 PM for AT&T) to 8 AM and all day Saturday*
ALLNET SPECIAL DISCOUNT RATE	*Monday through Friday, 5 PM to 8 PM*

from the bill if the service was kept for a year. When we called AT&T to ask for rate charts, a representative wanted to know the details of our personal calling patterns, since AT&T offers "17 or 18 different plans—one for every kind of caller"—and he clearly wanted to sell us one. He also knocked the quality of the competition's service.

Before we could pose our first question, every carrier we called to inquire about savings plans, calling cards, or 800 numbers asked for our name and phone number. To avoid undesired solicitation calls, ignore these requests. We did, and we still got the necessary information.

THE $MARTER CONSUMER

Call when it's cheapest. You can cut your bill by up to 20% by waiting until 5:01 PM, except on Saturdays.

If you call New York from San Francisco, you can save 44% with Allnet and 39% with Sprint by calling in the evening. (The basic time chart for the five major carriers is shown above.)

Watch out for rate changes and time-period changes. Some companies base the rate for an entire call on the rate when you placed it. This is preferable if you often start your calls at a cheaper time and end them in a more expensive time. On the other hand, if your calls often extend to lower rate hours, you would do better with a carrier that changes the rates when the time period changes.

Reassess annually. Rates and plans change constantly, so it makes sense to reconsider your long distance carrier and your calling plan at least once a year.

Pay with a credit card. Allnet, MCI, and Sprint allow you to pay for calls with a credit or charge card and AT&T allows payment with their Universal credit card. Paying with a credit card gives you the advantages of credit card payment, such as the "float." (See "Credit Cards," page 277, for an explanation of the "float.")

Avoid calling-card fraud. There's a new illicit profession, "surfing." "Surfers" are people who use your card number to sell heavily discounted long distance calls. They get your number by observing you punch it in or by listening to you recite it to an operator while using a public phone. To avoid being billed for thousands of dollars of calls to China, for example, try to punch in—rather than orally recite to the operator—your personal identification number. Use your free hand to cover or screen the hand that's punching in the numbers. Better yet, try to use phones that read the magnetic stripe on your calling card. If you must recite the number, do so in a soft but clear voice. Always be alert to anyone lurking about while you are placing a calling card call.

Don't get "slammed." To stop unauthorized switching of your long distance carrier, the Federal Communications Commission now prohibits local phone companies from honoring a request to switch your long distance service unless you are provided written confirmation of the switch, or you electronically authorized the change, or you received a follow-up mailing saying that you will be switched within 14 days unless you cancel, or there was an independent third-party verification of the switch. If you're unhappy about being slammed,

CALL FOR CREDIT

ALLNET	(800) 783-2020 for immediate credit
AT&T	Call the operator for immediate credit or (800) 222-0300 for bill adjustment
MCI	(800) 444-3333 for immediate credit
LDDS/ METROMEDIA	(800) 275-0100 for immediate credit
US SPRINT	Call the operator for immediate credit or (800) 877-4646 for bill adjustment

immediately ask your phone company to be switched back—for free.

Get credits for wrong numbers. Above are the five major carriers' phone numbers for getting a credit.

Try call accounting. Who's making those three-hour late night calls? If your kids won't 'fess up, consider getting Call Accounting. For a fee of $5 or so per month (AT&T has no charge), each caller will have to punch in a short special code when calling. There will be a separate page in your monthly statement for each caller.

■ **The Telecommunica-** tions Research & Action Center publishes **periodic rate comparisons** among the major carriers. For $2, they'll send you their *Tele-Tips Residential Long Distance Comparison Chart*. Send the money and a self-addressed, stamped envelope to TRAC at P.O. Box 12038, Washington, DC 20005.

■ **For answers to nearly all your** long distance questions, contact the experts at Tele-Consumer Hotline. Call (800) 332-1124. Available only to customers of Bell Atlantic, NYNEX, Pacific Bell, and Southwestern Bell.

■ **To complain about long** distance or international service, write to the Enforcement Division, Federal Communications Commission, Room 6202, Washington, DC 20554. Include copies of disputed bills and other documents to help them understand your complaint. To receive a written explanation of how to complain, call the FCC at (202) 418-0200.

PART 8

Children

CHAPTER 45

CHILD CARE

The Who, What, and Where

What's the problem with child care? There simply is not enough of it. Supply of any child care, let alone affordable, quality child care, has not kept pace with the demand of millions of parents in the work force and more and more single parents heading households. According to U.S. government statistics, one in four families with children have one parent at home, and the number of mothers—traditionally responsible for the prime burden of child care—who work outside the home has increased from approximately 30% to over 50% from 1970 to 1992.

If you feel bewildered and overwhelmed by your quest to find someone to care for your kids, you're not alone. Parents often must struggle with waiting lists for coveted day-care slots that can be years long or fees that are higher than one parent's salary. As a result, many settle for "whatever they can find," which often means a revolving door of child-care providers and arrangements that take an emotional toll on both parents and children.

Since your child's health and welfare are on the line, you can make your search for child care more sane and satisfying by treating it no less seriously than you do other major consumer purchases.

THE BASICS

The Three Child Care Models

There are many different child-care options, but only three basic models:

Day-care centers care for many children in a group or "school" setting. They are usually staffed by trained professionals under a significant amount of government regulation and oversight. Children can interact with many other children and are exposed to several different organized activities.

The disadvantages? Day-care centers can have child-to-provider ratios as high as 20 to 1; the best day-care centers tend to have extremely long waiting lists and tuition as high as some colleges; and many day-care centers have strict hours, vacation, and sick policies that may not fit with your work schedule.

After you consider the pros and cons of day-care centers, think carefully about the differences between for-profit and not-for-profit centers. About 40% of all centers are for-profit; they're either independent or franchise centers, such as "Kinder Care" or "Children's World." The rest are not-for-profits run by churches, synagogues, co-ops, businesses, research centers, or the government on a not-for-profit basis. According to a 1991 study published in the *Journal of Social Issues*, staff in not-for-profit centers tend to have more training and to receive higher salaries; not-for-profit centers have lower child-to-provider ratios, and parents participate more both as volunteers and in setting policy. Not surprisingly, the not-for-profit centers are rated "good" or "superior" twice as often as the for-profit centers.

Family day-care providers typically care for five to eight children in the provider's home. Besides being more personal, they are more flexible and tend to cost less than day-care centers. Another plus is that children are in a home rather than an institutional setting, yet are still exposed to other children.

On the other hand, family day-care providers tend to have less formal training; in many states, they are unregulated or less regulated than day-care centers. They can be hard to find and have more limited space than day-care centers.

In-home child-care providers (baby sitters or nannies) care for children in the child's home either

DAY-CARE CENTERS AT A GLANCE

PROS	CONS
■ Usually have trained professional staff. ■ More state regulation of both staff and facilities. ■ Often more educational and structured programming that has been shown to increase social competence, maturity, and intellectual development. ■ Offers changing experiences as children get older. ■ The opportunity for children to interact with many other children in a school-like setting. ■ More stable, less likely to close or quit than other day-care options. ■ Many center-based facilities offer basic health care.	■ Often high child-to-provider ratios. ■ Often high staff turnover. ■ Often long waiting lists to get in, especially for the best centers. ■ Strict, inflexible hours. ■ Many centers have no provisions for sick children. ■ More interaction with other children also means more exposure to infectious disease and viruses. ■ Centers are often inconveniently located in relation to the child's home and/or parents' place of employment.

FAMILY DAY CARE AT A GLANCE

PROS	CONS
■ Often the least expensive option because of low overhead and reasonable child-to-provider ratios. ■ More flexible and accommodating of parent's schedules than center-based day care. ■ More personal care and less provider turnover. ■ Opportunity for children to interact with a few, but not an overwhelming, number of other children, often of different ages. ■ Parents often have more input (and control) over the care and may more easily leave special instructions, when necessary. ■ Caregiver's home is often located close to the child's home.	■ Little if any government regulation and supervision of staff or facilities. ■ Often the provider has less training than providers in centers. ■ Less variety of activities and play materials. ■ Less structured and possibly fewer educational activities. ■ Family-based child-care can go out of business unpredictably. ■ No sick-child facilities or health care. ■ Since children are still interacting with other, albeit fewer children, there is still an increased risk of contagion.

on a full-time or part-time basis. In-home caregivers can live in their own homes or with the family. Their main advantage is that they provide the greatest flexibility for parents and the most continuity of care and personal attention for children. There may also be health benefits—especially for younger children and infants—in staying at home.

Of course, in-home providers are the most costly kind of child care, and typically they are less well trained and regulated than other caregivers. Also, children cared for at home may have less social interaction with other kids than do children at day-care centers or in family care arrangements, unless their

caregiver (or parents) structure regular social activities.

Making the Choice

There are pitfalls in each type of arrangement. You've probably heard at least one of the horror stories that pop up regularly on the evening news: a day-care center employee arrested for alleged child abuse; two children burned to death in a tragic fire in a Queens, New York, family day-care facility lacking smoke detectors and adequate emergency plans; and the Swiss nanny Olivia Weiner in Westchester County, New York, who was acquitted of murder charges in a

IN-HOME CHILD CARE AT A GLANCE

PROS	CONS
■ Most flexible hours. ■ Children can stay at home when they're sick. ■ Less opportunity for contagion by other children. ■ Most personal form of care. ■ Potentially more continuity of care. ■ Offers parents greatest degree of control over the child's care.	■ Most expensive option. ■ Providers may have little experience or formal training. ■ Lack of accountability; parents are the only enforcement and there are no legal mandates. ■ Children may not get the benefit of interaction with other children as much as children in family or center-based care. ■ Providers can quit unexpectedly, leaving parents scrambling. ■ Finding a qualified and affordable provider is often arduous.

case that sparked a national nanny debate as well as several made-for-TV movies.

Fortunately, tragedies such as these are rare. According to a comprehensive survey of all reported cases of sex abuse in day-care centers from 1983 to 1985, only 5 children out of 10,000 were abused in day care. During that same period, 9 of 10,000 were abused at home. Less than half of the day-care cases involved a professional child-care provider—the others involved janitors, bus drivers, and family members.

To prevent physical or sexual abuse, parents should look for facilities that:

■ Allow unlimited access to parents (and other caregivers, like grandparents and trusted friends).
■ Keep bathroom doors open while children are using them.

■ Do not allow providers to tease or physically punish children.
■ Have strict rules about who can pick up children.

Also, parents should be alert and perceptive: Do children at the center look fearful, anxious, or neglected? Be sure to ask plenty of extra questions if they do or if something "just doesn't feel right"; following your instincts may mean insuring your child's safety.

Day-care centers. The three key issues you should consider when you shop for a day-care center are staffing, policies, and facilities. Since day-care centers tend to be heavily regulated by state departments of health, facilities are usually up to par. Most are inspected for building code violations at least once a year. Still, it never hurts to check building maintenance and emergency procedures for yourself.

Staffing is also addressed by most state regulations, but training requirements tend to be loosely enforced and staff-to-child ratios tend to be high. Often, the director of the day-care center is required to have formal education and specialized training in child development, but the day-care workers—who have the most direct contact with your child—have far fewer requirements than the director. Some states require only a high school diploma. According to Carollee Howes, a developmental psychologist and Professor of Education at the University of California at Los Angeles, "When you are in a [day-care] center, you need that specialized knowledge of children to be able to manage groups and do developmentally appropriate activities."

In addition to training, turnover is a key staffing issue. If a well-educated caregiver quits after three months, then the children do not benefit. Often, centers either don't keep or refuse to discuss precise turnover statistics. To find out, ask other parents and get a sense of the work conditions by asking about the caregiver's salary and benefits. The center is less likely to have a revolving door if it treats its caregivers professionally.

But it is not enough for a center to have qualified, committed caregivers if it doesn't have enough of them. The Federal Intra-agency Day Care Requirements (FIDCR), established in 1980 but never implemented, suggest the following staff-to-child ratios:

- One caregiver to three babies
- One caregiver to four toddlers
- One caregiver to eight pre-schoolers

CHILD CARE FOR CHILDREN WITH DISABILITIES

Kerri D. enrolled her son Michael, who has juvenile diabetes, in a day-care program at the Indian Valley YMCA in Hartford, Connecticut. Even though it took the staff only a minute to check Michael's blood sugar, the YMCA forced Kerri to withdraw Michael because of concerns about liability, insurance, and regulations.

Fortunately, the federal Americans with Disabilities Act should help disabled children like Michael receive care. Centers must now determine whether they are *able* rather than *willing* to care for children with special needs. The Act took effect January 1, 1993, and applies to all child-care homes and centers except those operated by religious groups.

If your child has been unjustly excluded from day care, contact your state attorney general, the disability committee of your state's bar association, or the American Civil Liberties Union.

DAY-CARE CRITERIA

In 1980 the federal government established the Federal Intra-agency Day Care Requirements (FIDCR). Although these standards have never been implemented, FIDCR recommendations are a good guideline for parents. They require day-care facilities to:

■ Have a planned daily program of developmentally appropriate activities to promote intellectual, social, emotional, and physical development.
■ Train caregivers and provide an orientation including health, safety, and program procedures.
■ Give parents unlimited access to the care setting and regular opportunities to discuss the child's needs and participate in policy making.
■ Provide adequate and nutritious meals, as appropriate.

In addition, although there are no federally mandated child-to-provider ratios for day-care centers, and some states allow a ratio as high as 20 to 1, the FIDCR specifies that a center should have:

■ One caregiver for every three infants, and a maximum of six infants in total.
■ One caregiver for every four toddlers and a maximum of 12 toddlers in total.
■ One caregiver for every eight preschoolers and a maximum of eight preschoolers in total.

Family day-care providers. Family day-care providers working in their home appeal to many parents as an ideal middle ground between baby-sitters and full-fledged day-care centers. But according to the Child Care Action Campaign, a nonprofit advocacy group, there are only 1.5 million family day-care providers for the more than 5 million American children whose parents seek this kind of care.

Of central importance for parents seeking this option, about 80% of the family day-care providers are not regulated in any way. According to Barbara Reisman, executive director of the Child Care Action Campaign, this means that "basically, states are saying you're on your own if you use family child care. . . . Parents need to be very well-informed and very vigilant."

First, check with your state's health department to see what, if any, requirements family day-care centers have to meet. Then, if licensing, registration, or certification is required, make sure the center you're considering is operating legally.

Since any regulation for family

day-care centers is likely to be more lax than for formal day-care centers, take more time to check out the facility. Child Care Inc., a New York City referral agency, suggests the following checklist:

- Does the home have smoke detectors and fire extinguishers?
- Are medicines and household products kept locked up?
- Are toys safe and appropriate for the child's age?
- Do the children regularly go outside to play, when weather permits?
- Is there a clear schedule for meals, naps, and playtimes?

You should spend some time in the home observing various parts of the day, and you should spend a good deal of time talking with the child-care provider and checking his or her references. Reisman suggests that if you're not allowed to visit any time during the day, you should move on. Also, according to Sally Ziegler, executive director of the Child Care Council, another nonprofit referral group, "If children run hungrily to a visitor, it means they are not getting enough attention."

Finally, as with a day-care center, you should also check the number and ages of the children being cared for, the provider's vacation schedule (if any), sick day, and late-fee policies.

In-home child-care providers. Since your child will be cared for in your own home, you will set the rules. The only question is the qualifications of the provider. But finding a qualified provider is far easier

said than done—even if you're willing to pay top dollar and particularly if you want to hire a legal worker and pay her or him "on the books."

The question of not hiring illegal aliens and paying social security and other taxes has become a front-burner issue since the failed 1993 nomination of Zoë Baird for U.S. Attorney General simply because of her "nanny problem."

As the 1994 legislative session wound to a close, both the House and the Senate unanimously passed and President Clinton signed a "Nanny Tax" bill, H. R. 4278, the Social Security Amendment Act of 1994. It does two things: increases the exemption you're allowed before you have to pay taxes to $1,000, and simplifies the process, by allowing you to pay your employee's Social Security on your own W2 form.

Most families find caregivers by word of mouth: Once one family's children reach school age, they refer their nanny or sitter to another family. But if you're not so fortunately connected, you have two basic options: place "help wanted" ads or use a nanny agency. If you want to hire someone who is legal *and* willing to pay taxes, you may need to go through an agency. You especially need an agency if you aren't ready to spend lots of time screening scores of applicants yourself. (Remember Diane Keaton interviewing a parade of eccentrics in *Baby Boom*?)

No state specifically regulates in-home child-care providers. If anything, agencies that refer nannies and sitters are regulated as employment agencies, without any special requirements for referring people to care for children. They could just as well be screening gardeners or domestics. So while agencies are certainly helpful with preliminary screening, there is no way to avoid investing a significant amount of time and effort to find the most appropriate in-home child-care provider.

If you don't, the consequences could be disappointing or even tragic. In a story told to the NYC Department of Consumer Affairs, Kate L. said she was horrified to learn that the nanny caring for her infant—whom the agency had called "the perfect person"—had repeatedly lied: The nanny said she had worked for the De Beers diamond-baron family in South Africa and claimed to be a Cordon Bleu chef. The nanny's poor performance tipped Kate off that maybe this wasn't quite the case. And, at a dinner party, one of the guests recognized the nanny's "homemade" gourmet dessert as having come from the bakery around the corner. Before hiring the nanny, Kate had interviewed someone who she was told was Ms. De Beers. But even then she was somewhat suspicious when "Ms. De Beers'" accent slipped from South African to what sounded like Cockney.

> "We tell parents to spend at least as much time choosing child care as you would buying a car—you wouldn't buy a car over the phone. . . ."
>
> — PATSY LANE,
> Child Care Coordinator for the
> City of Los Angeles

And then there's the story of the mother from Westchester County, New York, who found out that her nanny had physically abused her three-year-old son when her son one day asked the new nanny whether she was going to "lock me in my room." The mother then found out that the previous nanny had routinely locked the child in until the mother got home from work.

If you decide to go through an agency, you have to choose one with almost as much care as you choose the actual provider. At anywhere from $500 to $2,000 per referral, it pays to make sure you're getting the referral service you're paying for. Following are some tips:

- Get a written contract that includes a specific job description for the provider you're trying to find. This will avoid wasting time on inappropriate referrals and also help prevent disputes about fees down the road.
- Ask specific questions about how the agency screens applicants. Do they do face-to-face interviews? How many references do they check? Do they keep and let you see written records of reference checks?
- Get and check the agency's own references. If the agency is not able or willing to refer you to other

parents who have used their services, you should strongly consider going elsewhere.

Whether you use an agency or go it alone, you have to do two things *yourself*: Interview the nanny and check her or his references. The whole process is so emotional and the stakes are so high that many parents end up relying on their "gut" or "instinct" and hoping they make the right choice. If you don't feel right about an applicant, don't bring that person into your home.

Child Care Inc. suggests asking a candidate the following questions in your interview:

- What do you like about working with children?
- How much television-watching do you think is appropriate?
- What would you do if my child disobeyed you?
- What would you do in an emergency if I couldn't be reached?
- Describe your typical day.

Check references after the interview, but be careful, advises Wendy Sachs, a representative for the International Nanny Association. Sachs owns a nanny placement agency and is a parent who employs a nanny. "The references you get are only as good as the person giving the references." One parent interviewed for a NYC Department of Consumer Affairs investigation of the nanny agency business, *Who's Watching the Kids?*, told of checking one reference with whom she shared a mutual friend and, only after an extended personal conversation, did

she get a true—and most unfavorable—picture of the applicant. One trick to checking references is to ask specific questions based on information you get from the nanny in an interview. If the answers don't agree, you can suspect a problem.

Indeed, the NYC investigators found widespread problems in reference checking. An undercover nanny "applicant" gave four agencies she visited the names of two Consumer Affairs staff members to call as "references." One of the agencies didn't even try to call the references and the others didn't try very hard, merely leaving messages but never actually talking to both parties. When contact was made, the questions were superficial, and the conversations only a few minutes long. Nonetheless, all four agencies told the undercover "applicant" that they had jobs for her, and two agencies lied to families, telling them that her references had been checked when they hadn't.

Finding the perfect provider is just half the battle: The other half is to retain your child's caregiver. Remember, you're the boss; you've got to take responsibility for supervising your sitter or nanny. The caregiver is a professional; no matter how cordial your relationship, she (or he) is not a member of your family and needs to be treated with professional courtesy. To establish and maintain a professional relationship with your caregiver, you should:

- Provide a written contract. Include specific job responsibilities, hours, salary, vacation/sick days policy, and car and telephone privileges.

■ Strongly consider providing benefits, such as health care and in-service training, for your provider and putting periodic opportunities for performance reviews and raises into your contract.

■ Meet with your provider regularly both to give feedback on job performance and to get feedback on your child's development.

WHAT TO WATCH OUT FOR

Special day-care center rules. Before you're satisfied that you've found the perfect child-care center, take a good look at any special rules. Many centers have prohibitively restrictive policies about who can drop off and pick up your child and when, and most charge at least half tuition on personal vacation or sick days, when your child does not attend. Before you sign up, make sure you know and can live within the rules.

Criminal background checks of nannies. Many parents seek criminal background checks before they hire a caregiver. Recent horror stories on the evening news have encouraged the creation of private-eye agencies such as Nanny Check in California that claim to do FBI and other criminal background checks. Unfortunately, no individual or organization has the authority to look at someone's state criminal record or FBI file without that person's permission. The only thing an

agency can do is county-by-county record checks, which tend to be both tedious and incomplete.

THE SMARTER CONSUMER

Shop around. Regardless of which option you choose—child-care centers, family day care, or in-home day care—both your child and your pocketbook will benefit from shopping around. Like buying a car, reliable and affordable child care requires both comparing the different models and regular maintenance to keep your child-care arrangements working. Here are five basic steps to steer you down the rocky road until your child starts school:

1. Consider your child and your lifestyle before you check out your options. Write out your priorities and take the list with you when you visit day-care centers or interview family or in-home providers.

2. Plan ahead. It's never too soon to start checking out your options. If you wait until a week before you have to go back to work, you'll be stuck with a snap decision.

3. Personally interview and check the references of whoever is going to be caring for your child, no matter what setting the care will be given in.

4. Make the transition as easy as possible for your children by taking extra one-on-one time and leaving them with the caregiver for a few hours at a time when the situation is still new.

5. Drop in unexpectedly every few weeks to make sure that your child is being cared for appropriately. Also, meet periodically with your care provider(s) to both give and get feedback on your child and child-care arrangements.

Have your prospective caregiver cleared by the FBI. You can ask a nanny candidate for her (or his) fingerprints and then send these, along with a cover letter and a $17 check, to the FBI Identification Division. It's also a good idea to ask for medical records, including a recent tuberculosis test and proof of childhood immunizations. If the candidate you prefer has no records, *you* should pay for the shots. Better safe than sorry, for both the caregiver and your child.

■ **For information on** family day care anywhere in the country, call *Child Care Aware* at (800) 424-2246.

■ ***The Complete Guide*** *to Choosing Child Care* by Judith Berezin, (Random House, $12.95), is a very good resource.

■ **For listings of nanny agencies and** nanny training programs around the country, call the *American Council of Nanny Schools* at (517) 686-9417.

■ **For information about your state's** laws and regulations regarding child care, contact your state department of health. Most have a special agency or bureau for child care.

■ **Child Care Action Campaign** is an advocacy group that also publishes a newsletter and other helpful reports for parents, such as *Child Care Primer, Liability Insurance and Child Care*, and *Tax Credit for Child Care*. To subscribe to the newsletter ($25/year, including membership) or for a list of publications, write them at 330 Seventh Ave., New York, NY 10001-5010, or call (212) 239-0138.

■ **For referrals to local child-care** resource and referral agencies, call the National Association for Child Care Resource and Referral Agencies, (800) 570-4543.

CHAPTER 46

TOYS

Not Just Child's Play

Play is the main work of childhood, and toys are the tools of the trade. However, each year nearly 150,000 children are injured playing with toys—more frequently than workers in many trades are injured on the job. In addition, many children spend more time watching toy advertisements than their parents spend watching their kids. And many of these ads are misleading, promising kids a product that just doesn't exist. Since kids can't unionize, it is up to parents to make their kids' playroom a safe and satisfying "work site."

THE BASICS

The toy industry spends nearly half a billion dollars on advertising to get consumers to purchase close to $13 billion dollars' worth of toys each year. Toys touting celebrity logos account for ever more expensive toys. But children are often disappointed by toys that do not live up to their glitzy advertisements. Far worse, thousands of children are rushed to emergency rooms each year because of toy-related injuries. Approximately 20 children die annually in accidents with hazardous playthings.

Two-year-old Betsy was playing with a teddy bear when she pulled off its hard plastic nose, popped it into her mouth—and almost choked to death on it. Lucky for Betsy, doctors removed the small toy part from her airways and she was fine; nonetheless, choking on small parts remains the leading cause of toy-related deaths.

The U.S. Consumer Product Safety Commission (CPSC) catalogs toy incidents like Betsy's and is the federal agency responsible for keeping hazardous playthings from endangering children. But the CPSC lacks the resources to adequately monitor and address the thousands of new toys introduced each year, many of which are imported from foreign manufacturers.

The U.S. Federal Trade Commission (FTC) monitors all advertising, including toy ads, but they too are outrun by the massive toy industry. The FTC catches a few deceptive ads each year, but many more misleading ads go unnoticed—except by the children they target.

The toy industry helps fund two pseudo-trade groups to monitor toy safety and advertising. The American Society for Testing and Materials (ASTM) develops voluntary toy

A TEST TUBE TOO SMALL

The CPSC defines a small part as a toy or part of a toy that fits entirely into a test tube 1.25 inches wide and 2.25 inches deep. However, children have choked to death on toys that pass the CPSC small-parts test.

In 1990, six children choked to death on the old version of Fisher-Price's Little People, which just barely exceeded the test-tube standard. In February 1991, Fisher-Price announced that it had increased the size of its Little People. But the CPSC has refused to enlarge the test tube.

Instead of the test tube, parents can use a cardboard tube from a toilet tissue roll, or the child's fist. If the object is smaller than the fist or fits into the cardboard tube, it should not be given to a child who still puts things in his or her mouth.

---

manufacturing guidelines and the Children's Advertising Review Unit (CARU), which is part of the Better Business Bureau, develops voluntary children's advertising guidelines. But since both the ASTM and CARU get much of their funding from the toy industry, they can be like foxes guarding the henhouse. The bottom line is that *you* need to protect your children from hazardous toys and misleading toy ads.

WHAT TO WATCH OUT FOR

Toy Safety

Don't assume that the toys on store shelves or that your kids receive as gifts from well-meaning friends and relatives are safe. There are just too many toys and not enough toy-safety cops on the beat to check each toy before it goes to market. Toys that are found to be unsafe can take months to recall, and recall notices rarely reach all consumers who have purchased the defective toy. So there's just no substitute for toy-safety vigilance. Here are some things to look for when shopping for safe toys:

Small parts. These are the leading cause of toy-related deaths and injuries to children under three. The CPSC considers anything smaller than 1.25 inches by 2.25 inches a small part, but children have choked on toys larger than this. Small parts can be either independent toys, such as tiny trucks or dolls, or parts of toys that can come off, like car wheels or doll shoes. Balloons and small balls are some of the potentially deadliest toys for young children.

Sharp points and edges. These can cut or puncture kids. Some toys have sharp points and edges by design; others are just poorly made. Toys can also develop sharp points and edges when they break, and many stuffed toys have sharp wires inside.

Cords and strings over 12 inches long. These can become a noose around a young child's neck and cause strangulation. Pull toys and crib gyms can be particularly hazardous when children roll around in confined areas, like cribs and playpens.

Loud noises. Noises from toy caps, toy guns, toy phones, radios, and other noisemaking games can injure a child's hearing. The CPSC bans toys that make particularly loud noises, but even quieter toys can impair hearing if used too close to kids' ears.

Electronic toys. These can cause shocks and burns if not properly constructed and maintained.

Toys with hazardous chemicals can be deadly to children. Some toys, such as chemistry sets, must include some chemicals, but others—such as model kits, children's nail polish, and some brands of spray "string"—contain some of the same substances found in toxic Superfund sites.

Toy chest lids have been known to fall onto children, hitting them in the head or trapping them inside the toy chest. Toy chests with hinged lids should be able to stay open in any position. Other options are toy chests without lids or with lightweight removable lids. All toy chests should have ventilation holes in case a child gets trapped inside.

Bikes, in-line skates, all-terrain vehicles, and other riding toys can be very hazardous if they are not the right size for the child and if children do not wear the appropriate protective gear. All-terrain vehicles injure one of every four riders and should not be used by children under 16. No child should use a bike, skateboard, roller skates, or roller blades, etc., without a protective helmet. More than half of the nearly 37,000 injuries related to in-line rollerskates reported in 1993 were suffered by children under 15. To help your kids skate safely, make sure they have the proper protective gear: padded helmets and wrist- and knee-guards.

Backyard play sets are no fun if they're not safe. Unlike many other children's products, there are no mandatory safety standards for play sets. Many are built excessively high with hard and heavy swing seats, sharp exposed bolts and edges, and overlapping play patterns. The most important aspect of a backyard play set, however, is what is on the ground below. Grass is not a safe play set surface: Kids need soft sand or wood chips to break their falls. The rubber mats under some schoolyard and city park play sets are OK, too—as long as they are properly maintained.

Toy Advertising

While some parents and consumer advocates have fought to ban all advertising to children, advertisers have been targeting younger and younger kids with ever more creative messages. The average TV show targeted to kids under eight has 12 minutes of advertising, compared with only eight minutes on adult programs. Furthermore, advertisements based on movies, TV shows, and other celebrities have skyrocketed. Kids not only see ads for such celebrity products as Batman action figures, but also see products like Reese's Pieces and Coke in movies like *Batman* and *ET.* The line between TV shows and commercials is also being blurred by infomercials and cartoons developed specifically to promote a licensed character or toy line. It's hard enough for adults to keep up with advertisers' antics, let alone help their kids through the maze of consumer messages. Here are some of the more common tricks of the trade to watch out for when watching TV:

Ads that make toys do things only Hollywood can make happen. Hidden wires and invisible hands can make airplanes and stuffed dogs seem to fly, and smoke and mirrors can make action figures conquer all. Each year some advertisers take special effects too far. For example, in 1993 Mattel was charged over $150,000 by the FTC for using special effects to enhance the performance of its G.I. Joe action figures and accessories.

Ads that show you more than you will get. Kids who get one set of a toy depicted in an ad with many sets or many different accessories are likely to be disappointed. A 1991 advertisement for the Domino Rally showed about five times as many dominos and accessories as a consumer would get in one box, making the game seem much bigger and more exciting than it is.

Ads for toys requiring parental supervision that don't show parents. If a child sees an ad for a toy like a ride-on electric car without parents around, then he or she will expect to be able to use that toy alone, even though the manufacturers suggest that safe play with the toy requires parental supervision.

Ads that blur the line between fantasy and reality. Kids have active imaginations but often expect a toy to do what it does on TV. A 1992 Treasure Trolls ad depicted the trolls laughing and making wishes come true. When kids found out the dolls didn't laugh, several complained to *Zillions,* the *Consumer Reports* for kids.

Ads enticing kids to buy toys just because of celebrity logos and look-alikes. While licensed toys account for about 10% of all toy sales, they make up almost 50% of toy profits, according to the Toy Manufacturers of America. For instance, a basketball with Michael Jordan's signature on it can cost three times as much as a basketball without it. Some toys with movie logos are marketed to kids who are too young to see the movies—but aren't too young for the marketing.

Ads that depict toys being used in violent ways. In particular, ads for guns and slingshots that show kids shooting other kids at close range send kids the wrong message for both play and real life.

Toy Safety

Read and heed toy age recommendations. Age labels on toys are not just developmental recommendations; they are often safety warnings. The Child Safety Protection Act of 1994 requires clearer and more prominent warning labels on potentially hazardous toys—and stricter penalties for manufacturers who ignore the law's warnings.

■ "Ages 3 and up" often means the toy has small (i.e., swallowable) parts.
■ "Ages 8 and up" often means the toy has electrical elements or hazardous chemicals.
■ "Ages 12 and up" often means that the toy can get excessively hot.

Don't buy a toy intended for an older child because you think that your child is exceptionally bright or will grow into it. Even exceptional two-year-olds put things in their mouths and can choke to death on toys with small parts.

Follow assembly instructions carefully and discard all packaging immediately. Safe toys can become unsafe if improperly assembled. Never allow children to play with packaging that is not part of the toy, or with toys before they are completely assembled and checked.

Check toys carefully and repeatedly for small parts, sharp points and edges, long strings, and other hazards. Not all toys are properly labeled, and toys that are safe when you buy them can become unsafe with use (and abuse). Be particularly careful with baby rattles, pacifiers, and other toys meant for babies and young children.

Remove crib gyms when infants can get up on their knees. Infants can and have choked to death by falling onto a crib gym strung across a crib.

Keep toys intended for older children out of the reach of younger ones. Teach older siblings about the hazards their toys pose to younger children. *Never* use balloons around young children who still "sample" small objects by mouth or who haven't the coordination to avoid inhaling a balloon while trying to inflate it.

Store all toys properly. Many toy-related injuries are caused by falling onto or over toys. Putting toys away can prevent these injuries as well as keep toys from breaking. Outdoor toys need to be protected from the elements to prevent rust and breakage that could cause serious injuries. Do not store toys in unsafe toy boxes or on shelving that children can climb.

Supervise children using toys and teach them to play safely. No matter how safe a toy is, children are creative and resourceful; they will often find ways to use toys in unintentional (and potentially hazardous) ways. Toys are not baby-

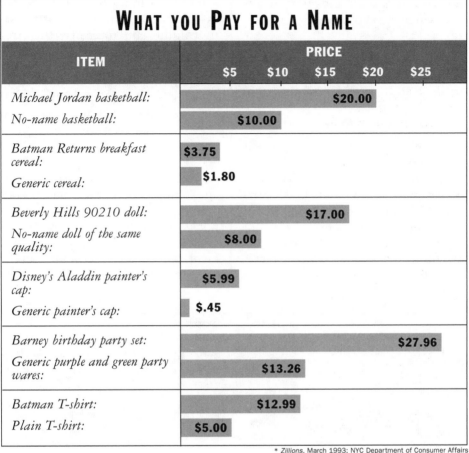

WHAT YOU PAY FOR A NAME

ITEM	PRICE				
	$5	$10	$15	$20	$25
Michael Jordan basketball:				$20.00	
No-name basketball:		$10.00			
Batman Returns breakfast cereal:	$3.75				
Generic cereal:	$1.80				
Beverly Hills 90210 doll:			$17.00		
No-name doll of the same quality:	$8.00				
Disney's Aladdin painter's cap:	$5.99				
Generic painter's cap:	$.45				
Barney birthday party set:					$27.96
Generic purple and green party wares:		$13.26			
Batman T-shirt:		$12.99			
Plain T-shirt:	$5.00				

* *Zillions*, March 1993; NYC Department of Consumer Affairs

sitters; there is no substitute for thoughtful adult supervision.

Check Recall Notice Boards at toy stores and call the CPSC Recall Hotline, (800) 638-CPSC. Toy recalls are often poorly publicized, so you have to take the initiative to find out if the toys you have bought are still considered to be safe. You can also report a potentially hazardous toy to the CPSC by calling the Hotline.

Watch out for toys used as prizes in cereal boxes and fast food kid's meals. These toys are often poorly constructed, overlooked by safety regulators, and almost always are small or contain small parts.

Play with your kids. This is the easiest way to both teach your kids how to play safely and check the toys for hazards. It's also fun!

Outsmarting Toy Ads

Watch TV with your kids. Use toy advertisements as tools to explain the difference between fantasy and reality and to teach kids to view advertisements skeptically.

Look—and, when you can, play—before you buy. Encourage kids to play with a toy at a friend's house or to look at it carefully in the store before buying it. The TV image of a toy is often quick to fade in real life.

Fight toy fads. It's tough to resist constant cries of "Buy me this" or "Buy me that," but a little will power will teach your kids some valuable consumer skills and could save you a considerable sum of money. Since most kids have short attention spans, one potential tactic is to wait a couple of weeks or even a month before deciding to buy—as celebrity marketing increases in volume and intensity, the time that particular products stay "hot" keeps getting shorter. When you do give in to a fad, try to buy useful items of good quality and teach kids to look more carefully at what they're buying than at the logo that's on it.

Finally, foster creativity. Encourage kids to draw their own "celebrity" logos on T-shirts, notebooks, party cups, and other products so they can identify with their favorite character without paying the premium price.

The No-Choke Testing Tube, a cylinder you can use to assure that small parts are big enough to avoid a choking hazard, can be purchased for $1 from Toys To Grow On, P.O. Box 17, Long Beach, CA 90801.

For tips for purchasing appropriate toys for children of different ages and abilities, write for *Which Toy for Which Child,* a free brochure published by the U.S. CPSC, Washington, DC 20207.

Request the Toy Recall List by writing to the CPSC at 5401 Westbard Ave., Bethesda, MD 20207.

A Parent's Guide: Adver*tising and Your Child* is available free from The Children's Advertising Review Unit (CARU) of the Better Business Bureau, 845 Third Ave., New York, NY 10022.

Zillions, the *Consumer Reports* for kids and their families, can be ordered through *Zillions,* Subscription Dept., P.O. Box 51777, Boulder, CO 80321-1777.

The Center for the Study of Commercialism publishes several guides for parents, and campaigns for better children's programming. Write 1875 Connecticut Ave. NW, Suite 300, Washington, DC 20009.

PART 9

Travel and Vacation

CHAPTER 47

AIRLINES AND AIRFARES

How to Avoid Flights of Fancy

L eaving on a jet plane? It was easier back when Peter, Paul, and Mary first sang their famous song. You simply bought a ticket and left. Since most tickets had no "time of travel restrictions" and didn't require buying a round trip to get a discount fare, you could readily head off without knowing when you'd be back again.

You still can give nary a thought to complicated airline ticket provisos, if you don't mind overpaying. But those who don't wish to make a charitable contribution to the airline industry need to understand the rules. Since the industry lost nearly $12 billion between 1989 and 1993, it's under tremendous financial pressure—thus, all the sales gimmicks, and new ways you can end up paying more than necessary.

THE BASICS

N ext time you're on a plane, look to the left of you, then look to the right. Both your neighbors probably paid a different fare than you did, even though you're seated in the same section of the plane, eating the same microwaved chicken breast and limp salad.

Fare disparities result from sudden changes in published fares, use of restricted discount tickets by some passengers, and from sales, coupons, commission rebates, consolidator tickets, frequent flier plans, and "yield management." What's "yield management?" To make as much money as they can on each flight, airlines use computers to constantly analyze the demand for each flight, with up-to-the-minute information on what's selling and what's not. When demand is low, they lower prices to attract passengers. If demand for a flight strengthens, the airlines curb discount ticket sales.

Getting the Lowest Possible Fare

I t's a good idea to let a seasoned travel agent search for you. Contrary to popular misconception, airline tickets do not cost more when purchased through a travel agent; the airline simply makes less. Still, you have to have your wits about you when using a travel agent, because of:

■ **Computer reservation system bias.** The first thing a travel agent does when you ask to book a flight from Point A to Point B is type your request on a keyboard connected to an airline computer reservation system (CRS) terminal. The CRS is then supposed to list all of the flights departing around the time you want to fly and the available fares. The agent processes your ticket through the same system. More than 80% of airline tickets are purchased through CRSs, and more than half of all airline tickets are purchased via the two dominant CRSs—Sabre, owned by American Airlines, and Apollo, owned by United Airlines.

Studies have questioned the fairness of CRSs. A report issued in 1992 by the consumer advocacy group Public Citizen estimated that consumers lose up to $1 billion a year because of built-in favoritism toward the CRS-owner's airline. So you may not be getting the absolute lowest fare or easiest connections when you book your flight from East Oshkosh to Podunk.

How can this happen? Lots of ways. CRSs are required to list every flight, and they do. But a 1992 congressional study found that CRS reservation information is typically more current for the owner airline's flights. It can also take longer to confirm a reservation for a seat on a non-CRS owner air-line. And the agent might have to make more keystrokes to book you on a non-owner airline, an important consideration when restless travelers are lined up at your travel agent's. Southwest Airlines, an expanding low-fare, no-frills carrier, has started its own CRS because its CRS-owning competitors are curbing travel agents' access to Southwest's schedules and fares.

■ **Agent commissions and perks.** Travel agents earn an average commission of about 10% per domestic flight ticket and 14.4% for international tickets. No problem with that. But airlines sometimes pay them bonuses (called "commission overrides") and "soft money" commissions (such as VIP club memberships) if they meet a sales target. Or they get permission to overbook, or sell more tickets than the plane has seats. And more tickets mean higher commissions. Such incentives may influence which airline the agent recommends.

Consolidator tickets may offer very significant savings. Consolidators are airline ticket wholesalers that buy large blocks of tickets at substantial discounts. They then resell these tickets to the public, travel agents, and travel brokers at less than the regular fare, pocketing some of the difference as profit. Most retail travel agents don't handle consolidator tickets on a regular basis—usually, you have to go to one of the discount agencies that advertise in back of the travel sections in Sunday newspapers.

Savings are especially significant on international flights, but consolidator tickets are not *always* cheaper. A 1992 survey by the Better Business Bureau (BBB) of Metropolitan New York found that on a roundtrip New York–Paris flight, a traveler would save anywhere from a few dollars off Tower Air's lowest fare, about $90 off United Airlines' best fare, $271 off British Airway's best, and $579 off Air France's cheapest ticket. The consolidator's tickets actually cost *more* than the cheapest American Airlines fare and there was no difference for Delta.

Consolidator tickets don't allow you to get an advance seat assignment or order special meals. They typically do not count toward frequent flier accounts, and it may be impossible to get refunds. They also have high cancellation and change penalties. On the other hand, there's a good chance that advance purchase requirements won't apply.

Another way to pay less is by going through a rebater. Rebaters earn the usual straight percentage commission from the airline but pass some of it along to you. For example, the high-volume Travel Avenue agency in Chicago gives customers a 7% cash rebate (less a $15 service fee for one ticket, $20 for two) off fares of more than $300. The rebate check is included with your ticket. However, since rebaters might not have the cheapest fares even after the rebate, you should still shop around if you use one.

If you're flexible about the exact date and time of day you fly and can leave on a moment's notice, then an international air courier ticket—which requires you to carry a package for someone else—might be

right for you (see **HELP** at the end of this chapter). You'll probably pay half the price of a regular ticket, and occasionally less.

What's the down side? You have to register with a courier company, which may require a small fee. You can't get tickets for two. You probably won't be able to check any baggage since your baggage allotment is taken up by the courier package—usually, financial documents. And there probably won't be much of a savings off discount fares during peak travel times.

But it is unlikely that you'll do any major schlepping; couriers usually just deliver and pick up documentation at both ends of the journey. What's in it for the company? Personal baggage is handled faster than freight, and probably more reliably. And sending a package with a person means it's far less likely to get waylaid or lost.

Finally, you can save by taking charter flights, for about the same price as a consolidator ticket. Some charter flights leave only once a week and there are few backup planes in case of a schedule disruption. Unfortunately, chores like boarding can drag on for hours. Charter passengers are protected by refunds in case of a departure time change of more than 48 hours or a more than 10% price hike.

Airfare Advertising: The Fine Print Says It All

Have you ever tried to read the fine print at the bottom of an airline advertisement? The advertising industry calls it "mice type"

GETTING THE BEST DEAL FROM YOUR TRAVEL AGENT

Use an agent you know and trust. For tips on finding a good one, see the box on page 459. The *Consumer Reports Travel Buying Guide* recommends working with agents who have the Travel Career Development Diploma on their office wall. The diploma, issued by the Institute of Certified Travel Agents (ICTA), affirms that the agent completed a course in how to get more information beyond that listed in airline CRS data banks.

Be fickle. Even if you have a long-standing relationship with a particular agent, nonetheless double-check whether you can get a better deal elsewhere.

Every time you book a flight, re-emphasize the importance of getting the lowest possible fare. Inform your agent that you don't mind making a stop or two or taking a no-meals, no-frills flight, if it will reduce your fare significantly.

Since airlines pay agents a commission consisting of a flat percentage of the fare, it can be tempting to neglect quoting you the super-cheap fare on the no-frills airline. The American Society of Travel Agents responds that agents would soon lose their customers if they started finding out about cheaper flights. Still, airfare structures are complex and fluid. If you don't show some initiative, your regular agent may not put in the extra effort to save you money.

As an antidote to "yield management," ask your travel agent to recheck the lowest fare a few days after you make your reservation or check with the airline yourself. You never know; the fare might have been cut. If it is significantly lower and there are no penalties or the penalties are minimal, ask to have your ticket reissued.

and it's so small you practically need a magnifying glass to read it. Since it has line after line of disclaimers about the low fare trumpeted in the banner headline, *ignore it at peril to your wallet.*

The ending of federal oversight of airfares in 1985—as part of Reagan's federal deregulation—opened the door to these small-print restrictions. Our current bifurcated fare system developed: Business travelers—who need flexibility—

pay high fares; other travelers enjoy lower fares but are now subject to many complicated travel time, advance reservation, and refundability restrictions, mostly revealed in the mice type. So either you get a reasonably priced fare and put up with myriad restrictions or pay three to four times as much for an unrestricted seat.

To illustrate, here are some of the small-print disclaimers found at the bottom of a full-page USAir advertisement for flights to Florida and several Caribbean islands published on September 28, 1993 in major U.S. daily newspapers. There were 11 lines of small type stretching the entire width of the page.

- *"Fares are each way based on round-trip coach travel. . . . Round-trip purchase required."* If, like most travelers, you are going round trip, you'll have to double the price quoted in the headline. Virtually every airline's ads have this disclaimer. And of course if you did want to go one-way, the price would be much higher than the "each way" price listed in the ad.

- *"Tickets are nonrefundable."* Watch out, because most bargain fares require you to purchase at least 14 days—some, 21 days—before departure; your plans could change in the meantime. Lately, airlines have eased this requirement slightly by allowing you a refund (or to reschedule) for a fee of $35 or so.

Proof that competition really does benefit consumers: Southwest Airlines has switched to free refundability for virtually all advance-purchase tickets and also has eliminated its requirement to stay over Saturday night for all but

> "*A*fter deregulation, there were all kinds of great prices and new competition. But unrestricted mergers all through the 1980s have led to a more consolidated industry than before deregulation. New competitors find it extremely hard to get a footing."
>
> —GERALDINE FRANKOSKI, Director, Aviation Consumer Action Project, Washington, D.C.

seven-day advance purchase discount tickets. (You still have to stay over one night—but it need not be Saturday.) United Airlines has followed suit, but only in areas where it competes with Southwest.

Furthermore, to compete with no-frills carriers like Southwest, Continental Airlines has dropped the refund fee for its "Peanuts" fares—their new no-meal, limited-baggage flights, now offered on approximately half of Continental's departures. And most airlines have begun to waive refund fees if you are exchanging a ticket for a lower fare on the same flight and you accept a voucher for the difference.

- *"A minimum first Saturday night stayover is required . . ."* (for Florida flights) and *"Day of week/time of day travel restrictions apply"* (for Caribbean flights). Often the really inexpensive fares are sold for the times that are least desirable.

- *Travel time ("blackout period")* restrictions, including: *"A minimum stay of 3 days is required. A maximum stay of 21 days is allowed"* (for Caribbean flights). A very significant restriction for those lucky enough to be thinking of a longer vacation. And *". . . all travel must be completed by 12/15/93."* So forget about these lower fares if you were hoping for a *mid-winter* break.

■ *"Reservations must be made at least 14 days prior to departure and tickets purchased within 24 hours of making reservations or 14 days prior to departure, whichever comes first"* (for advertised Florida flights). This has become normal procedure for discount fares. It may still be possible to get short-notice discount "bereavement" fares if you are attending a funeral, but according to travel agent Adriane Greene, president of the U.S. Association of Retail Travel Agents, airlines may actually call funeral homes for proof because so many travelers have lied. A Delta Airlines official told Ms. Greene about one man who tried to buy a bereavement discount ticket to Denver because his grandfather had passed away; he was charged the full fare at the airport because he was dressed in ski wear and carrying ski poles in the ticket purchasing line. So some airlines are phasing these fares out altogether.

■ *"Seats at these fares are limited and may not be available on all flights on all days."* Variations of this general disclaimer appear in nearly every airfare ad. This is the same as if a department store advertising $40 dresses at the bottom of the ad said in extremely small print, "Dresses at these prices may not be available when you arrive at the store." Department stores can't get away with it, but the federal government allows airlines to.

A call placed to USAir the morning of the ad inquired about a flight a month later from New York to one of the advertised destina-tions, Daytona Beach, Florida. Yes, the fare was available. (It came to $239 round trip.) But, the warning followed, there were a limited number of seats at this price—if too long an interval passed before booking the flight, the fare would jump to $270. When seats at that fare sold out, the round trip would cost $388. The reservations clerk was unable to say how long—days, weeks—the advertised fare would be available.

How easy is it to get a reservation on your preferred flight? *Consumer Reports Travel Letter* surveyed its readers in 1992 and found that only one in six callers got a seat on a first-choice flight; three out of four were at least able to get a flight on the preferred travel *date*.

A survey conducted in 1990 by the NYC Department of Consumer Affairs of major airlines' airfare ads in daily newspapers nationwide revealed that many advertised fares for the most popular routes weren't available even one day after the ads appeared. For example, on June 28, 1990, Consumer Affairs callers tried to make reservations in response to the previous day's Northwest Airlines ad in the *Los Angeles Times* for low-fare flights to Eastern cities. All flights on most of the days requested for flying from Los Angeles to New York or Cleveland were already sold out. The callers were also informed that most of the flights required connections with stopovers of at least two hours, which wasn't mentioned in the ad.

■ For good measure, just in case the "not available on all flights" disclaimer failed to cover every eventu-

YES, WE HAVE NO DISCOUNT AIRFARES

On the day in December, 1993, that a *Washington Post* ad for Northwest Airlines announced a $518 round-trip fare from Washington, D.C., to Paris, Jenny F. called to make a reservation. She was quoted a price of $1,584. "That must be the new fare," the reservation agent said, since "it's not pricing yet." After Jenny was put on hold for 25 minutes while the agent checked, she was offered a price of $593, still 14% higher than the advertised fare. And then the agent added that Jenny couldn't reserve even at that fare until seven days before the trip —and by then they'd probably be sold out. "Generally, the seats are all booked solid," Jenny was told.

In 1994, Northwest Airlines received a Harlan Page Hubbard Award from the Center for Science in the Public Interest "for advertising new low fares for travel between January and April, when the fares are actually only valid for 15 days during the advertised four-month period." (Hubbard was a famous 19th century snake-oil salesman.)

ality, the USAir ad mice type also said, *"Other substantial restrictions may apply"* and, *"Fares and schedules are subject to change without notice."* Most airline ads have similar all-purpose disclaimers.

Frequent Flier Benefits

Frequent flier benefits give the bigger airlines a competitive leg up on their smaller competitors that don't offer them. Giving away free flights is a powerful inducement to fly the same airline time and again.

The major variables to consider when comparing programs are the number of miles required for a free trip; the number of blackout days when you can't fly (average is about 30, mostly around holidays); how easy it is to use frequent-flier miles for a seat upgrade; how soon the miles expire (either after three years or unlimited); and how many destinations the airline serves.

Understand that airlines are not about to give away free seats on flights likely to be solidly booked with paying passengers. So seats to Hawaii, Florida, and Caribbean destinations are hard to get in the winter without reserving almost a year ahead of time. Europe in the summer is almost impossible. You may also have trouble getting seats on days just before and after the official blackout periods. Some airlines do allow free travel during blackout periods, but the mileage requirements may be much higher then. Generally speaking, it is becoming harder to redeem frequent flier miles—airlines are cutting back on aircraft and flights in an effort to keep all their planes flying full. And the increasing sophistication of yield-management computers has reduced the numbers of seats available for frequent fliers.

If you are a very frequent frequent flier, you'll qualify for the élite status most major airlines offer. Among the prequisites these loyal customers enjoy are bonus miles, free upgrades to business or first class, and greater accessibility to seats that are off-limits to run-of-the-mill frequent fliers. How far do you have to travel in one year to begin to qualify for special benefits?

The airlines giveth and the airlines taketh away: Early in 1995, most of the major airlines will increase the number of frequent-flier miles required for free tickets. For example, free domestic flights will require 25,000 miles, up from 20,000 miles, on American, Continental, United, and USAir. (Delta is cutting its requirement from 30,000 to 25,000 miles.) Higher levels cost 40,000 miles at Continental (red status), 50,000 miles at American (platinum status) and United (premier executive), and 60,000 at USAir (priority gold plus). You might go even higher. United, for example, offers "1-K service" for 100,000 miles or more. Of course, benefits vary from airline to airline; however, regardless of carrier, the greater the number of miles, the greater the benefits.

You don't have to fly to accumulate mileage. Nearly every major airline has teamed up with a Visa or MasterCard issuer to offer one frequent-flier mile for every dollar you charge on a card. Interest rates on outstanding credit card balances are competitive, although annual membership fees are higher than for regular credit cards. American Express's charge card has an advantage; members can choose to apply their mileage to five different airlines, and the miles don't expire as long as you keep your card. But you must charge a minimum amount each year to accumulate mileage.

You can also accumulate frequent-flier mileage when you use MCI or Sprint; AT&T also offers a frequent-flier plan. A stay in certain hotels can earn you 500 miles each stay. And when you rent a car, some agencies award 500 to 1,000 miles per rental.

Fly Safe

Don't read Ralph Nader's and Wesley Smith's 1993 book, *Collision Course: The Truth About Airline Safety*, while airborne. It could ruin your flight. But anyone who flies should read it when they're back on terra firma.

Actually, airline travel is very safe, relative to other ways of getting to where you're going. But the authors maintain that air travel could be even safer, and they lambaste the federal government for lapses in airline and airport safety. Nader and Smith have plenty of documentation to back up their findings and connect the financially precarious condition of many airlines with a drop in the number of mechanics per aircraft, a rapidly aging fleet, and increasing pilot fatigue. Overwhelmed air traffic

YOUNGSTERS ON THE GO

Bringing the family along? Kids love to fly—if they are kept entertained and comfortable. Here are some basic tips:

■ Most airlines offer special children's meals—hamburgers, hot dogs, etc. But, as with any other special meal requests (vegetarian, kosher) you have to call ahead to arrange them.

■ Bring along snacks like granola bars, bagels, and crackers—airline meals are served on a fixed schedule that may not match your kids' appetites. Also bring water and fruit juice.

■ Prepare packages with your kids' favorite entertainment, such as markers, paper, travel games, or dolls.

■ When you make your reservations, ask for a window seat: automatic entertainment (at least for awhile).

■ Check with a flight attendant about the airline's policy on kids visiting the cockpit.

■ With younger kids, request a bulkhead seat so they can move around more easily during flight.

Here are some tips for travel by unaccompanied children, provided by American Airlines spokesperson Joseph Crawley:

■ Arrive at the airport extra early. Each child will be given a packet to wear around his or her neck with tickets and other important information, such as medical conditions. You'll need time to fill out these forms. Also, it's a good idea to get to the departure lounge with enough extra time to familiarize your child with the airport and the personnel.

■ You must stay at the gate with your child until he or she has boarded.

■ A flight attendant will introduce himself or herself and make it clear to your child—in a way that nearby adult passengers can hear—that he or she is to be called if there are any problems. Your child *will* be monitored. One enterprising boy asked an American Airlines attendant for a Bloody Mary. She diplomatically asked for identification. He ended up with a glass of tomato juice.

■ At the destination, airlines will deliver your child *only* to a person specified previously, and that person absolutely must have photo identification. Sometimes people are very sloppy about this. In one situation Crawley related, a woman living on one coast reverted to her own name after a divorce from her husband on the other coast. When their child flew from one parent to the other there was confusion at the destination because of the name change.

Still, parents need not worry. American Airlines reservation personnel have gone so far as to take kids home for the night.

controllers working with outmoded equipment don't inspire much confidence, either.

The authors also point out that the hub-and-spoke route system—in which you are likely to be flown to a hub airport and then transfer to a second flight to your destination—has led to more small commuter aircraft on scheduled routes. These smaller planes are not as safe and their pilots often have less experience. According to the National Transportation Safety Board, propeller-driven "commuter" aircraft have nearly five times the number of fatal accidents per passenger as jets do.

How do you protect yourself? No one airline is appreciably safer than another. But for safety tips when flying any airline, see **The $marter Consumer** below.

Comfort and Quality

The incredible shrinking seat. Remember the old '50s game of seeing how many people could fit in a phone booth or a Volkswagen bus? Well, most airlines play that game, too, seeing how many passengers they can fit in the confines of an airplane fuselage.

Airlines traditionally offered up to 22-inch coach seat widths on their larger planes. The norm now is 19 inches or 20 inches.

Pitch describes how far seats are located from each other front to back; it has been sliced from 34 inches to 31 inches in much of the industry. These few inches make an enormous difference in comfort. In 1993, TWA received just acclaim for adopting a pitch of 34 inches to 36 inches on nearly all its planes.

If you're in a wide-body plane, such as an L-1011, a DC-10, or an MD-11 and the airline has ten seats abreast instead of the standard nine, there's a good chance you'll be very cramped if the plane is more than three-quarters filled. A more comfortable configuration is two aisles with five seats in the center and two on either side.

Other than going on a prolonged hunger strike before you fly, you can minimize discomfort by asking about the width and pitch of the seats on a plane you are considering flying. Remember, since seating configurations are determined by the airlines, the same model aircraft can be relatively spacious with one airline and like a cattle car with another.

Crack open a window? Have airlines been giving you headaches lately? No, not the headaches you might get trying to redeem your frequent-flier miles. We're talking about headaches after spending several hours aloft.

The New York Times reports that all of the air in the cabin is replaced with fresh air every three minutes in aircraft built before the mid-1980s. But newer planes provide only half fresh air—the rest is old air—and it is recirculated only every six or seven minutes. Since fresh air is introduced through the engines and must be cooled, giving passengers less of it saves fuel and money. The airlines, of course, say it makes no difference. But the *Times* reported that flight attendants are complaining of more air-travel related illness and the Association of Flight Attendants has commissioned a study. You might want to ask about the aircraft before you confirm your seat; older planes might actually be better for your health. With an average fleet age in 1993 of 12.7 years and 46% of planes at least 15 years old, you still have a pretty good shot at breathing fresh air.

WHAT TO WATCH OUT FOR

Code-sharing. Each airline is assigned a code for ticketing purposes. If you have to change planes, and if the code for the second leg of a flight is the same as for the first leg, then you might reasonably assume you'll continue on with the same airline.

Not necessarily. For the second leg of your trip, you might be scrunched up in a glorified crop-duster said to be owned by a subsidiary of the major airline you started out on. But according to *Collision Course*, most of the commuter airlines that share codes with a major carrier are not actually the same company as the major airline. For example, American Eagle—the commuter carrier for American Airlines—is actually four different companies: Executive Airlines, Flagship Airlines, Simmons Airlines, and Wings West Airlines.

Increasingly, you may end up with an entirely different major airline. You might think you're taking KLM all the way from Amsterdam

"TOWER TO FLIGHT 123 . . . ARE YOU AWAKE?"

Witnesses at a 1992 congressional hearing on pilot fatigue made some disturbing revelations. For example, Roberta Baskin, an investigative journalist who produced a television documentary, *Pilots: Dead Tired*, said she had found that most flying accidents are attributable to pilot error and that, in at least two recent highly publicized fatal accidents, pilot fatigue appeared to be a major factor. Many of the pilots she interviewed said that their tight schedules force them to fly on only four to six hours sleep. Commuter airline pilots tend to get the least amount of rest.

to Indianapolis, but you really are taking it only to Detroit, with a switch to Northwest for the rest of the trip. Or you could begin your journey with Air New Zealand and end up with Quantas. Travel agents and airlines are supposed to identify the name of the second airline, but they often don't.

Getting "bumped." This happens when the airline overbooks—takes more reservations than the plane has seats—and too many people with reservations show up at the gate. The law is on your side. If you are bumped from an aircraft and have to take another flight and you arrive at your destination more than an hour later than your originally scheduled arrival time, the airline *must* give you the cost of a one-way ticket (maximum value of $200). If you are more than two hours late, you get double the one-way ticket (maximum of $400). You should also be able to negotiate long-distance phone calls, free meals, and maybe a free hotel room, although your bargaining power is weak if numerous passengers volunteer to be bumped. Remember, though, that you get compensated only if you arrived at the gate at least 15 minutes before the scheduled departure time.

THE SMARTER CONSUMER

Take full advantage of airline fare wars. Buy discount "sale" tickets if they are at least 30% cheaper than the non-discount fare. This way, you'll be sure of locking in a good fare. If the fare goes even lower, airlines allow you to exchange for a cheaper ticket by paying a penalty of $35 or so, which may very well be worth it, given the additional savings you would realize.

Save money with upstart (and start-up) airlines. Southwest Airlines' very low fares are giving the major carriers tough competition in markets where they overlap. Among the very cheap new start-up airlines trying to steal business from the major carriers on selected routes are Kiwi Air (based in Newark, New Jersey); Family Airlines (of Newark, San Francisco, Los Angeles, Miami, Honolulu); Morris Air (Salt Lake City, Utah based); and Reno Air (of Reno, Nevada).

Guard your credit card number. Don't give a travel agent your credit card number without getting a ticket in return. Anne Marie M. called TFI Tours of New York City to inquire about flights to Florida. An employee said it was company policy that no information be given until the caller provided credit card numbers. Even though Anne Marie said she'd pay in cash, she capitulated when pressed. The next morning she called back to say the suggested flight was not convenient. TFI told her it couldn't cancel her "reservation" and that she had to pay the $335 airfare anyway.

Rack up the miles. If you want to benefit from frequent-flier programs, try to concentrate your flying with one airline. Then you'll have a chance not only of getting free flights for you and a companion, but maybe of qualifying for "élite" status—which gives bonus miles and VIP treatment. Also be aware that some airlines require more frequent-flier miles to get a free trip than others; compare requirements carefully and understand that airlines reserve the right to change the rules so long as mileage holders are given reasonable notice.

Here's another frequent-flier tip: If there are no free seats between say, Chicago and Los Angeles, ask if you can go through another city. Sure, it'll take longer—but it's free.

Seniors: Take advantage of discounts. All major airlines sell "senior coupons," which provide a very substantial airfare discount for persons 62 or older on all but short-haul flights. Senior coupons are typically sold in books of four ($596 at Delta, American, and United) and in books of eight ($1,032 at the same carriers). One coupon is needed for a one-way flight anywhere in the lower 48 states, which comes to as low as $90 or as high as $142 for one flight. You have to reserve 14 days in advance and travel day restrictions could apply.

Most U.S. airlines also offer a 10% senior discount off any published fare, except special short-term sale fares.

If using a consolidator, try to pay for the tickets with a credit card in order to preserve your right to withhold payment in case of a problem. Confirm reservations with the airline before and after paying. Make sure you're on a major carrier and not on a charter flight.

Buy split tickets when advantageous, if you don't mind making connections. Instead of buying one ticket from point A direct to point C, it might be cheaper to buy a discount or promotional fare from point A to point B, and a separate ticket from point B to point C.

Dealing with irretrievably lost baggage. Most lost luggage eventually turns up. But if your baggage is really gone, it's unlikely you'll get much in the way of compensation. By agreement among the airlines, you are entitled only to the depreciated value of what was lost, to a maximum of $1,250 for domestic flights ($9.07 per pound ceiling for international flights) and then only if you are able to produce receipts and other documents proving how much the lost items are currently worth. If you want more financial protection, you have to pay for it. Fortunately, most airlines are a little softer when it comes to giving you money for reasonable out-of-pocket expenses caused by losing your baggage.

While the airline is searching for your baggage, they don't have to but should advance you some cash for basic necessities—or at least provide you with a toiletries kit. If the news is good and they find your baggage, most airlines will deliver it to your destination address.

Smart seat trick. To increase likelihood of getting more wiggle room, ask for an aisle seat in the center row. Most of the empty seats on a plane that hasn't been fully booked will be the ones in the middle of the center row. If you're on the aisle, the seat next to you could very well be empty.

Fly safer. Avoid wearing synthetic fibers while flying; they tend to melt on your skin in case of fire.

Wear "sensible shoes" you can escape in easily. Scope out the scene as soon as you get to your seat. Where are the emergency exits? Read the safety briefing card. If it is winter and the weather is inclement, look out a window and check the wing for ice build-up; report any to a flight attendant. On March 22, 1992, ice build-up caused USAir flight 405 to run off the runway at New York's LaGuardia Airport, and 27 lives were lost. The local newspapers reported that one passenger noticed ice on the wing before the tragic attempted take-off and said, "We take off like this, we're all dead."

Stay alert during take-offs and landings, which is when most accidents occur.

■ To complain about air-line service, write to the Office of Consumer Affairs, U.S. Department of Transportation, 400 7th Street NW, Washington, D.C. 20590. You can also leave a recorded complaint on their voice mail, at (202) 366-2220.

■ To complain about airline safety or security, call the Federal Aviation Administration: (800) 322-7873. If it is a pressing safety issue, call the FAA Aviation Safety Hotline: (800) 255-1111; they will assign investigators to look into it. Anonymous calls to the Hotline are accepted, although the FAA encourages you to leave your name and contact information.

■ The *Consumer Reports 1995 Travel Buying Guide* is very helpful. It costs $8.95 at bookstores. To order direct, call (800) 272-0722.

■ Order the booklet, *Facts and Advice for Airline Passengers*, and a newsletter from the Aviation Consumer Action Project (ACAP). ACAP was formed by Ralph Nader and his associates to promote the interests of consumers in improved ground and air safety, environmental protection, affordable fares, and expanded passenger rights. It distributes passenger information leaflets and advocates passenger interests before regulatory bodies. Send $5.00 to ACAP, P.O. Box 19209, Washington D.C. 20036; call (202) 638-4000.

■ Want to know more about air courier services? If you can't find the book, *The Insider's Guide to Air Courier Bargains*, by Kelly Monaghan at your bookstore, order it from Inwood Training Publications, Box 438, New York, NY 10034. $16.95 includes postage and handling, or call (800) 356-9315.

■ To learn how each domestic airline ranks on flight delays, mishandled baggage, oversales (the percentage of ticket holders who are "bumped"), and consumer complaints, order the *Air Travel Consumer Report* published monthly by the U.S. Department of Transportation. Write to the Office of Consumer Affairs, U.S. Department of Transportation, 400 7th Street SW, Room 10405, Washington, D.C. 20590.

■ For the latest frequent-flier pro-gram developments, order the monthly *InsideFlyer* ($33 a year) by calling (800) 333-5937.

■ The July 1993 issue of *Consumer Reports* has a comprehensive seat comfort chart for every major airline.

TRAVEL

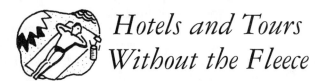

*Hotels and Tours
Without the Fleece*

One tour operator nationally advertised a $99 week-long cruise to the Bahamas that actually cost $700 once surcharges were added. Another operator, Jet Set Travel, used computerized telephone messages and direct mail to tell people they had been "specially selected" for a five-day, four-night Bahamas cruise package for only $328, *and*—if they purchased this package—two round-trip airfares to Hawaii at no additional cost. In fact, consumers taking this bait would have been required to buy 14 nights of lodging in Hawaii in order to get the free airfare. And if they gave the company their credit card number "to verify eligibility," as requested, they would have been billed instead.

These are but two examples of a rapidly spreading way of getting fleeced—travel and tour scams. One of every seven complaints received by the Federal Trade Commission (FTC) now involves the travel industry.

Of course, con artists represent only a small portion of the entire U.S. hotel and tour industry. If you know what to watch out for, you won't become a victim.

THE BASICS

A $mart Consumer Slept Here

If you're paying full price for a hotel or resort room and it's off-season at a not-yet-prime destination, you're doing something wrong. With a little bit of advance work, you can get rooms and even meals on your next trip for half price. Such big price breaks are available because hotel and resort owners spend almost as much running a half-empty hotel as a full one, and they use discounts to fill as many vacant rooms as they can.

But you can't just walk up to the registration desk of a $250-a-night hotel and announce that you'd like to pay only $125 tonight, including a free dinner in their award-winning restaurant. You have to go through a program, buy a voucher, or qualify for a special discount.

Membership programs that negotiate discounts with hotels and then pass most of the savings on to the general public offer what are probably the lowest room rates. Half-price rooms are the norm, and restaurant discounts of 25% are sometimes available as well.

Each program has its own roster of hundreds (or thousands) of hotels, motels, and resorts. You pay an annual fee of $20 to $100 for the roster and an identification card. The programs with lower annual fees tend to specialize in more modest lodgings—the Howard Johnsons, Holiday Inns, and Ramada Inns—while the $100 annual fee gets you discounts at tonier *habiliments*. After you've called ahead to see if discount rooms are available, you show the ID card at the check-in counter to claim your discount.

The modest pitfalls of these programs don't outweigh the potential for big savings. The lowest-priced rooms may be exempt from the program. Discount rooms are always "subject to availability," which typically is only when the hotel's occupancy rate is less than 80%.

The most comprehensive program, according to some travel writers, is "Travel America at Half Price," offered by Entertainment Publications (EP). You pay $50 a year for a card entitling you to discounts at any of the approximately 4,000 establishments in EP's directory. In addition, EP sells different coupon booklets for $32.95 each for 115 cities, offering 50% off room rates as well as restaurant discounts and a cut-rate Continental Airlines airfare. A special Europe booklet costs $42. Separate coupon books are also available for bed and breakfasts (25% discount). In January 1992, *Consumer Reports Travel Letter* called the program one of the "outstanding values" for travel that year.

(EP's phone number and names and phone numbers of additional discount travel services are listed in **HELP** at the end of this chapter.)

Another way to avoid paying a hotel's "rack" rate—the published full rate—is with vouchers. Here's how they work: You buy vouchers before you leave, either from a travel agent or directly from a voucher program. You make your own room reservations and use the vouchers to pay. Most voucher programs concentrate on hotels in certain areas of the world, such as Europe or Scandinavia. A few, such as the Holiday Inns voucher program, are worldwide. The big down side: You can't automatically assume that the voucher will save you money, because regular "rack" rates may be *less* than what you would pay using a voucher.

Hotel room discounts of 10% to 40% are available through hotel booking services or consortiums offering "preferred" rates. Your travel agent might be a member of such a service. The combined buying power of numerous agencies secures the lower rates. But be careful—you might pay less with a weekend discount or a half-price program. Room discounts can also be realized if you are a member of one of a wide range of organizations—from the American Automobile Association to labor unions—that have group discounts with hotel chains.

Aging has its benefits. Senior citizens—the age cutoff is either 55, 60, or 62, depending on the chain—qualify for 10% to 15% senior citizen discounts at many major hotel and motel chains. The

ROOM FOR SAVINGS

You can bypass travel agents, membership programs, and vouchers altogether if you call The Room Exchange, a wholesale agency that offers 20% to 50% off, depending on the season, at more than 22,000 U.S., Canadian, and Caribbean hotels. You simply call them at (800) 846-7000 (in NYC, (212) 760-1000) to check availability. Then you reserve by credit card and The Room Exchange mails you a voucher.

discount may increase to 25% to 30% if you make advance reservations. Some chains' senior discounts require membership in the American Association of Retired Persons (AARP) or give a greater discount to AARP members; you must be 50 or older to join AARP. Even if a hotel chain has no senior citizen discount, individual locations might, so always ask.

Hotel room discounts are available through hotel chains' frequent-stay programs, akin to the airlines' frequent-flier programs. You get credits based either on the number of nights you stay or how much money you spend. Savings may also be realized by reserving and paying well in advance—sort of like airlines' 21-day advance purchase tickets. Hyatt and Sheraton are two of the chains with such offers.

And don't forget about hotels' weekend rates, when they try to fill rooms empty of the usual business travelers with visitors enjoying a relaxing weekend.

Getting the Right Package Tour

A package tour is a combination of travel services—hotel, land, and air transportation, sightseeing tours—sold together for one price. Package tours have the potential to save you money because the tour operator purchases services in bulk. And by paying just once, before you leave, package tours make it easier to budget for your vacation and avoid surprise expenses.

Before you plunk down hundreds or thousands of dollars, you still have to have your wits about you, whether you're buying a four-day "weekend" in the Caribbean or going around the world in 80 days. Make sure you know exactly what the package includes, such as whether the airfare is from your home city or if you have to travel to a departure city—at your own expense.

Carefully study the proposed daily itinerary. Note the places you'll actually be visiting rather than just passing through on a tour bus. Be realistic in assessing your feelings about how much time you'll spend at each stop. Can you enjoy ten major European cities in only 15 days? And how much free time will you have? Some travelers prefer a regimented schedule, while others like to have half a day off now and then to do as they wish. What's your style?

Study the descriptions of the lodgings and the meals carefully. Are the proposed hotels in the center of the city you're visiting or close to the beach you hope to sun yourself on? What's their rating? Remember, a "deluxe" hotel in Timbuktu might be barely comparable to a budget chain motel in the U.S. How many meals are included? Are your menu choices limited?

Be sure to read the "conditions" section of the brochure. You'll learn the rules on cancellations, refunds, change penalties, and important restrictions or limits on meals, lodgings, baggage allowance, and extra items that might not be included in the total price.

Ask your travel agent or the tour operator a lot of questions. Far better to get the answers now—when you can still back out—than to find out later that you don't care for yak meat in the middle of the tundra and there's nothing else on the menu or the horizon.

Travel and Tour Pitfalls and Scams

Misleading or outright fraudulent travel offers are booming, and attorneys general and consumer affairs officials around the country report that travel scams are fast becoming one of the top consumer complaint categories.

While it's very unlikely that you'll encounter any sharks off the beach where you might next be vacationing, you have to watch out for them in the travel industry.

It's early March in a northern city. Over Sunday brunch you scan the newspaper travel section. The pictures of palm trees and couples walking hand in hand on deserted beaches are too alluring to resist. Monday morning, you call the phone number in one of the ads and after a few minutes of explanations you give your credit card number to make a reservation for a vacation package. You work hard. You deserve it.

What you don't deserve is for something to go wrong. It could be relatively minor, like a switch to a hotel not quite as nice as where you were supposed to stay. Or it could be disastrous, like $800 tickets that never arrive.

Let's start with the relatively benign package tour scams and pitfalls and work up to the real vacation-busters.

Understated vacation package prices. Consider the ad for Bermuda vacations by Travel Impressions, a group of 19 New York City travel agencies, that was published in a New York City daily newspaper in 1992. It mentioned only the lowest possible prices—"from $523 per person." After legal action by the NYC Department of Consumer Affairs, Travel Impressions paid a fine and changed its ads. A new ad for a Caribbean vacation package more realistically listed prices of "$808–$1,532."

Even the popular Carnival Cruise Lines was cited by the Department of Consumer Affairs for advertising a four-day Bahamas cruise for $449, when that was the rate for only the smallest, windowless room.

FINDING A GOOD TRAVEL AGENT

Too many people have been burned by fly-by-night travel agencies that go out of business before issuing ordered tickets, or by hotel vouchers bought through travel agencies that weren't honored when they presented them at the hotel desk—two examples of the difficulties you could encounter with a disreputable travel agency. The problem is that government only minimally regulates travel agencies. Almost anyone can open a travel storefront and start selling. In fact, only Rhode Island requires travel agents to pass a licensing examination.

So how do you find a well-established agency? Start by getting references from friends, relatives, and business colleagues. Avoid out-of-town agents who advertise locally, especially if their prices seem unusually low; if there's a catch or if something goes wrong, you will want to be able to visit the agency.

At the very least, make sure that the travel agent you use is licensed by the Airline Reporting Company to issue tickets. Much better, members of either the American Society of Travel Agents (ASTA; its 12,000 member agencies are about a third of all the agencies in the U.S.) or the Association of Retail Travel Agents (ARTA, with about 3,000 members) have been appointed by reputable airlines, cruise lines, or airline coordinating bodies that require agents to maintain a bond of at least $20,000. Both organizations have strict ethics codes. An agency must have been in business for at least three years before joining ASTA. In addition, ASTA offers a proficiency examination; look for the ASTA diploma on the agent's wall.

Tip: Find out from the agency if it gives you your money back if a tour operator or airline goes out of business. Some do, some do not, and some will partially reimburse you.

Practically worthless vacation certificates. You may get one of these in the mail as a sweepstakes or contest "prize." Some prize. Here's what will probably happen if you take the bait: You'll have to pay something, possibly as much as a few hundred dollars, for your "resort vacation." There could be a processing fee. It could be hard to actually redeem the certificate since you get to go on your vacation only on a "space-available" basis. Even after you get a reservation, the trip may be cancelled several times, and it may be difficult to get new reservations because of previously undisclosed time-of-travel restrictions. To add insult to injury, if somehow you manage to take the trip, you'll likely be put up in a second-rate hotel far from any resort.

Take a very close look at the next vacation certificate you see. Chances are, it is very carefully worded to make it *seem* like you'll get something for free, but it never actually says the trip is free.

And if it does say "free," it'll probably be linked to having to buy something. That "something" can be very expensive, cautions *Consumer Reports Travel Letter*. *Consumer Reports* gave an example of a department store's offer of free tickets to Hawaii or any one of three Mexican resorts. But you had to purchase seven consecutive nights of overpriced hotel accommodations at these destinations to qualify.

Your travel agent's refund check bounces. When Anu B. of Massachusetts paid Maharajah Travel $1,190 for an airline ticket to India but failed to get her tickets, the agency sent her a refund. Her bank rejected the check for "insufficient funds." Maharajah told her to redeposit it. It bounced again.

What you get barely resembles what you were promised. Gerry S. paid New Golden Horse Tours a total of $1,040 for a Florida vacation. The agent, the newspaper ad, and the brochure described a comfortable bus ride, a trip to Sea World, and a nice hotel. He got a bus with non-reclining seats and a broken toilet, a smelly hotel room with cockroaches and dirty sheets, and no Sea World.

The travel agent or tour operator doesn't send you the tickets you paid for or sends them late. Shaheen T. of Brooklyn needed to get to Kenya to visit a sick relative. She bought tickets from Maharajah Travel for herself and her four children, paying a total of $6,040 in cash, as required by the agency. She received no tickets—just a printout of her itinerary. Finally, after many phone calls, Maharajah said they'd meet her at the airport on the day of her flight. She went to the airport with her children and all their luggage. Yes, she got the tickets at the last minute. But when she was in Kenya and wanted to return, she discovered she hadn't been given tickets for the second leg of the return trip—London to New York. Eventually, tickets were express-mailed to her in London, but only after she was stuck there for two long days.

WHAT TO WATCH OUT FOR

Hotels, Motels, and Resorts

Using the phone. Hotels make a little extra money on the side by charging you a lot of money for phone calls made from your room. If you charge a call to your room, you'll probably be billed at high operator-assisted rates, even if you dial direct. On top of that will likely be a surcharge of as much as 50%.

Long-distance carriers provide access to their lines via a toll-free "800" number, which would allow you to circumvent the hotel's 75-cent fee. But some hotels are plugging this loophole by charging the fee for all calls, including "800" numbers. Carefully read the surcharge information that should be posted on the phone to find out your hotel's policy. If you're still unsure, ask the hotel desk staff before you dial.

Single supplements. Hoteliers charge single travelers supplements, which are typically 50% or even 100% of the per-person double room rate. *Travel and Leisure* magazine suggests that single travelers sign up for the guaranteed roommate offers of many tour operators and cruise lines. If the hotel doesn't come up with a roommate, you still get the room at the reduced, nonsupplement price.

Tour Packages

Adriane Greene, president of the Association of Retail Travel Agents, says that many savvy consumers who pride themselves on their shopping acumen lose their powers of critical judgment when a low-price luxury vacation is dangled before their eyes.

Warning bells and whistles should go off in your head when you see or hear any of the following:

Unsolicited telemarketing phone calls or postcards telling you that you "definitely won" a vacation or trying to sell you a discount vacation package. This is the most common travel scam vehicle. If you get such a postcard, rip it up. Hang up on anyone making such a phone call. It only means trouble; no reputable travel firm operates this way.

Florida-based Passport International is a good illustration. The FTC received 700 complaints about postcards telling recipients they had been "selected" to receive a trip. But complainants said it took months to get the trip vouchers they paid for—well beyond the 60-day time period allowed to dispute a credit card charge—and the trips that could be taken with the vouchers were nothing like what had been promised.

Often, the telemarketer or postcard sender is in business only long enough to rake in hundreds of thousands of dollars worth of certified checks and credit card charges. Trouble is, if you fork over money without first getting confirmed seats on a flight, confirmed reservations at a named hotel, or confirmed booking on a boat, there is little you can do.

Being "specially selected." Remember that "special" doesn't mean that only a few people were chosen; a million other people may have gotten the same postcard or inviting phone call.

Incredibly low prices. No one gives away $200 five-day Caribbean cruise packages. Any such offer probably doesn't mention a long list of additional fees and expenses, such as charges for ground transportation and processing.

Witness what happened to Cynthia and David Garast, as reported in 1993 in the *Chicago Tribune*. They responded to a classified ad for a full five-day, four-night Bahamas vacation, including a cruise between Florida and the Bahamas— all for the incredibly low price of

$239. Well, it *was* incredible. They soon learned that they would have to pay an additional "reservation deposit" of $139. Even then, their vacation date requests could not be guaranteed. After a year of trying, they were unable to get their $239 back.

And then there's the 1992 story of the "fabulous luxury vacation" for two in Florida and the Bahamas, all for only $399—including round-trip airfare to Florida, a rental car, and even free tickets to Disney World. Only after paying— with a check—did prospective vacationers learn they would have to fork over another $400 in "taxes" and other fees. Notably, credit cards were not accepted for payment.

High-pressure sales tactics, forcing you to decide "right then and there," or else the offer expires.

Taking your credit card number over the phone, especially after a high-pressure sales tactic was used. Never give your credit card number to someone asking for it merely to "verify" a free travel offer; it's nearly a sure bet that you'll have bought yourself the offer—whatever it may turn out to be.

Up-front "processing fees" or "refundable" deposits that cost more than the stated price of the trip.

"900" phone numbers. If you have to call a "900" number to learn the details of a vacation offer, typically you'll pay several dollars a minute for a few minutes and find out nothing—not even the "claim number" you were told to call for.

Failure to provide the name, exact address, and phone number of the company making the offer.

Call individual hotels to get the lowest room rate. Staff who answer a chain's national reservation number often don't know about the latest local discounts. Always ask about special deals.

In all travel transactions, always try to use a credit card. If you use cash and the agency or operator goes out of business, the chances of getting reimbursed are slim. But if you charged it, the protections for non-delivered merchandise or services afforded by the Fair Credit Billing Act may kick in (see "Credit Cards," page 277).

Book with reputable tour operators; those who belong to the United States Tour Operators Association must have 18 references from a variety of reputable travel agency organizations, must furnish the organization with a $250,000 indemnity bond, and must carry at least $1 million in liability insurance with worldwide coverage.

■ **Half-price programs.** Entertainment Publications can be reached at (800) 477-3234 or (313) 637-8400. Additional major discount hotel/resort services include: *The Privilege Card* has discounts ranging from 30%

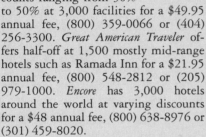

to 50% at 3,000 facilities for a $49.95 annual fee, (800) 359-0066 or (404) 256-3300. *Great American Traveler* offers half-off at 1,500 mostly mid-range hotels such as Ramada Inn for a $21.95 annual fee, (800) 548-2812 or (205) 979-1000. *Encore* has 3,000 hotels around the world at varying discounts for a $48 annual fee, (800) 638-8976 or (301) 459-8020.

■ **You can obtain hotel room dis**counts overseas by booking through your airline. For example, American Airlines offers 20% to 30% off at several hundred Best Western Hotels in Europe; call (800) 832-8383. To reach TWA's program, call (800) 438-2929. British Airways offers up to 50% off at 65 London hotels and more in other European cities, (800) 247-9297. Japan Airlines, Lufthansa, SAS, and Singapore Airlines also have programs.

■ **Has a travel agent or tour opera**tor "taken you for a ride"? Take *them* to the feds by writing to the Federal Trade Commission at 6th Street and Pennsylvania Ave. NW, Washington, D.C. 20580.

■ **The annual** *Travel Buying Guide* (issued by *Consumer Reports*) tells all you need to know about getting dis-

counts on airfares, hotels, car rentals, and more. Available at most bookstores.

■ **If you've been victim**ized by a tour or travel agent, call the consumer affairs division of the American Society of Travel Agents (ASTA) at (703) 739-2782. Or write to them at 1101 King Street, Alexandria, VA 22314. You'll get the most satisfactory result if your complaint is about something specific you were supposed to get and didn't.

Remember, ASTA is not able to force an agent to provide a refund, although a threat to expel them from the organization may prove persuasive. It exists primarily to benefit its members and is not a consumer advocacy organization.

■ **If you booked a tour through a** United States Tour Operators Association (USTOA) member and the operator totally fails to perform or goes insolvent, ask for a reimbursement claim form from the USTOA, 211 East 51st Street, Suite 12B, New York, NY 10022; call (212) 944-5727.

■ **Which hotels offer the best value?** To find out, consult the June 1994 issue of *Consumer Reports*. It separately ranked hotels in the luxury, high-priced, moderately priced, and budget categories.

■ **For a free copy of a guide to hotel** room safety, send a self-addressed, stamped envelope to American Hotel & Motel Association Tips, 1201 New York Avenue NW, Washington, D.C. 20005.

CHAPTER 49

CAR RENTALS

Avoid Trumped-Up Charges

B ettie H. of Manhattan called Budget Rent-a-Car several weeks in advance to reserve a car. She got a confirmation number. When she arrived on the travel day to pick up the car, she was told no cars were available. Bettie and her party had to wait for two hours.

Under a New York City law, the car rental firm was obliged to provide a car within half an hour of the reservation time. If no car was available, the rental outlet was required to transport her to an outlet where a car was available or replace the reservation with a car at least as large and suitable for her purposes at the originally quoted price.

The delay caused Bettie to miss her nephew's wedding dinner. To avoid the hassle and the heartbreak—and unnecessary additional expenditures—it pays to know your car rental rights. Because despite a recent major effort by the National Association of Attorneys General to reform car rental industry practices, tricks and heartaches still abound.

THE BASICS

I t's never been easy to figure out ahead of time how much a rental will cost. Beyond that, it's not as simple today as it once was to get a rental car. Rental companies are paring down their fleets to cut costs, refusing to rent to drivers with bad records, making up for lost profits with hidden charges, and trying to make you liable for the costs of escalating insurance claims.

Bad Drivers Need Not Apply

S everal years ago, major car rental companies began rejecting customers they judged pose the highest risk of getting into an accident. The policy is in effect in many Hertz, Avis, National, Budget, Enterprise, Thrifty, and Dollar rental locations in California, Florida, Maryland, New York, Ohio, Pennsylvania, and Washington, DC. And it's likely the policy will continue to spread. Almost 10% of rental customers are turned away for things like suspension or revocation of their driver's license, conviction for driving while under the influence of alcohol within the previous six years, or having been involved in the previous four years in an accident in which someone was killed or injured. The criteria vary slightly from one company to another.

Here's how the system works: You call to reserve a car. When you receive a confirmation number for your reservation, the reservations agent should tell you that your driving record may be checked when you come in to pick up the car. On that day, the counter attendant will ask to see your driver's license and will enter your name, driver's license number, and date of birth into a computer linked to a network of data bases containing state motor vehicle records. The computer then retrieves your record, analyzes it using criteria supplied by the rental company, and returns a verdict to the computer in the rental office where you are. Some companies will tell you exactly why you were turned down; others will simply give you a list of disqualifying criteria. The whole process takes less than a minute in most cases, a little longer when the driver's record is long.

While the concept is reasonable—no company should have to turn over a $20,000 car to a reckless driver—there are a few drawbacks. First, you won't know whether you will definitely get a car until you show up at the counter. Imagine getting off the plane (with your entire family in tow) for a weeks' vacation and finding that you cannot rent a car. In addition, in New York, where the system has been in use the longest, the Attorney General's office is investigating complaints that people have been turned away from the rental counter because of accidents in their record that were not their fault.

Young Drivers Need Not Apply

Most car rental firms will not rent cars to people younger than 21 (sometimes 25), saying that they can't get insurance for such "bad risks" and that there is a higher chance of younger drivers getting into accidents. People over 21 who have major credit cards or whose employers have corporate accounts with the rental firm generally have an easier time getting a car. Although turning down young drivers may be prohibited by state or local human rights laws, you'd have to sue the agency to find out—an unlikely vacation occupation. Younger drivers are better off securing an acceptable major credit card or traveling with an older companion who can more easily rent a car.

Collision Damage and Theft Coverage

In most states, the rental company will ask if you want to buy insurance that pays for damage to the car or replacement of the car in the event of theft. The most common option is the collision damage waiver (CDW). While this is not technically insurance, it is a provision in rental contracts that for a daily fee absolves the renter of responsibility for damage to or loss of the car. A few states, including New York and Illinois, have outlawed CDWs—most consumers don't need them, and car rental firms were coaxing, scaring, and deceiving as many as a third of their customers to buy the useless coverage. A reporter for *The Wall Street Journal* wrote in

1990 that a Florida Dollar Rent-A-Car agent handed him a contract with the "accept" box circled with no explanation and said, "Just initial for the waiver here."

Most people don't need collision coverage because credit cards or the insurance policy on the car they leave in the garage at home protects them. Credit card coverage, which is not as widespread as it once was, is most often "secondary coverage." This means that any personal automobile insurance kicks in first, leaving the credit card company responsible only for the deductible. For individuals who do not own cars or have their own automobile insurance, credit card coverage is primary.

Rental agents' protestations to the contrary, purchase of the CDW is optional *everywhere*. In Massachusetts, state law requires this fact to be disclosed prominently in all rental contracts. The notice must also inform Massachusetts renters that the CDW may duplicate their insurance, which might already cover them for damages to the rental car from collisions, theft, fire, or vandalism. In Florida, home of the largest leisure car rental market in the United States, state law requires insurance companies to say that they cover collision damage on vehicles rented for private purposes on the insurance identification cards routinely issued to policyholders.

On the small chance that you do not have collision or comprehensive coverage through your car insurance policy, your employer (if you're using the car for business), or the credit card on which you charged

the rental, it's a good idea to buy the CDW to protect yourself. You'll pay $10 to $14 a day for coverage, even though it only costs the company about $2 a day. If you got a sweet deal on a weekly rental, this can double the price.

Recently, cheaper variations have cropped up. If you decline the CDW, but don't want to pay your insurance company's deductible, you can buy $500 worth of coverage from Alamo for $3.

Liability Responsibility

Most of the major car rental firms—Alamo, Avis, Budget, Hertz, and National—are shifting the responsibility for and the price of liability coverage for injury, death, or damage to others and their property to the renter in many states. Check with each firm about its policy, but here is a partial list of the affected states: Alabama, Alaska, California, Colorado, Florida, Georgia, Hawaii, Idaho, Illinois, Indiana, Kentucky, Louisiana, Massachusetts, Maine, Maryland, Michigan, Mississippi, Missouri, Nevada, New York, New Jersey, North Carolina, Ohio, Oklahoma, Oregon, Pennsylvania, South Carolina, Tennessee, Texas, Utah, Washington, Wisconsin, and Wyoming. While in the past, car rental companies provided primary coverage for liability as part of the package, now your own policy must pay in the event of an accident that leads to a liability claim.

You have several choices: Rent from a company that does not charge for the coverage but provides it, rely on the liability coverage in your personal policy, rely on your employer's coverage if you are traveling on business, or buy the rental firm's coverage. This coverage is separate from collision coverage and the CDW, which only covers damage to or disappearance of the car.

Don't go without. Liability claims can involve millions of dollars. And the rental companies say liability claims costs and frequency are escalating, particularly in states with vicarious liability laws (California, Connecticut, Florida, Idaho, Iowa, Michigan, Minnesota, Nevada, New York, Rhode Island, and Washington, DC). These laws hold the owner, not the driver, of the vehicle responsible for damage. But don't assume that you don't need liability coverage just because the state you live or rent in has a vicarious liability law. Auto rental firms, regulators, and the courts are involved in a debate as to whether car rental firms can legally shift their liability responsibility to the renter in states with laws requiring the *owner* of the vehicle to take financial responsibility. Since the question has yet to be resolved and your entire net worth may be at risk, it's better to have double coverage than no coverage at all.

Coverage adds about $8 to the daily rental rate. Ask how much coverage this buys—or how much coverage the company provides if it comes *gratis*. Most rental companies provide only the minimum coverage mandated by the state, and this may not be enough to protect your assets in the event of a large claim against you. Some rental firms sell supple-mental coverage to fill in the gap. It's probably worth it if you have major assets that could be at risk.

WHAT TO WATCH OUT FOR

Hidden costs. The National Association of Attorneys General adopted advertising guidelines for car rental firms requiring them to include all *mandatory* charges and fees in the rates they advertise. Even so, there are plenty of *extra* hidden charges that can raise prices. If you are calling around to try to find the best deal, ask how much extra you will have to pay for:

■ *Additional drivers.* This used to be free, but many companies now charge $10, $15, or even $25 per rental for the option of letting someone other than the renter drive. (New York caps the charge at $5.) Many firms waive the charge for spouses and business associates.

■ *Upgrades to a larger class of car.* The prices quoted in ads are most often for the lowest class of car. If you need something bigger, it will probably cost you more.

Redlining. If you live in one of the five boroughs of New York City, it hurts to rent from Hertz anywhere in the metropolitan area, which includes all the airports (even Newark), Westchester County, and Long Island. If you live in the Bronx, Hertz tacks a whopping $56 onto your daily rate. For residents of Brooklyn, it's an extra $34. Queens means $15 more, and Manhattanites pay an extra $3. Hertz claims the

PUMP ME UP

Before you return the car, make sure it has a full tank of gas. Many rental companies will charge you more than twice the price at the pump if they have to put gas in the tank. One New Yorker complained to the NYC Consumer Affairs Department that he had returned a rental car to Avis at 5:30 AM. It was too early to find an open gas station. He had used about 10 gallons of gas, which at the time would have cost roughly $13.00 at the pump. Avis's bill for the gas came to $32.37.

additional charges reflect the cost of doing business in each of the boroughs as a result of New York State's vicarious liability law, which holds Hertz responsible for accidents involving its cars even if the renter was at fault. (New York City banned these additional fees for its residents, but while the law undergoes a legal challenge, Hertz continues to charge New Yorkers extra.)

Mileage caps. Some rental deals give you free mileage—but only up to a pre-set limit. Figure out if your itinerary will keep you within the allowance. If not, you could end up paying high additional charges for every mile you drive beyond the limit. About 30 cents a mile is not unusual. At this rate, if you drive 200 miles over the limit for a $35-a-day rental, you'll almost double the price for a two-day weekend getaway.

Damage. You'll be held responsible for any damage to the car, and car rental companies often pad their repair bills beyond what it actually costs to fix the damage. For instance, they may try to charge you for losses related to not being able to rent the car to someone else while it's in the shop. In 1988, 41 states got Hertz to refund more than $2 million to consumers and insurance companies it had overcharged for repairs.

Cancellation fees. They don't apply to all reservations—yet. But as of this writing, Avis, Hertz, and National had begun billing a penalty even if you never picked up the car. The policy varies a bit from one company to another, and even from one location to another, but it generally applies to minivans, convertibles, and other special cars. The fees range from $50 to $100. Reservations clerks are supposed to tell you about the cancellation penalty when you make the reservation. Ask how much notice you need to give in order to avoid the charge; it could be as little as a few hours or as much as a few days.

Look for bargains. Since many car rental locations are busiest during the week, serving business customers, they often offer low weekend rates to attract tourists. Just make sure you understand the restrictions. If you rent a car at a special weekly rate and decide you only want to keep it a few days, the price may revert to a much higher daily rate. In the end, you could end up paying significantly more for a few days than you would have paid for the whole week. Likewise, if you take a car for a few days and then decide you want to extend your trip, you probably won't be able to get the lower weekly rate, even if you keep the car a week.

Mileage caps can work against you if you will be covering a lot of territory, but they might work for you if you won't be traveling that far. Ask whether you can get a lower rate if you stay within a mileage allowance. And when the rental company offers two rates, figure out how far you will drive and calculate the most economical rate.

Make reservations ahead of time and get a confirmation number. This locks in the rate. If you reserve far enough in advance, you can avoid getting stung when rental firms boost their prices just before a holiday.

If a driver's license check means there's a chance you could be turned away, ask when you make your reservation if your record can be reviewed in advance.

Liability is a real issue if you rent cars often and have no coverage; you may want to consider tacking it onto your homeowner's insurance. If you don't cover yourself somehow, and you are involved in an accident in which someone is injured or killed, your personal assets may be at risk.

Make sure you have collision damage insurance from one source or another. Don't blindly count on your credit card for collision coverage. Chase no longer offers this perk with its standard Visa and Master-Cards. American Express, AT&T's Universal Card, and Diner's Club cards still cover you for collision damage as of this writing. For other bank cards, check with your issuer. This is particularly important if you will be renting a car overseas, where policies vary greatly.

If you have a car of your own, double-check that your collision insurance covers rental cars. If it doesn't, or if you wouldn't want to file a claim with your insurance

NOT SUCH A GREAT DEAL

Here's how a $69/week Florida rental could cost almost three times as much.

Weekly rental:	**$69.00**
Average daily charge for collision damage waiver:	
	$12.95 x 7 days = $90.65
Budget's daily rate for liability coverage:	
	$5.95 x 7 days = $41.65
	TOTAL $201.30

company because you'd have to pay a deductible or your rate would increase, you may want to buy the CDW. In fact, do not count on your personal automobile insurance to cover you in the event of a collision in a car you rent for business travel. Bob M. of Fort Lauderdale was told by his employer *not* to buy the CDW (if he did, the company wouldn't reimburse him for the expense). Trouble was, Bob's car insurance would only cover vehicles rented for his own private purposes. In the end, his employer assumed responsibility for damage to the rental car.

Read the CDW. If you buy one, make sure you understand the terms and restrictions, particularly the ones camouflaged in fine print. For instance, the CDW is most often void for accidents involving an unauthorized driver.

Check for scratches before you drive out of the rental lot. You will be charged for any dents or damage, no matter how minor. If pre-existing damage isn't noted in your rental agreement, you may be charged for a previous renter's scrape and your own carelessness.

Find an alternative. Drive your own car. Take a bus or a train. Use airport shuttles and cabs or limousines if you just need to get somewhere and wouldn't be using a rental car that much anyway.

▪ **If you have a problem with a** car rental: Report it to your state attorney general's office or to your local Better Business Bureau.

▪ **For more information, consult:** *Consumer Reports 1995 Travel Buying Guide* It's available for $8.95 at bookstores or call (800) 272-0722.

Other Services

CHAPTER 50

FUNERALS

The High Cost of Dying

Little is more painful than planning a funeral, especially during a time of mourning. And while a funeral is a religious or spiritual ceremony, it's also one of the most difficult consumer transactions the average American will make in his or her lifetime. It makes solid sense to plan ahead, difficult and distasteful as you may find it.

The elaborate funeral familiar to most Americans is a fairly recent tradition. Until the 20th century, funerals were considered intimate affairs, arranged mostly by the family of the deceased. But as Jessica Mitford, the Ralph Nader of the funeral industry, wryly noted, "We've come a long way, baby."

"Undertakers" became "funeral directors." Their responsibilities have expanded from supplying the coffin and transporting the body to the gravesite to protecting the public health and acting as grief therapists and planning directors. They brought back a practice dating to the Age of Pharaohs—embalming—in response to both alleged public health concerns and the emerging practice of "viewing" the body of the deceased, which was supposed to facilitate the healing process. Often, survivors bought package deals and entrusted most

decisions to the funeral director or were pressured into purchasing expensive caskets and glorious flower arrangements as a final show of affection and respect for their loved one. A typical funeral, according to Mitford, came to include:

"The display of the embalmed and beautified corpse reposing on an innerspring or foam-rubber mattress in an elegant "casket"; "visitation" of the deceased in the mortuary "slumber room"; an open-casket ceremony at which the mourners parade around for a last look; a burial vault that allegedly affords "eternal protection"; elaborate "flower tributes" from family and friends; a "final resting place" in a "memorial park" or mausoleum."

In 1963, Mitford published *The American Way of Death*, an exposé of abusive practices in the funeral trade that brought to light the myriad ways in which funeral directors foisted regal funerals on hard-up families. Mitford's landmark study generated seismic changes in the industry. After a 12-year battle, the Federal Trade Commission (FTC) in 1984 enacted the so-called Funeral Rule, for the first time establishing federal standards for funeral directors. The Rule is comprehensive and puts the onus on the provider to inform consumers of their rights. But it's no substitute for *knowing* your rights, especially since less than a third of funeral parlors are in compliance with all FTC regulations. And the Rule still does not apply to cemeteries, crematoria, or casket retailers.

As a result, complaints against the industry remain high. A summary of complaints filed with the New York State Bureau of Funeral Directing reveals a range of violations, from outright fraud (forging a consumer's signature on a contract to collect his or her insurance policy for payment) to poor professional practices (bodily fluids of the deceased leaking out of the casket) and flat-out inhumane treatment (cramming a body, hands bound together and wrapped in a hospital blanket, into an undersized casket). One complaint describes the body of the deceased displayed at the funeral as "unshaven, dirty nails, hair not combed, dirty shirt." One family reported that the funeral home misplaced their late son's ashes, another that the remains of the deceased were given to a person other than his widow.

> "*A funeral is, for most people, the third most expensive purchase they're going to make after a house and a car. Yet, in no other case are consumers at a greater disadvantage. They're beset by grief, for the most part ignorant about funerals . . . and under pressure to act quickly.*"
>
> —THOMAS NELSON,
> American Association of
> Retired Persons

THE BASICS

The range of choices for consumers has exploded in recent years. A lavish last homage or a minimalist memorial? Cremation or burial? Pre-plan, pre-pay—or procrastinate?

For the industry, the stakes are high. Remember the scene in *A Christmas Carol* where Scrooge visits the dying Marley and finds the undertaker already there? Scrooge asks him, "You don't believe in letting grass grow under your feet, do you?" The undertaker replies, "Ours is a highly competitive profession, sir." Funerals are a big business: Americans arrange over 2 million of them a year and spend over $9 billion annually on funeral and cemetery services, according to the National Funeral Directors Association.

But the stakes are no less high for consumers. The average funeral costs $5,000. Yet three quarters of families, when arranging a funeral, don't bother comparing prices and may end up spending far more than they should. For this reason, most experts, including the American Association of Retired Persons (AARP), strongly suggest that you

LIFE-GIVING GIFTS

According to the United Network for Organ Sharing, six patients die each day awaiting a liver or heart because no suitable donor is found. One of your lasting legacies could be the gift of life, or health, to one of the 31,000 Americans on waiting lists for organs around the country. Organs that can be transplanted are the kidneys, corneas, heart, heart/lungs, liver, pancreas, bone, bone marrow, and skin.

If you would like to donate your organs, inform your family and complete a Uniform Donor Card (signed by two witnesses) that can be attached to your driver's license. The card can be obtained from the Living Bank or the National Kidney Foundation (see **HELP** at the end of this chapter). The Bank also maintains a national registry of potential donors. All expenses are paid by the recipient and his or her health insurance.

---

plan your funeral in advance. Doing so has four benefits.

- It ensures that the ceremony will reflect your and your family's wishes.
- It lifts a tremendous weight from your survivors and leaves them free to grieve and mourn.
- It enables you to "comparison shop."
- It also lifts a burden from the person who is or may be ill to have funeral plans in place—one less worry.

"Pre-planning" your funeral means making a series of decisions regarding the disposition of the body, the type of ceremony you want, the selection of a site, and funding arrangements. You should strongly consider involving your family as well as a religious advisor or trusted friend who may not be as emotionally involved and can help

you make clear decisions. Write down your arrangements in a place easily accessible to relatives (*not* in your will—it won't be read until *after* the funeral).

Disposition of the Body

The most prevalent way to dispose of a deceased's body is burial in a cemetery, either in the ground (interment) or above-ground in a mausoleum (entombment). The latter is usually more expensive.

A second option is cremation, the choice of 18.5% of Americans and growing, according to the Cremation Association of North America. The body is reduced by burning to ash and "cremains," small bone fragments that are in turn pulverized into small particles. The ashes can be scattered—from the air, in the water, or over a field—or stored in an urn, to be buried in a cemetery, placed in a columbarium, or kept by the family.

Cremation can reduce your funeral expenses in a number of ways. By opting for "direct cremation," in which the body is taken directly from the place of death to a crematory, you eliminate the costs of embalming, cosmetic preparation of the body, use of the funeral home's facilities, and purchase of a casket. (Under the Funeral Rule, the funeral home is required to offer you in writing an inexpensive container in which the body will be placed for the cremation.) If you want a viewing prior to cremation, you may be able to rent an elegant casket for the ceremony for a third of its sale price.

A third option is donation of your organs or body to a medical school or hospital. Organ and tissue donation does not affect the need for funeral arrangements. But you may be able to eliminate almost all funeral expenses by donating your body to a medical school. However, you should make alternative funeral arrangements in case your body cannot be accepted. (See the box on the previous page for more information.)

Choosing a Ceremony

Whether you are planning your funeral or organizing the funeral of a loved one, don't meet with a funeral director until you have some idea of the type of funeral that suits you best.

The AARP recommends that you call or visit a minimum of two funeral homes to compare services and, especially, prices. Funeral directors are required to provide price information over the phone, and price lists of itemized services, caskets, and outer burial containers in person. The Funeral Rule gives you the option to buy only those services you want—not just "prix fixe" but also "à la carte." If a funeral provider claims that a certain good or service is required under state law, he or she must disclose the specific law requiring the purchase. Before signing an agreement, the funeral director must provide you with an itemized statement of the total cost, including a "good faith" estimate of any "cash advance" item, described below.

Here are some of the things to think about:

What type of service do you want? A funeral service can be held prior to the final disposition of the body (with or without viewing) or as a memorial service after burial, or both. The funeral service generally takes place at the funeral home, a place of worship, or the gravesite; the memorial service at the funeral home, a place of worship, or a private home.

Care of the body. Embalming—the replacement of bodily fluids with chemicals to slow the deterioration of the body—has long been routinely performed on public health grounds. It is, in fact, unnecessary. Embalming remains mainly as part of the process to prepare the body for one last display, or "viewing," before final disposition, along with clothing the body, or "dressing," hair dressing, and other cosmetic services. The Funeral Rule prohibits funeral directors from falsely representing that embalming is required, except, of course, for those rare cases where it is—such as when a body will be transported across state lines, if a funeral is delayed for a few days after the death, or when death occurred from a communicable, contagious disease. Some funeral homes require embalming to delay decomposition when a viewing is planned. If embalming was done without legal requirement or prior consent of the survivors, you don't have to pay.

Other services. All funeral homes charge a mandatory basic service fee that typically includes consultation with the family, preparation of legal documents and notices, care and shelter of the body before disposition, and overhead costs. Other charges may include transportation of the body, use of the facilities, or rental of tents and chairs if a gravesite service is held.

Caskets. Caskets vary based on their visual appeal, protective features—and price. Caskets can amount to half the cost of a funeral. According to Matthew Daynard of the FTC, they are a source of considerable profit for funeral directors, some of whom mark up the price from the wholesaler by as much as five- to tenfold. In response, some members of the industry have set up discount casket stores. And funeral providers are now prohibited from charging a "casket-handling fee" to consumers who buy a casket from another seller. Consider doing just that.

And remember—funeral directors (but not casket retailers) are required to provide a written price list of all caskets available.

Most caskets are made of metal or wood; some are fiberglass or plastic. While some sealed models can slow deterioration of the body, none preserve the body indefinitely. However, a 1988 Gallup poll found that 30% of customers had been told just that by funeral directors, in violation of the Funeral Rule.

Outer burial containers. Most cemeteries require a burial vault or concrete grave liner (or "rough box") to enclose the casket in a grave and prevent the ground from caving in as the casket deteriorates. (Arlington National Cemetery does not.)

Vaults are usually more visually elaborate (and twice as expensive) than grave liners and offer more protection—but here again, ignore all claims that a sealed vault will preserve the body indefinitely. It won't.

"Cash advance" items. These include flowers, fees for pallbearers, honoraria for clergy, memorial books, and obituary notices. Funeral directors, if they provide these items, must disclose any fee they charge or discount they receive.

Selecting a Site: The Final Resting Place

There is no Funeral Rule for cemeteries, and only 37 states require a license. Cemetery "pre-need" arrangements are typically far less regulated than funeral pre-need arrangements. Check with the Better Business Bureau (BBB) for a reliability report. The BBB also suggests that you look for a cemetery that has been in operation for a number of years. *Visit* several cemeteries yourself, not only to compare prices and make sure you like the setting but also to ensure that they are well cared for. (The prime complaint regarding cemeteries concerns maintenance.) In particular, walk around to find out how well maintained older graves are, and ask the cemetery for an audit of its perpetual care fund.

Read the fine print in your contract. If you buy a plot under a pre-construction plan, what happens if death occurs before the site is developed? If you purchase on time payments, what happens if death occurs before final payment is made? If you're shown a plot in a cemetery, your contract should specify whether you're buying the specific plot you were shown or merely the right to be buried in the cemetery. Does your contract include buy-back provisions? (Cemeteries are typically reluctant to offer refunds unless contractually bound.) Is the cemetery part of a credit-exchange program, enabling you to the cash equivalent in another participating cemetery? What are the limitations?

Cemetery costs range from $1,000 to $10,000 and up, including space, container, and marker. (A plot in the Westwood cemetery where Marilyn Monroe is buried will cost you $20,000.)

Most states require that the consumer make provision for maintenance of the grave. The perpetual care fee may be included in the sale of the plot, or you may be required to buy into a "memorial fund" or "special care fund" separately, payable upfront or annually.

Finally, if you are arranging the burial of a loved one, find out before you buy a plot if the deceased already owns a funeral plot—60% of the 65-plus population does. Veterans, their spouses, and their minor children are eligible for burial at one of the nation's national cemeteries, as well as a marker and a flag.

Funding Arrangements: Caveats About Pre-Paying

Life ain't cheap. But truth be told, neither is death. Carefully reviewing your assets, setting ample money aside, and shopping around may prevent an emotional heartache from becoming a financial heartburn.

First, find out if you can receive financial assistance for your funeral or that of a close relative by checking with Social Security, the Veterans Administration, a local General Assistance program, pension funds, or fraternal organizations.

The fastest growing trend in the industry is pre-payment, especially among senior citizens. While approximately 2 million Americans are buried annually, a million pre-paid (or "pre-need") funeral contracts were sold in 1990, up from 22,000 30 years ago. Such arrangements may bring you a certain peace of mind, but remember that you are making a major investment, and make sure that you know what you're paying for—and that you'll be getting it when the time comes.

Pre-payment takes two forms. You can plan the funeral with a funeral director, assess the cost, and pay the value of the funeral, which is then placed in a trust account. Or you can purchase an insurance policy from a funeral director or an insurance company in the amount of your planned funeral, name the funeral home as its beneficiary, and pay an annuity. Such plans are prohibited in certain states, including New York, Georgia, and Maryland.

Here's why: While the AARP strongly recommends that everyone "pre-*plan*" their funeral, it cautions consumers about *pre-payment*. Jessica Mitford was more blunt: "Stay away from them. You don't know what's going to happen to either your money or the company." Memorial societies offer the same advice. Instead, you may want to sign a non-binding pre-arrangement agreement to indicate your preferences. Lisa Carlson, a leading consumer advocate in the field and no friend of pre-payment, suggests only two reasons to pre-pay: First, depending on state law and the terms of your pre-payment contract, its value may not be counted against the asset ceiling for S.S.I. or Medicaid eligibility, whereas an individual account will; second, you may consider pre-paying if you have no survivors.

Still, setting funds aside can be a reassuring prospect for you and your survivors. Your safest bet may be to create a type of trust account, called a "Totten Trust" or "revocable living trust," which remains under your control but will upon your death pay funds for your funeral to a named beneficiary. (You may need an attorney to set up such a trust.) You can also set aside money in an interest-earning savings account designed as "payable on death" to the funeral home or your survivors, or open a joint savings account with a family member who has a "right of survivorship." Each of these options enables you to earn interest and lets your survivors keep any excess funds in the account. The interest earned, however, is taxable.

If you decide to pre-pay, read your contract carefully; make sure that it states clearly what goods and services you are paying for. And find out the following:

Is the contract "revocable"? If you change your plans, can you cancel your contract and get your full deposit back—and any interest earned? Is there a cancellation fee? Consumers who attempt to cancel a life insurance policy, in particular, may be severely penalized.

Is the contract "portable"? If you move out of state, can you transfer your plan to a funeral home in your new area? Again, will you be charged a fee?

Is the price of your funeral "guaranteed"? Will your estate be required to pay additional money if funeral inflation exceeds the interest earned on your payment?

Is your money secure? The main consideration is peace of mind: Are you getting what you paid for? When you contract with a funeral director, all states except Vermont,

Alabama, and the District of Columbia require that all or part of your payments—from 50% in Mississippi to 100% in most states—be placed in a trust account. But trust accounts are no panacea. Consumers in Ohio and Pennsylvania were left in the lurch after morticians in those states invested the trust funds in diamonds and rare coins.

While such investments are generally prohibited, "[r]egulations, investigations, and auditing are minimal in most states." The California Cemetery Board and Board of Funeral Directors, for instance, came under attack for lackluster supervision after a series of exposés in the *Sacramento Bee*—despite having among the toughest enforcement and auditing provisions in the country.

Ask your state funeral board if trust accounts are subject to regular audits, as in California, and if they are protected by state guarantee funds, as they are in Florida and a few other states. Life insurance policies are regulated and guaranteed in all 50 states—but not in the District of Columbia.

Installment payments raise a host of other issues. For instance: Are you being charged interest or a carrying fee? What happens if you fall behind on some of your payments? Who is liable if you pass away before payments are completed?

If you do sign a pre-need contract, make sure to give a copy to your next of kin or the friend or relative in charge of your funeral arrangements.

WHAT TO WATCH OUT FOR

Don't succumb to pressure sales tactics. Some funeral directors, for instance, will typically conceal from view or disparage as "welfare caskets" their lower-priced caskets to lure consumers to the highest-priced items. Ask to be shown the full variety of caskets available. Others may try to sell you an expensive memorial service if you opt for an inexpensive cremation.

Beware the door-to-door sales person. Mary B. of Phoenix, Arizona, and her husband both decided to pre-pay when a door-to-door salesman came to their house. Total cost: $10,000. Shortly afterward, they read an advertisement for the same funeral for $1,500 each. If you suspect fraud, you have three days to cancel your contract under the FTC's door-to-door cancellation rule.

THE SMARTER CONSUMER

If you find a casket you like, get the exact brand and model and call other sellers to find out about the price. Compare caskets and outer burial containers from various providers—the retailer you went to may not offer lower-priced items.

IF YOU'RE HIV POSITIVE

Lisa Carlson, author of *Caring For Your Own Dead*, found that early in the AIDS epidemic, funeral parlors frequently refused to care for the bodies of persons with HIV or AIDS. In addition, a 1989 study by the Gay Men's Health Crisis (GMHC) found that a lot of excessive billing and other abuses were taking place. AIDS activists and industry insiders believe that the industry has mostly cleaned up its act in recent years, but some establishments may still charge a higher fee for cer-tain services (e.g., extra disinfecting). The GMHC believes that the bodies of persons with HIV require no special handling or procedure, but individual state laws may require embalming.

Because the funeral director is likely to see the HIV status of the deceased on the death certificate, you may want to disclose the condition when planning for the funeral to avoid any last-minute complications. If you do not want the death certificate to mention the deceased's HIV status, most physicians will likely accommodate you—for instance, by listing instead the specific illness that was the immediate cause of death. (Most people with AIDS actually succumb to an opportunistic infection or invasive neoplasm.) If the physician refuses to change the death certificate, it can be appealed, but the process may take up to six months.

Consider memorial societies, which are volunteer-run, non-profit groups dedicated to dignified but inexpensive funerals. They can help you arrange the funeral of your choice at a significantly reduced cost. Membership usually requires a one-time $25 fee.

Forty-one states let you bypass funeral homes altogether. You will have to fill out a host of legal documents, arrange for final disposition with a crematory or cemetery, and attend to countless details on your own. Both Lisa Carlson's *Caring For Your Own Dead* and Ernest Morgan's *Dealing Creatively With Death: A Manual of Death Education and Simple Burial* provide useful information and checklists.

If you opt for cremation, the container with your remains will be destroyed during the process; you might prefer to buy an inexpensive container or unfinished wood box.

Save the cost of embalming and other cosmetic expenses with a closed-casket funeral.

Eliminate expenses for the use of the funeral home's facilities with a gravesite service. A memorial service at home will eliminate funeral expenses altogether.

Consider a weekday funeral, if your religious practice permits and if you're trying to keep costs down. Many funeral homes and cemeteries charge extra for services on weekends and holidays.

If you are concerned about relocating, don't pre-pay for a cemetery plot. Cemeteries are usually unwilling to buy back property. Or ask if the cemetery participates in a credit-exchange program, which enables you to transfer the value of your plot to another participating cemetery. Some 525 members of the American Cemetery Association in every state participate in such a program, but may impose restrictions.

■ To complain about a funeral parlor, contact your state regulatory board and the Federal Trade Commission, 6th Street and Pennsylvania Ave. NW, Washington, DC 20580; (202) 326-2000. For mediation (free) or binding arbitration, contact the Funeral Service Consumer Association Program, 2250 East Devon Avenue, Suite 250, Des Plaines, IL 60016; (800) 662-7666.

■ To complain about a cemetary, contact your state regulatory board, attorney general, or local consumer agency. For free, non-binding mediation, contact the Cemetery Consumer Service Council, Box 3574, Washington, DC 20007; (703) 379-6426.

■ Organ donation. The Living Bank, P.O. Box 6725, Houston, TX 77265; (800) 528-2971, and the National Kidney Foundation, 30 East 33rd Street, New York, NY 10016; (800) 622-9010. These organizations give out universal donor cards and provide information on organ donation and transplants.

■ Body donation. The National Anatomical Service, (800) 727-0700, will provide complete information about donating your body to science.

■ Memorial societies. To find a memorial society close to you, contact the Continental Association of Funeral and Memorial Societies, 6900 Lost Lake Road, Egg Harbor, WI 54209, or call them at (800) 765-0107.

■ The American Cemetery Association provides information on intrastate cemetary plot credit-exchange programs. Call (800) 645-7700.

■ Read *Caring For Your Own Dead,* by Lisa Carlson, (Upper Access Publishers, 1987). $12.95. Call (800) 356-9315 to order.

■ Get *Dealing Creatively With* *Death: A Manual of Death Education and Simple Burial,* by Ernest Morgan, (Barclay House, 1990). $11.95.

■ Read *Final Choices: Making End-* *of-Life Decisions,* by Lee E. Norrgard & Jo DeMars, (ABC-Clio, 1992). $45.

■ The American Association of Re- tired Persons has several free booklets: *Cemetery Goods and Services, Product Report: Funeral Goods and Services,* and *Product Report: Pre-Paying Your Funeral.* Call (202) 872-4880.

■ The FTC *publishes Funerals: A Con-* *sumer Guide* and *Caskets and Burial Vaults;* call (202) 326-2000.

CHAPTER 51

LAWYERS

Finding Affordable Representation

The problem of hiring a lawyer can be summed up by a 1973 *New Yorker* cartoon. A distinguished-looking attorney and an anxious prospective client are talking; the caption reads, "You have a pretty good case, Mr. Pitkin. How much justice can you afford?"

High prices for any product or service are a costly burden for cash-strapped Americans today. But paying too much for a TV is one thing. Paying too much for a lawyer, or having to pay so much that you can't afford the day in court due you, is quite another. One Westchester County, New York woman (she prefers not to be identified by name) with a doctoral degree in special education from Columbia University found herself in just such a bind: She paid her lawyers $15,000 to get the court to make the dead-beat dad she had divorced pay child support (awarded to her) for their three minor children. After three years she found herself embroiled in a fee dispute with her lawyers over $70,000 in accrued fees. On the eve of trial she refused to sign a note for the debt, and the lawyers abandoned her case. Rather than carrying out their mission of wresting child support from her unresponsive husband, they collected their fees by seizing and liquidating her retirement fund and entire bank account.

The legal profession not only perpetuates an aura of complexity and omniscience, but its esoteric mumbo jumbo—sprinkled generously with arcane Latin phrases like *sui generis* and *pro bono*, which simply mean "unique" and "cost-free" —can also hide feather-bedding and fee-hiking. It can also silence clients' questions about why three attorneys were needed in court for a seemingly simple case or how a one-hour phone call between lawyer and client could possibly have taken place when the client was atop Mount Kilimanjaro. (For the original, and still the best, book on how the legal profession converts complexity and esoterica into fat fees, see former Yale professor Fred Rodell's 1939 classic, *Woe Unto You Lawyers*.)

And in addition to the language barrier, there's the fabled superior attitude—perceived and proven— that surrounds all things legal. From the mid-19th century until 1975, the bar justified its rule *requiring* lawyers to charge no less than a minimum fee for specific legal services with the explanation that theirs was a profession and therefore not subject to the normal rules of the free market. No matter that the policy precluded price shopping and fee bargaining that might reduce huge fees. But what the bar called an "ethical rule" the Supreme Court unanimously called "price-fixing" and illegal in the *Goldfarb* v. *Virginia State Bar* decision of 1975. It took another unanimous *Bates and O'Steen* v. *State Bar of Arizona* decision from the Supreme Court in 1977 to knock down prohibitions against lawyers advertising—as if the provision of legal services were somehow not a commercial transaction. (Because many members of the established bar consider the *Bates* decision's "commercialization" of their "profession" demeaning and declassé, they often denounce TV, radio, or print ads for lawyers. The issue, however, should not be whether advertising offends their lawyerly sensibility but whether the ads tell the truth. As with any other product or service, legal advertising is fine unless it deceives or misleads.)

The laws may change, but the attitude lingers on. Florida legal secretary Rosemary Furman created a small business providing men and women with help filling out the legal forms necessary to obtain a divorce. The Florida bar challenged the legality of her business on the basis that she was not a lawyer and therefore should not be allowed to give what they perceived to be legal advice. The case dragged on for ten years; representation by the Public Citizen Litigation Group kept Rosemary out of jail, but it could not save her business. However, by the mid-1980s, the Florida bar and Supreme Court had relaxed their requirements enough so that people like Rosemary can now assist litigants with filling out forms. To the extent that courts require lawyers to do things that paralegals, court clerks, legal secretaries, or you yourself could easily do, you are paying these professionals something for nothing.

Such incidents fuel the current wave of anti-lawyer jokes and negative references in our popular culture—such as the lawyer-eating dinosaur in *Jurassic Park*, which provoked cheers in movie theaters around the country.

While the trend in the lawyer–client struggle may favor clients, it's also true that two-thirds of the public can't afford to hire a lawyer when they need one. In fact, new legal problems crop up in more than 40% of low- and moderate-income households each year—disputes between landlords and tenants or families and their health insurers over disallowed charges—but, according to a 1994 study by the American Bar Association, most people choose to avoid the formal legal system because they fear that it won't help them or that it will cost too much. Hence this chapter, which will guide you through the process of buying the best representation you can for whatever price your budget can bear, even if it means you represent yourself. (Nothing in the chapter should be construed as a *substitute* for legal advice, but instead as advice on how to pursue, procure, and evaluate professional legal services.)

THE BASICS

Purchasing legal services should be no more mystifying than buying any other product or service—a lawyer is there to serve you and help you get a job done. But getting good legal advice at minimal cost takes careful management of your own case and your relationship with your attorney—including choosing your lawyer carefully, hammering out a fair working (and billing) relationship, setting realistic goals, keeping track of your case, judicious use of telephone calls, and careful review of lawyers' bills.

Do You Need a Lawyer?

Many situations obviously require professional legal advice—dealing with criminal charges, filing a suit or being sued, drawing up a complicated will or trust, filing for bankruptcy or a contested divorce, buying a business or entering into a significant contract, adopting a child, or seeking redress for injuries sustained in a serious accident. And there are many less obvious situations in which a lawyer's advice or review of documents can easily pay for itself in avoided headaches and expenditures—contracts for significant home improvements or insurance agreements, for instance. But there are also situations in which a lawyer may not be necessary, for example in a dispute over a bill or a service. (For more on handling your own disputes, see the final chapter "How to Complain," page 603.)

The Selection Process

When you begin your search for an attorney, the two most important things to keep in mind are finding someone you feel comfortable working with and finding someone knowledgeable about the area of law with which you need assistance. Doing so will probably require talking to more than one attorney to see how each of them would treat both you and your matter. Even if you have to invest some money in these meetings (some lawyers charge for an initial consultation), it's probably well worth the investment in the long run.

The most common ways to find a lawyer include asking friends, family, and other attorneys. Surveys show that seeking names from such friendly sources is the most common way people find lawyers, and we recommend it, too. But make sure the recommendation fits your needs. Just because the young woman on *L.A. Law* was comfortable with Arnie Becker and happy with the divorce settlement he got for her doesn't mean her sister would be just as well-served by him, particularly if her sister wanted to bring a medical malpractice suit. Becker might, however, be able to refer the injured woman to an appropriate colleague. Be sure to choose a lawyer who knows the field your case falls in—for instance, if you want to adopt a child, pass over the kindly woman who wrote your mother's will (unless, of course, she also works as an adoption lawyer) and keep up the search for an attorney who specializes in adoptions.

Referral services. In the best of all worlds, using legal referral services, which are offered on a non-profit basis by virtually every state bar association, would give you the benefit of talking to experts who could assess your situation and make a referral to the appropriate attorney or another non-legal provider. "Most [bar association] referral services act as clearinghouses for social service agencies, government offices, and other services that may even be free," says Carol Woods, director of the San Francisco Bar Association's legal referral service. "What we provide is a knowledgeable person who can help you define your problem and help you figure out what resource is best. We get 85,000 calls a year and only 25% of them are referred to lawyers."

Each bar association runs its referral service differently. The basic service involves listening to your situation and referring you to the appropriate place. If you need an attorney, the service will give you the name of one who has agreed to participate and will provide you with a half-hour initial consultation at a fixed charge (anywhere from free to $25). Virtually all bar association referral services require their lawyers to carry malpractice insurance, and the best programs—like those in San Francisco, Los Angeles, and New York—require attorneys to demonstrate a certain level of experience in a given area before giving their name out. But there is a lot in between. Some have lawyers or spe-

cially trained interviewers answering the phone and making referrals, while others use paralegals or clerical staff.

To further confuse matters, for-profit referral services operate in Texas, Florida, California, and many other areas of the country. Some states—California, for instance—regulate them, but others don't. The danger is being referred to a lawyer who signed up with the service for a hefty monthly fee in return for getting every call—whether or not the lawyer is qualified and appropriate to handle the case—that comes from a designated zip code.

When using either kind of referral service, ask the following questions before you call any offered names:

- How did this lawyer get on your list? What were the specific qualifying criteria?
- Are the attorneys on your list required to have malpractice insurance?
- What happens if I'm not happy with the representation I receive? To whom would I complain or address grievances?

The first meeting of the minds. Take advantage of the free or low-cost initial consultations many lawyers offer to get information about the lawyer and a feel for his or her style. But don't feel obligated to hire the lawyer—if the consultation is free, it's free. Even if the lawyer charges for the consultation, it may be worth it if the lawyer spends a couple of hours with you going over the facts of the case, the documentation, where things stand now, and tries to apply the local law to the facts of your case.

To make the most of your visit, get organized before you go:

- Put together a file of all the relevant documents and study them. Bring copies with you to the initial meeting. For instance, if you want to declare bankruptcy, bring copies of all the bills you've received and a list of your assets and their fair market value; for a divorce, bring copies of all deeds, recent bank statements, and life, property, and health insurance policies.
- Write down a chronology of events, and make a copy to leave with the attorney.

Once you are there, you are simultaneously trying to size up the attorney's expertise, benefit from whatever advice you may be offered, and figure out how well you will work together. Here are some tips to make your evaluation easier:

- Ask how long the attorney has been in practice, how much experience he or she has with similar cases, how busy he or she is, and who else may be working on your case.
- Review the facts of your case and your document file. Run through the process step-by-step, and ask whether the lawyer anticipates any problems.
- Ask about the fee arrangement. An hourly fee is standard for most divorces, but bankruptcies or house closings are so rote that many lawyers charge a flat fee. If you will be billed by the hour, ask who will work on the case: The attorney? Other attorneys in the firm? Parale-

gals? Legal secretaries? Don't walk out in a huff if others will be working on your case; you might want an agreement that lets the expensive hot-shot do the expert legal work and uses a less experienced associate or legal secretary for more routine efforts, at an hourly rate that reflects their level of expertise. Less-skilled help should cost you less money per hour.

- Ask for an estimate of what it will cost you to resolve your legal situation—pre-trial, trial (if there is to be one), and possible appeal. Lawyers may be reluctant to give you an exact dollar amount, but they ought to be able to give you a range.
- Make sure you will receive a monthly, itemized bill.
- Ask for references.

The Written Fee Agreement

Once you have chosen a lawyer, work out an agreeable employment and fee agreement, and get it in writing. Make sure you understand the fee arrangement—read it carefully, ask questions about it, read it again when you get home, and ask more questions if you need to. Vague language can hide expensive traps. One retainer agreement we examined said, "It may be necessary to spend substantial amounts of time in obtaining the file." But it never defined "substantial amount," or what specific motions might be needed to fulfill this prediction, or what those motions usually cost. Another agreement included the following statement: "Because of mounting costs, it may be necessary from time to time for the applicable time charges to be increased, and such adjustments will be reflected in your billing." So the rate quoted could change at any time without advance warning and was essentially useless for the client trying to gauge future fees.

"It's truly remarkable how many people don't know how much they are being charged," says Allen Charne, director of the Legal Referral Service jointly sponsored by the New York City bar associations. That's why it's unremarkable that fee disputes sour so many lawyer–client relationships.

Make sure the written agreement accurately reflects your discussions and covers these crucial areas (explained in detail below): fees, expenses, retainer, billing procedure, dispute resolution procedures, and lawyer–client rights and responsibilities.

Fees. Lawyers use three billing methods: hourly fees, contingency fees, and flat fees.

■ *Hourly fees* are just what they sound like—you pay a set price for every hour (or fraction thereof) the lawyer spends on your matter. Lawyers most often bill in quarter-, sixth-, or tenth-of-an-hour increments. So no matter how long you meet or talk on the phone, the length of each conversation will be rounded up to the next increment. Thus, a five-minute phone call with a lawyer who charges $150 an hour will cost you $37.50 in quarter-hour increments, $25 in sixth-of-an-hour increments, or $15 in tenth-of-an-hour increments.

This arrangement provides a financial incentive for lawyers to put in time on your case. It may encourage them to do so even if the case doesn't warrant it.

If you will be billed by the hour, be sure your agreement stipulates reduced hourly fees for work done by associates, paralegals, or legal secretaries.

■ *Contingency fees*, most often used when the client cannot afford to pay the attorney if the case is lost, mean that the attorney "gambles" on the likelihood of winning. If you win, your lawyer gets an agreed-upon percentage of the settlement or judgment; if you lose, the lawyer gets no fee. Contingency fees are the norm for product liability, medical malpractice, and class action cases. Many states do not allow contingency fees for divorce and criminal cases, based on the belief that attorneys should be somewhat more objective and dispassionate on such matters.

While the percentage can be great (anywhere from 15% to 50%, but most often 33%), it theoretically makes up for the cases the lawyer works on but doesn't win (no fee). Still, you can usually negotiate a declining percentage for increasing damages. For instance, 33% of the first $500,000 in damages, 25% of the second $500,000, and 15% of anything beyond $1 million.

Even if you lose the case, you may be required to pay your lawyer's expenses. Make sure to investigate this ahead of time—get an estimate of what the bills might be—and hammer out an agreement about when these expenses will be payable.

■ *Flat fees* may be charged for routine matters that will take a fairly predictable amount of effort—for example, incorporating a business, drawing up a simple will, and uncontested divorces. Just be sure you ask about additional costs for expenses and court filing fees.

Expenses. No matter what kind of fee you pay, you will most likely be asked to also pay expenses for things like court filing fees, court reporters and transcripts, photocopies, postage and messengers, long-distance phone calls, private investigators, and expert witnesses. Make sure you understand which expenses are included in the fee and which will cost you extra.

Retainer. It is common practice for a lawyer to ask you to pay a sum of money up front from which he or she can draw payment as it's earned or pay court filing fees and other expenses. Ask whether this "retainer" is an advance on fees, expenses, or both and what happens if any is left at the end. Look for an agreement that refunds whatever is left.

If you don't, you could end up like the unhappy couple who sued Long Island, New York, matrimonial attorney Joel R. Brandes. He refused to refund a $15,000 retainer after the couple reconciled only a few weeks after the agreement was signed. The non-refundable retainer agreement was eventually struck down by the court, which found it "grossly excessive and shocking to the court's conscience" since "not one document was generated during the tenure of the agreement. Not one pleading or letter was pre-

pared by counsel. No appearance in court was made. No conference among counsel was scheduled, nor does it appear from the time-sheets submitted that the plaintiff was involved in negotiating a settlement with adverse counsel. . . . Thus to permit counsel to retain what he characterizes as the minimum fee would be to lend judicial approval to an hourly rate of $3,571.43 ($15,000 divided by 4.2 hours)."

Over the last two decades, non-refundable retainers have become prevalent in domestic, criminal, and, to a somewhat lesser degree, bankruptcy cases. New York is the only state that prohibits non-refundable retainers. If your lawyer insists on a non-refundable retainer, take your business elsewhere. And if your lawyer does no work, challenge him or her in court or through the disciplinary system run by the state bar associations.

Billing procedure. Ask to get an itemized monthly bill and get this spelled out in your fee agreement—not only that you will get a monthly bill but what it will include. You want a precise, itemized bill that lists each piece of work done on your case, the service performed, the individual who performed it, and the time it took, along with precise accountings of the amount of expenses and their purpose. An accurate monthly bill allows you to keep track of your case and keeps the lawyer accountable to you. A bill saying merely "For Services Rendered" should have gone out with hand-cranked adding machines.

Complaint resolution procedure.
Make sure the fee agreement spells out how you and your lawyer will work out any possible disputes between the two of you. This part of the negotiation may have an awkwardness like that between potential spouses who want a prenuptial agreement, but it can come in handy later. It also tells you something about the lawyer you are about to hire. Ask that you be allowed to discuss fee disputes without being billed for the time the discussion takes. And in the event you can't come to terms, ask if the lawyer will agree to fee arbitration or mediation.

Lawyer–client rights and responsibilities. This section of the written fee agreement should outline each of your rights and responsibilities. For instance, this is the place to get in writing the agreement that your attorney send you copies of all documents related to your case, that you receive periodic updates on how things are going, or that you have agreed to do some of the legwork yourself. It is also a place for the attorney to outline your responsibility to review your bills and pay promptly and keep him or her up-to-date on any developments that may affect your case. You also might want to ask your lawyer to append the "Client Bill of Rights" to the agreement (see the box on the facing page). New York requires a similar "Divorce Client Bill of Rights and Responsibilities" to be discussed with prospective clients and appended to all divorce retainer agreements.

Legal Service Plans

Legal service plans operate much like insurance—you pay an annual "membership fee" or "retainer," similar to an insurance premium, for access to legal services whenever you need them. Coverage varies from plan to plan and state to state, but most plans are geared to very basic legal needs—landlord–tenant disputes; bankruptcies; basic family matters (adoptions and simple divorces); and buying and selling homes. In addition to helping find a lawyer, they promise unlimited legal advice and counsel by phone, routine document drafting (wills and houseclosing contracts, for instance), document review, and access to lawyers who have agreed to work within a specified fee schedule for non-routine work. And like a health maintenance organization (HMO), most legal service plans promote preventive care by encouraging you to get advice before you find yourself with a significant legal problem.

And, not surprisingly, many middle-income consumers prefer to pay a couple of hundred dollars *a year* on the chance they'll need legal help rather than a couple of hundred dollars *an hour* when they actually do.

Pre-paid legal service plans started out as group benefits for union members that were paid for by employers. There are now also individual plans available, most often sold through the mail, telemarketing, or door-to-door. Group plans—which may be offered through your employer, union, or other member-

CLIENT BILL OF RIGHTS

1. You have the right to discuss the proposed rates and retainer fee with your lawyer and you have the right to bargain about the fees before you sign the agreement, as in any other contract.

2. You have the right to know how many attorneys and other legal staff will be working on your case and what you will be charged for their services.

3. You have the right to know in advance how you will be asked to pay legal fees and expenses at the end of the case. If you pay for a retainer, you may ask reasonable questions about how the money will be spent or has been spent, and how much of it remains unspent.

4. You are under no legal obligation to sign a Confession of Judgment or Promissory Note, or agree to a lien or mortgage on your home to cover legal fees. You are under no legal obligation to waive your rights to dispute a bill for legal services.

5. You have the right to a reasonable estimate of future necessary costs. If your lawyer agrees to lend or advance you money for preparing your case, you have a right to know periodically how much money your lawyer has spent on your behalf. You also have the right to decide, after consulting with your lawyer, how much money is to be spent to prepare your case. If you pay the expenses, you have the right to decide how much to spend.

6. You have the right to ask your lawyer at reasonable intervals how the case is progressing and to have these questions answered to the best of your lawyer's ability.

7. You have the right to make the final decision regarding the settlement of your case.

8. You have a right to any original documents that are not a part of your attorney's work product. For instance, if you gave your present attorney documents prepared by another attorney, you have the right to those documents. You have a right to ask your attorney to forward copies of documents to you in a timely manner as he/she receives them from the opposing attorney.

9. You have the right to be present at court conferences relating to your case that are held with judges and attorneys, and you also have the right to bring a family member or friend to all court proceedings, unless a judge orders otherwise.

10. You have the right to know the cost of bringing a motion. The cost may vary depending on the lawyer's rates and the circumstances of the case, but you have a right to a general estimate.

If at any time, you, the client, believe that your lawyer has charged an excessive or illegal fee, you have the right to report the matter to a disciplinary or grievance committee that oversees lawyer misconduct.

Source: Revision of the New York City Department of Consumer Affairs' Divorce Client Bill of Rights

ship organization—often cost little or nothing to join. Because they spread the risk over a large group, their operating costs are relatively low and they can pass the savings on to you. Many offer "comprehensive" benefits that cover practically anything and everything, including reimbursing you for things like expenses related to representing yourself in traffic court. Individual plans cost anywhere from $100 to several hundred dollars a year and most often provide "access" benefits—ie, the basic consultations and services described above. For more complex matters, individual plans will refer you to a lawyer who has previously agreed to provide legal services at a reduced price to the plan's members. Plans that give you more choice among lawyers typically cost more.

Whether a legal service plan makes sense for you depends upon your situation. If it's offered through your employer at little or no extra cost, it may be the perfect alternative to close the deal on a new house or to draw up a simple will. However, if you have to pay hundreds of dollars a year (commonly in monthly installments) just to join, ask yourself a few questions before you write the check:

- Do you have frequent or occasional legal questions?
- Do you have pre-existing legal problems? (Most plans exclude covering them.)
- Do you understand fully what out-of-pocket expenses you may incur or the difference between a "simple" matter and a more complicated one, for which you will have to pay? For instance, how simple is that will? Will your divorce *truly* be uncontested?
- Can you switch lawyers if you are unhappy with the one assigned to your case?
- Is there a satisfactory process for resolving any complaints you may have about the plan?

The laws governing legal service plans vary from state to state. Some 25 states, including Florida, Washington and Texas, have comprehensive statutes that either regulate legal plans as though they were insurance or assign jurisdiction to a state insurance department, since the plans operate so much like insurance plans. The laws require financial security, bonding, and reasonable complaint handling procedures. For more information, contact your state's Insurance Commissioner.

How to Avoid Lawyers

Small claims court. Small claims court was designed to allow a lay person to get a quick decision from a judge without paying big fees for minor disputes. The maximum amount disputable averages $2,000 but varies from state to state. (For more information on how to use small claims court effectively, see "How to Complain," page 603.)

Alternative dispute resolution. All parties have to be willing and you may still want an attorney's legal advice, but practically any conflict can be resolved more quickly and cheaply through mediation or arbitration than through litigation. Mediation and arbitration can also be more effective because they offer a less adversarial, non-judicial process that encourages deal-cutting and compromise rather than winning at all costs.

In arbitration, participants present their arguments to an impartial third party whose decision is final, binding, and most often not appealable. Parties are not bound by the rules of evidence, and the arbitrator is under no obligation to explain the final decision. Parties choose an arbitrator mutually, with the help of a judge, or through the American Arbitration Association. Since you usually cannot appeal an arbitrated decision, if you think you'll have trouble living with the result, arbitration isn't for you.

In mediation, parties work through the conflict themselves with the guidance of an impartial third party who simply facilitates a negotiation and allows the parties to hammer out a reasonable resolution.

WHAT TO WATCH OUT FOR

Get a second opinion. As with your physical health, a fresh evaluation can make all the difference.

Take the case of a New York City delicatessen worker who lost most of his arm when it got caught in a meat grinder. He went to one of the best-known personal injury lawyers in New York, who investigated the possibility of a product lia-bility suit. Because the grinder was 30 years old and had been manufactured in Italy, the lawyer believed that the deli man had nothing but a worker's compensation case, through which he could receive only a minimal settlement. A few years went by. When the deli man needed a lawyer to help with some trouble with his worker's compensation, he called the Legal Referral Service. (As it happened, there was just a week left before the statute of limitations was to run out on the case.) He was referred to a second personal injury lawyer who promptly filed a complaint and, after considerable legal maneuvering, settled the case out of court for over $1 million.

Overcharging, hidden charges, and phony bills. First, the profit motive behind the hourly billing fee structure encourages excess. "Most lawyers will prefer to leave no stone unturned, provided, of course, they can charge by the stone," wrote Stanford University Law Professor Deborah Rhode. And, effectively, they can. Efficiency is rewarded with lower fees, so where's the sense in keeping things moving as quickly as possible? A 1992 study of divorce actions by the New York City Department of Consumer Affairs found this to be particularly problematic for the non-moneyed spouse (typically women) in matrimonial cases. Excessive litigation, motion churning, and other delaying tactics drive up fees and delay justice. Take the observation of Justice Kristen Booth Glen of the New York State Supreme Court:

PRO SE: FLYING SOLO

If your financial situation limits your options—or to avoid legal feather-bedding—you are allowed to represent yourself, which is called going *pro se* in legal lingo. Ask the clerks in the courthouse how to fill out paperwork and to review the court's procedures with you. They may even help you prepare motions. Use local law libraries for legal research and local courthouses for records searches. Consumer activists have fought successfully in Florida, California, and Georgia to allow non-lawyers to assist people with simple legal matters, and Arizona has some of the most user-friendly courthouses in America. You can actually sit at a computer in a court clerk's office in Phoenix to fill out the necessary forms yourself!

Just don't forget Justice Louis Brandeis's commentary on an old axiom: "Long ago it was recognized that 'a man who is his own lawyer has a fool for a client.' The reason for this is that soundness of judgment is easily obscured by self-interest."

One emerging way to do some of your own legal work is through computer networks such as America Online, CompuServe, and others, many of which have legal bulletin boards. You can swap advice (or horror stories) and perhaps get a referral. You might even find your way into an electronic law library. The Legal Ease library of the state of Washington, for instance, has all of Washington's laws and regulations available via modem, as well as many standard legal forms. In the end, it's best to double-check whatever you've found out or done for yourself with a lawyer, but you may well prune back your bill by going solo at least part of the way.

Take Miles E. Crawford, for example. He used the Legal Ease library to draw up the papers necessary to set up a corporation. He then asked an attorney to review the matter. "He wasn't exactly pleased. I think he was expecting to make more money," Crawford told *The Wall Street Journal*.

"They come in for the conference and one lawyer says 'I want this and I want this' and the other lawyer says 'Why didn't you ask me?' And then the first lawyer says, 'Because seven weeks ago I tried to call you and you didn't call me back.' And I say to him 'Well, will you give it to him?' and he says, 'Of course I will.'

They've just spent three hours of the client's time over something that was not an issue at all—it was an absolute non-issue."

Second, it's relatively easy to bury hidden charges in bills or retainer agreements: One woman in the Consumer Affairs divorce study was billed for the time she spent organizing her own file at the lawyer's office; another was billed for phone calls she never received because she wasn't at home; and another told about a clause hidden in her lawyer's retainer agreement that would require her to pay a "penalty fee" if she and her husband reconciled.

Third is the fudge factor. Professor Rhode cites such abuses as billing two clients for the same time, charging for unnecessary work, or failing to disclose the basis of a bill. She cites a national survey of lawyers which revealed that a quarter of respondents had billed more hours than they actually worked. About half of those who responded denied that they had padded bills but believed that other lawyers did.

Unreturned phone calls and general unresponsiveness are among the most common and deserved complaints clients have about their lawyers. This can particularly be a problem with legal service plans. Ask whether the plan has lawyers on staff who actually handle members' questions or whether you'll simply be referred out to a lawyer on a list. Not surprisingly, the latter situation does not always provide the best incentive for the lawyer to answer your calls. John Prince of Fort Walton Beach, Florida, told *The Wall Street Journal* in 1991 that he called his lawyer three times in one week identifying himself as a member of Montgomery Ward's Signature Group legal services plan. He was told the lawyer was "out" each time and never received a return call.

On the other hand, at a price upward of $2 a minute and a mini-mum billing time of six minutes, ignoring your possibly overzealous calls may actually be saving you a bundle. Take the San Francisco man who complained to the San Francisco Bar Association's Legal Referral Service, from which he'd gotten his lawyer's name. He claimed the lawyer not only wouldn't return his calls but also that his bill was climbing too high too fast; when the director of the referral service called to investigate, the lawyer said that the man insisted on calling at least every other day and that there was no movement on the case because of the opposing party's delaying tactics. The lawyer wasn't returning the calls because he didn't want to add needless charges to the man's bill.

Fee-based arrangements, essentially kickbacks, between lawyers, doctors and lawyers, or mental health professionals and lawyers. If a professional of one kind or another recommends a lawyer to you, ask about the basis of the recommendation. It may be hard to get the truth, but you certainly won't get it if you don't ask. Look for legitimate recommendations: the lawyer who tells you that she's opposed her colleague yet been impressed with his understanding of the relevant legal precedent; the doctor who says that he's been an expert witness on cases the lawyer was arguing (and that he understands the medical aspects of cases like yours); the therapist who tells you that the lawyer has a good sense about how to deal with soon-to-be ex-husbands like yours and respects the privacy of clients. Ethical guidelines prohibit doctors from taking fees for making referrals, but lawyers' guidelines merely require that they affirmatively divulge the fact they are getting a fee.

People impersonating lawyers. Courts, bar associations, and attorneys general across the country receive complaints each year about people who misrepresent themselves as lawyers. Call your local courthouse or bar association to confirm that your lawyer is licensed to practice and in good standing. Or consult the *Martindale-Hubbell Law Directory*, available in your local library.

Legal services plans. Since the advantages of legal services plans are similar to those of HMOs, it's not surprising that some of the pitfalls are, too.

Ask about the qualifications of the plan's lawyers. If the plan will take any lawyer who agrees to the set fee schedule without screening them, you're simply paying a finder's fee rather than getting a well-thought-out referral to an appropriate professional. And don't sign up for a plan that won't let you switch lawyers if you are not satisfied with the work being performed on your case. Beware of additional charges; for instance, what happens if the contract you need reviewed runs over the eight-page limit?

Gerald Mann, former president of the American Bar Association–affiliated American Pre-Paid Legal Services Institute, cautions people to read the plan carefully: "Some plans never do a 'simple' will or divorce, which would be free, because the definition of what constitutes a

simple matter takes virtually all wills or divorces out of the classification."

Lawyers disciplining their peers and other deterrents of adequate lawyer discipline. If your attorney cheats or misadvises you, you have a right to sue for malpractice or breach of contract, complain to the bar association grievance committee, or submit to fee arbitration or a fee hearing in court. However, be forewarned that real redress through any of these means is rare.

More than 90,000 complaints are filed against lawyers each year, yet the vast majority are dismissed by bar-controlled attorney discipline committees that most often operate in secret and at a snail's pace. Even if your complaint gets heard and you "win," you won't get any money back. Sanctions run from private admonishment to disbarment, but your conflicts-of-interest-poisoned divorce settlement won't get any larger.

As for vengeance—or justice—know that just a handful of states have open disciplinary proceedings or records. Only West Virginia, Florida, and Oregon offer the public access to prior complaints about lawyers. Bar associations object to openness for fear of sullying individual lawyers' reputations. But in 1991, an American Bar Association commission found "in Oregon, Florida, and West Virginia ample evidence to demonstrate the public proceedings or public records of dismissed complaints do no harm to innocent lawyers' reputations. On the contrary, secrecy does great harm to the reputation of the profession as a whole."

As for initiating a lawsuit, if the root of your lawyer–client problem is that you couldn't afford your lawyer's legal fees, it's unlikely you'll be able to afford *another* lawyer to press charges. In any case, before you go ahead with another legal action, ask yourself if you have the stamina to withstand more motions, more court dates, and, inevitably, more lawyers.

Finding a lawyer you feel comfortable with and can trust is only the beginning. Managing the attorney–client relationship and looking out for your rights is just as important.

Approach your legal health the way you would your physical health. Don't wait until a legal crisis looms to seek counsel. A general practitioner can give you general advice and steer you to a specialist when a crisis arises. Many people end up overpaying "because they usually arrive in a panic" at a lawyer's doorstep, Ralph Warner, president of the consumer legal information publisher Nolo Press of Berkeley, California, told *The New York Times* in 1994.

Monitor the level of hostility between your lawyer and opposing counsel. Lawyers can sometimes increase the level of hostility between parties—and legal fees might increase along with it. This is often a problem in matrimonial cases, but it comes up in business and other kinds of cases, too. Keep in mind the story of a prominent hotel. A cleaning woman for the hotel was accused of stealing $30 from a hotel room. She insisted she didn't do it, and she took (and passed) a lie detector test. A hotel manager insisted on pressing charges. The woman was acquitted in a criminal trial. The hotel then sued the woman to get back the $30—and $15,000 in punitive damages. The cleaning woman countersued the hotel for malicious prosecution and won. The hotel was forced to pay her $300,000 over a $30 dispute.

Try to negotiate the fee. You lose nothing by asking. And although it's rare to get a truly uncontested divorce, if yours is, ask if the lawyer will do it for a flat fee.

Keep phone calls to a minimum. Instead, write down your questions and save them for a meeting. Limit your questions and discussion to legal matters; your attorney is a legal specialist, not a financial consultant or therapist. One focused, half-hour meeting could easily replace 20 random phone calls.

Put your goals or positions in writing and give a copy to your lawyer. For instance, if you are involved in a personal injury case, write down a realistic minimum below which you will not settle. If you are involved in a divorce, note the home, shared custody, or whatever else you consider non-negotiable. This decreases the possibility of a misunderstanding between you and your lawyer, and it protects both of you later. If necessary, you could show the court or a grievance committee that your lawyer ignored your wishes and, as well, counsel can remind you of what you said was a satisfactory settlement.

Work things out between yourselves if possible. If you and your ex-spouse are trying to work out a new visitation schedule for your children, for instance, try to come to terms without counsel and use the attorneys solely to draw up the papers. What's the point of threatening your ex with a schedule drawn up by an attorney if you know you won't be able to reach agreement?

Stay away from any lawyer who bills by the quarter hour. At $200 per hour, getting her on the phone (even for three minutes, to hear that there's no news on your case) will run you a minimum of $50. The most common billing interval is a sixth of an hour (ten minutes).

If your lawyer is working on a contingency basis, maximize your settlement or judgment by asking that expenses be deducted from the award *before* calculating the lawyer's fee—and get this understanding written into your fee agreement. To illustrate how much you can save, take the example of a $100,000 award in the chart below.

Be your own legal researcher or legal secretary. Don't be shy. You can do some of the legwork and trim your legal bills. For instance, you could ask your lawyer if you could go to municipal or local law school libraries to research the pertinent laws, or if you could go to the local courthouse to research and photocopy the incorporation papers of a local business.

Computer users can buy reasonably priced kits for bankruptcies, wills, and other simple legal forms themselves. It doesn't make much sense to spend $400 to hire a lawyer, or even $100 to hire a legal secretary to fill out forms, when the software to help you do the same thing costs only $40.

Expenses Before Fee:		Expenses After Fee:	
AWARD	$100,000	AWARD	$100,000
EXPENSES	-$10,000	LAWYER'S THIRD	-$33,333
BALANCE	$90,000	BALANCE	$66,667
LAWYER'S THIRD	-$30,000	EXPENSES	-$10,000
YOUR SHARE	$60,000	YOUR SHARE	$56,667

◾ Most local bar associations offer a legal referral service through which you can get the names of lawyers who specialize in the area of law you need. Usually, listed lawyers will see you for an initial consultation at no cost or for a relatively low fee of about $25. Check your phone book or call your courthouse for a listing.

◾ If you want information on prepaid legal plans, call the American Prepaid Legal Services Institute, (312) 988-5751.

◾ Read about lawyers in *The Frugal Shopper*, by Ralph Nader and Wesley J. Smith. (Center for Study of Responsive Law, 1992.) $10.00.

◾ Read *Smart Questions to Ask Your Lawyer*, by Dorothy Leeds for consistency. (Harper Paperbacks, 1992.) $8.99.

◾ Call or write to HALT: An Organization for Legal Reform, 1319 F Street NW, Suite 300, Washington, DC 20004; (202) 347-9600. In addition to many other books, they distribute a basic guide written by Kay Osteberg, deputy director of the organization, *Using a Lawyer . . . And What to Do if Things Go Wrong: A Step by Step Guide* (Random House, 1990). It's free to people who join HALT ($15/year) or $8.95 plus $1.80 for shipping and handling for non-members.

◾ Need information about a family matter? Call the Coalition for Family Justice, a self-help group that was founded by and is staffed by people (mainly women) who have been through difficult divorces and other domestic matters. The group offers infor-mation, advice, and support groups. Write to them at 821 North Broadway, Irvington-on-Hudson, NY 10533, or call (914) 591-5753.

◾ Want more information about alternative dispute resolution? Contact your local bar association or the American Arbitration Association at 140 West 51st Street, New York, NY 10020; (212) 484-4000.

◾ Refer to *The Consumer Reports Law Book: Your Guide to Resolving Everyday Legal Problems*, by Carol Haas and the editors of Consumer Reports Books. 1994; $29.95.

◾ Read *The Consumer's Guide to Understanding and Using the Law*, by Daniel Johnson. (Betterway Books, 1994) $14.95.

◾ Get *Representing Yourself: What You Can Do Without a Lawyer*, by Kenneth Lasson and the Public Citizen Litigation Group. (Farrar Straus Giroux, 1983.) It's available for $12.95 by writing to Public Citizen, Publications Department, Suite 600, 2000 P Street NW, Washington, DC 20036. A new edition is expected in late 1995 from New American Library/Dutton.

◾ Nolo Press, 950 Parker Street, Berkeley, CA 94710, is the largest publisher of self-help legal guides. Look for them in bookstores or call for a free catalogue: (800) 992-NOLO; (800) 445-NOLO in California.

◾ Your local bar association most likely has a grievance committee and/or a fee arbitration panel. Call your county courthouse or the bar association to inquire about the options in your area.

CHAPTER 52

EMPLOYMENT AGENCIES

Doing a Job on You

T he American job market is changing dramatically. The company man who got a job in a large manufacturing enterprise and rose through the ranks over the years has become something of a relic. Americans who are entering the work force now can expect to change jobs an average of eight times during their working lives. At the same time, corporations facing foreign competition are turning into leaner and meaner organizations in which every employee must show that his or her job is essential.

In this demanding market, Americans at all levels are likely to turn to employment agencies in record numbers. If you've seen the movie *Dave*, you may think it's a good thing: Kevin Kline plays the owner of a temp agency who fights hard—and with success—for the downtrodden who come to him. But outside Hollywood, things are not so simple.

Employment agencies fulfill a critical function; they bring together employer and job-seeker to the benefit of both. But some have

unconscionably chosen to hit people when they're down and out: Complaints against employment agencies rose 28% in New York City between 1990 and 1992. Having to look for a job in a recession or a tight job market is bad enough without the added insult of being tricked into paying a fee up front for no service or interviewing with an intermediary when you think you're talking to an actual potential employer.

THE BASICS

U nfortunately, you can't expect Uncle Sam to help you sort things out. Although federal laws govern such areas as employment discrimination and the minimum wage, employment agencies aren't subject to any federal regulations beyond basic consumer laws on deceptive trade practice. And regulations at the state level run the gamut from nonexistent (Florida) to comprehensive (Pennsylvania and Illinois).

Therefore, if you're not ready to familiarize yourself with your state or local laws—always a good idea—your best bet is to be vigilant and get to know the tricks of the trade. For all the complexity and diversity of the industry, it all comes down to one question: Who's offering what, and for how much?

Have You Found What You're Looking for?

The first issue is, what services does the company offer you? Agencies can help you obtain jobs in two different ways:

- *Employment agencies* will put you in touch with actual employers and/or provide job listings.
- *Career counseling services* generally try to help you sharpen your appeal to potential employers and become more "marketable." Services they provide include teaching you how to write a strong cover letter and resumé, helping you interview better, and counseling you in a new career path. They may require a fee for those services independently of finding a job.

Some companies, of course, offer both types of services. You should

> "**V**ictims of recession need a job, credit, and to save their home from foreclosure. You would think that these would be the last people con artists would prey upon. But because they are especially vulnerable, they're prepared to take risks to get the things they need, and that's what con artists take advantage of."
>
> —STEPHEN BROBECK,
> Executive Director, Consumer
> Federation of America

look for a firm with a track record in your line of business. If an agency actually presents you with lists of jobs or companies, find out where the listings are coming from. While most agencies will put you in touch with legitimate employers who are currently looking to fill positions that match your skills, beware of the following schemes:

- Some agencies offer little more than a "resumé service"—meaning they'll mail bundles of your (unsolicited) resumés to companies selected more or less at random. It doesn't take a genius to put together a lot of names: All you need to do is to go to the library and photocopy pages from corporate directories. If that's all the agency does for you, you can probably save yourself a fee by cutting out the middleman and doing the job yourself.
- An agency may present you with a list of actual job openings that fit your profile. The question is, how current is the list? Are the referrals to employers with *current* job openings or employers who listed job openings in the past? Where did they get the listings? Were they contacted by employers,

or did they simply pull the jobs from last Sunday's classified or other publicly available lists?

■ Finally, as the National Association of Consumer Agency Administrators and Consumer Federation of America have reported, "some companies sell unemployed workers lists of jobs that don't exist, and charge these individuals several hundred dollars each." Be especially wary of agencies that promise you the moon in some far-away land for a "modest fee." All you'll get is a castle in the air: Only an estimated 2% of customers of companies promising a job paying $70,000 or more in an exotic locale ever get one, and refunds are rare. Consumer watchdogs estimate that overseas-job scams rake in at least $100 million a year.

Shortly after Operation Desert Storm, Pennsylvania's attorney general at the time, Ernie Preate, went after two such companies, Jobs Overseas and Patriot Promotions, for selling lists for up to $24.50 that supposedly contained thousands of skilled and unskilled job opportunities in Kuwait, paying up to $87 an hour. In fact, the only link between the jobs listed and the Kuwaiti desert was that you could see mirages in both. The state's investigation revealed that most of the companies listed did not have contracts for work in the Persian Gulf, and the few that did hired only for highly specialized positions like oil field firefighter.

Similarly, in February 1993, Florida's attorney general filed suit against two employment agencies, New Career Services and Roblan, for promising high-paying jobs overseas for fees of $295 and $150 to $300, respectively. Of course, they were quick to collect the fees but unable to come up with any jobs.

Your Treat or Mine?

Before signing anything, be very clear about who'll pick up the tab.

Contingency-fee or retainer-fee agencies: The company looking to fill a position usually pays a fee to find someone for the job—often, a percentage of the new employee's first year's salary (25% to 45%). These are the so-called "headhunters," the executive-search companies that were an integral part of the go-go 1980s.

Employer-pay agencies are typically subject to little regulation. The theory, as one Michigan official explains, is that "businesses who pay the fees have the wherewithal to investigate companies and don't really need state government looking out for their interest in hiring a legitimate firm."

Be aware that if you obtain a job through a retainer-fee agency, you may be required to stay on the job for a certain duration—usually a year—or you will be responsible for all or part of the fee.

Applicant-pay agencies: Some agencies expect the job seeker to pay a fee—as much as 15% to 20% of the first year's salary. If you are required to pay, make sure you know what you're paying for. For instance, do you pay the fee to get your resumé in shape—or to find a

WHO'S THE BOSS?

You may end up contacting an employment agency without realizing it. In 1991, the NYC Department of Consumer Affairs revealed that many agencies run classified ads identical to those placed by employers. The goal: to lure job-seekers with a nonexistent job listing, then redirect them to another, perhaps less desirable, job opportunity. Some agencies failed to identify themselves even after undercover inspectors called.

But the *chutzpah* award goes to the Career Resource Center, which placed ads in newspaper "help wanted" sections for job openings with the Pennsylvania Turnpike Commission and U.S. Postal Service that were simply not available. Job-seekers who responded to the ads were asked to pay $40 for a job application and other purported employment information and they got nothing in return.

---

job? Do you pay before or after the services are provided? Do you have to pay even if you don't find a job? What if you find a job and it's not satisfactory? What is the agency's refund policy?

State governments are a lot more likely to regulate agencies when the applicant pays the fee. Regulations include licensing requirements, mandatory posting of bonds, refund requirement if the employee is terminated within a certain time, employment advertising disclosure requirements, and bans on advance fees or mandatory tie-ins with services like resumé preparation.

Finally, some agencies require *both* employer and employee to pay a fee.

Temp Agencies

Temporary help agencies are a breed apart in the world of employment agencies, even though many agencies offer both job referral and temporary assignments. You can become a "temp" by registering with a temp agency, filling out an application, taking any qualifying tests—such as word processing skills, for example—and receiving whatever training is required. You are then sent on assignment with another corporation. But as the fee structure makes clear, the "temp's" contractual relationship remains with the agency: The company for which the person works pays a fee to the temp agency, which in turn pays the worker.

One of the most striking phenomena of the changing labor market is the growth of temp services. Temporary employment has doubled since 1986 to become a $14 billion industry. According to the Bureau of Labor Statistics, nearly 1.5 million people were working through temp agencies on any given day in January 1993—and their ranks are predicted to rise 50% within five years.

Why are companies increasingly turning to temp work? For one, it gives corporations the flexibility to adjust their work force to shifting economic conditions. But in addition, corporations turn to temps to eliminate the costs of fringe benefits like vacations, pensions, and health care; federal mandates like equal opportunity and family leave; union representation; and other staples of a permanent work force. Bank of America, for instance, is restructuring its work force so that a mere 19% of its employees will remain full-time.

One consequence of this shift is that temps increasingly receive long-term assignments—and if the company that contracted for their services is afraid of losing them, they may get a permanent job offer. In a National Association of Temporary Services (NATS) poll, 54% of temps reported being asked to continue full-time at the company or organization where they were employed. As an agency manager explains, "It's kind of like dating before getting married."

Another consequence is that temp services are attracting a more qualified pool of workers: "temporary professionals." As John Fanning and Rosemary Maniscalco, explain in their book, *Workstyles to Fit Your Lifestyle: Everyone's Guide to Temporary Employment*, "No longer the domain of clerical staff, today's temporary workers include physicians and executives as well as word processors, bookkeepers, and data-entry clerks." Professional or highly-skilled work-

ers now account for 24% of temp workers, according to the NATS.

WHAT TO WATCH OUT FOR

Employment agencies have become increasingly sophisticated in their strategies to attract potential job seekers—and cash in on their credulous prey. In particular, watch out for:

Firms charging an advance fee. Chances are, you won't get a job, and you won't get your money back either. Diane Callis, president of the National Association of Personnel Services, argues that "no agency should accept a fee up front. No fee should be paid until the individual actually accepts a job through an agency."

Many states ban the practice, although agencies can get around the regulation by allocating the fee for a specific service. But Florida has no such regulations. The result: Cedric Gathwright of Mississippi answered an ad for a construction job after being several months out of work. He called a toll-free number and was offered a welder's job in Bermuda for $70,000 a year—more than he had made in the past five years combined. All he had to do to secure the job, he was told, was send a $295 security deposit to a Florida address. He borrowed the money from his parents and sent it to the company—but got neither a job nor his money back.

Other similar scams involve agencies offering job lists or access to some hidden job market for an advance fee of $2,000 to $10,000.

Classified ads by employment agencies. Classified ads are appealing, if only because your only up-front expense is the cost of the newspaper. But they're not always what they appear to be. Many employment agencies place alluring ads that appear to originate from a potential employer, then bait-and-switch the caller.

Stanley Wolfal answered such an ad touting a $9-an-hour job at the Tallahassee, Florida airport. He answered, expecting an interview for a food-service job, but found out that the ad was placed by Florida Employment Inc., an agency that charges cash fees for job leads. A representative of the agency promised him a job within a week in return for a $95 fee. What he got were job leads that had nothing to do with the original ad and that in many cases did not exist or that he didn't want.

The contract Stanley signed was heavy on jargon, promising access to "value-added data," but short on specific guarantees. The agency's oral promises, of course, were of little value.

Temp agency ads that don't deliver. According to Temple University professor Maureen Martella, workers are often lured to temp services by ads promising high wages and then pressured by recruiters to accept less. Often the advertised jobs are nonexistent.

"900" numbers offering job openings or job skills. Calling a "900" number is a de facto advance fee, regardless of the opportunities for job placement. You may not be able to find out how much the fee is before calling and could get a nasty surprise. In addition, if you're charged fraudulently, the phone company may not be able or willing to delete the charge.

Ernie Preate of Pennsylvania uncovered two such companies advertising their "900" job service line. Calls cost $24 and $10, respectively; neither out-of-state company offered a job in Pennsylvania. Preate was able to prosecute the firms under the state's Employment Agency Law, which prohibits charging a fee before the applicant has obtained employment, and to secure an agreement with the three major telephone long-distance companies to block such lines.

Nanny-gate. Here's a situation that turns the tables, leaving the potential employers at risk rather than the job applicants. Wanting to find out exactly whose hand rocks the cradle, the Department of Consumer Affairs in 1992 surveyed 50 nanny agencies in New York City. The result: 45 (90%) were in violation of state employment agency laws. The undercover investigation revealed that some companies lied to families by telling them that a potential nanny's references had been checked when they had not and that they guaranteed replacements for two months. Some companies also failed to even interview the nannies and illegally charged the family non-refundable registration fees (see the chapter on "Child Care," page 421).

BIAS AT THE JOB BANK

Some employment agencies have come under scrutiny in recent years for discriminatory practices or for accommodating discriminatory requests by employers. New York's attorney general and New York City officials found agencies using codes in job offerings, in clear violation of federal and state laws—for example, "all American," "front-office appearance," "mom-and-apple-pie," or "corporate image" meant white applicants only. In addition, CBS' *60 Minutes* sent a black and a white tester with similar resumés and skills to Cosmopolitan Care, a Manhattan employment agency, in 1989. You guessed it: The white candidate was given several referrals while the black candidate was told no positions were available.

THE SMARTER CONSUMER

After you've sorted out all the issues involved with using an employment agency, take a few extra steps to verify that you're dealing with a reputable firm.

Visit the premises to make sure that the agency is legitimate and not a fly-by-night operator or other scam artist. As *Time* magazine reporter Cathy Booth Hollywood explains, "even a small-time boiler-room operation with just three phones can take in $5,000 a day."

Get references. Ask if you can speak to a few clients who recently obtained jobs.

Check the agency's professional affiliations. Reputable associations include the National Association of Personnel Services (NAPS); the National Association of Temporary Workers, the Society for Human Resource Managers; and the American Management Association. The NAPS, for instance, offers a two-day certification exam for personnel consultants with at least two years' experience.

Take a copy of the contract home and read it carefully before committing to anything or making any payment. Again, make sure that all the promises and guarantees you received are in writing.

Before signing on with a temp agency, keep a few things in mind:

Look for a temp agency in your field of work. Some agencies are becoming highly specialized in such fields as health care support workers or electronics technicians.

Find out what benefits the agency offers. If you temp, the temp service *is* your employer. Therefore, you should look not just at how much cash you'll be making but what, if any, benefits you'll receive—vacation, health insurance, bonuses, pay raises, etc. The package you get will typically depend on the number of hours worked. While most temp services provide access to group-insurance policies, you may have to pay for it yourself. However, some agencies, trying to encourage the professionalization of the temp industry, are offering more generous benefits packages.

Manpower Inc., for instance, pays 50% of health insurance premiums for employees who have worked at least 300 hours. And MacTemps offers full benefits—health, dental, long-term disability, a 401(k) retirement plan, paid holidays, and vacation bonuses—to full-time temps (over 2,000 hours a year) and partial benefits to temps working at least 1,000 hours a year.

Keep looking for full-time employment. The main character of the 1993 film *The Temp* tries to kill her way to a permanent position with a paper shredder, a noose, and a bee with a wicked sting, among other weapons. While it doesn't have to be that bad, temp work is at best an inadequate substitute for a perma-

nent position—unless you need flexible assignments for personal reasons. Temps often receive lower wages and fewer benefits than full-time workers and lack the security of full-time employment—relative as that has become.

▪ Don't forget about free sources for employment opportunities: *legitimate* newspaper classified ads, local human resource agencies, library listings, and college placement offices. And possibly the most valuable of all: networking—with friends, former colleagues, or alumni groups, for instance.

▪ To complain or launch an investigation, contact your state attorney general, local consumer office, Better Business Bureau, the consumer office where the firm is located, or the Federal Trade Commission's Bureau of Consumer Protection.

CHAPTER 53

MAIL ORDER AND TELEMARKETING

Stamping Out Fraud

How does a Robot Culinaire food processor for just $12.79 sound? Or the luxury motor boat you've just "won"—that you can claim for a mere $159 freight charge? Or a telephone call saying you've won a free vacation in Hawaii?

Too good to be true? You bet. These are true offers—and truly scams. The "food processor" turned out to be a hand-operated gizmo with a rotary blade, and the motor boat was really just an inflatable raft with a battery-powered motor. The vacation in Hawaii didn't materialize—unless consumers first spent thousands of their hard-earned dollars on merchandise.

Millions of other consumers have received notification that they "will definitely receive either an S-10 Chevy Blazer or $5,000 CASH for attending a sales presentation," as promised by Precision Mailers of Minnesota. In fact, according to a Federal Trade Commission (FTC) investigation, consumers received prizes of minimal value, such as a 35-mm camera (worth about $10)

or a "wide-screen projection system" that turned out to be a mirrored plywood box and a 13" television for which consumers had to pay $200.

While outright misrepresentation is the exception rather than the rule, it's an all-too-frequent exception. The National Association of Attorneys General estimates that telemarketing and mail-order fraud of all kinds steal upward of $10 billion from consumers every year. Still, it's easy enough to avoid the scams if you shop through the mail and by telephone sensibly and defensively.

THE BASICS

Your Rights

Almost 100 million people order products or services by phone or mail each year. Most of these transactions go smoothly, thanks in part to FTC regulation. The FTC's Mail-Order Rule requires companies to send your order within 30 days or within the time frame promised in advertising or catalogues. The clock starts ticking as soon as the company receives payment from you, whether you order by mail, phone, fax, or computer. If the company cannot meet this schedule, it must notify you and send you a postage-paid reply card giving you the choice between canceling the order and getting a refund or agreeing to the new shipping date. If you cancel, the company must send your refund within seven days or credit your account within one billing cycle. If the company will miss the second shipping date, it must notify you again and give you the postage-paid option of canceling the order. (Transactions involving magazine subscriptions, book and record clubs, seed and plant purchases, photo processing, and C.O.D. orders are not subject to the Mail-Order Rule.)

> "*I*n the hands of a con artist, a phone is an assault weapon."
>
> —HUBERT HUMPHREY III,
> Minnesota Attorney General

If you pay for your purchase with a credit card, you are also covered by the Fair Credit Billing Act, which permits you to withhold payment of charges you dispute. You have 60 days to write to the credit card company explaining that you will not be paying the charge until the billing dispute is resolved. If the dispute is resolved in your favor, you do not have to pay the charges or any finance charges that accrued during the resolution process. If you were wrong, however, you have to pay both.

For the time being, you only have to pay sales tax if the mail order or telemarketing company has a "physical presence"—for example, a store or distribution facility—in the state in which you live, or if the laws of your home state require taxation. Thus, if you live in New York or Virginia and order something from the Lillian Vernon catalogue, you'll owe sales tax: Lillian Vernon has its headquarters in New York and a distribution center in Virginia Beach. However, if you live in any other state that does not require sales tax, you won't owe any sales tax on a Lillian Vernon order.

As for protection from scam artists, Congress passed and the President signed the Telemarketing and Consumer Fraud and Abuse Prevention Act in 1994, authorizing the FTC to draw up rules prohibiting deceptive telemarketing; it also allows state attorneys general to sue telemarketers on behalf of consumers.

WHAT TO WATCH OUT FOR

Mail or phone orders. Better Business Bureaus (BBBs) around the country handled over 22,000 complaints about mail and telephone solicitations in 1993. The most common problems were non-delivery of merchandise and goods or services that didn't live up to their advance billing—e.g., the "food processor" mentioned earlier.

When ordering, skip the postal "insurance." It's perfectly legal for firms to try to pass this charge on to you, but it's redundant. The company is legally responsible for making sure the merchandise arrives at your doorstep safely.

Also, be on the lookout for shipping and handling charges. Some firms calculate the charge based on the weight of your order; others charge a flat fee or calculate the fee based on how much you spend. When you take these fees into account, you might find you'd do just as well driving over to the mall.

Sweepstakes and prize promotions. You've seen these schemes. Perhaps you've even been taken in. You receive a call or a letter in the mail congratulating you on "winning" or being "chosen." All you have to do is buy something, or send a check, or call a "900" telephone number (at a rate of $10 per minute) to claim your reward. Ha!

Federal and state laws make it illegal to require a fee or purchase in a legitimate sweepstakes. All you legally have to do is lick a stamp. That's why you often find the disclaimer "no purchase necessary" somewhere in the mailing. And the odds of winning do not increase if you buy something. By law, everybody's chances must be the same.

Here's an example of how sweepstakes and prize promotion scams work. An outfit calling itself First National SweepsBank of America sent consumers a "facsimile passbook account that represents a worth of $10,000," according to

the company. The mailing was designed to induce people to buy things like jewelry and coupon books. No purchase was necessary, but Alfred Raffo, Jr. of Brooklyn, New York, didn't realize that. Raffo sent $15, as a mailing requested, to cover "venture processing, shipping, and handling" to collect what the mailing also said was a $10,000 prize. "Sure you'd like to be a winner. . . . But can it really be true that you . . . Alfred Raffo . . . WINS $10,000." Raffo got a zirconia "diamond" ring.

Not every sweepstakes is a swindle. If you read every word carefully, you'll often find that clever lawyers and layout artists have prefaced the enormous CONGRATU-LATIONS with a hardly noticeable "If you return the grand-prize-winning entry, we'll say . . ." Publishers Clearinghouse and American Family Publishers give away millions of dollars this way each year. Yes, someone really does become a millionaire overnight. But the chance that it will be you is infinitesimal. For one *Time* magazine sweepstakes, the odds were 1 in 900 million.

Chain letters. Any letter or telephone solicitation that requires you to send money to someone in return for more money later on should sound your alarm bells loud and clear. Since you can't win, don't even bother trying. These schemes typically induce you to send money to a person at the top of a list of names with the promise that you will receive many times the amount of money you lay out several weeks later. Lay off. Often the list is bogus, the names are fictitious, scam artists get the money, and your name never reaches the top of the list.

THE SMARTER CONSUMER

Ask telephone solicitors for a name and number to call back, or ask them to mail you more information. If they refuse, don't buy.

Never give your credit card number, bank account number, or social security number unless you are familiar with the company or have checked it out.

Check a company's reputation with the local BBB before you order anything through the mail in response to an unsolicited offer or from an unfamiliar company. Since mail order is one of the BBB's top complaint categories, they are likely to know about bad companies.

Keep records about everything you order, including the date, a tear sheet of the ad or the page out of

BEWARE OF BOGUS CHARITIES

Americans gave away $124 billion in 1992, and high-pressure telephone appeals on behalf of charities that take advantage of this goodwill, known as "telefunding," are an increasing problem.

"You are talked into donating large sums of money for what you believe are worthwhile causes. Too often, the bulk of the money goes to the company doing the soliciting, rather than to a charitable program," says Bennett M. Weiner, the director of the Council of BBB's Philanthropic Advisory Service.

To avoid getting taken in, know who you are giving to before you make a contribution. There's no need to suspect all charitable telephone solicitations, but do ask for additional facts, such as how much of your contribution or what portion of your purchase will be received by the charity and how much of the charity's income actually supports its programs and how much supports more fundraising. Consumer watchdogs suggest that an acceptable minimum ratio is 60% program to 40% fundraising. Ask for a copy of the charity's annual report or financial statement before you contribute and ask for an explanation of the solicitor's relationship to the charity. Send a check, rather than giving a credit card number.

You can check the charity's reputation with your local BBB or with your state's charity registration office (usually within the attorney general's office).

the catalogue, and either a copy of the order form or a written record of the items ordered, how much you paid, the company's name, address, and telephone number.

Familiarize yourself with the return policies. They vary from one company to another; some, like L.L. Bean, offer lifetime guarantees, while others have extremely limited return policies. This also means investigating who pays the shipping charges for returned items. Most often, you'll have to pay, especially if the problem is the item's fit. In cases where the product arrives damaged, significantly different than pic-

tured, or in error, the company should pay the return postage.

Open your packages promptly and make sure that you got exactly what you paid for and that it is in perfect condition. If you need to return anything, send it back by insured or registered mail with an explanation of the problem and your method of payment.

If you receive a notice that you have won a fabulous prize, read it very carefully. If you've won *anything*, it's almost certainly of considerably lower value than is likely to be represented in the headlines.

▪ **The National Fraud** Information Center, a project of the National Consumers League, (800) 876-7060, provides help in filing complaints.

▪ **The Direct Marketing** Association's Mail Order Action Line (MOAL) mediates disputes between consumers. Contact the Direct Marketing Association, MOAL, 1101 17th Street NW, Suite 705, Washington, DC 20036-4704.

▪ **For a copy of** *Too Good to Be True,* a free booklet on mail order and telemarketing fraud, write to the Consumer Information Center, Pueblo, CO 81009. For copies in Spanish, Chinese, or Korean, write to the U.S. Office of Consumer Affairs, 1620 L Street NW, Washington, DC 20036.

▪ **Fraudulent direct mail pieces may** be under the jurisdiction of the U.S. Postal Service. Address complaints to

the local postmaster or postal inspector. Look under "Postal Service U.S." in the U.S. government listings in your local phone directory.

▪ **Complain about what** you think are deceptive telemarketing practices to the Federal Trade Commission, Marketing Practices, 6th Street and Pennsylvania Avenue NW, Washington, DC 20580.

▪ **Address complaints about solici-** tors of charitable contributions to your local BBB or your state's charity registration office, often found within the attorney general's office.

▪ **The FTC publishes several free** fact sheets and brochures on telemarketing fraud, shopping by phone and mail, and credit billing. Contact the FTC, Public Reference Section, 6th Street and Pennsylvania Avenue NW, Suite 130, Washington, DC 20580; (202) 326-2222.

Trend Lines and Fault Lines

CHAPTER 54

WOMEN

Gypped by Gender

The incomes of women relative to those of men have crept up a bit since 1979 when a woman made 63 cents to a man's $1. Now women earn 75 cents to men's $1. That's progress in the *workplace*, however slow. But adding injury to injury, study after study has shown that American women in the *marketplace* pay more than men for many goods and services. Women, simply because of their gender, suffer the double financial blow of making less and paying more.

THE BASICS

The evidence of this gender gap is all around us. A New Jersey woman, for example, once wrote:

"Why is it that certain hair salons charge more to cut women's hair than men's? A friend of mine once asked a stylist why they insist on pursuing this practice, and he replied that it was because most men have shorter hair than most women.

"This, of course, is untrue; Manhattan is home to thousands of men with shoulder-length hair or longer, just as it is home to many women with short hair. These long-haired men require just as much shampoo, conditioner, and attention as their female counterparts."

One Phoenix woman who runs a van shuttle service opened a garage that caters to women because she was so fed up with male mechanics ripping her off. And legal challenges in Washington, DC; New York; San Francisco; Los Angeles; and Boston have shown that women have been losing their shirts because of dry cleaners' discriminatory price policies.

These sometimes-minor, day-to-day injustices don't "harm" women as obviously as workplace harassment, job bias, or discriminatory lending practices, but these overcharges add up to additional per-capita expenditures of hundreds of dollars a year. They create a commercial environment that simultaneously woos women with smooth sales pitches and targeted advertising but then discriminates against them in practice. Say we were talking about a car wash: Would anyone be able to get away with charging women more than men for a car wash? So why tolerate gender-based pricing for dry cleaning, haircuts, auto sales, or repairs?

WHAT TO WATCH OUT FOR

A mixture of outdated stereotypes, unscrupulous salespeople, "traditional" policies, and a lack of information conspires to require women to bargain harder to get the same deal a man would get more easily or to pay extra for identical service. This bias lurks beneath the rules of the supposedly impartial marketplace. So *caveat emptor*—let the buyer beware—applies especially if you're female.

Unfortunately, women face a lack of information about the prices paid by other consumers. If women car buyers, for example, have no way of knowing what prices men negotiate, they may not realize they are overpaying.

Similarly, service providers in many cities are not required to post their prices, making it nearly impossible for women to know that they pay more than men for identical service.

Don't Get Taken for a Ride

Car manufacturers and dealers have belatedly woken up to an economic truth—women not only drive cars, they buy them, too. Women buy and are the principal drivers of almost half the cars bought every year, and they participate in at least four out of every five new-car purchases. In an effort to appeal to this crucial consumer segment, the automobile industry developed special ad campaigns, offered training programs for the largely male staff of dealerships, and even used fewer shapely blondes in ads and annual automobile show promotions.

Still, women have good reason to dread car buying. Stereotypes persist: Dealers frequently assume women are pushovers and reward men, not for their superior knowledge or bargaining skills, but simply for being men. In a study conducted in Chicago, men were usually offered better deals on new cars than women, even at the outset before haggling began. And the women's disadvantage did not disappear as the negotiation continued. In the end, the prices for women included an extra 52% profit for the dealer, as compared to the price offered to white men for identical cars. Male and female "testers" used an identical bargaining strategy, designed to alleviate any advantage a superior bargainer would have.

A similar study of used car dealers in New York came to a similar conclusion. Undercover female car shoppers were quoted higher prices for used cars 42% of the time. When women were quoted higher prices, they were quoted an average of $396 more than men for the identical vehicle. In the 22% of cases when men were quoted higher prices, their additional charge averaged only $183. In one case, a female "buyer" was offered the same car as the male "buyer" but at a price nearly 11% higher.

While the evidence is indisputable, the motive is not. Car dealers and other vendors who use bargaining to set prices argue that

UNEQUAL TREATMENT

A woman posing as a prospective car buyer was sent by ABC's *PrimeTime Live* to test for discrimination; she was quoted a price $500 higher than a man was for the same 1992 Geo Tracker at a Cincinnati car dealership with the slogan, "Where salespeople treat gals as well as guys."

they don't explicitly discriminate on the basis of sex—the seller's goal is to get the highest price possible and the buyer's goal is to pay as little as possible, no matter what the gender of either party is.

Don't Get Fleeced

Long or short hair, straight or curly, elaborately styled or simply cut, women usually pay more than men for haircuts according to surveys in Boston, New York City, and California. In California, for instance, the State Assembly Office of Research estimated in 1994 that 40% of haircutters charged more for basic women's cuts than for men's. In a more extensive survey, two out of three New York City haircutters charged women more than men for a basic shampoo, cut, and blow dry—on average $4 more, a premium of 25% for a service that costs men an average of $16 and women an average of $20.

The practice is so prevalent and widely accepted that haircutters routinely splash their disparate prices in huge type across their shop windows. Millions of men and women walk past these displays daily never even thinking to question the price difference—or to question their own haircutter the next time they need a trim.

But, as the letter quoted earlier points out, the boundary between men's and women's hairstyles is fuzzier than ever today. Think about Fabio, the thick-maned model who graces the covers of many a romance novel and the occasional *People* magazine. And think about all the Fabio wannabes. Leave aside perms, coloring, or other special styling, and focus on the most basic service. It's hard to see much difference between putting a few layers in a man's hair and blowing it dry and doing the same for a woman. Or how trimming a guy's tresses so they can be pulled back into the perfect ponytail is any different from doing the same for a woman. Is the woman getting several dollars worth of extra time? More mousse? Is her blow dry consuming extra electricity? Or is she just getting clipped?

Most haircutters dismiss challenges to the dual price structure with flimsy excuses they can't back up: "Women are fussier," they say; or "women take longer"; or "women want a consultation before their cut." If these explanations were true, haircutters ought to happily give rebates to women with short hair and no need of a consultation. Or they'd collect a surcharge from men with complicated hairstyles. But they don't.

"How much time a client takes depends on how much hair they have," says the owner of a pricey Manhattan salon. "And I'm not referring only to length. A man's cut is just as much work as a woman's." A Boston haircutter gave a similar explanation to the *Boston Globe*: "We schedule just as much time for a man as for a woman. . . . Most men's cuts are short, but there are just as many details to attend to as a woman's. There's the back of the neck, the sideburns, etc."

The price gap seems to be a vestige of the days when men paid a barber a quarter for a cut and shave and women paid a few dollars to have their hair "done." Those days are long gone, but the discrimination often isn't.

Don't Get Taken to the Cleaners

Laundries in New York City charge women an average of 27% more than men to launder and press a basic white cotton shirt. For suits, women pay 5% more to have a lightweight dark wool suit dry cleaned than men. Surveys in Boston; Washington, DC; San Francisco, and the state of California have shown similar price disparities. In a 1994 survey of 25 dry cleaners, the California State Assembly Office of Research found that 64% charged more to launder women's cotton shirts than men's, and 28% charged more to dry clean women's suits.

A few cents here or there may not seem like much, but discriminatory cleaning and laundering prices cost American women mil-lions of dollars a year. New York City women alone pay between $1 million and $2 million extra every year. For example, the annual bill for a man who has three suits and ten shirts laundered monthly at one of the most biased shops in Manhattan would add up to only half what a woman with the same cleaning needs would pay: $828 vs. $432.

Cleaners say it's a pressing problem. Because of such fancy details as ruffles, pleats, tucks, fabrics, and linings, women's clothing requires some hand ironing that men's clothing does not. Even a plain, white, man-style woman's cotton shirt is more bother because, cleaners say, the pressing machines used by most cleaners and launderers were designed for men's shirts. But in fact, most women's shirts fit on the pressing machines, and some very large or small men's shirts do not. The deciding factor should be the characteristics of the shirt, not the gender of the character who brings it in, as was the case with Barbara Sobel of San Francisco. Her regular dry cleaner charges $2.50 to launder and press her button-down shirts when she brings them in. But when her boyfriend once brought the exact same shirts in for her, the same cleaner charged him *half* that price.

Don't Get Hemmed In

Although many in-house tailors at department stores and boutiques have changed their policies, others continue the long-standing tradition of charging women for alterations they offer men for free.

Michelle Fadelli of Sacramento, California, for instance, bought five suits for herself and four for her husband at Macy's one day in 1993. His alterations were free, and her similar alterations cost $142. When she complained, the charges were waived, according to *The Wall Street Journal.* So the next time you need your sleeves taken up, ask the store to apply the same policy to your jacket that they would a man's.

Divorce Lawyers Deplete the Marital Pot

Women are often denied a fighting chance for their rightful share of marital assets. The American adversarial legal system and equitable distribution laws in effect in many states (that result in lengthy investigations or litigation to evaluate marital assets) encourage enormous legal fees and financial exploitation of women when marriages are dissolved. Too often, divorce lawyers care more about fees than clients; consequently, the matrimonial law system either impoverishes women or prices them out of fair divorce settlements. A 1992 investigation of New York's divorce process by the NYC Department of Consumer Affairs identified the following trouble spots:

- Nonrefundable legal retainers;
- Overcharges and underperformance;
- Excessive litigation, delaying tactics, and motion churning;
- Perjury regarding assets valuation;
- Faustian bargains on the eve of a

trial, when the client has no choice but to sign a promissory note; and
- "Retaining liens," which essentially hold a client and her file hostage, even after the lawyer has been dismissed.

In response, the state's highest judge appointed a panel to examine the conduct of lawyers in matrimonial actions and eventually enacted a sweeping set of reforms that should protect women from losing their homes when their marriages end. (The chapter on "Lawyers," page 483, offers a more detailed discussion of this problem—and how to guard against it.)

Don't Get Denied Credit

Women, especially those widowed or divorced, often have a difficult time getting credit because they don't have a "visible" credit history. Even though most have made responsible credit transactions, their husband's name, not theirs, is the one on file with the credit reporting agencies that often serve as unworthy gatekeepers of credit.

To avoid becoming invisible in the financial world, married women should make a point of building their own financial history and credit ratings. Most credit card companies don't charge extra to put two names on an account. Even better, you can put some of the household bills—telephone, gas, electric, water, etc.—in your name. Be responsible and pay on time to build your own solid and independent financial history.

Savvy Savers

Since most women earn less than most men, they contribute less to pensions and Social Security. This, combined with the fact that most women outlive most men, increases women's need to save for their retirement. But it turns out single women are much worse off than married people or single men when it comes to retirement planning, according to Arthur D. Little financial consultants. And since social scientists predict that perhaps half of the marriages made since 1983 will end in divorce anyway, marriage does not necessarily provide cover.

Women must address this issue, but not at the risk of losing their savings or achieving only modest returns on their investments. Investment advisers have become aware of this fact and have begun offering seminars targeted at women. Be sure to do *independent* research before you buy anything. Read the chapters on mutual funds and retirement investing in this book to get started.

THE SMARTER CONSUMER

Civil rights laws enacted by the U.S. in the 1960s outlaw discrimination on the basis of race and gender in employment and housing. However, federal civil rights laws governing the sale of goods and services don't specifically protect women. State and local human rights laws, where they have been enacted, fill in the gap.

But even in places like New York, California, and Boston, where laws prohibit *de jure* gender-based bias, price disparities persist. Since every customer strikes her or his own deal, the nature of the car-buying process makes it difficult to document discrimination; although many haircutters post disparate prices on signs and in windows for all to see, the status has been quo for so long that it barely registers as bias, even to its victims. After the New York City Commission on Human Rights sued several dozen haircutters and cleaners, prices changed and the signs started coming down.

Educating yourself and speaking up for yourself are your best defenses against discrimination.

Buy on the merits of the deal, not the gender of the seller. A woman won't necessarily be any more sympathetic than a man, and she could be just as greedy as the next guy.

Don't go to a car dealer until you've done your homework, and don't be bashful about making it clear you know what you're talking about. (Read the chapters on buying new and used cars, pages 227 and 236, to get started.)

Understand before you sign. Don't sign any contracts to buy a car, retain a lawyer, or engage a home improvement contractor unless and until you have added clauses to protect yourself and understand every word. If you have any doubts, have someone you trust give it a second read.

Get an estimate before you authorize repair work on your car or home. And never sign a blank work order.

Don't be afraid to speak up. If you aren't happy with the price or the service being provided—whether it's a haircut, a routine transmission replacement, or a major legal matter like a divorce—you have an absolute right to complain. The provider will often drop the price or work a little faster to assure your repeat business or good reference, and to avoid having irate customers complaining to legal authorities or the media. If you can't settle the disagreement satisfactorily, go over the provider's head to the manager or to local and state consumer authorities, if you have to.

As for haircuts, dry cleaning, and tailoring, demand that you pay the same price a man would for the same service. If the establishment refuses, take your business elsewhere. You can also file a complaint with your state attorney general or human rights official; and you could also file a lawsuit.

Do your research. And don't invest your money in anything you haven't thoroughly sussed out. But at the same time, try not to be overly cautious. Taking greater risks can yield greater financial rewards.

■ *Why Women Pay More: How to Avoid Marketplace Perils*, by Frances Cerra Whittelsey, published by the Center for Study of Responsive Law, 1993; call (202) 387-8030 to order ($10).

■ *Gypped by Gender: A Study of Price Bias Against Women in the Marketplace*, is available from the New York City Department of Consumer Affairs for $5, 42 Broadway, New York, NY 10004.

■ *Women in Divorce: Ethics, Fees & Fairness*, is available for $5 from the New York City Department of Consumer Affairs (address above).

■ **If you think you've been** turned down for a loan on the basis of your sex, complain to your state's banking department.

■ **If you think you've been treated** unfairly simply because of your sex, report it to your attorney general's or other appropriate office.

CHAPTER 55

SELLING MINORITIES SHORT IN THE MARKETPLACE

 The Money of Color

In the movie *Boomerang*, in an example of art imitating life, Eddie Murphy received a chilly reception at a Fifth Avenue boutique—"We don't do layaway," says a salesman to Murphy and a group of young black executives as they walk into the store.

There's not much economic literature on the subject, but a bias operating throughout the marketplace injures consumers of color in their everyday commercial interactions. Just to shop for groceries, buy a compact disc, or get a haircut, people of color often encounter discriminatory prices, racial stereotypes, considerable inconvenience, and none-too-subtle surveillance. Take an instance in which the Manhattan restaurant check for a group of African-American diners included a 15% gratuity when the check for a white patron at the next table didn't, or the discovery by a female black lawyer shopping around for a haircut that several salons in Fairfax County, Virginia, charge African-Americans more than whites for a basic haircut.

When it comes to larger transactions like finding a home or buying a car, injustice is heaped upon insult and people of color must also face blatant bigotry or *de facto* redlining (in which companies draw a "red line" around certain areas and refuse to sell to people who live in those areas solely because of where they reside rather than how safely they drive or how big a down payment they've put aside).

For example, a 35-year-old male who lives in a comfortable suburban neighborhood pays $624 for mandated automobile insurance coverage, but a similar driver who lives in a poor, minority-dominated Brooklyn neighborhood pays $777, or 25% more. When producers for the television show *PrimeTime Live* sent an African-American and a white tester to look for apartments in St. Louis, the black man consistently received different treatment than the white man. In one building the white man was given keys to an apartment to look at and was encouraged to apply; when the black man came to look, he was told the only available apartment had been rented earlier in the day.

THE BASICS

It was just this kind of day-to-day consumer abuse of African-Americans that President Johnson's National Advisory Commission on Civil Disorders (commonly referred to as the Kerner Commission) cited back in 1968 as a significant contributing cause of riots in places like Watts, Newark, and Detroit in 1967. The applicable section of the commission's report could just as easily describe South-Central Los Angeles and, indeed, parts of most American cities today:

"Grievances concerning unfair commercial practices affecting Negro consumers were found in approximately half of the cities. . . . Beliefs were expressed that Negroes are sold inferior quality goods (particularly meats and produce) at higher prices and are subjected to excessive interest rates and fraudulent commercial practices."

The cost of such explicit or subtle marketplace bias is that those who have the least too often pay the most; even those who have plenty but are not white have a hard time buying the things they want or need. These irritating, frustrating, and humiliating marketplace practices compound the more well-known effects of poverty, educational inequity, and job discrimination.

This racial reality contradicts the popular assumption that capitalism is a judgment-free system that rewards merit and rejects private prejudices. Predominantly white, middle-class lifestyles are held up in advertising and the popular media as paragons of the American Dream—yet the image makers then turn around and deny the keys to the dream to those who seek them. Praising the market's "invisible hand," conservative business leaders attack government intervention in the economy as unnecessary and counterproductive, all the while they engage in private-sector prejudices that disadvantage non-white consumers.

For example, although people of color make up a sizeable minority of magazine readers, they are practically invisible in magazine advertising. (The few minority figures to appear in magazine ads are overwhelmingly children or cast in stereotypical roles of athlete, musician, menial worker, and object of charity.) While 25% of *Esquire's* and *GQ's* readers are black, for instance, in 1991 only 2.4% and 2.9% respectively of their ads had any blacks. Most mainstream magazines have similar omissions.

This visual belittling and virtual invisibility reinforces the small and large racial prejudices already

INVISIBLE PEOPLE

When corporate advertisers were surveyed in 1992, seven national firms—Calvin Klein, Perry Ellis, Gucci, Estee Lauder, Lancome, Giorgio Armani, and NordicTrack—had zero minorities in over 800 ads.

operating throughout society and the marketplace. Not seeing people of color in ads as consumers of clothes, cars, and computers contributes to the perception that people of color are an undifferentiated mass of bad credit risks, check-bouncers, and limited disposable income. In fact, a third of America's blacks are middle-class and live in the suburbs, and over the last 20 years the aggregate annual income of African-Americans has grown sixfold, to almost $270 billion. The black, Latino, and Asian communities spend over $500 billion a year on goods and services. Rather than cater to this market, however, advertisers and ad agencies bombard minorities with specially targeted ads for harmful products like cigarettes and malt liquor.

WHAT TO WATCH OUT FOR

Many businesspeople have answered charges of racism by saying the only color they care about is green—as in dollars. But the market cannot operate efficiently or freely if the immutable fact of skin color determines the outcome of everyday negotiations and situations.

People of color often face discrimination in the following six areas: grocery shopping, buying cars and car insurance, banking, finding and financing housing, making home improvements, and shopping for clothing and other durable goods.

Shopping for Groceries

Because there are no supermarkets in her South-Central Los Angeles neighborhood, a 69-year-old retired hospital worker walks 15 minutes to catch a bus to get to the nearest supermarket. She buys small bags of flour or sugar, even though bigger packages give better value, because she can't manage heavy grocery bags on the overcrowded bus trip home.

This anecdote illustrates the situation that residents of America's poor neighborhoods find themselves in day after day; they have so few choices about where to buy food that, as a result, they pay more and get less. In a 1991 study, the NYC Department of Consumer Affairs (DCA) found that while the most affluent areas in Manhattan had one supermarket for every 6,500 people, the most destitute neighborhoods of Brooklyn—populated mostly by people of color—had one supermarket for every 17,000 people. Because residents of lower-income neighborhoods are forced to shop in small convenience stores with higher prices and limited selection,

DCA calculated that residents of poor New York City neighborhoods pay an average of 8% more than people living in middle-class communities for a shopping cart loaded with the same grocery staples. That's an extra $350 a year for a family of four. One A&P in Harlem charged 13% more overall than an A&P in middle-class Queens. For example, in Queens, one pound of Oscar Mayer bacon cost $2.49; in Harlem it cost $3.29; in Queens, 13 ounces of Maxwell House coffee cost $2.69; the same can cost $3.59 in Harlem.

This pattern exists across the country, in big cities like Los Angeles, Detroit, Chicago, and in many smaller cities as well. In December 1991, the U.S. Conference of Mayors found that Cleveland and St. Paul were the only major cities that showed an increase in the number of supermarkets serving lower-income areas.

> "*I deals about equality and inferiority and superiority are not simply figments in people's minds. Such sentiments have an impact on how institutions operate, and opinions tend to be self-fulfilling.*"
>
> —ANDREW HACKER,
> in *Two Nations: Black and White, Separate, Hostile, Unequal*

Buying a Car and Auto Insurance

A 1991 study of scores of car dealerships in Chicago found that neatly dressed, articulate black testers were routinely quoted higher prices on new cars than neatly dressed, articulate whites, despite the fact that both customers used identical, rehearsed negotiating strategies to price a car of the same make and model with the same options. Based on over 550 visits to Chicago area car dealers by testers posing as middle-class car buyers, the study, published in the *Harvard Law Review*, found that black men were quoted prices that included more than double the markup offered white men, and black women were quoted an average price with a markup three times higher than that offered white men. So blacks pay as much as $150 million a year more for cars than whites.

Even after buying a car, minorities face an "insurance ghetto" when they try to purchase auto insurance. In spite of a New York State law prohibiting de jure red-lining, in 1992 DCA found de facto red-lining of lower-income communities by automobile car insurers. Simply by keeping company sales offices and agents out of low-income areas, car insurers force drivers who live in these neighborhoods to buy insurance from independent brokers who only can sell the exorbitantly priced "auto insurance plan," which was designed to insure people with bad driving records. This practice penalizes good drivers with clean records who happen to live in what the insurance industry considers "high-risk" *communities* and perverts the intent of the auto plan, which was designed to insure "high-risk" *drivers*.

As a result, many minority customers pay extra for state-required auto insurance based on their residence rather than their record. Aetna, for example, had one agent for every 22,000 registered vehicles in Queens and one for every 26,000 in Brooklyn; yet across the border, in suburban Nassau County on Long Island, Aetna had one agent for every 8,000 cars. Insurance that costs $669 a year in Brooklyn costs only $213 in Ithaca, New York. When New York City officials called insurance agents for an explanation, one with Allstate said, "Would you want to put *your* office in one of those neighborhoods?"

This problem is not peculiar to New York. The California Insurance Department has also found that car insurance is more expensive and more difficult to obtain in minority, low-income, and inner-city communities than in other communities in California. (See "Automobile Insurance," page 257, for tips on getting the best deal.)

Basic Banking Services

In 1992, 13 banks served the more than 250,000 residents of South-Central Los Angeles; in neighboring Melrose, which is 90% white, 15 banks served a community of 25,000.

The story is similar in minority and low-income communities across the country. The consolidation of the banking industry has left large, populous areas with few banks and extremely limited competition. In the Anacostia neighborhood of Washington, DC, for instance, only two banks serve the 69,000 mostly black and mostly poor residents, a resident-to-bank ratio six times worse than the national average of 5,000 residents per branch.

Even if people try opening a bank account at a branch in another neighborhood, they may well be thwarted by the "ten-block" rule. A study of major New York City banks by two state legislators found that most required applicants for checking accounts to live or work near the branch—most often within ten blocks. In effect, this rule deprives many people of color of one of the key tools for participation in the consumer economy—a checking account and an ongoing relationship with a bank that could be useful later for getting a loan.

All too often, no local bank means no savings accounts, no check-cashing, and no loans for individuals and businesses located in the area. When Bank of America closed a branch in the Vernon-Central neighborhood of South-Central Los Angeles in 1988, it shut down the last bank within a three-mile radius, according to Communities for Accountable Reinvestment, an advocacy group in Los Angeles. The customers, who had $31 million on deposit, had little choice but to use pawn shops and corner check-cashing outlets—which do not provide checking, savings, or lending services—for high-priced, bare-bones service.

Both pawn shops and check-cashing services have flourished since banks started fleeing the inner cities in the 1980s. Check-cashing businesses now outnumber banks seven to one in neighborhoods like South-Central L.A., but at an enormous cost to consumers. Checks worth about $43 billion were cashed at check-cashing outlets in 1990, for fees ranging from 3% to 20% of the check's value.

If you think the interest rate on your credit card is high, you haven't had to hock your watch lately. Pawn shop customers pay annual interest rates of 36% to 240% for short-term loans they can't get anywhere else. Here's how pawnbrokers rake in such astounding returns: You find yourself short of money for diapers and formula for your infant; the pawnbroker spots you $10 in return for your watch; 12 weeks later you exchange $14 for the watch; voilà, you've paid 40% interest to borrow $10 for less than three months.

The number of pawn shops in the country has grown over 60% since 1990, and outstanding loans have tripled to about $2 billion.

Finding and Financing a House

An annual Federal Reserve survey of 1991 home-mortgage data found that African-Americans were roughly twice as likely as whites to have their mortgage applications rejected. A *Washington Post* investigation of 130,000 deeds of sale in 1985 and 1991 showed that Washington-area banks and savings and loans extend mortgages in white neighborhoods at twice the rate they do in comparable black neighborhoods. What's more, a separate study by the Federal Reserve Bank of Boston found that even after adjusting for differences in credit history, debt-to-income ratios, and many of the other considerations that determine mortgage qualification, black mortgage applicants were 60% more likely to be rejected than similarly situated whites.

The disparity might be explained by income differences among groups, but the Federal Reserve's survey data showed that 21% of *high-income* blacks were turned down, compared with only 14% of *lower-income* whites. The Federal Reserve analysis also showed that as the percentage of minorities living in a community increased, the number of loan denials also increased, regardless of income levels.

"Everyone here has stories of being rejected [by local bankers]. After a while, you just give up trying to deal with them," said Neil G. to *The Washington Post* about Kettering, Virginia, a high-income, predominantly black suburban community, "In my whole block, I don't know anyone who has gotten their mortgage from a regular bank."

Making Home Improvements

Unscrupulous home improvement contractors and finance companies prey on lower-income, largely minority homeowners and

THE COLOR OF CREDIT		
Income	**Mortgage approval rates***	
	Whites	**Blacks**
LOW TO MODERATE (80% MFI)**	*69%*	*51%*
LOWER MIDDLE (80% TO 90% MFI)	*78%*	*61%*
UPPER MIDDLE (100% TO 120% MFI)	*80%*	*64%*
HIGH (MORE THAN 120% MFI)	*81%*	*66%*
ALL INCOME GROUPS	*76%*	*56%*

*Conventional mortgages approved in 1990; from U.S. Federal Reserve data.
**MFI = Median Family Income (of the area in which property is located).

trick them into taking high-interest second mortgages for shoddy and incomplete home repairs. An extensive DCA investigation of "equity theft" by contractors found that salesmen, acting, in effect, as agents for finance companies and banks, go door-to-door in areas of New York City where they know that homeowners can't afford repairs without financing and can't get reasonably priced financing directly from banks. As a result, many millions of dollars in equity have been transferred from the homes of poor and minority New Yorkers to the ledgers of banks via 20% mortgages or actual foreclosures.

Ironically, the banks that end up with the high-interest mortgages are many of the very same banks that wouldn't lend money to the homeowner in the first place. This has created a dual home-improvement-lending system—one for whites in middle-class neigh-borhoods and another for people in lower-income and/or minority neighborhoods. For instance, at the same time Citibank was charging 10% to 11% for mortgages it originated in middle-class neighborhoods, it was purchasing 16% mortgages from finance companies doing business in poor or predominately minority neighborhoods. (See the next chapter, "Seniors as Consumers," page 531, for more details on this scam and how to avoid it.)

Going Shopping

Shopping malls located in predominantly minority communities have trouble finding tenants, regardless of the income of area residents. Even though local family incomes averaged $38,522, southern California's largest shopping center developer had great difficulty filling a renovated 800,000-square-foot mall located in a predominantly minority community. A mall in Atlanta found similar resistance.

No wonder that 51% black Prince George's county, Maryland, lost out to 85% white Baltimore county for new Macy's and Nordstrom stores, even though Prince George's residents' median household income is 15% greater than Baltimore's.

If the stores won't come to you, go to the stores, some may suggest. But stores sometimes keep African-Americans out. Oprah Winfrey lived the experience Eddie Murphy acted out in *Boomerang*: She was actually denied entry to a Madison Avenue boutique after she buzzed to be let in. African-Americans report that they pretty much expect to be followed around or watched very carefully as they shop, and not because the salesperson has any intention of helping them find what they are looking for.

THE SMARTER CONSUMER

Most marketplace discrimination is not explicitly prohibited by existing law. The civil rights laws of the 1960s outlaw discrimination in a few specific and important areas—employment, housing, and public accommodations—but leave other markets for many goods and services uncovered.

Until there's a national debate on whether to extend civil rights laws to cover economic segregation generally, people must push for:

■ Strong enforcement of existing laws, such as the Community Reinvestment Act, the Fair Housing Act, and the Equal Credit Opportunity Act.

■ Stronger state insurance laws requiring insurers to charge based on driving record rather than personal residence, and financial penalties for firms that pull agents out of lower-income areas.

■ Broadening the use of local human rights laws against, say, haircutters or restaurants that explicitly charge minorities more than whites for the same services.

Individuals can arm themselves with the information they need to shop knowledgeably and wisely and band together to exert the strength of numbers:

Learn the law. Familiarize yourself with local human or civil rights laws. Know where to complain if you think your rights have been abridged.

Vote with your feet. If you're choosing between banks that are otherwise equal, pick the one with the best community reinvestment record. Avoid car dealers, haircutters, or other service establishments that base prices on race.

Organize protests or boycotts against grocery stores that charge higher prices in neighborhoods where consumers of color live.

Use community groups or religious organizations to take your concerns to local officials and business leaders who may be in a position to help bring supermarkets, department stores, and banks to your neighborhood by getting zoning variances or offering incentives to the owners of these kinds of establishments.

■ **The Federal Reserve** Bank's annual survey of home mortgage data is released every October. Look for summaries in *The Wall Street Journal*.

■ *Consumer Reports* publishes an annual car buying issue in April of every year. Look for it in your library, or send $5 to Consumers Union, 101 Truman Ave., Yonkers, NY 10703.

■ **Ask your state attorney** general or local consumer office about civil rights laws that may be in effect where you shop or live.

■ **For copies of the** *Poor Pay More* reports on shopping for food, home improvement contracts, and automobile insurance, write to the NYC Department of Consumer Affairs, 42 Broadway, New York, NY 10004.

CHAPTER 56

SENIORS AS CONSUMERS

Scamming the Elderly

Virtually every shady deal-maker targets seniors—tele-marketing scam artists selling phony medical cures, corrupt home improvement contractors selling over-priced financing, fast-talking insurance agents selling worthless policies. The stories are straight out of the tabloids—or your worst nightmare. Victimizing seniors is so commonplace that con artists have a name for it: "Getting Granny."

Take the following scam, clearly designed to appeal to seniors' deepest fears about medical emergencies: Life Alert Emergency Response Inc. used scare tactics and high-pressure in-home demonstrations of the personal emergency response systems to dupe elderly California and Arizona consumers into buying their exorbitantly priced systems. In extensive television advertising and sales presentations, the company said that it was staffed with former policemen and air-traffic controllers who had special access to "911" emergency services and that emergency services reacted faster to Life

Alert calls than to regular 911 calls. Not so. In addition, the company set prices artificially high so that they could be "dropped" for "special" customers, and Life Alert failed to inform customers of their right to cancel the contract.

THE BASICS

Why are seniors thought to be such easy targets? Two congressional investigations concluded that seniors are perceived as more vulnerable than younger consumers because:

- Seniors tend to live on fixed incomes, which makes many people more intent on cutting corners and getting bargains.
- Seniors can be lonely and isolated, which makes them more susceptible to doting salespeople.
- Many seniors live alone and can't easily turn to trusted family or friends for objective feedback and advice on consumer purchases.
- As a group, seniors have more

health problems and are often willing to try new things to alleviate pain and feel "young again."

To make matters worse, seniors often ignore or dismiss consumer fraud when it happens to them. Like anyone else, they don't like to admit they've been had. In addition, many seniors who are struggling just to get by refuse to entertain the notion that they could easily get taken, which, according to Robert N. Butler in his scholarly work *Why Survive: Being Old In America*, "often reflects the necessary illusions older people must maintain in order to survive as long as possible." Seniors interviewed for a New York City *Senior Consumer Watch Survey* indicated as much; one said "you can't do anything about [consumer rip-offs] . . . and you can't sit around all day worrying about these problems."

How can you and your loved ones be less vulnerable to consumer scams? First, recognize your own weak points—are you sometimes overzealous about saving money? Do you have access to a second opinion before you make major purchases? Do you try to get redress if you've been wronged, or are you more likely to turn the other cheek?

Second, learn to recognize the warning signs of various scams. According to former FBI Director William Sessions, "Illegal schemes are only limited by the imaginations of their perpetrators and by the susceptibility of the consuming public." It's certain that the schemers have proven their imaginative prowess, but you can make yourself less susceptible.

> "*The elderly are vulnerable because their memory is poor, they rarely take notes on phone conversations, and only occasionally ask for written guarantees. . . . Their most notable weakness is that once they recognize the deceit, they are often too embarrassed to relay the events to their offspring, friends, counsel, and law enforcement.*"
>
> —CONVICTED TELEMARKETER, testifying before a congressional committee

WHAT TO WATCH OUT FOR

Medical Quackery

A 1984 congressional report cited medical quackery as "a $10 billion scandal" and called it "the single most prevalent and damaging of the frauds directed at the elderly." Promotion and sales of useless remedies and cures for chronic and critical health ailments predates snake-oil merchants and covered wagons. No matter how many times quack remedies are exposed, vulnerable consumers—desperate for relief, or sometimes just hope—continue to

AARP's Rx for Spending Less

In 1989 the American Association of Retired Persons (AARP) surveyed hundreds of pharmacies across the country and found that "prescription drugs can cost more than twice as much from one pharmacy to the next in the same county—and more than 14 times from pharmacy to pharmacy across the country." Since then, several organizations, including the NYC Department of Consumer Affairs, the General Accounting Office, and the Visiting Neighbors Program, have confirmed these startling disparities.

It's no wonder, then, that prescription drug prices led the list of complaints in NYC's *Senior Consumer Watch Survey*. The AARP offers this checklist to help seniors get the best buy and the best care from pharmacies. Does your pharmacy have:

- Weekend hours
- 24-Hour service
- After-hours emergency service
- Free delivery service
- Personal medication records
- Medicine management aids
- Special labels and containers
- Free educational materials
- Prescription drug leaflets
- Free health screenings
- Discounts for senior citizens
- Generic drugs

spend their dollars on worthless do-nothing drugs.

Worse than do-nothing drugs that cost huge sums of money are quack cures that can actually damage your health. While most "miracle" remedies are harmless, some can be deadly. Algamar, for instance, was hailed by its hawkers as a wonderful new cancer cure, but it actually contained two potentially lethal bacterial organisms. The manufacturer raked in about $120,000 from 5,000 credulous customers before the U.S. Postal Service intervened.

Quack treatments can also inspire seniors to stray from the health regimen prescribed by their physicians. Lena R. of Philadelphia told a congressional committee that she spent over $2,000 and ignored the instructions of her husband's physician because "when he got sick, I was looking for magic." But the regimen of wheat grass juice, watermelon rind juice, and the juice of green vegetables prescribed by Dr. Haasz (who was actually a doctor of *engineering*) at a clinic called "The Beautiful Temple" did not cure her husband's cancer.

The Arthritis Foundation suggests the following tips for spotting unscrupulous promoters of phony cures:

- Beware of "special" or "secret" formulas or devices to cure ailments that are otherwise considered incurable.
- Be skeptical of case histories and

TELEMARKETING FRAUD

Chances are you've received a call from a company telling you that you've randomly been selected as a winner of some product or service—but before you can have it, you have to pay a fee. When the FBI investigated telemarketing fraud, the actual price paid by winners to get their "prizes" ranged from $29.95 to $599.

The FBI's three-year sting identified 548 individuals committing telemarketing fraud and 123 illegal telemarketing operations across the country. The elderly were the largest category of victims. Why? Convicted telemarketers testified before a congressional committee:

> "Retirees were easily accessible by phone, usually at home during the day, and thus easy to resell. We found the elderly intent on enlarging their nest egg, their limited income, and often interested in generating money for their grandchildren."

Once you've fallen for a scheme, you're more likely to be targeted again and again. Telemarketers often buy lists of people who have proven their vulnerability with other tricksters. So how can you end the cycle? Here are some tips:

- **Don't talk to sales agents who call you first.** If you want to buy something, seek it out yourself.
- **Keep your name off the lists.** Ask any organizations you belong to or contribute to not to include your name on any lists they might sell. This way you'll avoid the temptation of many unauthorized solicitations.
- **Look before you leap.** Before you reply to an offer, ask for the company's name, address, phone number, and references first. Beware of companies with only a P.O. box. Before you send any money or give out your credit card number, check out the company with the Better Business Bureau (BBB), your State Attorney General, or your local consumer protection office.
- **If you do get scammed, don't be embarrassed, get mad**—and get even! Report incidents of telemarketing fraud to the National Fraud Information Center at (800) 876–7060.

testimonials from satisfied patients. Look instead for confirmed results from clinical tests. If the promoter won't allow the remedy to be tested, don't use it.
- While there is a legitimate controversy between established and alternative medicine, watch out for promoters who accuse the medical establishment of deliberately thwarting their progress or persecuting them.

Home Equity Credit Scams

Many credit scams targeted to seniors are rooted in credit discrimination against seniors. For example, some finance companies have required seniors to pay off loans much more quickly than younger borrowers—sometimes within *three months*. Credit discrimination makes some seniors desperate for credit and thereby more vulnerable to credit scams. There are two major kinds of credit scams perpetrated against the elderly: home equity scams and credit repair scams.

Millions of seniors are house-rich but cash-poor. According to recent census statistics, more than 70% of seniors over 65 who head households own their own home, and more than 80% of these own it free and clear. Yet the mean income for seniors over 65 is under $20,000, almost $10,000 less than the national mean. Faced with mounting medical bills, costly home repairs, or just an eroding standard of living, these house-rich seniors are easily hooked by the promise of converting their castle's capital into cash.

But senior homeowners can quickly become homeless if they don't read the fine print on their home equity loans. For example, the Landbank Equity Corp. offered 79-year-old William J. a home equity loan to refinance delinquent medical bills. But after paying $7,731 in up-front points and fees and refinancing several times, William faced a $48,000 debt and imminent foreclosure on his home. The federal bankruptcy trustee suspects that Landbank stole some $17 million from vulnerable consumers before it went bankrupt in 1985.

Home equity loans offered by responsible lenders make good deals for millions of homeowners of all ages. However, home equity loans turn into life-time losses when legitimate lenders turn seniors down and a convincing con artist comes along to fill in the gap.

Seniors—especially minority seniors—have been particularly victimized by a recent wave of home equity theft by disreputable home improvement contractors working hand-in-glove with shady finance companies. Here's how it works when seniors are the targets: The senior citizen is visited at home by a home improvement contractor who offers to renovate the kitchen or bathroom or fix the roof or porch for very low monthly payments. Once the homeowner agrees, the contractor pulls out a thick sheaf of legal documents and asks, typically, for "a few signatures . . . just to get the work started." Only the lower right hand corner of each document is lifted, preventing the soon-to-be-victim from reading the full page. What the homeowner unwittingly signs, besides a home improvement contract, may be an application for a high-priced mortgage from the finance company.

These loans are often for far more than the homeowner had agreed to (typically, the contractor gets the homeowner to sign blank forms and an amount is filled in later), and interest rates of an extraordinary 18% to 21% have been the norm. And the contractors usually fail to complete the promised renovation work or do it so shoddily that it actually decreases the value of the house.

For example: In the Bedford-Stuyvesant neighborhood in Brooklyn, New York, an African-American woman named Louise B. was struggling to get by on a housekeeper's salary. She owns a home that needed repairs to the roof and kitchen, and she wanted to remodel to create a rental unit. A home improvement contractor who solicits in low-income minority neighborhoods agreed to do the work and arranged financing with Citibank. The contractor did $6,000 worth of work—and $15,000 worth of damage, rendering the home unlivable and unsafe. The contractor was paid in full by the bank, and Louise B. struggled to make the $760 monthly loan payments and eventually faced foreclosure.

In 1991, *The New York Times* reported on the growth in such home equity fraud in Alabama, Arizona, California, and Florida, concluding that as many as 100,000 people in 20 states had been victimized.

There are several home equity scam warning signs: First, beware of unsolicited offers, particularly from door-to-door home improvement sales people who conveniently carry around second mortgage applications. Be even more skeptical if the solicitor seems to be too much aware of your financial plight—some companies appraise your home and then send you an unsolicited loan offer. Many home equity scams begin with the scam artist promising to give the senior a break or "do them

a favor." Before any money changes hands the senior is made to feel in the huckster's debt. Finally, watch out for lenders who say that they're not concerned with your ability to repay the loan. Catch phrases like "no income or credit check" or "approval guaranteed" might be enticing, but they're sure signs of a scam. Reputable lenders want you to repay the loan; hucksters would rather get your house.

In addition to staying alert to these warning signs, you can avoid home equity scams by:

- Going to a reputable lender if you are interested in a home equity loan. Don't do business with lenders that come to you.
- Having an attorney or a trusted financial advisor review your loan agreement before you sign. Even sophisticated consumers have trouble deciphering the financial jargon and tedious technicalities of most loan papers. Have an outside expert recalculate the annual percentage rate (APR) to make sure it's accurate and to get a "bottom line" of how much your loan is going to cost.

In some states, certified public accountant associations and/or Elder Law Bar Associations provide some free services to seniors—check your telephone book for local listings. Low-income seniors can also try their local Legal Services for help. If you can't find a professional to help you for free, you can also ask finance professors at local colleges if they (or their students) would review your contract.

- Always check the reputation of your lender or home improvement contractor with your state attorney general, local consumer protection office, or the BBB *before* you sign on the dotted line. If the lender can't or won't wait, it's a sure sign that the loan has some serious loopholes.

Credit Repair Scams

Seniors who can't get a home equity loan, credit card, or auto loan are often vulnerable to credit repair scams. But there is nothing a credit repair service can do that you can't do for yourself—for free.

Credit repair services that promise "a new credit identity" or a "clean credit record instantly" are either lying or illegal. "New credit identities" are actually stolen personal identification numbers or social security numbers; using someone else's credit identity can land both you and the number dealer in jail.

There's simply no legal way to erase true records of missed payments or bankruptcy. You can start building a better credit profile by paying bills on time and taking on a manageable amount of debt. And if you dispute the accuracy or completeness of information in your credit file, the Fair Credit Reporting Act entitles you to add to your file a short explanation of your side of the story.

The best way to avoid credit scams? Know your rights. If you have been denied credit, you are entitled to a free copy of the credit report the lender used to make its decision. The lender legally has to tell you which company it used,

where to call, and the fact that you can get a free copy of your credit report if you call within 30 days. (See "Consumer Privacy," page 565, for a discussion of how to fix errors on your credit report.) If you believe that you've been discriminated against because you're a senior, contact the Elder Law Committee of your state's Bar Association or your local legal services office. They'll help you file a complaint with the appropriate agency or initiate legal action.

Finally, you can watch out for senior credit discrimination by being aware of what creditors are and are not allowed to do under the federal Equal Credit Opportunity Act (ECOA):

■ Creditors cannot discourage applicants from applying for credit because of age, race, color, religion, sex, marital status, or source of income.

■ Creditors cannot have a blanket policy based on age alone and cannot deny credit because the applicant is "too old" to qualify for credit insurance.

■ If creditors use age as one characteristic in a credit scoring system, people 62 and over cannot be scored lower for their age than people under 62.

■ If the consumer already has an account, creditors cannot change the terms of the credit or require a new application for credit when the account holder retires or reaches a certain age.

■ Creditors cannot assume that retirement income is always insufficient to repay a loan or discount or exclude income from part-time employment, annuities, retirement benefits, or public assistance benefits like Social Security.

- Creditors *can* ask about and evaluate the applicant's source(s) of income.
- If the credit is going to be used to buy or refinance a home, creditors *can* ask an applicant's age.
- Creditors *can* give seniors more favorable treatment.

Investment Fraud

Unscrupulous financial advisors promise sky-high investment returns—but the only thing that's aloft are the advisor's commissions. Bank interest rates sank to record lows in the early 1990s—often below the rate of inflation—and investment fraud has become more common. With 3% to 5% interest earned on bank Certificates of Deposit, many seniors are finding they can't cover their bills. This anxiety often pushes lifelong savers to become first-time investors. But since many seniors may be unaware of the risks associated with investing—and unfamiliar with the ways and wiles of Wall Street—investment fraudsters find them easy marks for their fly-by-night financial services. They all promise high, safe, and quick returns; require large investments, often as much as $100,000; and involve complicated prospectuses or forms that consumers are told they must sign but "don't have to read."

The Murphys of Missouri, for example, thought they were getting a great deal on a piece of retirement property in south Florida. But when it came time to retire, they found that their investment was literally under water—and their retirement savings with it.

An economy fueled by low interest rates is always tough for people who depend on interest income. Still, seniors who have to earn more on their money can find reasonable risks without falling for frauds. The most important thing to remember is that for every investor who's made a million overnight, there are likely to be many more who have lost as much as quickly. Don't be greedy. Increase your return with calculated risks that meet your investment objectives. To lower your risk:

Always read the fine print and understand what you're getting into before you move your money. Ask an attorney or a trusted financial advisor for help understanding mutual fund prospectuses and other financial contracts.

Be wary of financial fads. Like fads in fashion, various investment strategies tend to fall in and out of favor as quickly as poodle skirts and tie-dye. You'll be better off with an investment that's proved its performance over the long term.

Don't put all your eggs in one basket. Even the best pundits can't predict what the market will do tomorrow. Hedge your bets; accumulate a diversified portfolio that balances investments that do well under one set of market conditions with others that will do well under opposite conditions.

SOCIAL SECURITY SCAMS

Two words get the attention of almost every American over 65: Social Security. Every politician—and every scam artist—knows that a threat to Social Security will mobilize thousands of seniors to fight it. While there have been many legitimate threats to Social Security, and legitimate organizations formed to lobby to preserve seniors' interests, there have also been many phony threats and phony funds set up to steal from scared seniors.

Many of these groups are intended more for profit than politics. Several have been created by the same man: Richard Viguerie, figurehead of the New Right and founder of the modern-day direct mail operation. A 1992 *New York Times* article exposed several organizations with close ties to Viguerie, including the Seniors Coalition and the Taxpayers Education Association, which have raised tens of millions of dollars by sending direct mail to seniors with such claims as "All the Social Security Trust Fund Money Is Gone!" Senator David Pryor (D-AR), former head of the post office subcommittee, was quoted in the article as saying that Mr. Viguerie and his associates "appear to be opportunists who may have acted on the very fringe of the law—and at the expense of those for whom they claim concern."

Before you contribute to any cause, political or charitable, contact your state attorney general or the National Charities Information Bureau, a non-profit watchdog group, at (212) 929-6300. Beware of political groups' claims that contributions to them are tax deductible—support for most lobbying activities is not. Finally, while money can be key to political victories, don't forget to exercise your other political powers such as voting, writing letters to your elected representatives, and attending political forums.

So many different frauds are targeted to seniors; it's impossible to watch out for all of them all the time. Here are some general safeguards to make you a harder target for con artists of all stripes.

Avoid direct solicitations. If you want something, seek out merchants yourself. You will steer clear of both scams and costly impulse purchases.

Do your homework. Being a smart shopper is like being a smart student—but failing the "test" has a higher price than it did in school. Don't play multiple choice with your financial future or your health. Read the chapters in this book on prescription drugs, telemarketing, eyeglasses, and long-term health care to find out how to be a $marter consumer of these products and services.

Get a second opinion. Regardless of what they may claim, few salespeople put your best interests above their own. If the salesperson won't give you time to get advice and think over your purchase, don't give him or her the time of day, especially when fat commissions are at stake.

Complain if you get taken. Don't you wish someone had blown the whistle on the scam artist who scammed you? If you don't know who to call, look up your local consumer affairs office or state attorney general at the back of this book (they're also listed in the government section of your phone book), or contact one of the advocacy groups listed below.

■ **The American Association of Retired Persons** is both a potent lobbying force and resource for people over 50. Call (800) 424-2277 or write to 601 E Street NW, Washington, D.C. 20049, for a list of publications, campaigns, and local offices.

■ **Most state bar associations** have Elder Law committees that will help seniors use the courts to get redress. Look in the phone book for the number of your state bar association.

CHAPTER 57

CONSUMERS WITH DISABILITIES

Battling Barriers

Three letters of the alphabet separate the disabled from the rest of the population: A for Attitude, B for Barriers, and C for Communication. The disabled encounter ignorance and an unwillingness to communicate with them on the part of the general public, as well as physical barriers that impede their ability to get around. These two factors conspire to raise prices and limit choices for disabled consumers. The good news, however, is that this virtual wall is being torn down brick by brick, assisted by a fourth letter—T for technology.

As we approach the 21st century, reports of machines that read to the blind, "talk" to the deaf, and grant movement to the paralyzed seem to appear in the media almost daily. There was the day Bernice Connor turned on her television set and flicked a special switch. Words—the dialogue spoken by the actors, called closed captioning—appeared in white letters against a black band. For the first time in her life, as reported in a *TV Guide* article by her daughter Linda,

the hearing-impaired Mrs. Connor could follow and understand all that was happening on the screen. Computer smarts helped Chicago couple Bob and Joanne Greenberg, both completely blind, score with their business, the Bob Greenberg Sports Reports. They use a scanner that electronically captures printed information and stores it in the computer. They call up information on the computer as they need it, and additional technology, including a speech synthesizer, reads aloud what appears on the monitor. "Tasks such as billing and accounting," reports *The Wall Street Journal*, "which once could have taken them hours, can now be completed in minutes."

THE BASICS

As individual consumers, the disabled must chant the same mantras as anyone else: Comparison shop, get it in writing, beware the deal that sounds too good to be true, etc. But as a group, the disabled suffer from ignorance—that of the non-disabled.

The technology part is easy compared to public attitude. Although growing social awareness has opened doors for the disabled and led to empowering legislation, it has not yet led to a new age of enlightenment.

Many people with disabilities have been called "shut-ins," but they have really been shut out—of employment, education, mobility, expression, experience, and dignity. Education and economics have started to change this picture, as various state and local governments have passed laws that give access to the disabled.

ADA is A-OK

A major advance is the federal Americans with Disabilities Act of 1990 (ADA). Its major provisions started to take effect in 1992. In essence, this law says that people who are disabled cannot be treated differently than others. It also covers people who are in a situation associated with someone with a disability (e.g., the parent of a child with a disability), and it includes people who are perceived as being disabled (e.g., cancer survivors). They can't be barred from jobs for which they are qualified. They can't be refused hotel and restaurant accommodations that they can afford. They can't be re-

fused transportation, state and local government services, telephone and telecommunications service, or even the right to go in a store and buy what they please.

The first item on a disabled consumer's agenda is simply to get waited on. For example, for someone using a wheelchair, a store with steps and no aisle space in which to maneuver is truly a little shop of horrors. The ADA requires making barrier-free "if readily achievable" all "places of public accommodation"—which includes (but is not limited to) restaurants, bars, hotels, theaters, physicians' offices, pharmacies, retail stores, museums, libraries, parks, private schools, and day-care centers. Private clubs and religious institutions are exempt. Whether modifications are "readily achievable" depends on the ability of the establishment to reasonably afford them and on the difficulty in carrying them out. (If the establishment leases the premises, both the landlord and the tenant are responsible for complying with the ADA.) Installing offset hinges to widen doorways, making curb cuts, lowering pay telephones, and installing grab bars near toilets are examples of modifications that would probably be deemed "readily achievable." A modification that would probably not be deemed "readily achievable" in most cases is installing elevators.

> "**D**emand and they must provide. If you can't access the goods or services, they must be brought to you."
>
> —JIM WEISSMAN,
> Policy Counsel, Eastern Paralyzed
> Veterans Association

In 1993, in the first legal settlement involving the ADA's hotel guidelines, New York's swank Hotel Inter-continental agreed with the U.S. Justice Department to make $1.7 million worth of modifications such as adding ramps, widening doorways, and reconstructing rooms for the disabled.

All new construction must be accessible. And any renovations must make a facility accessible to the maximum extent feasible. For example, reconstructed bathrooms must be handicapped-accessible. The law caps the added accessibility expense at 20% of the total cost of the initial alteration.

At first, businesses groaned about compliance; many still do. Then some glimpsed an alluringly large "new" population of consumers—an estimated 34,000,000 Americans have activity-limiting disabilities—to woo. Trade organizations and publications in such fields as banking and the hotel and retail industries talked about the new legislation and stressed two points: Here's how you comply, and here's how you market. People with disabilities are now featured in all sorts of Madison Avenue cross-section-of-America ads.

Compliance can also come from creative solutions rather than from spending money. For example, if steps lead to a dry cleaner's entrance, the merchant can arrange for curb drop-off and pick-up. Instead of printing menus in Braille, a restaurant can have an employee read from a menu to visually impaired patrons.

Try to work it out with the establishment. Jane D. loves to dine at her favorite Manhattan restaurant, but as her diabetes began to worsen, she had to give herself insulin shots before starting to eat. So one evening she neatly and discreetly laid out her hypodermic needle and supplies on her restaurant table and proceeded to do what she had to do. The management was upset; she had "repulsed" the other diners and the staff.

Jane contacted the NYC Mayor's Office for People With Disabilities. They mediated an acceptable alternative: The restaurant would provide Jane with a clean, private

DID YOU KNOW?

■ Companies offering telephone service to the general public must offer telephone relay services to individuals who use telecommunications devices for the deaf (TDD) or similar devices.

■ Almost all TV sets now sold must contain a decoding chip. The chip provides access to closed-captioned programs.

■ According to the 1990 National Health Interview Survey, an estimated 33.8 million Americans of all ages had a limitation on activity—about 22.9 million were limited in a major activity and 10.9 million in a non-major activity. Some 7.8 million people aged 16 to 64 had a disability severe enough to keep them from working.

space—not an unsanitary bathroom—to adminster her injection. And she can continue to enjoy her favorite meals.

Know What You Buy

The world of the disabled is loaded with bureaucracy—government and private insurers; nonprofit organizations; federal, state, and local agencies; and the medical

---

CREATIVE COST-CUTTING

An ingenious cost-cutting tactic has emerged at the grassroots level—the equipment exchange. As the name suggests, people can borrow or purchase needed equipment and accessories (such as hospital beds) at substantially reduced costs.

The equipment exchange also helps people who need "loaners" while their own equipment is being repaired or readied. This means they don't have to be home- or bed-bound while waiting. Also, people who want to try out a brand before they purchase it get the opportunity.

Find out from your state or local office for people with disabilities if there is an equipment exchange in your area. Exchanges also advertise in the classifieds of national publications for the disabled.

---

establishment. In this rules-and-regs jungle, disabled consumers need to have sharp navigating skills and to know that they don't have to accept what they are told and how they are treated.

Take, for example, buying a wheelchair. A wheelchair is a hefty, complex, and expensive piece of machinery. It is customized and equipped with all sorts of appropriate appurtenances that fulfill the user's needs. Like a fine made-to-order garment, it must be fitted to the user's body.

The wheelchair process starts rolling when a doctor, occupational therapist, or physical therapist writes a prescription. The $mart consumer double-checks with the professional to make sure that the prescription includes every single item that is needed.

The consumer (or the consumer with his or her doctor) has to decide between motorized or manual. Motorized chairs are easier to use and less physically taxing to the user. But they cost more. And they're not really portable, since they can't be folded. They're also heavy—maybe too heavy to be tilted by another person, which can be a problem when negotiating curbs.

Another potential drawback to electric wheelchairs may be electromagnetic interference—from cellular phones, radio and TV stations, and CB radios. According to 1994 U.S. Food and Drug Administration (FDA) tests, radio waves caused brakes to release and wheelchairs to move uncontrollably. The FDA started requiring warning labels on motorized wheelchairs in

HELPFUL SERVICES AND PRODUCTS

There's no need to sit in the shadows when an age-related condition, drifts into one's life. Marvelous devices and/or skilled training that can help restore a full life are available from organizations such as *The Lighthouse*, government agencies that serve the aging, and private industry.

Design News magazine reports that at least 17,000 devices are available to assist the disabled, including hearing-aid amplifiers for telephones, a robotic arm for a quadriplegic to use on the assembly line, speech synthesizers, and special listening devices. *Business Marketing* magazine reported on DEC-Talk PC, developed by Digital Equipment in association with Children's Hospital. "When used with a laptop computer," said *Business Marketing*, "DEC-Talk PC becomes the voice of a nonspeaking person as they type into it."

AT&T specializes in two types of products: 1) amplification devices—handsets and adjuncts attached to telephones (including extra-loud ringers) and telephone sets that incorporate these capabilities, and 2) TDD telecommunications devices (also known as TTY), intended for the hearing-impaired or people with speech disabilities. The telephone set includes a keyboard and display screen. Department stores and other chains are more likely to discount these products, but the phone company stores also run sales. Call AT&T at (800) 233-1222 for information.

HumanWare, Inc. provides technology mostly for the blind and visually impaired, and for people with reading handicaps. These include laptop and notebook computer voice cards and an on-screen print enlarger that can translate printed material into Braille, a synthesized voice, and/or print enlargement. Call (800) 722-3393.

IBM manufactures or provides modified hardware and software for people with visual, auditory, or motor disabilities, including Voice Type (which recognizes simple spoken commands), Phone Communicator (which displays what is being said and also dials the phone), and alternatives to keyboard entry, such as joystick and mouth stick devices. Call (800) 426-4832.

Prentke Romich Co. makes communication devices for people who can't speak. The company's AlphaTalker lets the user press pictures to produce digitized speech; call (800) 262-1984. Additional manufacturers can be reached at *Apple Computer* (800) 776-2333; *Digital Equipment Corp.* (800) 344-4825; *Phonic Ear* (415) 383-4000; *Xerox Imaging Systems/Kurzweil* (800) 343-0311, ext. 231.

December 1994, including a numeric "rating" that indicates the wheelchair's radiowave resistance.

Even when all the decisions are made, the process is not over. Wheelchair dealers sometimes neglect to give a warranty at the time of purchase. This means that the customers have no idea for how long they can repair the chair without spending their own money. Be sure to ask.

When selecting a vendor for any product specially designed for the

---

TRAVEL SUPPORT

Disabled people who wish to go it alone might contact the Society for the Advancement of Travel for the Handicapped (SATH) at 347 Fifth Avenue, Suite 610, New York, New York 10016; by phone (212) 447-SATH or fax (212) 725-8253. SATH can give limited information over the phone—such as whether a particular hotel claims to be handicapped-accessible—and provides information sheets with more extensive information for $3. An annual membership is $45 ($25 for seniors and students), which entitles you to free help for a year and a quarterly newsletter. You might have to call a few times to get through to someone who can assist you. They are unable to return long-distance calls.

---

disabled, check their references. If the vendor is licensed, check with the licensing agency to see if any complaints have been filed. Be sure to find out how long it will take for the product to be delivered. When getting repairs, get an estimate that details costs for parts and labor and a completion date. Also try to get a ceiling on the price—it should not exceed the estimate by more than 10%. Request a loaner wheelchair or other product if the repairs will take time.

Disabled and on the Go

When following a daily routine, disabled people learn what obstacles they'll encounter and how to surmount or avoid them. But disabled travelers have to deal with all sorts of unanticipated obstacles—physical ones, such as a supposedly "accessible" hotel that really isn't, and human ones, namely discrimination against serving disabled people.

Fortunately, the situation is improving. The ADA is beginning to remove barriers on the ground, and the U.S. Air Carrier Access Act of 1986 (ACAA) is removing barriers to air travel. To start with, all terminals must be made fully accessible. Practically speaking, this means that disabled people must be able to use the primary ticketing area, that baggage areas—including gates and turnstiles—and the plane loading bridges and mobile lounges must be barrier-free. Each terminal must have a clearly marked telecommunications device for the deaf (TDD). Commuter aircraft with fewer than 30 seats are the big exception to the level-entry boarding requirement.

The ACAA also requires that all airplanes ordered after April 1990 or delivered to the airline after April 1992 to be wheelchair accessible. If the plane has more than one aisle, it must have a restroom accessible to someone using a wheelchair. Planes with more than 60 seats and an accessible restroom must have their own wheelchairs available—chairs that must have removable footrests and armrests to make transferring to the seat easier. If the plane has at least 60 seats and an inaccessible restroom, the disabled passenger must provide advance notice of the need for an aisle chair. By law, airlines are required to tell callers about restroom accessibility as well as any other pertinent information about disabled accessibility.

The ACAA prohibits airlines from requiring advance notice as a condition for receiving services and accommodations, other than what is required of all customers. The exceptions can be reasonably anticipated, such as connecting a respirator to the airplane's electrical system and carrying "hazardous material" packaging for a wheelchair battery.

Once on the plane, the ACAA prohibits airlines from denying disabled people seats in rows next to exits unless necessary to meet federal safety regulations. This means that such seats *can* be denied if it appears that the disabled person would be unable to perform the duties required by law of a person sitting in an exit row—basically, following oral and written instructions, opening the exit door, and moving quickly through it.

Disabled people are allowed to stow assistive devices, which are not counted in the carry-on quota, close to their seats. Mechanical wheelchairs get priority in the airplane's in-cabin stowage area, but electric wheelchairs have to travel with the baggage.

If an airline refuses to serve an individual because of a disability, it must provide a detailed written explanation within 10 calendar days of the refusal.

Accessibility improvements for train travel are still being phased-in. According to Amtrak spokesperson Steve Taubenkibel, by July 1995 at least one car on every train will meet ADA accessibility requirements, which includes a handicapped-usable restroom. And all new Amtrak cars now on order will be barrier-free—although people who use wheelchairs will still be limited to the lower level of the new Superliner cars. Amtrak has until the year 2010 to make their stations fully accessible.

A number of Amtrak stations now have lifts to get disabled, mobility-limited passengers up off the ground and into the cars. Taubenkibel suggests that disabled people with special travel needs—such as the wheelchair lift—call Amtrak 24 hours before their trip to make arrangements.

Many disabled people take vacations with tours organized especially for the disabled. The number of such tours has declined lately, to an estimated dozen or so. Why the de-

GUIDE TO GROUPS AND GOVERNMENT

Disabled consumers can get savvy advice from organizations that provide advocacy or assistance services. If you cannot find a local chapter, check with its national headquarters.

The *Center for Independence of the Disabled*, an advocacy group with chapters around the country, is headquartered in Alexandria, VA; call (703) 525-3406.

Disability Rights Education and Defense Fund in Berkeley, CA, provides information and assistance and legal advice regarding civil rights laws and protections related to disabilities; call (510) 644-2555.

Eastern Paralyzed Veterans Association at 75-30 Astoria Boulevard., Jackson Heights, NY 11370-1177 provides direct services and technical assistance; call (718) 803-EPVA.

The International Center for the Disabled in New York provides outpatient rehabilitation services, helps people with disabilities achieve independence, and provides information and training; call (212) 679-0100.

The Lighthouse in New York City serves the visually impaired by providing information, training, assistance in acquiring devices to aid employment, and an array of other services; call (212) 808-0077.

The National Association of the Deaf emphasizes communications skills, employment rights, and works in advocacy and legislation. Write to 814 Thayer Avenue, Silver Spring, MD 20910, or call (301) 587-1788.

The *President's Committee on Employment of People with Disabilities* provides educational materials and technical assistance. Write them at 1331 F Street NW, Washington, DC 20004, or call (202) 376-6205; TTY (202) 376-6205.

Department of Justice, Civil Rights Division, Office on the ADA provides legal and technical assistance. Write them at P.O. Box 6618, Washington, DC 20035.

The *Developmental Disabilities Bureau* (U.S. Department of Health and Human Services) assists with both information and advocacy services. Call them at (202) 690-5504.

cline? Curiously enough, two factors may be the ADA and ACAA, which are making domestic travel easier for the disabled. Another reason is that regular travel agencies are becoming more proficient at serving the disabled. A final factor in the decline of special tours for the disabled is that more disabled people wish to travel with the non-disabled. However, travelers who desire the company of other disabled people can find out about tours in the Mobility International publication, *A World of Options for the 90s.* (It costs $16 including handling; order from

Mobility International, P.O. Box 10767, Eugene, Oregon 97440; or call (503) 343-1284.)

When Bad Disallowances Happen to Good People

Life would be much simpler if insurers just approved all the invoices for reimbursement that landed on their desks. But they employ people whose job it is to review paperwork and routinely disallow, disallow, disallow. And then there are the errors that can occur. (For more information, see "Health Insurance in the 1990s," page 39, and "Doctors and Hospitals," page 63.)

You needn't accept the insurer's decree. Be meticulous about preparing your paperwork before submitting it. Then check the insurer's response against your records. Private insurers may have an internal appeals mechanism. If not, contact the local regulatory agency. The appeals process can be frustrating and time-consuming, but it is necessary to ensure that you get the full benefits of your coverage.

THE SMARTER CONSUMER

A sweet momentum favors the disabled. ADA is taking hold. So is the development and marketing of targeted helpful products. Both forces bring more disabled persons into the workplace and marketplace. And with a growing contingent of $mart disabled consumers holding fistfuls of dollars, the barriers will continue to fall. Here are some tips to help you advance the process:

Scout in advance. When getting ready to vacation, have your travel agent learn which hotels, restaurants, landmarks, etc. are accessible; where to get oxygen if needed; and what the ground transportation situation is. It can be difficult to obtain exactly what you want in a country where you don't speak the language. A useful book for you or your travel agent to consult is Helen Hecker's *Directory of Travel Agencies for the Disabled* (Vancouver, Washington: Twin Peaks Press, 1993, $19.95). It reports on 360 travel agencies that specialize in assisting the disabled.

You also can call the Convention and Visitor's Bureau, Chamber of Commerce, or government office for people with disabilities in the area you're planning to visit for a list of hotels, restaurants, theatres, and other establishments that are accessible to the disabled. A word of caution about the reliability of accessibility guides: Because standards vary and things change, always call first and ask *lots* of questions. Almost everyone who uses a wheelchair has arrived at an ostensibly "accessible" hotel only to discover steps at the entrance.

Speak up for your rights. If a restaurant or retailer is not wheelchair-accessible, tell the management about ADA, says Anne-Marie

Hugey of the Center for Independence of the Disabled. Let the proprietors know they can modify their establishment with advice from a local, federally funded technical assistance center. Point out that tax incentives might also be available.

File a complaint with the Feds if educating merchants doesn't help elicit ADA compliance. Mail written complaints to: Office on the Americans With Disabilities Act, Civil Rights Division, U.S. Department of Justice, P.O. Box 66738, Washington, DC 20035-9998. While there is no legal deadline, the Justice Department recommends doing this within 180 days of the alleged violation. It's a good idea to first write a letter to the offending establishment and give them time to answer. The person filing the complaint need not be the victim, but can act as a spokesperson or liaison.

Letters to the Justice Department should state the name and address of the establishment, the names of the owners and manager (if available), the violation (failed to provide accessible toilet, failed to provide a ramp, refused to allow a seeing-eye dog into the facility), how the establishment could remedy the situation, and whether the writer has spoken with and/or written to the owner, to no avail. Enclose a copy of any such letter. If you are alleging failure to remove archictectural barriers, try to include photographs or diagrams.

Don't expect a quick reply. Advocacy groups for the disabled have been complaining about extensive delays in conducting investigations. They urge that complaints also be filed with local or state human rights law enforcement agencies, if there are any where you live.

Insist on your air rights. Complain to the Department of Transportation about airlines that violate the ACAA. (Send the complaint to U.S. Department of Transportation, Office of Consumer Affairs, 400 7th Street SW, Washington, DC 20590, or call (202) 366-2220.)

Vote with your wallet. Anne-Marie Hugey says it's a powerful act to spend your money at a business that is accessible. Let other disabled people know which shops do the right thing. Reinforce the good behavior by telling the new recipients of your patronage why you have become their customer.

Go for the right fit. When buying a wheelchair or prosthesis, if it doesn't "feel right," it's not. Disregard retailers suggestions that you will get used to it. Advise the insurer that it's not a good fit. The manufacturer probably will say that they made it according to the prescriber's specifications and the prescriber will counter with a reasoned "did not." Bring them together and make them iron it all out—in your favor.

The "if it doesn't feel right" manifesto also applies to such equipment as crutches. The "notches" that make crutches adjustable are separated by different intervals, such that one brand might fit you better than another. It is not good to get used to a poorly fitting crutch.

Try before you buy. When buying specialized equipment, don't accept just the word of the salesperson. You need to know if the equipment works well for you. Try it out in a congenial setting—preferably at an organization or an equipment exchange that has the equipment up and running or with someone who already has the equipment.

Find out what the technical sup-port includes: Is there training? Is there an "800" number to call? Is there *any* number to call? Does the manual come in a format that *you* can use and refer to with convenience, such as large print, Braille, or on audiocassette?

Again, remember the warranty: What are the terms? Is there a service contract? How does that work for you?

• ***Ability,*** **a glossy four-**color magazine, offers information about new legal, technical, and social developments. It also features "human potential stories about people facing difficulties and living their life to the best of abilities."

The magazine is intended to be a bridge between people with disabilities and mainstream America. The bimonthly publication costs $29.70/yr. Contact *Ability* at 1682 Langley Ave., Irvine, CA 92714.

• ***Direct Link for the Disabled,*** **is a** nonprofit referral service that answers any disability questions. Typical queries deal with issues such as special needs and equipment. Although *Direct Link* deals with all disability issues, most questions seem to come from parents of children with very rare diseases. (805) 688-1603.

• **Easy Street offers a catalogue** that features 122 products, all aimed at making daily life easier. Items include "reachers" to extend one's reach (high or low) and doorknob levers that let you open a door by pushing instead of grasping; kitchen products that only require the use of one hand; wheelwalkers; and telephones for the hearing-impaired. Most products are low-tech and all are thoroughly tested before going into the catalogue; call (800) 959-EASY.

• **Handimail is an electronic mail** system for the disabled. There's lots of peer-to-peer information exchanged as well as some welcome communication between people, some of whom can't talk or move. With the Handimail program, people do a minimum number of keystrokes. Handimail membership is free, as is the software. Contact Harry Brawley, Sigea System, 19 Pelham Road, Weston, MA 02193, or call (617) 647-1098.

• **L.S. & S. Group offers a catalogue** of over 1,000 products for the visually impaired. These items include computer software, magnifiers, canes, "talking" kitchen scales, and liquid level indicators; call (800) 468-4789.

CHAPTER 58

PRODUCT SAFETY

 The Hidden Hazards in Everyday Products

In the summer of 1993, the Consumer Product Safety Commission (CPSC) required the makers of disposable lighters to make them child-resistant. Sounds like a major victory for the health and welfare of the nation, right? After all, children under five playing with lighters cause more than 5,000 fires in homes every year, which result in approximately 150 deaths and more than 1,000 injuries annually. Obviously, child-resistant lighters are an important advance for consumer safety. But what's troubling is that it took more than eight years to repair a safety defect the nation had known about for so long. "It is a shame, because the public believes the marketplace is safe because of this agency [the CPSC], and it is not living up to its part of the bargain," says David Pittle, technical director of Consumers Union and former Consumer Product Safety Commissioner (1973 to 1982).

The lesson is that although a product safety apparatus exists in the United States, you cannot count on it to protect you or your family from every hazard, even known hazards. For example, baby walkers caused 22,000 injuries in 1991.

Many consumer groups think baby walkers should be banned; Canada allows only baby walkers that cannot fit through doorways. Here's why: In April 1992, eight-month-old Chase W. fell down a flight of stairs in his baby walker and suffered a serious brain injury. Although his parents always kept the door to the stairway shut, relatives were visiting that day and the stairway door was mistakenly left open. Chase was cruising around in the low-slung frame on wheels and rolled through the doorway and down the stairs. Most injuries are not this serious, but 71% of them involve falls down stairs, 21% are simple tipovers, 5% result in burns, and 3% result in falls from the porch, according to a 1994 study published in *Pediatrics.*

In all, 22,000 product-related deaths and 29 million product-related injuries befall American consumers each year—at a cost of about $10 billion for emergency room treatment alone. Risks lurk around every corner, occurring where you'd least expect them nearly as often as where you'd most expect them. Toys, lawn mowers, household cleaning solutions, furniture, and power tools, to name a few, all pose hazards.

For instance, about 50 children under age two drown in 5-gallon buckets every year. In the summer of 1991, Tina E. used a 5-gallon bucket to wash her children's car seat covers on the lawn outside her home. Tina took the covers out of the bucket and walked around the side of her house to hang them on the clothesline. About 3 inches of soapy water remained in the bucket. She returned after less than a minute and found her 12-month-old daughter, Alora, missing. Tina called neighbors to help with the search for Alora. After several minutes, they found that Alora had toppled head first into the bucket and had drowned.

If you live or work with children or the elderly, it pays to be especially careful. Since young children cannot always recognize or avoid hazardous situations, they are especially vulnerable to household dangers. Likewise the elderly, who may recognize danger but cannot always respond as quickly as necessary. That's why the CPSC must issue strong industry-wide safety standards for hazardous products. The CPSC's often-slow pace notwithstanding, the standards work. In the decade following the establishment of the CPSC, accidental household injuries declined by 28%, as compared to the decade preceding the existence of the CPSC, when accidental injuries declined only 11%. Post-CPSC, accidental deaths declined by 27%; pre-CPSC, they declined only 13%.

THE BASICS

It's a Jungle Out There

The concept of consumer product safety dates back to the outrage and stir created in 1906 by the publication of Upton Sinclair's novel, *The Jungle*, which depicted the unsanitary and gruesome conditions under which America's meat was processed at the time. Enactment of the Food and Drug Act and the Meat Inspection Act followed shortly after.

Since then, Congress has given four federal agencies or departments responsibility for overseeing the safety of the products you buy: The Food and Drug Administration (FDA) oversees the safety of drugs, cosmetics, medical devices, and all food except meat, poultry, and produce; the Department of Agriculture ensures the safety of meat, poultry, and produce; the National Highway Traffic Safety Administration (NHTSA) regulates automobile, truck, and tire safety; and the CPSC looks out for the safety of virtually everything else.

Created in 1970 at the suggestion of Senate Commerce Committee Chair Warren Magnuson (D-WA), the National Commission on Product Safety finding that "the exposure of consumers to unreasonable product hazards is excessive by any standard of measurement" set the stage for the creation of the CPSC. The new agency opened in May 1973, at the tail end of the so-called Consumer Decade (1965 to 1975), during which Congress established or strengthened a number of federal agencies. The CPSC mandate: To "protect the public against unreasonable risks of injuries and deaths associated with consumer products" by developing voluntary industry-wide safety standards, issuing mandatory safety standards if voluntary standards were not established, conducting research, investigating the causes and volume of injuries, recalling and banning hazardous products, educating the public, and working with industry to create safer products.

To get an idea of the agency's reach, former CPSC commissioner David Pittle and Consumers Union board member Robert Adler suggest visualizing everything you'd find in a large shopping mall. "Except for guns, drugs, tobacco, food, and boats, the safety of virtually everything in the mall falls within CPSC jurisdiction." Estimates range from 10,000 to 15,000 product categories, and the businesses producing, distributing, or importing these products number well over a million.

One of its main functions is collecting data about injuries and deaths caused by consumer products through the National Electronic Injury Surveillance System

> "*It is essential that we act to revitalize the CPSC and stop the erosion of public confidence in the Federal Government's product safety activities. The CPSC is too important an agency to permit it to wither and die.*"
>
> —REP. ROBERT BYRD (D-WV)

(NEISS). Approximately 90 hospitals around the country report the incidence of emergency room visits that are related to a range of consumer products. The data allow CPSC to track broad trends and take action on some dangerous products—such as lawn darts, which were banned in 1988 after causing about 6,700 injuries between 1978 and 1987. Nobody else collects these data, and they support the work not only of the CPSC but also of activists and injury prevention researchers in and out of government and industry.

However, the CPSC's reach too often exceeds its grasp. Although the CPSC has nominal authority for ensuring the safety of a vast array of products, it lacks the clout—or the economic resources—to carry out its mission. For instance, in 1981 Congress required the CPSC to defer to voluntary industry-created, industry-wide standards of safe products rather than impose federally mandated standards, unless adequate voluntary standards were not forthcoming. This move essentially *required* the corporate foxes to guard the chicken coop—not to mention legitimized the idea. After evaluating this policy six years later, the Consumer Federation of America (CFA) concluded: "There were excessive time delays in developing voluntary standards, there was deferral to inadequate standards, there was reliance on non-existing voluntary standards, and there was inadequate monitoring of voluntary standards."

The NEISS data pose another hurdle. Since relatively few of the nation's hospitals are included in the sample, the data are incomplete and lack specificity. Mary Ellen Fise of CFA suggests that "to further understand and prevent childhood poisonings, CPSC could collect more specific information from hospitals that have emergency poisoning admissions—asking what type of containers held the substance and what type of closure was used."

Even worse, the CPSC is the only health and safety agency that restricts the release of reports of potential hazards. Under section 6(b) of the Consumer Product Safety Act (CPSA), before the agency releases information from which the identity of a manufacturer could be ascertained, it must first notify the manufacturer that the information may be released, permit the manufacturer to comment, and take steps to assure that disclosure is fair.

These cumbersome requirements allow manufacturers to intimidate the agency into withholding news of serious hazards with the threat of drawn-out, expensive lawsuits—during which time the hazard is still on the market. For instance, the CPSC began to suspect that a popular portable heater might pose a fire hazard in early 1988. In November of 1989, it issued a preliminary determination that the heaters might be risky, but it was not until August 1991, after negotiations with the manufacturer, that the public was alerted. In the 21 months between the CPSC determination and the public alert, eight people died in two fires that might have been caused by the heaters, according to the lawyer who represented some of the plaintiffs in the cases.

Another part of the CPSA requires manufacturers to notify the Commission if they receive information about defects in their products that could create a substantial hazard. This is similar to requirements of the automobile industry and the medical device industry that they report potential hazards to the National Highway Traffic Safety Administration (NHTSA) and the Food and Drug Administration (FDA), respectively.

Companies must report potential hazards to the CPSC if:

■ They receive information suggesting that a product fails to meet a consumer product safety standard or regulation.
■ A product has a defect or otherwise could create substantial risk of injury.
■ A product is the subject of at least three federal or state civil actions that allege the involvement of that product in death or grievous injury cases and that result in settlements or judgments which favor the victim.

These reporting rules apply to both domestic manufacturers and importers.

Although the public has immediate access to these reports as soon as they are filed with NHTSA or the FDA, access to CPSC reports is severely limited. Within the legally mandated CPSC operations, the public can see these reports only in relatively narrow circumstances, such as when the agency brings an imminent hazard lawsuit in court.

The CPSC has the power to ban and recall hazardous products. Most often, the Commission acts in cooperation with the manufacturer who agrees to recall the product voluntarily. To pick a typical example, in 1993 the CPSC and the Casablanca Fan Co. of City of Industry, California, issued a joint warning and voluntary recall of just about every ceiling fan sold under the Casablanca brandname since 1981. Of the more than 3 million fans sold by Casablanca in that interval, the company had received about 50 reports of falling fans that put people and objects below the fan at risk. Casablanca provided free repair kits with detailed instructions or free reinstallation to consumers who requested service.

WHAT TO WATCH OUT FOR

Rollover Risk

Minivans, sport vehicles, and light trucks are much more likely than passenger cars to flip over when you take sharp turns and corners—some vehicles are as much as 20 times more likely. Take this into account before you select a new or used car. Read *The Minivan, Pick-*

Up, and 4x4 Book (HarperCollins) to find rollover ratings for various models. You can also get the ratings free by writing Consumer Federation of America.

Mop Up—But Never Leave a Child Alone With a Bucket

Buckets, even if only partially full of water or other liquids— especially the 15"-high, 5-gallon buckets familiar at construction sites and in institutional kitchens— pose a drowning hazard to small children. After their original contents—spackle, canned peaches, or whatever—have been used up, many people reuse the handy 5-gallon containers for household chores.

If you have young children, don't leave any bucket unattended. In the short time it takes to answer the phone or to find a mop, a toddler can fall in, as was the case with Alora E. (described above). The bucket openings are large enough to permit easy entry, and the sides are not quite tall enough to prevent it; it's too easy for a young child to tumble in. And even if the bucket is only partially full, the liquid makes it extremely stable and unlikely to readily tip over— which is great for swabbing the back deck, but could be deadly for a child.

The Cook County, Illinois, Medical Examiners Office first brought the problem to the attention of federal regulators. Of the 25 bucket drownings the Cook County coroner investigated between 1984 and 1992, every one involved reusing

5-gallon shipping containers as household buckets.

Riding Mower Mishaps

The risk of an accident with a riding mower is almost twice that of a rotary push mower. Accidents have several common patterns: The machine tips over, the victim falls under or is run over by the machine, or the victim is thrown from or falls from the mower. Read and follow all the safety precautions that come with the equipment. If you've misplaced the literature, write to the CPSC to get a Product Safety Fact Sheet (Publication No. 588, Riding Lawnmowers).

Whether you're thinking about buying a car or a child's car seat, taking something for your cold, slathering on cosmetics or cooking a chicken, safety should

Annual Deaths and Injuries Associated with Selected Products		
Product	**Injuries**	**Deaths**
PACKAGING/POISONING	130,000	42
BICYCLES	58,000	1,000
RIDING LAWN MOWERS	25,300	75
ALL-TERRAIN VEHICLES, RIDDEN BY CHILDREN	19,400	77
FIREWORKS	13,240	5
HOME ELECTRICAL SYSTEMS FIRES	1,340	550
CARBON MONOXIDE/FUEL DETECTORS	1,000	350
HEAT TAPES	100	20
INFANT SUFFOCATION	N/A	200
CRIB TOYS	N/A	2
WOOD STOVES	N/A	24

Source: Consumer Product Safety Commission, 1992

CRIB SAFETY

The most dangerous item in the nursery is a child's crib. Each year, 50 children die in crib accidents. Over the years, the CPSC has ensured that new cribs are vastly safer than those of yore. But that won't protect your child from cribs that were manufactured before the CPSC's safety standards went into effect.

Watch out for bargain cribs you might pick up at a garage sale or have handed down to you. They may not meet current safety standards. And when your child is 36 inches tall, replace the crib with a bed.

For more information on crib safety, contact the Danny Foundation, which was named for a child who tumbled out of a crib, caught his undershirt on a post, and hung himself. Its number is (800) 83-DANNY.

always be a primary consideration—before price, before appearance, before keeping up with the Joneses.

Don't Toy Around

You cannot assume a toy is safe just because you see it for sale at the toy store. Thousands of children are injured seriously enough playing with unsafe toys each year to be hurried to the emergency room, and about 20 die. Choking on small parts is the leading cause of toy-related deaths.

There simply are not enough safety experts in the toy store aisles—or the warehouses of manufacturers, distributors, and importers. Recalls of hazardous playthings can take months, and it's rare that every purchaser can or will be notified. And no number of inspectors can stop or detect dangerous imported toys that are sold by street vendors without any federal review.

When recalls finally do take effect, they are usually so poorly publicized that it's prudent for you to check up periodically on your own to be sure that the toys your child plays with are considered safe. To find out about toy safety recalls, look for the Recall Notice Board at your toy store or periodically call the CPSC at (800) 638-CPSC.

Do your own legwork: Be on the lookout especially for small parts, sharp points and edges, cords and strings, loud noises, potential electric shocks, and hazardous bikes and all-terrain vehicles. (For more detailed information, read "Toys," on page 432.)

Wear a Bike Helmet

Over 50,000 children suffer head injuries while bike riding every year; another 300 under 14 die from bike-related head trauma. And tens of thousands of teenagers and adults suffer serious bike-related head injuries each year. In June 1993, 6½-year-old Bradley M., of Washington, DC, fractured his skull and suffered an epidural hematoma while riding his bike without a helmet. Another child playfully pulled on the back wheel of his bike and Bradley tumbled over the handlebars onto his head. He was in a coma for a week and then underwent surgery to drain the hematoma. After months of rehabilitation, doctors expect Bradley to fully recover.

Wearing a helmet can reduce your risk of head injury by as much as 85%. When shopping for helmets, look for ones that meet standards set by American National Standards Institute (ANSI) or the Snell Foundation (noted on the helmet itself and its packaging). Adults in the household should wear helmets, too—for safety, and as a good example to children.

Wear Your Seat Belt

While the federal government requires car manufacturers to equip all cars with "automatic crash protection," which means air bags or automatic safety belt systems (beginning with the 1987 model year), there is no federal law requiring people to actually use them. That is up to the states, most of which have passed laws requiring people to wear safety belts. However, the laws are relatively weak and almost uniformly unenforced. Even if your car has been equipped with automatic shoulder harnesses, as most new cars are, or air bags, as more and more new cars will be,

buckle up. The shoulder harnesses were not designed to work without the lap belt. And air bags will only pop out in a head-on collision of sufficient speed. In accidents involving slower speeds or side collisions, air bags provide no protection whatsoever. Your seat belt could save your life.

About six out of every ten people killed or injured in car accidents would have been saved had they been wearing safety belts. Still, only three in ten bother to buckle up.

Equip Your Home With a Smoke Detector

The risk of dying in a fire is twice as high in a home without a detector as in a home with one. For this reason, many states have laws requiring smoke detectors, which can increase the time you have to escape, as well as the time the fire department has to save your property. Although the devices have become ubiquitous, *Consumer Reports* (May 1994) estimates that one in three would not respond properly to a fire—primarily because of dead or missing batteries.

The U.S. Fire Administration suggests the following:

■ At a minimum, install a smoke detector outside each bedroom or sleeping area in your house, and keep bedroom doors closed when you sleep. It's also wise to have at least one detector on every level of the home. Be sure to install detectors away from air vents, windows, and other places where drafts may interfere with smoke detection.

- Don't forget to maintain your smoke detectors. Test them at least once a month. Clean the dust that collects with the vacuum cleaner at least once a year. Change the batteries every year, and use only the type of batteries recommended on the detector.
- If smoke from cooking causes the alarm to go off, do not remove the batteries or disconnect the power source. Simply fan the smoke away from the detector until the alarm stops. If this happens often, you might want to relocate the detector or install a different type.
- Develop a fire escape plan and review it with all members of your household. Don't forget to include a plan for children and elderly people who need special assistance.

While 90% of all homes were equipped with smoke detectors in 1994, only 30% had at least one fire extinguisher—even though both cost as little as $10. Since where there's smoke there's usually fire, your household should have at least one multipurpose extinguisher. Look for an A:B:C label, after classifications of the three types of materials that burn—A) ordinary combustibles, like paper and wood; B) flammable liquids, like cooking grease, gasoline, and paint solvents; and C) electrical fires, in wiring or television sets. In addition, you may want to invest in a B:C extinguisher for the kitchen, which will be much more effective on a grease fire than the multipurpose A:B:C: extinguisher.

To find out what kind of fire protection is required in your area, or to get further tips, check with your local fire department or your state's fire marshal. You might also want to contact the CPSC or read the May 1994 issue of *Consumer Reports*, "Protect Your Home."

Report Hazardous Products

Reporting dangerous products will save others from your misadventures or worse. Here's how:

Safety hazards associated with cars and tires should be reported to the NHTSA Auto Safety Hotline, (800) 424-9393. Through this number you can also get useful safety information on new and used cars, child safety seats, tires you may be considering, and the results of government crash tests.

Problems and questions related to food, drug, and cosmetics safety should be addressed to the FDA. If you experience food poisoning, an allergic reaction, product tampering, or other suspicious effects from drugs, medical devices, cosmetics, or foods other than meat and produce, contact the FDA at 5600 Fishers Lane, Rockville, MD 20857.

Problems with meat, poultry, and produce should be reported to the Department of Agriculture. The USDA Meat and Poultry Hot Line operates Monday through Friday from 10 AM to 4 PM EST, with extended hours in the days before Thanksgiving; call (800) 535-4555.

For most other products, call the CPSC hotline at (800) 638-CPSC and be prepared to give the following information:

- A description of the product.

- The company's name, address, and, if you know, whether the company is a manufacturer, distributor, importer, or retailer of the product.

- The nature and severity of the hazard and of the injuries that can result from using the product.
- Your name, address, and telephone number.

■ To report an unsafe consumer product or a product-related injury, or to request information, call the U.S. Consumer Product Safety Commission's toll-free hot line: (800) 638-2772; operators are on duty from 10:30 AM to 4 PM, Eastern time, Monday through Friday. There's also a teletypewriter for the hearing-impaired: (800) 638-8270 (everywhere but Maryland); (800) 492-8104 (TTY, Maryland only).

■ To find out about product recalls, read *Consumer Reports'* monthly feature, local papers, the Product Recall Notices at toy stores, or call the CPSC Hotline.

■ For information about the safety of baby and children, contact the National Safe Kids Campaign at (202) 884-4993.

■ For more specific information on fire safety, smoke detectors, and fire extinguishers, read the May 1994 issue of *Consumer Reports* or contact your state fire marshal or the U.S. Fire Administration, 16825 South Seton Avenue, Emmitsburg, MD 21727; (301) 447-1080.

■ Consumer Federation of America is a national non-profit consumer advocacy organization that has worked extensively on product safety issues. For their materials, write them at 1424

16th Street NW, Washington, DC 20036; (202) 387-6121.

■ National consumer, health, and insurer groups work together in the Coalition for Consumer Health and Safety to educate the public, identify and promote federal policy solutions to health and safety threats relating to motor vehicle safety, home and product safety, indoor air quality, food safety and nutrition, tobacco use, alcohol consumption and AIDS. For more information and for the brochure "Hidden Hazards," write to the Coalition for Consumer Health and Safety, 1424 16th Street NW, Suite 604, Washington, DC 20036.

■ For more safety information, see the following chapters in this book: "Water: Should You Be Worried About Yours?" "Getting the Lead Out of Your Diet: Dangerous Dishes," "Houses, Condos, and Co-ops: Buying and Selling the American Dream," "Airlines and Airfares: How to Avoid Flights of Fancy," "Cosmetics: The Truth Isn't Even Skin Deep," "Lawn Care: Toward a Sensible Greening of America," "Pharmaceuticals and Pharmacists: Prescription for Care," "Cold and Flu Remedies: Chicken Soup and . . ." and "Weight Loss Products and Programs: The Skinny on Dieting Deceptions and Dangers."

CHAPTER 59

CONSUMER PRIVACY

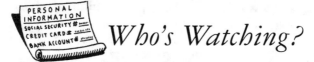

Who's Watching?

The word "privacy" never appears in the U.S. Constitution, yet it is "the most comprehensive of rights and the right most valued by civilized men," as Justice Louis D. Brandeis so aptly put it in his 1928 dissent in *Olmstead* v. *United States*. This is where the "right to be left alone" was first formulated, rooted in the Fourth Amendment protection of "persons, houses, papers and effects against unreasonable searches and seizures" and various other parts of the Bill of Rights.

In the computer age, it's nearly impossible to mind your own business without giving over all manner of personal information to people who are only too happy to mine your personal business for all it's worth. In the normal course of applying for a mortgage or a credit card, registering for a professional conference, filling out the warranty for a new television, renting an apartment, applying for health or life insurance, or applying for a check-cashing card at the supermarket, you surrender many of the most private details of your life. You also—largely unwittingly—part with control over who has access to this information.

No wonder public opinion surveys consistently show that most people—71% in a 1990 Louis Harris poll conducted for Equifax Inc., one of the biggest credit bureaus in the country—believe they have completely lost control over who sees personal information about them and how the data are circulated and used. They're right. Charles Z. of West Roxbury, Massachusetts, was charged 25% more than the standard rate for disability insurance because of a notation in his medical history that he was an alcoholic. Problem: He wasn't—but he had told an insurance investigator about attending meetings of Alcoholics Anonymous, for help in other areas of his life. Take advantage of the low-cost or free cholesterol testing at the local mall, and you may begin receiving solicitations from local hospitals and clinics for special diet programs.

Credit bureaus, government agencies—federal, state, and local—and marketers collect all kinds of information. Investigators for people like landlords, insurance providers, employers, and salespeople cull these public records and data banks to assess your value as a customer, adequacy as an employee. or risk as a loan.

They keep track of information

like how much you make, what magazines you read, how many children you have, where you went to school, where you live and work, your medical and psychiatric histories (and one day, perhaps, your genetic profile, including your tendency to inherit certain diseases), how credit-worthy or trustworthy you are, whether you've sued or been sued, how much debt you carry, your phone number (even if it's unlisted), and the last time you used a credit card. The list is endless.

Most often, you turned over the information for a legitimate purpose, but it's tempting—and in many cases legal—for data keepers to resell information for secondary purposes. You probably can't completely undo what's already been done to collect this information, but there are several steps you can take now to better protect your privacy. You can review the accuracy of the information that's out there, avoid giving too much more information to people who don't need it, and learn about your legal rights to privacy.

THE BASICS

At least 10 federal laws are supposed to protect individual privacy, but they are riddled with loopholes. Meanwhile, advances in computers, telecommunications, and other technologies have made it relatively simple to pass all kinds of information around. Such advances cut down the time it takes to approve a credit card purchase or process an order from a catalogue— which means you get what you want faster. However, new threats accompany the convenience. The same tools that speed your transactions also efficiently spread information about you. So without realizing it, you may have consented to this free flow of personal information when you signed release forms on credit card applications or health insurance claims.

Your Credit History

Credit reporting agencies, or credit bureaus, keep libraries of credit histories on 170 million individual Americans, anyone who uses credit to buy anything. These files come from public records as well as credit grantors such as banks and department stores, which periodically update the bureaus. Employers and credit grantors— banks, stores, or finance companies —use the information to evaluate the risks of lending money based on your history of making payments.

The Fair Credit Reporting Act (FCRA) of 1970 gives individuals the right to see and correct their credit reports and limits the rights of others to look at them. It also requires grantors of credit to explain to loan applicants why their requests were denied. The FCRA prohibits credit bureaus from divulging your credit record to just anyone, but it allows them to release it to those with a "legitimate business need." This is a large exception: For a small fee, a *Business Week* magazine reporter once got a copy of then-Vice President Dan Quayle's credit record. And a NYC Department of Consumer Affairs investigation showed that security hasn't gotten much better since then: In less than an hour, one investigator posing as a landlord obtained a fax copy of my credit history from a local reseller of credit information.

Furthermore, as we've seen, some of the information in these reports just isn't true and it can be damaging. More than one in five complaints to the FTC is about credit bureaus, and the FTC gets more complaints about inaccurate information in credit reports than about anything else. In a small but telling 1991 survey, *Consumer Reports* found that 48% of the 161 reports it examined contained errors, and 19% contained errors serious enough to cause the denial of credit, employment, or insurance. A larger survey undertaken by a credit bureau found errors in 43% of its own files.

Mrs. Lawrence of Boston had a typical complaint: She was denied credit because a complete stranger's bad debt appeared on her report. Just a few months earlier, her son and daughter's credit had been threatened when Mrs. Lawrence and her husband's entire credit history appeared in their children's reports. "Mistakes like these threaten 40 years of hard work and it has been a terrible ordeal trying to correct them," Mrs. Lawrence told the Massachusetts Public Interest Research Group.

It's likely that one or more of the three major credit bureaus—Equifax, Trans Union, and TRW—is tracking you. Periodically checking your records for inaccuracies will enable you to correct any mistakes before they can hurt you when you apply for credit, insurance, or a job. Since each bureau may have a slightly different profile of you, you need to contact all three of the major bureaus. (You'll find their addresses and telephone numbers in the **HELP** section at the end of this chapter.)

In your request, include your name, address, previous addresses for the past five years, Social Security number, your spouse's name (if you're married or divorced), signature, and a daytime telephone number. If you have been denied credit in the last 30 days, the report is free, as required by the FCRA. TRW will furnish your credit report to you once a year for no charge regardless of whether you have been turned down recently. Equifax charges $8, payable by check or major credit card, for residents of every state except Maine ($3), Maryland (one report per year free, additional reports $5), and Vermont (first report of the year free, additional reports $7.50). Trans Union charges $8 per credit

> "*With relative ease and for very little cost, anybody can learn anything about anybody.*"
>
> —ROBERT ELLIS SMITH,
> privacy advocate

record and $16 for a joint record. A copy should arrive within two to three weeks.

Your credit report may look like gobbledygook at first. Each agency uses its own coding system rather than plain English. Use the printed explanations they send with the report to help you decipher it. Essentially, these codes describe the status of your various credit accounts and your history of making or missing payments—what your credit limits are, whether you routinely pay late or scrupulously pay on time, etc. In addition to your credit record, the report will list every organization that has requested your report in the last two years. Sometimes the organization's name has been encoded, but the bureaus will tell you what the codes mean if you ask.

If you want to dispute any part of your credit record, write the bureau, explaining the inaccuracy. Under the FCRA, the bureau must reverify the information within a reasonable period, usually 30 to 60 days, or delete it from your file.

Negative information will remain in your file for seven years, bankruptcy information will stick around for ten. You may attach a written explanation to any negative information in your file that is in dispute. Keep your side of the story to fewer than 100 words and send it to the bureau.

Your Check-Bouncing History

You could be one of the seven million unsuspecting Americans unable to open a checking or savings account simply because your name is listed with ChexSystems, a nationwide data base containing the names of people accused of mishandling checking accounts. Many of the 54,000 banks that subscribe, including Citibank and Chemical Bank in New York and Wells Fargo and Bank of America in California, to name a few, automatically reject any checking or savings account application made by someone listed by ChexSystems; other banks take ChexSystems' information into account but do not necessarily use it to make a final determination.

It's understandable, and indeed laudable, that banks would want to reject check-kiters and other perpetrators of financial fraud, but ChexSystems also allows banks to disqualify the qualified. Take Jane R., a California grandmother of four who had bounced six checks over three years. After her branch closed down, she found she was not able to open a new account. Was she careless? Maybe. A profligate check-kiter? Hardly. But since there are no uniform standards for rating a ChexSystems report, one bank may add the names of people who bounced only two checks in one year, while others may require bouncing ten or more checks before reporting a problem customer.

To make matters worse, names remain in ChexSystems' file for five years, unless the offended bank makes a special request to have names removed—in other words, a few infractions in college could nix your application for an account four years later, even though your financial situation has stabilized.

Is inaccurate information a big problem? No one knows. Since few people know their files exist, few check their files and fewer dispute inaccurate information. The San Francisco advocacy group Consumer Action got a complaint from Shirley M. After she closed her account with a California bank, an old check came through and bounced. When subsequent statements showed no balance, she thought her account was squared away. Without her knowledge, the bank reported her name to ChexSystems and she found she was blacklisted when she tried to open a new account.

You can check your ChexSystems status for free. Send a letter—including your full name, Social Security number, signature, and a list of your home addresses over the last five years—to the address listed in the **HELP** section at the end of this chapter.

Your Driving Record

You probably haven't a clue about C.L.U.E. Personal Auto, but automobile insurers sure do. And as a consequence, they have plenty of clues about you and your driving record. Equifax Inc. compiled this data base, short for Comprehensive Loss Underwriting Exchange, which contains encoded information on claims going back three to five years—the policyholder's name, the driver's name, the vehicle involved, the nature of the claim, the status, and the cost to the insurer, no matter how small or large. Insurers use these claims histories to help decide whose premi-

ums to raise, whose policies not to renew, and who among new applicants is too big a risk or too costly to insure. C.L.U.E. catalogues eight out of ten personal automobile insurance policyholders in the country—about 107 million of the 134 million cars presently covered by liability insurance.

As with the credit bureaus that spawned it and that it resembles, C.L.U.E. offers a valuable service to consumers. It enables insurers to quickly figure out who to take on and who to slough off based on people's driving records and claims histories rather than on artificial and discriminatory factors such as where people live or their marital status. It also helps insurers to avoid frauders and fibbers, who raise premiums for honest and good drivers.

However, as with other data bases, the files are only as useful as they are accurate. Since very few people know about the files, even fewer check their records for accuracy—and it's nearly impossible to measure how straight the stories are. Furthermore, C.L.U.E. files contain *no* facts concerning the circumstances of any claims. "The amount of property damage and whether the person was at fault gives us a hint," said one underwriting supervisor at State Farm Insurance, "but it doesn't give us any facts." One Long Island, New York, woman was denied insurance after she had already canceled her old policy thinking she'd found a better deal. On the basis of one spurious claim that was cheaper for the insurance company to pay than to fight on her behalf, and two large vandalism claims that she filed when she lived in a dangerous neighborhood she had long since left, she couldn't get auto insurance.

Clearly, it's a good idea to check your C.L.U.E. record *before* you apply for auto insurance. Requests must include your name, address, signature, date of birth, Social Security number, name of your present insurance company, policy number, insurance companies for the last five years, your driver's license number, and the state that granted the license. If adverse action has been taken within the last 30 days, the report is free. For others, it costs $8.

When You Use a Credit Card or Pay With a Check

Many states have passed laws that make it more difficult for merchants to collect personal information when you pay for a purchase with a check or credit card. Some states prohibit a store from recording a credit card number on the back of a personal check. If the merchant insists, you can allow him or her to compare your signature, but no one can demand to write down your credit card number as a condition of making a sale. Another law prohibits a merchant from requiring excessive amounts of personal information, such as your address and phone number when you use a credit card to buy something. If your state does not have a similar law, remind any stubborn retailers that the major credit card companies actually *prohibit* a vendor from refusing a sale to a person who won't provide his or her address or telephone number.

Telephone Privacy

Many marketers have your phone number—credit card companies, catalogue companies, insurance salespeople, banks, etc. They got it because you gave it to them at an earlier time, or they bought it from another data base. They can frequently get it even before they answer the phone, when you call their "800" or "900" numbers. New telephone technology, called Automatic Number Identification (ANI), records your number for identification and future marketing purposes as soon as their phone starts ringing. Some organizations use this information immediately to link the number with a computer file describing you and previous purchases you've made. Used this way, this technology can help you order the right size of clothing or the right piece of luggage to match others you've bought in the past. Its efficiency also saves the vendor precious time, which means money. But without your consent, this service forfeits your anonymity and opens you up to aggressive future sales pitches.

Residential customers in some states can get a service similar to ANI to help screen local calls. Known as Caller ID, it enables you to see the phone number from which a caller is calling before you pick up the phone. If you decide not to answer, you can let an answering machine record a message and decide later whether to return it. This way you won't miss important calls from numbers you don't recognize.

Conversations you have on wireless communications devices such as cellular and cordless phones, baby monitors, mobile radios are not secure because they are transmitted over radio frequencies. What's more, federal law *permits* eavesdropping on all of the above—except cellular calls. If you use a baby monitor or a cordless phone, be aware that it's like bugging your own house; anyone with a scanner radio can listen in on the goings-on.

Swollen Mailboxes, Clanging Phones

Marketers—credit card companies, catalogue houses, diaper services, or the local hardware store—cull mailing and telephone lists from a wide variety of data bankers who eagerly scoop up infor-

GETTING OFF THE JUNK MAIL MERRY-GO-ROUND

The Direct Marketing Association (DMA), a trade group representing many of the nation's largest users of mail, telephone calls, and computers to sell things, also offers several services to the public. The DMA Mail and Telephone Preference Services give you the option to have your name removed from the lists used by DMA member companies. This move may thin out your bundle of mail, but it will not unclog your mailbox entirely. Plenty of businesses do not subscribe to the service, and the program is entirely voluntary, allowing a subscriber to participate as conscientiously as it wishes. However, a powerful incentive works in your favor: Because direct marketing costs a lot, it makes sense for a marketer to avoid contacting people it knows will junk unwanted mail.

To take yourself off the lists, send your name and address to the DMA address listed in the **HELP** section at the end of the chapter. Specify whether you would like to be removed from commercial or non-profit lists or both and also whether you would like to have your phone number deleted from telemarketing lists.

Under the Telephone Consumer Protection Act of 1991 and Federal Communications Commission rules, telemarketers who solicit you in your home must keep lists of people who do not want to be called again. The law allows you to file suit and collect damages for violations. Also be on the lookout for boxes you can check off on catalogue order forms to indicate your wish *not* to have your name sold.

mation from sources as varied as magazine subscription lists, warranty cards, market research surveys, and public records. For example, for the last 50 years New York State has made motor vehicle registrations available to Donnelly Marketing, the highest bidder. Women who checked into the hospital to give birth to a child probably signed a release form allowing the hospital to sell their names to marketers of infant formula, diaper services, and other baby products. Many non-profit groups and charitable organizations add significantly to their contributions by selling their lists. Catalogue companies routinely sell their lists to other companies; the names of people who have bought a product or service by mail are especially prized because these people have proven willing to shop through the mail.

Once they get your name, these marketers take to the phone (and mail) to deliver their pitch. You can keep these solicitations to a minimum by asking marketers you do business with or magazines you subscribe to *not* to sell your name to others. You can also minimize the amount of personal information they have on you by only giving that which is essential to do business with them.

Your Medical Records

Although no Federal law protects the privacy of your medical records, many states have laws that protect this information from being disclosed to anyone but you or someone you designate. How-

ever, insurance policy applications include a standard waiver that allows the insurer to obtain access to your health background and anything affecting it. The insurance company's investigators scour financial institutions, doctors, hospitals, medical labs, the workers' compensation board, employers, motor vehicles departments, and may even contact applicants' friends and relatives. University of Illinois political economist David Linowes points out that this practice effectively creates "a search warrant through your medical history without due process."

If something in your background suggests that the risk of insuring you is higher than average, an insurer may send a report to the Medical Information Bureau (MIB). Similar to the credit bureaus, MIB acts as a clearinghouse for 800 of the largest insurance companies in the U.S. and Canada. MIB stores both medical and non-medical information on more than 15 million people that helps insurers ferret out fraud and determine eligibility and premiums for life, health, and disability insurance. About 15% of insurance applications result in a report to the MIB. Once again, mistakes can creep into people's files. For instance, Jim G. of Palo Alto, California, once told a doctor during a routine physical exam that he drank a couple of six-packs of beer *a month*, which somehow wound up in his file as two six-packs *a day*. "Guess what happened when I applied for a disability insurance policy," Jim told *American Health* magazine.

Your medical records are sensitive personal information and are vulnerable to misuse. Do you want a potential employer to know that you are a recovering alcoholic or that you are HIV-positive?

It's a good idea to review a free copy of your file for errors. If you find any, write to MIB explaining the problem. The bureau will go back to the insurance company that supplied the information for verification. But if you and the insurance company disagree, it can be difficult—sometimes, impossible—to get a correction. It's possible, however, that you could add a statement to your file disputing or explaining the questionable information.

You also might want to check with your doctor(s) and insurer(s) to see what they have on you in their files and to get them to correct any mistakes you find.

When applying for insurance or filing a claim, try to revise the information release form, which most often is broader than the legal mumbo-jumbo suggests. Try to limit access and dissemination of information and add an expiration date after which information can no longer be collected or released.

THE SMARTER CONSUMER

Think twice before you give out any information about yourself that isn't absolutely necessary to complete a specific transaction. Do not write your driver's license number or credit card number on your personal check. Do not give your Social Security number unless absolutely necessary. Legally, you only have to give your number for tax or Social Security matters. However, there's nothing stopping a merchant from denying you service if you refuse to give the number.

Take a look at your file. Get copies of your credit reports from credit bureaus. Get copies of your medical records from insurance companies, your doctor(s), and the Medical Information Bureau. Check out your driving record on your C.L.U.E. report. If there's any information in any of the files that you dispute, write a brief letter explaining the error for inclusion in your file.

Give the bare minimum of information on warranty cards. Mailing and telephone marketing lists are culled from the cards. Virtually all warranties are valid as long as you have the receipt for the item.

Use an answering machine to screen unwanted phone calls.

Keep your name off the lists. Ask organizations whose mail you want to receive *not* to sell your name to others. This includes magazines, catalogues, and charities.

Send out your own change of address notes. Information from the U.S. Postal Service change of address form is sold to direct marketers who use it to update mailing lists.

If you are interested in privacy issues, two newsletters might interest you:

Privacy Journal
P.O. Box 28577
Providence, RI 02908

Privacy Times
P.O. Box 21501
Washington, DC 20009

If you want to check your credit report contact all three major credit bureaus to catch any and all errors and have them corrected. Equifax and Trans Union each charge a fee—about $8, but it may vary depending on where you live; TRW gives you a free report once a year. Contact:

Equifax National Consumer Center
P.O. Box 105873
Atlanta, GA 30348
(800) 685-1111

Trans Union Corp.
P.O. Box 390
Springfield, PA 19064-0390
(312) 408-1050

TRW National Consumer Assistance
  Center
P.O. Box 2350
Chatsworth, CA 91313-2350
(800) 392-1122

To dispute inaccuracies (you have to dispute in writing):

Equifax National Consumer Center
P.O. Box 740256
Atlanta, GA 30374-0256
Fax (404) 612-3150

Trans Union Corp.
P.O. Box 390
Springfield, PA 19064-0390

TRW
Dept. NCAC
P.O. Box 2106
Dallas, TX 75002
(800) 422-4879

For additional copies of your TRW report, beyond the free one you receive annually, write to (TRW NCAC, P.O. Box 2104, Allen, TX 75002, and send $8 per report.

If you have a problem with a credit bureau, report it to your state attorney general or to the Federal Trade Commission, Washington, DC 20580; (202) 326-2000.

To see your ChexSystems record, write to ChexSystems Inc., Attn: Consumer Relations, 1550 East 79th Street, Minneapolis, MN 55425.

To see what's in your C.L.U.E. auto claims report, contact C.L.U.E., Equifax Insurance Consumer Center, P.O. Box 105108, Atlanta, GA 30348; (800) 456-6004

To have your name removed from many mailing lists, contact Mail Preference Service, Direct Marketing Association, P.O. Box 9008, Farmingdale, NY 11735-9008

To have your name removed from many telemarketing lists, contact Telephone Preference Service, Direct Mail Association, P.O. Box 9014, Farmingdale, NY 11735-9014

To see your MIB file, contact Medical Information Bureau, P.O. Box 105 Essex Station, Boston, MA 02112; (617) 426-3660

The Direct Marketing Association publishes a brochure that explains why you get so much mail: *Direct Marketing: Opening the Door to Opportunity*. To request a copy, write the Consumer Services Department, DMA, 1101 17th Street NW, Suite 705, Washington, DC 20036-4704.

CHAPTER 60

ENVIRONMENTAL CLAIMS

Not Always Friends of the Earth

Biodegradable? Compostable? Ozone-friendly? Recyclable? Don't bet on it. The most degrading aspect of some products making these claims are often the claims themselves.

THE BASICS

Ever since Earth Day first energized consumers in 1970 to seek out and buy earth-friendly products, "green marketing" has become big business. The green marketing industry's revenues will reportedly be worth $95 million by 1997. And as of 1994, 55 million consumers based their buying decisions to some degree on environmental concerns. The Roper Organization reports that a quarter of the nation's population are "deep green" consumers who think about the environmental consequences of the products they buy.

By the mid-1990s, at least 300 stores across the country exclusively sold green products: earth-safe tile cleansers, earth-friendly cookbooks, bathrobes and slippers made of organically grown unbleached cotton, home composters, water-saving toilet flushers and shower heads, and super-efficient fluorescent light bulbs.

While some of these products actually reduce solid waste or save energy as they promise, the proliferation of green products has brought with it a cottage industry in misleading environmental advertising—what some consumer advocates call "green-collar fraud." Green-collar fraud poisons the well of public trust by making cynics out of consumers who want to be environmentally sensitive but can't distinguish between honest and false environmental claims.

WHAT TO WATCH OUT FOR

"Biodegradable" Plastic Bags

Some years ago a group of biochemists discovered that weaving cornstarch molecules with the plastic in a plastic bag caused the plastic to become brittle under certain laboratory conditions. In theory, the plastic might eventually crumble into smaller pieces of plastic. But "biodegradable plastic" turned out to be a term made up to describe something that doesn't really exist. Laboratory conditions are rarely replicated in garbage dumps, and the plastic portion of the bag will remain plastic—forever. Even in the few dumps where the bags were exposed to enough sunlight to break down, the wind picked up the scraps of plastic and blew them over to beaches and parks.

Don't be fooled by the term "biodegradable plastic" printed on the plastic bags in which supermarkets pack groceries. A coalition of Attorneys General from across the country and the city of New York have been investigating degradability claims for several years. Many bag companies have dropped their claims as a result, but some persist. Although the degradability claim has been discredited, stores continue to distribute the bags in an effort to seem sympathetic to the environment—and to their environmentally conscious consumers.

If you are still tempted to buy degradable bags, here's an additional problem: In tests conducted by consumer groups, they were among the weakest bags evaluated.

"Ozone-Friendly" Aerosol Cans

What should you make of the labels on aerosol cans asserting that the contents are "ozone-friendly" or contain "no chlorofluorocarbons"?

First, some definitions: Ozone is a very simple, electrically charged chemical molecule composed of three oxygen atoms. It forms a protective layer about 18 miles above the earth's surface. (Jet airplanes fly about six miles up.) The ozone layer protects us from skin cancer by blocking out harmful ultraviolet radiation.

Chlorofluorocarbons (CFCs) are more complex chemicals that for many years were used in refrigeration and aerosol devices (and are still used in refrigerators and air conditioners). When released into the air, CFCs make their way into the higher levels of the atmosphere and cause the ozone layer to thin, thus weakening the natural shield against harmful ultraviolet rays. Fortunately, though, CFCs have been illegal in most products since 1978.

Even so, many aerosol cans still boast that they contain "no CFCs" or are "ozone-friendly," leaving con-

> "To say a product is 'environmentally friendly' is inherently misleading. By virtue of its very existence, a product has had negative environmental ramifications."
>
> —JOHN TREVOR,
> Rhode Island environmental advocate and recycling official

sumers to scratch their heads and wonder what the claim could mean if CFCs are *already* illegal.

It's nonsense. In fact, virtually all aerosol cans that boast about being "ozone-friendly" actually contain harmful, flammable compounds called hydrocarbons that *form* ozone at ground level on sunny days. This type of ozone does nothing to repair *or* damage the protective layer high above, but it causes an important side effect: respiratory problems in elderly people, small children, and people with a history of respiratory illness. So much for our aerosol friends. Only the "pump" spray bottles that rely on old-fashioned finger power to create an aerosol mist are free of harmful hydrocarbon propellants.

"Compostable" Diapers

Not surprisingly, the disposable diaper industry is under siege by environmentalists: Disposable diapers take up about 1% of all the landfill space in the U.S., and it could take as much as 500 years for them to decompose in a landfill. Manufacturing diapers requires 1,265,000 metric tons of wood pulp and 75,000 metric tons of plastic each year. Over a billion trees are chopped down annually to make disposable diapers.

As municipal landfills began to fill up in the 1980s, thousands of environmentally minded consumers began switching to cloth diapers. On the defensive, the disposable diaper industry responded by bending the truth about diaper compostability. Procter & Gamble, the consumer products giant, sells about $1.75 billion worth of disposable diapers each year—all of which eventually wind up in our nation's landfills. But in 1990, the company began running print ads pretending that diapers turned into soil. The ads showed a handful of dirt and the caption, "Ninety days ago, this was a disposable diaper." The ads were bordered with pleasant images of trees and appeared in national magazines like *TV Guide*.

The ads should have included a headline that said, "This never happens." For the truth is that diapers might turn into soft, fertile soil only after their plastic liners are carefully removed, and only after the diaper is put into a huge, expensive, and experimental municipal composter, a device very few communities have. Moreover, the compost these behemoths produce is often too toxic to use as fertilizer anyway because it contains battery acid, mercury, and other toxic heavy metals. (One environmental group ran a parody of the P&G ad: a photo of a diaper with the headline, "Ninety days ago, this was a tree.")

But even some of the most savvy American consumers were fooled by the ads. In Los Angeles, after the ads appeared, consumers started leaving diapers out by the side of the road to be picked up by the city's recycling program. Problem was, Los Angeles had no composting facilities for the messy diapers, and so the county ultimately had to distribute 10,000 door-hangers asking residents to please not leave their diapers out with their recyclable newspapers,

GREEN PARENTING

Industries seeking the favor of green consumers have discovered something parents have known for years: Many family buying decisions are actually made by kids. So, in an attempt to win the hearts of school children, many industries target teachers with industry-sponsored messages disguised as "curriculum" materials. "Teachers are hungry for information, and with state budget cutbacks, companies are filling in the gaps," says Erica Guttman, a Rhode Island environmental official. According to Guttman, though, kids are getting mixed environmental messages.

For example, *Decision: Earth*, a booklet produced by Procter & Gamble, was sent to M.S. junior high school teachers in late 1993. The booklet drew the ire of environmentalists because it promoted disposable diapers with a deceptive "life cycle analysis" that 11 state attorneys general criticized in 1991.

Your children may also have encountered messages about drink box recycling. In 1992, students received glossy curriculum materials from the drink box industry inside their copies of *Scholastic* magazine, which ordinarily carries little or no advertising. The industry continues to claim that drink boxes are "recyclable," even though very few communities are able to recycle them at all.

bottles, and aluminum cans.

After the NYC Department of Consumer Affairs took legal action against Procter & Gamble, the company eventually agreed not to run the misleading ads. The lesson: Even the most ambitious and widely advertised environmental claims can be completely misleading.

Recycled/Recyclable

Cities across the country are closing landfill sites and are scrambling to find ways of reducing the amount of garbage their citizens produce. Recycling is a great way to help reduce solid waste. But in the rush to promote their products as "recyclable," many companies stretch the truth.

Take, for instance, the drink box industry, which produces more than two billion of those cute boxes of juice each year. Nowadays kids demand the little rectangular boxes that come with their own straw, and parents rely on their convenience and aseptic purity. Problem is, the bottles or cans you would have sent in your children's lunch box ten years ago were fully recyclable, while the plastic- or wax-coated juice boxes just accumulate in landfills.

In 1989, the juice box industry ran full page ads in national newspapers claiming, "This drink box is as recyclable as this page." True in theory, but there wasn't a city in the country—and there still isn't—where you could recycle juice boxes the way you recycle newspapers. (A few municipalities recycle drink boxes the same way they do milk cartons.) The NYC Department of Consumer Affairs accused the industry of deceptive advertising, and, ultimately, the ads were discontinued.

Be on the lookout also for "recycled" paper products. Much of so-called recycled paper actually contains wood shavings and scraps from paper mills, *not* true recycled paper. This method of "recycling" has been practiced for years by efficient paper mills, and doesn't represent environmental progress. If you want real recycled stationery, make sure that the product says it contains "post-consumer paper" or "post-consumer waste." That means that the product was made from paper products that were already used at least once by consumers.

The same holds for "recycled" plastic" bags. Plastic bag company Webster Industries got into some trouble several years ago when it apparently was the last to get the word that "biodegradable" plastic bags weren't. Now the company is selling "Renew" plastic bags labelled as "100% Recycled Plastic." The "100%" label suggests to consumers that the bags are composed entirely of recycled bleach bottles or other plastic garbage that would otherwise clog our landfills.

Not quite. Next to the word "recycled" is a tiny asterisk. If you hunt for it, you can find a dis-

claimer in fine print on the very bottom of the box. It says the bags are 60% post-consumer waste and 40% industrial waste, which includes plastic shavings and other scraps from the production process. While the company deserves kudos for selling recycled plastic bags, they ought to tell the whole truth about the product prominently.

THE SMARTER CONSUMER

Here are seven things you can do to be a green consumer and help preserve the environment:

Reduce solid waste. If you're an average American, you generate about 1,200 pounds of solid waste each year. That's garbage the size and weight of a small car, and a third of it is packaging you toss out immediately. One easy way to reduce waste is to carry a string shopping bag with you at all times, and ask for recyclable paper bags instead of plastic at the supermarket. If you're buying just one item, say "No bag, please."

Recycle paper. The American paper industry actually started as a recycling industry. The first paper mill, built in 1690 near Philadelphia, manufactured paper from second-hand linen and cotton rags. We now recycle only about 29% of the paper materials we use. Recycling would go a long way toward re-

REDUCE, REUSE, RECYCLE

Instead of this	Use this
1,000 paper towels	One cloth kitchen towel Crumpled newspapers
1,000 paper coffee filters	One gold-plated filter
1,000 polystyrene coffee cups	One ceramic mug
14 incandescent light bulbs	One compact fluorescent bulb
Toxic household cleaners	Vinegar, baking soda
Drink boxes	Thermos
Disposable diapers	Reusable cloth diapers

Comparisons based on expected useful life.

ducing our apparently insatiable appetite for trees: The average American uses about 580 pounds of paper each year (about 120 pounds of that is newsprint); in total, we consume about 850 million trees per year for paper.

So recycle those newspapers: One run of the Sunday edition of *The New York Times* consumes 40 acres of trees. Making new paper from old paper is also a great way to save energy. Turning old paper into new uses 30% to 55% less energy than making paper from trees—and it reduces air pollution produced by the manufacturing process by 95%.

Recycle aluminum and glass. Green consumers recycle all the aluminum cans and bottles they use—even the ones without deposits. And don't forget to recycle other types of aluminum—foil, pie plates, frozen food trays, window frames, and siding. Also, be sure to recycle any aluminum used in pack-

aging: 40% of all aluminum used in the U.S. is used for packaging.

Recycling these materials reduces solid waste *and* saves energy. The process of manufacturing aluminum from bauxite consumes so much energy that molten aluminum is "affectionately" known as liquid electricity. Making an aluminum can from recycled aluminum uses 90% less energy than making aluminum from scratch, and the energy saved will operate a television set for three hours.

Making new glass from recycled glass uses 32% less energy than starting from scratch, reduces air pollution created in the process by 20%, and cuts water pollution by 50%. The energy saved by recycling one glass bottle will light a 100-watt light bulb for four hours. And since glass doesn't crush that easily in a garbage dump, bottles tend to take up a lot of landfill space. So recycle every glass bottle you've got —clear, green, or even colored wine bottles. Some cities such as New York City actually crush colored glass, mix it with asphalt, and pave the streets with it. The result is that the streets sparkle with the new, brightly reflective surface, and the city preserves precious landfill space.

Convert to a green economy. The word "economy" originates in an ancient Greek word that means "the arrangement of a household." You can only hope political leaders will implement green policies in the national economy—and you can encourage those policies by lobbying and voting. Here are some things you can do to convert your own household to a green economy:

■ *Avoid household toxics.* You don't have to clean your oven with harsh oven-cleaner (usually containing lye); baking soda works fine. Use cedar chips instead of paradichlorobenzene, better known as mothballs, to winter-proof closets and drawers.

■ *Use unbleached paper coffee filters.* If you use coffee filters for your morning brew, be aware that the process of bleaching paper creates dioxin, a deadly toxic by-product, which often gets dumped into American waterways. You could also consider switching to a gold-plated coffee filter that doesn't require paper inserts at all. Depending on how much you like coffee, you could avoid using hundreds (if not thousands) of coffee filters over the life of the coffee maker.

■ *Use reusable containers* to save leftovers, rather than plastic wrap, which you'll just throw out afterward. If you must wrap a sandwich, use waxed paper instead of foil or plastic; it biodegrades.

■ *Use cloth kitchen towels* to dry hands and dishes instead of paper towels. They do the job better—and they won't wind up in the trash. You'll eventually save money by buying fewer paper goods.

■ *Here's a thrifty recycling tip:* Crumpled-up newspapers actually work a lot better at cleaning windows than paper towels, which can streak or leave little fibers. Spray your glass windows with a liquid glass cleaner, and wipe clean with yesterday's sports section.

Avoid using pesticides and insecticides on your lawn. Eventually, they will wind up in the water supply—yours, your neighbors', or both. Often, many lawn problems can be solved just by allowing your lawn to grow a little taller. It's not natural for a lawn to be as short as a putting green. Let it grow two or three inches; it'll be healthier and more resistant to fungus and insects. And if you leave the grass clippings after you mow, they help your lawn retain water naturally. (See "Lawn Care," page 209, for more information.)

Keep a ceramic mug on your desk at work. Use less Styrofoam—it's completely non-degradable. Even 500 years from now, that Styrofoam cup will still be a Styrofoam cup.

Let your voice be heard. You're not limited to voting once every four years. You can cast a vote for the environment when you write a letter, make a phone call, or send a fax or an e-mail communiqué. Urge legislators to pass stronger bottle bills. Urge your favorite fast food restaurants to reduce their use of packaging.

A massive letter-writing campaign recently convinced recording companies to abandon the bulky cardboard CD packaging for the less-wasteful shrink-wrap packaging. Never underestimate the power of the pen. And don't forget to send congratulatory letters, too. For example, if your neighborhood McDonald's is making an effort to reduce the packaging it gives to customers, let it know you notice.

Either way, keep in mind the corporate executive's rule of thumb: Every letter a company receives represents the views of 100 customers. So don't be shy, write to the CEO or President, and rest assured, your letter will get attention.

Design for a Livable *Planet*, by John Naar, Harper & Row, $12.95.

The Green Consumer, by Julia Mailer and Joel Makower, Penguin Books, $8.95.

The New York Environment Book, by Mark Izeman and Eric Goldstein, Island Press, $14.95.

Fifty Simple Things You Can Do to *Save the Earth*, the Earth Works Group, 1989, $4.95.

Making the Switch: Alternatives *to Using Toxic Chemicals in the Home.* Send $6 to Publication Department, Local Government Commission, 909 12th Street, Suite 205, Sacramento, CA 95814.

Nontoxic and Natural and The *Nontoxic Home,* by Debra Lynn Dadd. $11.95, available from the author at P.O. Box 1506, Mill Valley, CA 94942. Dadd also publishes a product-oriented newsletter called *The Earthwise Consumer,* available from the same address.

The Household Hazardous Waste Project, P.O. Box 87, 901 South National Ave., Springfield, MO 65804, (417) 836-5777. Send $8 for *The Guide to Hazardous Products Around the Home.*

For a pesticide-free lawn, read The *Chemical-free Lawn,* by Warren Schultz, Rodale Press, 1989.

For green kitchen products by mail, write to Seventh Generation, 10 Farrell Street, South Burlington, VT 05403.

For information on recycling contact: The Environmental Defense Fund, (800) CALL-EDF.

The Aluminum Association, 900 19th Street NW, Washington, DC 20006; (202) 862-5100.

Paper Recycling Committee, American Paper Institute, 260 Madison Avenue, New York, NY 10016; (212) 340-0600.

Glass Packaging Institute, 1801 K Street NW, Washington, DC 20006; (202) 887-4850.

Consumer Skills

CHAPTER 61

INSTALLMENT LOANS

Buying on Time, at a Price

Ageneration or so ago, few Americans bought on credit except when buying houses or, perhaps, cars. Credit cards were a novelty and cash on the barrelhead was the norm.

Look at us now! The total amount of consumer installment credit outstanding (not counting mortgage loans) rocketed from $105.5 billion in 1970 to $742.1 billion in 1991, a 600% increase in only two decades.

All this credit hasn't come cheap. A modest $13,000 car paid for with a five-year loan at 12.5% annual interest would end up costing $17,548.80.

THE BASICS

Credit Sales and Money Loans

Installment borrowing, also called closed-end credit, is a loan for a fixed amount that is to be repaid within a specific time in regular installments. Such loans are typically used to buy cars, furniture, or mobile homes, or to finance home renovations. A contract spells out the borrower's rights and obligations and the consequences of default. *Credit sales* and *money loans* are the two basic ways to obtain installment credit.

With a credit sale, you enter into a "retail installment contract" with the seller who extends the credit that you use to make a purchase—say, a new car. In most cases, this contract is immediately sold to another creditor to whom you then owe the money. In effect, the seller is the go-between for a creditor that the consumer has never met.

One important feature of a credit sale is that the sales terms and financing terms are tied together in one contract. This means that your obligation to pay the money back is conditioned on the seller's obligation to live up to the terms and conditions of the sale, including warranty obligations.

For many years creditors were able to use various legal dodges to make consumers pay even though the seller failed to honor the sales terms. The Federal Trade Commission (FTC) finally put an end to these practices by adopting what is called the "Preservation of Consumers' Claims and Defenses" Rule. This rule applies to all credit sales for $25,000 or less and to any credit sale secured by your dwelling or real property. It requires that the seller include this clause in every credit sale agreement printed in bold-faced type:

NOTICE

ANY HOLDER OF THIS CONSUMER CREDIT CONTRACT IS SUBJECT TO ALL CLAIMS AND DEFENSES WHICH THE DEBTOR COULD ASSERT AGAINST THE SELLER OF GOODS OR SERVICES OBTAINED PURSUANT HERETO OR WITH THE PROCEEDS THEREOF. RECOVERY HEREUNDER SHALL NOT EXCEED AMOUNTS PAID BY THE DEBTOR HEREUNDER.

If this notice is absent, don't sign and don't buy. Just keep in mind that if a seller is prepared to violate a federal mandate that creates important protections for you, what makes you think you can count on the seller to honor any other promises?

Tens of thousands of homeowners—mostly in lower-income, inner-city neighborhoods—have learned this the hard way. As described in earlier chapters, a wave of "equity theft" has swept the nation; dishonest home improvement contractors sell renovated kitchens, roofs, and newly created basement apartments by promising unrealistically low monthly payments. The work is rarely completed or is so shoddy that it has to be ripped out. To add insult to injury, the homeowners are often conned into signing a separate loan agreement for much more money than they were originally told—as well as a mortgage document.

In money loans, a creditor lends you money that you then use to pay for purchases. Banks, credit unions, or finance companies are the most common sources of such credit. Since the loan and a purchase you make with the money are separate transactions made under different agreements (and usually with different companies), the sales terms and financing terms are not locked together in the same closed-end loan agreement. This usually means that if you have a dispute about the purchase with the seller, you would have to repay the loan and separately settle up with the seller.

The FTC "Preservation of Consumers' Claims and Defenses" rule carves out an exception that can help you lock the terms of the sale into the loan agreement just like in a credit sale. This rule covers loans made in the following circumstances:

- The seller engages in a pattern or practice of referring purchasers to the creditor who makes the loan used to pay for the purchase, as when the seller arranged the loan, made out the papers for you, or sent you to the lender; or
- The seller and the creditor are affiliated for the purpose of making loans, as when the same company owns both.

The FTC locks the loan and sales terms together by requiring the seller to make sure that the lender includes the following clause in the loan agreement, as shown below:

NOTICE

ANY HOLDER OF THIS CONSUMER CREDIT CONTRACT IS SUBJECT TO ALL CLAIMS AND DEFENSES WHICH THE DEBTOR COULD ASSERT AGAINST THE SELLER OF GOODS OR SERVICES

OBTAINED WITH THE PROCEEDS HEREOF. RECOVERY HEREUNDER SHALL NOT EXCEED AMOUNTS PAID BY THE DEBTOR HEREUNDER.

This rule is likely to help you lock the sales and the loan terms together *only* if the lender includes the required clause in your loan contract.

Secured or Unsecured Installment Credit

Installment credit can be either secured or unsecured.

Secured credit simply refers to an extension of credit that is backed up by personal or real property or by a co-signer. With secured credit, a creditor has more than just your signature and income to fall back on to collect the debt. In case of default, a secured creditor also can use legal procedures to recover the collateral and sell it to pay off the debt. If the collateral brings more than the amount owing, it must be paid back to you; if not, the creditor could sue for the remaining amount, which is usually called the "deficiency balance."

The type of collateral used determines the legal procedures a creditor must employ to obtain the collateral upon default. The three most commonly used types of collateral are:

■ *Personal property,* like a car, boat, furniture, refrigerator, or household goods. A creditor obtains such collateral by getting what is called a "security interest" in the goods. The agreement that puts such goods up as collateral must be in writing, and is referred to as a "security agreement." In the case of credit sales, the retail installment sales agreement almost always includes the clauses a creditor needs to obtain a security interest in the goods you buy.

■ *Real property,* such as a home. To obtain such collateral, the creditor secures a first or a second mortgage on the property. A mortgage must be in writing. Someone, such as a contractor, who makes improvements to your home can, however, obtain a lien on it to secure payment. This lien does not have to be put in writing; the creditor acquires it because the law allows it.

■ *Liquid assets,* such as a bank savings account or a stock account at a brokerage firm. The creditor acquires a right to obtain the money or the stocks put up as collateral, and the assets are usually frozen until the loan is repaid. Such an arrangement must be in writing if the lender is not also the financial institution holding the account(s) you're using as collateral. If the lender is your own bank, however, a bank usually has what's known as a "right of set-off" which allows it to take from your accounts amounts for defaulted debts.

Borrowing with a co-signer is another way to obtain secured

> "**E**asy credit paves the road to bankruptcy."
>
> —ANONYMOUS

credit. Creditors usually require co-signers when an applicant doesn't have an acceptable credit record. The person who co-signs is then just as obligated to repay the debt as the person who actually received the money or the goods bought on the credit. If and when default occurs, it's the creditor's choice as to who will be made to pay.

Unsecured credit means the creditor has no additional collateral backing up the debt aside from your promise to pay. To collect, a creditor would first have to sue and then use legal procedures to enforce payment, such as garnishment of wages or attachment of property.

What the Law Says: Truth in Lending Act Disclosures

The federal Truth in Lending Act (TILA) requires creditors to clearly and conspicuously disclose in writing key credit terms. These disclosures must be made *before* you are legally bound to go through with the transaction.

TILA does not regulate the actual terms of a credit agreement. Such regulation is left to state law, and all states have various laws regulating the different types of credit you can get, such as bank loans, installment loans, finance company loans, retail installment contracts, etc. TILA has, however, simplified and standardized how creditors must disclose important financial terms. See the box on the next page for the key up-front disclosures creditors must make about closed-end credit transactions.

How Creditors Compute Finance Charges

Actuarial method. With this method, finance charges are computed bi-weekly or monthly by applying a periodic rate to a declining balance. A periodic rate may be expressed as "1.2% per month," for example.

The actuarial method can be used, to calculate the unpaid balance after any scheduled payment or the amount due in interest as of any payment. It can also be used to allocate what portion of pre-computed finance charges a creditor has to "rebate" if a loan is paid off early (see below).

When the actuarial method is used, finance charges are computed and owed as each payment becomes due.

Since the actuarial method calculates finance charges based on the time *between* scheduled payments, finance charges do not keep accruing if you pay late. But you also don't owe less if you pay early.

"Pre-computed" finance charges. Creditors "pre-compute" finance charges for many types of installment debts. This simply means they figure out in advance, assuming that all payments will be made on the scheduled due dates, the amount due for finance charges for the entire loan period and add it to the total amount owing under the contract. Finance charges do not accrue if you pay late, but you don't get credit for paying early. Creditors, however, collect late charges if payments are delayed beyond a

KNOW THE LINGO

Here are the key terms decoded that lenders must include in any credit agreement:

The "finance charge" and the "annual percentage rate" (APR). The finance charge is the cost of credit as a dollar amount for the entire loan period. The APR tells you the cost of credit expressed as a percentage of what you borrow. The rate is annualized so you can easily compare how much different creditors are charging regardless of differences in the amount borrowed or the length of the payment period.

The "amount financed" tells you the total dollar amount of credit being extended to you. This is the amount you must fully repay regardless of whether you pay the loan back before the originally scheduled term.

The "total of payments." This is the sum of all the payments scheduled to repay the debt. It is the sum of the amount financed plus the amount of the finance charge, or interest.

The "total sale price," in the case of credit sales, which is the sum of the total of payments plus any down payment.

The "payment schedule" is the amount, the number, and the date of the payments scheduled to repay the loan. If your schedule includes a balloon payment—one that is more than twice as large as other scheduled payments—it must be specifically identified.

Security interest. If the creditor is taking a security interest in products other than those being sold on credit, the property must be described in writing.

Late charges. Creditors assess such fees when your payment is late by between 10 to 15 days, depending on the law in your home state. The fee is usually 5% of the payment or a flat dollar amount, whichever is greater.

Prepayment consequences. What could happen if you pay your loan off early? This information also lets you know how the creditor computes finance charges on your debt.

The creditor indicates that you either "may" or that you "will not" have to pay a penalty if you pay the debt off early. Consumer credit laws in many states prohibit creditors from penalizing consumers for paying off installment debts early. If penalties are allowed in your state this disclosure tells you if you would have to pay the creditor an extra charge just to pay the debt off early. If the disclosure statement indicates there could be such a penalty, find out what the charge will be.

specified payment grace period (usually 15 days).

When finance charges are pre-computed, you could technically be obligated to repay the amount borrowed *plus* all the pre-computed finance charges. For example, in the car financing illustration given at the beginning of this chapter, the creditor who pre-computes finance charges adds the $4,548.80 that would be due in finance charges over five years to the $13,000 amount financed, to come up with $17,548.80—the total amount that is to be repaid in 60 payments of $292.48 each. Of course, creditors would collect huge windfalls if they could make you pay the entire $4,548.80 in finance charges even if you paid the loan off after only 30 months, for example. Here's why they can't:

Most state laws require creditors to "rebate" the portion of the pre-computed finance charges that are unearned by the creditor when a loan is paid off ahead of schedule. When a pre-computed debt is paid off early, you must pay the outstanding unpaid debt balance plus unpaid finance charges, only as of when you pre-pay. To come up with the right number, creditors must allocate how much of each $292.48 payment went to reduce the debt balance and how much went to pay finance charges. Since the loan balance is highest at the beginning of the loan, a much higher portion of each payment goes to pay finance charges at the beginning of the loan term than at the end; the amount due in finance charges is not directly proportional to the fraction of all payments that you had paid. For example, if you paid the loan back in full after making half the scheduled payments (30 out of 60, in our example), you would owe much more than just half of the $4,548.80 due in finance charges over the full term of 60 months.

The "Rule of 78s" is one method in frequent use for figuring out how much of the pre-computed interest a creditor has earned and how much the creditor must rebate upon pre-payment of the loan. The Rule of 78s produces a higher pay-off figure than the actuarial method described above, especially when the loan term is longer than five years and the APR is over 15%. That's why some states prohibit creditors from using the Rule of 78s to compute the rebate; others allow creditors to use it only for certain types of loans.

Daily simple interest method. With this method, creditors calculate the interest due on the debt on a daily basis by applying a periodic rate to the outstanding balance, as with credit cards. When using this method, creditors deduct from each payment the amount due for finance charges since the last payment and apply the remainder to reduce the debt balance. Most commonly used for computing interest due on mortgages, this method is becoming more widespread for other fixed-term installment debts because the increasing use of computers make the calculations easier for creditors.

Since the finance-charge meter keeps running each day from the last payment until the next one is made, your paying habits will affect how much you end up paying in finance charges. Borrowers who habitually pay early end up paying less than the amount disclosed as the total finance charges—the principal balance is reduced more quickly than estimated. On the other hand, borrowers who habitually pay late will end up owing more at the end of the loan term because the principal was reduced more slowly than estimated, especially if late payments occurred during the early part of the loan period.

WHAT TO WATCH OUT FOR

Loan consolidations and refinancing. Avoid consolidating or refinancing closed-end installment debts unless the APR for the finance charge on the consolidated loan is significantly lower than the rates charged for the debts you are consolidating. It's costly to consolidate installment debts because the pay-off amount for each account that you consolidate usually includes some left-over finance charges from the old contract—unless the old creditor computes finance charges on the unpaid balance on a "daily basis" method.

Adding new purchases to existing installment debts. It is seldom a good idea to add new purchases to an existing closed-end installment contract. First, the old purchases end up securing the new ones, sometimes long after you have repaid the amount owed for the old purchases. Second, it becomes very difficult to untangle what you owe for each purchase in case of a dispute about some of them; you can't safely withhold payment as you might be entitled to do if the disputed purchase was the only item financed under the contract.

Now you see it, now you don't: the "instant credit, no finance charges" trap. Newspapers are full of advertisments touting the availability of instant credit with no finance charges for from one to three months. These offers are made for both closed-end loans (such as for furniture) and open-end "revolving" loans (such as credit cards).

The hook is that you get the instant credit, but the "no finance charges" part disappears unless you repay the entire amount in full within the time allowed for "no finance charges"—that is, you have to pay it all back within one to three months of the date you made your purchase. If you don't do this, you will usually find you owe finance charges from that date.

Don't let the instant credit/no finance charge sugar-coating lure you into this credit trap. These deals are worth taking *only* if you are absolutely certain you'll pay the balance in full within the time allowed or if you have deliberately decided to assume the additional credit obligation that will result if you don't pay in full. Andy E. did this when he bought a $2,800 personal computer at New York City's J & R Music World on July 31, 1993. If he didn't pay the entire balance within three months, he would owe interest at an astounding 21.84%

APR, starting from the date of purchase. Fortunately, he did pay it all in time, in effect giving himself a free three-month loan. If he hadn't paid when he did, he would have immediately owed $52.14 in interest on his purchase.

Credit life or credit disability insurance. This insurance pays off the outstanding balance of the debt in case of the death or disability of the borrower. Creditors must include premiums for credit insurance in the finance charge unless they offer such coverage as an option. Disclosure documents, therefore, almost invariably include a statement indicating that you are aware you are not required to purchase the coverage, and a space where you must sign to indicate you have opted to buy any coverage that is included.

Credit insurance is almost always a bad buy. Stephen Brobeck, executive director of the Consumer Federation of America, summarizing his group's 1990 study of this product, called credit life insurance "the nation's worst insurance rip-off." A 1991 study by the Virginia Consumers Council found that nine of the top ten credit life insurance companies doing business in that state had an average loss ratio of an absurdly small 38.5%—in other words, less than 40% of what the companies took in was paid out in claims. If you really think you need such coverage, you can probably get much more protection for far less by purchasing a term life insurance policy. (See the chapter "Life Insurance," page 336.)

Credit disability insurance is even more expensive than credit life coverage, and is rarely worthwhile if you have sick leave at your job.

Property insurance. This insurance typically covers the property you have to put up as collateral against damage or loss. Creditors will invariably require you to obtain it for a car or other substantial collateral. While creditors can require you to have the coverage, they must give you the option to purchase it from other sources. You are better off shopping for your own coverage.

Some creditors are now pushing casualty insurance covering almost any collateral against loss or damage. Get such coverage through a homeowner or renter's policy rather than from your creditor.

THE SMARTER CONSUMER

Lessen the bite of auto and other closed-end loans. First, shop around for a lower interest rate or try your best to pay more up front in cash and finance less of your purchase. Take the example of the $13,000 car in the introduction. As explained, finance charges would add another $4,548.80 if the interest rate was 12.5% over a five-year period. You would have to devote $292.48 a month to pay back that loan and the car would end up costing you $17,548.80.

Assuming the loan period remains at five years, reducing the amount financed on the car to $10,000 would slash $1,050 from your total finance charges. Reducing the interest rate on $13,000 financed from 12.5% to 10% would slash total finance charges by $975.00.

Measure number two: Cutting the loan period from five to four years *lowers* the total finance charges from $4,548.80 to $3,585.92, a savings of $962.88—even if the interest rate remains the same. The car will end up costing $16,585.92. However, the period reduction *raises* each month's payment by $53.06, from $292.48 to $345.54. If you can handle the extra $53.06 a month, you can save a total of $962.88 in finance charges.

Reducing the dollar amount of monthly payments (instead of the actual number of payments) only makes the loan *seem* easier on your budget. So be careful about ads touting "low monthly payments."

With money loans, make sure you have the loan before you are committed to buy. Be sure that your purchase agreement includes a condition that obligates you to buy *only* if you obtain *acceptable financing* within a specified period. Alternatively, you could first obtain the loan and then make the purchase knowing you have the money to pay.

Doing it backwards can be costly. Suppose, for example, you put down a deposit and sign a purchase agreement expecting to pay for it with a loan but without including the financing condition in your purchase agreement. If you don't get the loan, you can't pay for the purchase; the seller will almost certainly treat it as a breach of contract and keep your deposit.

Wait at least 10 days after obtaining credit on any installment loan or purchase agreement before purchasing any products that you will pay for out of funds other than the credit being extended to you. The Uniform Commercial Code (UCC) section that governs security interests involving personal property in every state except Louisiana allows creditors to obtain a security interest in any personal property a debtor acquires after he or she receives the money. Creditors call this a security interest in "after acquired" property. In consumer transactions, however, the UCC sets a time limit on how many days "after" the agreement is signed a creditor can use this clause to reach personal property you acquire. This time limit is usually set at up to ten days after, but can vary depending on your state's law. A little patience is all it takes to beat "after acquired" security interest clauses that creditors exploit to get hidden leverage on consumers.

Don't co-sign for anyone . . . unless you won't mind having to pay. Since you will, if the primary signer does not, you are really extending that person credit but are getting none of the benefits of the loan. If the creditor—a professional judge of credit worthiness—is unsure about the primary signer's ability or willingness to pay, you must be doubly certain that the person you sign for will honor the debt.

Avoid late fees if at all possible. Make up skipped payments even if you have to get a cash advance on your credit card to do it. With late fees of 5% of each monthly payment, the creditor who "pyramids" late charges over the entire remaining loan period levies a finance charge at an incredible 60% APR.

Look beyond the APR to the total cost of the entire deal. The APR the creditor discloses does not tell the whole story, especially when there's a rebate involved. Manufacturers' rebates do not have to be counted as part of the finance charge. This practice makes it easy for credit sellers to team up with manufacturers to hide finance charges in the sales price. For example, if a bank charges 8% APR to finance a $12,000 car loan over four years, is that a better deal than the 6% APR deal the car manufacturer offers through a dealer on a car that would cost $13,000 if you financed it, but on which you would get a $1,000 rebate if you paid cash? The 8% loan on $12,000 would be cheaper (by $592.80) than the 6% rate on $13,000 you would have to pay without a cash-purchase rebate. It's smarter to borrow from the bank, pay in cash, and enjoy the rebate.

Always ask for an itemization of the charges for goods or services you are buying and/or payments the creditor is making on your behalf out of the credit being extended to you. For example, if the creditor is supposed to pay off an outstanding loan on a car you are trading in, make sure that's clearly identified as the creditor's obligation. Itemizing is also the only way for you to make sure the lump sum adds up to the prices you negotiated for each item. If there was an addition "mistake" but the lump sum is the only amount shown, that's what you will owe. If the costs are itemized, however, you will almost certainly owe no more than the sum of the itemized amounts rather than the mistaken total.

■ The pamphlet "Paying Off a Loan Early" explains the methods creditors use to calculate the pay-off amount when a loan is paid off ahead of schedule. Call 215-574-6458 to order, or write Federal Reserve Bank of Philadelphia, Public Information/Publications, P.O. Box 66, Philadelphia, PA 19106-0066.

■ *Usury and Consumer Credit Regulation* (1987, with a 1991 supplement), published by the National Consumer Law Center, includes tables and formulas for computing and checking interest rates and for calculating interest "rebates" that are due when a pre-computed loan is paid ahead of schedule. To order, call (617) 523-8010.

CHAPTER 62

LAYAWAY AND RENT-TO-OWN

Lending on the Fringe

Although layaway plans should be a relic from the distant past when consumer credit was not yet widely available, signs urging shoppers to "Ask about our convenient layaway plan" are still commonly seen in some discount furniture and clothing stores.

Rent-to-own (RTO) is a more recent phenomenon, a way to market primarily appliances, video, and electronic equipment to people who have trouble getting credit. Despite astounding mark-ups and astronomical rental charges, the RTO industry claims to have cornered 10% of the market for these products. The industry certainly leads in the race for the worst consumer deal in the 1990s, even when everything goes according to plan.

THE BASICS

Layaway Plans

Layaway plans allow you to pay in installments, but you don't get the goods until all the payments are made. It's the flip side of buying on credit. With layaway, *you* extend the credit to the retailer. That makes layaway plans risk-free for the seller and financially risky for consumers. Thousands of people lost their money and didn't receive their merchandise when Grant's, a national five-and-dime chain, went bankrupt in the 1970s.

So protect yourself. If you really must sign up for layaway, make extra sure the seller spells out these terms in writing:

Description of the goods. The goods should be described in detail. Be sure to include the brand name and model number.

Firm purchase price. The price should be firmly fixed in writing without the seller having any option to raise it later. Hijacking consumers for more money when they have completed their payments is like increasing the number of bombing missions needed to leave the service in *Catch-22*. It's unfair and it's one of the main tricks in this trade.

593

Payment period. The number and the amount of each payment should be clearly spelled out. Also, the plan should indicate how long the seller will hold the layaway once you start making payments.

Refund rights. Your right to a refund if you don't complete the payments within the specified payment period or if you change your mind about the purchase should be made explicit. State laws that specifically govern layaway plans and laws banning unfair and deceptive practices require that sellers clearly and conspicuously disclose their layaway refund policies. You are entitled to a refund of any payments made before the seller actually sets the product aside for you.

The Uniform Commercial Code (UCC), which governs the sale of goods, sets 20% of the purchase price or $500, whichever is less, as the maximum the seller can keep if you do not make all the required payments under a layaway plan. Sellers can keep more for seasonal items, such as winter clothing, or specially ordered goods, such as custom-designed furniture.

Rent-to-Own Plans

In December 1991, Ms. Angela P. "rented" a used four-head RCA video-cassette recorder from a Long Island rent-to-own company for 70 weekly payments of $19.99 each, plus tax. After making her 70 weekly payments, she would own the VCR. While it would have cost a few hundred dollars to buy new in a store, the VCR *cost $1,399.30 plus tax under rent-to-own.* This massive mark-up is the norm in the RTO business.

In RTO plans, you lease an appliance or furniture for a period of weeks or months. Once all of the scheduled rental payments are completed, you either own the product outright or have the option to buy it, for a nominal additional amount or for a substantial balloon payment (a large single payment at the end of the rental period). The RTO industry came up with balloon payments to avoid laws under which the transaction would otherwise have been deemed a credit sale, which would have triggered certain consumer protection laws the industry sought to avoid.

The RTO industry is woefully under-regulated. Of 31 states that have laws specifically governing RTO, only seven (Iowa, Michigan, Minnesota, Nebraska, New York, Ohio, and South Carolina) place a ceiling on lease charges. In these seven states, a portion of each payment, ranging from 45% to 55%, must be applied toward the actual purchase of the product. This still works out to an effective annual interest rate of 90% to 180%—a far

> *"Generally speaking, when a store fails, there is no recourse for the layaway customer."*
> —SUSAN KASSAPIAN, General Counsel, NYC Department of Consumer Affairs

cry from the 15% charged by most credit card issuers.

If you sign up for rent-to-own anyway, be sure the lease includes clauses with:

An accurate description of the item to be rented.

A payment schedule. This spells out the amount and timing of each rental payment.

The total cost. This identifies the total number of payments and the total amount you must pay to become the owner of the leased property. Compare total costs from RTO businesses to find out where you can get the best deal.

Additional charges. This usually includes taxes and charges for other services or insurance. Be sure you really want or need any additional services.

Late charges. Most states that regulate RTO transactions limit late charges. In New York, for example, it's $3 or 10% of the delinquent payment for weekly rentals, and $5 or 10% for monthly rentals, whichever is greater. You are usually allowed a grace period, generally a few days' duration.

Liability for loss. This spells out what you would owe in case the rented product is stolen or destroyed. RTO companies now sell "liability waiver" coverage under which they agree not to hold you liable for the theft or destruction of the product if you pay an additional charge. These charges can be high, but you could also owe a lot if the product is destroyed or stolen.

What happens in case of "excess wear and tear." Charges for excess wear and tear (usually defined in the contract) only matter if you cancel the lease and return the product or if you default and it is repossessed.

Ownership rights. What you have to do to become the owner of the leased product. Usually, you must keep up with the scheduled payments.

Cash price, which is what the RTO company would ostensibly charge if you bought it from them without renting. The rental charges are computed on the basis of it. The cash price is usually inflated. In the case of Angela P., believe it or not, the cash price for the used VCR was $699.95, probably three times what it would have sold for elsewhere.

Only a few states require that the cash price be disclosed. The difference between the cash price and the total cost of all the rental payments tells you how much extra you are paying in order to buy the item over time.

Early purchase option. Some state's laws, like New York's, entitle you to purchase the item at any time upon payment of the early purchase option price. Having an early purchase option is a big plus; you could save a lot in lease charges if you can buy yourself out of the lease early.

Reinstatement right. Explains how you can reinstate a lease after defaulting on the payments. This right usually lasts for only a few days unless you voluntarily return the merchandise. RTO companies

LAYING LOW, BUT NOT EXTINCT

Layaway may be on the wane, but it's still around. According to *The Wall Street Journal,* the 154-unit Hill Department Stores does nearly 12% of its business through layaways. And during the Christmas shopping season, nearly half of all purchases at Child's World toy stores in low-income communities are layaways.

are quick to repossess goods after payment defaults, which could result in losing all the payments made toward buying the product. The law in each state then spells out how many days you have to reinstate the lease after returning the merchandise.

RTO leases allow you to cancel the rental at any time. But then the company will cart the item away and all the rent you paid just goes with it.

WHAT TO WATCH OUT FOR

Old goods passed off as new. One of the most frequent RTO complaints is that a company furnished a used product when the consumer was supposed to get a new one. Under the laws in most of the 31 states that separately regulate RTO transactions, the item you are leasing

should be fully and clearly described, especially whether it is new or used. Insist that the agreement include a requirement that the product be delivered in its factory sealed container.

Balloon RTO payments or other conditions you would have to satisfy beyond making the periodic rental payments to become the owner. If there are any, you're looking at a worse than bad deal.

Used or missing manuals and warranties. These should be properly packed and sealed in their original envelope or wrapping. Booklets should not show any evidence of prior use.

THE SMARTER CONSUMER

Layaway Plans

Layaway your money for a rainy day. Since a layaway plan means saving money until you have enough to buy with cash, why let the seller hold your money without paying you interest? Instead, set up a bank deposit account that you use only for big-ticket purchases.

Use only well-known and established companies for layaway plans since you are lending *them* your money until you get the goods.

Rent-to-Own

Stay away. The smartest thing you can do is not to get involved with RTO in the first place. They're never a good deal.

If you return an RTO-leased item, have the company give you a written condition report that accurately describes the condition of the product when you returned it.

Promptly tell the dealer about defects or malfunctions. If the dealer cannot or will not quickly and properly correct the problem, the product will not improve with age. Your right to cancel at least gives you the chance to bail out quickly, before you get in too deep.

Immediately put your complaints in writing, clearly and fully spelling out the problems and making it clear that you expect the product to be promptly and properly serviced.

If you cancel early because of product malfunctions or defects, you should also insist on a refund of rental payments. If the dealer refuses, you could try to sue in small claims court. You have little to lose except the payments you have already made.

Canceling early and quickly may cost you the rental payments you have already made, but that's better than making more payments and getting nothing but grief.

Find out if you will be covered by the manufacturer's warranties. If such warranties are not extended to you until after you actually buy the product, be sure the agreement specifies that the dealer is responsible for servicing and repairing the product in the interim.

▪ Check with your state attorney general's office to find out about local RTO transaction requirements.

▪ If you run into problems with an RTO transaction, the book *Unfair and Deceptive Acts and Practices* by the National Consumer Law Center, 3rd edition, 1991, summarizes your protections under various state and federal laws; call (617) 523-8010 to order.

CHAPTER 63

COUNTERFEIT AND GRAY MARKET GOODS

 You Get What You Pay For

S everal years ago, the New York City Police Department confiscated 130 cases of ersatz Halston and Aramis fragrances in a Brooklyn warehouse. They looked exactly like the real thing, but any discerning nose would have known they were cheap knock-offs. And NYC residents weren't meant to be the only victims; the operation intended to ship to 30 different states.

Counterfeiting of high-quality luxury products has become a big business. But when buying name-brand products, counterfeits aren't the only scam to watch out for. You need also to be aware of "gray market" goods—products made by the manufacturer on the label but that are still not up to the manufacturer's usual standards.

THE BASICS

What Are Counterfeit Goods?

T he counterfeiter we normally hear about prints bogus bills and tries to use them to purchase genuine merchandise. Product counterfeiters do the reverse, producing bogus merchandise that they try to turn into genuine cash. Bogus goods or bogus bills, the result is the same—the person stuck with them usually ends up with garbage.

Product counterfeiters are really trademark pirates who slap counterfeit labels of respected manufacturers on their own products. They do a booming business, especially in places where tourists concentrate to look for bargains. In New York City alone, counterfeit sales amount to more than $2 billion annually.

And just as currency counterfeiters ignore the small stuff to concentrate on bigger bills like $20s, $50s, and even $100s, product counterfeiters go for high-priced, easy-to-move, high-demand items like watches, videotapes of first-run movies, or high-fashion apparel and accessories like sunglasses and handbags. According to the head of Rolex watches, over a third of all "Rolexes" sold are fakes!

As with most scams, trademark

pirates try to hook consumers with the "bargain-of-a-lifetime" lure—the Gucci handbag for $50 or "make me an offer;" the latest Bruce Willis action thriller on tape for only $5. The list is endless, but it's the same scheme—an incredibly low price for the genuine article, which is usually an inflated price for phony goods.

The only sure thing about buying counterfeit goods (assuming that you are unaware that you are buying a fake) is that you will be disappointed. The quality of the imitation is always vastly inferior to the genuine article. The $15 "Rolex" watch stops ticking after only a week. The bad stitching on the "Chanel" handbags is only one of the myriad quality differences with authentic Chanel handbags. The only way that you can effectively protect yourself is to avoid falling into the trap in the first place.

"Gray Market" Goods

Mary W. of Tulsa, Oklahoma, was upset when jewelers told her that parts for the watch she bought were unavailable because the watch had not been manufactured for distribution in the United States. William S. of Cincinnati, Ohio, was furious because the cam-

> "The gray market is the sale of goods with genuine brand names, but which are not intended for sale in the United States. It's actually legal, but it can hurt consumers badly."
>
> —BETTY FURNESS,
> WNBC Consumer Reporter

era and equipment he purchased by mail did not have warranties. Gerry C. of Durango, Colorado, was perplexed because the owner's manual for the product she bought was printed in French. Although they lived far apart, these consumers had one thing in common—each had unknowingly bought "gray market" goods.

Unlike counterfeit goods, which have phony brand names, "gray market" goods are genuine, brand-name products. But the goods are manufactured for sale outside the United States and are imported into the United States through illicit channels—that is, those other than the manufacturer's authorized distributor. The problem of gray market imports first cropped up in 1985, when price discounting came into fashion and their importation became more widespread.

Here's the rub: Because gray market goods are not made to be sold in the U.S., such products may not measure up to the standards that American consumers expect for the same brand-name product. So while the label is genuine, consumers can't immediately tell the quality of the product by the label consumers have come to know.

Consumers can stumble onto gray market goods in a wide range of consumer products—from toothbrushes and toothpaste to photographic equipment, soft drinks, and outboard motors. Cameras, batteries, electrical products, cosmetics, and watches are the most common.

Here is how consumers can be short-changed by shoddy gray market goods:

Warranties. The product is not covered by the manufacturer's warranty, is not eligible for warranty servicing by authorized repair sources, or is not covered by manufacturer's rebates.

Product differences. The product is not manufactured according to applicable U.S. health and safety standards, lacks qualities American consumers expect from that product, or includes parts or ingredients not found in the domestic version. Examples: Gray market cosmetics may contain additives like red dye #2 that are banned in the U.S.; Johnson & Johnson talc made in Brazil contains talc that is different from the U.S. version; detergents may have been formulated for water with a different mix of minerals than is usually found in the U.S.; or an electrical product may not operate on U.S. current, or may not be set for our radio frequencies.

Ingredient labels. The ingredient or contents labels may provide less information than is required for American products.

Is it ever worthwhile to buy gray market goods? Not if the price is close to what you would pay for a product made specifically for the U.S. market—why take a chance? But if the price of a gray market product is significantly lower than the product made for the U.S. market, it may be worth the risk of some difference in performance, unless the difference could matter a lot. It's unlikely to be worth gambling on possible quality or performance differences in the following situations:

The product interacts with your body, like food and cosmetics. Here you're taking chances with your health, and that's never a good gamble.

The product has moving parts that may require repairs, or you may need accessories to upgrade it. Everything you save on price could disappear with the first breakdown.

WHAT TO WATCH OUT FOR

Counterfeit Goods Warning Signals

Two sure-fire early warning signals usually go together: The price is "too good to be true." (In these cases, it always is.) And the product is sold by street vendors, at kiosks or small hole-in-the-wall-stores, or are not on display. The hallmark of quality products is that they are sold by established merchants from fixed locations. After all, the seller and manufacturer both seek to maintain an image for the product that matches its quality. You simply won't find high-quality products sold through shady locations.

The product lacks labels or hand tags that provide information about the company, the product's qualities, or references to licensing agreements (if it involves a licensed product, such as a fictional character, sports team, or movie). If the product is clothing, it should have sewn-in labels identifying the legitimate manufacturer.

The packaging is flimsy, the labels are made of inferior grade material, the printing on the package or labels is not sharp and detailed.

Written warranties are absent when you would normally expect them to be included, such as for a watch or a radio.

Gray Market Goods Warning Signals

Unfortunately, gray market goods do not come neatly labelled. New York is one of the few states that requires retailers to alert consumers that they might be buying gray market goods. But even New York's law only requires retailers to post signs telling consumers that some of the products they sell may not be covered by warranties valid in the U.S., may not be accompanied by instructions in English, or may not be eligible for manufacturer rebates. Here are warning signs that should alert you:

■ The product is not sold through a manufacturer's official or authorized representative.
■ The product is priced significantly lower than what you would expect to pay when purchasing from authorized sources.
■ The product labels or printing on

the package is entirely in a foreign language.
■ The owner's manual or other written instructions are entirely in a foreign language.
■ No warranty information is given for a product that would usually be covered by such a warranty.

You can't do much if you bought counterfeit goods. The manufacturers of the genuine articles might express their regrets, but they won't fix your problem—it is, after all, not their product. If you can find the seller, you could then try to get your money back because the seller engaged in deception or fraud by selling a product that was not, in fact, what it was represented to be. Sadly, this is easier said than done.

If you find out that you purchased gray market goods only after opening the package—such as by finding only foreign language instructions or a product that only runs on current not generated by your electric utility—take the product back to the seller and demand a refund, pronto. Tell the seller that the product is not fit for the usual purpose for which it is intended. In legalese, you can say that the product is "not merchantable" and the seller has "breached the warranty of merchantability" created by the Uniform Commercial Code.

■ For more information on counterfeit perfume and cosmetics products, read the "Toiletries, Fragrances and Skin Care" installment in *FDA Reports*, published October 22, 1984. It's available from the Food & Drug Administration, Consumer Affairs and Information, 5600 Fishers Lane, Rockville, MD 20857.

■ For more information on how the gray market operates, read the *Report on Drug Diversion*, prepared by the staff of the House Committee on Energy and Commerce, Committee Print, 1985.

■ If you buy an item that does not live up to the Uniform Commercial Code's requirement that it be fit to be used for the purpose for which it was sold, report the incident to the Attorney General of your state.

■ If you buy an item whose lack of a proper ingredient label leads you to suspect it to be counterfeit or from the gray market, report it to the Food & Drug Administration at the above address.

CHAPTER 64

HOW TO COMPLAIN

Talking Back

There's no need for a disgruntled customer to imitate Michael Douglas in *Falling Down* to get satisfaction. You may recall how Douglas' character attacked a convenience store's high-priced products with a baseball bat, saying, "I'm just standing up for my rights . . . as a consumer." Try submitting a formal complaint to a store or agency instead. As nearly all the prior chapters on specific products and services indicate, this tactic can work well.

Always shop with care—an ounce of preventive consumer education is worth many pounds of cure. But what should you do when disappointment invades even the smartest purchases? For instance, salespeople and advertisements make promises their products can't keep, an item that looks to be of superior quality turns out to be inferior, or a merchant's seemingly good intentions go bad. In fact, one federal study indicated that approximately one in four purchases results in one problem or another—yet only one in 25 people with problems actually takes the time and effort to complain. It pays to talk back in order to get your money back.

THE BASICS

Better Business Bureaus (BBBs) around the country handled 1.5 million consumer complaints in 1993. Be especially careful when you deal with the following businesses, which had the most complaints lodged against them: retail sales, home improvement companies, service firms, auto repairs and services, and ordered product (catalogue, telephone, and mail order) sales.

You have a good chance of getting redress if you take the trouble to address the problem. But you may never get what you paid for—and you might end up more frustrated than if you hadn't complained at all—if you don't complain in a firm and organized way. Wheels that know how to squeak will get the grease.

Correcting your problem helps others as well as yourself. When you complain to a business, your action may motivate merchants and manufacturers to change their ways. When you alert and seek help from a government or non-profit agency, you help them target the worst offenders for law enforcement and consumer education initiatives.

If you are fortunate enough to have a local or state government office with law enforcement authority, you have the extra benefit of legal clout and a better shot at speedy resolution of your problem. For instance, New York City has one of the broadest consumer protection

BUSINESS GROUPS RANKED BY COMPLAINTS

Group	Total Complaints	Rank
RETAIL	40,750	1
HOME IMPROVEMENT/REMODELING COMPANIES	31,750	2
SERVICE FIRMS (EXCEPT AUTO)	31,010	3
AUTO REPAIRS AND SERVICES	26,270	4
ORDERED PRODUCT SALES	22,240	5
VEHICLE DEALERS AND MANUFACTURERS	19,060	6
FINANCIAL SERVICES	9,640	7
TRAVEL/VACATION-RELATED SERVICES	8,560	8
PERSONAL AND PROFESSIONAL SERVICES	8,050	9
BUSINESS SERVICES	6,890	10
HEALTH AND MEDICAL	6,560	11
CREDIT/CREDIT SERVICES	6,290	12
REAL ESTATE SALES SERVICES	5,620	13
MANUFACTURERS AND WHOLESALERS	4,160	14
FRANCHISE AND BUSINESS OPPORTUNITIES	3,540	15 (tie)
HOME BUILDERS AND MANUFACTURERS	3,540	15 (tie)
DIRECT IN-HOME SALES	3,440	16
FOOD SALES AND SERVICES	2,590	17
ENTERTAINMENT	2,400	18
INSURANCE	2,310	19
SWEEPSTAKES, CONTESTS, AND GAMES	1,460	20

Source: Council of Better Business Bureaus, 1993

laws of any local government in the country. Every year, the city's Department of Consumer Affairs agency responds to some 150,000 New Yorkers and visitors with questions and problems, and formally handles an average of over 10,000 complaints. About 90% of consumers who file complaints get some satisfaction after Consumer Affairs staff helps them and the merchants work out mutually acceptable solutions to their disputes. Consumers receive an average of more than $1 million each year in money refunded and debts canceled. The one in ten complaints that are not resolved through Consumer Affairs mediation are referred to courts or dropped by the consumer. (See the appendix on page 611 for consumer offices or the attorney general's office in your state.)

THE SMARTER CONSUMER

The first step in becoming a $marter complainer is checking a seller's "return policy" *before* making a purchase—otherwise your complaint may be pointless from the start. Such policies should be posted on store premises and on sales receipts. They usually require that products be returned within a given time period, in good condition or in the original packaging, and with a receipt.

The Art of Complaining

Identify the problem. Go through the events leading up to your problem, including any attempts you made to resolve it.

Decide on an acceptable remedy. Do you want the item repaired? Replaced? Your money back? If you used credit, do you want your debt canceled?

Gather your records. Include all sales receipts, credit card statements or canceled checks, and contracts, and repair bills. You'll need them to support your case.

Start where you made the purchase. Call the business that sold you the item or performed the service. Describe the problem calmly and thoroughly. Politely tell the retailer how you would like the problem resolved. If you end up talking to the customer service representative, remember that you are dealing with someone other than the person actually responsible for your problem. So be firm while being polite and try to win them over. Ask for the manager or owner if the person you are speaking with is not helpful. You may need to move up the chain of command and call the company's headquarters to get satisfaction.

Contact the maker. To deal with a manufacturing defect, contact the manufacturer—ask for the consumer affairs director, the president, or the chief executive officer. (Phone numbers, sometimes toll-free, and addresses can be found on warranty cards, product boxes, or at the library.) A national firm may have

SAMPLE COMPLAINT LETTER

(Your address)
(Your city, state, zip code)
(Date)

(Name of contact person):
(Title)
(Company name)
(Street address)
(City, state, zip code)

Dear (contact person):

· Describe your purchase

· Name of product, serial numbers

· Include date and location of purchase

   On (date), I purchased (or had repaired) a (name of the product with serial or model number or service performed). I made this purchase at (location, date and other important details of the transaction).
   Unfortunately, your product (or service) has not performed well (or the service was inadequate) because (state the problem).
   Therefore, to resolve the problem, I would appreciate your (state the specific action you want). Enclosed are copies (copies, NOT originals) of my records (receipts, guarantees, warranties, canceled checks, contracts, model and serial numbers, and any other documents).
   I look forward to your reply and a resolution to my problem, and will wait (set a time limit) before seeking third-party assistance. Please contact me at the above address or by phone at (home or office numbers with area codes).

· State the problem

· Give the history

· Ask for specific action

· Enclose copies of documents

· Set time for action or response

· Include how you can be reached

Sincerely

(Your name)
(Your account number)

* Text in parentheses ( ) will change when you personalize your letter.
Source: US Office of Consumer Affairs

spent millions of dollars to create brand-name goodwill and be more concerned about not jeopardizing that good name than a local retailer would be. Before you contact the manufacturer, become familiar with the terms of your warranty. You also have rights under implied warranties that apply to all goods: Under the Uniform Commercial Code, which all 50 states have enacted in some version, a product must be fit to be used for the purpose for which it was intended—or you're entitled to restitution. You may also be protected by other local, state, and federal laws and regulations.

Put it in writing. If your problem cannot be settled over the phone, write a letter. Be brief and to the point. Let the company know that you believe the complaint can easily be resolved without any need for publicity or law enforcement action. In other words, adopt the admonition about a steel fist within a velvet glove.

Your complaint letter should include all the important facts about your purchase, the problem, and what you've done to try and resolve it:

- Your name, address, daytime and evening phone numbers, and account number, if appropriate.
- All important facts, including the date and place you made your purchase, and the serial and model numbers of the item, or the type of service you received and who performed it.
- A complete description of what you've already done to try to remedy the problem.
- Exactly what you want as a remedy, such as a replacement, repair, or your money back.
- A reasonable time frame for the merchant to respond and correct the problem.
- Copies—*not originals*—of all related receipts, invoices, and warranties.

Maintain a file. Keep copies of all your correspondence and make notes about the content of phone conversations with retailers and manufacturers. Be sure to get the names of everyone with whom you speak and the dates and outcomes of your conversations. Pay a little extra and send the letter by certified mail. Request a return receipt—it's evidence that the letter was received and shows the name of the person who signed for it. For extra protection against the letter being lost in the mail, you can pay a bit more to send the letter by registered mail.

> " *C*omplaining is important because you can not only help yourself but you can trigger an investigation, which can help many others as well."
>
> —BARBARA BERGER OPOTOWSKY, President of the Better Business Bureau of Metropolitan New York

The Next Step

If you still don't get satisfaction, it's time to contact your government consumer affairs office, trade association, or the Better Business Bureau. Send a brief cover letter outlining the problem and your attempts to resolve it on your own; include copies of your correspondence with the offending company. Send the company a copy of your letter to government authorities and you may get results even before the consumer affairs agency, trade group, or BBB takes action.

The government is there to help you. Really. In most parts of the country, local and state consumer affairs or attorneys general offices will be able to help you resolve your problem. These offices typically have the legal muscle—or at least the official letterhead—to persuade a firm to provide a fair result, or even to fine the company if it broke any laws or violated regulations. Federal agencies do not generally handle individual consumer complaints, but they keep track of your letters to help them target troublesome industries.

Tell the relevant trade association how you were tricked or unfairly treated. Some trade associations sponsor dispute resolution programs involving arbitration, conciliation, or mediation. Since the outcomes of these programs may be binding, get a copy of the program's rules *before* you file your case. (See **HELP** at the end of this chapter for information on these programs and refer to relevant chapters earlier in the book.)

Tell it to the judge. In those rare instances when all of the above efforts fail, consumers have one more option: suing the business in either small claims or civil court. Don't wait too long to exercise your legal rights: The laws where you live may limit the amount of time you have to file a lawsuit.

State and local consumer affairs offices usually offer advice on how to proceed in court, including how to get affordable legal help. Small claims courts handle disputes involving relatively small amounts of money, while civil courts handle cases involving bigger bucks. In small claims court, most people represent themselves without the help of lawyers. Civil court procedures can be complicated, and even though you may be allowed to represent yourself, you may not get very far without a lawyer.

Most often, the small claims process is convenient, fast, and saves you from having to pay a lawyer (although you can hire a lawyer simply to review your case with you or accompany you to court, if you like). Typically, small claims court is the place to take up cases involving broken contracts, negligent behavior that caused damage to your property, violation of your rights, and redress for purchases of defective merchandise or services. However, it's only worth the effort if the person or business you are suing can pay. The maximum amount disputable in small claims courts in the U.S. averages $2,000, but some states have a higher threshold: Alaska, California, Georgia, New Mexico, and Pennsylvania have raised their limits to $5,000; and in parts of Tennessee, the limit is $10,000.

To prepare your case, document your efforts to resolve the dispute yourself. Keep photocopies of all correspondence and a written log of all phone conversations. Before you go into court, get organized:

■ Prepare a written outline of the chronology of events. Keep it short and to the point.
■ If you have a problem with a local business, go to the County Clerk's office to research the full name, address, and owner of the business.
■ Make your own detailed estimate of what you are owed. Then, itemize your expenses and bills to determine what you think is fair compensation.
■ If visible evidence is relevant,

PLACES TO SEEK RESOLUTION

■ **Store.** Speak to or visit the original salesperson, the supervisor, a customer service representative, the manager, or the owner of the store.

■ **Manufacturer.** Write to the president or chief executive officer.

■ **Media.** Contact a consumer reporter, a letter-to-the-editor section, or media action line.

■ **Self-policing groups.** Convey the problem to the BBB, a trade association, or an industry-specific resolution group (eg, bar grievance committee, medical society, auto arbitration panels).

■ **Consumer groups.** Report the incident to one of Ralph Nader's groups, Consumers Union, or the Consumer Federation of America.

■ **Public agencies.** Inform the local consumer office or attorney general's office.

■ **Court.** Depending on the size of the claim, go to small claims or civil court.

■ **District attorney.** If the matter involves willful fraud, consider reporting it for possible criminal prosecution.

■ **Legislature.** Go to your city council or state legislature if a new law is needed.

---

photograph the place or item at issue for the judge.

When you go to court:

■ When you go before the judge, present your case and all the evidence. Listen to the story told by the opposing party and point out misstatements, misinterpretations of fact, and memory lapses. But don't lose your temper; the judge may take it as a sign that you're missing solid evidence.

■ Again, don't forget to bring all the supporting documents for your case with you to help the judge come to a fair decision.

■ Submit any evidence you have of your efforts to resolve the dispute outside court—ie, letters to the contractor who skipped town before finishing the job, canceled checks for payments you made that you thought were fair, notes to neighbors who insisted on letting their daughter practice the drums at 6:30 AM.

Speak Up and Out

If *The Consumer Bible* offers you anything, it's this—$marter consumers can save thousands of dollars a year if they compare prices and complain when aggrieved. Yet an estimated 24 of 25 purchasers who are dissatisfied but silent underestimate their power. Reputable stores and manufacturers survive and thrive if they get good word-of-mouth, avoid bad publicity and liability claims, and treat customers as advisors, not adversaries. These three elements actually stack the deck *in favor* of a committed complainant, so long as he or she energetically works through the alternatives described earlier. The goal of this book was to educate and empower you in the marketplace. Ultimately, only you can stand up for your rights as a consumer.

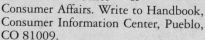 **To find listings of** local, state, and federal agencies, corporate consumer contacts, Better Business Bureaus and trade associations, consult the free *Consumer's Resource Handbook*, published by the U.S. Office of Consumer Affairs. Write to Handbook, Consumer Information Center, Pueblo, CO 81009.

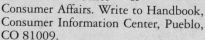 **Trade associations and their con-**sumer functions are also listed at your local library in *National Trade and Pro-* *fessional Associations of the United States*, published by Columbia Books, Inc.

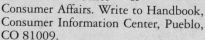 **If you just need the ad-**dress and/or phone number of a company, call the reference desk of your local library and ask them to look the company up in AT&T's directory of toll-free numbers or other directories of corporations they have, such as *Standard and Poor's Register of Corporations, Directors and Executives*, the *Standard Directory of Advertisers*, or the *Trade Names Directory*.

STATE CONSUMER OFFICES

Alabama

Office of the Attorney General
Consumer Affairs Division
11 South Union Street
Montgomery, AL 36130
(205) 242-7334
(800) 392-5658 (toll-free in Alabama)

Alaska

The Attorney General's Office refers complaints to the Better Business Bureau, small claims court, and private attorneys.

Better Business Bureau
2805 Bering Street, #2
Anchorage, AK 99503-3819
(907) 562-0704

Arizona

Office of the Attorney General
Consumer Protection Division
1275 West Washington Street
Room 259
Phoenix, AZ 85007
(602) 542-5763
(800) 352-8431 (toll-free in Arizona)

Office of the Attorney General
Consumer Protection Division
402 West Congress Street
Suite 315
Tucson, AZ 85701
(602) 628-6504

Arkansas

Office of the Attorney General
Consumer Protection Division
200 Tower Building
323 Center Street
Little Rock, AR 72201
(501) 682-2341 (voice/TDD)
(800) 482-8982 (toll-free voice/TDD in Arkansas)

California

California Department of Consumer Affairs
400 R Street, Suite 1040
Sacramento, CA 95814
(916) 445-1254
(916) 522-1700 (TDD)
(800) 344-9940 (toll-free in California)

Office of the Attorney General
Public Inquiry Unit
P.O. Box 944255
Sacramento, CA 94244-2550
(916) 322-3360
(800) 952-5225 (toll-free in California)
(800) 952-5548 (toll-free TDD in California)

Bureau of Automotive Repair
California Department of Consumer Affairs
10240 Systems Parkway
Sacramento, CA 95827
(916) 255-4300
(800) 952-5210 (toll-free in California, auto repair only)

Colorado

Office of the Attorney General
Consumer Protection Unit
1525 Sherman Street, 5th Floor
Denver, CO 80203
(303) 866-5189

Connecticut

Department of Consumer Protection
165 Capitol Avenue
Hartford, CT 06106
(203) 566-2534
(800) 842-2649 (toll-free in Connecticut)

Office of the Attorney General
Anti-Trust/Consumer Protection Division
110 Sherman Street
Hartford, CT 06105
(203) 566-5374

Delaware

Division of Consumer Affairs
Department of Community Affairs
820 North French Street, 4th Floor
Wilmington, DE 19801
(302) 577-3250

Office of the Attorney General
Economic Crime and Consumer Protection
  Division
820 North French Street
Wilmington, DE 19801
(302) 577-2500

District of Columbia

Department of Consumer and Regulatory
  Affairs
614 H Street, NW
Washington, DC 20001
(202) 727-7120

Florida

Department of Agriculture and Consumer
  Services
Division of Consumer Services
407 South Calhoun Street
Mayo Building, 2nd Floor
Tallahassee, FL 32399-0800
(904) 488-2221
(800) 435-7352 (toll-free in Florida)

Office of the Attorney General
Consumer Division
4000 Hollywood Blvd., Suite 505 South
Hollywood, FL 33021
(305) 985-4780

Office of the Attorney General
The Capitol
PL 01
Tallahassee, FL 32399-1050
(904) 487-1963

Georgia

Governor's Office of Consumer Affairs
2 Martin Luther King Jr. Drive, SE
Plaza Level-East Tower
Atlanta, GA 30334
(404) 651-8600
(404) 656-3790
(800) 869-1123 (toll-free in Georgia)

Office of the Attorney General
40 Capitol Square, SW
Atlanta, GA 30334-1300
(404) 656-4585

Hawaii

Department of Commerce and Consumer
  Affairs
Office of Consumer Protection
828 Fort Street Mall, Suite 600B
P.O. Box 3767
Honolulu, HI 96812-3767
(808) 586-2636

Department of Commerce and Consumer
  Affairs
Office of Consumer Protection
75 Aupuni Street
Hilo, HI 96720
(808) 933-4433

Department of Commerce and Consumer
  Affairs
Office of Consumer Protection
3060 Eiwa Street
Lihue, HI 96766
(808) 241-3365

Department of Commerce and Consumer
  Affairs
Office of Consumer Protection
54 High Street
Wailuku, HI 96793
(808) 243-5387

Office of the Attorney General
425 Queen Street
Honolulu, HI 96813
(808) 586-1282

Idaho

Office of the Attorney General
Consumer Protection Unit
Statehouse, Room 119
Boise, ID 83720-1000
(208) 334-2424
(800) 432-3545 (toll-free in Idaho)

Illinois

Office of the Attorney General
Consumer Protection Division
100 West Randolph, 12th Floor
Chicago, IL 60601
(312) 814-3000
(312) 793-2852 (TDD)

Indiana

Office of the Attorney General
Consumer Protection Division
219 State House
Indianapolis, IN 46204
(317) 232-6330
(800) 382-5516 (toll-free in Indiana)

Iowa

Office of the Attorney General
Consumer Protection Division
1300 East Walnut Street, 2nd Floor
Des Moines, IA 50319
(515) 281-5926

Kansas

Office of the Attorney General
Consumer Protection Division
301 West 10th
Kansas Judicial Center
Topeka, KS 66612-1597
(913) 296-3751
(800) 432-2310 (toll-free in Kansas)

Kentucky

Office of the Attorney General
Consumer Protection Division
209 Saint Clair Street
Frankfort, KY 40601-1875
(502) 564-2200
(800) 432-9257 (toll-free in Kentucky)

Office of the Attorney General
Consumer Protection Division
107 South Fourth Street
Louisville, KY 40202
(502) 595-3262
(800) 432-9257 (toll-free in Kentucky)

Louisiana

Office of the Attorney General
Consumer Protection Section
State Capitol Building
P.O. Box 94095
Baton Rouge, LA 70804-9095
(504) 342-9638

Maine

Bureau of Consumer Credit Protection
State House Station No. 35
Augusta, ME 04333-0035
(207) 582-8718
(800) 332-8529 (toll-free in Maine)

Office of the Attorney General
Consumer and Antitrust Division
State House Station No. 6
Augusta, ME 04333
(207) 626-8849 (9 AM to 1 PM)

Maryland

Office of the Attorney General
Consumer Protection Division
200 St. Paul Place
Baltimore, MD 21202-2021

(410) 528-8662 (9 AM to 3 PM)
(410) 565-0451 (Washington, DC area)
(410) 576-6372 (TDD in Baltimore area)

Eastern Shore Branch Office
Office of the Attorney General
Consumer Protection Division
201 Baptist Street, Suite 30
Salisbury, MD 21801-4976
(410) 543-6620

Western Maryland Branch Office
Office of the Attorney General
Consumer Protection Division
138 East Antietam Street, Suite 210
Hagerstown, MD 21740-5684
(301) 791-4780

Massachusetts

Department of the Attorney General
Consumer Protection Division
1 Ashburton Place
Boston, MA 02103
(617) 727-8400

Executive Office of Consumer Affairs and
  Business Regulation
1 Ashburton Place, Room 1411
Boston, MA 02108
(617) 727-7780

Department of the Attorney General
Western Massachusetts Consumer
  Protection Division
436 Dwight Street
Springfield, MA 01103
(413) 784-1240

Michigan

Office of the Attorney General
Consumer Protection Division
P.O. Box 30213
Lansing, MI 48909
(517) 373-1140

Bureau of Automotive Regulation
Michigan Department of State
Lansing, MI 48918-1200
(517) 373-4777
(800) 292-4204 (toll-free in Michigan)

Minnesota

Office of the Attorney General
Consumer Services Division
1400 NCL Tower
445 Minnesota Street
St. Paul, MN 55101
(612) 296-3353

Mississippi

Office of the Attorney General
Office of Consumer Protection
P.O. Box 22947
Jackson, MS 39225-2947
(601) 354-6018

Bureau of Regulatory Services
Department of Agriculture and Commerce
500 Greymont Avenue
P.O. Box 1609
Jackson, MS 39215-1609
(601) 354-7063

Missouri

Office of the Attorney General
Division of Consumer Protection
P.O. Box 899
Jefferson City, MO 65102
(314) 751-3321
(800) 392-8222 (toll-free in Missouri)

Montana

Consumer Affairs Unit
Department of Commerce
1424 Ninth Avenue
Box 200501
Helena, MT 59620-0501
(406) 444-4312

Nebraska

Consumer Protection Division
Department of Justice
2115 State Capitol
P.O. Box 98920
Lincoln, NE 68509
(402) 471-2682

Nevada

Commissioner of Consumer Affairs
Department of Commerce
State Mail Room Complex
Las Vegas, NV 89158
(702) 486-7355
(800) 992-0900 (toll-free in Nevada)

Consumer Affairs Division
Department of Commerce
4600 Kietzke Lane, B-113
Reno, NV 89502
(702) 688-1800
(800) 992-0900 (toll-free in Nevada)

New Hampshire

Office of the Attorney General
Consumer Protection and Antitrust Bureau
State House Annex
Concord, NH 03301
(603) 271-3641

New Jersey

Division of Consumer Affairs
P.O. Box 45027
124 Halsey Street, 7th Floor
Newark, NJ 07101
(201) 504-6534

New Mexico

Office of the Attorney General
Consumer Protection Division
P.O. Drawer 1508
Santa Fe, NM 87504
(505) 827-6060
(800) 678-1508 (toll-free in NM)

New York

Office of the Attorney General
Bureau of Consumer Frauds and Protection
State Capitol
Albany, NY 12224
(518) 474-5481

Office of the Attorney General
Bureau of Consumer Frauds and Protection
120 Broadway
New York, NY 10271
(212) 416-8345

New York State Consumer Protection Board
99 Washington Avenue
Albany, NY 12210-2891
(518) 474-8583

New York State Consumer Protection Board
250 Broadway, 17th Floor
New York, NY 10007-2593
(212) 417-4908 (complaints)
(212) 417-4482 (main office)

North Carolina

Office of the Attorney General
Consumer Protection Section
Raney Building
P.O. Box 629
Raleigh, NC 27602
(919) 733-7741

North Dakota

Office of the Attorney General
Consumer Fraud Section
600 East Boulevard
Bismarck, ND 58505
(701) 224-3404
(800) 472-2600 (toll-free in North Dakota)

Ohio

Office of the Attorney General
Consumer Frauds and Crime Section
30 East Broad Street
State Office Tower, 25th Floor
Columbus, OH 43266-0410
(614) 466-1393
(614) 466-1393 (TDD)
(800) 282-0515 (toll-free in Ohio)

Office of Consumers' Counsel
77 South High Street, 15th Floor
Columbus, OH 43266-0550
(614) 466-9605 (voice/TDD)
(800) 282-9448 (toll-free in Ohio)

Oklahoma

Office of the Attorney General
Consumer Protection Division
4545 North Lincoln Boulevard, Suite 260
Oklahoma City, OK 73105
(405) 521-4274

Department of Consumer Credit
4545 North Lincoln Boulevard, Suite 104
Oklahoma City, OK 73105-3408
(405) 521-3653

Oregon

Financial Fraud Section
Department of Justice
1162 Court Street NE
Salem, OR 97310
(503) 378-4732

Pennsylvania

Office of the Attorney General
Bureau of Consumer Protection
Strawberry Square, 14th Floor
Harrisburg, PA 17120
(717) 787-9707
(800) 441-2555 (toll-free in Pennsylvania)

Office of the Attorney General
Bureau of Consumer Protection
1251 South Cedar Crest Boulevard, Suite 309
Allentown, PA 18103
(215) 821-6690

Office of the Attorney General
Bureau of Consumer Protection
919 State Street, Room 203
Erie, PA 16501
(814) 871-4371

Office of the Attorney General
Bureau of Consumer Protection
Professional Building
P.O. Box 716
Ebensberg, PA 15931
(814) 949-7900

Office of the Attorney General
Bureau of Consumer Protection
21 South 12th Street, 2nd Floor
Philadelphia, PA 19107
(215) 560-2414
(800) 441-2555 (toll-free in Pennsylvania)

Office of the Attorney General
Bureau of Consumer Protection
Manor Complex, 5th Floor
564 Forbes Avenue
Pittsburgh, PA 15219
(412) 565-5394

Office of the Attorney General
Bureau of Consumer Protection
214 Samters Building
101 Penn Avenue
Scranton, PA 18503-2025
(717) 963-4913

Puerto Rico

Department of Consumer Affairs (DACO)
Minillas Station, P.O. Box 41059
Santurce, PR 00940-1059
(809) 721-0940

Department of Justice
P.O. Box 192
San Juan, PR 00902
(809) 721-7700

Rhode Island

Office of the Attorney General
Consumer Protection Division
72 Pine Street
Providence, RI 02903
(401) 274-4400
(401) 274-4400, ext. 2354 (TDD)
(800) 852-7776 (toll-free in Rhode Island)

Rhode Island Consumers' Council
365 Broadway
Providence, RI 02909
(401) 277-2764

South Carolina

Office of the Attorney General
Consumer Fraud and Antitrust Section
P.O. Box 11549
Columbia, SC 29211-1549
(803) 734-3970

Department of Consumer Affairs
P.O. Box 5757
Columbia, SC 29250-5757
(803) 734-9452
(803) 734-9455 (TDD)
(800) 922-1594 (toll-free in South Carolina)

State Ombudsman
Office of Executive Policy and Program
1205 Pendleton Street, Room 308
Columbia, SC 29201
(803) 734-0457
(803) 734-1147 (TDD)

South Dakota

Office of the Attorney General
Division of Consumer Affairs
500 East Capitol
Pierre, SD 57501-5070
(605) 773-4400

Tennessee

Office of the Attorney General
Division of Consumer Protection
450 James Robertson Parkway
Nashville, TN 37243-0485
(615) 741-3491

Division of Consumer Affairs
500 James Robertson Parkway
Nashville, TN 37243-0600
(615) 741-4737
(800) 342-8385 (toll-free in Tennessee)

Texas

Office of the Attorney General
Consumer Protection Division
P.O. Box 12548
Austin, TX 78711
(512) 463-2070

Office of the Attorney General
Consumer Protection Division
714 Jackson Street, Suite 800
Dallas, TX 75202-4506
(214) 742-8944

Office of the Attorney General
Consumer Protection Division
6090 Surety Drive, Room 113
El Paso, TX 79905
(915) 772-9476

Office of the Attorney General
Consumer Protection Division
1019 Congress Street, Suite 1550
Houston, TX 77002-1702
(713) 223-5886

Office of the Attorney General
Consumer Protection Division
1208 14th Street, Suite 900
Lubbock, TX 79401-3997
(806) 747-5238

Office of the Attorney General
Consumer Protection Division
3201 North McColl Road, Suite B
McAllen, TX 78501
(210) 682-4547

Office of the Attorney General
Consumer Protection Division
115 East Travis Street, Suite 925
San Antonio, TX 78205-1607
(512) 225-4191

Office of Public Insurance Counsel
333 Guadalope, Suite 3-120
Austin, TX 78701
(512) 322-4143

Utah

Division of Consumer Protection
Department of Commerce
160 East 3rd South
P.O. Box 45804
Salt Lake City, UT 84145-0804
(801) 530-6001
(801) 530-6601 (fax)

Vermont

Office of the Attorney General
Public Protection Division
109 State Street
Montpelier, VT 05609-1001
(802) 828-3171

Consumer Assurance Section
Department of Agriculture, Food and
  Market
120 State Street
Montpelier, VT 05620-2901
(802) 828-2436

Virginia

Office of the Attorney General
Antitrust and Consumer Litigation Section
Supreme Court Building
101 North Eighth Street
Richmond, VA 23219
(804) 786-2116
(800) 451-1525 (toll-free in Virginia)

State Division of Consumer Affairs
Department of Agriculture and Consumer
  Services
Room 101, Washington Building
P.O. Box 1163
Richmond, VA 23209
(804) 786-2042

Washington

Office of the Attorney General
Consumer Protection Division
P.O. Box 40118
Olympia, WA 98504-0118
(206) 753-6210

Office of the Attorney General
Consumer and Business Fair Practices
  Division
900 Fourth Avenue, Suite 2000
Seattle, WA 98164
(206) 464-6684
(800) 551-4636 (toll-free in Washington)

Office of the Attorney General
Consumer and Business Fair Practices
  Division
West 1116 Riverside Avenue
Spokane, WA 99201
(509) 456-3123

Office of the Attorney General
Consumer and Business Fair Practices
  Division
1019 Pacific Avenue, 3rd Floor
Tacoma, WA 98402-4411
(206) 593-2904

West Virginia

Office of the Attorney General
Consumer Protection Division
812 Quarrier Street, 6th Floor
Charleston, WV 25301
(304) 558-8986
(800) 368-8808 (toll-free in West Virginia)

Wisconsin

Division of Trade and Consumer Protection
Department of Agriculture, Trade and
  Consumer Protection
801 West Badger Road
P.O. Box 8911
Madison, WI 53708
(608) 266-9836
(800) 422-7128 (toll-free in Wisconsin)

Department of Justice
Office of Consumer Protection and Citizen
  Advocacy
P.O. Box 7856
Madison, WI 53222-3288
(608) 266-1852

Department of Justice
Office of Consumer Protection
Milwaukee State Office Building
819 North 6th Street, Room 520
Milwaukee, WI 53203-1678
(414) 227-4949
(800) 362-8189 (toll-free)

Wyoming

Office of the Attorney General
123 State Capitol Building
Cheyenne, WY 82002
(307) 777-7874

SOURCES

FOOD

1. GROCERY SHOPPING

Better Business Bureau A to Z Buying Guide. New York: Henry Holt & Co., 1990.

"A Common Sense Approach to Pesticides." Center for Science in the Public Interest's *Nutrition Action Healthletter*, September 1993.

Garman, Thomas E. *Consumer Economic Issues in America*. Boston: Houghton Mifflin, 1991.

Jacobson, Michael, Ph.D., Executive Director, Center for Science in the Public Interest. Comments made at Ralph Nader's Frugal Shoppers Week press conference. Aug. 31, 1992.

Newman, Stephen A. and Nancy Kramer. *Getting What You Deserve: A Handbook for the Assertive Consumer*. Garden City, NY: Doubleday, 1979.

New York City Department of Consumer Affairs. *Caveat Eater*. New York: May 1991.

——. *A Consumer Guide to Waxes on Fruits and Vegetables: Safer Choices for a Healthful Diet*. New York: Autumn 1991.

——. *Federal Trade Omission: False Nutritional Claims in Food Advertising*. New York: April 1992.

"Survival Guide to the Supermarket." *Consumer Reports*, September 1993.

U.S. Food and Drug Administration, with the American Heart Association. *How to Read the New Food Label*. (AHA 51-1052 (CP) and FDA 93-2260). Washington, DC: FDA, 1993; Dallas: AHA, 1993.

2. FAST FOOD OUTLETS

Jacobson, Michael F., Ph.D. and Sarah Fritschner. *Fast Food Guide*, 2nd ed. New York: Workman Publishing Co., 1991.

Leonard, Walter B. and the editors of Consumer Reports Books. *Consumer Reports Money-$aving Tip$ for Good Times and Bad*. Yonkers, N.Y.: Consumers Union, 1992.

Nutrition Action Healthletter. Washington, DC: Center for Science in the Public Interest, November 1993.

3. WATER

Blumenthal, Robin Goldwyn. "Water Bottlers Tap Resources to Prepare for FDA Label Rule; Consumers at Stake." *Wall Street Journal*, Mar. 12, 1993.

"Fit to Drink?" *Consumer Reports*, January 1990. *Get the Lead Out*. Oakland, CA: Environmental Law Foundation.

"How to Reduce Lead in Drinking Water." *New York Times*, Mar. 2, 1991.

Ingersoll, Bruce. "FDA Finds Bunk in Bottled Water Claims." *Wall Street Journal*, Apr. 10, 1991.

Ingram, Colin. *The Drinking Water Book*. Berkeley, CA: Ten Speed Press, 1991.

"Is There Lead in Your Water?" *Consumer Reports*, February 1993.

Milius, Susan. "Tapped Out." *Organic Gardening*, April 1988.

New York State Department of Law. *Consumer Guide to Water Treatment Devices*. New York: July 1990.

1991 Drinking Water Guide. San Diego: California Public Interest Research Group, January 1991.

"Quenching the Thirst for Safe Drinking Water." *NCL Bulletin*, March/April 1993.

Shabecoff, Philip. "EPA Adopts Stiffer Regulations to Protect Drinking Water Supply." *New York Times*, June 23, 1991.

Terry, Sara. "Troubled Water: Episodes in Milwaukee, New York and Elsewhere Show America What Must Be Done to Turn the Tap With Confidence." *New York Times Magazine*, Sept. 26, 1993.

U.S. Environmental Protection Agency. "Safe Drinking Water Hotline Factsheet." Washington, DC: February 1993.

Wald, Matthew L. "High Levels of Lead Found in Water Serving 30 Million." *New York Times*, May 12, 1993.

HEALTH

4. HEALTH INSURANCE IN THE 1990'S

Anders, George. "More Managed Health-Care Systems Use Incentive Pay to Reward 'Best' Doctors." *Wall Street Journal*, Jan. 25, 1991.

——————."Three HMOs Evaluate Themselves." *Wall Street Journal,"* Nov. 16, 1993.

"Are HMOs the Answer?" *Consumer Reports*, August 1992.

Bunis, Dena. "Medical Review Services Assailed." *New York Newsday*, Sept. 18, 1991.

Burton, Thomas M. "Firms That Promise Lower Medical Bills May Actually Increase Them." *Wall Street Journal*, July 28, 1992.

Freudenheim, Milt. "Many Patients Unhappy With HMO's." *New York Times*, Aug. 18, 1993.

Garland, Susan B., and Naomi Fruendlich. "Insurers vs. Doctors: Who Knows Best?" *Business Week*, Feb. 18, 1991.

Kessler, Glenn. "38.5M Without Health Insurance." *New York Newsday*, Dec. 15, 1993.

Kramon, Glenn. "Health Insurers in Trying to Save Find New Costs in Managing Care." *New York Times*, Aug. 25, 1991.

Luciano, Lani. "Getting the Most From Your Company Benefits." *Money*, May 1991.

Nader, Ralph, and Wesley J. Smith. *The Frugal Shopper*. Washington DC: Center for the Study of Responsive Law, 1992.

Public Citizen Health Action Group. "How You Can Make HMOs More Accountable." *Health Letter*, November 1991.

Ruffenach, Glenn. "Firms Use Financial Incentives to Make Employees Seek Lower Health-Care Fees." *Wall Street Journal*, Feb. 9, 1993.

Schultz, Ellen E. "Employees Find There Is Little Recourse When Denied by Company Health Plans." *Wall Street Journal*, Oct. 25, 1993.

——————. "Gaps in Coverage May Exist in Current Health Plans." *Wall Street Journal*, Sept. 29, 1993.

——————. "Medical Data Gathered by Firms Can Prove Less Than Confidential." *Wall Street Journal*, May 18, 1994.

Unger, Michael. "The Gatekeepers; A New Breed of Insurer Targets Rising Health Costs." *Newsday*, Dec. 3, 1991.

Winslow, Ron. "Health Care: HMOs May Impair Ties to Specialists." *Wall Street Journal*, July 9, 1993.

5. PHARMACEUTICALS AND PHARMACISTS

Colburn, Don. "How Drug Prices Vary." *Washington Post*, Dec. 15, 1992.

——————. "Drug Prices - What's Up?." *Washington Post*, Dec. 15, 1992.

Consumers Union. *The New Medicine Show*. Mount Vernon, NY: Consumers Union of the United States, 1989.

Gutfeld, Rose. "FDA Attacks Drug Makers' Ads to Doctors." *Wall Street Journal*, Aug. 3, 1993.

"How to Buy Drugs for Less." *Consumer Reports*, October 1993.

Long, James W., M.D., and James J. Rubacki, Pharm. D. *The Essential Guide to Prescription Drugs*. New York: Harper-Collins, 1993.

Miller, Roger W. "Doctors, Patients Don't Communicate." *U.S. FDA Counselor*, July/August 1983.

New York City Department of Consumer Affairs. *Pills and Potency—Why Prescription Drugs Need Expiration Dates*. New York: January 1993.

——————. *Comparison Shop for Less Expensive Prescription Drugs*. New York. February 1993.

Sloane, Leonard. "A Three-Part Prescription for Saving Money on Medications." *New York Times*, June 25, 1988.

Spalding, B.J. "Is Pharmacy Counseling a Myth?" *American Druggist*, May 1990.

Weber, Joseph, and John Carey. "Drug Ads: A Prescription for Controversy." *Business Week*, Jan. 18, 1993.

Wolfe, Sidney, MD *Worst Pills, Best Pills*. Washington, DC: Public Citizen Health Research Group, 1988.

6. DOCTORS AND HOSPITALS

Crenshaw, Albert B. "Making Fairness Part of Hospital Bills." *New York Newsday*, May 7, 1992.

"Hospital Costs." *Primetime Live*, ABC News. August 15, 1991.

Inlander, Charles B., and Ed Weiner. *Take This Book to the Hospital With You*. Allentown, PA: People's Medical Society, 1993.

—————150 Ways To Be a Savvy Medical Consumer. Allentown, PA: People's Medical Society, 1992.

Isaacs, Stephen L, J.D.,and Ava C. Schwartz, M.P.H. The Consumer's Legal Guide to Today's Health Care, New York: Houghton Mifflin, 1992.

Nelson, Lars-Erik. "Exec May Be Hazardous to Your Health." New York Daily News, Apr. 23, 1993.

New York State Department of Health. Cardiac Surgery in New York State, 1989-1991. Albany, NY.

Nicholson, Joe. "Doctors of Disaster." New York Post, Aug. 25, 1993.

Pennsylvania Health Care Cost Containment Council. A Progress Report, 1991-1993. Harrisburg, PA.

Public Citizen Health Action Group. "Unnecesary Casarean Sections: Halting a National Epidemic." Health Letter, June 1992.

—————. "Referral Profits Line Doctors' Pockets." Health Letter, October 1991.

—————. "Medical Records: Getting Yours." Health Letter, September 1992.

—————. "Ranking of Doctor Disciplinary Actions by State Medical Licensing Boards." Health Letter, July 1992.

Rosenthal, Elisabeth. "The Alert Consumer: Confusion, Errors and Fraud in Medical Bills." New York Times, Nov. 14, 1993.

—————. "Confusion and Error Are Rife in Hospital Billing Practices." New York Times, Jan. 27, 1993.

Sloane, Leonard. "Health Costs: Checking Bills Carefully to Catch Costly Errors." New York Times, Nov. 28, 1992.

Stutz, David R. M.D., and Bernard Feder, Ph.D. The Savvy Patient. Mount Vernon, NY: Consumers Union of the United States, 1990.

7. LONG-TERM CARE

Better Business Bureau A to Z Buying Guide. New York: Henry Holt & Co., 1990.

Brookings/ICF Long-Term Care Financial Model. Washington, DC: The Brookings Institute, 1993.

"Elder Care: The Insurer's Role." New York Times, Mar. 16, 1994.

"An Empty Promise to the Elderly?" Consumer Reports, July 1991.

Estes, Carroll L., and Thomas Bodenheimer. "Paying for Long-Term Care." The Western Journal of Medicine. Vol. 160, No. 1. January 1994.

Medicare: Entitlements and Advocacy Training. New York: Brookdale Center on Aging of Hunter College, Institute on Law and Rights of Older Adults. January 1992.

New York City Department of Consumer Affairs. Promise Them Anything: The Selling of Long Term Care Insurance for the Elderly. New York: 1993.

Nursing Home Input Price Index. Philadelphia, PA: The Wharton Business School of the University of Pennsylvania, 1993.

Nursing Home Insurance: Who Can Afford It? Washington, DC: Families USA. February 1993.

Pomeroy, Earl R. Testimony of the National Association of Insurance Commissioners Before the Labor and Human Resources Committee, U.S. Senate. Washington, DC: NAIC, 1992.

Ross, Jane L. Public/Private Elder Care Partnerships: Balancing Benefit and Risk, Testimony Before the Subcommittee on Human Services, Select Committee on Aging, House of Representatives. Washington, DC: GAO. July 9, 1992.

U.S. General Accounting Office. Long-Term Care Insurance: Risks to Consumers Should Be Reduced. Washington, DC: GAO. December 1991.

—————. Older Americans Act: More Federal Action Needed on Public/Private Elder Care Partnerships. Washington, DC: GAO. July 1992.

U.S. House Select Committee on Aging. Abuses in the Sale of Long Term Care Insurance to the Elderly. Washington, DC: June 1991.

Weissenstien, Eric. "Survey Casts Shadow on Long-Term Care Plans," Modern Healthcare, Apr. 27, 1992.

8. NUTRITIONAL SUPPLEMENTS

Barrett, Stephen, M.D., and the editors of Consumer Reports. Health Schemes, Scams and Frauds. Mount Vernon, NY: Consumer Reports Books, 1990.

Barrett, Stephen, M.D., and William T. Jarvis, Ph.D. The Health Robbers. Buffalo: Prometheus Books, 1993.

Brody, Jane. Jane Brody's Nutritition Book. New York: W.W. Norton, 1981.

Herbert, Victor, F.A.C.P., and M.S., Subak-Shurpli, eds. Mt. Sinai School of Medicine Complete Book of Nutrition. New York: St. Martin's Press, 1992.

New York City Department of Consumer Affairs. *Magic Muscle Pills!! Health and Fitness Quackery in Nutrition Supplements.* New York: May 1992.

U.S. Congress, Health and Environment Subcommittee of the House Energy and Commerce Committee, *Hearing: Regulation of Dietary Supplements, July 29, 1993.* 103rd Congress, 1st Session, Washington, D.C.: GPO, 1993.

9. WEIGHT LOSS PRODUCTS AND PROGRAMS

Barrett, Stephen, M.D. "Weight Control: Facts, Fads and Frauds," in *The Health Robbers,* Stephen Barrett, M.D. and William T. Jarvis, Ph.D., eds. Buffalo, NY: Prometheus Books, 1993.

Better Business Bureau A to Z Buying Guide. New York: Henry Holt & Co., 1990.

Brody, Jane E. "Fanatic Dieters May Shed Years Along with Pounds." *New York Times,* June 21, 1991.

——————. "Panel Criticizes Weight-Loss Programs." *New York Times,* Apr. 2, 1992.

Burros, Marion. "Eating Well." *New York Times,* June 16, 1993.

"Losing Weight: What Works — What Doesn't." *Consumer Reports,* June 1993.

National Institutes of Health. *Methods for Voluntary Weight Loss and Control.* Washington, DC: Technology Assessment Conference Statement, Mar. 30-Apr. 1, 1992.

New York City Department of Consumer Affairs. *A Weighty Issue: Dangers and Deceptions of the Weight Loss Industry.* New York: June 1991.

O'Neill, Molly. "In Fighting Shape, Three Diet Companies Mix It Up Over Advertising Claims." *New York Times,* June 8, 1991.

U.S. Federal Trade Commission and U.S. Food and Drug Administration. *The Facts About Weight Loss Products and Programs.* Washington, DC.

10. HEALTH CLUBS

Brenner, Elsa. "Fitness That Blooms in the Spring." *New York Times,* May 2, 1993.

Howard, T. J. "Gym-dandies: The Latest Craze in the Fitness Movement Is Not a Machine, but Personal Trainers Who Give TLC." *Chicago Tribune,* May 13, 1992.

IRSA, The Association of Quality Clubs. *50 State Summary: Sales Taxes, Bonding Regulations & Consumer Protection Laws Affecting the Health, Fitness & Racquet Sports Industry.*

——————. *The Economic Benefits of Exercise.*

——————. *The Guide to Choosing a Quality Health Club.*

Leary, Warren E. "If You Can't Run for Health, a Walk Will Do, U.S. Says." *New York Times,* July 30, 1993.

Leichter, Franz S. "Leichter Survey Shows Health Club Ads Are Deceptive; Calls for Passage of Needed Health Club Regulations." Press release. New York: Jan. 18, 1987.

Martin, Douglas. "Strictly Business: Fitness Clubs Vie for Market Share." *New York Times,* Feb. 1, 1993.

McCarthy, John. "IRSA's Quality Initiative—A Marketing Opportunity." *Club Business International,* August 1992.

——————. "The Question Is: What Business Are We In?" *Club Business International,* November 1991.

New York City Department of Consumer Affairs. *Choosing a Health Club: "Exercise" Caution.* New York: 1989.

——————. "Green Warns Against Health-Club Abuse in Post-Holiday Alert." Press release. New York: Jan. 5, 1992.

"92 on 1992—and Beyond." *Club Business International,* March 1992.

"Selling It." *Consumer Reports,* January 1991.

Sloane, Leonard. "Making Sure a Health Club Is on Strong Financial Ground." *New York Times,* Feb. 2, 1991.

U.S. Centers for Disease Control and Prevention & American College of Sports Medicine. *Summary Statement: Workshop on Physical Activity and Public Health.* Washington, DC: 1993.

Whitford, Ellen. "How to Pick a Health Club That is Just Right for You." *Atlanta Journal and Constitution,* Jan. 1, 1992.

11. INFERTILITY SERVICES

Berlfein, Judy. "Searching for Fertility." *Los Angeles Times,* Oct. 6, 1991.

Crier & Company. Cable News Network, June 19, 1992.

Dunkin, Amy, ed. "In Vitro Fertilization: Delivering that Ray of Hope." *Business Week,* Sept. 3, 1990.

Elmer-Dewitt, Philip. "Making Babies." *Time,* Sept. 30, 1991.

"Fertility Procedures' Track Records." *Washington Post,* Jan. 21, 1992.

Greenberg, Jon. "In-Vitro Fertilization Needs Regulation." National Public Radio's *All Things Considered,* Apr. 14, 1992.

Gutfeld, Rose. "FDA Says Labels of Fertility Drugs Must Warn Users." *Wall Street Journal,* Jan. 14, 1993.

Henry, Sarah. "The Courage to Conceive." *Parenting,* December/January 1990.

Hopkins, Ellen. "Tales From the Baby Factory." *New York Times Magazine,* Mar. 15, 1992.

Hotz, Robert Lee. *Designs on Life: Exploring the New Frontiers of Human Fertility.* New York: Pocket Books, 1991.

Miller, Annetta. "Baby Makers Inc." *Newsweek,* June 29, 1992.

New York City Department of Consumer Affairs. *Consumer Guide to Fertility Services.* New York: Fall 1992.

Pear, Robert. "Fertility Clinics Face Crackdown." *New York Times,* Oct. 26, 1992.

Resolve National Office. "The Ifs of IVF: The IVF Choice." Somerville, MA: May/June 1990.

———. "Questions to Ask About Assisted Reproductive Technology (ART) Programs."

Rothman, Barbara Katz, Ph.D. "The Frightening Future of Baby-Making." *Glamour,* June 1992.

U.S. Federal Trade Commission. *Facts for Consumers: Infertility Services.* Washington, DC: March 1990.

U.S. House of Representatives, Subcommittee on Health and the Environment of the Committee on Energy and Commerce. *Hearing: Fertility Clinic Services,* Feb. 27, 1992.

12. COLD AND FLU REMEDIES

"Another Way to Overtreat the Symptoms of a Cold." *Consumer Reports,* February 1991.

Brody, Jane E. "Personal Health." Column. *New York Times,* Oct. 1, 1986.

Cope, Lewis. "Fighting the Cold War." *Chicago Tribune,* Mar. 16, 1993.

New York City Department of Consumer Affairs. *Don't Be Left Out In The Cold: A Comparison of Cold and Flu Remedies.* September 1991.

Public Citizen Health Research Center. "Colds: How to Treat Them." *Health Letter,* February 1993.

Washington Post. "Cold Remedies Are a Hot Market." *New York Newsday,* Apr. 13, 1993.

13. EYEGLASSES AND CONTACT LENSES

American Association of Retired Persons. *The Eyes Have It!* Washington, DC: 1986. American Optometric Association Brochures.

Better Business Bureau A to Z Buying Guide. New York: Henry Holt & Co., 1990.

Brooks, Andree. "Yet Another High-Tech Innovation: Eyeglasses to Shake, Rattle and Roll." *New York Times,* July 31, 1991.

"Buying Glasses." *Consumer Reports,* August 1993.

Contact Lens Council. *What You Need to Know About Safe Contact Lens Wear.*

"Eye-Popping Price for New Contacts." *New York Newsday,* June 17, 1993.

"Q & A: Eye Protection." *New York Times,* Nov. 16, 1993.

Streitfeld, David. "Consummate Consumer; Law of the Lens." *Washington Post,* May 10, 1990.

U. S. Federal Trade Commission. "Eyeglasses."

Wald, Matthew. "Questions Arise on Methods of Filtering Ultraviolet Light." *New York Times,* Jan. 12, 1991.

Wasco, Dan Jr. "Eyewear Price Promotions Attract Increasing Scrutiny." *Minneapolis Star Tribune,* Apr. 12, 1992.

———. "Pearle Agrees to Revise Its Marketing Strategy." *Minneapolis Star Tribune,* Dec. 10, 1990.

14. GETTING THE LEAD OUT OF YOUR DIET

Environmental Defense Fund. *Legacy of Lead: America's Continuing Epidemic of Childhood Lead Poisoning.* Washington, DC: March 1990.

Environmental Defense Fund, California Department of Health, Office of the California Attorney General. *What You Should Know About Lead in China Dishes.* San Francisco: 1992.

New York City Department of Consumer Affairs. *Dangerous Dishes: Lead in Ceramics and What We Can Do.* New York: January 1993.

U.S. Centers for Disease Control. *Preventing Lead Poisoning in Young Children.* Washington, DC: October 1991.

———. *Strategic Plan for the Elimination of Childhood Lead Poisoning.* Washington, DC: 1991.

U.S. Food and Drug Administration. *Reducing Exposure to Lead from Ceramic Ware.* Washington, DC: November 1991.

15. HOUSES, CONDOS AND CO-OPS

Brooks, Andree. "Picking the Best Broker." *New York Times,* June 12, 1994.

——————. "Getting a Home Inspected." *New York Times,* Jan.y 23, 1994.

Bruss, Robert J. "Not All House Inspectors are Qualified." *Chicago Tribune,* Aug. 7, 1992.

Catalano, Joe. "What's Your House Worth?" *New York Newsday,* Dec. 11, 1993.

Eisenson, Marc. "25 Steps to a Penny Pinching Home Closing." *The Banker's Secret Bulletin,* Spring 1994.

Freedman, Alix M. "Power Lines Short-Circuit Sales, Homeowners Claim." *Wall Street Journal,* Dec. 8, 1993.

Glink, Ilyce R. *100 Questions Every First-Time Home Buyer Should Ask.* New York: Random House, 1994.

Harney, Kenneth. "Now You Have The Right to See Home Appraisals." *New York Newsday,* Jan. 1, 1994.

Irwin, Robert. *Tips & Traps When Selling a Home.* New York: McGraw Hill, 1990.

Kellerman, Vivian. "Buying a Home at a Government Auction." *New York Times,* Aug. 7, 1993.

Nader, Ralph, and Wesley J. Smith, *The Frugal Shopper.* Washington: Center for the Study of Responsive Law: 1992.

Rothstein, Mervyn. "When the Broker Works for the Buyer." *New York Times,* Sept. 19, 1993.

Sloane, Leonard. "When Buying a Home, Know About Escrow." *New York Times,* Apr. 4, 1992.

Smith, Anne Kates. "Heads Up, House Hunters —Here's a Guide to Recent Changes Affecting Buyers and Sellers." *U.S. News & World Report,* Apr. 5, 1993.

16. HOME IMPROVEMENT CONTRACTORS

Better Business Bureau A to Z Buying Guide. New York: Henry Holt & Co., 1990.

Brooks, Andree. "Repair Rip-Offs: Looking for Signs of a Scam." *New York Times,* July 4, 1993.

Buggs, Shannon. "Midwest Anticipates Flood of out-of-State Contractors; Officials Expect Price-Gouging and Scams to Multiply." *Dallas Morning News,* Aug. 6, 1993.

Burgio, Patti. Director of Government Affairs. National Association of the Remodeling Industry. Telephone interview. July 26, 1994.

Costanzo, Christie. "How to Pick a Remodeling Contractor." *Los Angeles Times,* Aug. 25, 1990.

Crowe, Rosalie Robles. "Building Cases Against Builders: Investigator Tracks Unlicensed Contractors." *Phoenix Gazette,* May 5, 1993.

Gilje, Shelby. "Not Quite at Your Service: Getting Home Repairs Done Can Be Difficult." *Seattle Times,* Mar. 6, 1990.

Giorgianni, Anthony. "Before You Hire a Contractor, Know What You're Getting Into." *The Hartford Courant,* May 22, 1993.

McCullough, David. *Truman.* New York: Simon & Schuster, 1992.

Melia, Marilyn Kennedy. "Rehab Resources: Funding Your Remodeling Project." *Chicago Tribune,* July 16, 1993.

Miller, Griffin. "Hiring a Home Contractor." *New York Times,* May 27, 1992.

Nader, Ralph, and Wesley J. Smith. *The Frugal Shopper.* Washington, DC: Center for Study of Responsive Law, 1992.

New York City Department of Consumer Affairs. *A Consumer's Guide to Home Improvement.* 3rd ed. New York: 1987.

——————. *Resolving Consumer Complaints 1990-1993: Who Complains, Why, and With What Results.* New York: February 1993.

——————. *The Poor Pay More for Less, Part III: Predatory Home Improvement Lending.* New York: February 1993.

Your Money: Home Improvement Scam Could Cost Homeowners Big Bucks. Cable News Network, July 10, 1993.

17. THE ENERGY EFFICIENT HOME

Brooks, Andree. "Talking: Fuel Co-ops: Shopping Around for Savings." *New York Times,* Sept. 23, 1990.

"Bulbs that Won't Charge Up Your Bills. *Business Week,* Sept. 16, 1991.

"Conservation Power: It Has a New Look That's Igniting an Energy Revolution." *Business Week,* Sept. 16, 1991.

"Cool It: A Survey of Energy and the Environment." *The Economist*, Aug. 31, 1991.

The Earth Works Group. *Fifty Simple Things You Can Do to Save the Earth.* Berkeley, CA: EarthWorks Press, 1989.

Goldstein, Eric A., and Mark D. Izeman. *The New York Environment Book.* Washington, DC: Island Press, 1990.

Incantalupo, Tom. "Oil or Gas? Burning Question Doesn't Have Easy Answer." *Newsday*, Sept. 9, 1990.

——. "Huddling With a Few Friends to Stay Warm," *Newsday*, Sept. 27, 1990.

New York Public Interest Research Group. "Conservation Tips" on Water, Appliances, Insulation, Cooling, Transportation, Heating, Lighting. New York: 1992.

——. "Weatherstripping and Caulking Tips," 1990.

Sloane, Leonard. "Oil vs. Gas: A Question of Cost Again." *New York Times*, Aug. 25, 1990.

Wald, Matthew. "And There's Always Natural Gas." *New York Times*, Aug. 9, 1990.

Walls, David. *The Activist's Almanac.* New York: Simon & Schuster, 1993.

18. HOME SECURITY SYSTEMS

Better Business Bureau A to Z Buying Guide. New York: Henry Holt & Co., 1990.

"Coping With Lighting: Tips From the Experts on How to Make the Home Safe, Inside and Out." *New York Times*, Oct. 27, 1990.

"How to Make Your Home Secure." *Consumer Reports*, February 1990.

Insurance Information Institute. "Home Security Basics." New York: April 1990.

Maxwell, Helen. *Home Safe Home: How to Safeguard Your Home and Family.* Far Hills, N.J.: New Horizon Publishing, 1992.

"Protect Your Home." *Consumer Reports*, May 1994.

"To Catch a Thief." ABC News *20/20*. Feb. 5, 1993.

19. FURNITURE AND MATTRESSES

Bernstein, Emily M. "All About: Ready-to-Assemble Furniture. *New York Times*, July 12, 1992.

Better Business Bureau A to Z Buying Guide. New York: Henry Holt & Co., 1990.

Crenshaw, Albert B. "Congress Eyes Curbs on Rent-to-Own Industry." *Washington Post*, 1993.

Friedman, R.S. "Tailor Your Furniture to Needs and Wallet." *St. Petersburg Times*, Nov. 8, 1992.

Gilgoff, Henry. "Carpet Scams Cited by City." *New York Newsday*, Aug. 11, 1993.

"Home Style: Getting the Right Home Furniture Takes Planning, Shopping Savvy, But You Can Have Fun Too." *Atlanta Journal and Constitution*, Oct. 3, 1992.

Kahn, Eve M. "To Pick a Sofa, Lift It, Squeeze It and Don't Forget to Sit on It. *New York Times*, Aug. 1, 1992.

New York City Department of Consumer Affairs. *Furniture: From Purchase to Delivery.* New York: April 1992.

——. *Mattress Buying: How Product Proliferation Confuses Consumers.* New York: March 1993.

Saunders, Tinah. "Let the Furniture Buyer Prepare." *Atlanta Journal and Constitution*, June 5, 1992.

Seymour, Liz. "Returning Furniture: Repent at Leisure." *New York Times*, Apr. 29, 1993.

U.S. Federal Trade Commission. "Guides for the Household Furniture Industry." Washington, DC: 1973.

20. ELECTRONIC GOODS AND APPLIANCES

Citibank. *Citibank Mastercard and Visa Offers Cardmembers Lifetime Warranty on Most Purchases.* Press release. June 9, 1993.

Des Ruisseaux, Richard. "Service Contracts Often a Bad Deal." Gannett News Service, July 7, 1993.

Flores, Delia. "Tug of Warranties: Deciding Whether Peace of Mind Justifies the Extra Cost." *Chicago Tribune*, Aug. 26, 1993.

Gill, Penny. "Buying Peace of Mind; Extended Service Contracts Expand Range of Goods Included, Types of Coverage." *HFD — The Weekly Home Furnishings Newspaper*, Mar. 15, 1993.

——. "Dispelling Consumers' Suspicions: Industry Addressing 'Bad Apples,' Cliche of Product Failure Upon Warranty Expiration." *HFD — The Weekly Home Furnishings Newspaper*, Mar. 15, 1993.

Giorgianni, Anthony. "Preparing for Battle in the Christmas Spirit of Giving." *Hartford Courant,* Dec. 12, 1992.

Glover, Mark. "Consider Value of Your Purchase Before You Pay for a Service Contract; The Stakes are High on Extended Warranties." *Chicago Tribune,* Mar. 23, 1993.

Hall, Carl T. "Service Contracts — Are They Worth It? Protection May Be Unnecessary." *San Francisco Chronicle,* May 17, 1993.

Major Appliance Consumer Action Panel. *Put New Appliances "To the Test" Soon After Installation* (Consumer Bulletin #3). Rev. ed.: May 1985.

O'Brien, Lisa Peters. "The Warranty Racket: Chances Are You Don't Need One, No Matter What the Salesman Says." *Working Woman,* July 1993.

Saladyga, John S. "Are Extra Warranties Worth It?" *New York Newsday,* Jan. 21, 1993.

Somerfield, Harry. "Getting Set: Shopping for a TV Doesn't Have to Be a Marathon Event." *San Francisco Chronicle,* July 15, 1992.

Wald, Matthew L. "Speaker-Shopping in New York's Bazaar." *New York Times,* July 28, 1990.

"Who Needs an Extended Warranty." *Consumer Reports,* January 1991.

21. CABLE TELEVISION

Bauman, Risa. "Selling in the Long Form." *Direct,* January 1993.

Cooper, Jean Duggan. "Cable Cuts." *New York Newsday,* Apr. 2, 1993.

Elliott, Stuart. "Some Big Marketers Join Audience for Infomercials." *New York Times,* June 5, 1992.

Farhi, Paul. "TCI Memo Called for Price Hikes." *Washington Post,* Nov. 16, 1993.

──────. "Television's Great Gray Area." *Washington Post,* May 13, 1994.

"FTC Promises Close Regulation to Ensure Infomercial Standards." *New York Newsday,* June 22, 1992.

Gilgoff, Henry. "You Might Not Get Lower Price for Cable." *New York Newsday,* Aug. 18, 1993.

Jefferson, David J. and Thomas R. King. "Slice It, Dice It: 'Infomercials' Fill Up Air Time on Cable, Aim for Prime Time." *Wall Street Journal,* Oct. 22, 1992.

Kolbert, Elizabeth. "States Act on Cable Rate Rises." *New York Times,* Nov. 19, 1993.

Landler, Mark. "The Infomercial Inches Toward Respectability." *Business Week,* May 4, 1992.

Lipman, Joanne. "Infomercials Attract Some Big Sponsors." *Wall Street Journal,* Jan. 14, 1992.

──────. "'Infomercial' Makers Try to Clean Up Act." *Wall Street Journal,* Mar. 4, 1991.

Marin, Rick. "The Stepford Channel." *New York Times,* Oct. 4, 1992.

Meier, Barry. "Standard Parts Debate Clouds Choices for Users of Cable TV." *New York Times,* July 7, 1990.

Nussbaum, Bruce. "'I Can't Work This Thing!'" *Business Week,* Apr. 29, 1991.

Perlow, Maris. "'Infomercial' Explosion." *New York Daily News,* Sept. 30, 1990.

Robichaux, Mark. "Scrambled Picture: How Cable-TV Firms Raised Rates in Wake of Law to Curb Them." *Wall Street Journal,* Sept. 28, 1993.

U.S. General Accounting Office. "1992 Survey of Cable Television Rates and Services." Report to the Chairman, Subcommittee on Telecommunications and Finance, Committee on Energy and Commerce, Washington DC: July 1991.

22. PETS

American Society for the Protection and Conservation of Animals. *Selecting the Family Dog: How to Find the Dog of Your Dreams.*

Crispell, Diane. "Pet Sounds." *American Demographics,* May 1991.

Dupuis, Mark A. "Pet Guarantee Bill Advancing." United Press International, Apr. 3, 1988 (Hartford, Ct; AM cycle).

Finnegan, Lora J. "Flying With Fido: Traveling With a Pet." *Sunset,* March 1993.

"Going Out in Style: Casketmaker Dennis Hoegh Sends Pets Packing in a Box of Their Own." *Time,* Feb. 1, 1993.

Gottlieb, Jeff. "No Resting for Her Pet: Cemetery Gives Dog Owner Deadline to Pay for Plot." *Houston Chronicle,* Apr. 18, 1993.

Green, Rany. "Is This You? — University of Oregon Study Reveals Psyches of Owners." *Seattle Times,* Apr. 8, 1993.

Jaegerman, Megan. "The Cost of that Dog in the Window." *New York Times,* June 13, 1992.

McIntyre, Ben. "Uncle Sam's Animal Crackers." *The Times* (London), Nov. 21, 1992.

McKey, Elizabeth and Karen Payne, "APPMA Study: Pet Ownership Soars." *Pet Business*, August 1992.

Patureau, Alan. "Pet Treats: When Most People View their Animals as Part of the Family, It's No Wonder There's a Market for Creature Comfort." *Atlanta Journal & Constitution*, Apr. 9, 1993.

"Picking the Best Vets." *St. Petersburg Times*, June 5, 1993.

"Stop Pet Breeding Voluntarily." Editorial. *St. Petersburg Times*, Apr. 5, 1993.

"Veterinary Service Market for Companion Animals, 1992 — Part II: Veterinary Service Use and Expenditures." *Journal of the American Veterinary Medical Association*, Oct. 15, 1992.

23. LAWN CARE

Baker, Jerry. *Jerry Baker's Lawn Book*. New York: Random House, 1987.

Rodale, Robert, et al. *Lawn Beauty - The Organic Way*. Emmaus, PA: Rodale Books, 1970.

Schneider, Keith. "Senate Panel Says Lawn Chemicals Harm Many." *New York Times*, May 10, 1991.

Slatella, Michelle. "Masters of the Turf; If you love you lawn (and we know you do), you either fret over it yourself, or pay a professional to do it for you." *Newsday*, July 29, 1992.

Stocker, Carol. "A few timely facts about fertilizer; Gardener's Notebook." *Boston Globe*, Apr. 8, 1993.

Stuart, Franklin, *Building a Healthy Lawn*. Pownal, VT: Storey Communications, 1988.

24. MOVING COMPANIES

American Movers Conference. Household Goods Carriers' Bureau. *Intrastate Regulatory Requirements*. May 21, 1993.

Brooks, Andree. "The Smooth Move." *New York Times*, June 6, 1992.

"Countdown: Planning Your Move." *Consumer Reports*. August 1990.

Crispell, Diane. "Movers of Tomorrow." *American Demographics*, June 1993.

Davis, Robert. "At White House, a Real Moving Day." *USA Today*, Jan. 21, 1993.

Fink, Ken. "Best Moving Deal Is to Do It Yourself." *Chicago Tribune*, May 1, 1993.

Gilje, Shelby. "Relocating? Some Tips That Will Move You." *Seattle Times*, May 16, 1993.

Goldberg, Jeffrey. "All the Wrong Moves." *New York Magazine*, June 7, 1993.

Miller, Griffin. "When It's Moving Day, Here's How to Handle It." *New York Times*, Oct. 10, 1992.

"Moving Cross-Country Without Professionals." *New York Times*, June 26, 1993.

Simross, Lynn. "Selecting a Reputable Moving Company Requires Homework. 'Get Everything in Writing,' Experts Advise." *Los Angeles Times*, June 12, 1991.

Sterritt, Kathleen. "Making Your Move: A Guide to Get You Going." *Washington Post*, Aug. 7, 1986.

Streitfeld, David. "Consummate Consumer — Space to Grow; The Move to Self-Service Storage." *Washington Post*, Nov. 12, 1990.

"Surviving Your Next Move." *Consumer Reports*, August 1990.

—————. *Your Rights and Responsibilities When You Move*. Washington, DC: GPO, 1992.

—————. Office of Compliance and Consumer Assistance. *1992 Annual Performance Reports of Interstate Movers Hauling 1,000 or More Shipments for Individual Shippers*. Washington, DC: 1993.

U.S. Senate. Committee on Investigations, Taxation, and Government Operations. *Abuses in the Moving Industry — Reforming a Troubled Business*. Washington, DC: GPO, 1992.

AUTOMOBILES

25. NEW CARS

"Annual Auto Issue," *Consumer Reports*, April 1992, 1993, 1994.

Bennet, James. "Buying Without Haggling as Cars Get Fixed Prices." *New York Times*, Feb. 1, 1994.

Better Business Bureau A to Z Buying Guide. New York: Henry Holt and Co., 1990.

Brown, Warren. "Letting Everyone in on the Secret." *Washington Post National Weekly Edition*, Sept. 30-Oct. 6, 1991.

Gillis, Jack. *The Car Book*. New York: Harper Perrenial, 1992.

Greater New York Automobile Dealers Association. *Car Buying or Leasing Made Simple: A Step by Step Consumer Guide*. New York: 1993.

Insurance Institute for Highway Safety. *Shopping for a Safer Car: 1994 Models*. Arlington, Virginia: September 1993.

Levin, Doron. "When It Pays to Complain: Detroit's 'Secret Warranties.'" *New York Times*, June 23, 1992.

McGinley, Laurie. "Traffic Cop: An Unlikely Advocate Has Helped Revive Auto Safety Agency." *Wall Street Journal*, Oct. 24, 1989.

Nader, Ralph, and Wesley J. Smith. *The Frugal Shopper*. Washington, DC: Center for Study of Responsive Law, 1992.

Nader, Ralph, and Clarence Ditlow. *Lemon Book: Auto Rights*. Mount Kisco, New York: Moyer Bell Limited, 1990.

National Automobile Dealers Association. *1993 NADA Data*. McLean, VA: 1993.

New York State Consumer Protection Board. *The Lemon Owner's Manual*. Albany, N.Y.: 1978.

Ross, James R. *A Former Car Salesman Tells All: How to Buy a Car*. New York: St. Martin's Press, 1992.

Schuon, Marshall. "Bags, Belts and the Safety Factor." *New York Times*, Oct. 17, 1993.

Sherman, Debra. "Ex-Car Dealer Tells All." *Ms.*, November 1988.

U.S. Department of Energy. *Energy Conservation Information for Vehicle Owners*. Washington, DC: GPO, January 1991.

U.S. Department of Transportation. National Highway Traffic Safety Administration. *This is NHTSA*. Washington, DC: GPO, December 1991.

—————. *1992 Traffic Safety Facts*. Washington, DC: 1992.

26. USED CARS

"Buying Used: How to Avoid the Lemons." *Consumer Reports*, April 1992.

Gillis, Jack. *The Used Car Book*. New York: Harper Perennial, 1992.

Knight, Jerry. "Lost but Not Leased? A Used-Car Glut Looms." *Washington Post*, June 5, 1994.

Lavin, Douglas. "Stiff Showroom Prices Drive More Americans to Purchase Used Cars." *Wall Street Journal*, Nov. 1, 1994.

Meier, Barry. "Buying Almost-New Cars With a Past." *New York Times*, Jan. 25, 1992.

—————. Buying a Used Car? There's Help Out There." *New York Times*, April 18, 1992.

Nader, Ralph, and Clarence Ditlow. *Lemon Book: Auto Rights*. Mount Kisco, New York: Moyer Bell Limited, 1990.

New York City Department of Consumer Affairs. "City Hits Auto Auctions with 9,000 Consumer Violations in First Law Enforcement Sweep Against Industry." Press release. Mar. 22, 1992.

—————. "Consumer Affairs Cracks Down on Every Auto Auction in the City for Mistreatment of Consumers..." Press release. May 8, 1993.

Quinn, Jane Bryant. "Lease a Used Car?" *New York Daily News*, May 22, 1994.

—————. "Stay in the Driver's Seat When Buying a Used Car." *Washington Post*, Jan. 19, 1992.

Ross, James R. *How to Buy a Car: A Former Car Salesman Tells All*. New York: St. Martin's Press, 1992.

27. CAR LEASING

Bennet, James. "Detroit Pushes Leasing but May Pay Later." *New York Times*, July 27, 1993.

Brown, Warren. "Auto Leasing's Looming Day of Reckoning." *Washington Post*, Mar. 11, 1994.

Gillis, Jack. *The Car Book*. New York: Harper Perrenial, 1992.

Gottschalk, Earl C., Jr. "When to Re-Lease or Release Your Leased Car." *Wall Street Journal*, Aug. 19, 1994.

Greater New York Automobile Dealers Association. *Car Buying or Leasing Made Simple: A Step by Step Consumer Guide*.

Herring, Hubert B. "How to Decide If Car Leasing is for You." *New York Times*, Dec. 26, 1992.

—————. "Driving a Hard Bargain." *Smart Money*, October 1994.

—————. "In the Driver's Seat: Car Leasing Is Hotter than Ever. Here's How to get the Best Possible Deal." *Smart Money*, November 1993.

New York City Department of Consumer Affairs. *Consumer Guide to Automobile Leasing*. New York: November 1992.

New York State Department of Law. "Abrams Announces Agreements Curbing Deceptive Auto Lease Ads" Press release. Apr. 8, 1993.

"Should You Lease? Maybe, but Beware of the Fine Print," *Consumer Reports*, April 1993.

U.S. Federal Trade Commission. *Facts for Consumers: Truth in Leasing*, February 1992.

Woodruff, David. "Is It a Deal? The Arithmetic of Leasing." *Business Week*, Feb. 7, 1994.

28. GASOLINE

Arendt, Phil. "How Octane Can Do a Number on You." *Chicago Tribune*, Aug. 16, 1992.

Brown, Warren. "Gasoline Ads Overstated, FTC Says; Sun Ordered to Stop Touting High Octane." *Washington Post,* Dec. 18, 1991.

Peyla, R.J. "Additives to Have Key Role in New Gasoline Era." *Oil and Gas Journal,* Feb. 11, 1991.

Wald, Matthew, "Amoco Begins the Sale of Cleaner Fuels," *New York Times,* Nov. 2, 1990.

—————. "It Burns More Cleanly, but Ethanol Still Raises Air-Quality Concerns." *New York Times,* Aug. 3, 1992.

White, Marybeth. "Consumers May Pump Gas Worthy of Old Glory." *USA Today*, July 2, 1992.

Wilkerson, Isabel. "Gas Tax Hits, and Drivers Aren't Happy." *New York Times*, Oct. 2, 1993.

29. AUTOMOBILE INSURANCE

Crenshaw, Albert B. "Car Insurance Costs Rising, But Slower; Survey Finds Location, Income Influence Rates." *Washington Post*, Dec. 8, 1991.

Delaware, State Department of Insurance. *The Guide to Delaware Automobile Insurance.* Wilmington: 1991.

Nader, Ralph, and Wesley Smith. *The Frugal Shopper.* Washington, D.C.: Center for the Study of Responsive Law, 1992.

—————. *Winning The Insurance Game.* New York: Knightsbridge Publishing, 1990.

Reich, Kenneth. "Survey Finds Car Insurance Rates Vary Widely." *Los Angeles Times*, May 23, 1990.

Taylor, Barbara. *How to Get Your Money's Worth in Home and Auto Insurance.* Insurance Information Institute, McGraw-Hill, Inc.: New York, 1991.

U.S. Department of Transportation. Consumer Information. *Insurance Discounts.* Washington DC: rev. August 1990.

30.CAR REPAIR

Better Business Bureau A to Z Buying Guide. New York: Henry Holt and Co. 1990.

California Department of Consumer Affairs. "Sears Auto Repair Registrations in Jeopardy Statewide." Press release. June 11, 1992.

Gillis, Jack. *The Car Book: The Definitive Buyer's Guide to Car Safety, Fuel Economy, Maintenance and More.* New York: Harper Perennial, 1993.

Hershey, Robert D. Jr. "Coping With an Ailing Old Car." *New York Times*, Dec. 22, 1990.

Incantalupo, Tom. "The Auto Service Schedule Debate." *New York Newsday*, July 20, 1993.

Kaye, Steven D., and Richard J. Newman. "Made-Up Maintenance." *U.S. News & World Report*, Sept. 14, 1992.

Konrad, Walecia. "Ten Things Your Mechanic Won't Tell You," *Smart Money*, August 1993.

New York City Department of Consumer Affairs. "Consumer Affairs Investigation Finds: Car Owners May Frequently Pay for Unnecessary Repairs." Press release. Nov. 8, 1989.

Spring, Justin. "How to Avoid Tow Trouble." *New York Times*, Jan. 6, 1994.

FINANCES

31. CREDIT CARDS

"Airline Charge Cards — Who Has the Best Deal?" *Consumer Reports Travel Letter*, August 1993.

Bankcard Holders of America. *Credit Cards: What You Don't Know Can Cost You.* Report., June 18, 1992.

—————. "Raising the Stakes in a War of Plastic." *New York Times,* Sept. 13, 1992.

Bryant, Adam. "It Pays to Stick to Basics in Credit Cards." *New York Times*, Oct. 31, 1992.

Eisenson, Marc. "Protect Yourself from the Plastic Monster." *The Banker's Secret Bulletin*, Winter 1990-91.

Gilgoff, Henry. "Merchants Push Credit Cards Hard, but Tactic Could be a Time Bomb." *New York Newsday*, Dec. 9, 1990.

—————. "Eating on Credit." *New York Newsday,* Sept. 30, 1991.

Kantrow, Yvette. "Banks Press Cardholders to Take Cash Advances." *American Banker*, Jan. 28, 1992.

—————. "Card Rate Wars: Bloodletting or Sleight of Hand?" *American Banker,* July 23, 1992.

Kleege, Stephen. "Ford, Citi Are Aiming to Pass GM in Cards." *American Banker*, Feb. 12, 1993.

Kristof, Kathy M. "Smart Money — Secret' and Costly Credit Card Fees." *New York Newsday*, June 18, 1992.

Lipin, Steven. "'No Fees Ever! Low Rates!' Firms Besiege Consumers With Credit Card Offers." *Wall Street Journal*, Nov. 10, 1993.

Morgan, Jerry. "Credit Card Wars — It's Getting Ugly Out There." *New York Newsday*, Dec. 7, 1992.

————— "More Credit Cards Give Cash Back." *New York Newsday*, May 17, 1994.

————— "Putting Plastic to the Metal." *New York Newsday,* Sept. 10, 1992.

Pae, Peter. "Watching for 'Traps' on Lower Rate Cards." *Wall Street Journal*, Feb. 21, 1992.

————— "Credit Card Issuers Give Consumers Holiday Incentives. " *Wall Street Journal,* Nov. 25, 1992.

————— "Cut-Rate Offers Reshuffle Game of Credit Cards." *Wall Street Journal*, Dec. 29, 1992.

Quinn, Jane Bryant. "Consumers Can Act to Cap Their Own Credit Card Rates." *Washington Post*, Nov. 1, 1991.

Quint, Michael. "Favored Credit Card Holders Quietly Given Lower Rates." *New York Times,* Nov. 13, 1991.

————— "Suits Pushing Banks to Obey State Laws on Credit Card Fees." *New York Times*, Feb. 23, 1992.

————— "Bank Robbers' Latest Weapon: Social Security Numbers." *New York Times*, Sept. 27, 1992.

Ramirez, Anthony. "A Citibank Promise to Shoppers." *New York Times*, Apr. 1, 1991.

Schultz, Ellen E. "Credit Card Crooks Devise New Scams." *Wall Street Journal,* July 17, 1992.

Schwadel, Francine. "Stores Offer Enticements to Encourage Shoppers to Charge Holiday Purchases." *Wall Street Journal*, Nov. 14, 1991.

————— "Rates on Store Credit Cards Stay High." *Wall Street Journal*, Oct. 29, 1992.

Sloane, Leonard. "Secured Credit Cards: Ask Before You Leap." *New York Times*, Mar. 16, 1991.

————— "How Thieves Try to Horn in on Your Credit Card Accounts." *New York Times*, Oct. 3, 1992.

Spiro, Leah Nathan, David Woodruff, and David Greising. "More Cards in the Deck." *Business Week*, Dec. 16, 1991.

U.S. Cong., House Committee on Banking, Finance and Urban Affairs, Subcommittee on Consumer Affairs and Coinage, *Hearing : Credit Card Disclosure Amendmensts of 1991*. 102nd Cong., 1st Session, Washington, DC: GPO, 1991.

————— *Give Yourself Credit (Guide to Consumer Credit Laws)*. 102nd Congress, 2nd Session, Washington, DC: GPO, 1992.

U.S. Federal Trade Commission, Office of Consumer/Business Education. *Choosing and Using Credit Cards*. Washington, DC: November 1991.

Willette, Anne. "Credit Cards Are Cash Cows for Issuers." *USA Today*, Apr. 28, 1994.

32. BANKING ON BANKS

Asinof, Lynn. "Looking for Better Rates and Lower Fees? Credit Unions Are Favorites These Days." *Wall Street Journal*, Sept. 2, 1992.

Bacon, Kenneth H., and Steven Lipin. "Under New Bank Law, More Large Depositors Face Losses in Failures." *Wall Street Journal*, Oct. 22, 1992.

Blykal, Jeff. "Finding the Best Bank for Your Dollar." *New York Magazine,* Dec. 7, 1992.

Cope, Debra. "If the Mutual Fund Bloom Fades, Can Banks Tough It Out?." *American Banker*, Mar. 29, 1993.

deCourcy Hinds, Michael. "Main Line Journal; Modern Crusade: Plight of the Rich." *New York Times,* July 2, 1991.

Federal Trade Commission, Office of Consumer/Business Education. *Lost or Stolen: Credit and ATM Cards*. Washington, DC: June 1987.

Haady, Robert. "The Deal on Debit Cards." *Chicago Tribune,* Apr. 13, 1993.

Kleege, Stephen. "Debit Cards Gain Favor With Merchants." *American Banker*, Feb. 10, 1993.

Mierzwinski, Edmund, and Paige Blankenship. *Up! Up! Up! ATM Fees Up!* Washington DC: U.S. Public Interest Research Group, 1991.

Nadler, Paul. "Customers Accept Higher Fees When Banks Use a Little Finesse." *American Banker*, Apr. 14, 1993.

Quinn, Jane Bryant. "Private Deposit Insurance May Not Be Worth Cost, Risks." *Washington Post.* Apr. 11, 1993.

Quint, Michael. "Charges for Accounts Grow More Expensive." *New York Times,* Dec. 12, 1992.

Replansky, Dennis. *Truth-in-Lending and Regulation Z/A Practical Guide to Closed-End Credit.* Philadelphia: American Law Institute, 1985.

Tobias, Andrew. "A Primer on Market Pitfalls." *Time,* May 3, 1993.

Updegrave, Walter L. *How to Keep Your Savings Safe.* New York: Crown Publishers, 1992.

33. MUTUAL FUNDS

Antilla, Susan. "Alternatives to CD's: The Ads Skip the Risks." *New York Times,* Nov. 7, 1992.

Black, Pam. "Reinvesting Your CD Without Leaving the Bank." *Business Week,* Apr. 19, 1993.

Clements, Jonathan. "Investors Can Benefit From Categories When Building a Diversified Portfolio." *Wall Street Journal,* Oct. 5, 1992.

Cope, Debra. "Bank Mutual Funds Target Big Batch of Maturing CDs." *American Banker,* Mar. 22, 1993.

Jasen, Georgette. "Be Wary When Buying Funds From Ads." *Wall Street Journal,* June 16, 1992.

Landerman, Jeffrey, and Geoffrey Smith. "The Power of Mutual Funds." *Business Week,* Jan. 18, 1993.

——————— "The Best Mutual Funds." *Business Week,* Feb. 15, 1993.

Money Magazine. *Money Guide — Mutual Funds.* New York: Time, Inc., Summer, 1993.

Morgan, Jerry. "Flood Into Funds Raises Concerns." *New York Newsday,* May 28, 1993.

Morris, Kenneth M. Alan M Siegel. *The Wall Street Journal Guide to Understanding Personal Finance.* New York: Simon & Schuster, 1992.

"Mutual Funds 1993, Part 1, Stock Funds." *Consumer Reports,* May 1993.

Myerson, Allen R. "No Front of Back Fees, But Watch That Middle." *New York Times,* May 29, 1993.

New York City Department of Consumer Affairs. *Making Sense of Mutual Funds.* Report. September 1993.

Quinn, Jane Bryant. *Making the Most of Your Money.* New York: Simon & Schuster, 1991.

Savage, Terry. *New Money Strategies for the '90s.* New York: Harper-Collins, 1993.

Wayne, Leslie. "Concern Over Bank Sales of Funds." *New York Times*, Dec. 31, 1993.

34. RETIREMENT NEST EGGS

Editors of Consumer Reports Books. *The Consumer Reports Money Book.* Mount Vernon, NY: Consumers Union, 1992.

Kaye, Stephen D. "Have I Got an Annuity for You." *U.S. News & World Report,* Feb. 17, 1992.

Morris, Kenneth M., and Alan M. Siegel. *Wall Street Journal Guide to Understanding Personal Finance.* New York: Simon & Schuster, 1992.

Quinn, Jane Bryant. *Making the Most of Your Money.* New York: Simon & Schuster, 1991.

Savage, Terry. *New Money Strategies for the '90s.* New York: Harper-Collins, 1993.

Williamson, Gordon K. *All About Annuities: Safe Investment Havens for High-Profit Returns.* John Wiley & Sons, 1993.

35. MORTGAGES AND HOME EQUITY

Asinof, Lynn. "How to Avoid the Pitfalls in Mortgage Refinancing." *Wall Street Journal,* Mar. 12, 1993.

Catalano, Joe. "There Are More Home Loan Options Than Ever — and More of a Chance for Trouble." *New York Newsday*, Aug. 22, 1992.

——————— "Is a New Mortgage In Your Best Interest?" *New York Newsday*, Mar. 14, 1993.

Chatzky, Jean Sherman. "Behind Enemy Lines." *Smart Money,* August 1993.

Crenshaw, Albert B. "Is Mortgage Refinancing the Right Move for You?" *Washington Post,* Apr. 11, 1993.

Dougherty, Timothy R. "Home Buyers Should Be Prepared to do the Paperwork Shuffle." *New York Newsday*, May 16, 1992.

Eisenson, Marc. *The Banker's Secret.* New York: Villard Books, 1991.

Glink, Ilyce R. *100 Questions Every First-Time Home Buyer Should Ask.* New York: Random House, 1994.

Gottschalk, Earl C. "What You Need to Know About Mortgage Brokers." *Wall Street Journal,* Apr. 9, 1993.

HSH Associates. *Understanding Mortgages — A Guide to Home Financing.* Butler, NJ: HSH Associates, 1989.

Irwin, Robert. *Tips & Traps When Buying a Home.* New York: McGraw Hill, 1990.

Kass, Benny L. "In Loan Terms, How 15 and 30 Add Up." *Washington Post,* Apr. 17, 1993.

Mandel, Mike. "Don't Jump Too Fast for That 15-Year Mortgage." *Business Week,* Sept. 20, 1993.

Middleton, Timothy. "High Hurdle — More Lenders Are Helping First-Time Home Buyers Overcome Their Biggest Obstacle: The Down Payment." *New York Newsday,* Mar. 6, 1993.

Morris, Kenneth M., and Alan M. Siegel. *Wall Street Journal Guide to Understanding Personal Finance.* New York: Simon & Schuster, 1992.

Pinder, Jeanne P. "Owners Refinancing Homes to Cut Debt, Not Payments." *New York Times,* Aug. 9, 1993.

Quinn, Jane Bryant. *Making the Most of Your Money.* New York: Simon & Schuster, 1991.

Savage, Terry. *New Money Strategies for the '90s.* New York: Harper-Collins, 1993.

U.S. Cong., House Committee on Banking, Finance and Urban Affairs, Subcommittee on Consumer Affairs and Coinage, *Give Yourself Credit (Guide to Consumer Credit Laws).* 102nd Congress, 2nd Session, Washington, DC: GPO, 1992.

36. LIFE INSURANCE

Belth, Joseph M. *Life Insurance: A Consumer's Handbook.* Midland Books, 1985.

Chatzky, Jean Sherman. "Everything You Ever Needed to Know About Insurance." *Smart Money,* October 1993.

Damato, Karen Slater, and Leslie Scism. "Insurer Warns of Premiums That 'Vanish'." *Wall Street Journal,* June 30, 1994.

Dutt, Jill. "Insurance Customers Steamed at Regulators." *New York Newsday,* Nov. 13, 1992.

Geer, Marilyn. "What Every Investor Should Know About Life Insurance." *Forbes,* June 22, 1992.

Harrigan, Susan. "Turning the Tables on Insurers." *New York Newsday,* Nov. 28, 1993.

Kaye, Barry. *Save a Fortune on Your Life Insurance.* New York: Simon & Schuster, 1991.

Lawrence, Jill. "The Pitfalls of Credit Life Insurance." *New York Newsday,* June 5, 1990.

Levin, Doron P. "A Solution to a Life Insurance Riddle." *New York Times,* Nov. 27, 1993.

Lieberman, Trudy, and the editors of Consumer Reports Books. *Life Insurance/How to Buy the Right Policy From the Right Company at the Right Price.* Mount Vernon, NY: Consumers Union of the United States, Inc., 1988.

"Life Insurance — How Much Coverage Do You Need?" *Consumer Reports,* July 1993.

"Life Insurance, Part 2, Choosing a Universal Life Policy." *Consumer Reports,* August 1993.

"Life Insurance, Part 3, Should You Buy a Whole Life Policy?" *Consumer Reports,* September 1993.

Nader, Ralph, and Wesley Smith. *Winning the Insurance Game.* New York: Knightsbridge Publishing, 1990.

New York State Insurance Department. *Consumers Guide for Life Insurance.* New York, 1989.

Quinn, Jane Bryant. *Making the Most of Your Money.* New York: Simon & Schuster, 1991.

Rowland, Mary. "Your Own Account; A Little Caution in Life Insurance." *New York Times,* Dec. 15, 1991.

Savage, Terry. *New Money Strategies for the '90s.* New York: Harper-Collins, 1993.

Sloane, Leonard. "Buying Life Insurance: Where to Start." *New York Times,* Mar. 2, 1991.

———————— "Life Insurance Isn't Just for the Healthy." *New York Times,* Feb. 1, 1992.

37. HOMEOWNER'S INSURANCE

Brooks, Andree. "Hiring an Adjuster for Damage Claims." *New York Times,* Apr. 24, 1993.

Insurance Information Institute. *Tenants Insurance Basics.* Pamphlet. 1989.

"Insuring Your Home." *Consumer Reports,* September 1989.

Marino, Vivian. "Homeowners Insurance Puzzles Many Who Must Purchase It." *Associated Press,* Sept. 7, 1993.

Morris, Kenneth M., and Alan M. Siegel, *The Wall Street Journal Guide to Understanding Personal Finance.* New York: Simon & Schuster, 1992.

Nader, Ralph, and Wesley Smith. *Winning the Insurance Game.* New York: Knightsbridge Publishing, 1990.

Salmon, Jacqueline. "How to Save on Insurance Premiums." *Washington Post,* Apr. 13, 1991.

Sherry, Christina. "Florida Homeowners Feel Pinch As Insurance Companies Bail Out." *Washington Post,* June 13, 1993.

38. DEBT COLLECTORS

"Debt Collection Agencies, Unfair Practices," in *Consumerism: New Developments for Business.* Chicago: Commerce Clearinghouse Inc., Sept. 24, 1980.

DeParle, Jason. "Poor Find Going Broke Is Too Costly." *New York Times*, Dec. 11, 1991.

Eiler, Andrew. *The Consumer Protection Manual.* New York: Facts on File, 1984.

Fair Debt Collection, 2nd ed. Boston: National Consumer Law Center, 1991 and supplement.

New York City Department of Consumer Affairs. *Merchants of Menace: Debt Collector Harassment.* New York: June 1993.

U.S. Federal Trade Commission. *Fair Debt Collection Practices Act.*

39. TAX PREPARERS

Adler, Barry. "The Smell of the Pencil, the Roar of the Calculator." *New York Times*, Mar. 1, 1992.

Block, Julian. "Tax Preparers Respect IRS — and Its Penalties." *Chicago Tribune*, Feb. 17, 1992.

Dougherty, Timothy R. "Tips to Ease the Taxing Task of Filing." *Newsday*, Mar. 14, 1993.

Esanu, Warren H., et al. *Guide to Income Tax Preparation.* Yonkers, NY: Consumer Reports Books, 1993.

Good Morning America. Interview with Tyler Mathisen. NBC, Feb. 5, 1992.

Griffith, Stephanie, and Evelyn Hsu. "Financially Strapped Residents Are Filing Early for Fast Cash." *Washington Post*, Feb. 24, 1992.

Jasen, Georgette. "If You're Confused by the Tax Forms, Here's Where to Find Professional Help." *Wall Street Journal*, Feb. 27, 1992.

Kantrow, Yvette D. "Court Directs a N.Y. Bank to Stop Lending Linked to Tax Refunds." *American Banker*, Mar. 27, 1992.

Ketron, Holly Wheelwright. "*Money* Ranks the Leading Tax Software." *Money*, March 1993.

MacDonald, Elizabeth M. "Many Preparers Make Errors on Returns Because They Haven't Kept Up With New Rules: Why Great Tax Pros Are Scarce." *Money*, January 1993.

Mansnerus, Laura. "Facing the I.R.S. Audit: When to Get an Expert." *New York Times*, June 26, 1993.

Morgan, Jerry. "Fast Tax Refunds Could Lead to Many Unhappy Returns." *New York Newsday*, Mar. 15, 1992.

———— "IRS Arrests Tax Preparer in Phony Refunds Case." *New York Newsday*, Apr. 16, 1991.

———— "Step 1: Figuring Out Who's the Best Tax Preparer for You." *New York Newsday*, Jan. 26, 1992.

Ross, John F. "Getting the Right Help From a Professional." *New York Times*, Mar. 1, 1992.

Shabecoff, Philip. "The IRS Tries to Clean Up its Act." *New York Times*, Mar. 3, 1991.

Sloane, Leonard. "Doing Taxes for the Lazy, the Nervous and the Rich." *New York Times*, Mar. 3, 1991.

Stern, Linda. "Finding the Right Tax Preparer." *Reuter Business Report*, Feb. 10, 1993.

Tritch, Teresa. "Keep an Eye on Your Tax Pro." *Money*, March 1993.

Watterson, Thomas. "Time to Find Tax Preparer Never Better." *Boston Globe*, Jan. 17, 1991.

"What to Do After Panicking." *New York Times*, Mar. 1, 1992.

WHAT YOU WEAR

40. JEWELRY AND WATCHES

Better Business Bureau A to Z Buying Guide. New York: Henry Holt & Co., 1990.

Diamond, S.J. "Watch Out for Dangled Karat of Fool's Gold." *Los Angeles Times*, July 27, 1987.

"Everyone's Best Friend." ABC News *PrimeTime Live*, Nov. 4, 1993.

Jewelers of America. *What You Should Know About Buying a Diamond.* New York: 1992.

————. *What You Should Know About Colored Gemstones.* 1992.

————. *What You Should Know About Cultured Pearls.* 1992.

————. *What You Should Know About Karat Gold Jewelry.* 1992.

————. *What You Should Know About Jewelry Appraisals.* 1976.

"Little White Lies." *7 Days*, Mar. 8, 1989.

Sloane, Leonard. "Jewelry: Admire Glitter, but Count Karats." *New York Times*, Jan. 18, 1992.

U.S. Federal Trade Commission. *Facts for Consumers: About Fine Jewelry.* Washington, DC: GPO, June 1989.

41. COSMETICS

American Academy of Dermatology. "Facts About Sunscreens." Shaumburg, IL.

Being Beautiful: Deciding for Yourself: Selected Readings on Beauty, Beauty Products, Health, and Safety (with an introduction by Ralph Nader). Washington, DC: Center for Study of Responsive Law, 1986.

Better Business Bureau A to Z Buying Guide. New York: Henry Holt & Company, 1990.

Brumberg, Elaine. *Save Your Money, Save Your Face: What Every Cosmetics Buyer Needs to Know.* New York: Facts on File and Perennial Library, 1986, 1987.

Castleman, Michael. "Beach Bummer." *Mother Jones*, May/June 1993.

"Competitive Media Reporting." New York: A joint venture of Arbitron and Leading National Advertisers.

Foulke, Judith E. "Cosmetic Ingredients: Understanding the Puffery." *FDA Consumer*, May 1992.

New York City Department of Consumer Affairs. *The Cosmetics Trap: When Truth Is Only Skin Deep.* New York: June 1992.

————. *A Study in Hype and Risk: The Marketing of Skin Bleaches.* New York: August 1992.

Schoen, Linda Allen, and Paul Lazar, M.D. *The Look You Like: Medical Answers to 400 Questions on Skin and Hair Care.* New York: Marcel Dekker and sponsored by the American Academy of Dermatology, 1990.

Stehlin, Dori. "Cosmetic Safety: More Complex Than at First Blush." *FDA Consumer*, November 1991.

Winter, Ruth. *A Consumer's Dictionary of Cosmetic Ingredients.* New York: Crown Publishers, 1984.

42. DRY CLEANING

Better Business Bureau A to Z Buying Guide. New York: Henry Holt & Co., 1990.

Collins, Clare. "Wash It or Clean It? Read the Fine Print." *New York Times*, Mar. 21, 1992.

International Fabricare Institute. *Trouble Spots.* Silver Spring, MD, 1991.

"Natural Clothes Cleaning Presses Case." *New York Times*, Nov. 29, 1993.

Neighborhood Cleaners Association. "Questions and Answers About the Ecoclean Alternative."

New York: May 1993.

New York City Office of the Public Advocate. *Clothed in Controversy.* New York: Aug. 30, 1994.

U.S. Federal Trade Commission. "Court Upholds FTC Charges Against New Jersey Clothing Company." Press release. Washington, DC: Oct. 7, 1992.

TELEPHONES

43. TELEPHONES

Brooks, Andree. "Who's the Phone For? Depends on the Ring." *New York Times*, Feb. 29, 1992.

Crenshaw, Albert B. "Making a Call for Saving on Telephone Service; Study Shows Most People Don't Know Costs of Choice." *Washington Post*, Dec. 6, 1992.

Dahl, Jonathan. "Before You Use the Hotel Phone, Read This." *Wall Street Journal*, Aug. 2, 1994.

Gellene, Denise. "Home 800 Numbers: Talk of the Town?" *Los Angeles Times*, Sept. 21, 1991.

Keller, John J. "Are They Safe? Nobody knows. But Studies Are Underway to Determine the Health Effects of Cellular Frequency Radio waves." *Wall Street Journal*, Feb. 11, 1994.

———— "Decisions, Decisions." *Wall Street Journal*, Feb. 11, 1994.

———— "Cellular Phone Safety Concerns Hammer Stocks." *Wall Street Journal*, Jan. 25, 1993.

Lazzareschi, Carla. "Saving on Long Distance? Now There's a Cause." *Los Angeles Times*, Aug. 16, 1992.

Martin, Justin. "Phone Card Boom." *Fortune*, Aug. 23, 1993.

Meier, "Speak Your Phone-Card Number Softly." *New York Times*, Aug. 15, 1992.

Miller, Michael. "If You Don't Like Hearing All the Dirt, Don't Get a Scanner." *Wall Street Journal*, Oct. 9, 1990.

Mott, Patrick. "Dial `M' For Making Sense of Choices in Phone Technology." *Los Angeles Times*, Mar. 6, 1993.

San Francisco Consumer Action. "The Phone Page." *Consumer Action News*, February 1993.

Sims, Calvin. "The California Phone Rush Is On." *New York Times*, Aug. 8, 1993.

———— "New York Gets Chance to Save on Phone Bills." *New York Times,* July 15, 1989.

Sloane, Leonard. "Making Sense of Telephone Services." *New York Times,* May 11, 1991.

Sturm, Paul. "Phoning Home Without Going Broke." *Smart Money*, August 1993.

44. CALLING LONG DISTANCE

Berkowitz, Harry. "No More Mr. Nice Guy — AT&T Starts Getting Tough to Keep Center Stage." *New York Newsday,* Mar. 13, 1994.

Davis, Kristin. "1-800 Collect Calls: Cheap, but Not the Cheapest." *Kiplinger's Personal Finance Magazine,* November 1993.

Kansan, Dave. "AT&T Seeks Residential Rate Boost, Says New Discount Plan to Offset Gains." *Wall Street Journal,* Dec. 29, 1993.

Ramirez, Anthony. "Plastic Keys to Phone Wizardry." *New York Times,* May 5, 1992.

———— "Battle Is Fierce on the Phone Front." *New York Times,* Nov. 27, 1993.

Telecommunications Research and Action Center and the Consumer Federation of America. *Long Distance Selection Guide.* Washington, DC, rev. April 1993

CHILDREN

45. CHILD CARE

Better Business Bureau A to Z Buying Guide. New York: Henry Holt & Co., 1990.

Clarke-Stewart, Alison. *Daycare.* Cambridge, MA: Harvard Univ. Press, 1993.

Collins, Clare. "Nanny Background Checks Have Big Limitations," *New York Times.* Mar. 17, 1994.

Improving Child Care Through the Child Development Associate Program. Washington, DC: Council for Early Childhood Professional Recognition. June 1992.

Kagan, S.L. "Examining Profit and Non-Profit Child Care: An Odyssey of Quality and Auspices," *Journal of Social Issues,* Vol. 47, 1991.

Kassler, Jeanne. "The Great Nanny Hunt: The Definitive Guide to Finding Someone You Can Trust." *New York Magazine,* July 19, 1993.

Lauerman, Connie. "Who's Watching the Children?" *The Chicago Tribune,* Apr. 26, 1992.

New York City Department of Consumer Affairs. *Who's Watching the Kids?* New York: 1992.

O'Connell, Martin and Amara Bachu. *Who's Minding the Kids? Child Care Arrangements: Fall 1988.* Washington, DC: U.S. Department of Commerce, Economics and Statistics Administration, Bureau of the Census, 1992.

Pelletier, Elaine S. *How to Hire a Nanny: A Complete Step-by-Step Guide for Parents.* New York: Andre & Lanier, 1994.

Ward, Anthony Ph.D., Toni Porter and Nancy Kolben. *A Child Care Primer: Basic Facts About Child Care in New York City.* New York: Child Care Inc., 1990.

46. TOYS

Better Business Bureau A to Z Buying Guide. New York: Henry Holt & Co., 1990.

Children's Advertising Guidelines. New York: Childrens' Advertising Review Unit (CARU) of the Council of Better Business Bureaus Inc, 1994.

Clear & Present Danger: Statistical Support for Choke Hazard Warning Labels. Trenton, NJ: New Jersey Public Interest Group, 1991.

NAS Case Report. New York: National Advertising Division, Council of Better Business Bureaus, Inc. 1986-94.

"Playing for Keeps: Kids, Toys, and Danger." *Consumer Reports*, November 1990.

Standard Consumer Safety Specification on Toy Safety, Designation F 963-86. Philadelphia, PA: American Society for Testing and Materials, 1986.

Toy Industry Fact Book. New York: Toy Manufacturers of America. 1992-3; 1993-4.

"Tricky Ads." *Penny Power, A Consumer Reports Publication.* Vol. 7, No. 3, December 1987/January 1988.

Trouble in Toyland. Washington, DC: U.S. Public Interest Group, 1994.

U.S. Consumer Product Safety Commission. *For Kids' Sake Think Toy Safety.* Washington, DC: U.S. CPSC, 1994.

————. *National Electronic Injury Surveillance System (NEISS) All Products Summary Report.* Washington, DC: 1994.

————. *Product Safety Fact Sheet No. 47: Toys.* Washington, DC: U.S. CPSC, August 1986.

————. *Product Safety Fact Sheet No. 61: Electrically Operated Toys and Children's Articles.* Washington, DC: U.S. CPSC. May 1988.

—————. *Product Safety Fact Sheet No. 74: Toy Boxes and Toy Chests*. Washington, DC: U.S. CPSC, September 1989.

—————. *Merry Christmas With Safety*. Washington, DC: U.S. CPSC, 1985.

U.S. Federal Trade Commission. *Toy Ads on TV*. Washington, DC: FTC, April 1993.

"The Zap Awards." *Zillions, The Consumer Reports for Kids*, November 1992.

TRAVEL

47. AIRLINES AND AIRFARES

Better Business Bureau of Metropolitan New York, Inc. *Airline Ticket Consolidators: Bargain or Bombast?* Press Release. New York: July 28, 1992.

Busche, Linda. "Airlines Stretch to Give More Room in Coach." *USA Today*, May 11, 1993.

"Frequent Flier Programs—The Pick of the Pack." *Consumer Reports Travel Letter*, November 1992.

Hirsch, James S. "Code Sharing Leaves Fliers Up in the Air." *Wall Street Journal*, Mar. 11, 1993.

—————. "Some Clever Travelers Beat Sky-High Fares By Knowing where to Look on the Ground." *Wall Street Journal*, Mar. 12, 1993.

—————. "Takeoff Is Bumpy for Start-Up Airlines As They Try to Grab a Piece of the Sky." *Wall Street Journal*, July 1, 1993.

—————. "Frequent Flier Plans: Turbulence Ahead." *Wall Street Journal*, Sept. 20, 1993.

Kobliner, Beth. "38 Ways to Be a Smarter Flier." *Money*, November 1990.

Nader, Ralph, and Wesley Smith. *Collision Course/The Truth About Airline Safety*. Blue Ridge Summit, PA: TAB Books, 1994.

Nelson, Janet. "Airlines Relaxing Policy on No-Refund Tickets." *New York Times*, Sept. 22, 1991.

Perkins, Ed. "Beat the Crunch, Few Airlines Respect Your Kneecaps." *Chicago Tribune*, Aug. 22, 1993.

Popkin, James. "Superdiscounts for Flexible Fliers." *U.S. News & World Report*, July 16, 1990.

Price, Wayne. "Plan Now to Cash in Frequent-Flier Miles." *USA Today*. May 25, 1993.

Public Citizen Health Action Group. "Pilot Fatigue Could Kill You." *Health Letter*, May 1992.

Rice, Faye. "Be a Smarter Frequent Flier." *Fortune*, Feb. 22, 1993.

Scherreik, Susan. "An Upgrade for Air-Courier Travel." *Business Week*, Aug. 23, 1993.

Schmit, Julie. "Flying First Class Cheaper but Not Easier." *USA Today*, July 13, 1993.

"The Seat Squeeze Aloft." *Consumer Reports Travel Letter*, September 1991.

"Snug Seats in the Sky—Avoiding the Coach Crunch." *Consumer Reports Travel Letter*, July 1993.

Sommers, Carl. "Q and A." *New York Times*, July 7, 1991.

Tolchin, Martin. "Frequent Fliers Saying Fresh Air Is Awfully Thin at 30,000 Feet." *New York Times*, June 6, 1993.

Wade, Betsy. "Frequent Fliers Feeling Squeezed." *New York Times*, May 22, 1994.

Weiner, Eric. "Decoding Ads for Special Fares." *New York Times*, Nov. 18, 1990.

"Which U.S. Airlines Are Best?" *Consumer Reports Travel Letter*, August 1991.

"Winning the Upgrade Game." *Consumer Reports Travel Letter*, July 1991.

Yom, Sue-Sun. "Fliers Feel the Pinch in Tighter Seats." *Wall Street Journal*, June 27, 1990.

48. TRAVEL

Adler, Jack. "If the Deal Sounds Unbelievable, Don't Believe It." *Los Angeles Times*, Oct. 25, 1992.

American Society of Travel Agents. *Hotel Tips*. Alexandria, VA: 1989.

—————. *Avoiding Travel Problems*. Alexandria, VA: 1990.

Gordy, Molly. "Travel Con Artists Take No Vacation From Crime." *Newsday*, Oct. 31, 1991.

Grossman, Kathy Lynn. "Beware of Those Selling Cheap Trips." *USA Today*, July 8, 1992.

"Half-Price Hotels in '93 — What's New? What's Best?" *Consumer Reports Travel Letter*, April 1993.

"Hotel Vouchers: Deals and Gouges." *Consumer Reports Travel Letter*, June 1993.

"Hotel Vouchers: Watch Your Step." *Consumer Reports Travel Letter*, August 1992.

Kobliner, Beth. "How To Complain on the Road." *Money*, December 1992.

McGinley, Lauri. "Offers of Luxury Trips at Low Prices Lure Many Consumers Into First-Class Scams." *Wall Street Journal*, May 13, 1992.

New York City Department of Consumer Affairs. *Travel Scams: The Road to Nowhere.* Report. New York City: June 1993.

Potter, Everett. "How Much Will You Pay for This Hotel Room?" *Smart Money,* August 1993.

U.S. Federal Trade Commission. FTC News. *FTC Charges Florida Firms in Deceptive Travel Certificate Scheme.* Washington, DC: Apr. 6, 1992.

——————*Richmond, Virginia Firms Agrees to Pay $15,600 to Settle Federal Trade Commission Charges Tied to Jet Set Travel Scheme.* Washington DC: Apr. 17, 1992.

Wade, Betsy. "Dialing Away Dollars in Hotels." *New York Times*, July, 18, 1993.

——————"Rebating Travel Agencies: For Plan-It-Yourselfers." *New York Times*, July 25, 1992.

——————"Tightening Up On Agencies." *New York Times*, Apr. 18, 1994.

Washington Post. "Gripes: What to Do About Them." *Washington Post*, Jan. 3, 1993.

"What's the Price, Anyway?" *Consumer Reports Travel Letter*, October 1992.

Why Won't Travel Scams Go Away? Transcript of a conference by the American Society of Travel Agents. Dec. 3, 1992. Washington, D.C.

Yenckel, James T. "Gobbling Over Turkeys: Where to Complain, & When." *Washington Post*, Nov. 22, 1992.

49. CAR RENTALS

Dahl, Jonathan. "Car Rental Firms Leave Drivers Dazed by Rip-Offs, Options, Misleading Ads." *Wall Street Journal*, June 1, 1990.

——————. "Rental Counters Reject Drivers Without Good Records." *Wall Street Journal*, Oct. 23, 1992.

"Final Report and Recommendations of the National Association of Attorneys General Task Force on Car Rental Industry Advertising and Practices." *Antitrust & Trade Regulation Report*, Mar. 16, 1989.

Hirsch, James. "Chase Cuts Off Its Car-Rental Insurance Perk." *Wall Street Journal*, June 8, 1993.

Lavin, Douglas, and Robert Johnson. "Prices for Rental Cars Are Set to Climb Sharply — Again." *Wall Street Journal*, Sept. 29, 1993.

Meier, Barry. "When a Reservation Doesn't Get You a Car." *New York Times*, Jan. 18, 1992.

Pearl, Daniel. "Airport Shuttles and Limos Compete With Rental Cars." *Wall Street Journal*, Sept. 20, 1993.

Sims, Calvin. "Bias by Age and Credit Is Found in Car Rentals." *New York Times*, Aug. 20, 1994.

U.S. Public Interest Research Group. *Taking Consumers for a Ride: A Report on Collision Damage Waivers.* Washington, DC: May 1990.

Wade, Betsy. "Liability Is Being Shifted to Auto Renters." *New York Times*, Aug. 8, 1993.

Wald, Matthew L. "Car-Rental Computers Rejecting High-Risk Drivers." *New York Times*, Sept. 9, 1993.

——————. "Car Rentals Hide Welcome Mat." *New York Times*, Jan. 15, 1992.

——————. "For Car Renters, New Options for Insurance." *New York Times*, Dec. 21, 1991.

OTHER SERVICES

50. FUNERALS

American Association of Retired Persons. *Product Report: Funeral Goods and Services.* Washington, DC: AARP, July 1989.

——————. *Product Report: Pre-Paying Your Funeral?* Washington, DC: AARP, August 1992.

Babbitt, Wendy. "A Business You'd Rather Ignore — But Shouldn't." *Public Citizen*, July/August 1991.

Burkins, Glenn. "Protecting the Bereaved." *Chicago Tribune.* Mar. 10, 1993.

Colburne, Don. "Need Spurs Study of New Sources of Organ Donors." *New York Newsday*, June 22, 1993.

Continental Association of Funeral and Memorial Societies, Inc. *Wholesale Casket Price List.* November 1990.

"Death and Deception." Editorial. *Sacramento Bee*, Apr. 11, 1993.

"Debate Rages Over Funeral Rules." *Chicago Tribune*, Jan. 9, 1989.

Dietz, Jean. "Senior Set: Still Keeping Watch on the U.S. Funeral Industry." *Boston Globe*, Dec. 11, 1988.

Gilje, Shelby. "The Cost of Dying — Cremation or Burial? What Sort of Service? Arranging a Funeral Can Be Perplexing." *Seattle Times*, Oct. 25, 1992.

Glover, Mark. "A Fresh Approach to Funeral Prices." *Sacramento Bee*, May 9, 1993.

"Itemized Price List Required." Gannett News Service, Apr. 28, 1993.

Long, Scott A. "Basic Consumer Tips Apply When Arranging a Funeral." Gannett News Service, Apr. 28, 1993.

Mitford, Jessica. "The Funeral Salesman." *McCall's*, November 1977.

National Kidney Foundation. *The Organ Donor Program*. New York City: National Kidney Foundation, Inc.

Norrgard, Lee E, and Jo DeMars. *Final Choices: Making End of Life Decisions*. Santa Barbara, ABC-CLIO Inc., 1992.

U.S. Federal Trade Commission, Office of Consumer/Business Education. *Funerals: A Consumer Guide*. Washington, DC: GPO, September 1991.

51. LAWYERS

American Bar Association Public Education Division. *The American Lawyer: When and How to Use One*. Chicago: ABA Press, 1993.

Brooks, Andree. "To Get Legal Advice Without Overpaying, Handle Some of the Tasks Yourself." *New York Times*, Mar. 26, 1994.

——————. "On Winning Big in Small Claims Court." *The New York Times*, Oct. 19, 1991.

Green, Mark, and John F. Berry. *The Challenge of Hidden Profits: Reducing Corporate Bureaucracy and Waste*. New York: William Morrow Co.

Green, Mark, and Ralph Nader, eds. *Verdicts on Lawyers*. New York: Thomas Y. Crowell Co. 1976.

Haas, Carol and the editors of Consumer Reports Books. *The Consumer Reports Law Book: Your Guide to Resolving Everyday Legal Problems*. Yonkers, NY: Consumer Reports Books, 1994.

Hernandez, Raymond. "The People's Court — Notes From the Small Claims Front: Wringing Justice, With Peace, From the Maddening Fabric of Everyday Life." *New York Times*, Mar. 20, 1994.

Johnson, Daniel. *The Consumer's Guide to Understanding and Using the Law*. Cincinnati: Betterway Books, 1994.

Lasson, Kenneth, and the Public Citizen Litigation Group. *Representing Yourself: What You Can Do Without a Lawyer*. New York: Farrar Straus Giroux, 1983.

Leeds, Dorothy, with Sue Belevich Schilling. *Smart Questions to Ask Your Lawyer*. New York: Harper Paperbacks, 1992.

MacCaulay, Stewart. "Lawyers and Consumer Protection Laws." *Law & Society Review*, Fall 1979.

Nader, Ralph, and Wesley J. Smith. *The Frugal Shopper*. Washington, DC: Center for Study of Responsive Law, 1992.

New York City Department of Consumer Affairs. *Women in Divorce: Lawyers, Ethics, Fees & Fairness*. New York: March 1992.

Pinckney, Michael J. "Arguing Your Case: Some Counsel From the Bench," *New York Times*, Mar. 20, 1994.

Simon, Stephanie. "Mixed Verdict: Prepaid Legal Services Draw Plenty of Customers and Criticism," *Wall Street Journal*, Aug. 6, 1991.

Stevens, Amy. "Uneasy About 'Dial-a-Lawyer' Services, Attorneys Seek Cure to 'Refer Madness.'" *Wall Street Journal*, Jan. 2, 1991.

Torry, Saundra. "Airing Disciplinary Laundry in Full View of the Public." *Washington Post*, May 27, 1991.

——————. "Many With Legal Needs Avoid the Court System." *Washington Post*, Feb. 6, 1994.

Woo, Junda. "Electronic Bulletin Boards Furnish Legal Information to Non-Lawyers," *Wall Street Journal*, Jan. 18, 1994.

52. EMPLOYMENT AGENCIES

Berkowitz, Harry. "Nanny-Agency Violations: City Survey Finds Deceptive Practices at 45 out of 50." *New York Newsday*, Nov. 25, 1992.

Buder, Leonard. "Employment Agency Accused of Bias." *New York Times*, Feb. 21, 1990.

Caporale, Patricia. "Executive Search Companies Pick Up Pace." *Orlando Sentinel Tribune*, Feb. 9, 1993.

Consumer Federation of America. News Conference by Stephen Brobeck, Executive Director, at the National Press Club (transcribed by Federal News Service). Washington, DC: July 14, 1992.

"'Contingent' Workers Deprived of Benefits, Wages, Senate Panel Hears." *Pension Reporter*, June 21, 1993.

Diesenhouse, Susan. "In a Shaky Economy, Even Professionals Are 'Temps.'" *New York Times*, May 16, 1993.

Furfaro, John P., and Maury B. Josephson. "Temporary Employees." *New York Law Journal*, May 7, 1993.

Gilgoff, Henry. "City Targets Job Agencies." *New York Newsday*, Mar. 5, 1993.

Hollywood, Cathy Booth. "Nice Work If You Can Get It." *Time*, Mar. 8, 1993.

Kane, Mary. "More People Forced to Turn to Temporary Work." *Minneapolis Star Tribune*, Apr. 18, 1993.

Kilborn, Peter T. "New Jobs Lack the Old Security in a Time of 'Disposable' Workers." *New York Times*, Mar. 15, 1993.

MacTemps. "MacTemps Introduces the Industry's First Full Benefits Program for Temporary Help". Press release. Mar. 8, 1993.

Ozemhoya, Carol U. "Agencies Charged With Deceptive Practices." *South Florida Business Journal*, Feb. 9, 1993.

Pennsylvania Office of the Attorney General. "Lists of Job Opportunities in Kuwait Were Bogus, Preate Alleges." Press release. Harrisburg, PA: July 8, 1991.

—————. "Preate Orders Business to Stop Allegedly Deceptive Help Wanted Ads" Press release. Harrisburg, PA: Feb. 12, 1993.

—————. "Telephone Carriers to Block Pay-per-Call Job Information Services". Press release. Harrisburg PA: Oct. 23, 1991.

Rosen, Jan. "Looking for Work." *New York Times*, May 23, 1992.

Ross, Sherwood. "Temp Agencies Mislead Workers, Study Finds." *Reuter Business Report*, Dec. 29, 1992.

Suris, Oscar. "Check Out Job Services Before You Pay." *Orlando Sentinel Tribune*, Oct. 27, 1992.

Zeff, Pat Sullivan. "Jobs That Fit Bill, for Now: Temporary Posts Meet Needs of Workers in Transition." *Chicago Tribune*, July 11, 1993.

53. MAIL ORDER AND TELEMARKETING

AT&T. *Be Aware of Phone Fraud*. New York: 1993.

Better Business Bureau. "Dialing for Dollars: Advice on Holiday Phone Appeals." Press release. Nov. 19, 1993.

Better Business Bureau A to Z Buying Guide. New York: Henry Holt & Co., 1990.

Cummins, H.J. "Check Out Charitable Organizations." *New York Newsday*, Dec. 9, 1993.

Direct Marketing Association. *Tips for Telephone Shopping*. Washington, DC: 1991.

Gilgoff, Henry. "Watch the Mail — and Fine Print." *New York Newsday*, Apr. 5, 1993.

Klein, David, Marymae E. Klein and Douglas Walsh. *Getting Unscrewed and Staying That Way*. New York: Henry Holt & Co., 1993.

Kuntz, Mary. "Catalog of Mail-Order Rights." *Newsday*, Oct. 2, 1987.

Louis Harris and Associates. "Telephone-Based Fraud: A Survey of the American Public. New York: April-May 1992.

Meier, Barry. "FTC Adds Safeguards for Shoppers." *New York Times*, Sept. 21, 1993.

Ramirez, Anthony. "Curbing Machines That Phone to Solicit." *New York Times*, Nov. 5, 1992.

Slagle, Alton, "Tough New Tone on Phone Fraud." New York *Daily News*, Jan. 23, 1992.

U.S. Federal Trade Commission and the National Association of Attorneys General. *Telemarketing Fraud: How to Spot It, How to Avoid It*. Washington, DC.

TREND-LINES AND FAULT LINES

54. WOMEN

Ayres, Ian. "Fair Driving: Gender and Race Discrimination in Retail Car Negotiations." *Harvard Law Review*, Vol. 104, No. 4, February 1991.

Commonwealth of Massachusetts. "Attorney General Harshbarger Warns Dry Cleaners Not to Charge Women Higher Prices." Press release. Sept. 12, 1991.

Myerson, Allen R. "Wall Street Addresses Women's Distinct Needs. *New York Times*, July 31, 1993.

New York City Department of Consumer Affairs. *Gypped by Gender: A Study of Price Bias Against Women in the Marketplace*. New York: June 1992.

—————. *Women in Divorce: Ethics, Fees & Fairness*. New York: March 1992.

Rigdon, Joan E. "State May Ban Bias in Pricing Hairdos, Wash." *Wall Street Journal*, May 11, 1994.

Swisher, Cara. "Pressing Charges: Law Students Fight Discriminatory Fees." *Washington Post*, June 29, 1989.

Whittelsey, Frances Cerra. *Why Women Pay More: How to Avoid Marketplace Perils*. Washington, DC: Center for Study of Responsive Law, 1993.

55. SELLING MINORITIES SHORT IN THE MARKETPLACE

Ayres, Ian. "Fair Driving: Gender and Race Discrimination in Retail Car Negotiations." *Harvard Law Review*, Vol. 104, No. 4, February 1991.

Braitman, Ellen. "As Pawnshops Thrive, Banks Steer Clear." *American Banker*, Nov. 15, 1991.

Brenner, Joel Glenn, and Liz Spayd. "A Pattern of Bias in Mortgage Loans." *Washington Post*, June 6, 1993.

Canner, Glenn B. and Dolores S. Smith. "Bias in Home Lending." *Federal Reserve Bulletin*, November 1991.

Dent, David J. "The New Black Suburbs." *New York Times Magazine*, June 14, 1992.

Freedman, Alix. "An Inner-City Shopper Seeking Healthy Food Finds Offerings Scant: Producers Neglect the Market While Stores Say They Just Carry What Sells." *Wall Street Journal*, Dec. 20, 1990.

Milbank, Dana. "Finast Finds Challenges and Surprising Profits in Urban Supermarkets." *Wall Street Journal*, June 8, 1992.

New York City Department of Consumer Affairs. *Banking on Merging*. New York: October 1991.

—————. *The Poor Pay More for Less, Part 1: Grocery Shopping*. New York: April 1991.

—————. *The Poor Pay More for Less, Part 2: Automobile Liability Insurance*. New York: July 1992.

—————. *The Poor Pay More for Less, Part 3: Equity Theft*. New York: February 1993.

New York City Public Advocate's Office. *The Poor Pay More for Less, Part 4: Financial Services*. New York: April 1994.

Quint, Michael. "Racial Gap Detailed on Mortgages." *New York Times*, Oct. 22, 1991.

Schwadel, Francine. "Poverty's Cost: Urban Consumers Pay More and Get Less, and Gap May Widen." *Wall Street Journal*, July 2, 1992.

Siverstein, Stuart, and Nancy Rivera Brooks. "Shoppers in Need of Stores: South Los Angeles Has Been Tagged by Businesses as a Place to Avoid." *Los Angeles Times*, Nov. 24, 1991.

Spayd, Liz, and Joel Glenn Brenner. "Area Blacks Have Worst Bank Access." *Washington Post*, June 7, 1993.

Thomas, Paulette. "Persistent Gap: Blacks Can Face a Host of Trying Conditions in Getting Mortgages." *Wall Street Journal*, Nov. 30, 1992.

56. SENIORS AS CONSUMERS

American Association of Retired Persons. "Credit Discrimination: Knocking Down the Barriers." *Senior Consumer ALERT*. Washington, DC: March/April 1989.

—————. "Home Equity Scams: The Cruelest Consumer Fraud." *Senior Consumer ALERT*. Washington, DC: Spring 1987.

—————. "If It Quacks Like a Duck, Don't Trust It: Fraud in the Sale of Health-Related Products." *Senior Consumer ALERT*. Winter 1990-91.

—————. "Investment Fraud: The Subtle Scam." *Senior Consumer ALERT*. Spring 1990.

Butler, Robert N. *Why Survive: Being Old in America*. New York: Harper and Row, 1975.

Eckholm, Erik. "Alarmed by Fund-Raiser, the Elderly Give Millions." *New York Times*, Nov. 12, 1992.

New York City Department of Consumer Affairs. *Seniors As Consumers: An Analysis of the Senior Consumer Watch Survey*. New York: April 1993.

Tsiantar, Dody, and Annetta Miller. "Dipping Into Granny's Wallet: Marketers Woo Seniors." *Newsweek*, May 10, 1992.

U.S. Department of Justice Bureau of Investigation. *Operation Disconnect: Press Briefing Material*. Washington, DC: March 1993.

U.S. House of Representatives Select Committee on Aging, Subcommittee on Health and Long Term Care. *Quackery: A $10 Billion Scandal*. Washington, DC: May 31, 1984.

57. CONSUMERS WITH DISABILITIES

Bureau of National Affairs. *Title II of the Americans With Disabilities Act: Technical Assistance Manual*. Washington DC: April 1992.

Eastern Paralyzed Veterans Association. Removing Barriers in Place of Accomodation. Jackson Heights, NY: 1992.

Field, Robert. "Phones Drive Wheelchairs Up the Wall." *New York Post*, Aug. 3, 1994.

New York Lawyers for the Public Interest, Inc. *Your Rights Under the Americans With Disabilities Act to Access to Public Accomodations*. New York.

U.S. Department of Education, National Institute on Disability and Rehabilitation Research. *Disability Statistics Report*. Washington, DC: March 1993.

U.S. Equal Employment Opportunity Commission and U.S. Department of Justice, Civil Rights Division. *The Americans With Disabilities Act—Questions and Answers*. Washington, DC: September 1992.

58. PRODUCT SAFETY

Asch, Peter. *Consumer Safety Regulation: Putting a Price on Life and Limb*. New York: Oxford Univ. Press, 1988.

Claybrook, Joan, and David Bollier. *Freedom From Harm*. New York: The Democracy Project, 1985.

Fise, Mary Ellen. "Statement to the Consumer Product Safety Commission on the CPSC Long Range Plan." Washington, DC: June 18, 1992.

Green, Mark, et al. eds. *Changing America: Blueprints for the New Administration*. New York: New Market Press, 1992.

"A Major Recall of Ceiling Fans." *Consumer Reports*, February 1994.

Meier, Barry. "Product Safety Commission Is Criticized As Too Slow to Act." *New York Times*, Sept. 21, 1991.

U.S. Consumer Product Safety Commission. "Alert: Hidden Hazards in the Home: Large Buckets Are Drowning Hazards for Young Children." Washington, DC: April 1992.

——————. *National Electronic Injury Surveillance System Product Summary Report for Calendar Year 1993*. Washington, DC: 1994.

——————. "Product Safety Fact Sheet on Riding Lawnmowers," Publication No. 588. Washington, DC: revised spring 1988.

59. CONSUMER PRIVACY

Carnevale, Mary Lu. "Fighting Fraud." *Wall Street Journal*. May 18, 1992.

Consumer Action. *Consumer Alert on ChexSystems*. San Francisco: September 1991.

Lacayo, Richard. "Nowhere to Hide." *Time*, Nov. 11, 1991.

Louis Harris & Associates and Dr. Alan F. Westin. *The Equifax Report on Consumers in the Information Age*. Atlanta: 1990.

Massachusetts Public Interest Research Group. *For Their Eyes Only*. Boston: April 1990.

Miller, Annetta, and John Schwartz. "How Did They Get My Name?" *Newsweek*, June 3, 1991.

Miller, Michael. "Patient's Records Are Treasure Trove for Budding Industry." *Wall Street Journal*. Feb. 27, 1992.

New York City Department of Consumer Affairs. *Prying Eyes*. New York: November 1991.

——————. *Secret Files and Consumer Rights*. New York: April 1992.

Rothfeder, Jerry. "Is Nothing Private." *Business Week*, Sept. 4, 1989.

"Sellers of Government Data Thrive." *New York Times*, Dec. 26, 1991.

Smolowe, Jill. "Read This!!!!!!" *Time*. Nov. 26, 1990.

U.S. Public Interest Research Group. *Credit Bureaus: Public Enemy #1 at the FTC*. Washington, DC: June 1991.

——————. *Don't Call; Don't Write; We Don't Care*. Washington, DC: October 1993.

"What Price Privacy?" *Consumer Reports*, May 1991.

"Who's Reading Your Medical Records?" *American Health*, November 1993.

60. ENVIRONMENTAL CLAIMS

Brown, Patricia Leigh. "A Symbol of the Fast-Food Culture." *New York Times*, Nov. 2, 1990.

Center for Science in the Public Interest. "Worst Ads of the Year Named." News release. Washington, DC: Jan. 27, 1994.

Dadd, Debra Lynn, and Andre Carothers. "A Bill of Goods? Green Consuming in Perspective." *Greenpeace*, May/June 1990.

Dold, Catherine. "Green to Go: Shopping Well is the Consumer's Best Revenge Against Environmental Degradation." *American Health*, April 1990.

The Earth Works Group. *Fifty Simple Things You Can Do to Save the Earth*. Berkeley, CA.: EarthWorks Press, 1989.

Eleven Attorneys General. *The Green Report II: Recommendations for Responsible Environmental Advertising*. May 1991.

Environmental Action staff. *Solid Waste Action Paper # 5: Drink Boxes*. Washington, DC: Environmental Action Foundation, 1991.

Environmental Defense Fund. "Recycle. It's the Everyday Way to Save the World." Washington, DC: 1990.

Goldstein, Eric A., and Mark D. Izeman. *The New York Environment Book*. Washington, DC: Island Press, 1990.

Gutfeld, Rose. "Americans Flunk Test on Environment." *Wall Street Journal*, Nov. 8, 1991.

Holusha, John. "Industry Seeks U.S. Rules Covering Environmental Ads." *New York Times*, Feb. 20, 1991.

——————. "Learning to Wrap Products in Less — Or Nothing at All." *New York Times*, Jan. 19, 1992.

——————. "So What Is 'Environmentally Friendly." *New York Times*, Jan. 26, 1991.

——————. "Some Smog in Pledges to Help Environment." *New York Times*, Apr. 19, 1990.

Horovitz, Bruce. "'Green' Honeymoon is Over." *Los Angeles Times*, May 12, 1992.

Lublin, Joanne. "Agencies Are Joining the Rush to Give 'Green' Marketing Advice." *Wall Street Journal*, Jan. 25, 1991.

Martin, Douglas. "Save a Planet, Make a Buck: The 'Green' Industry Ripens." *New York Times*, June 14, 1993.

"Old Cans Get a New Life, in Sleek Automobiles." *New York Times*, Feb. 20, 1991.

Ramirez, Anthony. "Soap Sellers' New Credo: Less Powder, More Power." *The New York Times*, Feb. 1, 1991.

Rule, Sheila. "Smaller CD Boxes Promised Amid Clamor About Waste." *New York Times*, Feb. 28, 1992.

Schneider, Keith. "As Recycling Becomes A Growth Industry, Its Paradoxes Also Multiply." *New York Times*, Jan. 20, 1991.

Stipp, David. "Lunch Box Staple Runs Afoul of Activists." *Wall Street Journal*, Mar. 14, 1991.

Ten Attorneys General. *The Green Report: Findings and Preliminary Recommendations for Responsible Environmental Advertising*. November 1990.

Walls, David. *The Activist's Almanac*. New York: Simon & Schuster, 1993.

CONSUMER SKILLS

61. INSTALLMENT LOANS

Eiler, Andrew. *The Consumer Protection Manual*. New York: Facts on File, 1984.

National Consumer Law Center. *Truth in Lending* (and 1993 supplement). Boston: 1989 and 1993.

U.S. Federal Reserve Board of Governors. *Consumer Handbook to Credit Protection Laws*. Washington, DC: December 1991.

62. LAY-AWAY AND RENT-TO-OWN

Better Business Bureau A to Z Buying Guide. New York: Henry Holt & Co. 1990.

Unfair and Deceptive Acts and Practices, 3rd ed. Boston: National Consumer Law Center, 1991.

63. COUNTERFEIT AND GRAY MARKET GOODS

"Importing of 'Gray Market' Goods Upheld; Decision Likely to Save Consumers Millions of Dollars." *Los Angeles Times*, May 31, 1988.

"Inside the Gray Market." *Time*, Oct. 28, 1985.

Ioannou, Lori. "Shopping the Gray Market." *New York Daily News*, Sept. 29, 1985.

New York City Department of Consumer Affairs. "Green and Designer Companies Launch Biggest Anti-Counterfeit Sweep." Press release. Feb. 27, 1991.

64. HOW TO COMPLAIN

Better Business Bureau A to Z Buying Guide. New York: Henry Holt & Co. 1990.

Garman, E. Thomas. *Consumer Economic Issues in America*. Boston: Houghton Mifflin, 1991.

Klein, David, Marymae E. Klein and Douglas Walsh. *Getting Unscrewed and Staying That Way*. New York: Henry Holt & Co. 1993.

Nader, Ralph, and Wesley J. Smith. *The Frugal Shopper*. Washington, DC: Center for Study of Responsive Law, 1992.

New York City Department of Consumer Affairs. *Resolving Consumer Complaints 1990-1993: Who Complains, Why, and With What Results*. New York: February 1993.

U.S. Office of Consumer Affairs. *Consumer's Resource Handbook*. Washington, DC: 1992.

INDEX

B

ALSO BY MARK GREEN

Changing America: Blueprints for the Clinton Administration (1993, editor)

America's Transition: Blueprints for the 90's (1988, editor)

Reagan's Reign of Error: The Instant Nostalgia Edition
(1987, 2nd Edition, with Gail MacColl)

The Challenge of Hidden Profits (1985, with John Berry)

Who Runs Congress? (1984, 4th Edition)

Winning Back America (1982)

The Big Business Reader (1980, edited with Robert Massie, Jr.)

Taming the Giant Corporation (1976, with Ralph Nader & Joel Seligman)

Verdicts on Lawyers (1976, edited with Ralph Nader)

The Other Government: The Unseen Power of Washington Lawyers (1975)

Corporate Power in America (1973, edited with Ralph Nader)

The Monopoly Makers (1973, editor)

The Closed Enterprise System
(1972, with Beverly C. Moore, Jr. & Bruce Wasserstein)

With Justice for Some (1971, edited with Bruce Wasserstein)